BUILDING CONSTRUCTION

MATERIALS AND
TYPES OF CONSTRUCTION

BUILDING CONSTRUCTION

MATERIALS AND TYPES OF CONSTRUCTION

Donald C. Ellison
PROFESSOR OF BUILDING CONSTRUCTION
PURDUE UNIVERSITY

W. C. Huntington

Robert E. Mickadeit
ARCHITECT AND CIVIL ENGINEER
ALAN HANCOCK COLLEGE

Sixth Edition

John Wiley & Sons
NEW YORK   CHICHESTER   BRISBANE   TORONTO   SINGAPORE

Chapter Opening Photo Credits

Chapter 1:   Werner H. Muller/Alpha Press — Jeroboam.
Chapter 2:   Fred Bodin/Stock Boston.
Chapter 3:   Carol Palmer/The Picture Cube.
Chapter 4:   Patricia Hollander Gross/Stock Boston.
Chapter 5:   Robert Kalman/The Image Works.
Chapter 6:   Stuart Rosner/Stock Boston.
Chapter 7:   American Plywood Association.
Chapter 8:   Courtesy Dow Chemical Corporation.
Chapter 9:   Mark Antman/The Image Works.
Chapter 10: Bruce Kliewe/Jeroboam.
Chapter 11: Courtesy Composite Technology, Inc.

Library of Congress Cataloging-in-Publication Data

Ellison, Donald C.
    Building construction.

    Rev. ed. of: Building construction / Whitney Clark
Huntington, Robert E. Mickadeit.   1981.
    Bibliography: p.
    Includes index.
    1. Building. 2. Building materials. I. Huntington,
Whitney Clark, 1887 –   . II. Huntington, Whitney
Clark, 1887 –   . Building construction.
III. Mickadeit, Robert E., 1923 –   . IV. Title.

TH145.E45 1987   691   86-19071
ISBN 0-471-85052-7
ISBN 0-471-87427-2 (pbk.)

Printed in the United States of America

10 9 8 7 6 5 4 3 2 1

PREFACE

This text introduces building nomenclature and construction methods to students of architecture, building construction, and construction technology. The sixth edition provides a thorough updating of the entire book, and several specific additions. To facilitate understanding and learning of the contents, we have added: an introduction at the beginning of the chapter to introduce the material to be presented, learning objectives to enable the reader to focus on the important concepts being presented, a summary at the end of the chapter to review the material, a set of review questions to reinforce learning of the concepts and information, and a list of key terms that are defined in the body of the chapter and/or in the glossary at the end of the book.

Several new illustrations have been added, primarily in the areas of subsurface exploration, excavation, backfilling, compaction, and cast-in-place concrete. A genuine effort has been made to expand descriptive material on construction methods. Examples include text material on site preparation, excavation, pier construction; and mixing, batching, and transportation of concrete. New chapter subheadings include metal building systems, single membrane roofing, and drywall construction. A new chapter on fiberglass reinforced plastic structural element applications has been added. Chapter 2, Sitework in the previous edition was divided into two chapters with the headings of Soil (new Chapter 2) and Foundations (new Chapter 3).

Chapters have been arranged in a sequence that parallels the sequencing of the divisions in the Construction Specifications Institute format. However, some deviation was necessary to accommodate the chapter division and the new chapter on fiberglass reinforced plastic structural elements.

This text is intended as an introduction to construction materials, systems, and methods. It is by no means exhaustive and sources for further study are listed in the references. A listing of appropriate professional and trade associations for each chapter is also included as a source of additional material.

Several reviewers and a number of my colleagues in the Department of Building Construction at Purdue made valuable suggestions for this edition, and the consensus of their views has been incorporated. I regret that it was not possible to accommodate all of the constructive suggestions I received. Their effort is greatly appreciated. Also, I want to acknowledge my two secretaries, Patricia Borders and Carol Kirts, for their efforts above and beyond the call of duty in getting this manuscript ready for publication.

Donald C. Ellison
Purdue University

CONTENTS

CHAPTER 1
BUILDING PROCESS

1.1 Building Process
1.2 Codes and Standards
1.3 Building Loads

1.4 Building Elements
1.5 Building Costs
1.6 Selection of Materials

The building process begins once the need for a building is established. The need may be a new school in a population growth area, a new hospital to replace an outdated health clinic, a new hotel to better serve visitors to a convention center, or a high-rise office building. Generally, the ultimate user of the building has established the need. The building process is the series of actions and operations necessary to make the need a reality. There are four general phases in the building process; the preliminary phase, the design phase, the contractor selection phase, and the construction phase. The decisions made in each of the phases determine what materials and methods will be used.

Most municipalities have adopted building codes to safeguard the public. These codes set minimum standards for quality of materials, imposed loads, allowable stresses, mechanical and electrical equipment, and fire safety.

Although buildings come in a variety of shapes and sizes, they will all have, in one form or other, each of the following major elements: foundations that transfer the total load of the building to the supporting soil or rock; structural frames that support and transfer all imposed loads to the foundation; protective barriers that keep out the weather; and interior finishes to enhance the well being of the occupants. The total life cost of the building will depend on the quality and suitability of the materials and methods used for each of the major elements.

Objectives

1. Define each of the general phases in the building process.
2. State the purpose of building codes.

3. Describe the function of each of the major elements in a building.
4. Describe how the selection of materials and methods affects the total life cost of a building.

1.1 Building Process

The need or desire of building may set in motion a number of steps and processes that will affect many people in order to fulfill the construction requirements. An overview of the *building process* is outlined here.

PRELIMINARY PHASE

Clients (individuals desiring a building) usually require the services of an architect or possibly an engineer. During the preliminary phase of the building process the architect is responsible for gathering and coordinating data that will be required for the construction process; often clients themselves supply this information. But the larger proportion of required information will be supplied by manufacturers, their technical organizations, professional organizations, and various codes.

Information on materials must be obtained from manufacturers or their representatives. Expert consultants may supply information that must be relevant, timely, and appropriate to the project.

Factual information about the building site should include contours, soils tests, weather, geologic evaluation, and availability of transportation and water.

The preliminary phase usually includes a report that lists likely solutions, alternative approaches, and costs, and may include economic feasibility studies.

Preliminary Estimate

Preliminary estimates are required to determine the approximate cost before detailed plans and specifications are prepared. Such an estimate may be used by the prospective owner to obtain the necessary financing to successfully complete the project or to determine how much of the planned facility can be completed with available funds.

A common preliminary estimate is the cost per square foot estimate. It is made by multiplying the floor area of the proposed building by a cost that is based on historical costs of similar types of buildings. These costs are based on an architect's experience, a contractor's suggestions, or published values.

A similar method multiplies the volume of the building by a historical cost that is obtained from the sources previously mentioned. Another method uses the cost per unit of capacity, such as the cost of a school per pupil or classroom, a hospital per bed, or a hotel per room.

Environmental Considerations

Environmental impact reports are now required in many municipalities and states. Environmental studies are now more universal in application, whereas formerly they were thought of as involving only mechanical equipment of buildings — heating, ventilating, plumbing, and illumination.

The current concerns for environmental issues do increase construction problems and the cost of buildings. Environmental requirements for building construction are debatable as to what precisely constitutes environmental impact. A project in one locality may create a different environmental controversy than a nearby project.

Geological reports (in addition to soils reports) are now required in areas of high earthquake probability and of doubtful geologic stability. Prepared by engineering geologists, these reports should include, but not be limited to, information on rock core samples, the location of known faults, caverns, the bearing values of rocks, rock informations and their extent, and the classification and types of rocks.

Environmental aspects may be classified broadly as those that are of only temporary concern (the construction period) and those which have long-lasting effects, including the ecological balance of the area. Some short-term concerns might be classified as public nuisances: riveting, pile driving, and other noises of the building process and dust, which may be controlled by water spraying or using a dust palliative.

The demolition of existing structures or the removal of rock overburden may require the use of explosives. This activity, closely regulated by governmental agencies, may require blasting mats and scheduling of blasting shots at certain times only.

The removal of unsightly construction debris, especially in demolition work, may be a problem. The rupture of gas lines and underground power lines can prove fatal. The rupture of water lines can cause flooding of the site and adjacent property.

Some long-term factors causing concern for the environment are: traffic congestion, parking availability, the utilization of ground surface for parking, landscaping, obstruction of views, unsightly and oversized signs, destruction of sites that have intrinsic, archaeologic or historic values, disruption of plant and animal life, water demands, sewage disposal, overhead utility lines, exposed pipelines, malodorous emissions and abusive noise levels that are produced by a manufacturing process, and brush fire potential.

The effects of the building operations and the building itself may be detrimental to the natural life of the area (the ecological balance) and may require studies and reports by experts.

Radiation hazards are a factor in certain structures. Flooding, causing floods, mud slides, and earth movement in such a manner that would abuse the public or a neighbor is a matter for concern.

Schematics

Concluding the preliminary phase are schematic plans of the project based on the data gathered. These drawings frequently include spatial concepts, delineated sketches that depict the project in plan, elevations, and perspective, as well as building models. These drawings may form part of a report required by other appropriate governing bodies such as a coastal commission, planning department, or a commission wielding architectural (design) control.

With the approval of schematics the preliminary phase is completed and the planning process enters into the design phase. Data gathering usually continues in an effort to deal with problems that arise.

DESIGN PHASE

Various consulting engineers are engaged to solve specialty problems, such as mechanical, electric, structural, landscape, acoustics, and site gradings. These engineers and the architects prepare the working drawings that are used for the construction of the building.

Working drawings require constant reference to and consultation of building codes and standards.

A number of legal approvals may be required, depending on the complexity and nature of the project. Usually local building officials have jurisdiction and should be consulted on code interpretations. State or federally controlled projects will require the appropriate stamps of approval, including state fire marshal approval or a seismic design check in some jurisdictions. Usually city or county building departments that exert control have a requirement that they must check plans for code conformity. The specifications usually follow the Specifications Format, published by the Construction Specifications Institute.

The widely adopted Uniform Construction Index provides three interrelated formats: the Specifications Format, the Data Filing Format, and the Cost Analysis Format. These formats follow a systematized classification of building materials and processes in 16 headings known as divisions. These divisions are arranged in a sequence that outlines in a most general way the order that would be followed in conducting a construction project.

Below is the complete Specifications Format.

CONTRACTOR SELECTION PHASE

Written specifications are prepared along with the working drawings. Generally, specifications supplement the working drawings by stating quality, color, and other factors desired that cannot be stated conveniently on the working drawings.

Contracts are prepared that state the expectations required of the building contractor, owner, and architect. These include a number of bonds that must be furnished: the bid bond, which assures that the chosen bidder will accept the offered contract; performance bond, which assures that the contractor will perform functions faithfully according to the terms of the contract; and a labor and material payment bond, which assures that the contractor will pay for all labor and materials used on the project and will deliver a lien-free completed project.

Contract documents are sent to qualified contractors, usually for a printing and handling fee.

Contractors prepare their estimates usually based on a material survey called a take off that has been "extended" to include unit prices, labor, supervision, and transportation.

At a specified date, place, and time, the contractor's bid is opened and recorded. The successful bidder is then offered the bid and asked to provide the necessary bonds previously mentioned.

MASTERFORMAT Broadscope Section Titles Reprinted from MASTERFORMAT, CSI Document MP-2-1, copyrighted June 1978, Construction Specifications Institute.

DIVISION 0—BIDDING AND CONTRACT REQUIREMENTS

00010	PRE-BID INFORMATION
00100	INSTRUCTIONS TO BIDDERS
00200	INFORMATION AVAILABLE TO BIDDERS
00300	BID/TENDER FORMS
00400	SUPPLEMENTS TO BID/TENDER FORMS
00500	AGREEMENT FORMS
00600	BONDS AND CERTIFICATES
00700	GENERAL CONDITIONS OF THE CONTRACT
00800	SUPPLEMENTARY CONDITIONS
00950	DRAWINGS INDEX
00900	ADDENDA AND MODIFICATIONS

DIVISION 1—GENERAL REQUIREMENTS

01010	SUMMARY OF WORK
01020	ALLOWANCES
01030	SPECIAL PROJECT PROCEDURES
01040	COORDINATION
01050	FIELD ENGINEERING
01060	REGULATORY REQUIREMENTS
01070	ABBREVIATIONS AND SYMBOLS
01080	IDENTIFICATION SYSTEMS
01100	ALTERNATES/ALTERNATIVES
01150	MEASUREMENT AND PAYMENT
01200	PROJECT MEETINGS
01300	SUBMITTALS
01400	QUALITY CONTROL
01500	CONSTRUCTION FACILITIES AND TEMPORARY CONTROLS
01600	MATERIAL AND EQUIPMENT
01650	STARTING OF SYSTEMS
01660	TESTING, ADJUSTING, AND BALANCING OF SYSTEMS
01700	CONTRACT CLOSEOUT

DIVISION 2—SITEWORK

02010	SUBSURFACE INVESTIGATION
02050	DEMOLITION
02100	SITE PREPARATION
02150	UNDERPINNING
02200	EARTHWORK
02300	TUNNELLING
02350	PILES, CAISSONS AND COFFERDAMS
02400	DRAINAGE

02440   SITE IMPROVEMENTS
02480   LANDSCAPING
02500   PAVING AND SURFACING
02590   PONDS AND RESERVOIRS
02600   PIPED UTILITY MATERIALS AND METHODS
02700   PIPED UTILITIES
02800   POWER AND COMMUNICATION UTILITIES
02850   RAILROAD WORK
02880   MARINE WORK

DIVISION 3—CONCRETE

03050   CONCRETING PROCEDURES
03100   CONCRETE FORMWORK
03150   FORMS
03180   FORM TIES AND ACCESSORIES
03200   CONCRETE REINFORCEMENT
03250   CONCRETE ACCESSORIES
03300   CAST-IN-PLACE CONCRETE
03350   SPECIAL CONCRETE FINISHES
03360   SPECIALLY PLACED CONCRETE
03370   CONCRETE CURING
03400   PRECAST CONCRETE
03500   CEMENTITIOUS DECKS
03600   GROUT
03700   CONCRETE RESTORATION AND CLEANING

DIVISION 4—MASONRY

04050   MASONRY PROCEDURES
04100   MORTAR
04150   MASONRY ACCESSORIES
04200   UNIT MASONRY
04400   STONE
04500   MASONRY RESTORATION AND CLEANING
04550   REFRACTORIES
04600   CORROSION RESISTANT MASONRY

DIVISION 5—METALS

05010   METAL MATERIALS AND METHODS
05050   METAL FASTENING
05100   STRUCTURAL METAL FRAMING
05200   METAL JOISTS
05300   METAL DECKING
05400   COLD-FORMED METAL FRAMING
05500   METAL FABRICATIONS
05700   ORNAMENTAL METAL
05800   EXPANSION CONTROL
05900   METAL FINISHES

DIVISION 6—WOOD AND PLASTICS

06050   FASTENERS AND SUPPORTS
06100   ROUGH CARPENTRY
06130   HEAVY TIMBER CONSTRUCTION
06150   WOOD-METAL SYSTEMS
06170   PREFABRICATED STRUCTURAL WOOD
06200   FINISH CARPENTRY
06300   WOOD TREATMENT
06400   ARCHITECTURAL WOODWORK
06500   PREFABRICATED STRUCTURAL PLASTICS
06600   PLASTIC FABRICATIONS

DIVISION 7—THERMAL AND MOISTURE PROTECTION

07100   WATERPROOFING
07150   DAMPPROOFING
07200   INSULATION
07250   FIREPROOFING
07300   SHINGLES AND ROOFING TILES
07400   PREFORMED ROOFING AND SIDING
07500   MEMBRANE ROOFING
07570   TRAFFIC TOPPING
07600   FLASHING AND SHEET METAL
07800   ROOF ACCESSORIES
07900   JOINT SEALANTS

DIVISION 8—DOORS AND WINDOWS

08100   METAL DOORS AND FRAMES
08200   WOOD AND PLASTIC DOORS
08250   DOOR OPENING ASSEMBLIES
08300   SPECIAL DOORS
08400   ENTRANCES AND STOREFRONTS
08500   METAL WINDOWS
08600   WOOD AND PLASTIC WINDOWS
08650   SPECIAL WINDOWS
08700   HARDWARE
08800   GLAZING
08900   GLAZED CURTAIN WALLS

DIVISION 9—FINISHES

09100   METAL SUPPORT SYSTEMS
09200   LATH AND PLASTER
09230   AGGREGATE COATINGS
09250   GYPSUM WALLBOARD
09300   TILE
09400   TERRAZZO
09500   ACOUSTICAL TREATMENT
09550   WOOD FLOORING
09600   STONE AND BRICK FLOORING
09650   RESILIENT FLOORING
09680   CARPETING
09700   SPECIAL FLOORING
09760   FLOOR TREATMENT
09800   SPECIAL COATINGS
09900   PAINTING
09950   WALL COVERING

DIVISION 10—SPECIALITIES

10100   CHALKBOARDS AND TACKBOARDS
10150   COMPARTMENTS AND CUBICLES
10200   LOUVERS AND VENTS
10240   GRILLES AND SCREENS
10250   SERVICE WALL SYSTEMS
10260   WALL AND CORNER GUARDS
10270   ACCESS FLOORING
10280   SPECIALTY MODULES
10290   PEST CONTROL
10300   FIREPLACES AND STOVES
10340   PREFABRICATED STEEPLES, SPIRES, AND CUPOLAS
10350   FLAGPOLES
10400   IDENTIFYING DEVICES
10450   PEDESTRIAN CONTROL DEVICES
10500   LOCKERS
10520   FIRE EXTINGUISHERS, CABINETS, AND ACCESSORIES
10530   PROTECTIVE COVERS
10550   POSTAL SPECIALTIES
10600   PARTITIONS
10650   SCALES
10670   STORAGE SHELVING

10700	EXTERIOR SUN CONTROL DEVICES
10750	TELEPHONE ENCLOSURES
10800	TOILET AND BATH ACCESSORIES
10900	WARDROBE SPECIALTIES

DIVISION 11—EQUIPMENT

11010	MAINTENANCE EQUIPMENT
11020	SECURITY AND VAULT EQUIPMENT
11030	CHECKROOM EQUIPMENT
11040	ECCLESIASTICAL EQUIPMENT
11050	LIBRARY EQUIPMENT
11060	THEATER AND STAGE EQUIPMENT
11070	MUSICAL EQUIPMENT
11080	REGISTRATION EQUIPMENT
11100	MERCANTILE EQUIPMENT
11110	COMMERCIAL LAUNDRY AND DRY CLEANING EQUIPMENT
11120	VENDING EQUIPMENT
11130	AUDIO-VISUAL EQUIPMENT
11140	SERVICE STATION EQUIPMENT
11150	PARKING EQUIPMENT
11160	LOADING DOCK EQUIPMENT
11170	WASTE HANDLING EQUIPMENT
11190	DETENTION EQUIPMENT
11200	WATER SUPPLY AND TREATMENT EQUIPMENT
11300	FLUID WASTE DISPOSAL AND TREATMENT EQUIPMENT
11400	FOOD SERVICE EQUIPMENT
11450	RESIDENTIAL EQUIPMENT
11460	UNIT KITCHENS
11470	DARKROOM EQUIPMENT
11480	ATHLETIC, RECREATIONAL, AND THERAPEUTIC EQUIPMENT
11500	INDUSTRIAL AND PROCESS EQUIPMENT
11600	LABORATORY EQUIPMENT
11650	PLANETARIUM AND OBSERVATORY EQUIPMENT
11700	MEDICAL EQUIPMENT
11780	MORTUARY EQUIPMENT
11800	TELECOMMUNICATION EQUIPMENT
11850	NAVIGATION EQUIPMENT

DIVISION 12—FURNISHINGS

12100	ARTWORK
12300	MANUFACTURED CABINETS AND CASEWORK
12500	WINDOW TREATMENT
12550	FABRICS
12600	FURNITURE AND ACCESSORIES
12670	RUGS AND MATS
12700	MULTIPLE SEATING
12800	INTERIOR PLANTS AND PLANTINGS

DIVISION 13—SPECIAL CONSTRUCTION

13010	AIR SUPPORTED STRUCTURES
13020	INTEGRATED ASSEMBLIES
13030	AUDIOMETRIC ROOMS
13040	CLEAN ROOMS
13050	HYPERBARIC ROOMS
13060	INSULATED ROOMS
13070	INTEGRATED CEILINGS
13080	SOUND, VIBRATION, AND SEISMIC CONTROL
13090	RADIATION PROTECTION
13100	NUCLEAR REACTORS
13110	OBSERVATORIES

13120	PRE-ENGINEERED STRUCTURES
13130	SPECIAL PURPOSE ROOMS AND BUILDINGS
13140	VAULTS
13150	POOLS
13160	ICE RINKS
13170	KENNELS AND ANIMAL SHELTERS
13200	SEISMOGRAPHIC INSTRUMENTATION
13210	STRESS RECORDING INSTRUMENTATION
13220	SOLAR AND WIND INSTRUMENTATION
13410	LIQUID AND GAS STORAGE TANKS
13510	RESTORATION OF UNDERGROUND PIPELINES
13520	FILTER UNDERDRAINS AND MEDIA
13530	DIGESTION TANK COVERS AND APPURTENANCES
13540	OXYGENATION SYSTEMS
13550	THERMAL SLUDGE CONDITIONING SYSTEMS
13560	SITE CONSTRUCTED INCINERATORS
13600	UTILITY CONTROL SYSTEMS
13700	INDUSTRIAL AND PROCESS CONTROL SYSTEMS
13800	OIL AND GAS REFINING INSTALLATIONS AND CONTROL SYSTEMS
13900	TRANSPORTATION INSTRUMENTATION
13940	BUILDING AUTOMATION SYSTEMS
13970	FIRE SUPPRESSION AND SUPERVISORY SYSTEMS
13980	SOLAR ENERGY SYSTEMS
13990	WIND ENERGY SYSTEMS

DIVISION 14—CONVEYING SYSTEMS

14100	DUMBWAITERS
14200	ELEVATORS
14300	HOISTS AND CRANES
14400	LIFTS
14500	MATERIAL HANDLING SYSTEMS
14600	TURNTABLES
14700	MOVING STAIRS AND WALKS
14800	POWERED SCAFFOLDING
14900	TRANSPORTATION SYSTEMS

DIVISION 15—MECHANICAL

15050	BASIC MATERIALS AND METHODS
15200	NOISE, VIBRATION, AND SEISMIC CONTROL
15250	INSULATION
15300	SPECIAL PIPING SYSTEMS
15400	PLUMBING SYSTEMS
15450	PLUMBING FIXTURES AND TRIM
15500	FIRE PROTECTION
15600	POWER OR HEAT GENERATION
15650	REFRIGERATION
15700	LIQUID HEAT TRANSFER
15800	AIR DISTRIBUTION
15900	CONTROLS AND INSTRUMENTATION

DIVISION 16—ELECTRICAL

16050	BASIC MATERIALS AND METHODS
16200	POWER GENERATION
16300	POWER TRANSMISSION
16400	SERVICE AND DISTRIBUTION
16500	LIGHTING
16600	SPECIAL SYSTEMS
16700	COMMUNICATIONS
16850	HEATING AND COOLING
16900	CONTROLS AND INSTRUMENTATION

The above system of selecting a contractor is the traditional *design-bid-construct* method. The owner could elect to hire a contractor without competitive bidding. Instead of asking for bids from several contractors, the owner might negotiate with a few selected contractors or with an individual contractor and arrive at an acceptable price for both parties. Often owners who have ongoing projects may find that it is advantageous to have continuing contractual agreements with a contractor who has demonstrated the ability to complete projects on time, within budget, and according to the contract drawings and specifications.

Other systems include the *design-build* process, where one organization enters into a contract with the owner to perform all of the phases previously discussed; *construction-management* process, where a construction management firm is contracted to assist the architect during the preliminary and design phases and to oversee the construction phase. Compensation for these services is generally on a cost-plus basis. They are reimbursed for agreed upon costs plus a fee.

CONSTRUCTION PHASE

Mobilization of the contractor's work force proceeds by moving onto the site, ordering materials and equipment, hiring, and awarding subcontracts. Building layout proceeds with the employment of a surveyor or civil engineer, and sitework commences, followed by the substructure of foundations and basements. The coordination of the project is handled by the general contractor's project manager. Success in this area requires a manager who can orchestrate several subcontractors and his or her own forces simultaneously with the least lost effort.

The architect usually has the responsibility to inspect the project at appropriate times, such as the placing of the foundation, while framing is erected, during installation of finishes, and at the close of the contact.

Supervenient inspections are frequently made.

Engineers seldom inspect unless called in for a special problem. City, state, county, and federal inspectors may conduct on site inspections if the project is in their jurisdiction.

1.2 Codes and Standards

The purpose of **building codes** is to regulate the design and construction of buildings in a manner that safeguards the general public.

Building codes usually include types of construction, function of the structure called *occupancy,* quality of materials, the imposed loads, allowable stresses, mechanical and electrical equipment, and other requirements related to buildings with special emphasis on fire safety.

Basically, the codes issued by various agencies are quite similar. There are, however, significant differences; therefore, the code adopted by a given municipality must be satisfied by buildings constructed within its jurisdiction. The requirements of various codes may be included in this text for instructional purposes, but for a specific application the governing code should be consulted.

MODEL BUILDING CODES

Most municipalities have building codes. Jurisdictions that do not originate their own building codes often adopt, by reference, all or parts of certain established model codes.

Today there is a tendency in model codes toward the **performance code.** This type of code requires a specified result. The advantage of this approach, as opposed to the rigid specification type code, is that newer materials and methods of construction may be permitted.

Many states have established building codes which may control all building construction within the state; however, individual communities may adopt their own codes. An example is the State Building Construction Code adopted by the State of New York. As stated therein: ''The municipalities of the state have the option to accept or not to accept the applicability'' of this code.

Several regional agencies have formulated *model building codes.* These have been prepared to assist municipalities in preparing codes, or a municipality may adopt such a code, by reference, if authorized by the statutes of the governing state. The following are examples of model codes.

The International Conference of Building Officials, Whittier, California, publishes the *Uniform Building Code.* This model code has been widely adopted by various communities — over 2,000 municipalities in 44 states. This code, known as the *UBC,* is kept current by constant review, with a new edition published every three years. Additionally, this organization publishes a volume of building standards that defines various building tests, a fire code, fire code standard, and material qualities.

The Basic Building Code is published by Building Officials and Code Administrators International, Chicago, Illinois. This model code, a performance code, is continually updated by annual supplements and revisions, as required. BOCA publishes several other model codes such as *The Basic Fire Prevention Code* and *The Basic Housing Code.*

The Standard Building Code is published by the Southern Building Code Congress, Birmingham Alabama.

The National Building Code is recommended by the American Insurance Association, successor to the National Board of Fire Underwriters. This code contains appendices covering hurricanes and earthquakes. The American Insurance Association also recommends the *Fire Prevention Code* as a companion document.

OTHER CODES AND STANDARDS

There are a number of organizations that advance the knowledge of materials and methods of construction and promote codes and standards. Some of these organizations are concerned with several materials, while others are involved with only one material and its applications. These organizations produce literature that is of interest to a technical audience — architects, engineers, students, and inspectors. A partial description of the activities and contributions of some of these organizations follows.

Among authoritative organizations is the American Society for Testing and Materials of Philadelphia. The work of this society includes the development of standards, test procedures, criteria, and specifications and definitions for a vast number of materials. ASTM standards cover most building materials, including soils and rock. ASTM standards are frequently cited in building specifications as the basis upon which quality decisions will be judged. Their standards are reviewed (if necessary, revised) and published annually.

The Construction Specifications Institute (CSI), Washington, D.C., promotes the standardized specifications that cover the field of building construction. Their format for construction specifications and materials classifications has been widely adopted in the industry. Its literature covers not only specifications but includes commentary on the uses of materials.

The American Concrete Institute (ACI) of Detroit, Michigan, is an organization that disseminates information for the improvement of design, construction, manufacture, use, and maintenance of concrete products and structures. Its interests encompass all aspects of concrete production. The ACI *Building Code Requirements for Reinforced Concrete* (ACI 318), which is revised annually, serves as a building industry standard.

The American Institute of Steel Construction, Chicago, advances the use of fabricated steel framed structures. It performs research and development and serves to further the use of steel by technical publications, seminars, awards, scholarships, and the promotion of quality and safety in shop and field. Its *Manual of Steel Construction* is used as the industry standard for the design of structural steel. Also, the *AISC Specification for the Design, Fabrication and Erection of Structural Steel for Buildings* is usually referenced by engineers in building specifications and is adopted by reference in building codes.

The American Iron and Steel Institute, New York, has established standards and produces technical information on steel and the industry. This includes information on uses, processes, and standard designations.

The Copper Development Association, Inc., New York, provides technical information regarding copper, bronze, and brass for building use.

The Aluminum Association, New York, provides standards and technical information that covers structural, mechanical, physical properties, uses, specifications, coatings, finishes, and building products of aluminum.

The National Fire Protection Association, Boston, Massachusetts, publishes the *Fire Protection Handbook,* which gives not only essential information on fire prevention and protection but details the reasons and with background information. Additionally, NFPA publishes the standards known as the *National Fire Codes* in seven volumes averaging 900 pages each. Most of these standards are published separately in pamphlets. Other publications of NFPA include an inspection manual and books covering particular occupancies.

The Asphalt Institute provides engineering, research, and educational programs for the asphalt industry and its users. The Institute produces extensive literature and audiovisual aids on the uses of asphalt in the building industry. Research engineers of the Institute are engaged in a number of programs such as thickness design of asphalt pavements, testing, and developing of paving mixes, soil beneficiation and stabilization, aggregate studies, airfield pavements, linings for hydraulic structures, and energy conservation.

Several regional lumber associations encourage regeneration of the forests, establish standards and sizes for lumber, and supply technical data to specifiers, builders, and users.

Among these associations are:

▶ The Western Wood Products Association, Portland, Oregon, is the largest of these associations. It is an association of softwood lumber manufacturers of 12 western states grading pines, firs, spruces, and cedars.

▶ West Coast Lumber Inspection Bureau, Portland, Oregon, grades and inspects Douglas fir, hemlock, cedar, and other softwood lumber of California and the regions of Washington and Oregon west of the Cascade Summit.

▶ Redwood Inspection Service, San Francisco, California, grades and inspects products of *Sequoia sempervirens*.

▶ Southern Pine Inspection Bureau, Pensacola, Florida, covers longleaf pine, slash pine, shortleaf pine, and loblolly pine produced in the southeastern states from Maryland to Texas.

▶ Northeastern Lumber Manufacturers Association, Inc., Glens Falls, New York, grades northern and eastern pines, cedars, spruces, balsam fir, and other softwoods of New England, New York, New Jersey, and Pennsylvania.

▶ National Hardwood Lumber Association, Chicago, Illinois, performs services for the hardwood products industry parallel to those performed by the softwood associations. Among the myriad hardwoods that are its concern are walnut, maple, oak, birch, ash, hickory, and cypress, a softwood.

▶ The American Institute of Timber Construction (AITC), of

Englewood, Colorado, tests and disseminates information on the structural aspects of timber construction, including laminated timber.

▶ The American Plywood Association of Tacoma, Washington, produces literature on plywood. This includes, but is not limited to, testing, grades, systems, specifications, physical qualities, and the structural and finished uses of plywood.

Various agencies of the United States government, especially the Bureau of Standards, Washington, D.C., and the Forest Products Laboratory, Madison, Wisconsin, resemble the above associations.

Much information can be obtained, often at little or no cost, by writing these agencies. Publications by agencies of the federal government are obtained by writing the U.S. Government Printing Office, Washington, D.C.

FIRE-RESISTANCE RATINGS

Building codes commonly classify buildings according to the Fire Zone in which the building is located, location on property, type of construction, and according to use or occupancy. The most important factor in the classification according to the type of construction is the resistance to fire exposure. In classifying buildings according to fire endurance, it is necessary to measure the performance of the various structural parts of a building under exposure conditions. It is necessary that the fire-resistive properties of materials and members be measured and specified according to a common standard expressed in terms which are applicable to a wide variety of materials, situations, and conditions of exposure.

The "*Standard Fire Test,*" known also as the fire endurance test, accomplishes these objectives. This test is designated by the Underwriters' Laboratories as UL 263 and by the American Society for Testing and Materials as ASTM E119. It consists of exposing samples of the material, a building member, or an assembly to a fire of specified intensity and duration. In some cases, a 2½ in. fire hose stream is applied to a heated sample from a distance of 20 ft. Performance is defined as the period of resistance to standard exposure elapsing before the first critical point in behavior is observed, and it is expressed in hours. For example, a material is given a 2-hour rating if it withstands the test for a period of 2 hours.

Most of the common building materials and assemblies of materials have been tested, rated, and the results published by the Underwriters Laboratory. For this reason, it is not usual to make fire tests in connection with the design of individual buildings.

Fire endurance tests on a bearing wall assembly are required for a specified time in hours. Bearing walls are required to support their loads without penetration by flame or gases sufficient to ignite cotton wastes. The hose stream test (for assemblies that are to be rated for 1 hour or more) is conducted on the loaded assembly in a heated condition. The assembly, in a cooled state, must also support specified loads. In no event may heat that penetrates through the wall assembly produce a temperature rise of more than 250°F on the unexposed surface.

The fire endurance tests for nonbearing walls are similar to those conducted on bearing walls. Naturally, the nonbearing wall assembly is not required to carry imposed loads during the fire endurance test.

Floor and roof assemblies carry imposed loads during the fire endurance test. Acceptance as a fire rated assembly requires that the fire and temperature transmission requirements be similar to the forementioned bearing wall assembly. The hose test is not required.

The fire protective material that surrounds beams and columns may also be tested for endurance. The protective assembly must limit the rise in temperature in the steel member to not more than a specified amount.

Another fire test is the Test Method for Fire Hazard Classification of Building Materials, which is known as the Underwriters' Laboratories UL 723. This tests the flame spread ability of a material. The test determines "the comparative burning characteristics of the material under test by evaluating the flame spread over its surface, fuel contributed by its combustion, and the density of the smoke developed when exposed to a test fire." The flame spread classification (FSC) of a material is graded on a scale from 0 to 100. As a basis, the classification of 0 is assigned to asbestos cement board and a classification of 100 is designated to select grade red oak flooring.

Flame spread ratings are usually specified for materials which are interior surface finishes, such as plastics, plywood, acoustic materials, and wall coverings.

FIRE LIMITS, ZONES, OR DISTRICTS

The New York State Code includes the following definition: "*Fire limits.* Boundary line establishing an area in which there exists, or is likely to exist, a fire hazard requiring special fire protection."

Two classes of fire limits are included in this code.

Fire limits A comprising the areas containing highly congested business, commercial and, or industrial occupancies, wherein the fire hazard is severe; and or, Fire limits B comprising the areas containing residential, business and, or commercial occupancies or in which such uses are developing, wherein the fire hazard is moderate.

All of those areas not included in fire limits A or B are designated herein as outside the fire limits.

The areas within fire limits are often called fire zones or fire districts.

BUILDING CLASSIFICATION

Building code requirements are based primarily on building occupancy or use, type of construction, and location.

Classification According to Occupancy

The classification of buildings according to occupancy, as included in the National Building Code, is as follows.

Assembly occupancy means the occupancy or use of a building or structure or any portion thereof by a gathering of persons for civic, political, travel, religious, social, or recreational purposes.

Business occupancy means the occupancy or use of a building or structure or any portion thereof for the transaction of business, or the rendering or receiving of professional services.

Educational occupancy means the occupancy or use of a building or structure or any portion thereof by persons assembled for the purpose of learning or of receiving educational instruction.

High hazard occupancy means the occupancy or use of a building or structure or any portion thereof that involves highly combustible, highly flammable, or explosive material, or which has inherent characteristics that constitute a special fire hazard.

Industrial occupancy means the occupancy or use of a building or structure or any portion thereof for assembling, fabricating, finishing, manufacturing, packaging, or processing operations.

Institutional occupancy means the occupancy or use of a building or structure or any portion thereof by persons harbored or detained to receive medical, charitable, or other care or treatment, or by persons involuntarily detained.

Mercantile occupancy means the occupancy or use of a building or structure or any portion thereof for the display, selling or buying of goods, wares, or merchandise; except when classed as a high hazard occupancy.

Residential occupancy means the occupancy or use of a building or structure or any portion thereof by persons for whom sleeping accommodations are provided but who are not harbored or detained to receive medical, charitable, or other care or treatment, or are not involuntarily detained.

Storage occupancy means the occupancy or use of a building or structure or any portion thereof for the storage of goods, wares, merchandise, raw materials, agricultural or manufactured products, including parking garages, or the sheltering of livestock and other animals, except when classed as a high hazard.

Classification According to Type of Construction

Buildings are classified in building codes according to types of construction based on the *fire resistance* of their structural members or assemblies. Codes vary in the details of such classifications, but the objectives sought are similar. The *New York State Building Construction Code* will serve as an example.

According to this code, if the temperature required to ignite and support combustion of a material, or combination of materials, is below 1382°F., the material is designated as combustible, and if a higher temperature is required, it is designated as noncombustible.

The principal combustible materials used in buildings are wood, organic fiber boards, and plastics. The principal noncombustible materials are steel, aluminum, concrete, and masonry materials such as brick, stone, and structural clay tile, as well as plaster and glass.

According to the New York State Code, buildings are classified into five types as follows.

Type 1. Fire-Resistive Construction. That type of construction in which the walls, partitions, columns, floors, and roof are noncombustible with sufficient fire resistance to withstand the effects of a fire and prevent its spread from story to story.

Type 2. Noncombustible Construction. That type of construction in which walls, partitions, columns, floors, and roof are noncombustible and have less fire resistance than required for fire-resistive construction.

Type 3. Heavy Timber Construction. That type of construction in which the exterior walls are of masonry or other noncombustible materials having an equivalent structural stability under fire conditions and a fire resistance rating of not less than 2 hours; in which interior structural members including columns, beams, and girders are timber, in heavy solid or laminated masses, but with no sharp corners or projections or concealed or inaccessible spaces; in which floors and roofs are of heavy plank or laminated wood construction, or any other material providing equivalent fire-resistance and structural properties. Noncombustible structural members may be used in lieu of heavy timber, provided the fire resistance rating of such members is not less than ¾ hour.

Type 4. Ordinary Construction. That type of construction in which the exterior walls are of masonry or other noncombustible materials having equivalent structural stability under fire conditions and a fire resistance rating of not less than 2 hours, the interior structural members being wholly or partly of wood of smaller dimensions than those required for Heavy Timber Construction.

Type 5. Wood Frame Construction. That type of construction in which walls, partitions, floors, and roof are wholly or partly of wood or other combustible material.

Each of the five types of construction which have been described, except Type 3, is divided into two subtypes which vary according to the degree of fire resistance required. The requirements for subtypes *a* are more severe than those for subtypes *b*.

The fire-resistance ratings required for the various types and subtypes are shown in Table 1.1.

From Table 1.1, it will be noted that the highest required fire rating is 4 hours. This rating is required in the higher type of fire-resistive construction for exterior bearing walls, for party walls, and for interior firewalls, bearing walls, and partitions. It is also required for columns, beams, girders, and trusses supporting more than one floor. These are the most important structural elements in a building. It is also required for the party walls and fire walls of heavy timber construction.

The lowest fire rating required is ¾ hour. It is required for panel and curtain walls in fire-resistive construction and in the higher type of noncombustible construction, and interior partitions and nonbearing walls for all types of construction except fire-resistive. It is also required for bearing walls and nonbearing walls for the higher type of wood frame construction and for various other members in ordinary and wood frame construction. Noncombustible construction without a fire rating is required for various members in the lower type of noncombustible construction. Combustible construction is permitted in some parts of heavy timber construction and in several parts of ordinary and wood frame construction.

The highest type of construction, designated as fire-resistive in Table 1.1, is often designated as fireproof. However, it is not feasible to construct a building which is really fireproof, and therefore that term is being replaced in building codes by the term fire-resistive. The term mill construction, which often is used instead of heavy timber construction, had its origin in New England where construction using heavy timber was developed many years ago to decrease the fire hazard in textile mills. This type of construction is also called slow-burning construction for obvious reasons. These terms are occasionally used in building codes. The types of construction known as heavy timber construction, ordinary construction, and frame construction are used in nearly all codes. A classification not given here but often found in codes includes buildings with unprotected steel structural members. It is considered to have a fire resistance lower than ordinary construction because the strength of steel decreases at high temperatures. Such a classification is designated as unprotected metal, metal frame, or light incombustible frame.

Classification According to Fire Hazard

All codes recognize the differences in fire hazard as determined by the kind of occupancy within each general occupancy class. For example, the New York State Building Construction Code includes the following classifications according to fire hazard.

Low hazard. Business buildings.

Moderate hazard. Mercantile buildings. Industrial and storage buildings in which combustible contents might cause fires of moderate intensity as defined in the code.

High hazard. Industrial and storage buildings in which the combustible contents might cause fires to be unusually intense, as defined in the code, or where explosives, combustible gases, or flammable liquids are manufactured or stored.

Other Regulations

Codes include requirements such as those for exits, stairways, elevator shafts, corridors, roofs, protection of openings in exterior walls, interior finish, flooring materials, doors and doorways, and building contents.

Many references are made in this book to code requirements for various parts of buildings. The code requirements for the loads carried by buildings are considered in Section 1.3. Codes include allowable working stresses for the many materials included in a building. They are of great importance in structural design but do not fall within the scope of this book. The allowable bearing pressures for foundations, illustrated by Table 2.5, are included in codes.

Codes also include requirements for ventilation, sanitary features, electric wiring, and mechanical equipment, which are not covered in this book.

1.3 Building Loads

The loads to which buildings are subjected may be divided into four classes: dead loads, live loads, lateral loads, and other loads.

Dead loads include weights of all parts of the building such as walls, structural frame, permanent partitions, floors, roofs, stairways, and fixed equipment.

Live loads include the weights of the occupants, furniture, movable equipment, stored material, and snow that may accumulate on the roof.

Lateral loads include distributed horizontal loads which act above the ground level and are assumed to have effects equivalent to those produced by wind pressures. For some regions they include lateral loads which are assumed to have effects corresponding to those produced by earthquake shocks. Also included are horizontal loads on foundation walls caused by earth pressure and water pressure.

DEAD LOADS

The magnitudes of dead loads to be used in design are determined by the weights of the building materials, the assemblies of materials, and the fixed equipment which are used in the construction of buildings.

Table 1.1 Miminum Fire-Resistance Requirements of Structural Elements (By types of construction; fire-resistance ratings in hours)

Structural Element	Type 1 (fire resistive)		Type 2 (non-combustible)		Type 3 (heavy timber)	Type 4 (ordinary)		Type 5 (wood frame)	
	1a	1b	2a	2b		4a	4b	5a	5b
Exterior									
Bearing walls	4	3	2	nc	2	2	2	¾	c
Nonbearing walls	2	2	2	nc	2	2	2	¾	c
Panel and curtain walls	¾	¾	¾	nc					
Party walls	4	3	2	2	4	2	2	2	2
Interior									
Fire walls	4	3	2	2	4	2	2	2	2
Bearing walls or partitions	4	3	2	nc	2	¾	c	¾	c
Partitions enclosing stairways, hoistways, shafts, other vertical openings, and hallways									
On outside exposure	2	2	2	2	2	2	2	¾	¾
On inside exposure	1	1	¾	¾	¾	¾	¾	¾	¾
Nonbearing walls and partitions separating spaces	1	1	¾	¾	¾	¾	¾	¾	¾
Columns, beams, girders, and trusses (other than roof trusses)									
Supporting more than one floor	4	3	2	nc	c	¾	c	¾	c
Supporting one floor	3	2	¾	nc	c	¾	c	¾	c
Floor construction, including beams	3	2	1	nc	c	¾	c	¾	c
Roof construction, including purlins, beams, and roof trusses	2	1	¾	nc	c	¾	c	¾	c

Key: nc = noncombustible, c = combustible.

The code includes special requirements and exceptions that are not included in this table.

Example: This may vary with different codes.

LIVE LOADS

The magnitudes of the live loads on floors are determined by the types of occupancy of the various units into which a building is divided. There is a marked uniformity in building code requirements for the minimum live loads for which the floors of buildings are to be designed. These loads refer to normal conditions. Any special conditions to which a floor may be subjected must be considered. The floor loads recommended by the Uniform Building Code are given in Table 1.2. Note that the floor load for offices included in this table is 50 lb per sq ft. Some codes require 80 lb per sq ft for this occupancy. An additional load of 20 lb per sq ft is often included for masonry partitions not included in the initial plans, if there is a possibility that such partitions may be installed at a later date. Many codes provide for a concentrated load on any 2½-ft sq area if such a load on this otherwise unloaded area produces stresses greater than the required uniform load. Other special provisions for live loads are included in various codes.

Codes include requirements for minimum live roof loads. The simplest requirement is a load of 20 lb per sq ft of horizontal projection in addition to the wind load regardless of the slope of the roof. In most parts of the United States, provision must be made for a snow load. It may cause a greater load than the required minimum. Of course, the possible snow load varies widely throughout the country. According to the New York State Code, the required snow load on a flat roof varies from 20 to 60 lb per sq ft according to the building's location on a snow map included in the code.

Another factor in the snow load is the slope of the roof. In the New York State Code, no load is required for slopes of 60 degrees or more with the horizontal. The required load varies for roof slopes between 0 and 60 degrees in a specified manner which is somewhat higher than would be given by a linear variation.

If a roof is also to be used as a floor, it must be designed for the live load it is to carry but for not less than the minimum live load required for floors, the magnitude depending upon the type of use of the roof.

WIND PRESSURES

The wind pressures, or wind loads, on buildings vary with the geographical location and, for a given location, with the height above the ground surface. Winds are assumed to act in any horizontal direction in spite of the direction of prevailing winds. There are positive pressures on the windward

Table 1.2 **Uniform and Concentrated Loads**

Use or Occupancy		Uniform Load[a]	Concentrated Load
Category	Description		
Armories		105	0
Assembly areas[d]/and auditoriums and balconies therewith	Fixed seating areas	50	0
	Moveable seating and other areas	100	0
	Stage areas and enclosed platforms	125	0
Cornices, marquees, and residential balconies		60	0
Exit facilities, public[e]		100	0
Garages	General storage and/or repair	100	c
	Private pleasure car storage	50	c
Hospitals	Wards and rooms	40	1000[b]
Libraries	Reading rooms	60	1000[b]
	Stack rooms	125	1500[b]
Manufacturing	Light	75	2000[b]
	Heavy	125	3000[b]
Offices		50	2000[b]
Printing plants	Press rooms	150	2500[b]
	Composing and linotype rooms	100	2000[b]
Residential[f]		40	0
Restrooms[g]			
Reviewing stands, grand stands, and bleachers		100	0
Schools	Classrooms	40	1000[b]
Sidewalks and driveways	Public access	250	c
Storage	Light	125	
	Heavy	250	
Stores	Retail	75	2000[b]
	Wholesale	100	3000[b]

[a] See Section 2306 for live load reductions.

[b] See Section 2304(c), first paragraph, for area of load application.

[c] See Section 2304(c), second paragraph, for concentrated loads.

[d] Assembly areas include such occupancies as dance halls, drill rooms, gymnasiums, playgrounds, plazas, terraces and similar occupancies which are generally accessible to the public.

[e] Exit facilities include such uses as corridors and exterior exit balconies, stairways, fire escapes and similar uses.

[f] Residential occupancies include private dwellings, apartments, and hotel guest rooms.

[g] Rest room loads shall be not less than the load for the occupancy with which they are associated but need not exceed 50 pounds per square foot.

Reproduced from the 1979 edition of the *Uniform Building Code,* copyright 1979, with permission of the publisher, the International Conference of Building Officials.

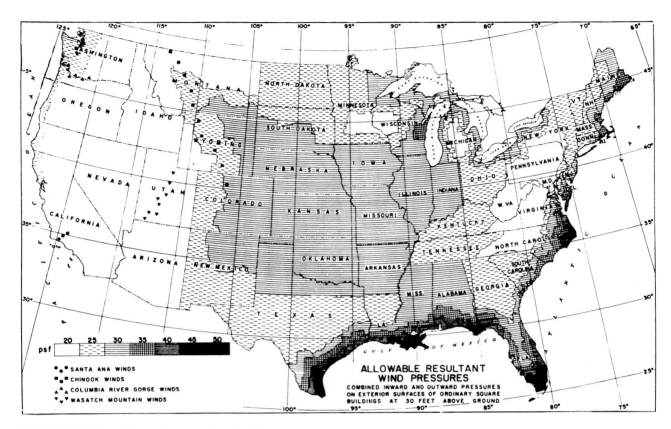

FIGURE 1.1 Allowable resultant wind pressures.

side of a building and negative pressures, or partial vacuums, on the leeward side. Design pressures are based on the total resultant pressure, which is equal to the sum of these pressures.

Extensive studies of wind pressures by the National Bureau of Standards form the basis for the Building Code Requirements of the American Standards Association. The comments in this article are based on these studies.

The recommended design pressures are computed from measured velocities of gust winds, and the rectangular shape of exposed building surfaces and many other factors that affect wind pressures are taken into consideration.

The minimum allowable resultant wind pressures for various parts of this country at a height 30 ft above the ground surface are shown on the map in Figure 1.1.

The design wind pressures for various height zones above the ground surface and various minimum wind pressures for the height of 30 ft above this surface are given in Table 1.3. For example, if the pressure at the height of 30 ft as given on the map in Figure 1.1 is 30 lb per sq ft, the design wind pressure at a height of 100 ft is 45 lb per sq ft as shown in the table.

As stated in the studies above:

The wind pressures and suctions in the immediate path of tornadoes are considered to be so great that construction strong enough to withstand them is not economically feasible. Therefore, in recommending design wind pressures, building codes do not take into consideration the violent forces that can be expected within the narrow path of a tornado.

Experience has shown, however, that buildings designed for wind pressures even less than those recommended have not collapsed but have survived without irreparable structural damage and relatively few, if any, casualties.

Wind pressures tend to overturn buildings as a whole and parts of buildings above any elevation. To avoid this, codes require that the resistance of the dead load of a building to overturning above any elevation be one and a half times the overturning effect of wind, both factors being measured by their moments about the leeward edges. For the condition

Table 1.3 Design Wind Pressures for Various Height Zones

Height Zone Above Ground Level, ft	Wind Pressures Map Areas, lb per sq ft						
	20	25	30	35	40	45	50
	Design Wind Pressure, lb per sq ft						
Less than 30	15	20	25	25	30	35	40
30 to 49	20	25	30	35	40	45	50
50 to 99	25	30	40	45	50	55	60
100 to 499	30	40	45	55	60	70	75
500 to 1199	35	45	55	60	70	80	90
1200 and over	40	50	60	70	80	90	100

which includes the effects of wind loads in the computed stresses in the resisting members, codes permit the allowable stresses to be increased one-third. However, the allowable stresses must not be exceeded for the condition that does not include wind load.

Building codes include factors for adjusting horizontal wind loads to sloping roofs and for the uplift pressures on roofs caused by wind loads.

EARTH AND WATER PRESSURES

A portion of a foundation wall may be below the ground surface (Figure 1.2A). For this condition, the lateral earth pressures may be assumed to equal one-half of the corresponding water pressures.

If there is a uniform vertical pressure of p_v lb per sq ft on the ground surface, the unit lateral pressure p_s acting on the height h may be assumed to equal one-third of p_v.

If the groundwater level is above the bottom of the wall (B), the additional pressures caused by the water may be assumed to equal four-fifths of the water pressures which would act on the submerged portion of the wall if no soil were present.

The reduction of one-fifth in the water pressure is assumed to offset the reduction in earth pressure on the submerged portion of the wall owing to the buoyant effect of the water on the submerged soil.

Foundation walls retaining expansive clay soils may be subjected to very large earth pressures because of their increase in volume as their moisture content increases, even if they are entirely above the groundwater level. If these are thin walls supporting low buildings, they may fail under the action of such pressures. It may not be feasible to construct a wall thick enough to resist these pressures. Under these conditions, a wall should be backfilled with a nonexpansive soil for a considerable distance from the wall.

Earth pressures against free-standing walls require special consideration.

If the groundwater level is above the bottom of a basement floor and the ground water is in contact with this

surface, the floor must be designed to resist an uplift pressure equal to the water pressure to which it is subjected. This is equal, in pounds per square foot, to 62.4 times the vertical distance, in feet, between the groundwater level and the bottom of the floor.

SEISMIC FORCES

Few portions of the United States have not witnessed at least minor earthquakes in recorded history, the most severe earthquake damage occurring in Alaska and California. The fact that seismic activity has not been evident in an area does not preclude the possibility of future destructive earthquakes, although the probability may be minimal. The procedures and investment necessary to design and build conforming structures that meet earthquake resistant criteria is little compared to the reassurances gained. Perhaps a thoughtful passage from the Brick Institute of America publication, *Reinforced Brick Masonry and Lateral Force Design* will clarify:

All buildings, whether so designed or not, have some inherent resistance to lateral forces. This has been shown by the survival of some buildings of little or no designed resistance to severe earthquakes, tornadoes, and bombing attacks. The fact of such a survival does not guarantee future survivals, no more than does a soldier coming from a battle unwounded guarantee him to be bullet-proof.

The probability of earthquakes of a destructive severity is determined from geological and historical data. The susceptibility to earthquakes of areas in the United States is indicated in Figures 1.3, 1.4, and 1.5.

Earthquake loads, which are also called seismic loads, are treated as lateral loads that involve the entire structure. The seismic load is applicable to all parts of the structure, whereas other lateral loads (wind loads) are applicable to only portions of the structure. It is for this reason that earthquake resistant structures must be designed with connections capable of resisting seismic forces. For example, beams and columns per se seldom fail as a result of seismic stress, although the connections to them are more likely to fail. Thus, seismic forces require careful design and analysis of the entire structure, especially its connections. Seismic forces, often thought of as a lateral force, are unpredictable in their application; they may actually be a vertical acting force in severe earthquakes.

Listed below are several definitions of building components relating to earthquake resistant construction. These definitions, from the National Building Code, are similar to terms found in most building codes that have earthquake resistant provisions.

Space frame means a three-dimensional structural system composed of interconnected members, other than shear or bearing walls, laterally supported so as to function as a

FIGURE 1.2 Lateral pressures due to earth.

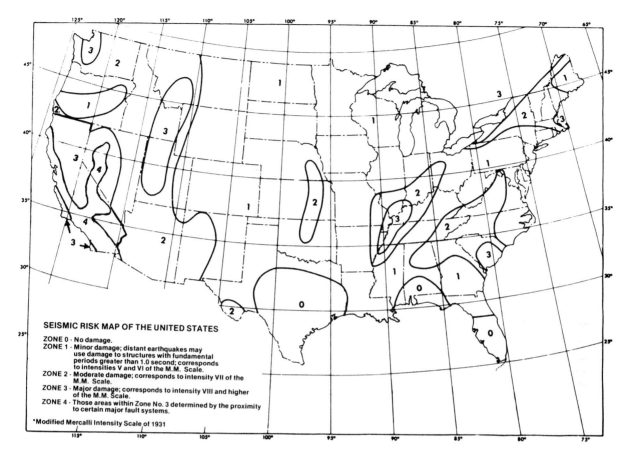

SEISMIC RISK MAP OF THE UNITED STATES

ZONE 0 - No damage.
ZONE 1 - Minor damage; distant earthquakes may use damage to structures with fundamental periods greater than 1.0 second; corresponds to intensities V and VI of the M.M. Scale.
ZONE 2 - Moderate damage; corresponds to intensity VII of the M.M. Scale.
ZONE 3 - Major damage; corresponds to intensity VIII and higher of the M.M. Scale.
ZONE 4 - Those areas within Zone No. 3 determined by the proximity to certain major fault systems.

*Modified Mercalli Intensity Scale of 1931

FIGURE 1.3 Seismic risk map of the United States. Reproduced from the 1979 edition of the *Uniform Building Code,* copyright 1979 with permission of the publisher, the International Conference of Building Officials.

FIGURE 1.4 Seismic zone map — Alaska. Reproduced from the 1979 edition of the *Uniform Building Code,* copyright 1979 with permission of the publisher, the International Conference of Building Officials.

FIGURE 1.5 Seismic zone map — Hawaii. Reproduced from the 1979 edition of the *Uniform Building Code,* copyright 1979 with permission of the publisher, the International Conference of Building Officials.

complete self-contained unit with or without the aid of horizontal diaphragms or floor bracing systems.

Space frame — vertical load-carrying means a space frame designed to carry all vertical loads.

Space frame-moment resisting means a vertical load-carrying space frame in which the members and joints are capable of resisting design lateral forces by bending moments. Such moment resisting space frames may be enclosed by or adjoined by more rigid elements which would tend to prevent the space frame from resisting lateral forces, where it can be shown that the action or failure of the more rigid element will not impair the vertical or lateral load-resisting ability of the space frame.

Space frame-ducile moment resisting means a moment resisting space frame with the necessary ductility provided by a frame of structural steel conforming to ASTM A7, A36, A441 with moment-resisting connections or by a reinforced concrete frame. The provisions for more rigid elements used in combination with moment resisting space frames also apply to ductile moment resisting space frames.

Box system means a structural system without a complete vertical load-carrying space frame. In this system, the required lateral forces are resisted by shear walls as hereinafter defined.

Shear wall means a wall designed to resist lateral forces parallel to the wall. Braced frames subjected primarily to axial stresses shall be considered as shear walls for the purpose of this definition.

Examples of code requirements to resist earthquake shocks are included in the following:

▶ The *National Building Code* of the American Insurance Association.

▶ The *Uniform Building Code* of the International Conference of Building Officials, of which the Pacific Coast Building Officials Conference is a subsidiary.

Structural engineers well versed in earthquake-resistant design should be consulted on the design of major buildings to be constructed in regions subject to severe earthquake shocks.

1.4 Building Elements

The structural elements of buildings may be composed of various combinations and forms of foundations, walls, columns, beams, girders, trusses, arches, rigid frames, cables, and domes.

Walls are constructed of all the traditional construction materials, that is, masonry, wood, and concrete. Additionally, walls are made of manufactured materials in various combinations.

Columns and beams are constructed of wood, steel, masonry, or reinforced concrete; however, stone columns are used for ornamental purposes.

Trusses are usually constructed of steel, although wood is used extensively and reinforced concrete occasionally. Reinforced concrete is not considered an appropriate material for truss construction, although there are examples of its successful use.

Rigid frames, which are a form of arch, are constructed of wood, reinforced concrete, and steel. Arches, vaults, and domes of long span are frequently constructed of wood, steel, reinforced concrete, and occasionally of aluminum. Masonry arches are constructed of brick or stone. Steel twisted-wire strand cables are sometimes used to support long-span roofs and cantilever projections of roofs.

The assembling of the various structural elements so that each may perform its function is known as **framing**. One classification of buildings is on the basis of the function of the walls. If the walls support the dead, live, and other loads (in addition to keeping out the weather), the building is classed as wall-bearing construction; but if the loads, including the weight of the walls, are carried by the structural frame of columns, beams, and girders, the building is classed as skeleton construction. This term is usually applied to office and similar structures but not to industrial buildings.

The classification of buildings according to type of construction, as included in building codes, should be reviewed, for example, frame, heavy timber, ordinary, etc.

Steel construction consisting of steel beams, girders, columns, and trusses supporting floors and roofs of light joist construction, of heavy timber construction, or of fire-resistive construction is extensively used on all classes of buildings except dwellings. The exterior walls may be bearing walls for the lower buildings, but for buildings of more than three or four stories, skeleton construction is usually used. In more expensive buildings, fire-resistive construction is used throughout. For buildings up to about 60 stories high, steel and reinforced concrete are competitive; but for higher buildings, steel construction is without rival because faster erection is possible. Sometimes the structural frame and floor slabs have been constructed at the rate of a story a day.

Reinforced concrete construction may be used for nearly all classes of buildings. Private dwellings are rarely of this type, although apartment houses, hotels, office buildings, schools, warehouses, and industrial buildings are often built of reinforced concrete. In buildings with a steel framework, the floors and roofs are usually of reinforced concrete. For tall buildings, steel construction has the advantage of smaller columns for the lower floors. Even for the lower buildings, skeleton construction may be used because of faster erection time. When bearing walls are used, each floor must await the bearing wall to carry it; but with skeleton construction, the structural frame and floors may be constructed rapidly.

The part of a building below the ground surface is called the foundation or substructure, and the portion above ground is called the superstructure. Herein, the part of a building bearing directly on the supporting soil or rock is called the foundation, whereas the supporting rock or soil is referred to as the foundation material. The function of the foundation is to transmit and distribute the building loads and other imposed loads to the foundation material. Walls below the ground surface resting on the foundations are foundation walls.

Codes use various terms to describe foundation design. The *bearing pressure* is the pressure intensity between the foundation bottom and the foundation bed. The allowable bearing pressure is the recommended design bearing pressure that will safely ensure against excessive settlement or rupture of the foundation material. If the foundation material is soil, allowable bearing pressures are called allowable soil pressures. *Bearing capacity* is a general term referring to the ability of a foundation material to support loads safely. The ultimate bearing capacity is the maximum bearing pressure that a foundation material can sustain without rupture.

The difference between the ultimate bearing capacity and the allowable bearing pressure is a safety factor. These values are usually expressed in pounds per square foot. The ultimate bearing capacity divided by the allowable bearing capacity yields the *factor of safety*. This is a number usually from 2 to 3.

FOUNDATION MATERIALS

Foundations may be supported on soil or bedrock, consisting of bedding planes exposed on the surface or underlying several hundred feet. Bedding planes may be horizontal, as originally formed, or inclined. Marked variations of rock classes and properties may occur within short distances or at different depths. Soils are also subject to wide variations in general type and in physical properties. A soil with a high bearing capacity may be underlaid by a soil with low bearing capacity. Layers of peat (or other highly compressive soil) may cause excessive settlement if not discovered and conditioned. Clay soils may cause extensive heaving due to swelling and contraction if exposed to alternate wetting and drying cycles. When possible, expansible clays should be avoided as foundation materials.

SUBSURFACE EXPLORATION

Because of uncertainties in underground conditions, adequate subsurface explorations should be made before the foundations are designed or the site purchased. Methods for making proper subsurface explorations are described in Chapter 2.

FOUNDATION TYPES

Building loads and other imposed loads are transmitted to the earth in the following ways:

1. By *spread foundations* bearing over a sufficient area preventing undue settlement or rupture. Foundations of this type consist of individual footings under walls or columns, as shown in Figure 1.6, or a single, heavy reinforced concrete slab called a mat or raft, which may cover the entire foundation area and support all building loads. Foundations of the latter type are often called floating foundations, although this term is commonly applied to all types of spread foundations.

2. By *pile foundations,* which are slender vertical members of timber, concrete, steel, or a combination of these materials. The load is distributed into the soil by friction piles or transmitted directly to hardpan or rock by end bearing piles. Pile foundations require not less than three piles to a footing to ensure stability. Groups of piles are called clusters and are joined at their tops by a cap that is designed to distribute the imposed loads to the piles. Batter piles are driven at a slope. (See Figure 1.7.)

FIGURE 1.6 Reinforced concrete column footing.

FIGURE 1.7 Pile foundations.

FIGURE 1.8 Pier foundations.

3. By *pier foundations* in which concrete piers pass through soil of low bearing capacity until a satisfactory foundation bed is reached. This may be a firm soil or hardpan, requiring the pier to be belled out at the base to increase the bearing area. Piers resting on rock seldom require belled out bases. If soil characteristics preclude belling out, or if dimensions of the superstructure determine the dimensions of a pier, piers may be hollow. Hollow piers are frequently used for bridge piers but rarely for buildings. (See Figure 1.8.)

MINIMUM DEPTHS

The foundation depths depend upon the building space requirements, the adjacent foundation depths, the imposed loads, the foundation material characteristics, and the climatic conditions. Except where bearing on solid rock, foundations exposed to freezing temperatures must be placed below *frost line* to prevent heaving. A minimum depth of 1½ ft below the frost line is recommended. The frost line is the maximum depth that the ground freezes — varying with the locality. In colder regions, the frost line may be 6 ft or more below the surface, whereas in Southern climes the ground never freezes. In most cities or localities, the depth of the excavation required to prevent frost heaving is well established by codes.

Subsurface explorations should be carried to sufficient depth and with adequate investigation to establish clearly the foundation material characteristics. This investigation should establish that no soil layers of low bearing capacity underlie to cause excessive foundation settlement and that no rock cavities, fissures, or faults exist. Layers of peat below pile tips have been known to cause excessive settlement of pile foundations.

EXCAVATIONS AFFECTING ADJOINING PROPERTY

In excavating the foundations of new buildings, provisions must be made to prevent damage to nearby land and buildings. Bank cave-ins may cause personal injury or damage to property by serious undermining of adjacent building foundations. Prevention may require extensive shoring, discussed in Chapter 2.

Because the responsibility for the protection of adjacent property varies, a careful investgation of local requirements should establish this responsibility prior to estimating or before initiating construction operations.

WALLS

Wall construction is classified according to functions, positions, and methods of construction. These classifications do not always meet clearly defined demarcations because some walls meet more than one classification.

Walls enclose buildings, exclude weather, functionally subdivide floor areas, and serve as one of the oldest architectural components — the bearing wall. As bearing walls, they carry vertical loads of the building; as nonbearing walls, they support only their own weight; as shear walls, they resist the lateral loads caused by seismic forces or wind parallel to the axis of the wall. These loads may be transmitted to a foundation wall which is built below ground level, below curb level, or below the floor level immediately above the ground level.

Curtain walls sometimes called panel walls or enclosure walls, enclose the building and are supported and anchored to the structural frame. A special type of curtain wall is the sandwich panel wall. It consists of two thin slabs, usually reinforced concrete, separated by a core of rigid insulating material such as lightweight concrete, cellular glass, or plastic foam. The slabs are connected by metal ties. Although sometimes made of masonry, this type of wall is more frequently made of lighter materials, such as glass and metals.

Similar to the curtain wall is the solar screen made of perforated material that must be supported by a structural frame. The solar screen functions as a visual barrier for privacy, as a sunshade, and mercifully, as a screen to hide poor architecture. It should be used with caution on the lower floors because it serves as a wonderful ladder for playful children and adventurous second-story burglars.

Some walls, called area separation walls, divide the floor area of a building into separate parts for fire protection, for different uses, or for restricted occupancy. A fire wall, or more properly a fire-resistive wall, is made of fire-resistive materials and is given a fire rating from 1 to 4 hours. It subdivides the building by a continuous barrier from the foundation through the roof, restricting the spread of fire. Such a wall that extends through the roof is classed as a parapet wall — that portion above the roof is the parapet. An area separation wall is similar in function to a fire wall, but it is not necessarily continuous from the foundation through the roof and is called a partition.

A number of walls are identified by their method of construction. Frequently, faced walls, or veneered walls, are built with a facing material that is adhered or anchored to the backing. This facing, also called a veneer, is usually of material more durable and attractive than the backing to which it is anchored. Although bonded to the backing, it may not contribute structurally to the wall. These walls are sometimes called composite walls.

COMPRESSION MEMBERS

Columns support beams and trusses and resist compressive stresses. They are constructed of wood, masonry, steel, or reinforced concrete.

Forces that tend to shorten or compress a member are called compressive forces, and the stresses set up in a member by these forces are called compressive stresses.

The vertical members of a structural frame, called columns, transfer floor and roof loads to the foundations. Such loads cause stresses in the columns which are chiefly compressive; however, eccentric loads, rigidity of joints, wind loads, earthquake shocks, and lateral loads subject columns to bending stresses which may be of considerable magnitude. Bending or flexural stresses are set up in a member when it bends.

Classes of Columns

Columns are divided into three general classes according to the ratio of the longitudinal dimension to the least radius of gyration.

If the length of a column is relatively small when compared with its lateral dimension (Figure 1.9A), the column does not tend to bend to any extent when carrying a load; and if the load is appied so that its resultant load is on the axis of the column, the stresses are assumed to be uniformly distributed over each cross section of the column. If the length of a column is great when compared with its lateral dimension, the column will tend to fail by bending or buckling (Figure 1.9C) even though the magnitude of the direct compressive stress is small. A third class includes columns intermediate in ratio of length to lateral dimension to the classes just mentioned; such columns tend to fail by a

FIGURE 1.9 Classes of columns.

combination of direct stress and bending or buckling. Reinforced concrete columns are usually of the first class if there are not lateral loads. Timber and steel columns may be in either the first or third class. Columns of the second class are not used to any extent.

Other Terms Used

Columns are often called posts, especially when made of timber. Truss members carrying compressive stresses are called struts, but their action is the same as that of columns. In general, members that carry compressive stresses are called columns, posts, struts or props.

The light, closely spaced, vertical compressive members used in walls and partitions in wood frame and light steel constuction are called studs. Stone or brick columns are sometimes called pillars, but this is not a technical term. The term pier has about the same meaning as pillar and is more commonly used.

BEAMS AND GIRDERS

A *beam* is a horizontal member supported at one or more points along its length and carrying loads acting perpendicular to its length. The reactions at the supports are parallel to the direction of the loads (Figure 1.10).

If the line of action of the loads is not perpendicular to the axis of the beam, these loads are resolved into components acting perpendicular to the length of the beam and components acting parallel to the length of the beam (B). In supporting the transverse components, the beam performs its primary function; while carrying the components parallel to its length, it acts as a column.

A beam may be curved or bent (C) if the supports are so arranged that the reactions at the supports will be vertical for vertical loads. This may be accomplished by placing one end on rollers (C) or, to a certain degree, by using plates which permit sliding. If the ends are so arranged that horizontal movement is restricted as the structure deforms, the reaction will no longer be vertical, and the structure will be an arch (D).

FIGURE 1.10 Types of beams.

FIGURE 1.11 Reinforced concrete framing.

FIGURE 1.12 Lintels for a masonry wall. TM5-742, *Concrete and Masonry,* Department of the Army, June 1970.

Flexural Stresses

There are two general classes of stress set up in a beam by the loads: flexural or bending stresses and shearing stresses. As a beam deflects under a load, the material on the upper side of the beam shown in *(A)* is compressed or shortened, and that on the lower side is elongated. The stresses causing the shortening are called compressive stresses, and those causing the elongation are tensile stresses. Taken together, they are termed flexural stresses. These stresses are greatest at the extreme surfaces of the beam and are zero at the neutral axis near the center of the section. For a beam composed of one material, the neutral axis passes through the center of gravity or centroid of the cross section. The variation of stress is illustrated by the

triangles in *(E)*, the intensity of the stress usually varying directly as the distance from the neutral axis, as indicated by the lengths of the horizontal lines in the triangles.

Shearing Stresses

It is evident that the forces acting on a horizontal beam tend to cut it along vertical cross sections, as shown in *(F)*. The stresses set up in the beam by this action are called shearing stresses. Another stress is horizontal shear, which acts across the transverse section of the beam through its neutral axis. This form of shear is quite evident in wood beams of short spans with heavy concentrated loads.

Classification According to Support

Beams are divided into classes according to their method of support. A simple beam is supported at two points near its ends. (Figure 1.10G). A special case of the simple beam is the overhanging beam, which is supported at two points but projects beyond or overhangs one or both supports (H). Similar in some respects to the overhang beam is the cantilever beam, supported and rigidly held in position at one end only (I). The propped cantilever beam is supported at two points and rigidly held in position at one of them (J), whereas the fixed beam is supported at two points and rigidly held in position at those points as shown in (K). A beam supported at three or more points as shown in (L) is referred to as a continuous beam.

Classification According to Use

Beams are also classified according to their function. When any distinction is made between beams and girders, the beam is the smaller member and may be supported by the girder (see Figure 1.11). A lintel is a beam with a short span supporting masonry or other loads over an opening (see Figure 1.12). Rafters are closely spaced beams supporting the roof and running parallel to the slope of the roof (see Figure 1.13). Although rafters for flat roofs are called joists, joists are usually closely spaced beams supporting a floor or ceiling.

A purlin supports the roof sheathing while spanning between the principal roof supports, such as the roof trusses or arches. Girts, placed horizontally on the sides of a building, function similar to purlins. They are attached to the columns and support the sheathing and siding of buildings.

They are used a great deal on mill buildings (see Figure 1.14).

Framed openings in floors for stairwells or duct openings require members with special names. The beams that frame the side of the opening parallel to the floor joists are called the trimmers, while those that frame the other side and frame into the trimmers are called headers. Tail beams are the members that were cut out to make the opening. They frame into the headers (see Figure 1.15).

Materials

Beams are constructed of wood, steel, or reinforced concrete, as described in the following articles. Stone is occasionally used for lintels; but its low structural strength usually demands that it be supported by a steel lintel, which is frequently concealed.

TRUSSES

A *truss* is a framed structure consisting of a group of triangles arranged in a single plane so that loads applied at the points of intersection of the members will cause only direct stress (tension or compression) in the members. Loads applied between these points cause flexural stresses. The framework shown in Figure 1.16A will illustrate the essential features of a truss, although a truss of this type is of no practical use.

In a truss, the ends of a framework must be supported so that the reactions at the supports are vertical for vertical loads. This result is accomplished by arranging one end so that horizontal movement may take place by sliding or roll-

FIGURE 1.13 Roof framing terms. TM5-551B, *Carpenter,* Department of the Army, July 1971.

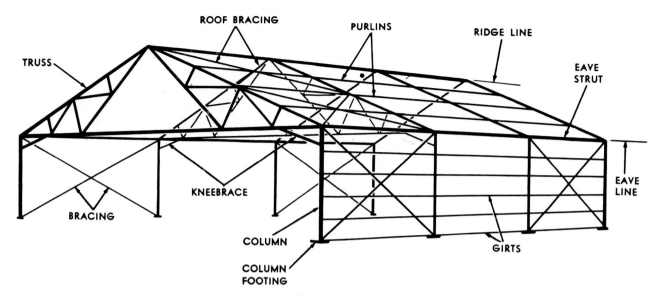

FIGURE 1.14 Framework of a typical mill building. TM5-744, *Structural Steelwork,* Department of the Army, October 1968.

FIGURE 1.15 Double headers and double trimmers. TM5-551B, *Carpenter,* Department of the Army, July 1971.

ing on the bearing plate *(B)* when loads are applied, or when changes of length occur due to temperature changes.

If the ends are so arranged that horizontal movement is restricted, the reactions will be inclined and the framework will act as an arch *(C).* It is not customary to provide sliding or rolling bearings for trusses whose span does not exceed 40 or 50 ft.

Parts of the Truss

The points of intersection of the truss members are called joints, or sometimes panel points. The upper members form the upper or top chord; and the lower members, the lower or bottom chord. The web members connect the joints on the upper chord to those on the lower *(A)* by gusset plates. Web members carrying compressive stresses are struts, and those carrying tensile stresses are ties. The terms end post, vertical post, hip vertical, and panel apply to special forms of trusses and will be defined later. The distance from center to center of the supports is called the span.

Materials

Trusses may be built wholly of wood, of wood and steel rods combined, or of rolled-steel sections. Concrete is used to a limited extent, but it is not usually suitable material for trusses.

Types of Trusses

Since a truss is composed of a group of triangles, it is possible to arrange innumerable types; but certain types have proved more satisfactory than others, and each has its special uses. The various types of trusses used in building construction are illustrated by line diagrams in Figure 1.16 and 1.17. The members indicated by heavy lines normally carry compressive stresses, and those indicated by light lines normally carry tensile stresses for vertical loads. The types shown with parallel chords may have gently sloping top chords that permit roof drainage without changing the truss type. The number of subdivisions or panels will depend upon the length of span and the type of construction.

The more common forms of trusses will be discussed in the following paragraphs.

The king-post truss (Figure 1.16 D), the queen-post truss (E), and the inverted king-post and queen-post trusses (F) and (G) are all used for short spans in wood construction. The members indicated by heavy lines are made of wood, and those indicated by light lines are usually steel rods. The inverted king-post and queen-post trusses are often called trussed beams. The lower chords of the trusses in (D) and (E) carry tensile stresses but are usually made of wood and therefore are indicated by heavy lines.

The Howe truss may be constructed with inclined top chords (H) or with parallel chords (I). Howe truss members that are always constructed with wood are indicated by heavy lines. Those indicated by the light lines may be steel rods. The truss with sloping chords is usually used for pitched roofs, whereas the truss with parallel chords may be used to support flat roofs or floors. Howe trusses may be divided into any number of panels to suit any span or purlin spacing.

The Pratt truss, of wood or steel, may be constructed with inclined top chords (J), with parallel chords (K), or with broken upper chord, forming a camel-back Pratt truss. The truss with sloping chords is used for supporting sloping roofs, and the type with parallel chords is used for supporting flat roofs or floors. Pratt trusses may be divided into any number of panels to suit any span or purlin spacing.

The Fink truss is always constructed with inclined chords (L), and all the members are made of steel sections or of wood. Fink trusses are very widely used in supporting sloping roofs. They may be divided into any number of panels to suit any span or purlin spacing. A modified form of Fink truss is shown in (M), and a fan Fink or fan truss is shown in (N).

The Warren truss, widely used for supporting floors or flat

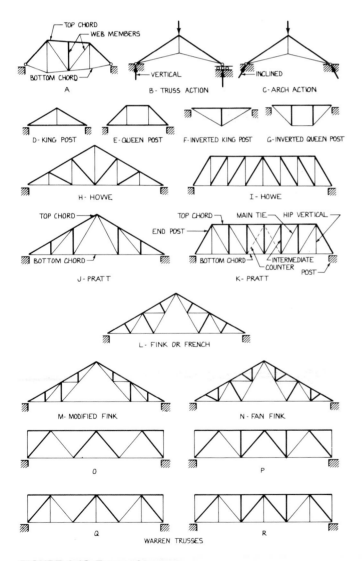

FIGURE 1.16 Types of trusses.

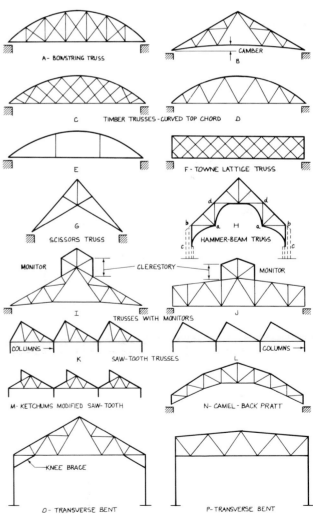

FIGURE 1.17 Types of trusses and transverse bents.

roofs, is always constructed with parallel or nearly parallel chords *(O)*. Vertical members may be provided to reduce the distance between joints on the upper chord *(P)*, on the lower chord *(Q)*, or on both chords *(R)*. The Warren truss is very widely used for supporting floors or flat roofs.

The bowstring truss (Figure 1.17A) is usually constructed of wood.

A truss is said to be cambered when the bottom chord is raised at the center, as in the cambered Fink truss shown in *(B)*. Camber improves the appearance of a truss and prevents sagging and the illusion of sagging.

Various special forms of wood roof trusses are shown in *(C)* to *(H)*. The trusses shown in *(C)* and *(D)* have curved upper chords; the various members are built up of 1- or 2-in. lumber. A curved trussed beam or tied arch is shown in *(E)*. This beam is built up of light lumber and steel rods. A scissors truss is shown in *(G)*, a hammer-beam truss shown in *(H)*, and a Towne lattice truss in *(F)*. In the hammer-beam truss shown in *(H)*, the parts of the truss marked *A-B-C* act as brackets to reduce the span to *D-D*. These brackets must be securely fastened to the wall along the vertical member *B-C*, and the wall must be capable of withstanding the outward thrust produced at the point *C*. The structural action is complicated.

Other special forms of roof trusses are shown in *(I)* to *(N)*. Monitors are placed on top of roof trusses *(I)* and *(J)* to give better light and ventilation. The vertical face of a monitor, called the clerestory, is provided either with glass in sash, which will open to provide light and ventilation, or with louvers for ventilation only.

The sawtooth truss shown in *(K)* and *(L)* is used to provide light and ventilation; the steeper face of the roof is covered with glass so that a part of the sash will open. This face is usually turned toward the north to secure a uniform light. The type shown in *(K)* is constructed of steel, and that in *(L)* is constructed of timber and steel rods.

Another form of sawtooth truss is shown in *(M)*. Its vertical face is provided with top-hung sash. This type is always constructed of steel sections.

A camel-back Pratt truss with a heavy cambered lower chord is shown in *(N)*.

Steel or timber roof trusses secured to columns give lateral rigidity *(O)* and *(P)*. Such combinations of trusses and columns are called transverse bents. In the transverse bent shown in *(O)*, the braces between the truss and columns are called knee braces. They are provided to give transverse or lateral rigidity.

A type of truss which is rarely used is the Vierendeel truss (Figure 1.18). It does not satisfy the definition of a truss but is given that designation. Trusses of this type are advantageous where it is necessary to keep unobstructed openings between the vertical posts. They are built of reinforced concrete or steel. Because of the omission of diagonals, all the members are subjected to bending stresses, and the joints must be rigid to ensure structural stability.

ALL JOINTS ARE RIGID
ALL MEMBERS DESIGNED FOR DIRECT STRESS AND BENDING

FIGURE 1.18 Vierendeel truss or girder.

ARCHES, RIGID FRAMES, AND DOMES
Arches

Traditionally, *arches* were constructed entirely of masonry; thus, many arch terms relate to masonry, although all arches generally have certain properties in common. The curved arch ring forms an opening width called the span and a height called the rise. In the opening, the underside or concave surface is the soffit or intrados. The upper or convex surface is the back or the extrados. The exposed vertical surfaces or sides of the arch ring are the faces, and the highest point in the arch ring is the crown. In masonry construction, the unit of which the arch is composed is termed a voussoir, and the voussoir at the crown is called the keystone. Each end of an arch is supported by an abutment, which is a mass of material that resists any lateral thrust imposed by the arch. Arches that are a part of a wall do not have well-defined abutments because the wall itself serves in this capacity. A series of arches in sequential order forms an arcade.

Brick and stone arches are one of the traditional forms of construction. These arches have a structural function, but their design is determined largely by appearance.

Arched roofs may have barrel arches or ribbed arches. A barrel arch resembles a segment of a barrel without longitudinal curvature. The cross sections perpendicular to the length of the roof are identical. A barrel arch, continuous from one end of the roofed area to the other, forms a vault. A ribbed arch is one of a series of arches providing structural support for a roof deck which spans between arches. The deck is continuous from one end of the roofed area to the other.

There are two general types of arch ribs (Figure 1.19). The solid rib *(A)* is subjected primarily to compressive stresses but also to flexural and shearing stresses. The trussed or framed rib *(B)* is made up of members arranged in triangles, as in trusses, each of which is subjected to either tensile or compressive stresses. Arch ribs are also called arch rings.

(A) SOLID RIB ARCH   (B) TRUSSED OR FRAMED RIB ARCH

FIGURE 1.19 Arch ribs.

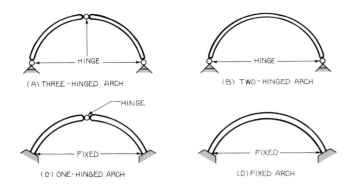

FIGURE 1.20 Types of arches.

FIGURE 1.21 Support for ends of arches.

Some types of framed arches are not arranged in the form of ribs.

Arched roofs consisting of two or more intersecting arched units are called groined roofs, vaults, or arches. The lines of intersection of the arched units of the structural members in these locations are called groins.

Arched roofs are used chiefly for the long spans required for such structures as armories, exhibition halls, field houses, gymnasiums, and assembly buildings. Barrel arches are usually constructed of reinforced concrete; solid arch ribs of steel or wood.

Arches are constructed with their ends securely fixed to their foundations or abutments so that no rotation can take place at these points. Hinges may be installed to permit rotation and expansion. In the three-hinged arch, there is a hinge at each abutment and one at the crown; however, the ends of the arch ring are securely fixed at the abutments (Figure 1.20C); and in the no-hinged or fixed arch, no hinges are provided, leaving the ends of the arch rigidly anchored

to the abutments (D). Steel and wood arches are usually three-hinged or two-hinged. Reinforced concrete arches may be of the three-hinged, two-hinged, or fixed type. The one-hinged arch is rarely used. Actual hinges may be provided for long-span arches, but often arrangements which offer negligible resistance to rotation are used.

The horizontal component of the thrust at each end of an arch may be transmitted through the foundation to the supporting soil if it has adequate capacity to carry this component as well as the vertical component. Otherwise a steel tie placed below the floor level and encased in concrete forms a tie beam (Figure 1.21A).

If desired, the enclosed area is restricted by vertical side walls, shown by dashed lines in the figure, the ends of the arches left exposed or enclosed, thus increasing the building space. The ends of the arch may be supported on rigid abutments (B), but occasionally their construction is similar to that of the framed arch.

Curve of Arch Ring

Curves and combinations of curves are used in forming arches. When strength and economy of material are principal factors, as they are in arch bridges, the curve of the arch ring is determined by the span and rise of the arch and the loading characteristics. For the ordinary arches over openings in walls, appearance determines choice in design rather than strength and economy of material. The failure of arches is caused by the spreading of the abutments or of the material that serves as abutments. Spreading occurs when arched window or door openings are placed too close to the wall corners or when the abutments at the ends of the arcade are insufficient.

Types of Arches

The curve of the intrados is often a portion of the arc of a circle or a combination of the arcs of various circles with different radii and centers. Four types that have one center, shown in Figure 1.22, are the semicircular; the segmental, which includes less than a semicircle; and the stilted, which consists of a semicircular arch ring with straight vertical sections on each side.

Two-centered arches are shown in (B). The three types —blunt, equilateral, and lancet—differ only in the relation between the radius and the spacing of the centers. In the blunt or drop arch, the centers are within the arch. In the equilateral or Gothic arch, the radius of the intrados equals the span, and the centers are therefore on the springing lines. The centers of the acute or lancet arch are outside the arch.

There are two types of three-centered arches (C). In the first, one center is used for the arc of the central portion of the arch and two centers for the arcs at the ends of the arch

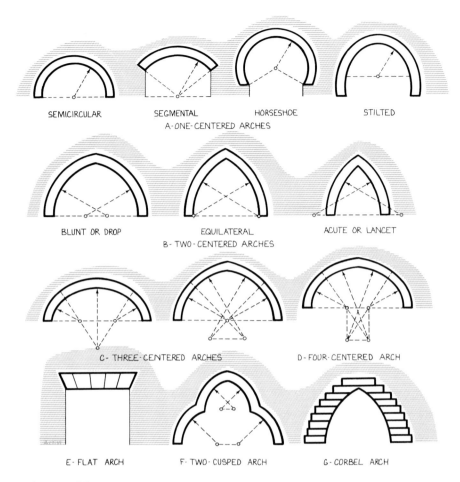

SEMICIRCULAR   SEGMENTAL   HORSESHOE   STILTED

A-ONE-CENTERED ARCHES

BLUNT OR DROP   EQUILATERAL   ACUTE OR LANCET

B-TWO-CENTERED ARCHES

C-THREE-CENTERED ARCHES   *D-FOUR-CENTERED ARCH*

E-FLAT ARCH   *F-TWO-CUSPED ARCH*   *G-CORBEL ARCH*

FIGURE 1.22 Types of arches.

ring. In the second, one center serves for the two arcs at the ends of the arch ring, and two centers are required for the central portion of the arch ring.

The four-centered or Tudor arch *(D)* is similar to the second type of three-centered arch, but the centers for the lower section of the arch ring do not coincide as in the three-centered arch. The vertical alignment of centers shown in the figure is not essential to this type.

The flat arch *(E)* may be supported by arch action, but it is usually carried on a concealed lintel.

The two-cusped arch is illustrated in *(F)*. Many forms of cusped arches have been used for effect. Structurally, they are inefficient.

The elliptic arch is similar in shape to the three-centered arch shown in *(C)*; however, the intrados is parabolic with its axis vertical.

The corbel arch *(G)*, although not truly an arch, is called an arch because of its shape. There is no real arch action; each course is corbeled or cantilevered but over the course below until the two sides meet. This, the oldest form of arch, is not used in modern building construction. A stepped arch is one whose back is stepped to correspond with courses of masonry units in the wall above the openings.

Rigid Frames

The structural action of *rigid frames* resembles that of arches. However, arches are so proportioned that the stresses in the principal members are primarily compressive, whereas rigid frames are proportioned to provide adequate ceiling height over the entire area, even though the structure is supported by foundations located just below the ground surface and not elevated, as the arch shown in Figure 1.21B. Rigid frames are subjected to large bending and shearing stresses because of their form, illustrated by the several types in Figure 1.23. Rigid frames are often called arches, because their structural action is similar to that of an arch. Several types of single-story rigid frames are illustrated in Figure 1.23. Multistory rigid frames are also constructed.

The vertical members of rigid frames are called the legs. The top members are sometimes called rafters. The portion of the frame adjacent to the junction of a rafter and a leg is called a knee, or the haunch. If two rafters of adjoining frames meet on a leg, the adjacent portions of these members form a Y. The center of the top member of a symmetrical frame, or a single break in the direction of the top member, is called the crown.

FIGURE 1.23 Types of rigid frames.

Three single-span rigid frames are illustrated in Figure 1.23(A), (B), and (C), the only differences being the types of connections at the bottoms of the legs and at the crown. The frame in (A) is called a three-hinged frame because of the hinges at the bottoms of the legs and at the crown; the frame in (B) is called a two-hinged frame because there are hinges only at the bottoms of the legs; and the frame in (C) is called a hingeless, no-hinged, or fixed frame because of the absence of hinges. Actually, no real hinges are provided at any point but, at points where it is assumed in the stress computations that hinges are present, the detail or arrangement provides a negligible resistance to rotation. When it is assumed that bottoms of the legs are fixed, the connection of the leg to the foundation and the foundation itself are so designed that there will be negligible rotation of the legs at these points. The usual assumption is that the connections at these points are hinged.

Steel ties (A), (B), and (C) may be provided under the floor if necessary to carry the horizontal components of the thrusts of the legs.

Balconies may be cantilevered out from the vertical legs to provide for spectators (H), or running tracks may be provided in gymnasiums in this manner. The top members may be cantilevered outward beyond the legs (I) to provide canopies for protection over loading platforms or other areas.

Rigid frames are used extensively in gymnasiums, field houses, assembly halls, churches, and industrial structures requiring large unobstructed floor areas and ceiling heights.

Domes

Domes (Figure 1.24) are frequently used as roofs over large circular floor areas for assembly halls, gymnasiums, field houses, and other buildings. They are constructed of self-supporting, reinforced concrete shells as described in Chapter 4, or the structural members may be various types of wood, steel, and aluminum sections arranged in a great variety of patterns.

A dome exerts outward thrusts continuously around its perimeter. These are resisted by a tension ring, as shown in the figure. The dome and tension ring are usually supported on columns spaced around the perimeter and braced to provide lateral stability for the structure. Bearing walls are also used for support. Purlins are commonly provided to span the space between ribs and support the roof deck.

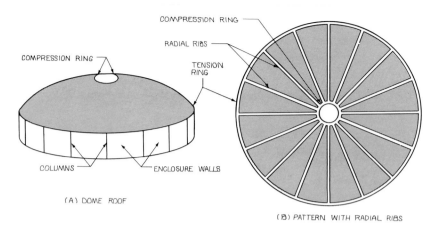

FIGURE 1.24 Circular dome roof.

Cables

The roofs of buildings may be supported by steel cables. Each cable consists of a strand of several wires. The wires in a strand are arranged in a helical form. The cables used in supporting roofs are made up of wires produced by cold-drawing steel rods through steel dies. The process of cold-drawing produces wires with very high tensile strengths.

1.5 Building Costs

The construction cost is only a fraction of the *total life cost* of a building. More and more owners consider the total life cost of a proposed facility when making the decision whether to build or not. Generally, the total life cost of a building will include costs associated with the following activities; information gathering, design, land acquisition, construction, financing, and maintenance and operating expenses of the completed facility. Experience has determined that over 50% of the total life cost of a building are the costs of maintaining and operating the completed building.

The selection of materials and methods of construction has significant influence on the cost of maintaining and operating the finished structure. The uncertainty of future energy costs make it imperative that consideration be given to building systems that have proven their ability to minimize energy consumption. Finishes that endure and are easy to maintain may be selected over those that are more aesthetically desirable. Location on the site can influence energy consumption and outside maintenance expenditures, but may require more extensive site preparation costs.

The decisions made during the preliminary and design phases will affect the total life cost of the building. They should be made only after a careful study has been made of the many alternatives that are available. It is important that the time value of money be included in making comparisons between alternatives that have costs occurring during different time frames.

1.6 Selection of Materials

When evaluating a building material the selection of the material must be based on several factors, which may be classified roughly as economic criteria, mechanical properties, and aesthetic qualities. Selection depends on the intended function or application, which is based on the materials' performances in these three classifications.

Product evaluation is seldom the same for any two applications. There may be similarities between projects, but each project's priorities and conditions must be evaluated. Although mechanical properties and aesthetics could make material selection seem obvious, economics frequently dictates. Usually the mechanical properties or behavior of a material are the bases for the economic rationale. Seldom is a choice of a material based on a single factor, but selection is based on a combination of factors. Rarely is aesthetics the sole determine except perhaps in monumental architecture, but even then the property of durability is a consideration.

Economically materials may be evaluated on cost, maintenance, fire resistivity, availability, replaceability, and perhaps durability.

Material classification that may be measured as mechanical includes the structural properties of shear, tension, compression, creep, plasticity, and elasticity, also hardness, softness, resistance to corrosion, the elastomeric ability for expansion and contraction, and certain acoustic and electrical properties. Impermeability to the passage of moisture is usually desirable, as well as certain thermal properties. In some cases the density of a material may exclude it as a choice, whereas in other applications a dense material may be desirable. For example, clay roofing tile requires a substantial supportive structure that may be expensive for the contemplated spans; a material lighter than clay tile might be more appropriate. Dense materials are necessary in some locations such as foundations, in ground water, in radiation shielding applications, and in meeting certain acoustic requirements.

Clearly, the qualities of a material viewed for texture and color are aesthetic.

Summary

The completion of the building process has made an established need a reality. The requirements of the owner have been satisfied and the appropriate codes and standards adhered to. Through careful study of the needs of the owner and the existing site conditions, the designer selected a foundation system that will successfully transfer the total load of the building to the supporting soil or rock. He or she specified a structural framing plan that supports and transfers all imposed loads to the foundation. The protective barriers chosen protect the interior from the weather, present an aesthetic appearance, and are easy to maintain. Interior finishes have been used that create an environment in which people can work, rest, study, or recover without being distracted by the activities around them.

The costs to design the building, acquire the site, perform construction, provide financing, and to operate and maintain it make up a total life cost that is economical and within the owner's budget. The owner can expect to have a serviceable facility for many years to come.

Key Terms

building process
design-bid-construct
design-build
construction-
    management
building codes
occupancy

performance code
model building codes
fire limits
fire resistance
framing
bearing pressure
bearing capacity

factor of safety
spread foundation
pile foundation
pier foundation
frost line
walls
columns

beams
trusses
arches
rigid frames
domes
total life cost

Review Questions

1. List the four phases of the building process and describe the actions and operations that take place in each phase.

2. How do building codes usually classify buildings?

3. List the major elements in a building and describe their function.

4. What four classes of loads are buildings subjected to?

5. What types of costs are included in the total life cost of a building?

CHAPTER 2
SOIL

2.1 Subsurface Exploration
2.2 Soils and Soil Testing
2.3 Soil Pressures

2.4 Bearing Areas of Spread Foundations
2.5 Foundation Settlement
2.6 Settlement of Pile Foundations

The first material encountered in the building process is soil. It is the one material that has a continuing effect on the serviceability of the proposed structure. The nature of this material is such that any universal standard only partially describes what the expected performance might be. Because soil plays such an important role in the building process, it is necessary to determine its nature, composition, physical properties, and suitability as a structural material before any commitment can be made beyond the preliminary phase.

During the preliminary phase, subsurface exploration is conducted on the proposed site, often before the site is secured. Samples of the soil are obtained and soil testing is done to determine the nature, composition, and physical properties. The results of these tests enable the designers to establish allowable bearing pressures and select the appropriate type of foundation system.

The soil may be capable of supporting the imposed loads with the use of spread footings. When the soil beneath the elevation at which a spread foundation would normally be established is too weak to provide adequate support, piles are used to transfer the imposed loads to a firmer soil at a greater depth. In some cases the imposed loads are of such a magnitude that piers or caissons are needed to carry the loads to bedrock. The information gained from the subsurface exploration and soil testing allow the foundation engineer to provide the right foundation for the intended structure.

Objectives

1. Become familiar with the various methods used for subsurface exploration.
2. State what tests are done on soils and how they relate to the performance of the soil as a structural support.
3. List the factors that influence the settlement of spread foundations and pile foundations.

2.1 Subsurface Exploration

Preferably before a building site is purchased, and certainly before the foundation plans are prepared, an investigation must be conducted to determine the character of the underlying material, including the depth to the groundwater table. Even though groundwater may not affect building design, it may have adjunct effects resulting in costly construction difficulties. Major structures located on soils of little known properties require calculations and estimates of expected foundation settlement and investigation of swelling and shrinkage probabilities. Settlement predictions necessitate securing soil samples at various depths below the foundation levels. Soil samples should be taken in a manner that will preserve them in their natural, intact state. These are undisturbed samples. Various devices have been developed to secure such samples.

Loading tests are made to determine the soil bearing capacity. Before conducting such tests, their informative value should be carefully considered. As will be mentioned later, these tests may be of limited or of no value because the bearing capacity of some soils does not vary in direct proportion with the area; the unexposed soil underlying the test area may be of very different character from the soil contributing to the test results. In a loading test conducted over a small area (usually 1 sq ft), only the soil immediately underlying transmits sufficiently high stresses to affect the results significantly, whereas the soil characteristics for a considerable depth below an actual foundation contribute to foundation settlement. The larger the foundation, the greater the depth affected. This depth is usually about 1½ times the width of the foundation.

METHODS OF SUBSURFACE EXPLORATION

The usual methods that determine the character of the material underlying a building site are:

1. Test pits
2. Sounding rods
3. Soil auger borings
4. Wash borings
5. Hollow stem borings
6. Churn drilling
7. Diamond drilling
8. Shot drilling
9. Geophysical methods

Test pits, sounding rods, soil auger borings, wash borings, hollow stem borings, and churn drilling are appropriate methods for soil explorations, whereas rock investigations are conducted by test pits, churn drilling, diamond drilling, and shot drilling. Where buildings are to be founded on bedrock, it is necessary to drill into bedrock far enough to ensure the solid rock is thick enough to support the proposed loads. Wash borings and churn drillings are used to penetrate boulders in soil. Test pits can be used in rock, but the information necessary for examining rock can be secured more economically by diamond drilling, churn drilling,

and shot drilling. Geophysical methods determine distinguishable subsurface conditions in the properties of rock and soil formations by analyzing their ability to transmit sound and electricity. This method is not used in building site investigations but more for geological and oil exploration. Each of these methods, except the geophysical method, will be explained briefly, with a concluding statement devoted to methods of obtaining soil samples. Surface soil tests are discussed briefly in Chapter 3.

Test Pits

The most satisfactory method for securing reliable information concerning subsurface soil conditions is *test pits,* for this procedure permits soil examination in its natural undisturbed state. This method is relatively expensive because the pits must be large enough to work in. They are shored and lined by properly supported horizontal and vertical members to prevent caving (see Figure 2.1).

Sounding Rod

The *sounding rod* is a steel rod or pipe about ¾ in. in diameter, in about 5 ft lengths, joined by standard couplings and provided with a pointed lower end. It is hand driven with a maul or drop weight, lubricated with water, and turned with a pipe wrench to reduce sticking. The number of blows required to drive the rod indicates the nature of the underlying soil. Driving should continue until the rod "refuses" further penetration. This may mean that rock has been struck, particularly if the rod "brings up" with a sharp ring. Because the effect is the same when hitting a large boulder or a rock ledge, other probings should be made nearby to determine if refusal is at about the same elevation or if the rod penetration had been stopped by a boulder. After driving has been completed, the rod is removed by a lever and chain. The sounding rod yields no soil samples, but experienced operators can estimate the soil character by observing the manner by which the rod penetrates the soil. The results offer little value beyond indicating the presence of rock (within reach of the rod).

FIGURE 2.1 Test pit.

(A)   (B)

FIGURE 2.2 Hand-operated augers. (A) Helical auger. (B) Post-hole auger. *Foundation Engineering,* R. B. Peck, W. E. Hanson, and T. H. Thornburn. Copyright © 1974, John Wiley & Sons, Inc. Reprinted by permission of John Wiley & Sons, Inc.

Soil Auger Boring

Holes bored into soil with *soil augers* are rotated by hand or power driven. Augers are of various types, one type being similar to the wood auger. See Figure 2.2. Diameters vary from 1½ to 12 in. The type selection depends upon the material to be penetrated and the power system employed. Augers are mounted on sections of pipe with new sections added as the boring progresses. If the penetrated material is damp sand or contains considerable clay, the hole may not cave; but if caving occurs, the auger is operated inside a metal casing which sinks or is driven as the boring progresses. If the soil adheres to the auger, indications of the soil's nature can be obtained by examining this soil. Below the groundwater level in sand or in silt, it may be necessary to bail out the soil. Sometimes this method is employed above the groundwater level by adding water and mixing it with the soil to be removed from the hole. If boulders are present, they are drilled with a churn drill or shot with explosives.

Wash Boring

One method for boring test holes into unconsolidated materials is *wash boring* (see Figure 2.3). A bit is mounted on the lower end of a pipe called a drill rod through which water is forced. The drill rod is worked up and down or churned and rotated slowly. The bit strikes the soil or rock, gradually penetrating it. Various types of bits are used, selection depending upon the material to be penetrated, but all are provided with holes permitting water to pass from the drill rod through the bit and against the sides of the hole. For

FIGURE 2.3 Apparatus for making wash borings. *Foundation Engineering,* R. B. Peck, W. E. Hanson, and T. H. Thornburn. Copyright © 1974, John Wiley & Sons, Inc. Reprinted by permission of John Wiley & Sons, Inc.

clearance, the width of the bit is greater than the diameter of the drill rod. Cuttings are washed by water rising to the surface in the annular space between the rod and sides of the hole. The process derives its name from this operation. In soil, the drill is removed and the casing is installed before caving occurs. The casing is driven at intervals as the drilling proceeds. The nature of the soil penetrated is often judged by examining the borings or cuttings surfaced by the wash water, but such information is questionable. Experienced operators may form some estimate of the soil characteristics by the "feel" of the equipment. A more satisfactory sampling method relies upon removing the bit and the drill rod and replacing the bit with an open-ended pipe or with special forms of samplers. The apparatus is again placed in the hole and the pipe is driven into the soil at the bottom. The pipe or sampler is brought to the surface; the sample removed and examined. Although not dry, the sample is called a dry sample to distinguish it from the samples brought up in wash water. Such a sampling procedure is, of course, not adaptable to rock. But this boring method is used for penetrating sand, gravel, clay, boulders, and solid rock.

Hollow Stem Borings

Wash boring equipment has been largely replaced by mobile drilling equipment capable of drilling to greater depths,

FIGURE 2.4 Mobile drill model B-30. Courtesy of Mobile Drilling Company, Inc.

at faster speeds, and obtaining intact samples of soil (see Figures 2.4 and 2.5). *Hollow stem boring* augers are used to penetrate the soil and serve as a casing to keep the hole open (see Figure 2.6). When the desired depth is reached, the plug is withdrawn and replaced with a soil sampler.

Churn Drilling

The *churn drilling* or dry churn drilling method used in soil, boulders, and rock is similar to the wash boring method, though the means of cuttings removal is different. In removing the cuttings, only enough water to fill the bottom of the hole is used. The cuttings mix with the water as the churning proceeds, and at intervals the drill stem is withdrawn; a sand pump or bailer removes the cuttings and water. The samples obtained from the bailer are unreliable indicators of the material penetrated. Reliable samples may be obtained in the same manner as "dry samples" in the wash boring method; or core samples of rock may be secured at intervals with diamond drills, shot drills, or saw-toothed drills, with the churn drill removed while obtaining cores.

Diamond Drilling

The *diamond drill* is suitable only for rock drilling. The drill is a hollow, steel cylinder with embedded black diamonds outside and inside the bottom edges, forming a bit. The diamonds are set to provide a small clearance between the bored hole and the outside diameter of the drill cylinder, and as a result, the core will be slightly smaller than the inside diameter of the cylinder. The drill is rotated by power-driven equipment cutting into the rock by abrasion. Water forced down the drill rod to the bottom rises in the annular space between the drill rod and the sides of the hole. This water removes the cuttings and cools the bit. The bit is not attached directly to the drill rod, but a cylinder called a core barrel is intermediate, providing space for a core length up to 10 ft. The drilling apparatus with the sample in the core barrel is removed periodically (see Figure 2.7). The core lifter automatically grips the core so that it is removed in the barrel. At its best, the core provides a plausible record of the material penetrated. Gaps usually exist in the record because core recovery is often incomplete. Diamond drilling is expensive but rapid. The core size is commonly 1⅛ in., with a 2 in. hole. Larger holes can be drilled, but the cost increases rapidly with the diameter of the hole. The diamond drill can drill in any direction.

Shot Drilling

The *shot drill* obtains cores from rock. It is a hollow cylindrical bit rotated by an attached drill rod cutting a circular groove in the rock. The cutting is by chilled steel shot, which is fed into the hole and which find their way under the rotary bit. A core barrel is provided between the bit and the sides of

FIGURE 2.5 Mobile drill model B-61. Courtesy of Mobile Drilling Company, Inc.

the hole, as in the diamond drill. The cuttings are washed from the cut surface by pumped water surging through the drill rod and bit orifices. The water rises in the annular space between the drill rod and the sides of the hole. The drill rod has a considerably smaller diameter than the core barrel and bit; thus, the velocity of water flowing upward is decreased above the core barrel. For this reason, the cuttings accumulate in a space provided on top of the core barrel and are removed when each section of core is withdrawn.

The presence of cavities delays drilling because the shot disappears into the spaces, losing contact with the lower edge of the bit. After filling the spaces with cement grout, drilling is resumed with the bit cutting through the hardened grout. Holes are usually 4 or 5 in. in diameter. This is similar

to a widely used method of taking in-place concrete core samples on structural slabs, such as highway pavements.

SOIL SAMPLING

As has been stated, the information obtained about the soil penetrated by some exploratory methods is usually inadequate for foundation design. To obtain information about the properties of the soil at various depths, the bits attached to the drill rods are replaced at intervals by various types of samplers forced or driven into the bottom of the hole. The objective of the sampling operation is to obtain an undisturbed soil sample.

The simplest type of sampler, which is suitable only for cohesive soils such as clay, is a thin-walled seamless steel tube not less than 2 in. in diameter and from 2 to 3 ft long; the tube is filled with soil by forcing it into the bottom of the hole. In the testing laboratory, the tube with its contents is cut into lengths of about 6 in. The soil is forced from these short lengths to obtain specimens for testing.

Another device is an open-ended cylinder referred to as a split barrel sampler and especially designed for either sand or clay. The cylinder is driven into the ground and filled; when extracted, it provides a soil test specimen (see Figure 2.8).

2.2 Soils and Soil Testing

FORMATION OF SOILS

The earth's surface is solid rock, called **bedrock,** either exposed as outcroppings or overlaid with water or unconsolidated material formed by the weathering of the solid rock. This unconsolidated material (mantle rock, soil, or earth) rests on the rock from which it is derived and gradually grades into that rock, or it erodes and is redeposited by wind, water, or glacial ice. **Residual soil** remains over the rock from which it was formed. Soil transported in water and redeposited at another site is called **alluvial soil** or **alluvium.** The sizes of the particles in alluvial soil depend on the water velocity with grain size decreasing as water velocity decreases. Changes in velocity may occur gradually along the water course resulting in fairly uniform deposits over an extensive area, whereas rapid flow within short reaches may produce deposits with marked variations. As a result, alluvial soil deposits usually are stratified. Loess is a soil type formed of fine windblown material. Rock fragments and particles picked up by glaciers and redeposited by the melting glaciers form sizeable **moraines.** These deposits may

FIGURE 2.6 Hollow stem auger. (A) Plugged while advancing auger. (B) Plug removed and sampler inserted to sample soil below auger. *Foundation Engineering,* R. B. Peck, W. E. Hanson, and T. H. Thornburn. Copyright © 1974, John Wiley & Sons, Inc. Reprinted by permission of John Wiley & Sons, Inc.

FIGURE 2.7 Schematic diagram of core barrels. *(a)* Single tube. *(b)* Double tube. *Foundation Engineering,* R. B. Peck, W. E. Hanson, and T. H. Thornburn. Copyright © 1974, John Wiley & Sons, Inc. Reprinted by permission of John Wiley & Sons, Inc.

FIGURE 2.8 Split barrel sampler. *Foundation Engineering,* R. B. Peck, W. E. Hanson, and T. H. Thornburn. Copyright © 1974 John Wiley & Sons, Inc. Reprinted by permission of John Wiley & Sons, Inc.

be ridges crossing valleys, called terminal moraines and formed where the glacial movement had a balanced melting rate for an extended period. Lateral moraines are ridges paralleling the valley formed by debris deposited along the sides of melting glaciers. Debris deposited to a considerable depth over a wide area by a melting receding glacier forms ground moraines. Unless modified by subsequent water erosion, the glacial deposit of mixed size material forms an unstratified mass called till. Fine particles, ground-off bedrock by abrasive glacial action, are known as rock flour.

CLASSIFICATION OF SOILS

Soils are formed by the disintegration of rocks. For engineering, the principal types of soil may be divided into two general classes according to the grain sizes. The *coarse-grained soils* are gravels and sands; *fine-grained soils* are silts and clays.

For comparative simplicity, the discussions in this article contrast the properties of sands and clays. Other soils and other terms applied to soils are considered briefly.

Soil deposits usually consist of mixtures of various classes of soil. They may contain organic materials such as peat, which is partially decomposed, highly compressed vegetable fibers, and muck (often found with peat), which is fine clay or mud.

There are various systems for classifying soils. A system of grain size classifications of grain soils, adapted from that of the U.S. Department of Agriculture, indicates the following (Table 2.1).

This classification should not be confused with the grain size separation between fine and coarse aggregates used as concrete aggregates.

This classification of soils according to grain size is convenient because grain size analyses are relatively simple. However, this means of classification is unsatisfactory because grain size is only one factor in determining the behavior of soils. Sand may be ground to a fineness leading to a classification as clay according to grain size; however, finely ground sand will not possess the other properties usually associated with clay.

Table 2.1 **Classification of Soils by Grain Size**

Gravel, 1/12 in. and over	Silt, 1/12,500 to 1/5000 in.
Sand, 1/500 to 1/5000 in.	Clay, less than 1/12,500 in.

FIGURE 2.9 Formation of sand and clay deposits.

Although the grains of sand may be granite, basalt, and other rocks, most sands and gravel grains are silicon dioxide and quartz. The grain shapes vary from angular to round. Table 2.1 shows that the grain size of clay is comparatively small. The grains are composed of hydrous aluminum silicate and various compounds such as quartz and iron oxide. Particle shape is flat or flakelike, similar to mica.

Silt has properties intermediate between fine sand and clay. The grain size of silts is not a true indication of their behavior. Some silts or rock flour resemble rounded sand grains in shape and behavior. They are usually silicon dioxide. Other silts resemble clay in their composition, particle shape, and behavior. Some soils intermediate between silts and clays in composition and behavior are called silty clays.

Structure of Soil

The structure of a soil deposit bears a direct relation to its properties. Sand grains deposited in water gravitate to relatively dense deposits, whereas fine clay grains adhere to other clay grains without dense consolidation. These processes are illustrated in Figure 2.9. A clay deposit resembles a network of solid grains with the intervening water-filled spaces called voids or pores. Applied loads are transmitted through the deposit along the network. The transformed network results in increased water pressure in the pores termed pore pressure.

If the network is broken or disturbed, the grains become wholly or partially surrounded with water and the soil mass loses all or partial rigidity and is called disturbed, remolded, or recompacted. Samples of soil obtained intact are undisturbed samples.

Voids in Soils

The voids may be filled with air, other gas, water, or a combination of these materials. The specific gravity of soil grains varies between 2.5 and 2.8, regardless of composition or size. Even though the specific gravity of most soil grains is fairly constant, a cubic foot of soil may vary from 70 to 150 lb. This results from differences in proportions of voids to solids which are dependent upon the grain size gradation; moisture content; and the degree of *consolidation* or compression by overlying material and superimposed compaction, tamping, and vibrating loads.

In a volume occupied by equal spheres, the voids between spheres may vary from a minimum of one-fourth to a maximum of one-half the total volume. This variation in the void percentage is dependent on the arrangement of the spheres, not upon the sphere size. If the spheres are mixed sizes, the percentage of voids is reduced — the smaller spheres progressively filling in the voids between the larger spheres. The volume of voids in a soil sample to the total volume of the sample is called the percentage of voids. This ratio is expressed as a percentage. The ratio of the volume of voids to the volume of the solids is the *void ratio.* The percentages of voids, and therefore the void ratios of sand, are relatively small compared to those of clay.

From Table 2.2, it is obvious that, in a sample of sand, the volume of voids is less than the volume of solids, whereas in a sample of clay, the volume of voids may exceed the volume of solids manifold. The voids in sand above ground water will be filled mostly with air; however, if below the groundwater level, they will be filled with water. Except near the surface, the voids in most natural deposits of clays are filled with water irrespective of the groundwater level. Placed and compacted clay fills may contain considerable trapped air. Sometimes gases other than air occupy the voids of clay. Occasionally these are flammable and form explosive mixtures with air. Natural clays and silts do not contain measurable volumes of air if located below the zone where temporary drying by evaporation occurs.

Table 2.2 Percentages of Voids and Void Ratios

	Percentage of Voids	Void Ratios
Sands	30 to 45	0.43 to 0.82
Clays	35 to 95	0.54 to 19.00

Classification Tests

Various soil classification systems are in use throughout the country. They have been developed by different organizations to determine the suitability of a soil for specific engineering applications. The American Association of State Highway and Transportation Officials classification system is used to predict the behavior of soil subgrades under highway pavements. The Federal Aviation Administration uses a separate classification system to establish the thickness for airport pavements. The most widely used system of soils classification for building applications is probably the United Soil Classification System. This system, which is based on the grain size of soils, divides soils into two major groups, fine-grain soils and coarse-grain soils. Initial sieve analysis of a soil specimen classifies it as fine grain if one-half or more of the sample passes the No. 200 sieve or coarse grain if 50% or more is retained. Fine-grain and coarse-grain soils are classified by further sieve analysis and by their behavior with water as determined by the Atterberg limits (see Table 2.3).

Coarse-Grain Soils

Additional sieve analysis of a coarse-grain soil sample determines the proportion by weight retained or passed. If the greater percentage of the sample is retained on the No. 4 sieve, the soil is a gravel (G), otherwise a sand (S). The gravel or sand sample is then classified according to the percentage that passes the No. 200 sieve. If less than 5% pass, the gravels are classified as well-graded gravels (GW) or poorly graded gravels (GP), while the sands are classified well-graded sands (SW) or poorly graded sands (SP). If 5% to 12% pass, the specimen, a borderline soil, is a mixture of sand or gravel with silt or clay. If more than 12% passes the No. 200 sieve, the Atterberg limits determine the clay or silt on a representative sample. These results are plotted on a chart called the plasticity chart in Figure 2.10 which classifies the soil.

Fine-Grain Soils

Fine-grain soils (50% or more passing the No. 200 sieve) are classified by their position on the plasticity chart as determined by the Atterberg limits tests. The Atterberg limits consist of the *shrinkage limit,* liquid limit (LL), and plastic limit (PL). The limits test determines the boundary or limits of a soil in its various physical states: solid to liquid and plastic to nonplastic.

The liquid limit is the moisture content of a soil at the boundary between its liquid to plastic states. The test procedure requires a mechanical liquid limit device (Figure 2.11) and a grooving tool. A moist sample of soil placed into the brass cup to a depth of 1 cm is separated into halves by a grooving tool. The device handle is turned rapidly, causing a notched cam to drop the cup 1 cm until the separated soil

Table 2.3 **Auxiliary Laboratory Identification Procedure**

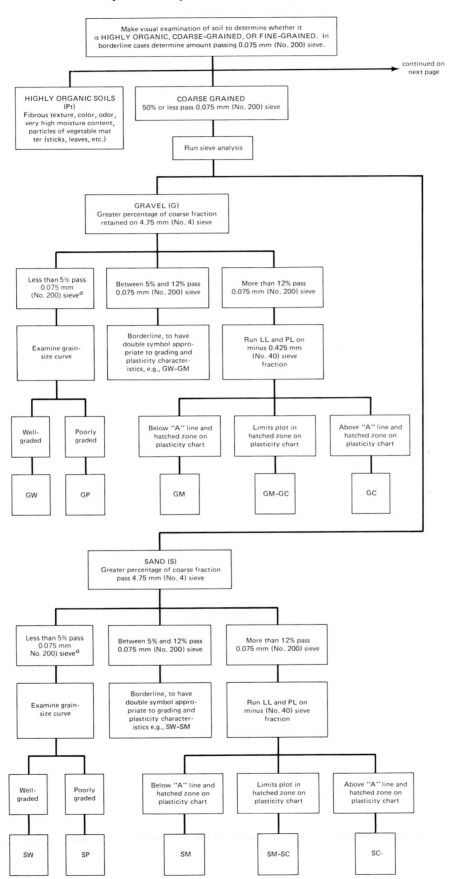

continued on next page

Table 2.3 **Continued**

(continued from previous page)

Courtesy of The Asphalt Institute. Note: Sieve sizes are U. S. Standard.
[a] If fines interfere with free-draining properties, use double symbol such as GW-GM, etc.

halves flow together and the number of drops (called blows) is recorded. A specimen that includes soil from each half of the cup at the point of contact is taken and its moisture content determined. Ideally, the first trial should record about 15 blows and the final trial 35 blows. These data are plotted on semilog graph paper, and a straight line graphed through points of blows versus moisture content. At a point where the graphed straight line intersects the 25-blow abscissa line, the corresponding ordinate identifies the moisture content at which the soil reaches the transitional state between solid and liquid, known as the *liquid limit.*

A distinction is made between material that has a liquid limit (an Atterberg limit) more or less than 50. Clays have a greater plasticity than silts, so if a liquid limit of more than 50 registers, the specimen falls onto the clay side of the chart. Gravels would be either silty gravels (GM), clayey gravels (GC) or a combination of silty gravel-clayey gravel (GM-GC). If the specimen had been classified as a sand, then the results of the Atterberg limits are plotted on the plasticity chart and the sand specimen is classified as a clayey sand

(SC), silty sand (SM) or the combination silty-sand-clayey sand (SM-SC).

Here it is best to note that in identification of soils, the first term identifies the qualifying or descriptive adjective (well-graded, clayey, silty) and the second term the principal or predominant soil classification (clay, sand, silt, gravel). Note that the reverse is true when identifying the soil by letter symbols, SW, GW, etc.

The plastic limit test, which is also used to classify fine-grain soils, requires a soil to be rolled back and forth rapidly on a firm nonporous surface such as glass. The soil is rolled into a threadlike cylinder ⅛ in. in diameter. In this state, the soil is plastic. The test requires several trials. After rolling, the soil is kneaded into a ball and rerolled. At some point, enough moisture evaporates from the soil causing it to lose its plasticity. The soil will no longer roll into a single long thread, but will break into several pieces when rolling is attempted. A moisture content determination is made on these broken pieces. Thus the *plastic limit* is the moisture content at which the soil loses its plasticity.

FIGURE 2.10 Plasticity chart. The Asphalt Institute.

The plasticity index, which is the ordinate on the plasticity chart, is simply the liquid limit minus the plastic limit.

The liquid limit versus plastic limit index data then is plotted on the plasticity chart, and the fine-grain soil classification determined. The significant boundary areas on the plasticity chart are liquid limit values less than 30, 30 to 50, and more than 50, and plastic index valued above or below the "A-line" (see Figure 2.10). Liquid limits below 30 indicate silts and clays of low compressibility, and values above 50 indicate values of high compressibility.

Fine-Grain Size Analysis

Material that is finer than the No. 200 sieve is also graded for grain size. The microscopic grains cannot be classified by conventional sieve analysis. Therefore, fine-grain cohesive

FIGURE 2.11 Liquid limit device.

soils are placed into a defloccuating solution; hydrometer and temperature readings are taken and the results calculated by Stokes' law.

According to Stokes' law, the largest particles in suspension will settle first, while the finer particles will remain in suspension longer. As this settlement continues, there is a decreasing density of the mixture, due to the sedimentation of the denser particles. Thus the temperature/hydrometer/ time relationship measures the changing mixture density. The results of these readings are used to calculate the particle sizes by Stokes' law. A grain size curve will indicate if the soil is well-graded or gap-graded.

Testing for Water Content

The most noticeable property that affects a soil's behavior is its water content. Thus, the water content determination is usually an important part of most soils tests. The water content is determined by (ASTM D 2216) taring, weighing the moist soil, drying it in an oven at 110°C and then weighing the dried solid, Ws. The difference between the wet and dry weights is the water that was evaporated, Ww. When tested for water content, the moist soil is kneaded through the hand and compressed. Its characteristics and properties are noted: cohesiveness, adhesiveness, glister, odor, and color. Its water content is estimated because after several tests one can confirm the water content test of a given soil within 2% or 3%.

SOIL WATER

Water exists in soil in four states: capillary, gravitational, hygroscopic, and adsorbed water. Capillary water is contained in minute pores small enough to cause capillary action. It is considered further below. Water that percolates through soil and that can be drained or pumped out is called gravitational water. Water that surrounds the individual grains with a thin film that cannot be removed by air drying is hygroscopic or film water. It can be removed by oven drying. Adsorbed water clings to the surface of the soil grains and cannot be removed by drying. The soil grains themselves do not absorb water but contain chemically combined water, not considered here. In a given sample of soil, the ratio of the water weight to the dry soil weight is the moisture content. This is expressed as a percentage.

The water in the voids or pores of soil is called pore water, and the pressure exerted by this water constitutes pore pressure. Pore pressure resists external pressures tending to compress or consolidate the soil. By partially holding the soil grains apart, pore pressure diminishes the frictional resistance between grains and therefore reduces the shearing strength. For this reason, tests of soil shearing strength that neglect the pore pressure are not valid. Because sand is very permeable, its pore pressure nearly equals the hydrostatic pressure resulting from the head in static water above

the determined pressure point. Because clay is very impermeable, the pore pressure under a loaded area may indicate
higher values than the surrounding soil. This inequality is
gradually reduced as the pore water is forced from the
pores in the loaded area and assimilated pressure equilibrium approached. This process may require centuries.

The density or weight per cubic foot of clayey soil in
compacted fills is dependent on the soil moisture content.
For every soil sample, there is a moisture content with a
given compaction that will result in a maximum density. The
optimum moisture content is the amount of moisture in a
given soil sample that will produce the maximum density
with a given compaction.

CAPILLARITY

In a soil where pore water contacts air, a concave surface is
formed called a meniscus. This adsorption is often called a
film. The surface tension in the adsorbed water binds the
grains, amply illustrated by damp sand. The soil voids also
serve as capillary tubes, causing the water to rise above the
groundwater level. This *capillary rise* is the height above
groundwater level that water is elevated by capillary action.
In soils, the amount of capillary rise varies with the diameter
of the pores, which is a function of the grain size. The grain
size of sand is large with resultant large pore size, causing
this type of soil to possess practically no capillarity; but in
clays, the small grain size contributes to a large capillary
rise. For this reason, the pores of subsurface clays are
usually filled with water, though the groundwater level may
be many feet below. The rate at which capillary water per-
meates a soil depends upon the size of the pores; it is very
slow in clay. Capillary water cannot be drained out of soil by
any system of drainage.

SWELLING AND SHRINKING

The volume of clay soils tends to change as the moisture
content changes, even though no change occurs in the
external load. This volume change may be a *swelling* or a
shrinking. The change results from stresses exerted by
capillary action in the soil pores. The pores may be considered as bundles or networks of irregularly shaped capillary
tubes permeating the soil. At each point where a pore is
exposed to air, a meniscus forms on the water in the pore
and over the end of the pore. As water evaporates across
the surface, the volume of water in the pore decreases while
the menisci remain at or near the ends of the pore. This
combined action in all pores results in a pulling together,
compressing, or shrinking of the soil. If menisci contact
water from rains, floods, or other causes, the menisci are
destroyed and swelling occurs. There is a limit to the
amount of shrinkage that can take place.

The pore size of sands is so great that no volume change
occurs because of this capillary effect; but in clays, this

phenomenon is pronounced, as manifest by the deep
cracks that form in clay deposits as they dry out and then
dissipate after rains.

The effects of swelling and shrinking are most pronounced in the upper few feet of soil and therefore are a
concern in the design of buildings supported on shallow
footings. Tests are conducted on soil samples to predict the
extent of volume change in the soil with corresponding
changes in water content. The effects of swelling and
shrinking will be discussed in greater detail later in the
chapter.

PERMEABILITY

A significant property of a soil is its *permeability* — that
property of a soil that permits water to pass through its voids
or pores. Because of its large grain and large pore size,
sand offers little resistance to the passage of water. In contrast to sand, the grains of clay are microscopic and the
pores minute; consequently, clay has greater resistance to
the passage of water. Sand, therefore, is very permeable
and clay is very impermeable. Silts are intermediate in permeability. Because of compositional variations, wide latitudes exist in the permeabilities of different clayey soils —
for example, the presence of a small amount of clay may
greatly affect the permeability of sand. Some clays are a
thousand times more permeable than others. The permeability of a soil has a marked effect on the rate that a soil
compresses or consolidates under foundation loads and
also on the watertightness of the foundations.

SHEARING STRENGTH

The *shearing strength* of soils depends upon several factors, namely, the frictional resistance between soil grains
referred to as internal friction, the mutual molecular attraction of the soil grains called true cohesion, and apparent
cohesion, which is the binding of the soil mass by capillary
action of the pore water. Molecular attraction is a negligible
factor in the cohesive strength of sands because the distance between the centers of gravity of sand grains is comparatively large, the sand grains being large for a given
volume. Conversely, clay has small, flat grains and relatively
numerous particles in a given volume, resulting in a molecular attraction that is a factor in the cohesive strength. Additionally, the large grain size and correspondingly large pore
sizes produce little capillary activity; thus, apparent cohesion is not a factor in the shearing strength of sand. However, clay has small particles and small pore size contributing to a large capillary action and therefore great apparent
cohesion. Therefore, the shearing resistance of sand is due
only to internal friction, while the shearing resistance of clay
is due to both internal friction and cohesion. If clay is submerged, capillary action is destroyed, and as a result, apparent cohesion disappears. Submerging has little effect on

internal friction in sand. There are many difficulties in determining the shearing resistance of clay, but this is beyond the present discussion.

The shearing strength of a soil affects its ability to support imposed loads without heaving and prevent sliding due to its own weight or other loads. Various tests are conducted in the field and laboratory to determine the probable shearing strength of the soil under conditions similar to those present during and after the construction of the proposed structure.

COMPRESSIBILITY

The magnitude of foundation settlement depends to a large extent on the *compressibility* of the underlying soil. For the unit pressures under foundations, the unit stresses are relatively low considering the materials that make up the soil grains. The amount of internal deformation of the soil grains is negligible, leaving the decreased volume of the soil due to the decreased volume of the voids. For sands, there can be relatively little decrease in the voids unless their bulky grains are rearranged by a sudden shock or by vibration. For clays, with their scalelike grains and high percentages of voids, a large decrease in the volume of voids may result from foundation pressures. The compressibility of dense sand is therefore quite low, but for clays it is quite high. For some clays, such as those in Mexico City with void ratios as high as 14, the compressibility is very large. Because the compressibility of water is negligible, any settlement resulting from compression may be due to the squeezing of water from the turgid voids. Because of its permeability, sand offers little resistance to the passage of water, and the final degree of compression is reached almost as soon as the load is applied, even though the pores may be water filled. Conversely, clay is quite impermeable, with the pores of natural deposits normally water filled with compression taking place slowly and continually over an extended period. Air is forced from the voids of sand almost instantaneously by applied pressure while offering little resistance. This is called initial consolidation.

In clay, entrapped air and pore water may lie dormant for a considerable time, compressing when pressure is applied; therefore, a certain amount of settlement can occur instantaneously if air is present in the voids. The process of squeezing water out of soil and thereby decreasing its volume is known as primary consolidation. This is caused by the application of a sustained applied load. Consolidation can take place only when the stresses are large enough to break the cohesive bond between soil particles. Fixed consolidation takes place after imposed loads are transferred from the pore water to the solid soil grains.

CONSOLIDATION TEST

This is one of the more widely conducted and more significant soil tests. This test, which is usually performed on a saturated, undisturbed sample, determines the rate and the amount of consolidation of a soil; also, it indicates the expected rate and magnitude of building foundation settlement. The test is conducted upon a cylindrical specimen placed in a consolidometer (there are several types) and subjected to a vertical or axial load that simulates the overburden and building loads. This is done by adding increments of increased loads to the soil with each load increment imposed for at least 24 hours. Settlement readings are recorded at specified times starting at 0.1 minute up to 24 hours or more for each load increment. Tests may be conducted for days.

ELASTICITY

When a body is stressed, its dimensions change. A body that returns to its original form and dimensions when applied stresses are released is elastic, possessing the property of elasticity. Sands are not elastic. Clays have considerable elasticity when the stress values are small compared with the rupture values.

PLASTICITY

The property of a material permitting it to undergo changes in shape or to flow when subjected to steady forces without noticeable change in volume is called plasticity. Sands are not plastic. Clays are plastic at high stresses.

SOLUBILITY

Solubility is not a major factor in soil used to support building foundations. The most soluble material found in soil is gypsum. Limestone is moderately soluble.

CONTRASTING PROPERTIES OF SAND AND CLAY

Sand and clay are two soils with properties that are at either extreme, as shown in Table 2.4. Their properties are of special interest to the architect and engineer. Sands, and especially clays, exhibit variations in compositions and properties while possessing certain aforementioned characteristics, but to varying degrees.

USES OF SOILS

Soil is used directly or processed as a building material. Naturally, it serves as the foundation support for most structures if rock beds are not readily accessible. Some foundations of major structures are carried to bedrock.

Clay is the principal material in the manufacture of fired brick, adobe brick, structural clay tile, vitrified clay pipe, terra-cotta, roofing tile, ceramic floor and wall tile, and porcelain plumbing fixtures. Clay deposits selected for a particular purpose are processed into the finished product primarily by heat.

Table 2.4 Contrasting Properties of Sand and Clay

Property	Sand	Clay
Grain size	Large and bulky	Minute and scaly
Pore size	Large and wide	Small and narrow
Void ratio	Relatively small	Usually high
Internal friction	Large	Very small[a]
Cohesion	Small	Usually large
Capillary effects	Very small	Very large
Permeability	High	Low
Compressibility	Low	High
Shrinkage	Very low	High
Elasticity	Low	High for low stresses
Plasticity	None	High for high stresses

[a] Internal friction of clay is large when no pore water is pesent. Pore water is usually present and holds the grains apart, causing the "apparent" internal friction to be low.

Clay is an ingredient of portland cement, in which the clay is mixed with the proper amount of limestone, pulverized, burned to a clinker, and repulverized.

Sand is an essential ingredient in masonry mortars and plasters. Used thusly, it is mixed with a cementing material such as portland cement, lime, or gypsum plaster and water. Sand is the principal component of concrete. Sand and gravel are used as a free-draining base material under concrete floor and pavement slabs and as a cushion under brick floors and pavements to secure an even bearing. Sand is one of the principal constituents of window and structural glass.

Gravel is a soil grain-size term that applies to rock particles that range in diameter from ¼ in. to 6 in. They are chiefly quartz but may be other types of rocks. The term pebble applies to gravels with diameters up to 3 in. The larger (rock) particles sized 8 in. up to diameters measured in feet are called boulders.

Gumbo is a dark-colored sticky clay. Adobe is a light-colored sandy calcareous clay that is used for sun-dried or kiln-fired masonry products. Bentonite is a highly expansive clay formed by the weathering of volcanic ash. It swells perceptibly up to 10 times its original volume when wet and is used in slurry or in panels to impede the passage of water.

2.3 Soil Pressures

Spread foundations and settlement design computations are based on the pressure distribution between the foundation bed and the underlying soil. Investigators have measured these pressures and have developed methods for computation. The measured soil pressures, subject to the uncertainties in most pressure cell methods, correlate experiment and theory with reasonable satisfaction. The computed pressures, determined by analytical methods, assume that soils have certain properties which they possess only to a limited degree.

A widely used method, developed in 1885 by Boussinesq, is for a homogeneous, isotropic, elastic solid with an applied normal surface load. Various proposals attempt to modify Boussinesq's solution for application to soils, but no approach is generally recognized. The pressures of interest in foundation computations are the unit vertical pressures on horizontal surfaces at various depths. The calculation of these pressures, using Boussinesq's method directly, is quite laborious; however, Newmark developed a procedure that has greatly simplified the computations. Boussinesq's solution applies to soil pressures produced by superimposed loads — pressures of interest in settlement computations.

CONTACT PRESSURES

The distribution of the normal pressure on the surface of contact between the bottom of a footing and the soil is worth noting. The analytical solution based on idealized properties, assuming the footing to be perfectly rigid, gives the stress distribution in Figure 2.12A with infinite, unit normal pressures at the edges. Actually, no material could be perfectly elastic for infinite stresses, and therefore, the pressure under the edges will have some large finite value.

The distributions for rigid plates on clay and sand have been determined experimentally, with the results shown in Figure 2.13B. The contact pressures for clay were found to have a distribution similar to that given by the analytical solution. As the depths of the footing increased, the proportionate difference between the edge pressures and the center pressure decreased. Probably the pressure distribution in clay will gradually become more uniform as the clay consolidates under pressure. The contact pressures for sand were found to be a maximum at the center and zero at the edges, where the footing was on the surface. This would be expected because the sand grains under the edge of the footing have no lateral support and so can carry no vertical stress.

With clay, cohesion provides this lateral support. When

FIGURE 2.12 Contact pressures on surface.

FIGURE 2.13 Contact pressures below surface.

the footing is below the surface, edge pressures are developed because the sand grains under the edge now have lateral support which is proportional to the depth below the surface. Lateral support increases, however, as the center of the footing is approached, and the pressures increase accordingly. The usual practice in the design of footings is to assume a uniform pressure distribution (Figure 2.13A). The effect of other distributions should be considered, especially in combined and continuous footings and in raft

foundations as well as the elastic deflection of the foundation on the distribution of foundation pressures.

The effect of the distribution of contact pressures on the unit vertical pressures under a footing does not extend deep enough to be of any importance in settlement computations.

PRESSURE BULBS

The unit vertical pressures under a square footing, as computed by Boussinesq's solution, are shown in Figure 2.14A and experimental values for a circular plate on sand, determined by Kogler and Schedig, are shown in Figure 2.14B.

In each of these figures, the values are for unit vertical pressures at points in a vertical plane through the center of the loaded surface. The magnitudes of the pressures are indicated by lines, sometimes called isobars, drawn through points of equal vertical pressure. These figures are called *pressure bulbs* because of their form. The dimensions of computed pressure bulbs are directly proportional to the width of the loaded area. It is assumed that this proportion applies to pressure bulbs in actual soils, but the variations in the soil do affect the dimensions of the bulb. The distribution of the contact pressures is different for clay and sand, but the effect of this difference extends only below the immediate surface. The upper portions of the pressure bulbs for clay and sand are therefore different, but in other respects they are considered identical.

The isobar for zero stress is at the surface for Boussinesq's solution (Figure 2.14); but for the experimental bulb, it extends downward and outward from the edge of the footing (Figure 2.14B). Note that the isobar does not close. It

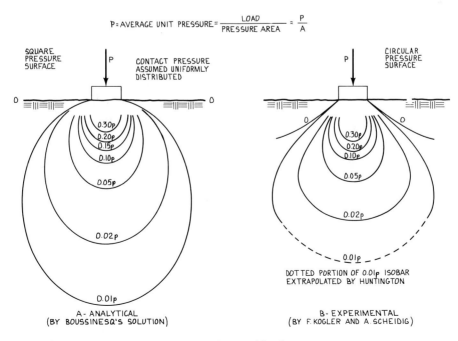

FIGURE 2.14 Bulb pressure for isolated spread footing.

FIGURE 2.15 Bulb of pressure for a group of spread footings.

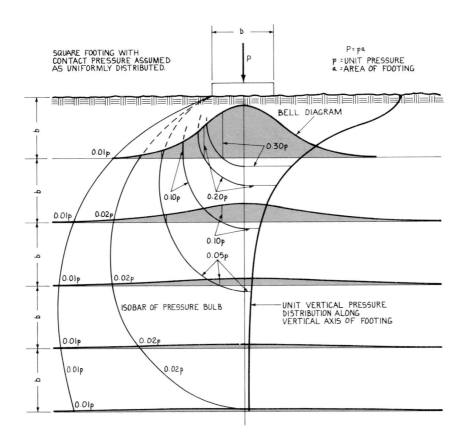

FIGURE 2.16 Relation between bell diagrams and bulb of pressure.

cannot pass under the footing, as do all other isobars, because nothing would be supporting the load along the surface of which this line is a trace.

Buildings are usually supported on several footings. The pressure bulbs for the individual footings gradually merge into a single bulb for the entire foundation (Figure 2.15).

The pressure bulb for a square mat supporting all the columns of a building is identical to that for a square footing (Figures 2.14 and 2.16).

Most of the settlement of a footing, a group of footings, or a mat is due to the unit vertical pressures included within the bulb for pressures of 0.2p. For convenience, this will be referred to as the significant bulb of pressure. Pressures outside this bulb can be neglected.

BELL DIAGRAMS

The distribution of unit vertical pressures along horizontal planes at various depths is illustrated in Figure 2.16. These are bell diagrams. The "stress volume" included under each of these diagrams is equal to the load. The pressure bulb corresponding to the bell diagrams is shown. At each point where an isobar crosses the corresponding horizontal line, the ordinate of the bell diagram is equal to the pressure represented by the isobar. The distribution of unit vertical pressures along a vertical line through the center of a footing

is shown in Figure 2.16. The abscissas in this figure are equal to the corresponding midordinates of the bell diagram. A pressure bulb is analogous to a contour map; and a bell diagram, to a profile.

2.4 Bearing Areas of Spread Foundations

The bearing areas of spread footings must be proportioned to satisfy the following requirements:

1. There must be an adequate factor of safety against failure of the underlying soil, which ruptures when the shearing stresses produced by the footing loads exceed the shearing strength of the soil. The factor of safety commonly required for stresses caused by dead and live loads only is 3. If stresses produced by wind loads or earthquake shocks are included, the factor is reduced to 2; these loads are not considered to act simultaneously.

2. The settlement of any footing from the compression of the underlying soil must not be more than use conditions permit.

3. The relative, or differential, settlement between any adjacent footings must not be excessive. The differential set-

tlement permitted depends on the consequences of such settlement. In the absence of complete information, differential settlement is often limited to ¾ in.

CODE VALUES FOR ALLOWABLE SOIL BEARING PRESSURES

The most common procedure for selecting values for the *allowable pressures* on various soils is to consult the governing building code or values recommended by appropriate agencies (see Table 2.5). This information is sometimes supplemented by bearing capacity tests conducted in accordance with specified procedures, described later. Usually, appropriate subsurface investigations, previously described, should be made. The extent of these investigations depends upon occupancy, economic importance of the building, and general knowledge of difficulties anticipated at the site.

Uncertainties in the selection of appropriate values for the allowable soil pressures from such tables are due partially to the indefinite descriptions of the soils. They are subject to differences in interpretation. This is true especially for clays. Factors not recognized in code values or in the conventional procedure for proportioning the bearing areas may have significant effects on the behavior of foundations. Some of these are summarized in Section 2.5.

The allowable soil pressure for an underlying stratum, as determined by settlement, is in some instances less than that of the soil on which a foundation rests. This discrepancy is provided for by the requirement that the unit pressure due to the footing load computed on the top surface A-A of the weaker stratum (Figure 2.17) shall not exceed the allowable soil pressure for the material in that stratum. The load here is considered uniformly distributed over the area intercepted on the top surface of the weaker stratum by planes sloping from the edges of the foundation 60° with the horizontal, as shown in the figure. This is an arbitrary assumption and does not follow the form of the bell diagram in Figure 2.16. However, the procedure is considered sufficiently accurate for its intended purpose and is simple in its application.

Table 2.5 Allowable Foundation and Lateral Pressure

Class of Materials[b]	Allowable Foundation Pressure[c] lbs/ft sq	Lateral Bearing lb/sq ft/ft of Depth Natural Grade[d]	Lateral Sliding[a]	
			Coefficient[e]	Resistance lb/sq ft[f]
1. Massive Crystalline Bedrock	4000	1200	.79	
2. Sedimentary and Foliated Rock	2000	400	.35	
3. Sandy Gravel and/or Gravel (GW and GP)	2000	200	.35	
4. Sand, Silty Sand, Clayey Sand, Silty Gravel and Clayey Gravel (SW, SP, SM, SC, GM and GC)	1500	150	.25	
5. Clay, Sandy Clay, Silty Clay and Clayey Silt (CL, ML, MH and CH)	1000[g]	100		130

[a] Lateral bearing and lateral sliding resistance may be combined.

[b] For soil classifications OL, OH and PT (i.e., organic clays and peat), a foundation investigation shall be required.

[c] All values of allowable foundation pressure are for footings having a minimum width of 12 inches and a minimum depth of 12 inches into natural grade. Except as in g below, increase of 20% allowed for each additional foot of width and/or depth to a maximum value of three times the designated value.

[d] May be increased the amount of the designated value for each additional foot of depth to a maximum of 15 times the designated value. Isolated poles not supporting buildings such as flagpoles or signs may be designed using lateral bearing values equal to two times the tabulated values.

[e] Coefficient to be multiplied by the dead load.

[f] Frictional value to be multiplied by the contract area. In no case shall the frictional resistance exceed one-half the dead load.

[g] No increase for width is allowed.

Reproduced from the 1976 Edition of the *Uniform Building Code* copyright 1976, with the permission of the publisher, the International Conference of Building Officials.

FIGURE 2.17 Assumed distribution of vertical pressures under a footing.

FIGURE 2.18 Comparison of significant bulb pressure for test load and for actual load.

In estimating settlement, the allowable pressures on underlying soil are considered as pressures that the building can add to those already there. This is equivalent to neglecting the weight of the soil in determining the pressures on underlying soil for comparison with allowable values.

BEARING CAPACITY TESTS

Tests help select the allowable soil pressure. The tests are conducted in a pit bottom several feet below the ground surface. Test loads are usually applied in pits which have bottoms at the identical elevation as the bottoms of the proposed footings. Loads are applied to a test area at least 1 ft square on the bottom of the pit. There should be no other loads on the bottom of the pit.

In one procedure, a load equal to the proposed allowable soil pressure is applied and settlement readings taken at least every 24 hours. The test is continued until there is no more settlement during a 24-hour period. The load is then increased 50% and the settlements observed. The proposed allowable soil pressure is considered satisfactory if the initial settlement is not more than ¾ in. and if the additional settlement is not more than 60% of the initial settlement due to the load equal to the proposed soil pressure. The settlement resulting from the load equal to the proposed soil pressure is sometimes limited to ½ in. The test is repeated, if required, until an appropriate allowable soil bearing value can be selected.

A test area of 4 sq ft is sometimes required, especially for soils with the lower allowable soil pressures. Tests for several test areas are required for selecting allowable soil pressures when there are major differences in the proposed footing sizes.

Procedures for interpreting loading-test data are arbitrary and not entirely satisfactory. The results are affected by the relation between the test area and the area of the pit bottom. If the test area occupies a large portion of the pit bottom, the loaded soil receives considerable support from the soil surrounding the pit, but if only a small portion of the bottom is loaded, this support is minimal. Experienced judgment,

guided by examination and tests of the underlying soil, must be used in the interpretation of test results.

This type of test may have little value in determining allowable soil pressure. The soil pressures under a footing that account for most of the settlement are those included within the pressure bulb equal to $0.2p$ (Figures 2.14 and 2.16). The pressure bulb extends to a depth approximately one and one-half times the width of the footing. This is the significant bulb of pressure (Figure 2.18). For a load test, this bulb extends only a short distance below the loaded surface, but for an actual footing (Figure 2.18B), the bulb extends much deeper. If the actual bulb passes through an underlying soft stratum, much of the footing settlement might be due to the compression of the stratum. The settlement (due to the soil compression under a given unit pressure) varies directly with the dimensions of the loaded area, similar to pressure bulb increases.

ULTIMATE BEARING CAPACITY

The bearing capacity of a building foundation may be determined by the permissible settlement or by actual rupture of the soil. When a load is placed on soil, shearing stresses set up in the soil cause the grains to move in relation to each other. This fact is demonstrated by the photograph in Figure 2.19; a time exposure is taken as a rod was forced into sand contained in a box with the exposed side made of plate glass. A flat side of the rod was placed next to the glass. During the test, the path of each sand grain movement in contact with the glass is photographed by time exposure. The exaggerated vertical movement of the rod is greater relatively than permissible footing settlement, but the photograph illustrates the tendency for the soil to displace laterally and upward. A similar phenomenon has been observed in clay. The soil grains near the rod move outward and upward

FIGURE 2.19 Displacement of sand by surface load.

along curved paths, and heaving occurs at the surface. Outside a fairly definite boundary, the soil is not displaced.

In the disturbed region, the shearing stresses along the curved paths exceed the shearing resistance of the soil, but in the undisturbed region the shearing resistance exceeds the shearing stresses. The displacements are illustrated in Figure 2.20. Analytical solutions have been devised for computing the maximum load that a soil with a known shearing strength will carry.

FAILURE OF EARTH SLOPES
Earth slopes of cohesive soil may fail by rupture with no load except the weight of the earth itself, as manifested by landslides. Buildings placed on or near a sloping earth surface may contribute to slide failures and be damaged or destroyed. Some earth slopes fail very slowly, and failure is foretold by excessive cracking in the buildings or by gradual settlement. In other earth slopes, the failure may be sudden because of the weakening of the soil by absorbed rain-

water, the increased soil weight, and the force exerted by percolating water. The effect of earthquake shocks compounds the situation.

A common failure of earth slopes is diagrammed in Figure 2.21. A portion of the earth embankment designated as *ABCD* tends to slide on the curved surface *BC* (a weakened shear plane) and to pile up as shown by the irregular lines. If a part or all of a building occupies the horizontal surface affected, the building will be damaged or will collapse. Experience has shown that earth slopes, except clean sand or gravel, fail on roughly curved surfaces. In computations of earth slope stability, the assumption is usually made that failure will occur on a smooth arc, called a slip circle. The portion of the slope that slides is considered to rotate about *O*, the center of the arc. The resistance to failure is offered by the shearing strength of the earth along the arc. If the moment $W \cdot a$ (in Figure 2.21), representing the forces tending to cause failure, exceeds $T \cdot r$, the moment of the resisting forces, failure results. If $W \cdot a$ is less than $T \cdot r$, the slope is stable, the factor of safety is measured by $T \cdot r \div W \cdot a$.

The arc *BC,* on which failure is most likely, must be located by trial, because the arc will give the least factor of safety in the computations. If a building is on the summit of a slope, or within the slip circle (Figure 2.21*A*), the weight *W'* with the moment arm, *b,* must be included in the computations. Where forces other than these exist, they must be considered. A slope that is stable prior to building may fail because of the added building load. Buildings should not be on or near clay slopes unless measures are taken to prevent failure from the causes outlined in this paragraph. Instead of passing through a building (Figure 2.21*B*), the rupture surface may emerge a considerable distance behind the build-

FIGURE 2.20 Causes of settlement of footing.

FIGURE 2.21 Failure of earth slopes.

ing, as in deep-seated failures. The sliding block of soil carries the building to destruction. Analytical methods for investigating the stability of earth slopes are recommended.

BEARING CAPACITY OF ROCK

Rock gradually grades into soil, and therefore no definite value can be given for the bearing capacity of rock. The bearing capacity of rock is given in Table 2.5. Sound bedrock usually will support any load transmitted by a concrete pier because the allowable unit compressive stress in the concrete is less than the allowable bearing stress in the rock. A given material is stronger in bearing when the load is applied to a small portion of its surface than when formed in a prism such as a pier. Failure in bearing could occur only by shear, in a manner similar to the failure of soil that carried a surface load (Figure 2.20). As stated in Section 2.2, some shales yield by plastic flow when subjected to bearing pressures. Thus, shales should always be carefully investigated before subjected to heavy bearing pressures.

When rock is considered for foundation support, compression tests should be made to determine a safe bearing value. Allowable bearing pressures given in Table 2.5 are in general terms.

Other accountable factors in examining rock for proposed foundations are the direction of stratification or dip as illustrated in Figure 2.22, structural defects, such as excessive fractures, caverns and solution channels in limestone,

FIGURE 2.22 Tendency to slide along bedding plane.

faults and fissures, and possible weak underlying strata. If a fault crosses the building site, the possibility of movement along the fault and possible consequences should be considered.

As previously stated, a test hole drilled 10 ft or more in the bottom of a rock excavation may yield a core that would reveal any objectionable structural defects or unsatisfactory underlying material.

2.5 Foundation Settlement

All foundations settle except those on sound rock. When the supporting soil is dense, coarse sand or gravel, the amount of settlement is relatively small, unless the loads are excessive and unless the settlement occurs as soon as the load is applied. In contrast to sand and gravel, settlement of clay may be large and may continue over many years. In extreme cases, the settlement of structures founded on clay is measured in feet.

Settlement may not be objectionable if the entire foundation settles uniformly, if the settlement is not excessive, and if the settlement is predictable within reasonable limits. Such settlement causes no structural damage. However, *differential settlement,* or different amounts of settlement in adjacent parts of a foundation, introduces internal stresses that may seriously weaken a building by throwing various parts of the building out of plumb. Differential settlement produces unsightly cracks, causes floors to be out of level and uneven, causes roofs to leak, interferes with door operation, and unbalances mechanical equipment.

In the design of spread foundations, it is usually assumed that, if the supporting soil is fairly uniform over the building site, settlement will be uniform when the unit pressures exerted are the same for all parts of the foundation. In computing pressures, only the weight of the building and imposed long-term static loads are considered to cause settlement. Additionally, the maximum unit pressure in any part of the foundation for any possible condition of loading is usually limited to some arbitrarily adopted allowable soil pressure — that this practice is unsatisfactory, particularly for cohesive soils such as clays, has become increasingly evident. Experience with actual foundations supported by experimental and theoretical investigations show that, within certain limits, the settlement for a given unit pressure on a given soil increases as the lineal dimension of that area increases. This practice has also been unsatisfactory because of the inadequate and faulty methods used for determining the allowable bearing pressures for soils.

CAUSES FOR SETTLEMENT

The possible causes of foundation settlement are:

1. Reduction in the volume of the voids of the supporting

soil and, therefore, in the volume of this soil, which is the compressibility. This is the principal and usually the only important cause of foundation settlement.

2. Actual rupture of the soil.

3. The lateral displacement of the soil is so small that it need not be considered unless the lateral support of the soil is reduced by adjoining excavations or unless shallow foundations bear on soft clay.

4. The compression of the soil grains themselves is negligible because the unit stresses in the soil grains, in relation to the loads placed on foundations, are too small to be of any consequence.

As explained in Section 3.1, the most effective method for reducing the settlement of foundations supported on a deep bed of soft clay is to excavate the basement of the building to a depth sufficient enough to make the weight of the soil removed equal to the weight of the building and its permanent contents. Thus, increased soil pressure from the building load is avoided.

SETTLEMENT PREDICTIONS

Settlement predictions for structures founded on clay are based on the consolidation phenomenon mentioned in Section 2.2. They are made by computing the unit vertical pressures, caused by the building loads, below the foundation and by making consolidation tests at various depths on representative samples of the soil that supports the building. The procedures followed in computing the unit vertical pressures were considered in Section 2.3. The consolidation test is made in a specially designed apparatus in which the soil sample is compressed and the time rate at which the sample deforms under a given unit pressure is observed, provision being made for water to escape at the top and bottom surfaces of the sample. Mathematical relationships have been developed that enable the settlements to be estimated from the unit foundation pressures and the consolidation characteristics of the samples, due consideration being given to the location of the porous strata. These samples in the test apparatus should be undisturbed samples. Settlement predictions require specialized knowledge and experience and are the province of an engineer soil specialist.

GROUND WATER

A large portion of our land surfaces are underlaid with *ground water* occupying the pores and other spaces in the soil and rock. The groundwater surface is called the groundwater table or simply the water table. Generally, the groundwater table is not horizontal but follows roughly the contour of the ground surface. The groundwater table elevation at a given point is termed the groundwater level. Reference is often made to the permanent groundwater level, but in most locations, no permanent groundwater level exists. The water table elevation fluctuates with the amount of rainfall and with the depletion by pumping for water supply. The water table may be lowered markedly by the construction of sewers, drains, subways, and other underground works.

The location of the groundwater table is of particular concern in selecting the type of foundation, in foundation design, and in planning construction procedures.

LOWERING OF WATER LEVEL

The groundwater elevation may affect the settlement of foundations bearing on soil. The water level often lowers after a building has been completed. It may occur because sewer or drainage systems are installed or subways, depressed highways, and other underground works are constructed. Many years may elapse before this groundwater decline occurs.

If foundations are on sand or gravel with an underlying stratum of clay and the water level is in these permeable materials, the pressures on the underlying clay stratum may be increased by lowering of the water level because of the reduced buoyant effect of water or the effective weight of submerged sand or gravel.

If the foundations are on clay, lowering the groundwater level will promote the consolidation of the clay. Also, the clay soil may be compressed further by the increased capillary tension in the soil, as explained in Section 2.2.

EFFECTS ON ADJOINING BUILDINGS

Foundations of existing buildings supported on waterbearing sand or silt may be undermined by adjoining excavations because of pumping operations to control the water. Soft clay soils may squeeze into excavations for piers and walls. This condition is shown by the excess of the excavated material over the volume of the excavation. Excess of excavation, or lost ground, may result in a corresponding settlement of adjoining foundations.

Even though a building is constructed only to the limits of its own site, it causes vertical as well as lateral pressures in the soil of the adjoining sites. The increased vertical soil pressures under the foundations of an existing building due to the construction of a new building on an adjoining site may cause the existing building to settle.

Upheaval of the soil resulting from the reduction of soil pressures when an adjoining building is removed may damage a building, but soils that will produce this effect are rare.

SHRINKING AND SWELLING

As explained previously, clay soils shrink and swell as the moisture content varies markedly during long periods of drought or rainy weather or with seasonal changes. These effects are most pronounced in the upper few feet of soil and therefore involve buildings on shallow foundations. Some clays are more susceptible to this action than others; those with high percentages of bentonite are especially objectionable. Shrinking and swelling tend to be more pronounced on exterior footings than on interior footings because of the greater protection given to the latter by the building. Extensive damage might occur only many years after construction.

Some exterior footings have settled considerably more than the interior footings because of shrinkage, and in others, the exterior footings have risen considerably above the interior footings because of soil expansion. The possibility of heaving and settlement should be considered when building in regions where this has taken place or where expansive clays exist.

The only apparent means of avoiding these difficulties is to carry the foundations to depths where they will not be affected.

COMMENTS

1. For footings bearing on a given soil and causing equal soil pressures on the bearing area, the following relationships prevail for uniform deposits of sand, gravel, and clay foundation materials.

(a) The settlements are approximately proportional to the widths of wall footings and to the linear dimensions of isolated footings which have the same ratios between their lateral dimensions.

(b) The settlements of wall footings are greater than those of isolated footings.

2. The settlement of footings founded on sand or gravel occurs during a short period of time and then ceases, but for those founded on dense clays, the settlement may continue for many years.

3. For uniform deposits of sand or clay, most of the settlement of a footing acting independently is due to the vertical soil pressures included in a depth equal to one and one-half times the width of the footing, as indicated by the pressure bulb for $0.20p$ in Figures 2.14A and 2.16, which may be called the significant bulb of pressure.

4. In uniform sand or clay deposits, most settlement of one row isolated footings is indicated by the significant bulb of pressure shown on the left side of Figure 2.15. The pressure bulb for several rows of isolated footings is shown on the right side of Figure 2.15.

5. If the underlying deposits of soil are more compressible than the soil on which a footing is founded, the underlying deposits may contribute significantly to the settlement of the footing or to a foundation consisting of several isolated footings, especially if they lie within the significant bulbs of pressure.

6. The settlement of shallow footings founded on some clays may significantly increase because of a diminution of the moisture content during periods of drought, or such footings may heave during periods of heavy rainfall.

7. Foundations of unconsolidated sand or gravel may settle owing to a decrease in void spaces caused by excessive vibrations within a building or by operations adjacent to the building. Foundations on clay are not affected.

8. Foundations on clay or soil underlaid with clay deposits may settle if the groundwater is lowered.

2.6 Settlement of Pile Foundations

For convenience, it is usually stated that piles support foundations; however, piles are intermediate members which transmit foundation loads to the underlying soil or rock. Such piles are called *bearing piles* to distinguish them from sheet piles and other kinds of piles, such as fender piles and guide piles. Interlocking sheet piles are driven juxtaposed to form a continuous barrier or sheet, retaining earth or forming an effective watertight diaphragm. Fender piles and guide piles have special functions as indicated by their names.

The bearing capacity of the soil into which piles are driven may be fairly uniform throughout the length of the piles which transmit the load from the pile to the surrounding soil. The piles may pass through soft soil with little or no bearing capacity and then penetrate into firmer soil to which the load is transmitted by friction, or the piles may pass through soft soil to hardpan or rock to which the load is transmitted by the pile tips. The entire load on a pile foundation is considered to be transmitted through the piles with no load transmitted directly to the soil by the pile cap.

DESIGN REQUIREMENTS

Pile foundations must satisfy the following requirements:

1. The pile caps or mats must be structurally adequate to transmit the building loads to the piles.

2. Each pile must have adequate strength to carry its load and adequate bearing capacity to transmit its load to the supporting foundation material.

3. The entire foundation must be proportioned so that excessive building settlement is prevented.

4. The differential settlements between adjacent footings must not exceed permissible values. The consequences of these settlements are the same as they are for spread foundations, as explained previously.

5. The shearing stresses in the supporting soil must not exceed an adequate factor of safety against rupture of the soil. A safety factor of 3 is adequate for dead load plus full live load, and a factor of 2 is adequate when wind loads or

earthquake shock are included; the design is based on the most critical condition.

6. To ensure stability, a minimum of two rows of piles should support a continuous or wall pile footing, and a minimum of three piles should support an isolated or column footing.

CAUSES OF SETTLEMENT

Some causes of friction pile foundations settlement are:

1. An individual pile may settle by moving through the sur-rounding soil, as shown in Figure 2.23A. An isolated pile normally settles because of the compression of the sur-rounding soil to which it transmits stress, as indicated by the pressure bulb *(B)*. However, piles are not used individually.

2. A pile footing and the surrounding soil will settle because the foundation load transmitted by the piles will compress the soil, as indicated by the pressure bulb (Figure 2.23C).

3. A cluster of piles supporting a footing together with the enclosed soil may settle by yielding as a unit and moving downward with respect to the surrounding soil (Figure 2.23D).

FIGURE 2.23 Bulbs of pressure and settlement of piles and pile footings.

4. An entire pile foundation of several pile footings will settle because the soil underlying the structure as a whole compresses. This condition is normal for building foundations having a number of isolated footings; but unexpected settlements of large magnitude may be caused by undetected layers of low bearing capacity soil, such as peat. To avoid this difficulty, adequate subsurface exploration of the soil should be conducted for a considerable depth below the pile tips. Foundation settlement is caused by the compression of the soil and results from the stresses transmitted to it by the piles, as indicated by the pressure bulb in Figure 2.23E.

Other causes of settlement are the lateral movement of soil under a foundation, removal of lateral support or undermining, compacting of loose sand by vibrations, and damage to piles during driving.

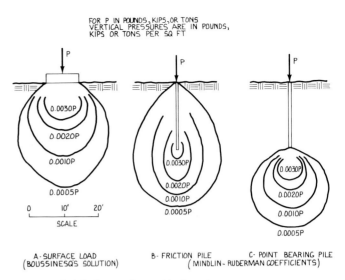

FIGURE 2.24 Comparison of bulbs of pressure.

PILE ACTION

Unless resting on hardpan or rock, a pile is supported by skin friction along its length and point resistance at its tip, both exerted by the soil that surrounds the pile. A pile supported primarily by skin friction is called a *friction pile* or a *floating pile*, and one supported principally by point resistance is a point-bearing or end-bearing pile. The distribution of the load between skin friction and point resistance depends upon the type of soil penetrated and is discussed subsequently. Below the pile tip, the load is supported entirely by the underlying soil. A pile, therefore, increases the bearing capacity of a soil by distributing the load through a wider area and deeper into the soil. A footing on the ground surface, a friction pile, and a pile that transmits its load primarily by point resistance illustrate their pressure distributions in Figure 2.24.

Piles driven in deposits of loose sand compact the sand and thereby increase its bearing capacity. Piles driven for this purpose only are called compaction piles.

PILE CLUSTERS OR GROUPS

Piles are not used singly but are arranged in groups or clusters centered under the loads. These loads are distributed to the individual piles by rigid *pile caps* or reinforced concrete similar to spread footings. A footing bearing on piles is called a *pile footing.*

It is sometimes assumed that the bearing capacity of a pile group is equal to the bearing capacity of one pile multiplied by the number of piles. This is true when the piles bear on rock or if the piles are spaced so far apart that the overlapping of pressure bulbs is of no consequence. Generally, bearing piles can be spaced more closely than friction piles. The spacing factors are the compressive strength of the piles and the bearing capacity of the supporting foundation material.

There is no entirely satisfactory criterion for the spacing of friction piles. It is sometimes considered that the perimeter of the pile group should equal at least the sum of the perimeters of the individual piles. This conclusion is based on the assumption that the shearing resistance per unit of surface area is the same for the piles as for the prism of earth included within the perimeter of the pile group (Figure 2.23D). The center-to-center spacing of piles is usually required to be not less than 2½ or 3 times the diameter of the round piles or the diagonal of rectangular piles, but the minimum of 2 ft 6 in. is often used.

The distribution of vertical pressures on a horizontal plane at the points of the piles is somewhat as shown in Figure 2.25. In this figure, it is assumed that the piles act independently and that the total vertical pressure at any point on the horizontal plane is equal to the sum of the vertical pressures at that point produced by the individual piles. On this basis, the settlements of the center piles would obviously be greater than those of the outside piles. However, the rigid cap would cause all of the piles to settle nearly the same amount. This tends to increase the pressure under the outer piles and decrease it under the center pile, but the pressure under each center pile would still be greater than it would be under a single pile. Mat footings founded on piles as shown in Figure 3.10 tend to settle more at the center than at the end due to this effect.

A simple useful procedure assumes that the load from a group of piles is distributed outward and downward at an angle of 60° with the horizontal; the load extending from the perimeter of the group of piles is at an elevation where the piles enter a stratum that has satisfactory bearing capacity. The soil pressures are considered uniformly distributed on the portions of horizontal planes included within the 60° limiting planes. This procedure is illustrated in Figure 2.26.

A - STRESSES UNDER SINGLE PILE   B - STRESSES UNDER ROW OF FIVE PILES

FIGURE 2.25 Vertical pressure distribution at elevation of pile points.

Each pile is assumed to carry by point resistance a load equal to the allowable unit soil pressure at the point of the pile multiplied by the area of the point. The remainder of the load is assumed to be carried by skin friction and to be transmitted to the surrounding soil at a uniform rate along the pile. The actual soil pressures at the depths where the soil type changes are computed and compared with allowable soil pressures stated by the code. These allowable soil pressures must not be exceeded. Only the pressures due to the foundation load are included. Overlap of planes of adjacent footings must be considered.

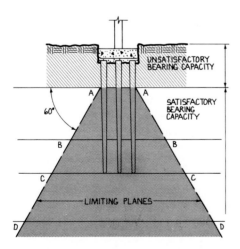

FIGURE 2.26 Assumed distribution of vertical pressures under pile footings.

EFFECT OF WIDTH OF FOUNDATION

Half pressure bulbs for a spread footing and a friction pile footing are compared in Figure 2.27A indicating that the piles lower the pressure bulb significantly and thereby increase the bearing capacity. Half pressure bulbs for a mat or raft foundation supported on the ground surface and on friction piles are shown in Figure 2.27B. It is evident that the piles have little effect on the pressure bulb, except near the ground surface, and therefore are not effective in reducing the settlement or increasing the bearing capacity of the mat footing.

EFFECTS OF TYPE OF SOIL

When a pile is driven, it occupies a space made available only by compressing the surrounding soil or by displacing the volume of soil equal to the pile volume. To compensate for this volume displacement, the soil surrounding the pile rises or heaves. In some soils, the pile occupies a space that results partially from compression and partially from heaving.

The bearing capacity of loose sand or other compressible fill may be improved by compacting it with piles. The pile spacing required to produce the necessary bearing capacity by compaction is determined by trial.

It is difficult to drive piles into dense sand or gravel without the aid of jetting. The water jet decreases the point resistance and, in some instances, decreases the frictional resistance along the length of the pile. The jet washes the

FIGURE 2.27 Relation of width of foundation to effectiveness of piles.

sand grains away from the point and up along the pile surface to the top of the ground. If a jet is used, the final penetration of the pile should be secured by driving with the hammer only. Jets are not as effective in clay soils. If heaving must be reduced, possibly because it affects adjacent piles, holes may be bored or cored out with driven open-end pipe to receive the piles which are driven into final positions. The depth of the holes is usually less than the length of the piles.

The point resistance of a pile driven into clay does not contribute significantly to its bearing capacity, but it is a factor in the bearing capacity of the piles driven into dense sand.

When piles are driven through a layer of partially consolidated soil and into firm soil, the load on the piles may be gradually increased as the layer consolidates and settles. The increase is caused by the frictional drag on the piles as the settlement progresses and may result in increased settlement of the foundation or even failure of the piles.

The bearing capacity of a pile may increase or decrease after the driving is completed. If the pile is driven into coarse sand that can drain freely, there is little change after a period of rest. In fine sand and silt, which are less permeable than coarse sands, and in clay, the displacement of soil by the pile will build up pressure in the water in the voids of the soil surrounding the pile. This pressure resists the penetration and increases the point resistance. Since the soil is slowly permeable, however, water pressure will gradually be dissipated and the point resistance will decrease accordingly. Piles driven into clay displace the corresponding volume of clay, causing heaving and compressing the clay very little, but a small amount of water is squeezed out of the clay adjacent to the pile tip and rises around the pile. This lubricates the pile surface and reduces its frictional resistance.

The vibration of the pile during driving makes the hole slightly larger than the pile and forms a space around the pile into which the water can flow. After driving, the clay surrounding the pile gradually reabsorbs the water and "sets" around the pile, thereby increasing the skin friction. Since most bearing capacity of piles driven in clay is due to skin friction, the increase in skin friction after a period of rest increases the bearing capacity. This is the reason that piles driven in clay "freeze up" after driving operations have been suspended for a short period. The resumption of driving will be more difficult and require breaking this frictional bond before further penetration is made.

Except in clean sands and gravels, the adhesion between the soil and the pile is usually greater than the shearing strength of the soil itself, so that the resistance along the sides of the pile is usually the shearing strength of the soil immediately surrounding the pile. This shearing resistance depends upon the internal friction and the cohesive strength of the soil. Because of the compacting effect of the pile during driving, the shearing strength of the soil close to the pile may be greater than that of the soil at some distance from the pile. The shearing area, of course, increases as the distance from the pile increases.

When clusters of piles are driven in clay soils, the driving of one pile may cause adjacent piles already in place to rise and become unseated. If this occurs, all of the piles so affected must be seated by partial redriving.

BEARING CAPACITY OF INDIVIDUAL PILES

The bearing capacity of individual piles is estimated by pile formulas or measured by applying loads to *test piles.* The formulas may be static or dynamic. These formulas calculate the resistance of a pile to loads tending to cause movement with respect to immediate surrounding soil and not to the bearing capacity of the surrounding soil. Pile settlement is movement of the pile through the soil or movement of the pile and the surrounding soil as a unit. The latter is caused by the compression of the soil under the action of the pressures induced in it by the load transmitted from the pile to the soil.

Static formulas estimate the bearing capacity by computing the shearing resistance along the surface of the pile and the bearing point resistance. The shearing resistance and point resistance are obtained experimentally. The extreme variation in soils of the same general class makes it difficult to determine suitable values for the pertinent properties in estimating shearing and bearing resistance.

Dynamic formulas compute the pile bearing capacity from its behavior during driving. The factors used in all formulas are the energy used in driving and the average penetration produced by the last few blows. Other factors may be the pile weight, its cross-sectional area, its length, and its modulus of elasticity. These factors compute the energy lost during the hammer impact on the pile.

There are a plethora of driving formulas available to serve

some expressed or assumed soil condition. Any formula must be used with caution and measured judgment and only after a careful investigation of the prevailing conditions.

The frictional resistance and the point resistance of a pile in permeable materials, such as sand, gravel, and permeable fills, are nearly the same during driving as under static load. When a pile is driven into these materials, a theoretically sound, dynamic formula can be expected to give good results. The frictional and point resistances that prevail during driving, however, differ greatly from resistances that act when a pile is at rest if a pile is driven in relatively impermeable materials, such as fine-grained silts and soft clays. As explained in the previous section, skin friction in soils of this type is reduced during driving by water squeezed out of the soil, which lubricates the surface between the pile and the soil, and point resistance is increased by the pressure built up in the pore water as the point displaces the soil. After a period of rest, the water along the pile surface is absorbed by the soil and frictional resistance is restored, but point resistance decreases because the excess water pressure at the point is dissipated as water gradually moves from the region in which the pressure is built up by driving.

Dynamic pile driving formulas are applied to cast-in-place concrete piles. The formula may be logical when applied to shell piles where the shell is rigid enough to maintain the compression in the soil surrounding the pile. With shell-less piles, the conditions are changed so radically by removing the casing that such a formula is not a good indicator of bearing capacity.

The most satisfactory method of determining the bearing capacity of individual friction piles is by actually loading piles and observing their behavior during driving and under static load. These are called test piles. Enough test piles should be used to certify that the variations in the soil conditions in different parts of the site are determined. A common requirement is that the allowable load causes no settlement for 24 hours, and the total settlement shall not exceed 0.01 in. for each ton of test load. Another requirement is that the design load shall not be greater than 50% of the load, which causes a permanent settlement of ¼ in. in 48 hours. There are other modifications of this requirement. To be of value, the test loads should not be applied immediately after the pile is driven. Sufficient time should elapse enabling the soil to adjust itself to static conditions, thus avoiding the temporary effects of driving on frictional and point resistance. The bearing capacity of a pile may increase after a period of rest if driven in some soils; it may decrease if driven in others; or it may not change at all. In driving a test pile, the penetration per blow or the average penetration for several blows should be observed. When the penetration per blow of the other piles is equal to or less than the final penetration per blow of the test pile driven in the same material, those piles can be assumed to have a bearing capacity at least equal to that of the test pile. In using the test pile as an index of the bearing capabilities of other piles, the piles them-

selves, the kind of soil, the hammer, and the driving procedure must be the same as those associated with the test pile. This comparison of the final penetrations of piles with that of the test pile is not usually followed.

The procedure just described is satisfactory for determining the bearing capacity of individual piles as controlled by permissible settlement; but as has been explained, the bearing capacity of a group of friction piles is not always equal to the bearing capacity of one pile multiplied by the number of piles because of the overlapping of their pressure bulbs. Occasionally, groups of three or four piles are loaded with test loads, but the cost of applying loads to pile groups is so large that pile groups are not often tested. Any adjustment of the design load for the number of piles in a group is based on judgment, although building codes include formulas for this purpose.

SETTLEMENT PREDICTION

The procedure for predicting settlement of pile foundations supported by clay is similar to that for spread foundations outlined briefly in Section 2.5. The vertical pressures in the soil supporting the foundation are computed on the basis of Boussinesq's method (Section 2.3). Representative undisturbed samples of the soil are subjected to consolidation tests, which give data about the amount that they are compressed when subjected to given pressures. By mathematical procedures, the total compressive effect of all the soil under a building producing settlement is predicted from the vertical pressures and from the behavior of the samples. Piles complicate the situation in regions covered by the depth to the pile tips. Below that elevation, the conditions are identical with those under a spread foundation. It is necessary only to include the soil to a depth twice the entire foundation because at greater depths the soil pressures are so low that they have very little effect on the settlement, provided that there are no layers of peat or other soft soil at greater depths.

Formulas for the bearing capacity of piles can only give information about the loads that individual piles will carry without the pile moving through the soil that surrounds it. They give no data concerning the settlement. A loading test gives data concerning the settlement of an individual pile under a given load produced by any movement of the pile with reference to the soil and to a compression of the soil surrounding the pile during the relatively short period covered by the test. Because clay compresses very slowly, the total settlement of test piles driven in clay is not obtained from the tests. Furthermore, the overlapping pressure bulbs of the individual piles and pile groups form a composite pressure bulb for the entire foundation, as indicated in Figure 2.23; therefore, the settlement of an isolated test pile due to the soil compression is not an index of the settlement when that pile is under a foundation. The loads on adjacent piles contribute to settlement because of the overlapping pressure bulbs. The pressure bulbs indicate that deep-lying strata would have no effect on the settlement of isolated piles or on individual pile footings but contribute to the foundation as a whole. This condition may be particularly significant if deep-lying soil strata yield excessively. Friction piles are ineffective in reducing raft foundations settlement as illustrated in Figure 2.27. The same situation exists in buildings supported on several isolated, friction pile footings. There are cases in which settlement has greatly exceeded the settlement of an individual pile carrying the same load during a loading test. The common assumption that settlement will be uniform if all piles are loaded equally is but a dream.

Buildings founded on prepared sand or gravel usually have little settlement, and friction piles are not often used for these buildings except when the sand is unconsolidated and vibrations from machinery may cause the sand and the building to settle. Any settlement will take place within a relatively short period. Present methods for computing settlements are based on the theory of consolidation and apply to soils such as clay, in which settlement is due to the squeezing of water out of the soil.

Summary

During the preliminary phase of the building process, subsurface exploration was conducted at the proposed site and soil samples were secured. The samples were tested to ascertain if the soil and subsoil were suitable for carrying the total load of the proposed structure. The soil was tested to determine its permeability, compressibility, shearing strength, and susceptibility to swelling and shrinkage. The results of the soil testing enabled the foundation engineer to establish allowable bearing pressures to be used for the final design of the foundation system. The specified foundation system was selected because it supported the total load of the building, minimized the effects of settlement, controlled the effects of groundwater, and maintained the structural integrity of adjacent buildings. With the design completed, contractors can be selected and construction started.

Key Terms

test pits
sounding rod
soil augers
wash boring
hollow stem boring
churn drilling
diamond drilling
shot drilling
bedrock
residual soil

alluvial soil
moraines
coarse-grained soils
fine-grained soils
consolidation
void ratio
shrinkage limit
liquid limit
plastic limit

optimum moisture
  content
capillary rise
swelling
shrinking
permeability
shearing strength
compressibility
pressure bulbs

allowable bearing
  pressure
differential settlement
groundwater
bearing piles
friction piles
pile cap
pile footing
test piles

Review Questions

1. What is the purpose of subsurface exploration?
2. List two methods of obtaining soil samples.
3. What is the purpose of soil classification?
4. What causes swelling and shrinking of a clay soil?

5. What is permeability?
6. What requirements have to be satisfied to ensure a spread foundation has an adequate bearing area?
7. What factors influence the settlement of foundations?

CHAPTER 3
FOUNDATIONS

The construction phase begins soon after the contractor has been selected. The soil and rock that will support the building have been analyzed and the foundation system designed. The construction of the foundations generally presents the most difficult aspect of building construction. There is always an element of the unknown present during this phase of construction. Careful planning of the operations can keep the unknown from causing undue disruption in the construction sequence. The planning must consider the location of existing utilities, proximity of adjacent structures, disposal of demolition refuse and excess excavation, and access to the construction area.

Before the construction of the foundations can be started, the site is readied and the necessary excavation starts. If the sides of the excavation have to be braced, methods will be used that will permit the construction to proceed in an orderly fashion. After the construction of the foundation is finished, the areas that were overexcavated to accommodate construction operations have to be backfilled. The compaction of this material is vital to the finished appearance and durability of sidewalks, parking areas, roadways, and other permanent site improvements.

The care taken in the construction of the foundation will set the tone for the construction operations that follow. It is important to remember the foundations support all the loads imposed on the building and transfer them to the supporting soil and rock. A number of different types of foundations may be used on any one building site. The discussions that follow include spread foundations, pile foundations, pier foundations, and deep basement walls.

Objectives

1. Become familiar with the operations included in site preparation.

2. Understand how the different types of foundations transfer the building loads to the supporting soil and rock.

3. Understand how the moisture content of soil affects the compaction effort.

4. Become familiar with the specialized equipment used in foundation construction.

3.1 Sitework

Sitework, as a necessary adjunct to the building process, includes a number of items that are temporary or permanent.

Temporary measures include the building of storage facilities, offices required for the prosecution of the work, roads and parking, testing facilities, and equipment. Security measures may include temporary fencing as well as lights, alarms, and fire protection equipment.

Permanent sitework may include sidewalks, roads, parking lots, fencing, signs, landscaping, and utilities. Utilities consist of electric power entrance, distribution, manholes, pullboxes, and perhaps transformer stations, water supply, landscape irrigation systems, fire hydrants and supply, and sewage disposal manholes, telephone and television cable lines, pullboxes, gas lines, and valve housing.

FIGURE 3.1 Temporary supports for existing utilities.

SITE PREPARATION

Before site operations begin, the location of all existing underground utilities should be established and overhead lines noted. Most utility companies provide assistance in locating their underground services. If utility services cannot be temporarily shut off or relocated, special provisions have to be made to support and maintain these services during the construction phase (Figure 3.1). Hand excavations may be required to verify the location of the underground utilities.

The site is then cleared of all structures, foundations, debris, unwanted vegetation, and top soil. The plans usually specify in detail what is to be removed, stockpiled, or left intact. Initial layout is performed to locate the building lines and to delineate the spaces on the site that are to be used for contractor offices, contractor employee parking, storage areas, access roads, and other facilities required for the prosecution of the work. Hopefully, the contractor established a working site plan during the estimating phase that will allow the construction operations to proceed with minimal interruption.

EXCAVATION

The foundations for most structures are established at an elevation below existing ground level. In order to accomplish the construction of the foundations, the soil above the founding elevation must be excavated. Shallow excavations can usually be made without supporting the surrounding material if there is adequate space to establish slopes at which the soil can stand. The steepness of the slopes is a function of the type and nature of the soil, weather conditions, depth of excavation, and the length of time the excavation must be left open (see Figure 3.1).

If the building under construction extends to the property lines or existing structures are adjacent to the excavation, sloping of the material may not be possible and the sides of the excavation will have to be supported. Two common

methods for bracing the sides of shallow excavations are shown in Figure 3.2. Deeper excavations require more extensive bracing systems and will be discussed in more detail in Section 3.5. In both cases, sheeting is driven to an elevation below the bottom of the proposed foundation. Then excavation is done in stages to facilitate the placing of the wales and struts or rakers, depending on the method of bracing being used. If the excavation is deeper than approx-

FIGURE 3.2 Common methods for bracing sides of shallow excavations. *Foundation Engineering,* R. B. Peck, W. E. Hanson, and T. H. Thornburn. Copyright © 1974, John Wiley & Sons, Inc. Reprinted by permission of John Wiley & Sons, Inc.

FIGURE 3.3 Excavation sides retained by steel-sheet piles.

imately 10 ft, steel sheeting will be used in place of the wood sheeting shown (see Figure 3.3).

BACKFILLING

After the foundations have been completed, it is necessary to fill the voids that were created by the overexcavation needed to accommodate the slopes and the bracing, or both, used during the construction of the foundations. This operation is called backfilling. It is one of the least controlled operations in construction, especially in residential and light commercial applications. This material often supports traffic areas adjacent to the completed structure. Unless this material is compacted or consolidated to about the same density as the undisturbed soil next to it, differential settlement of and cracks in the sidewalk or paving will occur.

COMPACTION

The backfill is usually placed and compacted in lifts of 6 to 8 in., depending on the material, using small compaction equipment similar to the one shown in Figure 3.4. *Compaction* specifications usually state that the in-place density of the backfill reach a "percentage of the compaction" or "relative compaction" or "relative density" of the soil's *maximum dry density* at optimum moisture content when compacted. The percentage is frequently 90% for parking lots and up to 95% for service roads that are expected to support heavy trucking. The compaction test most commonly used in building work is the Standard Proctor Test.

Standard Proctor Test

Compacted soil is measured in terms of density in pounds per cubic foot. To determine the density value of a soil from a given job site, a sample of the soil is taken to a soil test lab and a Standard Proctor Test is performed. The purpose of the test is twofold. The Standard Proctor Test measures and expresses the density attainable for any given soil as a

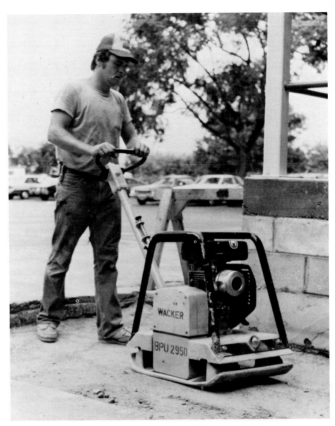

FIGURE 3.4 Hand-operated vibrating plate. Wacker Corporation, Milwaukee, Wisconsin.

standard and determines the effect of moisture on soil density.

In this test, a sample of soil is compacted in a standard container 4 in. in diameter and 4.59 in. high which has a capacity of $\frac{1}{30}$ cubic foot. The container is filled in three layers. Each soil layer is compacted using a 5.5 lb weight which is lifted 12 in. and dropped 25 times evenly over each soil layer, yielding a soil sample which has received 12,375 foot-pounds of energy per cubic foot, determined as follows:

1 ft × 5.5 lb × 25 drops × 3 layers × 30
$$= 12,375 \text{ ft lb/cu ft}$$

After striking off the surface of the container, the soil sample is weighed immediately after the test (wet weight) and then weighed again after drying the soil in an oven (dry weight). The difference between the wet and dry weights represents the weight of the water that was contained in the soil. The density of the dry soil can be expressed in terms of pounds per cubic foot. The amount of water may also be expressed as a percentage.

For example, for a given $\frac{1}{30}$ cu ft soil sample:

Wet Weight = 4.6 lb
Dry Weight = 4.0 lb
Weight of Water Lost = 0.6 lb

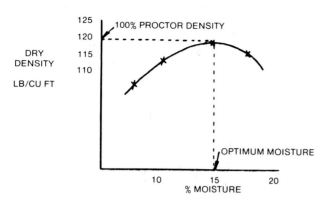

FIGURE 3.5 Moisture-density curve. Wacker Corporation, Milwaukee, Wisconsin.

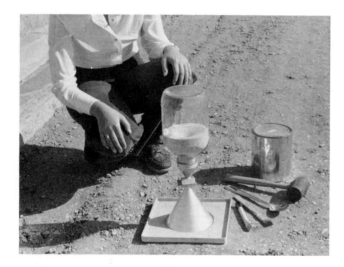

FIGURE 3.6 Sand-cone density test.

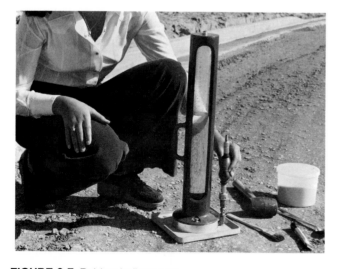

FIGURE 3.7 Rubber balloon test.

Then:

$$\text{Soil Dry Density} = \frac{4.0 \text{ lb}}{\frac{1}{30} \text{ cu ft}} = 120 \text{ lb/cu ft}$$

$$\text{Percentage of Moisture} = \frac{0.6 \text{ lb}}{4.0 \text{ lb}} \times 100 = 15\%$$

The procedure is repeated, adding different amounts of water to the soil with each repetition and the soil weights and percentage of moisture are recorded as described previously. Plotting the data on a graph, a curve similar to the one shown in Figure 3.5 is obtained. The curve is referred to as the *moisture-density curve* and reveals the following:

1. At a certain moisture, the soil reaches a maximum density when a specific amount of compaction energy is applied.

2. The maximum density reached under these conditions is called maximum dry density or 100% compaction.

3. The moisture value at which maximum density is reached is called optimum moisture.

4. When compacting soil at above or below the optimum moisture and using the same compactive effort, the density of the soil is less than when compacted at optimum moisture.

5. The 100% compaction value obtained above is used as a standard for measuring the degree of compaction obtained during the compaction operation.

Field Compaction Tests

The compaction of the backfill is measured by determining the in-place density by using the sand-cone density test (Figure 3.6) or the rubber balloon test (Figure 3.7). In either test, a small hole is excavated, the excavated material is weighed, and its water content determined. The volume of the excavated hole is determined (using the sand-cone apparatus) by filling the hole with a sand whose weight, volume, and bulk density is known. When the rubber-balloon device is used, a water-filled balloon lines the excavation and the volume of the water measures directly the volume of the hole.

The results of this in-place density test, expressed in terms of a dry unit weight, will reveal the degree of compaction that is compared to the 100% compactive effort. The sought-after density, expressed in terms of the dry unit weight, is the maximum density at optimum moisture content.

If the dry density of the material tested above is 115 pounds per cubic foot, the degree of compaction obtained would be:

$$\frac{115 \times 100}{120} = 96\%$$

The soil has been compacted to 96% of the maximum dry

FIGURE 3.8 Nuclear density-moisture meter. Seaman Nuclear Corporation, Oak Creek, Wisconsin.

density. This result can be compared to the specified degree of compaction to determine if the compaction specification has been met or if more compactive effort is required. Since the samples obtained during the compaction operation have to be taken to a lab to determine the dry density, several hours will pass before the results are known. Because of this, it is not feasible to take tests after each compaction pass and too much or too little compaction is a possibility.

Faster results can be obtained using a Nuclear Density-Moisture Meter (see Figure 3.8). The meter operates on the principle that dense soil absorbs more radiation than loose soil. The meter is placed directly on the soil to be tested and activated. Gamma rays from a radioactive source penetrate the soil, and, depending on the number of air voids present, a number of the rays reflect back to the surface. These reflected rays are registered on a counter. The counter reading is referred to a chart which gives the soil density in pounds per cubic foot. The density is compared to the maximum dry density from the Standard Proctor Test and the degree of compaction is obtained as before. These faster results, in less than 3 minutes, allow for constant monitoring of the compaction operation and ensures the compaction requirement is being met without overcompaction, which wastes equipment time and personnel. The Nuclear Density-Moisture Meter is expensive and may not be economical for smaller operations.

Parking Lots and Service Roads

The usual procedure for parking lot, access, or service road construction involves layout, clearing, grading, compacting; subbase, base course preparation, priming, paving,

sealing, and marking. There may be appurtenances to be constructed such as utility boxes, curbs, sidewalks, gutters, and spillways.

Parking lots and service roads frequently are paved with asphaltic concrete (see Figure 3.9). After the area is surveyed and staked out, it is cleared of debris and undesirable growth. Desirable plants and trees, if too large for removal, are clearly tagged and protected from damage by erecting temporary warning barriers.

Subbase preparation usually requires stripping and grubbing, which consist of topsoil removal to a depth of from 4 to 12 in. The soil is bladed off and stored for future landscaping or disposal. Scarifying by heavy equipment to a depth up to 2 ft is sometimes required in order that cohesionless soil may be imported, mixed in, watered, and compacted. The procedure provides for a bonding of the new subbase to the existing base material.

The procedure requires compacting the soil in thickness of 6 to 8 in. lifts, using sheepsfoot rollers and heavy rubber-tired and vibrating type rollers.

Base aggregates that are retained on the No. 4 sieve are classified as coarse, otherwise they are classified as fine, and those that pass a No. 200 sieve are termed mineral dusts. The base course material, usually of well-graded coarse aggregate of about ¾ in. maximum size, is compacted by rolling with equipment that weighs from 2 to 200 tons. The base course is usually compacted in lifts of

Asphalt concrete wearing surface
Aggregate base subgrade

FIGURE 3.9 Typical asphaltic concrete pavement section.

FIGURE 3.10 Wall footing.

FIGURE 3.11 Column footings.

6 in. with a total thickness from 6 to 24 in. Final thickness depends on expected loads and subbase conditions.

It is essential that the finished grade elevations of the compacted base course be level, smooth, and as near to the predetermined finished grade as possible. Any deviation from a smooth, even, uniform slope will be reflected in the finished asphaltic concrete wearing surface that is to follow. Poor drainage and undesirable depressions known as "birdbaths" will result if an even base course is not achieved. All dips and high spots must be smoothed out and compacted, because paving specifications may require that no dip exceed ½ in. within a 10-ft straightedge. The base course is usually required to meet compaction standards that are determined by the Proctor compaction test or a modification of the test.

3.2 Spread Foundations

Spread footings distribute the building loads over a sufficient area of soil to secure adequate bearing capacity. They may be classified according to the manner in which they receive the loads.

WALL FOOTINGS

Wall footings supporting light loads may be simple footings constructed of plain concrete that do not project more than about 6 in. beyond the edges of the wall. The minimum footing depth is usually equal to twice the projection. Minimum code requirements state that light longitudinal reinforcement in simple concrete wall footings shall be embedded to minimize shrinkage and objectionable temperature cracks and to bridge over soft foundation material.

The most common wall footing is the reinforced concrete

slab footing of constant depth called a T-footing (see Figure 3.10). The main reinforcement on a spread wall footing is perpendicular to the wall and near the slab bottom to keep projections from cracking off near the wall. The reinforcing bars tend to slip in the concrete because of high bond stresses. This necessitates a large surface area on the reinforcing bars which is obtained by using small, closely spaced bars.

COLUMN FOOTINGS

Column footings are the most common type of isolated or independent footings. For light loads, the simple type may suffice, but most column footings are constant depth slab footings with two-way reinforcing (Figure 3.11A). As in wall footings, small closely spaced bars provide greater bond strength. Timber grillage footings constructed in tiers, similar to the steel grillage footing in Figure 3.11B, are permitted only for temporary buildings and for frame buildings with footings below the "permanent" groundwater level.

In steel grillage footings, Figure 3.11B, the beams are held by spacers placed between them; a layer of concrete 6 or 8 in. thick is placed under the lower beams, and the entire footing is encased in concrete with a minimum edge thickness of 4 in.

COMBINED FOOTINGS

This type of footing frequently supports walls and columns near the property line. If such a column were centered on an isolated footing, the footing would project over the property line. If the column were near the edge of such a footing, the foundation pressures would not be symmetrically distributed, and the footing would tend to settle unevenly or to rotate. This is solved by combining the wall column footing and the nearest interior footing into a single footing, as in

FIGURE 3.12 Combined footings.

Figure 3.12*A*. To avoid rotation, combined footings are proportioned so that the centroid (of the area that bears on the soil) is on the line of action of the resultant column loads. *Combined footings* are usually trapezoidal in plan. It is assumed that this produces uniform pressure distribution under the footing.

The footing for a wall column and two adjacent interior columns may be combined, particularly at the corners of the buildings. Combined footings are usually reinforced concrete, although grillage footings (Figure 3.12*B*) have been used. A combined footing may be rectangular in plan. If the interior column load is greater than the wall column load, a rectangular footing can be proportioned so that the centroid will be on a line of action of the column loads. In order to simplify the foundation construction, some building codes permit adjacent foundations to project into streets and alleys.

CANTILEVER FOOTINGS

These footings serve as combined footings by permitting a wall column load near the edge of a footing. The principle of the *cantilever* is illustrated in Figure 3.13*A*. The load is supported near the end of a beam which has one support over the center of the wall footing and the other support at the adjacent interior column. Because the beam projects beyond its support, it is "cantilevered." Cantilever footings, (*B*), are usually reinforced concrete, but steel grillage footings have been used. The cantilever is not evident in actual footings because a fulcrum is not used, and in the reinforced concrete footing, the beam is merged into the slabs. However, it is evident that the beam prevents uneven settlement by holding the wall footing in a horizontal position. The beam connecting the footings is called a strap beam, and footings of this type are often called connected footings.

FIGURE 3.13 Cantilever footings.

CONTINUOUS FOOTINGS

Continuous footings of reinforced concrete slabs extend continuously under three or more columns, as in Figure 3.14. They tend to reduce the differential settlement between columns. This action is more effective if the foundation wall is constructed as a reinforced concrete girder (Figure 3.14*B*). If the footing and the wall are poured separately, as is usually done, the lower reinforcing should be at the bottom of the wall; but if monolithic, this steel is more effective near the bottom of the footing. Transverse reinforcing must be near the bottom of the slab. Corresponding steel is required in the footing illustrated in Figure 3.14*A*. Continuous foundations shown in (*B*) may support bearing walls as well as columns. This is desirable because it reduces differential settlement caused by variations in the soil and reduces cracking in the walls bearing on the foundation wall, as well as in the foundation wall itself. If there are windows in the foundation walls, the upper band of reinforcement should be placed below the windows, with light reinforcement over the openings, and reinforced diagonally at the corners of the openings. Cast-in-place concrete foundation

FIGURE 3.14 Continuous footings.

REINFORCED-CONCRETE MAT FOOTINGS

FIGURE 3.15 Raft or mat foundations.

walls reinforced in this manner are appropriate even for small structures such as residences. The additional cost is small and the results worth many times the cost. Two-way continuous footings may reduce differential settlement more effectively than one-way continuous footings. Foundations tied together in this manner resist earthquake stresses.

RAFT OR MAT FOUNDATIONS

Raft or mat foundations are usually reinforced concrete slabs from 4 to 8 ft thick covering the entire foundation area

(Figure 3.15*A*). These slabs or mats are reinforced with layers of closely spaced bars oriented at right angles to each other and placed 6 in. below the top and bottom surface of the mat. To avoid construction joints through lateral dimensions, the entire slab *(B)* may be poured in one operation. Another form of raft or mat is the reinforced concrete inverted T-beam, with a slab covering the entire foundation area *(C)*. The beams are two-directional, intersect under the columns, and are poured integrally with the slab, forming a monolithic structure. Before the basement floor is placed, the space between these beams is filled as shown in the figure. If the slab is placed at the top of the beams and monolithic with the mat, the mat serves as the basement floor and saves excavation and filling, *(D)*. This construction is suitable for a soil that will stand without caving so that the space occupied by the beams can be excavated and the whole mat poured without forms. Raft or mat foundations are used when the bearing capacity of the soil is so low that other footing cannot be used and where piles cannot be used advantageously or are not necessary. Foundations of this type are commonly called *floating foundations.*

RIGID FOUNDATIONS

In recent years, there is a tendency to use the term floating foundations in a more restricted sense. It applies to foundations where the weight of the earth excavated will equal, or about equal, the building load. In such a case, the total vertical pressure on the foundation material is about the same after the building is completed as it was before the excavation was started, and thus settlement is held to a minimum. All settlement may not be eliminated because there may be an elastic rebound in the soil when the earth load is removed and a corresponding deformation when the building load is added. If a foundation is not rigid and is below the ground surface, the central portion of the building will probably settle more than the outer portion.

To minimize differential or uneven settlement, foundations must be constructed rigidly. Two methods may be needed to accomplish this. One method employs a rigid reinforced concrete box-like structure consisting of outside and cross walls in the basement (Figure 3.16*A*). The other method uses the basement floor and the first or second floor as chords and the columns as posts of rigid frames, *(B)*. These frames are called Vierendeel girders or trusses. They are not trusses in the traditional sense because they are not composed of triangular frames. The joints must be designed to take bending stresses because the diagonal members have been omitted. In order to secure the required rigidity, girders may extend through two or more floors. This is conveniently done where a subbasement is required.

Reinforced concrete trusses with diagonals have been used instead of Vierendeel girders. Reinforced concrete interior walls restrict the use of basement space. Openings in these walls reduce the rigidity of the walls and introduce problems in design. Reinforced concrete trusses with diagonals also restrict the use of the space, but Vierendeel girders do not.

3.3 Piles and Pile Foundations

TYPES OF PILE FOUNDATIONS

Pile foundations are similar to spread foundations in some respects. Spread foundations transmit loads directly to the soil, whereas pile foundations transmit loads first to the piles which, in turn, transmit the load to the soil or rock. The upper

FIGURE 3.16 Rigid foundations.

end of a pile is called the head or butt, and the lower end the point, the tip, or the nose. An isolated or independent pile footing is illustrated in Figure 3.17. The member into which the butt ends of the piles are embedded is called the pile cap. A cantilever pile footing is illustrated in Figure 3.18 and a raft or mat in Figure 3.19. Combined and continuous pile footings, corresponding to these spread footings, are used extensively. Several types of pile are used: wood piles, precast concrete piles, cast-in-place concrete piles, structural steel piles, and steel pipe piles. The following paragraphs briefly discuss each type.

Wood or Timber Piles

Wood piles are tree trunks with the branches trimmed and bark stripped. They are driven with the small end down, except under special conditions, such as in permafrost. The tip may be cut square or pointed or provided with a metal point called a shoe, or a pilot. Metal tips may be cast iron or rolled steel. Pointed or blunt, metal tips may have fins that give more assurance for straight driving. A steel pile ring may protect the butt end of the pile from damage. When driving is not difficult, unpointed piles are used, especially if the points rest on a hard stratum, as in the *end-bearing* or point-bearing piles. Driving through firm clay may be made easier by using blunt-tipped piles. If the material penetrated contains boulders or other obstructions, brooming and splitting are avoided by installing metal shoes and pile rings.

Those portions of wood piles permanently below the ground water will last indefinitely, but consideration must be given to the possible lowering of this level. Those portions of wood piles above the groundwater level may be weakened or destroyed by decay or damage caused by insects and marine borers. Preservative treatments, such as creosote, make piles more resistant to decay.

Almost any kind of sound timber that will withstand driving and that has adequate strength for the imposed loads can be used for piles below the "permanent" groundwater level. The most commonly used woods are the cedars and cypress (which are very decay resistant), Douglas fir (very long piles of excellent quality can be obtained from Douglas fir), southern pine, red oak, white oak, and spruce. Douglas fir, southern pine, and red oak respond better to treatment processes than the other woods. In general, heartwood is more resistant to decay than sapwood, but better treatment process results are secured with sapwood than with heartwood.

Wood piles are classified by ASTM D 25 according to use as friction piles or as end-bearing piles. Further classification is made with respect to bark peeling, namely, clean-peeled, rough-peeled, or unpeeled.

Wood pile quality is based on the presence and severity of wood defects such as size, soundness and frequency of knots, holes, splits, checks, and the amount of grain twist.

Other requirements specify a relationship of butt diameter to tip diameter. The tip diameter is rarely less than 6 in. or the butt less than 8 in. Wood piles should be free from short or reversed bends and have a uniform taper, and a straight line extending from the center of the butt to the center of the tip should lie wholly within the pile. Limbs and knots should be trimmed flush with the surface of the pile.

The dimensions for wood piles are determined by the load to be carried and the nature of their use.

Precast and Pretensioned Concrete Piles

Piles constructed of concrete, both reinforced and pretensioned, are used extensively. Sizes vary from 9 in. to 54 in. in diameter, with lengths up to 300 ft. Tapered or of uniform section, piles are usually square or octagonal; but they may be cylindrical (hollow core or solid), triangular, or rectangular

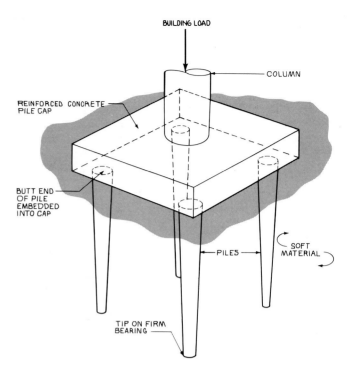

FIGURE 3.17 Isolated pile foundation.

FIGURE 3.18 Reinforced concrete cantilever footing on piles.

FIGURE 3.19 Reinforced concrete mat foundation on piles.

FIGURE 3.20 Precast concrete pile and cast-in-place shell piles.

(tongue and groove sheet pile). The piles must be designed for erection stresses and the stresses produced by the subjected loads. In general, the bearing capacity is the resistance of the soil to the load that moves the piles through the soil, rather than by the strength of the pile itself.

The reinforced pile has longitudinal bars with hoops or spirals (Figure 3.20A). If the reinforcing is provided only because of the handling and driving stresses, the concrete coverage outside the reinforcing need only exceed 1 in. Reinforcing required by the service loads should be protected by at least 1½ in. of concrete; in extreme exposure conditions, 3 in. coverage is required. The top and point should be provided with additional lateral reinforcement to withstand the driving stresses. For piles driven in plastic clay soils, a blunt or flat point is preferable, whereas a long tapering point should be used in sand or gravel or for those that must penetrate hard strata. Where conditions are extremely severe, a metal point or shoe is desirable. If piles are jetted into position, as will be described later, a pipe is cast into the pile along its axis, with the pipe end contracted to a nozzle.

Precast piles are sometimes pretensioned in the same manner as columns. The principal advantage of prestressing piles is to avoid cracks that could lead to corrosion of the reinforcement by ground water.

Precast concrete piles may be spliced by bars embedded in epoxy grout or by embedded steel welded together.

Pretensioned concrete piles are exceptionally well adapted for passing through water. Their durability, which assures less corrosion, ideally suits them for waterfront construction.

Cast-in-Place Concrete Piles

Concrete piles that are cast-in-place, or in situ, in the ground

are of two general types: the shell or cased piles, and shell-less or uncased piles.

A *shell pile* is formed by driving a closed point sheet steel shell or casing into the ground and filling it with concrete. In the Raymond pile, shown in Figure 3.20B, the tapered shell is made of relatively thin sheet steel with an 8 in. minimum diameter. Straight-sided shells are also used. This pile is formed by: (1) inserting a steel mandrel or core inside the shell and driving the mandrel and shell; (2) removing the mandrel and inspecting the shell interior; and (3) filling the shell with concrete. For piles up to 40 ft in length, the shell is in 8-ft sections with overlapping joints; for piles with lengths exceeding 100 ft, the shell consists of sections screw jointed. The Union or Monotube pile (Figure 3.20C), is formed by: (1) driving a heavy, fluted, sheet steel, tapered shell into the ground and inspecting the interior; and (2) filling it with concrete. For piles up to 40 ft, the shell is one piece; and for piles to 100 ft or more, sections are factory welded or field welded. The MacArthur cased pile is formed by: (1) driving a heavy steel casing with an inserted core; (2) removing the core and inspecting the casing; (3) inserting a corrugated steel sheet; (4) filling the shell with concrete; and (5) placing the core on top of the concrete and withdrawing the casing, leaving the concrete-filled shell in the ground.

A *shell-less pile* is formed by: (1) driving a shell with an inserted driving core; (2) withdrawing the core; and (3) filling the shell with concrete while withdrawing the shell. This type is the Simplex pile in Figure 3.21 and the Pedestal pile in Figure 3.22. As the casing is removed, the concrete in the Simplex pile is forced against the soil by the fluid pressure of the concrete and by impact during placing. Greater pressure may be exerted, if desired, by tamping the concrete.

The Pedestal pile, which may also be a pressure injected footing (Figure 3.22), is formed by: (1) driving a casing with a core into the ground; (2) removing the core and placing concrete in the bottom of the casing; (3) replacing the core and pulling the casing up 1½ to 3 ft while exerting pressure on concrete with the core; (4) ramming concrete to form a pedestal; and (5) removing the core, filling the casing with concrete, replacing the core to exert pressure on concrete, and pulling the casing to form the finished pile.

The Franki (Figure 3.23) concrete foundation is a ***pressure injected footing.*** The completed footing features an enlarged compressed concrete bulbous tip which is forced into intimate contact with the surrounding densified soil. This unique footing forms by compacting a charge of 3 to 5 cu ft of no-slump concrete through a steel sleeve or

"drive-tube" that guides a free-falling ram. The concrete plug is rammed into the earth, followed by the guide sleeve. At the desired depth, the penetration of the guide sleeve is stopped and the concrete is bulbed-out by compressing it against the bearing soil by further ramming. In the uncased shaft, the pipe is then withdrawn in stages of 12 to 24 in. increments. The ram is withdrawn while the pipe guide-sleeve is recharged with concrete—concrete which is rammed into close contact with the surrounding soil, compressing and forming a dense compact shaft. The piles are usually unreinforced; however, reinforcement can be added to meet design requirements.

FIGURE 3.21 Simplex pile.

FIGURE 3.22 Pedestal pile or pressure injected footing.

FIGURE 3.23 Cast-in-place shell-less piles of pressure injected footing.

Another method, used by the Franki Foundation Company, employs a cased shaft, which is a steel casing that is inserted through the drive guide sleeve after the bulbous tip has been formed. This steel casing is embedded into the compressed pressure injected footing, and then the guide sleeve is withdrawn. If reinforcement is required, it is placed in the casing, and then the casing is filled with concrete. Easy to form and construct, this pressure injected footing has the distinct advantage of great resistance to uplift.

These piles, which may be battered (sloped) or vertical, have been seated in soils ranging from fine sands to coarse gravels.

Composite Piles

Wood piles and cast-in-place concrete are combined to form *composite piles* (Figure 3.24) to take advantage of the lower cost of wood piles for the portion below ground water and durability of concrete piles for the upper portion. If the Raymond pile is used, a wood pile is first driven nearly full length. The shell and mandrel are then placed on the wood pile and driven. The mandrel is removed and the shell filled with concrete, forming a concrete pile on top of a wood pile. The joint must be designed for driving and for excluding water and soil. The joint must withstand separation due to heaving soil when adjacent piles are driven. If the MacArthur cased pile is used, the wood pile is driven inside the casing and the concrete pile is formed in the usual manner.

Pipe Piles

Piles of this type consist of heavy steel pipe filled with concrete (Figure 3.25A). Pipes are driven with open ends or, for the smaller sizes, with the bottom end closed. The usual types of pile hammers are used, or hydraulic jacks are used if there is a load to jack against, as in underpinning.

The resistance to penetration is reduced by cleaning out open-end piles as the driving progresses. This is particularly true for piles driven through sand because the sand plugs the end of a pile and the resistance offered is the same as though the end were closed. Cleaning out is usually accomplished by pushing a 2½ in. pipe into the soil within the pile and forcing compressed air through at a pressure approaching 100 lb per sq in. This air pressure blows the soil out of the pile. Water may be mixed with the soil to facilitate its removal. *Pipe piles* are also cleaned with small orange-peel buckets and earth augers. Clay cores that enter open-end pipe piles have been removed by withdrawing the pipe and core, forcing the core out with a plunger, and redriving the pipe. The pipes may be placed in sections with joints holding the sections in position, assuring good bearing between the ends of the sections, and no projecting on the outside of the pipe. Concrete is placed by dumping it at the top of the pile, but the bottom portion of long piles should be placed with drop-bottom buckets to avoid segregation. Water should be removed from the pipe before the concreting, but if dewatering is impossible, a concrete seal is placed by a drop bucket. After sealing, the water can be pumped out and the remainder of the concrete placed in the dry. After the concrete is set, a steel bearing plate may be grouted over the upper end of the pile to secure good bearing on the steel and the concrete. In determining the bearing capacity of pipe piles, both the steel and concrete are considered as carrying stress with allowance for the different moduli of elasticity or stiffnesses of the two mate-

FIGURE 3.24 Composite pile.

rials. The pipe walls are commonly ⅜ in. thick but may be thicker. The diameters vary from a 10 in. minimum. In calculations, a deduction of ¹⁄₁₆ in. is sometimes made in the thickness to allow for corrosion. Available information indicates this is unnecessary for piles driven in undisturbed soils.

STRUCTURAL STEEL PILES

Hot rolled-steel H-sections, called H piles, (Figure 3.25*B*) are increasingly used for bearing piles. This type of pile is particularly advantageous in driving to bearing on sound rock passing through soil where driving is difficult because of boulders or thin strata of hardpan or rock which are underlaid with weaker strata and therefore do not have adequate bearing capacity. Because of their small sectional area, steel bearing piles displace only a small volume of soil and are ineffective in compacting loose sands or increasing their bearing capacity. They are uneconomical as ordinary friction piles. Moreover, the full surface area is unavailable for frictional resistance because soil wedges between the flanges, causing the pile to act as a square pile. Available information indicates that corrosion is not a serious factor and that protection against corrosion is required only for structural steel piles driven in disturbed soils. Steel H piles range in depth from 8 to 14 in. and weigh up to 177 lb per linear ft.

COMPARISON OF TYPES

The life of wood piles can be prolonged by impregnating them with creosote under pressure. Untreated, fire resistant wood piles should be used only below the permanent groundwater level. Concrete and steel piles do not have this limitation. The use of concrete piles results in considerable reduction in excavation, masonry, and imposed loads.

Where the piles project above ground surface, precast concrete piles are usually more suitable than cast-in-place piles, although the shell type can be reinforced longitudinally to give satisfactory service. Precast piles must be reinforced to withstand the flexural stresses which occur during handling and the stresses due to driving, but the stresses are usually compressive after the piles are in the ground and do not require reinforcing. Tensile stresses may be induced, however, by soil heaving brought on by driving adjacent piles, causing the rupture of shell-less, cast-in-place, underreinforced piles. The rebound of the soil and the driving of adjacent piles may reduce the section or may otherwise damage the piles before the concrete has set. The driving of adjacent piles may collapse the shells of shell-type cast-in-place piles before the concrete is placed or may damage the piles themselves immediately after the concrete is placed. To avoid damage to cast-in-place piles by adjacent driving operations, all the shells for removable casings for a pile group are usually driven before any of the

FIGURE 3.25 Pipe pile footing and structural steel pile footing.

concrete is placed or no pile is filled within 5 ft of a future pile location. The shell-type cast-in-place pile excludes water and earth from contact with the fresh concrete of the pile.

The required lengths of precast piles must be determined before they are ordered. They must be cut off in the field and excess length wasted if they cannot be driven to the required depth. Withdrawing the casing in forming shell-less cast-in-place piles, or encased piles in which the shell is inserted in the casing before withdrawal, releases the stesses set up on the soil during driving and makes any dynamic pile driving formula inapplicable.

To develop their full capacity, pipe piles and structural steel piles are usually founded on rock or hardpan and are usually used to support heavy loads. Structural steel piles can penetrate hard strata and gravel. Corrosion of pipe or sheet piling in structural piles is not a consideration.

The allowable load on individual piles varies from 15 tons to 150 tons, mainly depending upon the type of pile and the supporting material. The minimum value is for a wood-friction pile; the maximum value is for a large steel pipe pile bearing on rock. Larger loads can be carried by steel-encased concrete cylinders constructed in the same way as pipe piles, but cylinders with 24 in. or larger diameters are sometimes classed as piers.

Almost any type of pile can be secured or constructed in lengths as great as 140 ft. Structural steel H-bearing piles 200 ft long were used to support an office building in New Orleans.

Further comparisons are made later in this chapter.

PILE DRIVING

Piles of various types and dimensions are driven by a pile driver operating in conjunction with a power hammer or water jet.

The steam hammer is used extensively. It rests on the head of the pile continually while its driving power, derived from the reciprocating parts of the hammer itself, strikes blows in such rapid succession that the pile is kept in almost continuous motion. Steam hammers are single-acting and double-acting. A single-acting steam hammer is a heavy ram which is raised 2 to 4 ft by steam admitted under pressure to a cylinder located above the ram, which falls by gravity when the steam is exhausted. The steam pressure acts against the underside of a piston connected to the ram by a piston rod. The ram is guided in its fall, and the various parts are held together by a frame (Figure 3.26A). The hammer is positioned on top of the pile by using a pile driver or by suspending it from the boom of a derrick or from a gin pole. A double-acting steam hammer is similar to a single-acting hammer. The ram is raised 4 to 20 in. by steam admitted under pressure to the cylinder on the lower side of the piston, but instead of falling by gravity alone, as in the single-acting hammer, the ram is forced down by steam under pressure admitted to the cylinder on the upper side of the piston synchronous to the exhaustion of the steam on the lower side. The principle of the double-acting hammer is shown in Figure 3.26B.

Steam hammers can be operated with compressed air as pneumatic hammers. Some types are converted to operate under water. Steam hammers may be inverted for use in pulling sheet piles and sheeting. Power hammers drive piles more rapidly and with less damage than drop hammers.

One of the most noteworthy developments in pile driving has been the invention of the vibratory pile driver-extractor. In soils that previously caused driving difficulties — particularly sands and gravels — pipe, H piles, and sheet piles have been driven with dramatic ease. The theoretical principles supporting this vibratory hammer are not discussed here, although the mechanical device is briefly described.

This hammer, which features relatively silent operation, drives and extracts piles or caissons with amazing speed. An example of the capabilities of this hammer is illustrated by one project using 355 HP 14 × 177 lb by 55 ft piles, where each pile was driven to refusal in about 7 minutes — by other methods this would require nearly 1½ hours for each pile.

Two motor-driven eccentric weights rotating in opposite directions impart a vibratory motion to a driving head. Undiminished, this vibratory motion is transmitted to the pile and then to the soil, which is displaced by the pile tip (see Figure 3.27).

The pile vibrates vertically with a frequency equal to the revolutions per minute of the rotating eccentric weights — or vibration ranges to 1800 cycles per minute. The vertical motion or amplitude of the pile ranges from ¼ in. to about 2 in.

In addition to the stated advantages, the vibratory driver does not distort or batter unprotected pile butts as an impact hammer would. It is easily operable in cold weather, and power requirements may be satisfied by available or portable high voltage supply.

Because of their simplicity, efficiency, and capabilities, diesel hammers are becoming a wider and much preferred

FIGURE 3.26 Steam or air hammers.

FIGURE 3.27 The vibratory hammer. L. B. Foster Co.

choice for many pile driving jobs. Water-cooled or air-cooled, they may be used for vertical or inclined driving. The energy ratings range from about 868 ft-lb for the smallest hammer to 117,175 ft-lb for the largest.

The extremely simple operating principle is described and illustrated (see Figure 3.28):

1. Free Fall and Compression. The gravitational fall of the ram activates the cam on the fuel injector, which injects fuel into the cup-shaped head of the impact block. The free falling ram automatically closes the air intake-exhaust ports

and compresses the entrapped air. This compression gives an initial downward thrust to the pile.

2. Impact and Combustion. The descending ram strikes the impact block of the driver, resulting in a direct positive downward thrust to the pile. Simultaneously, the atomized fuel is forced into an annular combustion chamber where the highly compressed air ignites the fuel. The combustion results in further pile penetration and a reaction to the ram.

3. Power Stroke. The reaction causes the ram to recoil upwards. Exhaust ports open, and burnt gases are expelled.

FIGURE 3.28 Diesel pile hammer. The Foundation Equipment Corp. and Delmag-Maschinenfabrik.

4. Air Intake. As the ram elevates to its summit, it opens the air intake ports and activates the fuel system. The injector is refueled for the next cycle.

The water jet or *jetting* is used in driving piles. It consists of a pipe (placed at the side of a pile) with water under pressure washing the material away from the tip of the pile. The pipe is about 2½ in. in diameter, with the lower end decreasing to form a 1½ in. nozzle. The upper end of the pipe is connected to a force pump by a hose. The pile drops into the space formed by the water jet. Some water from the jet rises to the surface and lubricates the sides of the pile and decreases the friction of the surrounding earth, thus assisting materially in driving. A load placed on the pile

Cross of DELMAG–D22

Oil tank

Tripping device

Ram weight (piston)

Fuel tank

Guide jaws

Pump lever

Exhaust ports

Fuel pump

Shrunk-on mantle
and pump guard

Impact block

Helmet

Pile

Cross-section of DELMAG Diesel pile hammer.

FIGURE 3.28 *(continued)*

assists in forcing it down, or else light blows are struck with a pile hammer. In addition to the jet that delivers water to the point of the pile, jets may be used to deliver water along the side of the pile to assist in decreasing the frictional resistance to correspond with that developed in driving without the jet. The final penetration is usually given with a pile hammer after the jet has been turned off.

Concrete piles often have the jet pipe cast in place along the axis of the pile. Piles driven with a water jet are not damaged in driving, and therefore this method is particularly suitable for precast concrete piles. The water jet may be used in many classes of material, but it operates most successfully in sand. Building codes restrict or ban the jetting except by special permission because soil may be disturbed around adjacent foundations, thus causing settlements.

The pipe for pipe piles used in underpinning is often forced into position by hydraulic jacks that act against the building. This operation requires less space than a pile driver and causes less disturbance.

3.4 Piers

Buildings are frequently supported on circular concrete piers extended to a material, such as dense sand or gravel, firm clay, hardpan, or bedrock, having the necessary bearing capacity. Such buildings, usually of steel or reinforced concrete, have foundations supporting columns rather than bearing walls. The column load is distributed over the pier by grillage beams or by reinforced concrete pier caps. The top 2 or 3 ft of each pier is usually reinforced with steel spirals or hoops. If the height does not exceed 12 times the diameter, or if the diameter is 6 ft or more, heavy reinforcement is not required; but special reinforcement is sometimes used to reduce the pier size. Piers deeper than 12 diameters and less than 6 ft in diameter shoud be reinforced with vertical steel spaced uniformly around the pier not less than 3 in. from the surface.

If a pier is to rest on bedrock, the uniform section shown in Figure 3.29A is used. If supporting material is clay or hardpan, the bearing area must be increased; therefore, the pier is belled out (Figure 3.29B). Firm clay or hardpan will stand without support while the bell is excavated. The side slopes of the enlarged section usually make an angle of about 60° with the horizontal. The sides are again made vertical for about 1 ft at the bottom. The bell should be designed as a spread footing, with reinforcing near the bottom to carry tensile stresses if they exceed allowable values for plain concrete footings.

Various excavation methods are used. In these methods, some device, such as sheeting, sheet piles, or caissons, holds back the earth and keeps out water. In one method, soil-laden water in the excavation prevents caving of clay until some form of casing is provided. The sheeting or sheet piles may be removed as the concreting progresses, but they are frequently left in place. Caissons are always left in place, becoming a part of the piers. Formerly, piers were constructed of brick and stone; now concrete is used exclusively. Timber and steel, used during the excavating process and left in place, will not deteriorate excessively in ground water.

CONSTRUCTION METHODS

The methods used for constructing concrete piers can be divided into two general classes; the open-well method and the caisson method. In the open-well method, the construction is performed under atmospheric conditions using various methods to prevent unwanted soil and water from entering the open well.

Caissons are a structural element, cylindrical in shape, with a hollow core down the center, and a cutting edge around the perimeter on the bottom end. They are sunk to the desired elevation by excavating the soil under the cutting edge, allowing the caisson to sink under its own weight or in combination with other applied forces. Caissons are constructed of steel, concrete, or a combination of the two. They may be classed as open or pneumatic. Open caissons are used where ground water can be held back by an earth plug in the bottom of the caisson. In the pneumatic caisson method, water is held back by compressed air while workers carry on the excavation in a pressurized atmosphere.

Though piers can have any geometrical configuration, the cylinder or the circular shaft are used almost exclusively for building construction applications. In the discussions that follow, the concrete pier being constructed is assumed to be a circular shaft. However, most of the methods being discussed could also apply to rectangular piers.

Some factors determining the construction method adopted are: (1) the nature of the soil; (2) the depth of the excavation; (3) the construction clearances on the building site; and (4) the type of foundation under adjacent buildings.

TYPE OF SOIL

The simplest material to excavate is firm clay, which is usually sufficiently watertight to excavate below the groundwater level by open-well methods. Any water leakage or seepage is pumped out. Firm clay will stand unsupported without caving while excavation proceeds several feet and will give ample time to provide support. Some open-well caissons excavated in clay more than 100 ft deep have stood unsupported for several hours. Water-bearing seams of sand and gravel introduce complications that may necessitate a different procedure than would normally have been followed; however, it may be impossible to control and seal off these seams.

Hardpan presents no unusual difficulty in excavating if

reasonably watertight and will normally stand unsupported until the concrete is poured.

Saturated sand offers little resistance to the penetration of caissons, but special methods must be used to keep the surrounding soil from flowing into the excavation. Excavated soil in excess of the volume required by the pier may enter from under adjacent foundations, causing them to settle. This is called lost ground. Every effort should be made to avoid lost ground, although this may not be serious if the piers are isolated or are not located adjacent to water mains, sewers, or subways.

Layers of boulders are often on rock strata that support piers. Boulders may be difficult to remove and may interfere with lowering the caisson and establishing the necessary seal between the caisson and the bedrock.

Usually piers founded on rock rest on the rock surface or are embedded into the rock except for deep basements. Two or more excavation methods are frequently combined in a single well where different types of soil are uncovered during excavation.

The various methods used in excavating for piers will now be described.

OPEN-WELL METHODS

The construction used in open-well methods can be classified as cofferdams if ground water is present. A *cofferdam* is a structure built to exclude water and cave-ins from entering a given area enabling work to proceed under atmospheric conditions. This allows working in the dry. Some leakage usually occurs, but it is controlled by pumping. A cofferdam may be a temporary installation or part of a permanent structure. Sometimes the difference between a cofferdam and a caisson is difficult to distinguish. In general, a self-contained structure independent of the surrounding soil for support is a caisson; but if the structure requires lateral support, it is a cofferdam, as in the case of sheet piling and sheeting. In some localities, all foundation piers are referred to as caissons regardless of the meaning of the term. Foundation piers are sometimes called subpiers to distinguish them from piers above ground.

Excavations usually require support on exposed vertical faces to prevent caving. Thus, a diaphragm, ordinarily made of wood planks, is braced against the exposed face. Various terms designate the diaphragm or its components, some having identical or similar meanings. The most common term is *sheeting,* also called sheathing; it is usually vertical, but may be horizontal. Vertical sheathing is often called lagging, but this term implies that the members are parts of a curved diaphragm, such as the staves of a barrel or drum. Occasionally, lagging members are called poling boards. Horizontal sheeting members are often called breast boards because they are placed against that face or breast of an excavation as the work proceeds. They are also called cribbing if they form a rectangle.

FIGURE 3.29 Concrete piers.

The diaphragm retaining the earth is often constructed of vertical members designated *sheet piles* made of wood, steel, or occasionally of reinforced concrete. Sheet piling is distinguished from vertical sheeting because sheet piling is driven in advance of the excavation.

Wide-flange steel beams are often driven vertically into the ground spaced a few feet and along the edge of a proposed excavation. These are called *soldier beams* because they stand erect rather than in the usual horizontal position of beams. As the excavation progresses, horizontal sheeting, or breast boards, is supported on the beam flanges.

Vertical sheeting, sheet piles, and soldier beams are supported by horizontal members called *wales,* or waling, or rangers placed at horizontal intervals along the height of the soldier beam. The wales are in turn supported by one end of transverse struts or braces; the means of support for the other end depends upon prevailing conditions. Inclined *struts* or braces supporting wales are also called rakes, or rakers, and spur bracing.

Chicago Method

Hand-excavated wells with timber sheeting were once common and may still be used to advantage where limited construction clearances exist. The best known method originated in Chicago in 1892 and is particularly appropriate for clays in which water-bearing inclusions are not present. In

FIGURE 3.30 Chicago board method for open wells.

the *Chicago method,* a circular hole is excavated by hand for a depth of 4 to 5 ft (see Figure 3.30). The walls of the hole are then lined with vertical sheeting or lagging. The lagging is retained by two steel rings placed inside which force the lagging against the earth. The well must be accurately excavated to avoid lost ground. After the first set is placed, another section is excavated, and another set of sheeting is placed. This process is repeated until the desired depth is reached. If difficult material is excavated, the sections may be as short as 18 in. Excavation may proceed manually.

The sheeting is 2-in. or 4-in. tongue and groove lumber with edges beveled to fit the curve, and with the metal rings varying in size from 3 in. by ¾ in. to 4 in. by 1 in. The rings are divided into semicircles with bolted flanges at the ends and joined in pairs to complete the circle. In the wells where soil squeezed into the excavation, threatening to collapse the lining, a disaster was prevented by inserting, where necessary, heavy wooden drums divided into two segments and forcing them against the lining by jack screws. These drums were removed as the wells were filled with concrete (see Figure 3.43 later in this chapter).

When using this method below groundwater level, pumping will be necessary because water will enter through seams in an otherwise impervious clay. Because it is mandatory to supply fresh air to the workers, the exhaust of pneumatic spades may supply sufficient air for this purpose. Occasionally poisonous or explosive gases are encountered, and it is necessary to supply a large amount of air by blowers which force the air through lines extending to the bottom of the well (Figure 3.43).

An example of a deep foundation placed by this method was sixteen piers for the Cleveland Union Terminal Building, which was excavated 262 ft below the curb and nearly 200 ft into ground water. A combination of horizontal sheeting, steel sheet piles, and sheeting was used (Figure 3.43).

Sheet Piling

Instead of retaining the earth with sheeting, as in the above methods, sheet piling may be driven around the perimeter of a well in advance of the excavation (Figure 3.31). Excavation is conducted manually. If driving is easy, the sheet piling may be driven its entire length before excavating, but in all cases, the piles are kept in advance of the excavation. The piles are braced by horizontal and transverse frames as progress permits.

The simplest form of wood-sheet piling is wood planks driven side by side (Figure 3.31). This type of piling will retain earth but will not keep out water. A common form of wood-sheet piling is the Wakefield piling (Figure 3.32), which is three planks spiked to form a tongue and groove. Other forms of wood-sheet piling are shown in Figure 3.32. With the exception of the simple planks, all the forms are intended to keep out water and to hold back earth. Two forms of interlocking steel piling are shown in Figure 3.32. If wood piling is used, the well should preferably be square or rectangular (Figure 3.33), but if steel piling is used, a circular plan gives good results. Wakefield piling will withstand the impact of drop hammers, but steel sheet piling is usually driven with steam or air hammers or with resonant, vibratory, or hydraulic hammers.

For wells more than 25 ft deep, two or more sections of piles may be driven offset as shown in Figure 3.33. The second section is a few inches inside the first section, after excavating to the bottom of the first section, and so on for other sections, which allows sufficient overlap to provide a water seal.

Wells to 60 ft deep have been excavated by this method. Some forms of water-tight steel piling are used in this method for digging wells below ground water where water that enters the excavation neither exceeds pumping capabilities nor washes material under the piling into the well. Frequently, the piles are driven through porous water-bearing material until the ends of the piles are embedded in clay, which effectively seals the bottom.

Telescoping Steel Cylinders

Telescoping steel cylinders from 5 to 8 ft long may supplant vertical sheeting or sheet piling. These cylinders differ in diameter by 2 in. increments. The largest cylinder is sunk (Figure 3.34A) by excavating below the cutting edge and driving the cylinder down. The excavation is by hand. After the first cylinder is positioned, the second, which is telescoped inside, is sunk in the same manner and others in succession to the desired depth.

A bell is excavated if the soil permits (Figure 3.34B). After the excavation is completed, the bell is filled with concrete (Figure 3.34C), and the cylinders are withdrawn as concreting proceeds until the pier is completed (Figure 3.34D). The excess concrete conforming to the increased section can be avoided by using a smaller cylindrical form. The annular spaces between the concrete and the earth walls are then filled with sand. Telescoping cylinders can be used in

FIGURE 3.31 Sheet piling for open wells.

FIGURE 3.32 Types of sheet piling.

water-bearing soil that will not hold its shape, as required by the Chicago method, and where the cylinders are driven in advance of the excavating to avoid lost ground. A bell cannot be formed unless the final excavation is a suitable material such as clay. This is one form of Gow pile and might be classed as an open caisson.

Drilling Methods

Various types of maneuverable equipment, truck or crawler mounted, are used in drilling wells for poured concrete foundation piers. The material penetrated is loosened or broken up and removed by drills, which are suspended from power cranes and guided by the cylindrical steel casings.

FIGURE 3.33 Use of sheet piling.

FIGURE 3.34 Telescoping steel cylinders.

FIGURE 3.35 Earth drilling equipment.

There are three types of drill used, namely, the auger and the bucket, both penetrating by rotation, and the grab-hammer or hammer-grab, which penetrates by vertical impact.

In some wells, partial protection is required; and in others, precautions are required to the full depth. Protection against caving is provided by vertical lagging or steel cylinder casings. Casings are ¼ in. to ¾ in. thick, as described later. If water-bearing formations are present, water is deterred from entering the well by steel cylinder casings, as will be explained.

AUGER DRILL

An auger drill (Figure 3.35A) is similar to a wood auger. It is mounted on the lower end of a power-driven solid or telescoping vertical shaft, called a Kelly bar (Figure 3.36). When drilling operations start, the drill tip is placed on the ground. As the shaft rotates, the drill bores a hole into the ground. The auger has two cutting edges and from three to five helical turns or flights. After the drill rotates sufficiently to fill the helical turns, the earth-laden auger is raised to the surface and spun rapidly to throw the earth from the auger by centrifugal force. This forms a ridge of loose earth around the hole. The earth is removed. Reaming devices attached to the drill are employed for excavating holes larger than the drill or for excavating bells at the bottom. Drills range in diameters to 20 ft with capabilities of drilling to depths of 160 ft.

The auger drill is suitable for excavating clay, sand, some hardpans, and other material that will remain on the helical turns while the auger is withdrawn.

Although piers are usually for large structures, small-di-ameter piers are sometimes used for small buildings such as residences. Piers may be desirable if suitable foundation material is at a considerable depth and especially if the soil is an expansive clay, the bottoms are often belled out. Wall bearing buildings are supported by **grade beams** on top of piers (Figure 3.53).

BUCKET DRILL

A bucket drill is a short steel cylinder or bucket mounted with its axis vertical on the lower end of a Kelly bar (Figure 3.36). The bottom of the bucket is so constructed that, when rotated in contact with the soil, it scoops up the soil, fills the bucket, and advances into the ground. One type of bucket is illustrated in Figure 3.35. When the bucket fills, the shaft and bucket are raised and rotated horizontally to clear the hole. The load is then dumped through the movable bottom, and the bucket is lowered and refilled. Buckets have diameters up to 20 ft and are capable of drilling to a depth of 200 ft. Wells with enlarged diameters and wells belled at the bottom can be drilled by attaching adjustable reamers or trimming arms to the bucket or shaft so that the trimmed earth falls into the bucket as illustrated in Figure 3.36.

The bucket shown in Figure 3.35B is called a core barrel. It has replaceable teeth around its bottom edge. This type of bucket is suitable for excavating into solid or broken consolidated material in intermediate hardness.

The bailing bucket in Figure 3.35C is designed to remove water or mud that may contain small rocks. A valve at the bottom opens and admits the material while the bucket is lowered, closes as it is hoisted, and can be opened to discharge. It is not rotated.

PROTECTION AGAINST CAVING AND GROUND WATER
Caving of soil penetrated by auger and bucket drilling operations is prevented by installing vertical wood lagging when necessary, as in the Chicago method, Figure 3.30, or by inserting steel cylinder casings. These linings are placed in sections as the drilling progresses or after the excavation is completed, depending upon conditions. Steel casings are also employed where required to exclude ground water as the drilling progresses. When they are used, the bottom of the casing is kept far enough in advance of the excavation so that a plug of earth which excludes the water is formed. A steel casing can be driven in advance of the excavation until it penetrates an impervious formation to form a water seal which excludes ground water. Penetration into impervious formations is obtained by impact on top of the casing. Rock is sealed by cutting a circular seam while rotating a saw-

FIGURE 3.37 Benoto hammer grab.

FIGURE 3.36 Well bored in clay with bucket drill.

toothedged drill casing during vertical thrust. The latter procedure is facilitated if the casing is somewhat smaller than the well. To avoid lost ground, it is necessary to fill the annular space solidly between the casing and the well. Wood wedges have been used for this purpose below the permanent groundwater level.

Lagging or steel casings may be left in place, or they may be removed for further use if economical. Some installations have characteristics of cofferdams and others of open caissons.

HAMMER-GRAB
The Benoto drill (Figure 3.37) is a grab-hammer or hammer-grab that is several feet long and weighs a ton or more. The hammer is similar to a drop hammer used in pile driving but has a grab at the lower end similar to an orange-peel or clam-shell bucket. The unit, alternately raised and dropped by a power driven cable hoist, is guided by a steel cylinder casing. When the hammer-grab is dropped, the jaws are

open. They penetrate or chop into the material by impact. When the cable is hoisted, the jaws close, grab a load of soil, hoist and dump it. In addition to guiding the hammer-grab, the casing prevents caving and groundwater penetration. The tube or casing is extended by adding sections that are joined by special interlocking devices or by butt welding. In material difficult to penetrate, the jaws are locked open temporarily and the grab is dropped several times.

The lower end of the casing has a toothed cutting edge. It may be kept 3 or 4 ft ahead of the grab, forming an earth plug that excludes water from the well in water-bearing soil; or if hard dry material is being penetrated, the grab is kept slightly ahead of the casing to facilitate the downward progress of the casing. After the well excavation has been completed, the bottom is prepared to receive the pier and concrete. The casing is extracted progressively while the concrete is placed. Hydraulic rams withdraw the casing and exert longitudinal forces combined with partially reciprocating rotary motions.

The hammer-grab is suitable for excavating any type of material, including solid rock. In a large-diameter well containing water, a short vertical steel cylinder with an air lock on top, called a diving bell, can be lowered into a well to provide a working chamber where one or two men can work with pneumatic drills or place explosives. This arrangement can be used for the excavation of very hard ground or rock.

PIER DEPTHS

The diameters and depths of piers depend upon the structural criteria, the depth to a formation capable of sustaining the loads, other geological conditions, and the drilling equipment available. There are no arbitrary limits on the diameters or depths of wells. When conditions are favorable, drilling is usually the most rapid method. In selecting a method for a specific project, relative costs and the time requirements are major considerations. Wells can be drilled in any type of material with appropriate equipment. A firm clay not requiring support against caving and containing no water-bearing seams is the ideal soil for drilling, but ideal conditions are rarely found. Auger and bucket drills are suitable only in soil and hardpans, but the hammer-grab can penetrate rock. Churn drills and special rotary drills excavate rock.

Open Caisson Method

The open caisson method consists of the following operations (Figure 3.38):

Constructing the caisson and preparing the site to receive it, placing the caisson over the site, excavating the soil on the interior of the caisson, advancing the caisson so that its cutting edge contacts or sinks below the bottom of the excavation and continuing this process to the foundation

FIGURE 3.38 The open caisson method.

stratum, sealing the bottom of the caisson to exclude water and soil, preparing the excavated space to receive concrete, examining the foundation bed, and placing the concrete to form the pier.

CONSTRUCTION

Caissons are usually cylindrical, from 2 ft or more in diameter, and are made of welded steel plates or of reinforced concrete. The thickness of the steel plate depends mainly upon the caisson, upon the material to be penetrated, and upon the method of advancing. Place thickness varies from ¼ in. to about ¾ in. The cutting edges are often reinforced with steel bands placed on the inside. A steel caisson may be a full length single unit or its length increased by adding section units as the sinking progresses.

PLACING

A caisson is usually started in a sheeted starting pit above the groundwater level. To maintain the caisson in a vertical position, it may be propped against the sides of the pit, but it is often necessary to erect towers to maintain vertical alignment.

EXCAVATING

Excavation within a caisson depends upon the method used to advance it; therefore, these two phases must be considered together. Each operation, however, is listed separately. The soil is removed from the interior of the caisson by manual and mechanical methods. A pick or pneumatic spade is used to loosen the soil, which is then shoveled into buckets that are hoisted to the surface. Such a method is suitable above the groundwater level and is suitable below the water table only if the water flowing under the cutting edge and into the caisson can be controlled by pumping (Figure 3.39*B*). Mechanical methods employ the orange-peel and small clam-shell buckets which can be operated through water (Figure 3.39*A*). These are often grab buckets because they "grab" the soil and are self-filling.

ADVANCING

Methods of advancing the caisson are as follows:

▶ By the weight of the caisson itself — always a factor in advancing the caisson; and in some soils, reinforced concrete caissons may weigh enough, requiring no other applied force.

▶ By loads applied to the top of the caisson, such as concrete blocks, steel rails, pig iron, etc.

▶ By driving the caisson with pile hammers. This procedure is applicable only to steel tubular caissons reinforced at the top and thick enough to withstand driving. One hammer, acting on a beam across the top of the caisson, may be sufficient; or two hammers acting simultaneously, but not necessarily synchronized, may be required.

A - EXCAVATION THROUGH WATER   B - WATER EXCLUDED BY EARTH PLUG EXCAVATION BY HAND

FIGURE 3.39 Methods of excavating in open caisson method.

▶ By reducing the resistance to penetration with water jets around the cutting edge to loosen and displace the soil. This is called jetting and is usually restricted by codes. Water jets supplement the caisson weight and are often used with loaded caissons or caissons driven by hammers.

▶ By drilling and blasting below the cutting edge to break up material that is difficult to penetrate, and by blasting near the cutting edge to jar the caisson loose momentarily and permitting it to fall a short distance. These procedures are occasionally used to supplement other methods.

▶ By driving the caisson with hydraulic jacks. This is possible only when there is a load to jack against, as there usually is in underpinning.

The usual procedure advances the caisson by placing loads on its top and excavating by hand to groundwater level. Below this level, water will usually enter the caisson under the cutting edge at such a rate that it cannot be controlled satisfactorily by pumping. The excessive inflow will wash large quantities of soil into the caisson. A serious objection to jetting and pumping is the possibility of undermining adjacent footings by the lost ground brought into the caisson by the incoming water, even when excavating through water. If the penetrated soil is fine sand, this action is quite pronounced, but it may cause no difficulty in some clays. Excavation is, therefore, continued by means of an orange-peel or clam-shell bucket. If the penetrated soil is clay with seams of permeable water-bearing soil, it may be possible to hand excavate the clay and to resort to grab buckets only while penetrating the permeable seams. Penetration may be facilitated by jetting if excavation is through water. In some soils, water jets make the addition of loads to the top of the caisson unnecessary.

If the caisson is driven with pile hammers or is forced down with hydraulic jacks, the cutting edge may be driven far in advance of the excavation. The soil plug in the bottom, as shown in Figure 3.39, reduces the inflow of water, allowing control by pumping and resulting in little lost ground, thus permitting manual excavation.

SEALING
If the pier is founded on firm clay or hardpan, the caisson is socketed into the material to form a seal, as shown in Figure 3.38B. Seepage is pumped out. Bells for the enlarged pier bases are excavated in the dry. If clay or hardpan overlies a rock foundation bed, the seal is established (Figure 3.38) and excavation is carried on through these materials to rock, using the procedure just given. If necessary, clay walls are supported by sheeting. Usually no support is required in hardpan.

If the porous water-bearing soil continues until rock is reached, a seal is formed between the bottom of the caisson and the rock.

PREPARING THE BEARING SURFACE
Where the excavation has been carried through a water-filled caisson, the rock is cleaned with a grab bucket or other device. A diver may make preparations and visual examination of the foundation bed. A concrete seal is then placed in the bottom of the caisson using a bottom-dump bucket. After this seal hardens, the caisson is pumped out and is ready for concreting.

When the caisson has been driven or forced with a hydraulic jack, an effort is made to socket the bottom of the caisson far enough into the rock to form a seal. If a plug of soil has been maintained to retard water inflow (permitting manual excavation), the plug cannot be removed until the seal is established. Cement grout pumped around the cutting edge may assist this operation. An uneven or sloping rock surface compounds the difficulty.

If the various methods for sealing between the bottom of a caisson and bedrock are unsuccessful, or if sealing through water is considered unsatisfactory because of the inability for preparing and examining the foundation bed, the open caisson can be converted into a pneumatic caisson. A top is placed on the caisson and air locks attached. Water is removed and investigating, preparing, and sealing the foundation bed is carried on under compressed air. The pneumatic caisson method, fully described later, may be necessary to employ before bedrock is reached if boulders or other obstructions are uncovered that cannot be passed in a simpler way.

CONCRETING
After the seal is established, water is pumped out and the caisson is filled with concrete using bottom-dump buckets.

FIGURE 3.40 Concrete pier with structural steel core.

CONCRETING PIERS WITH STRUCTURAL STEEL CORE
The load capacity of concrete piers in steel-plate open caissons can be increased by encasing a structural steel W or HP section (Figure 3.40A). Because of the inserted steel core, the bearing capacity of the rock stratum surface may be insufficient to carry the load transmitted by the pier. The required additional capacity is secured by drilling a hole into rock, the hole having a diameter equal to that of the outside of the shell. The bearing pile section is carried several feet below the surface of the stratum. The shell and the hole in the rock are then filled with concrete as shown (Figure 3.40B). By this means, the pier load is distributed over a much greater area at the bottom than if the pier were supported solely on the rock surface. The assumed stress distribution in the rock is shown in the figure. The stress distribution is determined by the allowable bond strength between the pier and the surrounding rock and by the assumed direction of the lines of stress.

In constructing this pier in water, the steel caisson shell is driven to rock. A hole in the rock is drilled deep enough to form a watertight seal after the caisson has been driven down into the rock. The caisson is then pumped out and the remainder of the rock excavation carried on in open air.

Pneumatic Caissons Method
The pneumatic caisson is used for constructing building and pier foundations through water-bearing material to bedrock. It consists of the following operations.

FIGURE 3.41 Pneumatic caisson method.

CONSTRUCTION AND PLACING

The essential parts of the pneumatic caisson are the working chamber, the shaft, the air locks, and perhaps the cofferdam. The working chamber and cofferdam may be constructed of timber, steel, or reinforced concrete. The shaft is usually constructed of steel. See Figure 3.41A and B.

The pneumatic caisson process is illustrated in Figure 3.41. The lower end of the caisson, including the working chamber, is first constructed and placed on the ground surface or in an excavated hole as shown in Figure 3.41C.

EXCAVATING AND ADVANCING

Excavation proceeds in the working chamber and the caisson advances by sinking of its own weight or because of an imposed load. As soon as the cutting edge reaches the ground water, water rises in the working chamber; therefore, the air locks are at the upper end of the shaft as shown in Figure 3.41D, and sufficient air pressure is applied to the working chamber to force out the water. People who have been acclimated to the increased air pressure can now work in the working chamber without interference of water. As the caisson sinks, the pressure in the working chamber must be increased to balance the increased water pressure.

The part of the caisson above the working chamber may be surrounded with a cofferdam, as shown in Figure 3.41A, to retain the earth and water as the caisson sinks. Concrete is placed in the cofferdam to form the pier and as a weight to assist in forcing the caisson down. Removable forms may be used instead of the cofferdams, as shown in Figure 3.41*B*. The level of the concrete is always kept above the top of the ground. Frequently, the entire pier is completed before the sinking starts.

The earth exposed in the working chamber is excavated by any convenient method and is hoisted to the surface in buckets passing through air locks. If the material is quite fluid, it may be blown to the surface through a pipe, the air in the chamber providing the necessary pressure. Soil that is blown out is heaped over the end of a stiff hose placed on the bottom of the working chamber and connected to the pipe leading to the surface. A valve is provided to close this pipe when not in operation.

WATER SEALING AND CONCRETING

When the cutting edge of the caisson has reached bedrock, as shown in Figure 3.41*E,* the surface of the rock is prepared to receive the pier. A layer of concrete heavy enough to resist the hydrostatic pressure is placed in the bottom of the working chamber. This seals the caisson to exclude water. The air pressure is released, the air locks and possibly the shaft are removed, and the concrete is carefully placed under atmospheric pressure in the remaining portion of the working chamber and the shaft, as shown in Figure 3.41*F.* Care must be exercised to avoid air pockets and to overcome shrinkage in the hardening concrete.

REMOTE CONTROLLED EXCAVATION

A system of excavation has been tested, permitting a 30 ft diameter caisson to be sunk 165 ft. This system, invented by Mitsubishi Heavy Industries, controls television cameras and excavating equipment remotely. A remotely controlled backhoe excavates and moves the material to the center of the caisson while a clamshell on a cable hoist removes the material. The clamshell passes through a set of air locks. As excavation proceeds, the concrete sinks of its own weight as a conventional caisson does (see Figure 3.42).

The system permits safe continual monitoring and final inspection during excavation and concreting. The hazards of working on a pneumatic caisson are eliminated, as are the depth limitations imposed by manual excavation.

ADVANTAGES AND DISADVANTAGES

The virtues of the pneumatic process are:

1. The only excavation required is that of the volume of the pier.

2. Adjacent foundations are not undermined as they might be in the open caisson method.

3. An opportunity is provided for proper examination and preparation of the foundation bed to receive the pier. This is not always possible in the usual form of the open caisson method.

The disadvantages are as follows:

1. The depth below ground water is limited to about 110 ft because it is not safe to work in the air pressure required by

greater depths. The working period that people can endure without ill effects decreases as the required pressure increases.

2. The labor cost is relatively high compared with other methods.

Combined Methods for Pier Construction

Usually it is unfeasible to excavate a well exclusively by one method. Two or more methods may be employed.

If a stratum of water-bearing material, such as water-bearing gravel or sand, overlies a thick stratum of clay which is underlaid with hardpan or rock, sheet piling may be driven through the top stratum of sand into the clay a sufficient depth to form a watertight seal. The clay may then be excavated by the Chicago method.

At the site of the Cleveland Union Terminal Building, this condition existed, but the ground water was a few feet below the level at which the well excavation started. The upper part of the well down to the groundwater level used

FIGURE 3.42 Self-sinking caisson unit. Reprinted with permission of *Engineering News-Record.*

FIGURE 3.43 Horizontal sheeting, steel-sheet piling, and lagging in a single hole.

horizontal sheeting (Figure 3.43). Below this and extending into the clay, steel-sheet piles were used; the remaining depth employed the Chicago method.

Another combination of methods, illustrated in Figure 3.44, meets the situation in which a thick layer of clay overlies a stratum of water-bearing gravel and boulders lying on a rock stratum on which a pier is to rest. The Chicago method is used in the clay. Before water-bearing gravel stratum is reached, the well is stepped out, as shown to give sufficient room to drive steel-sheet piling through the gravel to bedrock. The bottom of the lagging is kept far enough above the top of the gravel stratum that the remaining clay

acts as a seal to exclude water. The sheet piling is driven into the excavation and extends to bedrock. The piles are driven to form a seal between their lower ends and the rock; the enclosed earth, gravel, and boulders are cleaned out; the foundation bed is prepared; and the concrete is poured. Water-bearing strata between layers of clay can be passed with sheet piling following this procedure (Figure 3.44) or can be sealed off with steel cylinders with inside diameters large enough to clear the sheeting.

Because of their relatively low cost, open caissons are used to penetrate water-bearing stratum of sand, gravel, or silt; caissons can be equipped with locks converting them

FIGURE 3.44 Combined vertical wood lagging and steel-sheet piling.

FIGURE 3.45 Lateral bracing for sheeting or sheet piling.

into pneumatic caissons, a precautionary procedure adopted when encountering material that the open caisson will not penetrate, or it may be desirable to secure the advantages of the pneumatic caisson method in preparing the foundation bed and in filling the caisson with concrete.

3.5 Deep Basement Walls

Tall buildings may have basements that extend several floors below the ground level and even below the ground water. The methods employed in constructing basements are similar to construction methods explained for pier foundations. Procedures for bracing basement walls to resist

lateral pressures while the permanent building frame is erected, however, are quite complex. After the frame is in place, it resists these pressures.

The construction methods include vertical and horizontal sheeting, sheet-pile cofferdams, and pneumatic caisson cofferdams that surround the area to be excavated. Open caissons are rarely used for buildings because of the impending danger of undermining adjacent foundations and other underground works by excessive lost ground. They may be suitable, however, for undeveloped areas or in some built-up areas if special precautions are taken to avoid settlement of adjacent buildings.

A combination of methods may be used. The excavation above the ground water may be protected by a single diaphragm of sheeting or sheet piling; the lower portion, by a double-wall steel-sheet piling cofferdam within which the basement wall is constructed or by a pneumatic caisson cofferdam.

METHODS OF BRACING

For relatively shallow excavations, vertical sheeting or sheet piling may be supported temporarily by rakes or rakers. The upper end of each raker bears against a wale and the lower end against a timber foot block, Figure 3.45, all struts bearing against a single foot block.

Before the bracing, the interior is excavated to the level below which another construction method is employed. Portions to be excavated, called *berms,* are undisturbed until the wales and inclined struts can be placed successively to support the sheeting or sheet piling. The basement wall is then constructed within the confines of the sheeting or sheet piling, the bracing altered as required to serve as a temporary bracing. The bracing must be wedged tightly to minimize movement. Actually, berms are horizontal surfaces that form breaks in earth slopes. The term, however, is often used as indicated above.

The bracing method just described is not usually used for deeper excavations. For deep excavations, the bracing spans the entire well, extending to the opposite pit wall. Thus, the pit walls give mutual support to prevent caving (Figure 3.45). This is called *cross-lot bracing.* Normally, it extends in both directions across the excavation. Temporary bracing must be arranged to clear the members of the permanent structure. The excavation is conducted as shown by the dashed lines in the figure, leaving temporary beams for lateral support while the bracing is installed progressively downward. To reduce the cost, members of the permanent structure may serve as temporary bracing. In both cases, the supporting members must be stressed with wedges or jacks to minimize lateral movement.

SOLDIER BEAMS AND BREAST BOARDS

A common retaining method for basement excavation uses wide-flange soldier beams driven full length before excavating. Horizontal timber breast boards or sheeting inserted between them are supported on the beam, Figure 3.46.

The soldier beams are spaced a few feet apart. The breast boards are timber planks, from 2 to 4 in. thick and long enough to provide end bearings on the flanges of the beams. Breast boards, placed as the excavation progresses, are supported against the inner flanges, *(A)* and *(B)*. Wedges driven between the flanges and the breast boards force them against the trimmed earth.

The soldier beams are supported laterally by wales at vertical intervals. The wales are supported by spur or cross-lot bracing (Figure 3.45).

In Figure 3.46B, the wall is cast between the soldier beams, and for that shown in *(A),* in front of the beams to

A BREASTBOARDS SUPPORTED BY INNER FLANGES

B BREASTBOARDS SUPPORTED BY OUTER FLANGES

FIGURE 3.46 Soldier beam and breastboard construction.

FIGURE 3.47 Tiebacks supporting soldier beams. *Engineering News-Record,* April 18, 1961.

which it is anchored. The wall is reinforced to resist lateral pressures.

Where rock is available for tieback anchorage, soldier beams may be braced by *tiebacks.* One end is anchored in rock outside the area to be excavated, and the other end attached to a wale beam (Figure 3.47). First a hole is drilled through the soil and into the rock surface. After the soldier beams are driven and excavation and breast boards placed to a depth just below the top line of wales, a pipe that serves as a sleeve is driven at a 45° angle from the wale to the rock formation surface. A socket is then drilled into the rock formation by a drill operating through the pipe. The pipe sleeve and socket are cleaned out with air or water jet. The lower end of the wire tendon tieback is grouted in the socket with high early strength cement grout. The tendon is prestressed by jacks and anchored to the wale. This procedure is repeated for each tieback located at each soldier beam. The lower ends of the soldier beams are anchored, as shown. The apparent advantage of this procedure is that unobstructed working space is available. It was originated by Spencer, White, and Prentis, Inc.

DOUBLE-WALL STEEL-SHEET-PILE COFFERDAM

As illustrated in Figure 3.48, a deep basement and foundations are constructed at a site where explorations indicate underlaid filled material, an unconsolidated permeable water-bearing formation, a relatively impervious rock formation with low bearing capacity, and finally, sound bedrock on which the foundation is supported. The basement extends into the impervious rock with low bearing capacity.

The fill is supported by a single row of steel-sheet piles with spur bracing installed as the enclosed area is excavated, as shown in (A). Two rows of interlocking steel-sheet piles are driven through the permeable water-bearing formation until their bottoms form a water seal in the relatively impervious rock. Steel diaphragms driven at intervals between the two rows of piles form cells from which the material then is excavated. As the excavation proceeds, I-beam wales and braces are installed to resist the lateral pressure of the earth and water. In this manner, a double-wall steel-sheet-pile cofferdam is constructed completely around the area. Finally, a trench requiring no lateral support is excavated through the relatively impervious rock to bedrock.

All the preparations required for constructing the outside wall, as shown in (B), are now completed. First, the trench is filled with concrete, using forms on the exposed face in the basement. Above this point, the wall forms are constructed in sections in the cofferdam and concreted, the original wales and cross braces removed progressively and replaced with wales and shorter braces bearing against the completed concrete and the exposed row of sheet piles. The keyed horizontal construction joints between successive wall sections are provided with water stops.

While the construction of the outside walls is underway, the interior portion of the basement is excavated, leaving berms of unexcavated material to provide lateral support. These berms and the top of the general excavation are lowered progressively to permit the installation of the cross-lot bracing, as illustrated in Figures 3.45 and 3.48C: the spur bracing is supported by the cross-lot bracing. Spur bracing can be avoided by extending the top of the outer row of sheeting to the ground surface, if conditions permit.

After placing the cross-lot bracing, the piers supporting the interior columns can be constructed, and finally the basement floor, as shown in (D), together with the necessary waterproofing and underdrainage, can be installed as described in Section 3.6. The remainder of the building is then constructed (D).

PNEUMATIC CAISSON COFFERDAMS

The exterior walls of deep basements may be constructed by the pneumatic caisson method using a cofferdam of rectangular reinforced concrete caissons (Figure 3.49). Each caisson is sunk to rock, sealed, air locks removed, and the working chamber and shafts filled with concrete. Excavation and bracing can then proceed.

WELL POINT METHOD

A *well point* is a pipe with a pointed lower end and with a screen or filter along the lower 3 or 4 ft of its length. The well point method for dewatering in water-bearing material surrounds the area to be excavated by one or more rows of closely spaced well points placed along each side. The water table is lowered by pumping the water through the well points. The excavation within the area can then be in the dry. Some well points are placed by driving with a maul, whereas others are positioned by jetting. The well points are spaced about 3 ft apart; the top is connected to a header pipe connected to a pump. The water level may be lowered as much as 20 or 30 ft. Additional lowering may be accomplished by arranging well points in two or more vertical stages. This method is used chiefly in trench excavation and in dewatering an entire building site and is also applicable to pier excavation. To keep banks from caving, sheeting may be necessary, but it need not be watertight (see Figures 3.50 and 3.51).

GROUTING SOIL AND ROCK FORMATIONS

Certain soils can be stabilized and made more impervious. Structural defects in rock formations, such as cracks, joints, fissures, and cavities which weaken them or cause them to be permeable, can be filled by pressure injected grout. The grouts used may be chemical solutions or mixtures of water and portland cement, portland cement and finely ground sand, or clay.

Various methods are used for chemical grouting. In general, each makes use of two solutions which react chemically when mixed and gel or solidify. They may be mixed in the formation by injecting one and then the other. This is called a two-shot method. In the one-shot method, the two chemicals are mixed immediately before or during injection and gel at a predetermined time after injection. Injections by specially designed pumps force solutions into the formation through a driven pipe, a cased or uncased drill hole, de-

FIGURE 3.48 Double-wall steel sheet pile cofferdam.

pending upon the character of the formation. Techniques confine the grout to desired locations. After the grouting, the formations treated become more stable and relatively impermeable.

One chemical grouting method uses a mixture of sodium silicate and calcium chloride. Another utilizes a mixture of acrylamide and methylenebisacrylamide and is called AM-9 Chemical Grout. Chemical grouting may be effective in gravel and sand formations but not in silt or silty sand. It has been used successfully in some hardpans.

Portland cement, portland cement and fine sand, and clay grouting are extensively used to make rock foundations for dams more impermeable or more stable, but these methods are rarely, if ever, used in constructing foundations

for buildings. The grouts formed by mixing these materials with water are pumped into holes drilled in rock foundations.

Injection procedures are expensive and involve uncertainties because of unknown subsurface conditions, and the results are sometimes disappointing. The operations are complex and require skill and experience.

BENTONITE SLURRY

In some areas, a groundwater table cannot be lowered because any groundwater drawdown from dewatering would cause settlement to the surrounding buildings. This prevails as a potential hazard where surrounding buildings have foundations resting in the soil rather than extending to

FIGURE 3.49 Caisson cofferdam.

bedrock. Dewatering by conventional well points is usually possible; but if the groundwater table is lowered, the soils lose their buoyancy. Soil consolidation follows with possible disastrous results to structures adjacent to the excavated site.

If a building foundation is to be built on such a site, piles or caissons might be an obvious solution. If, however, a basement is to be excavated, a cut-off wall must be built to maintain the existing groundwater level. This protects the surrounding soils while excluding the ground water from the excavation site so that operations may proceed in the dry. Conventional underpinning methods to adjacent structures may be prohibitive or impossible.

A method devised to permit working in the dry is the *slurry-trench*, also called the diaphragm wall or slurry-wall.

A trench about 3 ft wide is excavated in sections about 20 ft long to bedrock or to a depth below the intended basement or foundation. This trench is then filled with a mixture of water and bentonite. This slurry prevents the collapse of the trench walls. A prefabricated, welded cage of deformed reinforcing bars is lowered into the slurry. Tremie concrete is then placed in the trench, displacing the bentonite slurry, which is pumped out and stored in tanks for future use.

Because a mechanical bond between the concrete and the rebars is deterred by the residual bentonite slurry, it is necessary to use deformed bars that are welded and made into a cage. Trenching and constructing the diaphragm wall along the entire perimeter of the building site proceeds in increments. After the wall sections have been made watertight, the site is dewatered. The excavation of the founda-

FIGURE 3.50 Details of well-point assembly. *Foundation Engineering*, R. B. Peck, W. E. Hanson, and T. H. Thornburn. Copyright © 1974, John Wiley & Sons, Inc. Reprinted by permission of John Wiley & Sons, Inc.

tions or basement walls then progresses in the dry while maintaining the integrity of the groundwater level and soil conditions outside of the excavation.

This is basically the procedure; however, since its initial use in Milan, Italy, in 1961, there have been improvements in technique and procedural variation.

One of the greatest difficulties has been to effect a tight seal between adjacent slurry panels to prevent the tremie concrete from entering the adjacent panels. This seal has been accomplished by the cored-in large steel soldier

beams spaced about 20 ft between slurry panels. This separates and forms the ends of the panels. The piles are concreted after they are placed.

A notable example of the method was the excavation of the World Trade Center in New York, in conjunction with the wall tieback system, using four rows of tiebacks. The concrete wall was anchored into bedrock as the site excavation proceeded. The completed wall was used as the perimeter basement wall. A full and interesting account of this procedure can be read in the April, 1969 and December, 1967 issues of *Civil Engineering*.

3.6 Basement Walls and Dampproofing

Basement floors above ground water must be protected against dampness and infiltrating rainwater that penetrates permeable backfills. This protection is called *dampproofing*. Basements below the groundwater level must be waterproofed to resist water infiltration and hydrostatic pressure equal to the unit weight of water (62.4 lb/cu ft) multiplied by the depth (in feet) of the point below the groundwater level. Unless alleviated, the pressure is exerted on the underside of basement floors.

DAMPPROOFING

Water infiltrates basement walls through cracks, defective joints, and through small continuous passages in permeable concrete or masonry units. Moisture from backfills may also penetrate walls by capillary action through continuous channels causing damp interior walls.

FIGURE 3.51 Multiple-stage well-point setup. *Foundation Engineering*, R. B. Peck, W. E. Hanson, and T. H. Thornburn. Copyright © 1974, John Wiley & Sons, Inc. Reprinted by permission of John Wiley & Sons, Inc.

FIGURE 3.52 Dampproofing and water proofing basements.

Dampproofing is accomplished by any of the various procedures listed below. Some may be omitted where walls are not adversely affected by dampness, or where an arid climate or impermeable backfill exists. These methods are illustrated in Figure 3.52.

1. Drainage of surface water away from the building by sloping the ground surface and by conducting the rainwater from downspouts that discharge on the ground surface into paved channels.

2. Applying a dampproof coating to the exterior surfaces below the ground level. This coating may be one of several materials:

(a) Bituminous materials or silicones applied in liquid form by brushing or spraying or in plastic form by troweling.

(b) One or two coats of portland cement mortar, including a water repellent that is troweled or pneumatically placed, giving a smooth finish.

The bituminous coating can be applied directly to smooth concrete surfaces, but if the surface is rough or if the coating is intended for a masonry wall, a smooth mortar coating should be applied first. The mortar coating may suffice without requiring the bituminous application.

The coatings will seal a wall against moisture penetration by capillary action from a damp backfill or from infiltration through minor defects, but coatings are, of course, ineffective in sealing cracks that develop after the coatings are applied.

3. Providing granular fills under floors and installing vapor seals. Concrete floors laid directly on fine-grained soils tend to draw moisture from the soil by capillary action. Such a floor should always be on a tamped granular base from 4 to 6 in. thick made of gravel, crushed rock, or cinders. As an additional precaution, a layer of heavy roll roofing or a 4 to 6

mil polyethylene film is laid on a sand bed over the granular base. Care should be taken to avoid puncturing the vapor barrier during concrete placement. The sheeting is usually lapped but taped and sealed when free water is present (see Figure 3.52A).

4. Installing a backfill drainage system to keep rainwater and wet soil away from basement walls. Included in this system are the *footing drains* which discharge into a storm sewer, or when feasible, into a drywell. A drywell is a pit excavated in permeable soil, or a pit with a bottom in such soil, and filled with gravel or crushed rock. Sometimes it is a lined empty pit with a cover and a soil bottom.

The footing drains are 4-in. or 6-in. vitrified clay drain tile perforated or plain laid with open joints. The upper half of open joints is covered with strips of roll roofing to exclude soil. The drain tiles are surrounded with gravel or crushed rock. A blanket drain of this material, at least 12 in. thick, is placed against the wall extending upward to within a foot of the ground surface. The remainder of the backfill is ordinary tamped soil—the topsoil supporting vegetation and preventing free access of surface water into the blanket drain. The latter objective is accomplished more effectively by placing a strip or roll roofing over the top of the blanket drain and extending it into the ordinary soil (see Figure 3.52). This accomplishes the further objective of preventing the ordinary soil from working into the drain.

Other factors deserve consideration. In residence construction, the basement may occupy only a portion of the area under the first floor, thereby leaving an exposed ground surface. Fine-grained soil may serve as a "wick" in drawing moisture into the basement from the underlying soil by capillary action. This can be reduced or prevented by covering the exposed wall with a heavy polyethylene film held in place, especially at the joints, by earth. Crawl spaces should be treated in the same manner.

Dampproofing coatings are sometimes placed on the inside surface of exterior walls. Such coatings of either bituminous materials or cement mortar may eventually lose their bond with the wall and fail. If used, special care should be taken to insure good bonding.

WATERPROOFING WALLS

A basement in the ground water must be designed to exclude water and to resist the earth and hydrostatic pressures. Prevailing conditions determine procedures.

An effective method for waterproofing basements provides a continuous membrane around the outside walls below the groundwater level and on the underside of the basement floor (Figure 3.52B). This membrane is built up of three to five or more layers or plies of bituminous saturated felt, or cotton fabric, or a combination of these materials. It is sealed and held to the wall surface with coal-tar pitch hot mopped similar to constructing a built-up roofing surface. Care in backfilling must be taken to prevent rupturing the membranes.

PARGING

A surface prepared for membrane application should be smooth and dry. A unit masonry surface will require a coat of smooth troweled portland cement plaster ⅜ to ½ in. thick. This is called *parging.* The surface is hot pitch mopped before the first ply is applied, and the exposed outer surface of the in-place ply is mopped (see Figure 3.52B).

A wall membrane should be protected from puncture caused by rock backfill and by rupture caused by backfill settlement. A coat of portland cement mortar, a layer of asphalt-impregnated fiberboard, or, preferably, a single wythe of masonry, will protect the membrane.

WATERPROOFING FLOORS

Before placing a floor membrane, a tamped base of gravel or crushed rock 4 in. or more thick must be provided. A sand bed or a cement mortar or concrete leveling bed at least 1 in. thick is placed on this base to receive the membrane. The membrane is placed, and then the concrete basement floor slab is poured. The membrane must be continuous under all columns, interior walls, and exterior walls, as shown in the figures. The membrane must also be continuous across the joint between the floor and exterior wall membranes.

Construction joints in walls not protected by membranes must be sealed with noncorrosive metal or neoprene waterstops which permit movement without rupture, as in Figure 3.52.

The wall must be designed to resist the lateral earth and water pressures, and the floor designed to resist any hydrostatic uplift pressures.

Obviously, the basement cannot be excavated nor these procedures accomplished if the ground water cannot be pumped out and lowered below the basement floor level.

If the exterior surface of the basement wall is accessible, the membrane and its protection are applied to this surface (Figure 3.52B). If inaccessible, the procedure is reversed as shown in Figure 3.52C.

According to the modified procedure, the protective wythe of brick masonry is placed, rigidly supported against outward movement and plastered with a coat of portland cement mortar. The membrane is then applied to this surface. Finally, the wall is constructed with the protective layer serving as one side of the form if the wall is of concrete. If it is a masonry wall, any spaces between the outer surface of the wall and the masonry must be filled tightly with mortar or grout.

The quantity of water pumped from a basement excavation depends upon the groundwater level and the soil permeability. If the basement walls enter clay stratum acting as a water seal, the quantity may be relatively small. To discharge this ground water, the built-up membrane under the basement floor can be replaced with a vapor seal and by providing a tile drainage system in the granular base. The water discharges into a pit called a sump, and the collected water is elevated by an automatic electric sump pump discharging intermittently into a storm sewer. This system alleviates uplift pressure on the underside of the basement floor.

BENTONITE PANELS

One method of dampproofing takes advantage of the expansive qualities of bentonite clay. Kraft paper bags, made into thin 4 ft square panels, are filled with a bentonite compound. Secured against the basement wall and back filled, the kraft paper deteriorates, exposing the bentonite compound. This material, when contacted by water, swells to about ten times its original volume, forming a positive moisture barrier.

Loose bentonite compounds placed under slabs are covered with a temporary sheet preventing premature wetting. The bentonite swells when wet, forming an impenetrable barrier that dampproofs the basement slab. This application should be supplemented by installation of area drainage that will deter a build-up of water that would impose a condition of hydrostatic uplift.

3.7 Slabs on Grade

Slabs on grade are frequently used for light buildings such as residences and those requiring only shallow foundations.

The usual methods of constructing slabs on grade are the slab with grade beams and the slab with thickened edges, called a *thickened slab.* Thickened slabs are constructed in a manner that enables them to serve as a foundation — a foundation integral with the slab. Slabs on grade are also constructed with grade beams supported on piers, piles, or pedestal types of footings. In either case, the slab floats on the prepared subbase.

FOUNDATION BED PREPARATION

Using a bulldozer, grader, or scarifier, the top 8 to 12 in. ground surface is first skinned of all organic material, and the topsoil removed and stockpiled for possible future use. Any new soil required for fill or subbase is then imported and spread, watered, and compacted to the required density with the use of sheepsfoot rollers and rubber tired compactors. Testing is conducted as compaction proceeds. Tests are usually performed by using the sand cone density method or the Modified Proctor compaction test, ASTM D-1557. A density of 90% is normally specified.

The limits of compaction are the entire area of the building slab plus a 5 to 10 ft perimeter border. This includes the area that will be occupied by the foundations, which are to be excavated later.

After a subbase has been compacted to the specified density, well-graded rock or gravel is spread over the entire subbase, including perimeters. This rock base is usually 4 to 6 in. thick and is compacted to a density of about 95% compaction. A sand bed spread over the rock serves to cushion and protect the waterproof film from puncture.

With the foundation bed compacted, excavation proceeds, using backhoes and trenchers, or bucket drills. The excavation for footings, piers, pedestals, and trenches for grade beams or thickened slabs are cut through the compacted rock base and into the compacted subbase.

GRADE BEAMS

After excavation, the grade beams are formed where required on each side, reinforced, and the concrete poured. The grade beams may form the entire perimeter of the building and support the exterior walls and the imposed loads. The walls may be of masonry, or framed of steel or wood.

Rigid insulation, such as asphaltic impregnated fiber boards or plastic foam types, may be placed on the interior side of the grade beam.

Grade beam depths are determined by the structural requirements designed to resist the imposed loads. The bottom of grade beams should extend below the frost line (see Figure 3.53).

THICKENED SLABS

Thickened slabs are poured integrally with the floor slabs. The interior side of the perimeter trench footing is sloped or

FIGURE 3.53 Grade beams.

FIGURE 3.54 Thickened slab for exterior walls.

FIGURE 3.55 Thickened slab for interior walls.

battered 1 to 1. Only the exterior side of the trench may require forming. The slab is then reinforced and poured, as in Figure 3.54. The thickened portion extends below the frost line.

These economically constructed slabs are used only on light construction and carry only moderate loads.

REINFORCEMENT

Because these slabs support minimal loads, very little reinforcing is required. In most installations, electric Welded Wire Fabric (W.W.F.) is specified; the most common type is a fabric with 10 gage rods in both directions, forming 6 in. square holes, designated $6 \times 6 - W1.4 \times W1.4$ (see Figure 3.54).

INTERIOR WALLS

The interior walls of slabs on grade are supported by thickening the slab. A shallow trench is excavated with sloping sides; the trench is reinforced and poured integrally with the floor slabs (see Figure 3.55).

Opinions differ upon the use and value of membranes under slabs on grade. Some hold that membranes are of limited value because they are invariably punctured during installation and, moreover, that a compacted 6 in. layer of 1½ to 2 in. rock under a dense, well-graded, low slump concrete will deter water entry, as in Figure 3.55. Again opinion varies, and the student is alerted to differing construction techniques that seem opposed but accomplish the intended task.

Summary

The construction of the foundations for the building has been completed. They will support all of the loads imposed on the building and transfer these loads to the supporting soil and rock. Construction methods used provided protection to adjacent structures during the construction phase and will continue to do so throughout the life of the building.

If the soil at the elevation of the foundation and below was capable of providing support, spread foundations that distribute the loads over the bearing area were used.

When the soil at the bottom of the foundation was not able to support the loads with spread foundations, piles were added to carry the loads to firmer soil or rock at a lower elevation. Concrete piers founded on hardpan or bedrock were used when the loads of the structure could not be carried by a spread foundation or pile foundation or when these piers were needed to provide protection to nearby structures.

Careful planning was done to ensure that the unknown element in foundation construction did not cause any undue delays in the construction sequence.

Key Terms

compaction
maximum dry density
moisture-density curve
spread footing
column footing
combined footing
cantilever
raft or mat foundation
floating foundation

end-bearing pile
shell pile
shell-less pile
pressure injected footing
composite pile
pipe pile
jetting
caisson

cofferdam
sheeting
sheet pile
soldier beam
wale
strut
Chicago method
grade beam

berm
cross-lot bracing
well point
slurry trench
dampproofing
footing drain
parging
thickened slab

Review Questions

1. List the operations included in site preparation.

2. Describe how the foundations listed below transfer the building loads to the supporting soil and rock.
   a. Spread foundation.
   b. Pile foundation.
   c. Pier foundation.

3. Describe how the moisture content of soil affects the compaction effort.

4. List and describe three pieces of specialized equipment used in foundation construction.

CHAPTER 4
CONCRETE

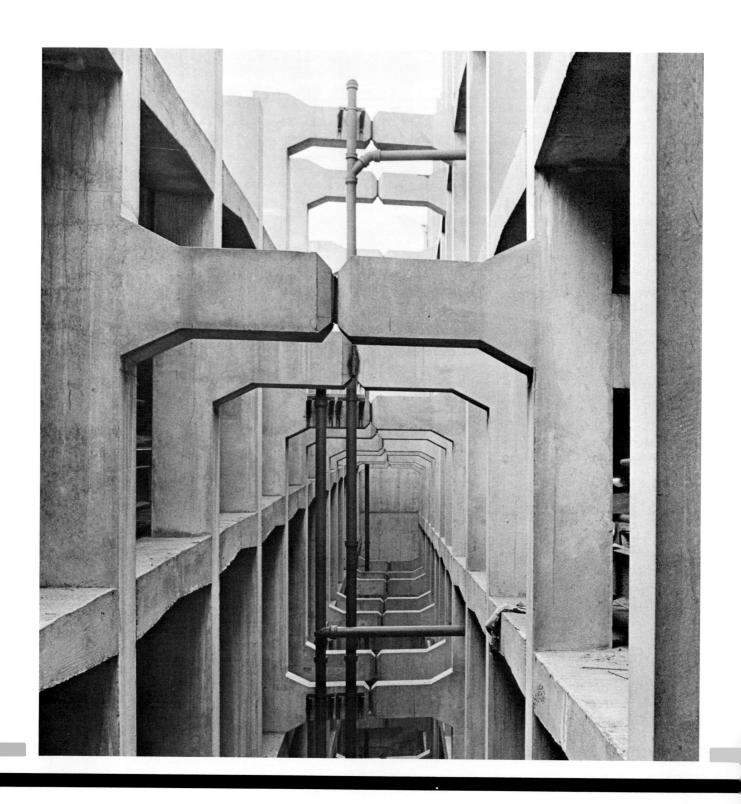

4.1 Concrete Materials
4.2 Cast-in-Place Concrete
4.3 Concrete Framing
4.4 Concrete Formwork

4.5 Concrete Accessories
4.6 Precast Concrete
4.7 Concrete Shell Structures

Concrete is the most versatile material used in building construction. It is basically a mixture of two parts, aggregates and paste. The paste, comprised of portland cement and water, binds the aggregates together in a hard mass as the paste hardens because of the chemical reaction between the cement and water.

In its plastic state, concrete can be molded to any desired shape and finished to a smooth hard surface. In its hardened state concrete has strength, durability, abrasion resistance, and watertightness. Concrete is used almost exclusively as the main material in foundation construction. It is used for walls, beams, girders, and columns in the building's structural framework. Concrete is often the specified material for site improvements including sidewalks, planters, curbs, and parking areas. Concrete is one of the few building materials that can be manufactured on the site using readily available raw materials.

Despite concrete's versatility and desirability as a material for building construction, it is more susceptible to permanent damage by the contractor than other construction materials. Care must be exercised in batching, mixing, transporting, placing, and finishing operations to ensure that the specified mixture is obtained and that it remains a homogeneous mixture until it comes to rest in its final position in the structure. Concrete needs time, a constant temperature, and moisture for proper hydration of the cement and strength gain of the concrete. If the contractor ensures that the specified mix is delivered, places the concrete without segregation, keeps the hardened concrete at a constant temperature, and prevents evaporation for the specified time, the owner will be provided with a material that is strong, durable, and able to meet the requirements.

Objectives

1. Understand how cement, water, and aggregates are transformed into a hard rocklike mass.

2. Become familiar with the properties of plastic and hardened concrete.

3. Understand how the water-cement ratio affects the properties of plastic and hardened concrete.

4. Become familiar with the equipment used to transport concrete on the construction site.

5. Understand the principles of reinforced concrete.

6. Become familiar with the various forming systems used to mold and support plastic concrete.

7. Become familiar with various concrete structural elements commonly used in building construction.

4.1 Concrete Materials

Concrete is a mixture of *portland cement* and water combined with inert materials called *aggregates* — sand, gravel, and crushed rock. The cement and water combine chemically, forming a paste that sets and hardens, binding the aggregates into a rocklike mass.

CEMENT MANUFACTURE

The materials necessary to the manufacture of portland cement are lime, silica, and alumina. These ingredients are obtained by processing a mixture of limestone with impure limestone that contains considerable clay, or with clay or shale, or with blast furnace slag. They must be mixed in the proper portions as determined by analysis.

At the risk of oversimplification, the process is as follows. Quarried materials, such as limestone, are introduced to the primary crusher, where they are reduced to about 6 in. material. Further crushing and grinding in the secondary crusher brings the material down to about ¾ in. Measured portions of raw materials, mentioned above, are then blended. This blend is subjected to fine grinding and further mixing in ball mills and tube mills, a step accomplished by a dry process or a wet process in which water is added to the raw materials, forming a slurry.

The raw materials are then submitted to a rotary kiln for about 4 hours, where they are subjected to temperatures of about 3000°F. The resultant clinker is cooled. Gypsum, to control the time of set, is then added, and the mixture is pulverized by a series of grindings to an extremely fine powder — cement.

The cement is then cured and prepared for shipment in bulk or in the familiar 1 cu ft paper bags weighing 94 lb.

TYPES OF CEMENTS

Portland cement should conform to ASTM C 150. All cement types are not alike in behavior and properties. Special portland cements satisfy specific requirements.

There are five types of portland cement that are generally used for construction. Type I cement is called standard or normal, and is used for constructing columns, beams, floor slabs, and other general construction purposes. Type II cement is modified. Similar to Type I, it has a lower content of tricalcium of aluminate and is intended for the same usage as Type I but in localities where a light sulfate resistance is required. This cement, which has a lower heat of hydration (see below), is used in structures of larger dimension and massive pours, such as dams. High early strength cement is Type III and attains an accelerated strength, as is desired for precast concrete. The increased tricalcium silicate content accelerates the heat of hydration. This makes Type III cement most suitable for cold weather concreting. This type of cement should not be used in pouring members of large dimension because the high heat of hydration tends

to cause expansion and subsequent cracking. Type IV cement, termed low heat, is used in massive pours to diminish cracking. Type V cement is sulfate resistant. It is used in areas where excessive sulfate activity is expected. Type V cement should be used for sewage treatment plants and for concrete drainage structures that are expected to carry waters with a high sulfate content.

Air-entrained cements produce concrete that has innumerable microscopic air bubbles. This permits the concrete effectively to resist scaling and spalling, which are deterioration caused by the contraction and expansions of freezing and thawing cycles. *Air-entrained concrete,* identified as Type IA, IIA, and IIIA, is also characterized by improved workability, reduced segregation, and negligible bleeding. In addition to their air-entraining properties, Type IA possesses the usual properties associated with standard; Type IIA, those associated with modified; and Type IIIA, those associated with high early strength cements.

A special type of cement is white portland cement, which is produced in Types I, III, and IA. This nonstaining cement is used effectively with coloring agents or as plain white cement in terrazzo, precast concrete, masonry mortar, stucco, or in any other building component suitable for gray concrete.

MIXING WATER

Water should be free from excessive amounts of oils, acid, sugar, alkali, organic matter, or other deleterious substances, but potable water is usually satisfactory for making concrete. Seawater can be used for concrete, but requires a richer mixture. Surface water, which is nearly always present on aggregates even though they appear dry, must be considered in determining the amount of mixing water. When calculating the amount of water required for a concrete mixture, determination of the aggregate moisture content must be made for mixture control. Moisture content will depend upon the absorbency and porosity of the coarse aggregate. The desired condition is called saturated surface dry (SSD), a condition rarely found in the field. Also, if dry aggregate is used, volume corrections must account for the water that the aggregate will adsorb. In any event, the quantity of water required is the net amount that enters the cement paste.

SETTING

When water is added to portland cement, a chemical reaction, *hydration,* transforms the materials into a product that possesses cementatious properties. As this mortar sets, it releases heat, known as the heat of hydration. The process of setting is an initial set, followed by the final set. The rate of the setting is measured by the penetration of weighted Gillmore needles, or by the Vicat device. Initial set should not occur before 45 minutes, nor should final set require more than 10 hours.

Infrequently, a premature setting, known as false set occurs in a few minutes. Its cause is thought to be due to improper manufacturing and curing of the cement, with gypsum as the culprit.

AGGREGATES

The inert material, called aggregate, is usually divided into two classes according to size. Usually, all aggregate passing a sieve with ¼ in. openings is fine aggregate and that retained is coarse aggregate but other grading criteria are in use. Aggregates graded so that the finer particles progressively fill the voids surrounding coarser particles have a smaller percentage of voids than aggregates consisting of uniform particles. Therefore, well-graded aggregates are more economical because a smaller amount of cement paste is required to fill the voids. Specifications ordinarily state the size grading of each aggregate by conforming to ASTM C 33.

Fine aggregate is usually sand, and coarse aggregate is gravel or crushed stone; but when sand is unavailable, fine aggregate can be made by crushing rock. Crushed, air-cooled, blast-furnace slag is sometimes used.

Some aggregates produce lightweight concrete. Cinders and coke breeze, because of their sulfur content, tend to corrode steel reinforcing and embedded steel pipes. Burned clays and shales, which expand, become vitrified during the burning process. Vermiculite ore is micaceous aluminum. Magnesium silicate greatly expands by sudden heating, causing the water between its thin layers to vaporize, forming greatly expanded lightweight cellular granules. Perlite is a volcanic siliceous rock crushed and heated to a high temperature, causing combined water to vaporize and form innumerable tiny bubbles inside the lightweight glassy particles. Others are natural lightweight stones such as lava, pumice, and tuft. Nailable concrete is produced by using sawdust and cinder aggregates.

Sometimes aggregates are natural mixtures of sand and gravel just as they come from a gravel pit, without grading or washing. This is called pit-run gravel, bank gravel, or bank run. It is not a satisfactory aggregate because of the uncertain quality of the resultant concrete. Better and more economical concrete can normally be produced by carefully graded aggregate because a saving in cement will be realized.

Aggregates should be rounded, insoluble, clean, strong, hard, and durable particles, which are not coated with dust, clay, silt, or other substances. They should not expand or contract when wet with water or react chemically with the cement. Shale and some cherts are particularly objectionable because of their volume change and unsoundness. Flat, elongated, and angular particles, if present in large quantities, reduce the workability of concrete. Aggregates are screened to secure the desired gradings and are washed to remove impurities.

The maximum usable size of aggregate depends upon the character of the work. The size should not exceed one-fifth the width or thickness of the form in which it is being placed or three-fourths the clear space between reinforcing bars. A maximum size of 3 in. is often specified. Questionable aggregates should be tested because there is the possibility of producing inferior concrete, regardless of the proportions used. The tests may include a sieve analysis (ASTM C 136), analyses for organic impurities (ASTM C 40) and soundness (ASTM C 88), and the Los Angeles Rattler test (ASTM C 131) to determine aggregate hardness. The compressive strength of concrete is a good index of the quality of the aggregates used and of the durability, water tightness, and other desirable qualities of the concrete itself.

Heavyweight aggregates are used in concrete for nuclear structures requiring radiation shielding and other purposes requiring dense concrete. Such natural occurring heavyweight aggregates are barite, limonite, and magnitite. Steel products such as steel chips, nuts, bolts, shot, filings, and punchings are also a type of heavyweight aggregate. This type produces the densest concrete, weighing nearly 300 lb per cu ft.

AGGREGATE GRADATION AND SIEVE ANALYSIS

Well-graded aggregate produces an economical concrete that requires a minimum of cement paste while attaining optimum workability. Concrete that consists mostly of ungraded large aggregate is harsh and unworkable; and concrete with excessive fines is uneconomical due to the large amount of cement paste required.

There are a number of gradation curves that serve as guides. Most are based on ASTM C 33, the concrete industry standard. If used intelligently, these standards will usually produce well-graded aggregates.

Laboratory aggregate specimens are sampled from crusher plant or batch plant stockpiles that supply the aggregate used in the eventual field mix. Proper sampling requires portions to be taken from several points around each stockpile: base, center, and top. Excessive portions taken from one location will result in unrepresentative samples because the larger aggregates tend to collect at the bottom while the fines remain near the top or are windblown to one side of the pile.

Sample weights should be about 100 lb, then reduced to workable specimens by the mechanical splitter.

A mechanical sample splitter reduces large samples efficiently and accurately by one-half.

The quartering method requires the field sample to be placed on a clean hard surface and turned over five times, then scooped into a conical pile that is flattened. Two cuts at right angles through the center divide the sample into quarters. The opposite quarters are retained, the others discarded. The process is repeated until a desirable size sample is obtained.

Table 4.1 Grain Size Analysis of Coarse Aggregate and Fine Aggregate for Concrete

Sieve No.	ASTM C 33 Limits %	Passing — Accumulated (1) %	Passing — Accumulated (2) WT	Retained — Accumulated (3) WT	Retained — Accumulated (4) %	Retained — On Individual (5) %	Retained — On Individual (6) WT
Coarse Grain: 2 to No. 4					*Sample Wt. = 750 g*		
2	100	100			0	0	0
1½	95–100	96			4	4	30
¾	35–70	55			45	41	307
⅜	10–30	25			75	30	225
4	0–5	4			96	21	158
Pan		0			100	4	30
Fine Grain:					*Sample Wt. = 500 g*		
⅜	100	100					
4	95–100	98	490	10	2	2	10
8	80–100	85	425	75	15	13	65
16	50–85	65	325	175	35	20	100
30	25–60	45	225	275	55	20	100
50	10–30	21	105	395	79	24	120
100	2–10	3	15	485	97	18	90
Pan				500		3	15
				F.M. =	2.83	100%	500

1. Assume % in Col. 1
2. Determine % in Col. 4 (100% − Col. 1).
3. Determine % on each sieve in Col. 5 (45% max. on any two adjacent fine sieves.)
4. Determine weights passing and retained accumulative and on each sieve.

$$\text{Fineness modulus (F.M.)} = \frac{\text{retained accumulative \%}}{100} = (2.30 - 3.10 \text{ limits})$$

NOTE: The weight and percentage and weight retained on fine individual sieves will frequently not total 100%.

Reprinted from the *Annual Book of ASTM Standards, Part 14,* copyright American Society for Testing and Materials, 1916 Race St., Philadelphia, PA 19103.

COARSE AGGREGATE GRADING

According to ASTM C 33 grading specifications, coarse aggregate sizes range from those passing the No. 16 sieve up to those retained on the 3½ in. but passing the 4 in. sieve. Well-graded aggregates are produced if specified percentages of aggregate pass through a specified combination of five sieves (see Table 4.1). These percentages passing have a range for each sieve. There are 10 combinations of sieve stacks, with choice dependent on the intended location and function of the concrete product, and the available aggregate stockpiles.

FINE AGGREGATE GRADATION

Only one combination of sieves is used for fine aggregate distribution. This series of eight nested sieves consists of the ⅜ in., Nos. 4, 8, 16, 30, 50, and 100, which are each one-half the size of the sieve above. To produce an acceptable fine aggregate distribution, the percentage of material passing must be within a defined range. As a guideline for proper distribution, the percentages passing these sieves are totaled and the sum divided by 100. The result is known as the *fineness modulus,* which should fall between 2.10 and 3.10. As a rough guide, fine sand has a fineness modulus from 2.10 to 2.60, medium sand from 2.60 to 2.90, and coarse sand from 2.90 to 3.20.

Grading specifications further prohibit more than 45% of the total sample to accumulate on any two adjacent sieves.

All material must pass the ⅜ in. sieve.

Table 4.1 shows a grading chart. Note that the percentages passing do not always tally to a neat 100%. Up to 1½% of the total sample may stick on finer sieves and be unrecoverable.

BULKING

The volume of a given quantity of damp sand is much greater than the same volume of dry sand. This volume increase is due to an increase in the moisture content and is called *bulking.* When the weight of the moisture reaches about 6% of the weight of the sand, the bulking may be as high as 20% to 30%. Further moisture additions tend to decrease the amount of bulking until the sand is completely inundated when there is practically no bulking. The bulking of fine material is more for a given percentage of moisture than that of coarse material. Coarse aggregate bulks very little. Methods of measuring sand should be such that bulking can be avoided.

ADMIXTURES

Admixtures are materials added into the standard concrete mixture for the purpose of controlling, modifying, or imparting some particular property to the concrete mix.

Some additives have more than one effect on the concrete. These effects may be desirable or detrimental, depending upon conditions and requirements. For example, an admixture may retard the set, permitting improved finishing while reducing the water content, or an additive that accelerates the time of set may have adverse effects by producing excessive cracking.

Functionally, admixtures are implemented for a number of reasons, which are clearly summarized by ACI committee 212, as follows:

1. To increase workability without increasing water content or to decrease the water content at the same workability.

2. To accelerate the rate of strength development at early ages.

3. To increase the strength.

4. To either retard or accelerate initial setting.

5. To retard or reduce heat evolution.

6. To modify rate of or capacity for bleeding, or both.

7. To increase durability or resistance to severe conditions of exposure including application of ice-removal salts.

8. To control expansion caused by the reaction of alkalies with certain aggregate constituents.

9. To decrease capillary flow of water.

10. To decrease the permeability to liquids.

11. To produce cellular concrete.

12. To improve penetration and pumpability.

13. To reduce segregation particularly in grout mixtures.

14. To reduce or prevent settlement, or to create slight expansion, in concrete or mortar used for filling blockouts or other openings in concrete structures, and in grout for seating machinery, columns or girders, or for filling post-tensioning cable ducts or voids in preplaced aggregate.

15. To increase bond of concrete to steel.

16. To increase bond between old and new concrete.

17. To produce colored concrete or mortar.

18. To produce fungicidal, germicidal, and insecticidal properties in concrete or mortars.

19. To inhibit corrosion of embedded corrodible metal.

20. To decrease the unit cost of concrete.

An accelerating admixture increases the rate of set and the rate of strength gain. Accelerated strength development, a decided advantage in precast concrete work, is desirable where early form removal and erection are necessary for economy. A further advantage of accelerators is a reduction of the curing time. Calcium chloride is the most widely used of the several accelerating admixtures.

Air-entraining admixtures are certain detergents, as in the salts of wood resins, petroleum acids, sulfonated lignum, proteinaceous materials, and fatty and resinous acids. These admixtures cause numerous air bubbles about 1 mm in diameter to form in the concrete. This produces a concrete with an improved workability that permits a reduction in the quantity of water required for placement. With the improved water-cement ratio that results, some increase in concrete strength is realized. The microscopic bubbles result in improved resistance to freezing and thawing cycles and decreased spalling and deterioration caused by the weathering cycles. Air-entrainment is particularly desirable in concrete used for highway work in colder regions.

Admixtures are further classified as water-reducing, retarding, water-reducing and retarding, and as water-reducing and accelerating.

These water-reducing admixtures reduce the water requirement while producing a concrete that retains its workability and consistency. Retarders and accelerators modify the setting times of concrete. This permits increased working time for finishing operations, especially exposed aggregate finishes. Retarders, such as ligno sulfonate, are also useful in obtaining crack-free surfaces, particularly in pours of large volumes. Sugar and citric acids have a similar effect on concrete. They should not be used as admixtures, and precautionary measures should avoid the use of mixing waters or form boards that have any contact with these materials.

Finely divided mineral admixtures are known as relatively chemically inert materials, cementitious materials, and pozzolans. The inert materials include ground quartz, ground limestone, bentonite, hydrated lime, and talc. Some of the cementitious materials are natural cements, hydraulic limes, slag cements, and granulated iron blast furnace slag. ASTM C 219 defines *pozzolan* as "a siliceous or siliceous and aluminous material, which in itself possesses little or no cementitious value but will, in finely divided form and in the presence of moisture, chemically react with calcium hydroxide at ordinary temperatures to form compounds possessing cementitious properties." Fly ash, a diatomatious earth, volcanic glass, and some shales or clays are pozzolanic materials.

These admixtures produce a concrete that has excellent workability. If properly proportioned, they are beneficial in concrete that is pumped through pipelines. Mineral admixtures vary in their effect on concrete. Generally, they may improve sulfate resistance, effect a lower temperature rise in the mix, prevent excessive expansion, and reduce permeability. However, these properties are more or less marked in their effect depending upon the particular mineral admixture, the proportions used, and the cementitious materials used. These admixtures supplement or improve the proportions of finer aggregates required for a mix. They are also used for special concrete mixtures, such as preplaced aggregate construction.

There are several other admixtures that are occasionally used to produce special effects. Gas-forming admixtures, such as hydrogen peroxide and powdered aluminum, release gas bubbles in fresh concrete. Aggregate settlement and bleeding are thus minimized, and increased bond to reinforcing may be realized.

Expansion-producing admixtures, such as granulated iron, produce a grout that has a nonshrink property.

Bonding admixtures, which are frequently two-component epoxy compounds, are mostly used for patching and bonding for anchorages.

Various color admixtures provide black, red, brown, buff, green, and white concretes. These reliable and stable earthen colors are preferred choices among architects. Blues and greens are elusive.

Certain copper and chemical compounds have been used, although with mixed results, as an admixture for fungicidal, germicidal, and insecticidal deterrents. More research is definitely needed in this area.

Soaps, stearate, mineral oils, asphalt emulsions, and certain cut-back asphalts are used as dampproofing admixtures. They do have side effects detrimental to concrete strengths. The effectiveness of dampproofing admixtures may be gravely questioned, as results do not substantiate expectations. Architects frequently prohibit any dampproofing admixtures.

Admixtures are made in liquid, paste, or powder. Accuracy in batching concrete proportions is essential, especially the additions of admixtures. Admixtures that are mixed in as liquids are air-entraining agents, water reducing agents, retarders, and those that have a two-fold function, such as water reducing retarders and water reducing accelerators. Pozzolans, gas forming agents, coloring materials, grouting, and some retarding admixtures are produced in powdered form. These types should be mixed in a dry state with the cement.

Admixtures should be of only the finest quality. When using additives, caution should be taken by using the product of only one manufacturer and by following their printed instructions without deviation.

PROPORTIONING

The proportioning of concrete ingredients has been the subject of much research, and several methods for proportioning have been devised. A method in vogue for years called for arbitrary proportions that neglected the characteristics of the materials or the amount of water used. For example, a 1:2:4 concrete consisted of one volume of cement, two volumes of fine aggregate, and four volumes of course aggregate. This is not an entirely satisfactory method and is not recommended for engineered construction.

Emphasis is now placed on the water-cement ratio method of proportioning. The strength of the cement paste that binds the aggregate particles together to make concrete is determined by the proportion of water to cement used in making the paste. In order to obtain a workable plastic paste, more water is used than is actually necessary to satisfy the required chemical changes while the paste sets and hardens. However, by increasing the proportion of water (beyond that required to produce the plastic mixture), the paste is diluted and its strength and durability reduced. The result is a strength reduction in the concrete produced from dilute paste because the strength of the aggregates is usually greater than the paste and is therefore not the determining strength factor. Restated, and to paraphrase the

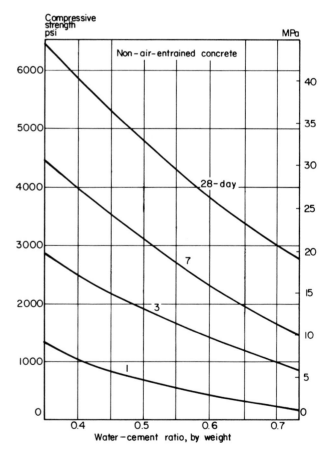

FIGURE 4.1 Typical age-strength relationships of concrete with different water–cement ratios. *Design and Control of Concrete Mixtures,* Twelfth Edition, Portland Cement Association.

Table 4.2 **Maximum Permissible Water-Cement Ratios for Concrete (when strength data from trial batches or field experience are not available)**

Specified Compressive Strength f'_c, PSI[a]	Maximum Permissible Water-Cement Ratio			
	Non-Air-Entrained Concrete		Air-Entrained Concrete	
	Absolute Ratio by Weight	U.S. Gal. Per 94-lb Bag of Cement	Absolute Ratio by Weight	U.S. Gal. Per 94-lb Bag of Cement
2000	0.66	7.5	0.62	7.0
2500	0.65	7.3	0.54	6.1
3000	0.58	6.6	0.46	5.2
3500	0.51	5.8	0.40	4.5
4000	0.44	5.0	0.35	4.0
4500	0.38	4.3	0.30	3.4
5000	0.31	3.5	b	b

[a] 28-day strengths for cements meeting strength limits of U.B.C. Standard No. 26-1, Type I, IA, II, or IIA and seven-day strengths for Type III or IIIA; with most materials, the water-cement ratios shown will provide average strengths greater than indicated in Section 2604 (c) 2 as being required.

[b] For strengths above 4500 p.s.i. with air-entrained concrete proportions should be selected by the methods of section 2604(c) 2.

Reproduced from the 1976 edition of the *Uniform Building Code,* copyright 1976, with permission of the publisher, the International Conference of Building Officials.

maxim, the concrete is only as strong as its weakest ingredient. The weakest link in the "concrete chain" is the paste, and the strength of the paste is determined by the proportion of water used (see Figure 4.1).

The ratio of the quantity of water to the quantity of cement is called the *water-cement ratio* — a ratio that may be expressed in terms of United States gallons of water to a sack of cement but preferably by the weight of the water to the weight of the cement (see Table 4.2). Increasing the proportion of cement paste beyond that required to produce a workable mix does not increase the strength or durability of concrete. The proportion of cement paste required to produce a workable mix depends upon the aggregate gradation. For a given volume of aggregate, coarse particles present less total surface to be covered by the cement paste than finer particles do. It is therefore desirable to use the lowest proportion of fine aggregate that will fill the voids in the coarse aggregate. However, an excess of coarse aggregate causes the mixture to be harsh and difficult to place. To correct this situation, there is a tendency to increase the amount of water, thus reducing the strength and durability. The proper procedure is to increase the workability by better grading of the aggregates, but if this is not possible, the proportion of cement paste must be increased. For a given water-cement ratio, rounded aggregates produce a more workable concrete. Angular shaped aggregates produce a concrete difficult to place. In other words, for the same workability, concrete composed of rounded aggregates requires a paste with a lower water-cement ratio and therefore produces a higher strength than concrete made from angular aggregates.

As stated, the strength and durability of concrete are dictated primarily by the water-cement ratio. The proportioning of concrete requires a water-cement ratio that will produce a strong and durable concrete meeting the required conditions of exposure. The next step is to determine the amount of cement paste to produce a workable mix. The consistency, or state of fluidity, that gives concrete the required workability depends upon the placement conditions. Concrete required for a large mass without reinforcing bars can be stiffer than concrete placed in confined, reinforced members. Also, vibrating the concrete in the forms, by special equipment, permits stiffer mixtures.

The lower values of water-cement ratios, such as 0.50, produce a cement paste that has good adhesive quality. To give some idea of a water-cement ratio:

$$\frac{1 \text{ cu ft water} = 62.4 \text{ lb}}{1 \text{ cu ft cement (one bag} = 94 \text{ lb)}} = 0.66$$

This ratio would probably produce a cement paste of low adhesive quality.

The cement by its nature requires only a minimum of water to form an adhesive that will bind the inert aggregates together into a mass called concrete. If more water is added to the cement than is necessary to make the paste, excessive voids result. The result is a weak concrete.

SLUMP OF CONCRETE

The *slump test* determines the consistency and workability of plastic concrete. In the laboratory, the test, ASTM C 143, evaluates a mix design for its expected consistency and workability at its intended placement; whereas field tests

(A)

(B)

(C)

(D)

FIGURE 4.2 Slump of concrete.

(A)

(B)

FIGURE 4.3 Kelly ball test.

(A)   (B)

FIGURE 4.4 K-Slump test.

substantiate laboratory design expectations. The test is conducted by placing a representative concrete sample into a stabilized, truncated, sheet metal cone that rests upon a damp, level platform. The concrete, placed in three equal volumes is tamped 25 times (each layer) with a bullet-nosed ⅝ in. by 24 in. rod. The last layer is struck level and the cone raised in a steady, even motion. The vertical distance from the 12-in. metal cone down to the center of the slumped concrete measures the slump (see Figure 4.2A, B, C, D).

A reliable supplementary test is the ball penetration test, ASTM C 360, sometimes called the "Kelly ball test." The device, shown in Figure 4.3A, B, is a 30 lb hemispheric chunk of steel with a stem calibrated in inches. The ball, placed upon the level surface of freshly deposited concrete, penetrates the concrete. The depression is measured directly on the stem. The values, in inches, compare to one-half the values of the slump test.

A recent development simplifies the matter. The K-Slump device is a ¾ in. perforated tube that contains a floating scale (see Figure 4.4A, B). The tube is pushed into plastic concrete; after 1 minute the float is released and the consistency (comparable to slump) is read directly. The probe is withdrawn from the concrete and a second float reading measures the workability. This test has proved to be comparable to the traditional slump test and in time may replace it.

Besides the obvious simplicity, the K-Slump tests in-place concrete in nearly any location or member that is 6 in. or more deep and wide.

Any experienced engineer or technician can estimate the slump of plastic concrete within an inch; nevertheless tests must be conducted and the results recorded. This test is of limited value. It is of some benefit to the technician during the mix design process in the laboratory, but as a field test it only confirms what is obvious.

COMPRESSIVE STRENGTH TESTING

The results of tests on molded concrete cylinders determine the ultimate *compressive unit strength* of concrete, f'_c. In the laboratory design mix process, ASTM C 192 is followed to determine the compressive unit strength of trial batch mixes. During the construction phase a similar test, ASTM C 31, confirms laboratory mix designs and monitors the strength requirements of jobsite concrete.

Cylinder specimens, which are based upon the maximum aggregate size, have diameters of 2, 4, 6, 8, 12, and 18 in. and lengths twice their diameters. The most commonly used are 6 in. in diameter by 12 in. long, which are the smallest permitted for field specimens. Molds are made of waxed paper, steel, and plastic. For some unknown reason steel molds produce specimens with higher compressive strengths.

Concrete is placed into the mold in three equal layers and each layer rodded a specified number of times (25 times for each layer for 6 in. diameter molds) with a bullet-nosed rod. The top layer is struck or floated level and then protected from rapid evaporation by a suitable top plate such as glass.

Generally, three specimens are molded for a test. Tests are usually conducted daily or for every 100 cu yd of concrete.

The specimens are cured in a moist condition for a specified number of days known as "test days" or "breaks." The test ages are usually 3, 7, and 28 days; however, 1-day test breaks are now gaining favor.

After moist curing, the specimens are capped with a molten sulphur compound or a high-strength cement. The capping assures that the cylinder ends are parallel, smooth and even, so that equal load distribution is attained. The capped cylinders are compressed to failure in a compression machine and the results expressed in compressive units, psi, or MPa (megapascals).

If the average cylinder strength on jobsite concrete falls below the specified strength, there is usually a reexamination of specifications, test data, and structural member analysis to determine if the in-place concrete will be acceptable —lots of conferences. If ordered, drilled core samples of the questionable concrete are taken and tested. If core samples fail, load tests may determine if the concrete member supports loads without undue deflection.

AIR CONTENT

Air-entrained concrete is characterized by innumerable microscopic air cells that significantly improve the concrete workability and durability. In the plastic state, air-entrained concrete has tiny air bubbles that contribute to better consistency, which results in a more workable mix — the aggregates slide over each other during placement. In hardened concrete, small cells, formed by the air bubbles, provide space for expansion when water freezes. This prevents

Table 4.3 **Concrete Air Content for Various Sizes of Coarse Aggregate**

Nominal Maximum Size of Coarse Aggregate (in.)	Total Air Content, Percent by Volume
⅜	6–10
½	5–9
¾	4–8
1	3.5–6.5
1½	3–6
2	2.5–5.5
3	1.5–4.5

Reproduced from the 1976 edition of the *Uniform Building Code,* copyright 1976, with permission of the publisher, the International Conference of Building Officials.

damage by spalling and scaling due to freeze-thaw cycles (see Figure 4.5).

Furthermore, air entrainment decreases bleeding and aggregate segregation. Bleeding is manifest by water rising to the surface of the concrete, or by collecting in pockets below large aggregate particles, whereas *segregation* is the separation of fine aggregate from the coarse aggregate. Usually the coarse aggregate gravitates to the bottom of the form while the fines collect at the top. Segregation has a number of causes: overvibrating, moving plastic concrete laterally, poor aggregate gradation, excessive water-cement ratio, and improper mixture proportions.

The disadvantage of air entrainment is a loss of 28-day compressive strength. For example, a concrete with a water-cement ratio of 0.48 could produce a strength of 5000 psi, but with entrained air 4000 psi would be expected.

Air gained through normal mixing, known as entrapped air, ranges from approximately 0.3% to 3%. However, a mill-mixed air-entrained cement or an admixture will produce air entrainment up to 8% (see Table 4.3).

Concrete placed in highways or any structural members that will be subject to severe weathering require entrained air.

AIR CONTENT TESTING

The air content on plastic concrete may be made by any of several methods: the volumetric method, the gravimetric method, the air indicator, and the pressure meter methods that feature a high silhouette or low silhouette apparatus.

The volumetric method employs a bronze apparatus called a "Roll-a-meter." It consists of a measured bottom bowl and a top section that has a stem with a window (see Figure 4.6). Concrete is rodded in the bottom bowl in three equal layers with each layer rodded 25 times and the last layer struck even.

After the top section is clamped over the bowl, a long, bottom-baffled funnel is inserted, through which water is added to the zero mark.

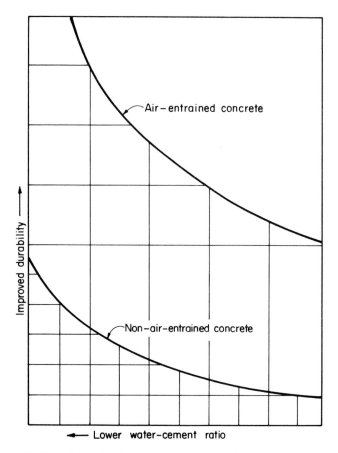

FIGURE 4.5 Idealized relationship between freeze–thaw resistance and water–cement ratio for air-entrained and non-air-entrained concrete. *Design and Control of Concrete Mixtures,* Twelfth Edition, Portland Cement Association.

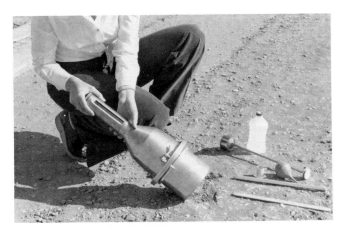

FIGURE 4.6 Air content testing.

The apparatus is capped, inverted, rocked, and rolled. This agitation liberates the entrained air, which rises through the water and into the stem of the device. The water, which has replaced the entrained air, recedes on the scale.

Because a foamy surface usually renders the liquid level indistinct, isopropyl alcohol in 1.0% increments may be added until a clear reading is possible. The level of the receded liquid (water and alcohol) indicates the volume of air that has risen to the top. The liquid level plus the number of increments of alcohol are read directly as the percentage of entrained air.

The relative simplicity, reasonable accuracy, and versatility for field and laboratory account for the method's popularity. This method is capable of testing concrete with aggregates of any weight.

QUALITY CONCRETE

Quality concrete is the product of strong, well-graded aggregates that are bound together by a cement paste of a minimum water-cement ratio. To be of value, the concrete must be workable and economical.

Good concrete as it comes from the mixer appears as a dry, chunky, rocky mass in which the coarse aggregate particles are discernible but coated by the cement paste and when troweled the chunkiness disappears and smooth surface results.

4.2 Cast-in-Place Concrete

Concrete is a versatile material that can, in its plastic state, be molded into any desired shape. This property makes concrete an ideal material for cast-in-place applications. Once it has hardened, concrete is strong, durable, resistant to abrasion, and watertight. To ensure that the desired end product is obtained, care must be taken in each operation in the production of concrete. The ingredients must be of the quality specified and measured accurately for each batch. The concrete must be mixed thoroughly until it is uniform in appearance and all ingredients evenly distributed. Equipment used to transport the concrete to the job site must be able to maintain the homogeneous mixture and deliver it in a timely fashion. The method used to convey the concrete, from the delivery point on the job site to the point where it will be placed in the structure, must do so without causing segregation of the mixture or delay in the placing operation. The placed concrete must be consolidated to mold it within the forms and around reinforcement and to eliminate rock and air pockets. Finally, the concrete must be cured by preventing the loss of moisture and maintaining the concrete temperature for a definite time.

BATCHING

To produce quality concrete, the ingredients must be measured accurately for each batch. Most specifications require that batching be done by weight rather than volume because of the inaccuracies in measuring aggregates by volume. Small jobs around the home and in remote areas are usually batched by volume, but uniform quality cannot be assured. Specifications generally require that materials be measured in batches within these percentages of accuracy: cement, 1%; aggregates, 2%; water, 1%; admixtures, 3%. Equipment should be capable of measuring quantities within these tolerances. The accuracy of the batching equipment should be checked on a regular basis and adjusted when necessary. Most specifications on public work require the accuracy of the batching equipment to be certified.

MIXING

Concrete can be mixed in a stationary mixer at the job site or at a ready-mix plant. They are available in sizes from 2 cu ft to 12 cu yd. Mobile truck mixers with revolving drums, available in sizes from 6 cu yd to 12 cu yd, are the most commonly used in building construction (see Figure 4.7). Generally the ingredients are batched at a central plant, loaded into the truck mixer, and the concrete is mixed en route to the job. If the central plant has a stationary mixer, the concrete may be mixed at the plant and then loaded into a mixer truck for transportation to the job. The mixer truck will operate at a slower agitating speed and is capable of hauling a larger quantity than their rated mixing capacity. Another form of mobile mixer is the mobile batch-mixer. Generally mounted on a truck chasis, it is a combination materials transporter and batching-mixing plant. Cement, aggregate, and water are transported in bulk form in compartmented bins and tanks. The ingredients are then batched and mixed at the point of delivery as needed.

FIGURE 4.7 Truck mixer-agitators equipped with chutes.

TRANSPORTING

Concrete is transported from the mixer to the forms by wheelbarrows, two-wheeled buggies, power buggies, bottom-dump buckets, conveyors, dump trucks, and chutes; or it may be pumped through hoses and steel pipes. Before selecting the mode of transport, factors that must be considered are the quantity, the job layout, and the equipment available. The method employed must prevent the separation of the materials, called *segregation,* and ensure quality concrete. Following are some of the more common methods of transporting concrete on building construction job sites. Where production figures are mentioned, they are averages and assume that delivery is adequate and that the amount can be handled at the point of placement.

Chutes

The most economical method of transporting concrete is with open trough chutes. Most mixer trucks have chutes that are capable of moving the concrete for a distance of up to 20 ft. Care must be exercised to prevent segregation. If the slope is too steep, the larger aggregate will run ahead of the rest of the mixture. The slope should be steep enough to allow the concrete to flow at a sufficient speed to keep the chute clean but not so fast that the materials will separate. Chutes longer than 20 ft should only be used if separation of the concrete can be prevented (see Figure 4.7).

Wheelbarrows and Buggies

Wheelbarrows are one of the oldest methods of transporting concrete on the job and are still used for small placements and for placement to areas that are inaccessible to other equipment (see Figure 4.8). Capacities range from 2 to 4 cu ft and one person can place up to 1½ cu yd of concrete per hour. Suggested maximum horizontal travel is 200 ft. Smooth runways are important for ease of movement.

Buggies are similar to wheelbarrows, but have capacities of 6 to 8 cu ft and one person can place an average of 3 to 5 cu yd per hour. Maximum travel is 200 ft, and smooth, level, and rigid runways are required (see Figure 4.8).

Power buggies are capable of handling larger quantities of concrete and yet have the ability to reach inaccessible areas. Capacities of 9 to 12 cu ft are available and can move 15 to 20 cu yd per hour over a 600 ft travel distance. They are also able to climb grades of up to 35%. Runways must be smooth and firm (see Figure 4.8).

Buckets

Several kinds of concrete buckets are available, and the choice depends on the size of aggregate used, consistency of the concrete, and the capacity of the equipment used to lift the bucket. Standard buckets are available in sizes of ⅓ cu yd up to 4 cu yd. The most common size in building construction is the 1 cu yd bucket. Gates on the buckets are usually of the self-closing, double clamshell type and are controlled manually by levers for hand or rope pull opening. Self-closing and nonjamming features in the gate are important to allow partial discharge of the load at the will of the operator (see Figure 4.9).

Buckets cannot transport concrete without the use of another piece of equipment to do the lifting. The crane is the usual choice because it is normally found on most construction sites. There are three types of cranes that are used most frequently. They are the crawler mounted crane, truck mounted, and the tower crane. The vertical and horizontal distance that a crane can move the concrete will depend on its capacity and the length of boom. Cranes may have boom lengths up to 400 ft and capacities of 175 tons and more. This capacity may be misleading since it is the capacity with the boom nearly vertical. For example, a 70 ton crane with a 200 ft boom has a capacity of 2 tons at a radius of 120 ft. One cubic yard of concrete weighs about 2 tons. The production rate will vary depending on many factors including the capacity of the crane, positioning of the buckets for loading and discharging, size of the bucket, and the skill of the operator. Thirty to forty cubic yards per hour can be expected under average conditions.

Conveyors

Conveyors are used to transfer concrete horizontally and for limited distances vertically. Most conveyors used in building construction are 18 in. wide and from 25 to 60 ft in length. Conveyors can be linked in series to increase the horizontal distance. They can be equipped with radial-spreading discharge units that can be rolled back and forth and swung up to 360 degrees around a pivoted support (see Figure 4.10). Capacities of up to 300 cu yd/hr are possible, but the conveyor capacity seldom determines the actual placing rate. On thin slabs, the ability of the placing crew to spread,

FIGURE 4.9 Concrete bucket. Gar-Bro Manufacturing Co., Heber Springs, Arkansas.

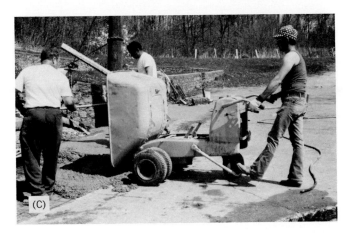

FIGURE 4.8 (A) Wheelbarrow. (B) Buggie. Gar-Bro Manufacturing Co., Heber Springs, Arkansas. (C) Power buggie. The Prime-Mover Co., Muscatine, Iowa.

vibrate, and strike the concrete will determine the placing rate. Sixty cubic yards per hour would be average for slabs 6 in. or less in thickness. On placements for thick mat foundations, the maximum capacity can be reached only if there is a steady supply of concrete to feed the conveyors.

Pumps

Pumping has become one of the most popular methods of transporting concrete on the job site. Pumping is a point to point delivery system in which concrete is moved under pressure through rigid pipe, flexible hose, or a combination of both, to its final destination. The use of pumps in conjunction with articulating booms can accommodate almost any placing situation. Pumps are capable of moving concrete horizontally to distances of 1000 ft and vertically to 300 ft. Capacities of 100 cu yd/hr are possible, but 40 to 60 cu yd/hr are average depending on placement conditions. Pumps are able to deposit concrete directly to the point of use without the aid of additional equipment (see Figure 4.11).

PLACING

Before concrete is placed, the forms should be carefully cleaned; and except in freezing weather, the forms should be thoroughly sprinkled unless oiled forms are used. The concrete should be placed to avoid segregation. Dropping concrete above a height of 5 ft is objectionable because it causes segregation and entrapped air. The concrete next to the forms should be spaded and tamped to prevent honeycombing and to improve the appearance of the exposed surface, but excessive spading or tamping will result in segregation.

Concrete is honeycombed when it contains air pockets where the coarse aggregate is not surrounded with fine aggregate and mortar.

FIGURE 4.10 Conveyor belts operating in series supply concrete to a radial spreading unit. Morgen Manufacturing Co., Yankton, S.D.

The quality of concrete can be improved by consolidating it by vibration. Some types of vibrators are attached to forms, others are placed on the surface of the freshly deposited concrete, such as slabs and pavements, and still others are inserted into the concrete (see Figure 4.12). They may be driven by electricity or compressed air. If vibrators are used, a stiff, low slump, low water-cement ratio concrete can be placed satisfactorily. Thus, stronger and more durable concrete can be formed from the same materials. Vibration also facilitates the flow of concrete around closely spaced reinforcement and into places that would be difficult to reach by ordinary methods, although, as a practice, concrete should not be moved laterally by vibrators.

Partially hardened concrete or concrete that has attained

FIGURE 4.11 Truck mounted boom and pump combination. Morgen Manufacturing Co., Yankton, S.D.

initial set should never be used even though its plasticity is restored by retempering, which means adding water and remixing.

Underwater concrete placement should be avoided. However, if concrete must be placed under water, it must not be allowed to fall through the water because the mortar would wash out. Two devices for depositing concrete under water are in use: the bottom-dump or drop-bottom and the tremie. The drop-bottom bucket is constructed with a bottom that opens when it touches the surface on which the concrete is to be deposited. The tremie is a steel pipe long enough to pass through water to the required depth of placement. In starting operations, the pipe bottom is plugged to exclude water and to retain the concrete with which it is filled. It is then positioned at the point where the first concrete is to be deposited. The plug is then forced out, and concrete flows out of the pipe to its place in the forms without passing through the water. Concrete is supplied at the top of the pipe at a rate sufficient to keep the pipe continually filled. The flow of concrete in the pipe is controlled by adjusting the depth of embedment of the lower end of the pipe in the deposited concrete. The upper end of the pipe may have a funnel shape or a hopper which facilitates feeding concrete to the tremie. Care must be exercised to keep the tremie from losing its charge, otherwise it will fill with water, necessitating a recharge with the plugged tremie. If a richer concrete is used, however, some engineers permit the operation to continue while the water is forced from the tremie by the concrete; the additional cement takes the place of that washed out of the concrete by the water in the tremie. After the concrete is placed, it is not spaded or puddled.

CURING

The chemical reaction that transforms cement into hardened concrete continues for a long period if conditions remain favorable. This results in a gradual increase in the strength of the concrete and an improvement in other properties. For these reactions to continue, moisture must be present and the temperature favorable. An excess of water is always present when the concrete is placed. If the evaporation of this water is prevented or reduced, the water necessary to continue the chemical operations will be present. Evaporation is reduced by covering the surface with wet burlap or plastic film, by sprinkling, by coating the surface with a waterproof paint, spraying with various liquids, or by covering slabs with sand which is kept moist. This protection against evaporation should be continued for 7 days or longer (see Figure 4.13).

COLD WEATHER CONCRETING

Concrete must be protected from freezing at least during the first 7 days after placement. The heat generated by the

chemical reactions is an important factor in maintaining desirable temperatures. The mixing water may be heated and, if more heat is required, the aggregates may also be heated, especially to remove the frost and ice. Type III cement may be used. Specifications often require that concrete be maintained above 50°F for the first 7 days after placing, but the materials should not be heated enough to raise the temperature of the concrete above 70°F. After concrete has been placed, it can be protected by enclosing it in a plastic film enclosure and maintaining heat in the enclosed space. Covering a temporary framework with canvas tarpaulins is a common method. The heat may be supplied by steam which is allowed to escape into the enclosed space to provide moisture for curing. Salamanders, which are commonly oil-burning stoves, are also used to provide heat. The freezing point of concrete can be lowered by the use of salt or other chemicals; however, this practice is objectionable.

Concrete should never be placed on frozen ground because settlement may occur when the ground thaws. All ice and frost should be removed from forms before concrete is placed.

FIGURE 4.12 Internal vibrator. Wacker Corporation, Milwaukee, Wisconsin.

FIGURE 4.13 Concrete strength increases with age with favorable temperature and varying durations of moist curing. *Design and Control of Concrete Mixtures,* Twelfth Edition, Portland Cement Association.

HOT WEATHER CONCRETING

Precautionary measures must be taken during hot weather. Concrete that generates excessive heat may lose strength and exhibit excessive plastic shrinkage cracking. These detrimental effects may be alleviated by lowering the temperature of the concrete. Aggregates are cooled by sprinkling them with cold water, and chilled water or ice is used in the mixing water. Retarding admixtures, judiciously used, are beneficial in lowering the heat of hydration while permitting a longer curing time. Proper concreting practice will assure a measure of success in hot weather, especially proper and prolonged curing, protection from direct sunlight and warm breezes, and scheduling that will assure afternoon placements.

PNEUMATICALLY APPLIED CONCRETE

Concrete or cement mortar can often be advantageously placed by a pneumatic procedure to coat concrete or masonry surfaces, to fill small spaces without using forms, or to patch or repair defects in concrete surfaces. In this procedure, a dry mixture of cement and sand is forced through a hose by compressed air. At a hand-held nozzle, water is supplied to the mixture in a mixing chamber. Directing the nozzle deposits the mortar in the desired place. Because

the apparatus resembles a gun, the product is often called gunite and, because it is "shot" into place, it is also called shotcrete.

If properly proportioned mixtures are skillfully applied, the finished product will be strong, dense, and highly impermeable to water penetration.

DRY PACKED MORTAR

It is often necessary to place cement mortar beds which will be strong and have a minimum shrinkage in small, relatively inaccessible spaces. Examples of such spaces are: the construction clearances required between the bottoms of column bases and the tops of footings; open spaces provided at construction joints so that overlapping bars which project from the ends of adjacent members can be welded to establish continuity; and other small spaces provided for any purpose. Bolt holes in concrete and surface defects caused by improper placing must also be filled or patched.

The mortar used to fill such spaces usually consists of a relatively rich mixture of sand and cement with a minimum moisture content of putty-like consistency which will not develop surface moisture when pressed nor shrink when setting. It is commonly placed by hand tamping and protected against premature drying. It is often referred to as dry pack, although some moisture is present.

CAST-IN-PLACE REINFORCED CONCRETE

Cast-in-place concrete, as its name implies, is cast in its permanent position and location in contrast to precast concrete, which is cast at some other location. Prestressed concrete is reinforced concrete in which the reinforcement has been stressed, before the concrete is loaded, to counteract partially the expectant stresses caused by the anticipated loads. Most prestressed concrete is precast; precast and prestressed are considered together in Section 4.6.

Concrete with a minimum of reinforcement, that is, with only enough reinforcement to resist shrinkage and temperature changes, is classed as plain concrete. *Reinforced concrete* contains enough reinforcement to act effectively with the concrete in resisting forces.

PREPLACED AGGREGATES

Heavyweight concretes are placed in the conventional manner, or by the preplaced aggregate method, which is also known as the prepacked method, grout intrusion, or grouted concrete method. In this method, the coarse aggregate is placed in water-tight forms, and grout is then pumped in to permeate through the aggregate. Proper vibration of the framework assures a smooth surface free from honeycomb.

Well-suited for the heavyweight aggregates, this system has been employed for surface and underwater heavy foundations, and for wall panels, especially those that require exposed rock or aggregate surfaces. Rock aggregates that possess the qualities mandatory for exposed surfaces may be set as form liners that are held in place with wire mesh, or by wire mesh assemblies.

Heavy, well-constructed watertight formwork is required to contain the grout mixture and to resist the imposed hydrostatic pressures. Reinforcement is conventional. Grouting pipes, spaced at about 5 ft intervals, are then placed in the formwork. Wet, clean, coarse aggregate is then consolidated into the formwork by tamping.

Grout, specially prepared, is usually mixed with a pozzolan and a fluidity agent that contributes to a fluid grout, while acting as a water reducing and set retarding agent. The grout, mixed to a creamy consistency by high-speed mixers, is then pumped through the piping into the aggregate mass. The level of the grout, which must be monitored, should be maintained above the pipe outlet. Grout level is ascertained by several methods, of which a sounding well is one simple method. This contains a float that continually indicates the grout level.

This method of construction is one of the newer evolutionary developments in concrete technology. Its proper implementation requires expertise. The system is well outlined in a report by the American Concrete Institute (ACI), "Preplaced Aggregate Concrete for Structural and Mass Concrete," from which this description is drawn.

LAITANCE

When excess water is used, fine inert particles from the cement aggregate, called *laitance,* accumulate in the water on the top surface of concrete. As the water evaporates, this fine inert material forms a residue and, if unremoved, forms a plane of weakness. Because of the excess water or water gain, the concrete below the thin layer of laitance is usually porous and lacks durability. The formation of laitance should be prevented by avoiding excess water rather than trying to remove the laitance after it has formed. Laitance may be removed by wire brushing or sandblasting.

CODE REQUIREMENTS

The Building Code Requirements for Reinforced Concrete, prepared and adopted by the American Concrete Institute, have been included in many building codes and represent the best concrete practice. Specific comments about design in this treatise are based chiefly on these requirements.

PLAIN AND REINFORCED CONCRETE WALLS
Uses

Concrete has largely replaced stone and brick for foundation walls, for it is generally more economical, more substantial, and more watertight than brick or stone masonry.

However, brick masonry will withstand uneven settlement without serious cracking better than plain concrete. Bearing walls above grade may be constructed of concrete. Attractive buildings with concrete exterior walls are being constructed. In some, the exposed surfaces are left as they come from the forms, with very little touching up; but in others, special surface treatments are used.

If the interior of a building is to be of reinforced concrete construction, the usual practice is to use the skeleton type of building with wall columns and beams, and enclosure walls of concrete, brick, structural clay tile, or some special type of curtain wall. This section will deal only with concrete walls; the other types are considered elsewhere.

Concrete is used to an extent for bearing partitions and fire walls, but it is unsuited for nonbearing partitions because of its weight, the cost of forms, and the difficulty of installation after the floors are built. Concrete partitions cannot be poured much thinner than 4 in.; therefore, other forms of construction, some hollow and some thinner, have distinct advantages in weight and cost and are at least as satisfactory in other respects.

Concrete Foundations or Basement Walls

Foundation or exterior basement walls are of several types. The simplest is that shown in Figure 4.14, which supports the vertical load and withstands the lateral pressure of the earth. Ordinarily, the earth pressure is not considered in this type of construction because its effect is small compared to the vertical loads; but for low buildings with deep basements, the earth pressure is a factor in design. Walls of this type are frequently unreinforced except in the footings, but longitudinal reinforcement is desirable to reduce objectionable cracking produced by temperature changes, shrinkage, and uneven settlement. This reinforcement is placed near the top of the wall and near the bottom just above the footings. Longitudinal reinforcement placed in the footings is not fully effective in the beam action of the wall because of the construction joint between the footing and the wall. Special provision made for earth pressure may require a thicker wall than would otherwise be necessary. Vertical steel reinforcement placed near the inner surface of the wall will cause the wall to act as a vertical slab supported at the bottom by the basement floor and at the top by the first floor constructions.

The type shown in Figure 4.14B is designed to carry the concentrated loads of columns instead of the uniform load of a wall. Since there is now a definite beam action, the wall must be designed as a continuous reinforced concrete beam. The effect of earth pressure and the provisions for such pressure are the same as in the walls of the first type.

Instead of resting the columns on a bearing wall, they may be carried to a continuous footing (Figure 4.14C). The walls are required to carry only the lateral earth pressure and possibly a load contributed by the first floor. The lateral earth

FIGURE 4.14 Reinforced concrete foundation walls.

pressure may be provided for by reinforcing the wall as a vertical slab supported by the basement and first floors, as shown in the figure, or the main reinforcement may be placed horizontally; the necessary support is provided by the columns.

In Figure 4.15A, the columns are supported on independent footings, and the wall carries only the lateral earth pressure and possibly a load contributed by the first floor. The wall is designed as a vertical slab supported at the top by the first floor and at the bottom by the basement floor; the main reinforcement is placed vertically near the inner face. In *B*, the wall is supported by the columns, and the main reinforcement is place horizontally near the inner face. Windows or other openings in the wall will determine the most

desirable method of support, or it may be economical to design the wall as a slab supported on four sides.

Deep basement walls of larger buildings are described in Section 3.5.

Concrete Walls

All walls constructed of concrete should contain some reinforcement to provide against cracks caused by temperature changes, shrinkage, or unequal settlement. This is particularly true at corners and around openings. Building codes divide concrete walls into two classes, plain and reinforced.

According to the Building Code of the ACI 318-71, rein-

FIGURE 4.15 Reinforced concrete foundation walls.

forced concrete walls are required to have a horizontal reinforced area equal to at least 0.0020 of the vertical cross-sectional area of a wall and a vertical reinforced area equal to at least 0.0012 of the horizontal cross-sectional area. Walls with less reinforcement, or none, are classed as plain concrete.

Plain Concrete Walls above Grade

In exterior walls classed as plain concrete, horizontal reinforcement is much more essential than vertical reinforcement. It is frequently desirable to place a band consisting of one or two bars all around the building just above the window opening and another band just below these openings. It is also desirable to place a similar band of steel near the bottom of the wall.

Reinforced Concrete Walls above Grade

Reinforced concrete is extensively used for panel walls in skeleton construction and to a lesser degree for bearing walls. In skeleton construction, the exterior walls rest on wall beams or grade beams and are carried by the structural frame. They are called panel walls and are usually installed after the structural frame is completed.

Panel walls are required to carry only the wind loads, and thus their thickness is usually determined by the minimum thickness which can be poured and which will be watertight and still satisfy requirements. The thickness should not be less than 4 in. and will rarely be more than 12 in. Precast enclosure walls are reinforced with wire fabric or small rods. A weathertight joint between the column and the wall is secured by a metal diaphragm or by a polysulphide sealant. A turned-up spandrel beam may serve as a panel wall.

Structural Requirements for Reinforced Concrete Walls

The design requirements for reinforced concrete bearing walls may be satisfied by certain empirical requirements. These requirements apply when the wall dimensions are determined by other than structural analysis. Moreover, these empirical requirements apply only when the loads are reasonably concentric with the walls. They are adapted with permission from Section 14.2, "Building Code Requirements for Reinforced Concrete (ACI 318-71)," a copyrighted publication of the American Concrete Institute.

1. The length of the wall to be considered as effective for each concentrated load shall not exceed the center-to-center distance between loads, nor shall it exceed the width of the bearing plus four times the wall thickness.

2. Reinforced concrete bearing walls shall have a thickness of at least one-twenty-fifth of the unsupported height or width, whichever is the shorter.

3. Reinforced concrete bearing walls of buildings shall be not less than 6 in. thick for the uppermost 15 ft of their height; and for each successive 25 ft downward, or fraction thereof, the minimum thickness shall be increased 1 in. Reinforced concrete bearing walls of two-story dwellings may be 6 in. thick throughout their height, provided that the permissible load is not exceeded.

4. The area of the horizontal reinforcement of reinforced concrete walls shall be not less than 0.0025 and that of the vertical reinforcement not less than 0.0015 times the area of the wall. These values may be reduced to 0.0020 and 0.0012, respectively, if the reinforcement is not larger than ⅝ in. in diameter and consists of either welded wire fabric or deformed bars with a specified yield strength of 60,000 lb per sq in. or greater.

5. Walls more than 10 in. thick, except for basement walls, shall have the reinforcement for each direction placed in two layers parallel with the faces of the wall. One layer consisting of not less than one-half and not more than two-thirds the total required shall be placed not less than 2 in. nor more than one-third the thickness of the wall from the exterior surface. The other layer, comprising the balance of the required reinforcement, shall be placed not less than ¾ in. and not more than one-third the thickness of the wall from the interior surface. Bars, if used, shall not be less than No. 3 bars, nor shall they be spaced more than 18 in. on centers. Welded wire reinforcement for walls shall be in flat sheet form.

6. In addition to the minimum as prescribed in (4), there shall be not less than two No. 5 bars around all window or door openings. Such bars shall extend at least 24 in. beyond the corner of the openings.

7. Reinforced concrete walls shall be anchored to the floors, or to the columns, pilasters, buttresses, and intersecting walls.

8. Panel and enclosure walls of reinforced concrete shall have a thickness of not less than 4 in. and not less than one-thirtieth the distance between the supporting or enclosing members.

9. Exterior basement walls, foundation walls, fire walls, and party walls shall not be less than 8 in. thick.

10. Where reinforced concrete bearing walls consist of

Table 4.4 **Minimum Wall Reinforcement No. 3 Bars Assumed**

Thickness (in in.)	Spacing of Horizontal Bars	Spacing of Vertical Bars
6	7¼	12
8	5½	9
10	4½	7¼

FIGURE 4.16 Reinforced concrete columns.

studs or ribs tied together by reinforced concrete members at each floor level, the studs may be considered as columns.

As an example of the reinforcing that would be required, the number and spacing of rods given in Table 4.4 satisfy the requirements (4) of this code. They should be placed as specified.

CONCRETE COLUMNS

Unreinforced concrete columns will crack from bending stresses induced by differential settlement, temperature changes, or unbalanced loads on the surrounding floors. Consequently, unreinforced columns are not used except where the least width is large compared to the length; then they would be classed as piers rather than as columns. Vertical bars placed near the surface of concrete columns provide resistance to bending; however, the principal load on columns causes compressive stresses that will cause the vertical bars, if used alone, to tend to kick out or buckle and spall off the surrounding concrete. To avoid this, circumferential or lateral reinforcements are used as ties spaced 8 to 12 in. apart (Figure 4.16) or in the form of closely spaced hoops.

Because it is difficult to make individual hoops, a single rod is bent into a helix *(B)* that acts in the same manner as individual hoops. It is called a spiral hoop or simply a spiral, although it is really a helix. Columns with ties are called tied columns, and those with spiral hoops, usually called spirally reinforced columns, are sometimes termed hooped columns. The spiral reinforcement serves another purpose. By confining the concrete core within the spiral, it prevents sudden and complete column failure, therefore making it more dependable. Ties are not as effective as spirals; the allowable load on a tied column is taken as 85% of the allowable load on a spirally reinforced column with the same area and vertical reinforcement.

Other types of columns composed largely of concrete are the composite column and the combination column. A composite column is a steel or cast-iron structural member completely encased in concrete with spiral and vertical reinforcement (see Figure 4.16*L* and *M*). A combination column is a structural steel member that supports the principal load and which is wrapped with welded wire mesh and encased in concrete that supports some additional load. This type of column resembles the composite column shown in Figure 4.16*(L)*. Another type of combination column is the concrete filled steel pipe column.

The load on a column is considered to be distributed between the concrete and the vertical reinforcement — structural steel, steel pipe, or cast iron included in the column in accordance with specified relationships. Some of the specific requirements for the various types of columns are considered in the following paragraphs.

Spirally Reinforced Columns

This type of column is illustrated in Figure 4.16*B, D, E,* and *F.* They are formed with wood or metal and filled from the top; or in the case of long columns, they are filled at pocket openings in the form. The vertical reinforcement, with an area between 1% and 8% of the overall or gross cross-sectional area of the column, must be at least four No. 5 bars. The vertical bar spacing requirements are the same as for spirally reinforced columns. Lateral ties must be at least No. 2 bars spaced not more than 16 bar diameters, 48 tie diameters, or the least dimension of the column. Columns that require more than four vertical bars require additional ties so that each bar is held firmly in position. The minimum cross

sectional dimension of a rectangular column is 8 in., with a gross area of not less than 96 sq in.

Composite Columns

This type of column, illustrated in Figure 4.16*A, C, D, E, F,* and *I,* must not have a metal core cross-sectional area exceeding 20% of the gross area of the column. Hollow metal cores must be filled with concrete. All reinforcement values including spacing, splices, and protective cover must conform to the limitations required of spirally reinforced columns. A minimum 3-in. clearance between the spiral and the metal core is required, except 2-in. clearance is permitted when a structural steel wide-flange (W) column is used.

Metal cores must have milled splices that are in alignment. Other requirements include the unified action between the concrete and its reinforcement with the metal core. The metal core must support erection loads or any other imposed loads before it is encased in concrete.

Combination Columns

A combination column requires a minimum of 2½ in. of concrete cover over all metal parts except rivet or bolt heads. The concrete must have reinforcement equal to 4 × 8/W1.4 × W1.4, with the 8 in. wires parallel to the column axis. The mesh, which surrounds the column, must be lapped at splices and covered with a minimum of 1 in. of concrete. The steel column, like the composite column, is designed to carry any erection loads before it is encased in concrete. This type of column, similar to Figure 4.16*M,* is used in lower floors of reinforced concrete buildings, thereby reducing the required column size.

Another form of combination column is a steel pipe filled with concrete. Concrete filled steel pipes that are unprotected do not have a fire rating. However, they may have a concrete protective covering that will permit a fire rating. The concrete is frequently covered with a finish for aesthetic expression.

Irregularly Shaped Section

Column cross sections are usually square, circular, or octagonal. However, conditions may require columns with other cross sections, such as the section in Figure 4.16*(H)* with interlocking spirals and the sections in *(G), (J),* and *(K).* The ties are arranged to support the longitudinal rods, including the vertical rod in the middle of each side of the square section.

CONCRETE BEAMS AND GIRDERS

Concrete is strong in compression but weak in tension. This deficiency is overcome by placing steel bars in the concrete

TENSILE REINFORCEMENT

A- CONCRETE BEAM REINFORCED WITH STEEL RODS

COMPRESSION REINFORCEMENT

NEUTRAL AXIS

BEAM B   TENSILE REINFORCEMENT   TEE BEAM C   TEE BEAM D   BEAM E

SECTIONS

F - BEAM SHOWING DIAGONAL TENSION CRACKS (SIMPLE SPAN)

G - PART OF TENSILE BARS BENT UP TO PREVENT DIAGONAL CRACKS

H - VERTICAL STIRRUPS TO PREVENT DIAGONAL CRACKS (SHEAR STRESSES)

I - COMBINATION OF BENT UP BARS AND STIRRUPS TO PREVENT CRACKS

BENT BAR

J - ENDS OF BARS HOOKED OR BENT TO INCREASE RESISTANCE TO SLIPPING

FIGURE 4.17 Reinforced concrete beams.

on the tensile side of a beam (Figure 4.17A) so that they will resist the tensile stresses; a very efficient form of beam results. A sufficient amount of steel reinforcement usually makes the beam as strong in tension as is required.

The simplest form of beam is rectangular in section (B), but because the concrete on the tensile side of the beam is not considered to resist any tensile stress, some of this concrete may be omitted in wide beams, leaving only enough to carry the steel rods and to provide for the shearing stresses. This forms the T-beam shown in (C). The corresponding rectangular beam is shown by the dashed lines. Usually some of the concrete on the compressive side near the neutral axis is also omitted (D). By referring to Figure 1.10, it is evident that the stress resisted by material near the neutral axis is small so that its omission only slightly reduces the strength of the beam.

Frequently, it is necessary to design a beam of given

strength in a limited depth which is smaller than would be required for an ordinary rectangular or T-beam. The tensile strength is provided by the required amount of tensile reinforcement, but the amount of concrete available for compression is limited by the space to be occupied. The additional compressive strength necessary is secured by placing steel bars on the compression side of the beam, forming a double-reinforced rectangular beam (Figure 4.17E) of balanced design. Steel is about 15 times as effective in compression as the same amount of concrete. Because of relative costs, however, it is more economical to use concrete to carry compressive stresses.

Thus far, only tensile and compressive stresses have been considered, but it is necessary to provide for shearing stresses also. These stresses combined with the tensile stresses cause diagonal tension stresses that result in diagonal cracks near the ends of a beam (F). Where shear stresses are large, it is necessary to provide reinforcement to prevent cracks. Shear reinforcement is provided by bending up some of the tensile bars (G), or by spacing vertical U-shaped stirrups that envelop the tensile steel at not more than one-half the depth of the beam. Usually a combination of bent-up bars and stirrups is used (I). In rectangular beams, stirrups also retain the top reinforcement steel in position; they overcome the tendency of these bars to kick out — a function similar to column ties or hoops. The ends of stirrups are usually hooked to increase their resistance to slipping. In beams reinforced for compression, they are bent around the compressive steel. Steel reinforcement does not prevent the formation of small cracks on the tensile side of a beam, for if the steel is not overstressed, the cracks are minute and unobjectionable.

Still another form of very serious stress is bond stress, which is caused by the tendency of the steel to slip within a loaded concrete member. To increase the bond strength, deformed bars are used and are usually adequate. Further resistance to slippage is increased by end anchorage or by hooking the ends (J).

The reinforcement in continuous beams must be arranged differently from that in simple beams. If reinforcement is provided only at the bottom of the beam, it is evident that tensile stresses in the upper part of the beam will cause cracking over the intermediate supports (Figure 4.18A); if the ends are continuous over columns, cracks will develop on top, at or near the columns. To prevent these cracks, steel is introduced near the top surface of the beam near the supports (B). Instead of using separate bars at the top, it is more efficient to bend up some of the bottom bars where they are no longer needed (C). At least one-fourth of the bottom reinforcement should remain in the bottom except in end spans, where this proportion should be one-third. Usually the bar splices are made over the supports and the bars are arranged as shown in (D), although they are usually aligned. The ends of plain tensile bars must be hooked to increase their resistance to slipping; however, hooks are

FIGURE 4.18 Reinforced concrete beams.

usually not required on deformed bars. The inclined portions of the bent-up bars effectively resist diagonal tension stresses, although it is usually necessary to use stirrups where shear reinforcement is not provided by bent-up bars. It may be desirable to have several points at which the bottom bars individually or in pairs are bent up as shown in *(E)*. This figure illustrates a completely reinforced concrete beam built monolithic with the supporting columns, which are reinforced to resist any induced bending stresses.

In building construction, floor slabs are usually cast monolithic with the beams and girders, as shown in Figure 4.19C. This slab effectively resists the compressive and flexural stresses in the upper part of the supporting beam at midspan; however, near the beam supports the compressive stresses are in the lower part of the beams. At these points, the bars which run straight through near the bottom of the beam carry a part of the compressive stresses. Continuous beams which are cast monolithic with the floor slabs are therefore T-beams in the central part of the span and double-reinforced rectangular beams over the supports.

CONCRETE SLABS
Ordinary Slabs
For design considerations, reinforced concrete slabs are considered as wide shallow beams. As floors and roofs, they are supported by masonry bearing walls or by reinforced concrete or steel frames. Building codes as a general rule do not permit timber beams to support concrete slabs except as nonstructural slabs; however, in composite construction, timber is used for structural slab support.

The simplest example is that of separate slabs simply supported on beams (Figure 4.19A), although such construction is uncommon. Usually slabs are continuous over the beams *(B)*. It is necessary to provide steel reinforcement near the top of the slabs over the supporting beams be-

FIGURE 4.19 Reinforced concrete slabs.

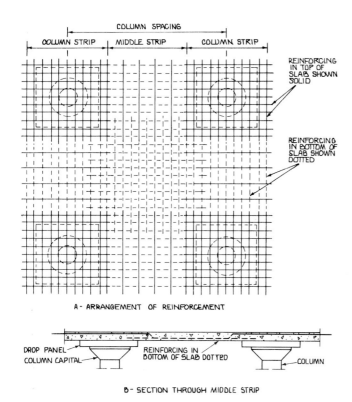

FIGURE 4.20 Two-way flat slab construction.

FIGURE 4.21 Flat-plate and slab-band floor construction.

cause the tensile stresses are at the top at this point. This is provided by bending up some of the steel from the bottom of the slab or by installing short bars over the supports. Although no tensile stresses exist at the bottom of the slab over the supports, it is desirable to continue at least one-fourth of the bottom steel straight through. The steel required at the top of the slab over the supports is about equal to the amount required at the bottom at midspan (see Figure 4.20).

Reinforced concrete slabs, monolithic with reinforced concrete beams and girders (C), span between the beams while acting as the flange of the supporting T-beams. The slabs, continuous over the beams, require tensile steel near the top over the beams. The code permits the portion of the slab extending a distance eight times its thickness on each side of the beam to be considered as the flange of the T-beam. The total width of the slab so considered, however, cannot exceed the distance center to center of the beams or be greater than one-fourth of the span of the beams. It is sometimes possible and desirable to support a slab on four sides by beams or bearing walls (D).

The principal reinforcement for slabs, of course, runs perpendicular to the supporting members, but it is necessary to provide a small amount of temperature reinforcement parallel to the supports to prevent cracks produced by temperature changes and shrinkage. The reinforcement usually consists of No. 3 bars spaced on about 18-in.

centers, but light slabs may be reinforced with welded wire mesh (E) or expanded metal lath (F). The ribbed metal lath shown in (G) is used under light slabs poured without the usual forms. The ribs are sufficiently rigid to span between supports and the mesh so fine that the concrete will not run through but will form a substantial grip on the mesh.

Flat-Slab Construction

The ACI code defines a *flat slab* as a concrete slab reinforced in two or more directions, generally without beams or girders to transfer the loads to its supports. The supports are usually columns. To assist in transferring the loads to the columns, the upper portion of each column may be enlarged to form a column capital (Figure 4.20). The portion of the slab immediately surrounding each column or column capital is strengthened to resist better the intensified stresses in this region. The slab may be thickened in this area by forming a drop panel on the bottom (Figure 4.20), which is cast monolithically with the remainder of the slab. Flat-slab construction is suitable for bays which are approximately square. The reinforcement is usually arranged in the two directions parallel to the sides of the panel. Slabs reinforced in this manner are called two-way flat slabs.

For purposes of design, a two-way flat slab, indicated in Figure 4.20, consists of strips in each direction as follows:

A *middle strip,* one-half panel in width, symmetrical about the center line of the panel.

A *column strip,* of two adjacent quarter panels on either side of the column center line.

Longitudinal reinforcing within each strip is usually made constant in size and spacing. The bars, located near the bottoms or the tops of the strips, as shown in Figure 4.20, resist the tensile stresses caused by the loads.

The minimum permissible thickness of slabs with drop panels is one-fortieth of the longest span but in no case is it to be less than 4 in. The side of a drop panel must be at least one-third the parallel span. The maximum effective central angle of a column capital is 90°. The bottom portion of flat slabs may include recesses or pockets formed by permanent or removable fillers between reinforcing bars, as described later and illustrated in Figure 4.23F. Many other factors, such as openings and length of reinforcement, are considered in the regulations.

Flat-slab construction as described is used extensively for warehouses and industrial buildings with heavy floor loads. For buildings that are subdivided by partitions, the interference of column capitals and drop panels presents partition framing problems.

Flat-Plate Construction

For lighter floor loads, such as those in office buildings, apartment houses, hotels, and dormitories, flat slabs, called *flat-plate construction,* are designed without column capitals or drop panels (Figure 4.21A). Flat-plate construction, which is used extensively, gives a flat, uninterrupted ceiling, well-suited to subdivision. For the same clear ceiling height, flat-plate construction results in a story height lower than other forms of floor construction. Such slabs are designed in accordance with flat-slab principles. The shearing stresses in the portions of slabs close to, and surrounding, the columns limit the loads for which this type of construction is feasible. The slab thickness, which varies from about 6 to 10 in., depends upon the column spacing, the loading, and the allowable stresses.

Slab-Band Construction

Slab-band construction consists of wide shallow beams, called bands, running continuously along each longitudinal row of columns and supporting one-way slabs spanning between bands and cast monolithically with them (Figure 4.21B). The space under the bands may be devoted to closets, washrooms, etc., locating the principal rooms under the slabs to achieve flat ceilings. To accomplish this, the band is sometimes located off center with the columns. A column may also be set somewhat off center from the other columns in a row. Rectangular columns located in partitions may have a width equal to the width of the band and a thickness sometimes as small as 8 in. The slab thickness, which varies from about 5 to 8 in., depends upon the column spacing, the band width, the loading, and the allowable stresses.

A combination of ribbed slabs, described in the following paragraph, and slab-band construction (Figure 4.21C) may be used to form a flat ceiling. This type of construction is adaptable to longer spans and heavier loads than would be possible with flat-plate construction.

Ribbed Slabs

In reinforced concrete beams and slabs, the concrete between the neutral axis and the tension face contributes nothing to the flexural strength, but it is effective in resisting a part of the shearing stresses, as explained earlier. The shearing stresses in slabs are usually low; therefore, all this concrete is not necessary. To save concrete and to reduce the weight of the slab, a large part of the concrete on the lower side of the slab is eliminated, leaving only the ribs or joists (Figure 4.22A). The bottom of the corresponding solid slab is at the bottom of the ribs. These ribs are made wide enough to resist the shearing stresses and to carry the necessary tensile steel. Practically the same amount of steel is required for a solid slab, except for the saving in steel

FIGURE 4.22 Ribbed slabs of reinforced concrete.

FIGURE 4.23 Cores for ribbed slabs and grid flat-slab construction.

resulting from a reduction of the dead load. The remaining flange may extend down to the neutral axis, but usually it does not. This results in a reduction in the compressive resistance, but this is small because the concrete near the neutral axis carries very little stress. The solid slab would be reinforced with relatively small bars closely spaced, but in the ribbed slab, two larger bars are ordinarily used in each joist. This results in increased bond stresses, but such stresses are not often a controlling factor. Some conditions require solid bridging between joists, spaced not more than 15 ft apart, for some types of joist floors. This bridging is commonly 4 in. wide and the full depth of the joists. It is reinforced with one rod near the top and one near the bottom. The primary function of bridging is to distribute heavy loads into several joists. The minimum permitted width of joists is 4 in., and the depth below the bottom of the slab is

sometimes limited to three times the width. The clear spacing between the joists is limited to 30 in. The thickness of the top slab varies from 1½ to 3½ in., depending upon the span and loading.

The detail of a ribbed slab supported at a bearing wall is shown in Figure 4.22B. The details used for slabs continuous over bearing walls, concrete girders, and steel girders are shown in (C) to (E).

Occasionally, it may be advantageous to support a slab on four sides and provide ribs in two directions, as shown in (F).

Ordinary wood forms would be so expensive for ribbed slabs that their cost would be prohibitive. For this reason, various formwork types have been devised. The sides of the joists and the bottom of the slab are formed by structural clay tile, hollow gypsum tile, or sheet-steel cores (Figure 4.23A to C), or special forms of concrete block called tile fillers or simply fillers. Wood forms are constructed for the bottoms of the joists. These are usually made of 2 in. material and are sufficiently wider than the joists to support the edges of the clay or gypsum tiles or the steel pans. The formwork is therefore very simple.

The fillers provide a plaster base for the ceiling formed by the underside of the slab. Special forms of tile or block cover the ceiling. The ends of the end tile may be closed by a thin slab made for that purpose by using pieces of sheet-metal or wire screen.

The sheet-steel cores may be made of heavy material, which can be removed after the concrete has set and reused several times. They may also be thinner material to be left in place. If removable forms are used and the ceiling is plastered, metal fastened to the underside of the joists serves as a plaster base for the ceiling below. Various types of anchors can be cast in the underside of the joists to receive the metal lath. If the sheet-steel cores are to remain in place, metal lath is laid over the formwork before the cores are set. The metal lath is wired to the reinforcing bars in the joists. In one type of steel core, the lath is fastened to the core as shown in Figure 4.23D before the core is placed. Sheet-metal closers or end caps are made for the end cores. Because of excessive shearing stresses, it is sometimes necessary to widen the joists at the ends by using tapered cores. The most common widths of metal core are 20 and 30 in., used with joist widths of 4, 5, and 6 in. Core depths vary by 2 in. increments from 6 to 14 in. They are usually corrugated to increase their stiffness and are lapped one or one-half corrugations, or more if necessary, to provide the required lengths. The cores are supported on forms that form the bottom of the joists. No forms are necessary between the joists. The costs of removing cores must be considered, as must the greater cost of placing the lath. The type most suitable for a given case can be determined only by studying all the factors involved.

For all types of core, the reinforcement in the top slab must be adequate to resist the loads on the slab and to provide for temperature changes and shrinkage of the concrete. Temperature reinforcement usually consists of wire mesh of ¼ or ⅜ in. rods normal to the joists and spaced from 6 to 12 in. No temperature reinforcement is required, however, parallel with the joists because the reinforcement in the joists is adequate.

Ribbed slabs are suitable for spans varying from 10 to 35 ft. In constructing long-span slabs, camber should be provided to offset the deflections caused by elastic deformation and time yield or plastic flow, called creep.

Special types of tile and sheet-steel cores are available for two-way construction. A steel core for two-way construction is shown in Figure 4.23*E*.

A form of flat slab construction has been devised to make use of the ribbed slab in place of the flat slab. This is known as the grid flat slab, or waffle slab and is illustrated in Figure 4.23*F*. The reinforcing is not shown in this figure, but would be similar to that used in the two-way system shown in Figure 4.20 with the rods placed in spaces between the cores (see Figure 4.24).

4.3 Concrete Framing

In framing a reinforced concrete building, the forms are first constructed, the reinforcing steel is placed, and finally the concrete is placed. After the concrete sets, the forms are removed, and curing procedures continue. It is obviously impossible to place the concrete for an entire building of any magnitude in one operation; therefore, construction joints cannot be avoided. These should be located and constructed so as not to impair the strength or appearance of the building. The joints in slabs, beams, and girders should be, preferably, vertical and at the center of the span where the shearing stresses are small. The column concrete should be placed to the underside of the floor girders for beam and girder construction so that the shrinkage of the concrete columns may precede the placement of the floor above.

Forms are usually constructed of wood, but steel forms are extensively used, especially for buildings of flat-slab construction. The reinforcing steel is held in position by wiring the bars together at their intersections. The bars for each beam, girder, and column are usually wired together forming a frame which is set in position as a unit. Various devices such as chairs, high chairs, and spacers have been designed to hold reinforcing steel in position.

Reinforced concrete buildings may be of bearing-wall construction or of skeleton construction. The bearing walls may be constructed of brick, stone, structural clay tile, concrete block, plain concrete, or reinforced concrete, described earlier.

The cross section of a reinforced concrete building with flat-slab construction is shown in Figure 4.25*A* and one with beam and girder construction in *B*.

FIGURE 4.24 Waffle slab or grid flat-slab in library.

FIGURE 4.25 Types of reinforced concrete framing.

FIGURE 4.26 Beam and girder construction.

Typical details for a building of the beam and girder type are shown in Figure 4.26. All reinforcing is deformed bars. The features which should be noted in this figure are as follows:

1. The reinforcing in the slab is at the bottom near the center of the span and at the top where the slab crosses the beams. Some of the bottom steel continues through the bottom.

2. The reinforcing in the beams is similar to that in the girders. The horizontal bars in the bottom of the girder are bent up from the bottom to the top in the region near the supporting columns.

3. Shear reinforcing is provided by bent-up bars and vertical stirrups.

4. Dowels extend from the spread footings into the columns. These dowels, equal in size and in number to the longitudinal bars in the column, transfer the stress in the column bars to the footing. They extend into the column and into the footing a sufficient distance so that their bond stress will not be excessive.

5. The longitudinal bars in the interior columns are arranged around the edge of the columns and are surrounded with closely spaced spiral reinforcing. To avoid confusion, all the longitudinal bars are not shown in the section, but they are shown in the plan view.

6. The longitudinal bars of the wall columns are held in position by lateral reinforcement ties that are not as closely spaced as the spirals of the interior columns.

7. The columns are spliced by extending the longitudinal bars from one column upward into the column above. To accommodate the smaller size of the upper columns, the bars are bent inward in the part of the column occupied by the floor construction. They are again made vertical at the floor level.

8. The slope of the roof is obtained by a lightweight concrete fill that receives the built-up bituminous roofing. The lightweight concrete fill also serves as heat insulation. An expansion joint provides space between the filling and the parapet wall so that the fill can expand as it becomes heated. If this provision were not made, the topping would either buckle or push the parapet wall out. Similar expansion joints should be provided at other points. It is usually desirable to slope the roof for drainage, although good results have been secured with decks that do not slope to drains. Such decks require an impervious surface. Dead level roof decks should be avoided because shallow pools of standing rainwater that may accumulate will bring eventual damage to a built-up roof.

9. The panel walls consist of aluminum sash that occupy the entire width between coumns and below which a spandrel masonry wall is placed.

10. The parapet wall is capped with a coping, the top of which slopes and drains onto the roof and not over the face of the building.

Typical details of a building of the flat-slab type are shown in Figure 4.27. The features that should be noted in this figure are as follows:

1. The substitution of flat-slab construction for the beam and girder construction shown in the previous figure.

2. The drop panels and the column capitals of the interior columns.

3. Brackets and drop panels of the exterior columns.

4. The spiraled interior columns. For clarity, only a part of the longitudinal bars are shown in the section but they are all shown in the plan view.

5. The tied wall columns. Since these columns are rectangular, they are provided with intermediate ties.

Other features are the same as the corresponding features of the beam and girder type which have just been explained.

LATERAL RESISTANCE

The problems involved in designing tall buildings with steel frames to resist the lateral forces caused by wind and earthquake shock is considered in Section 6.2. As with steel frame buildings, nonbearing masonry walls and partitions contribute to the lateral rigidity of a reinforced concrete building, but the magnitudes of such contributions are uncertain and they are usually neglected in design. The only resisting elements that are considered are the integral structural parts. Members subject to stresses produced by wind and earthquake forces combined with other loads may be proportioned for unit stresses one-third higher than the allowable stresses for dead and live loads only, but the size of a member must not be less than is required for these loads.

The horizontal deflections from lateral loads tend to distort the rectangular partitions constructed between the columns and floor systems and cause them to crack. A similar phenomenon occurs in door and window openings with objectionable results. Therefore, even though a frame may be structurally adequate as far as stresses are concerned, it may not be satisfactory. For that reason, horizontal deflections of a frame as well as stresses must be considered.

A significant factor in determining the special structural requirements for resisting lateral loads of given intensities is the ratio of the height, or the portion of a building above the elevation being considered, to the width, or smallest lateral dimension. Another significant factor is the type of floor construction. Construction with girders framing into the columns and running the width of a building offers considerable resistance to lateral forces without exceeding allowable stresses in the columns or girders, but construction with flatplate floors are less effective in this respect.

Usually tier buildings only a few stories high, or the upper few stories of tall buildings, do not require special provisions for wind unless they are very narrow in at least one dimension. It will be obvious to experienced designers that under some conditions no special provisions are required and that under other conditions they are certainly necessary. Between these two extremes, each case must be given specific consideration.

Tall buildings with long narrow plans require special provisions to resist wind loads acting against the broad side of the building but do not normally require such provision to resist the wind load against the narrow side. This condition results from the smaller wind load and the greater lateral strength of the building in the direction parallel to the longer dimension. When the usual types of construction prove inadequate to resist the lateral forces (after permissible increases have been made in the allowable stresses), a common solution includes reinforced concrete *shear walls* in some of the vertical bents bounded by continuous columns and the floor systems. Shear walls are made integral with the other structural members by tying them together with reinforcing bars. They are designed to resist the lateral forces on the portions of the building that contribute to the lateral loads.

A simple arrangement of shear walls to provide transverse rigidity is illustrated in Figure 4.28. Pairs of columns in every third row in each story are connected by shear walls forming wind bents. To provide for a longitudinal corridor, shear walls are not placed between the two interior columns in each transverse row.

The lateral loads are transmitted horizontally to the wind bents by the floor systems as explained for steel tier buildings. The usual types of reinforced concrete floor systems transmit these loads, but sometimes special provisions require additional reinforcement or increased sections.

Preferably, shear walls are continuous from the foundation to the maximum height at which they are required. When this is not possible, the lateral loads are transferred

FIGURE 4.27 Flat-slab construction.

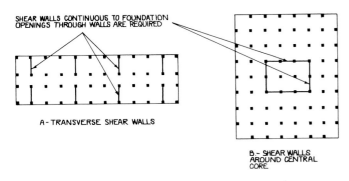

SHEAR WALLS CONTINUOUS TO FOUNDATION
OPENINGS THROUGH WALLS ARE REQUIRED

A - TRANSVERSE SHEAR WALLS

B - SHEAR WALLS
AROUND CENTRAL
CORE

FIGURE 4.28 Shear walls.

horizontally between discontinuous shear walls by the floor systems where the discontinuities occur. The vertical loads are transmitted directly downward.

The simple patterns of shear walls illustrated in Figure 4.28 may not be possible in all buildings. Shear walls are frequently located in walls that enclose elevator shafts and stairwells, or they are located in other positions that do not interfere with usable floor space.

Shear walls vary from 6 to 12 in. thick depending upon structural conditions. As has been stated, their function is to resist horizontal shearing forces produced by lateral loads, which in many regions may include seismic shocks as well as wind. Generally, shear walls are not considered to support dead and live loads. Reinforced concrete bearing walls do resist lateral forces in a manner similar to shear walls. Such walls carry the dead and live loads in addition to the lateral loads and, for that reason, must be thicker than shear walls. Usually, such construction is uneconomical.

Another means of increasing lateral rigidity and strength is by orienting the longer dimension of rectangular columns parallel with the short dimension of the building plan and framing deep floor girders into them.

Under any conditions, the provisions to resist lateral forces must be such that the resultant resistance at any elevation is colinear with the resultant lateral force at that elevation. Otherwise, the building tends to twist.

Restated, lateral resistance is often provided by a rectangular core bounded by shear walls. In each building of the twin Marina City Towers in Chicago (Figures 4.29, 4.30, and 4.31), a cylindrical reinforced concrete core provides resistance to lateral forces. Each core, which has an internal 32-ft diameter to its full height of 64 stories, rises 588 ft above the circular reinforced concrete pad or mat on which it bears. The thickness of the core walls varies from 30 in. at the bottom to 15 in. at the top.

The diameter of each foundation mat is 58 ft. Originally, the design thickness of each mat was 3 ft; but because of construction difficulties, one mat was made 6 ft thick. Each mat is supported on two concentric rings of piers passing through soil and hardpan to rock about 115 ft below. The inner ring includes 8 piers located directly beneath the core

wall, and the outer ring includes 16 piers, each directly beneath a column located as is described and illustrated in Figure 4.31.

The structure surrounding the core has a height of 60 stories. Supported primarily on two rings of 16 columns each, column centers are located on circles concentric with the core. One ring has a radius of 23 ft 6 in.; the other, 54 ft 8 in. The inner ring of columns bears on the mat, as has been stated, and each column in the outer ring is supported on a foundation pier extending to rock. Each pier in the outer ring is anchored to the mat by a radial tie beam, and the piers are tied together by circumferential beams.

The upper portion of each pier is reinforced, some throughout their entire depth, with vertical bars. A 6-ft square steel bearing plate 2 in. thick on top of each pier in the outer ring facilitates the transfer of the column load to the caisson. The top ends of the reinforcing bars in the column are welded to the top of the plate. Full bearing is assured by placing the concrete in the top of the pier through a hopper extending through a hole in the center of the plate providing a hydrostatic head.

The lower 4 stories of each building are occupied by shops and services. The next 16 stories provide parking for 448 cars with access to the building. The next 40 stories provide 448 apartments of varying sizes, and the upper 4 of the 64 stories in the core of the building house the elevator machinery, air conditioning equipment, and other mechanical equipment. The elevators, stairways, and various other services are located in the core, which is surrounded at each floor level by a corridor.

The core walls, columns, and foundations are of ordinary stone concrete. The ramps and the floors of the apartments are lightweight concrete slabs integral with wide shallow beams radiating from the core and over the columns in the two rings (see Figure 4.31). The parking ramps occupy the space between the core and the outer row of columns and cantilever out 9 ft 2 in. beyond their centers. On the apartment floors, a semicircular balcony cantilevers out in each bay beyond the columns in the outer row. The apartments are enclosed between exterior columns with floor-to-ceiling glass curtain walls which include sliding glass doors providing access to the balconies. The balconies are open except for railings.

The maximum height of the parapet wall above street level is 581 ft.

EXPANSION JOINTS

The following material on expansion joints is quoted from the Joint Committee Report.

a. Expansion joints are expensive and in some cases difficult to maintain. They are, therefore, to be avoided if possible. In relatively short buildings, expansion and contraction can be provided for by additional reinforcement. No arbitrary spacing for joints in long

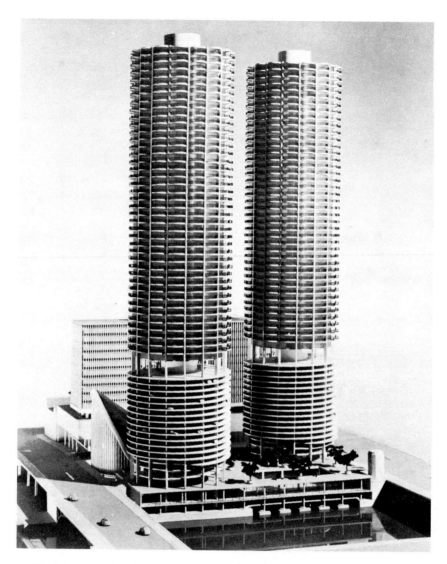

FIGURE 4.29 Model of Marina Towers in Chicago. Architects and Engineers: Bertrand Goldberg and Associates. Consulting Engineers: Severud-Elstad-Krueger Associates. Foundation Consultants: Moran, Mueser and Rutledge and R. B. Peck. Sponsors: Building Service Employees International Union.

buildings can be generally applicable. In heated buildings joints can be spaced farther apart than in unheated buildings. Also, where the outside walls are of brick or stone ashlar backed with brick, or where otherwise insulated, the joints can be farther apart than with exterior walls of lower insulating value.

b. In localities with large temperature ranges, the spacing of joints for the most severe conditions of exposure (uninsulated walls and unheated buildings) should not exceed 200 ft. Under favorable conditions buildings 400 to 500 ft long have been without joints even in localities with large temperature ranges.

c. In localities with small temperature ranges, the spacing of joints for unheated buildings or with uninsulated walls should not exceed 300 ft. In such localities buildings up to 700 ft long have been successfully built without joints where other conditions were favorable.

d. In roof construction, provision for expansion is an important factor. The joints in the roof may be required at more frequent intervals than in other portions of the building because of more severe exposure. In some cases expansion joints spaced 100 ft apart have been provided in roofs and not in walls or floors.

e. Joints should be located at junctions in L-, T-, or U-shaped buildings and at points where the building is weakened by large openings in the floor construction, such as at light wells, stairs, or elevators. Joints should provide for a complete separation from the top of the footings to the roof, preferably by separate columns and girders.

FIGURE 4.30 Marina Towers in Chicago during construction.

FIGURE 4.31 Partial plans of Marina Towers.

CONCRETE RIGID FRAMES, ARCHES, AND DOMES
Rigid Frames

A single-span two-hinged rigid frame is shown in Figure 4.32. The structure, supported on spread footings, has a tie rod under the floor that carries the outward horizontal components of the thrusts on the footings. The roof deck is wood plank sheathing supported by reinforced concrete purlins. Haunched ends improve the lateral support they provide for the frame. Exterior walls, constructed of concrete reinforced for temperature changes and shrinkage, are supported by the frame. Concrete slabs might have been used instead of the wood roof sheathing shown.

Usually, rigid frames can be constructed more economically by precasting rather than casting in place.

Arches

Long-span reinforced concrete arches support the roofs of

FIGURE 4.32 Reinforced concrete rigid frame.

hangars, auditoriums, field houses, and other structures requiring unobstructed floor areas.

The cross section of a reinforced concrete thin-shell arched roof with stiffening and carrying ribs supported on cantilever abutments for the War Memorial of Onondaga County in Syracuse, New York, is shown in Figure 4.33. The arch rib spans 160 ft and the cantilever projects 27 ft on the abutments. Twelve identical bays spaced 19½ ft center to

center and arranged in pairs with the dimensions as shown in the figure comprise the structure. Each alternate rib is divided into two half-ribs separated by cane fiber insulation board. This joint, which provides for expansion and contraction produced by temperature changes, serves as a construction joint, enabling two bays to be poured in one operation. The same forms were so arranged that they could be moved easily from bay to bay to cast the six pairs

FIGURE 4.33 Thin-shell concrete arched roof supported on cantilever piers. *Engineering News-Record.*

FIGURE 4.34 Thin-shell concrete arch roof of Denver, Colorado, Coliseum. Structural Engineers: Roberts and Schaefer. Courtesy Denver Convention and Tourist Bureau.

of identical arch bays. The cantilever abutments were cast about a month in advance of the arches, allowing them to gain sufficient strength to support the arches.

A wood fiber insulation board 1 in. thick deck covers the entire roof, over which a 4-ply asbestos-felt built-up roofing is applied. The ceiling was sprayed with 1 in. of acoustical material. Edgarton and Edgarton, Architect-Engineer Associates, prepared the design and were responsible for the supervision. Ammann and Whitney were consulting structural engineers. F. S. Merritt, Senior Editor of *Engineering News-Record,* wrote the article on which this description was based and from which the illustration was taken.

An exterior view of a thin-shell arch coliseum is shown in Figure 4.34.

Domes

Reinforced concrete is used extensively in the construction of roof domes, which usually cover circular areas. The simplest form of dome would be generated by revolving a solid arch about a vertical axis through its center. Arches of this type are illustrated in Figure 4.63. A common form is the ribbed arch, illustrated diagrammatically in Figure 1.19. The spaces between ribs are spanned by purlins that support the roof deck. A simple folded-plate domed roof is shown in Figure 4.66.

A thin-shell dome roof for a theater in San Diego, California, was constructed by compacting a man-made mound of earth 36 ft high shaped to serve as the form for the underside of the dome. The dome is a pierced concrete shell 190 ft in diameter. It is supported on its periphery by five thrust blocks. Arches between these supports form openings 9 ft high. The major portion of the dome is 4 in. thick but

increases to 16 in. at the thrust blocks; the edges between thrust blocks are stiffened with edge beams.

The compacted fill was covered with a skim coat of concrete that formed a smooth surface which was oiled to prevent bonding. After placing the reinforcement, the lightweight concrete of the dome was placed pneumatically. Finally, after the concrete had cured, the earth fill and the skim coat of concrete were removed. Architects were Richard Wheeler and Associates; structural engineers were S. J. Blaylock and Associates; and the contractor was Peter Kiewit Sons.

The domed roof illustrated in Figure 4.35 consists of 32 arch ribs with the outer end of each supported by an inverted L-shaped pier. The inner end of the ribs is supported by a centrally located compression ring into which the ribs frame. The ring carries the inward thrusts of the ribs at the crown. The outward thrusts, through the lower ends of the ribs which are carried directly by the piers, transfer to an upper tension ring which encircles the roof structure between the horizontal portions of the piers. The lower outward thrusts of the piers are carried by a lower tension ring located below the ground surface. The spaces between ribs are spanned by purlins spaced about 10 ft concentrically. Bulb tees spaced about 33 in. span radially between purlins and support noncombustible compressed fiberboard roofing plank 3 in. thick. The roof plank serves as an excellent heat-insulating and acoustic material when used as decking.

The dome, with a span of 250 ft and horizontal legs of each pier 35 ft long, has an overall diameter of 320 ft. The ribs and purlins of the dome are constructed of lightweight concrete, and the remainder of the structure is constructed of regular concrete. The piers and the columns supporting

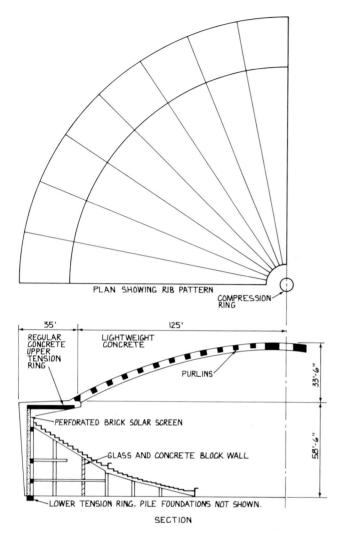

PLAN SHOWING RIB PATTERN

COMPRESSION RING

35' — REGULAR CONCRETE UPPER TENSION RING

125' — LIGHTWEIGHT CONCRETE

PURLINS

33'-6"

58'-6"

PERFORATED BRICK SOLAR SCREEN

GLASS AND CONCRETE BLOCK WALL

LOWER TENSION RING. PILE FOUNDATIONS NOT SHOWN.

SECTION

FIGURE 4.35 Concrete ribbed dome, Jacksonville, Florida, Coliseum. Architects: George R. Fisher and A. Eugene Cellar. Structural Engineer: Grumar E. Kraus.

the seating area have pile foundations. The facade is a solar screen of perforated brick, and the interior walls are glass and concrete block. The building encloses basketball, ice hockey, trade shows, and other events.

4.4 Concrete Formwork

Concrete, a plastic material, must be formed. *Formwork* means the containment or support of plastic concrete that allows the concrete to shape and attain its final form.

Formwork must have several qualities beyond the required or intended shape. It must be economical and strong enough to support the imposed dead, live, and erection loads. The forms should be reusable and easily erected and

removed. A versatile formwork will meet any jobsite conditions or special design requirements. The essential problem in formwork design is to assemble a temporary structure that can be disassembled in a relatively short period of time, that is economical, and that will support the excessive dead and live loads. It may be uneconomical to assemble the formwork structure by means which ignore the fact that the structure may be disassembled to permit reuse of most of the materials.

Class I formwork is generally regarded as temporary, or for the support of light loads requiring a plywood of an inferior quality compared to the plywood required for Class II formwork. Class II formwork is for the type of structure that will be supporting the heavier loads, and formwork of concrete is for the larger, more permanent structures.

Economy in formwork is achieved by implementing a number of factors. Foremost is overall jobsite planning and control. This should include the designing of forms and a planned sequential coordinated movement of large sectional components or assemblies. Preconstruction planning should include a careful selection of forming materials. This may include panelized materials or sheathing boards, plastic-faced plywoods, hardboards, steel panels, or other materials that will assure a high reuse factor.

The proper supervision and the effective employment of experienced workers while erecting efficiently constructed forms will permit fast erections and form removal, which is called stripping. The vertical members that support horizontal formwork are called *shores;* however, the vertical bracing members are generally referred to collectively as the falsework or centering. After forms are stripped from floor slabs, the slabs are reshored by replacing the shore braces against them, thus preventing deflection and cracking.

There are several systems that assure economical erection and stripping. Specially designed metal clamps and metal wedges and assortments of these may be used for assembly.

Formwork, to be safe and economical while molding the concrete to the desired shape, should be structurally adequate. Formwork failures by collapse are frequent enough to warrant the attention of engineered design. Usually collapse failures are caused by one or a combination of the following: localized overloading of placement equipment; lack of lateral support; defective form materials; poorly assembled and misaligned materials; and undersized and overspaced supporting members.

Collapse of poorly planned but adequately constructed formwork may be initiated by bumping a vertical supporting member with a loading buggy, crane booms, or buckets. A chain reaction on poorly planned formwork layouts may result in eventual complete collapse.

One of the more troublesome aspects of concrete form construction is locating and installing embedded items. Embedded items are usually materials that penetrate into the concrete, although this includes materials that pass through the concrete, such as pipes. Requirements frequently include blockouts for various equipment, pipe sleeves, passage openings, inserts and anchorages, waterstops, electrical boxes and conduits, and other mechanical equipment. The proper location and alignment, termed interface, is essential with mechanical equipment. If provision is not made for these items, or if they are mislocated in the formwork, embedment by drilling and cutouts into the hardened concrete will be required — often at great expense. Coordination between the formwork designer-constructor with the various crafts is mandatory. A thorough examination of all drawings is essential.

MATERIALS

Form materials that are in contact with the concrete must be supported by frames, shores, braces, studs, and walers, which are usually made of wood or steel. The usual forming materials are strip boards (sheathing), plywood, hardboard, steel, and reinforced plastic. In some cases, compacted earth, formed or sculptured sand, and even other concrete are used as forms for reinforced concrete.

Most forming systems employ wood in some degree. Generally, the most economically available wood is used. Frequently, Douglas fir or southern yellow pine serve this purpose, although western hemlock, ponderosa, northern white sugar, and Idaho pine are used. Wood that contacts the concrete should be nonstaining and free from organic substances that may impart detrimental effects to the concrete.

LUMBER

Sheathing boards are either centermatched Tongue and Groove (T&G), shiplapped, or square edged and surfaced on all sides (S4S). Square edged sheathing leaves a rough surface that effects a texture.

Early efforts at formwork used mostly solid wood, which usually consisted of 1x, S4S, or centermatched T&G sheathing in contact with the concrete. In wall forms, these are nailed to vertical members called studs, which in turn are supported by a double row of horizontal walers that are spaced about 3 ft on center (see Figure 4.36). This formwork usually impresses the grain of the form boards on the surface of the finished concrete. If S4S material is used, a rougher texture that is characterized by bulges, depressions, deflections, knot holes, grain, and imprints of the form imperfections is impressed in the finished concrete surface. Formerly, these surfaces were frequently ground smooth and given a grout coat of cement that covers all traces of the formwork. Today, this type of rough textured surface is desired for special effects, and some architects make a special effort to gain this effect.

FIGURE 4.36 Typical wall form showing main components. (From *Formwork for Concrete,* Fourth Edition by M. K. Hurd. Copyright © 1979. Courtesy of American Concrete Institute.)

PLYWOOD

Plywood is the most common forming material. Plywood for formwork is classed according to usage as Class I and Class II. The latter class includes that which is intended for heavy construction, that which entails great expense, and that which is planned for high reuse. These classes of plywoods are usually D.F. (Douglas fir), and southern yellow pine. They are made with faces of grade B materials in ⅝ in. and ¾ in. thicknesses in the standard plywood dimensions.

Plywood cohered by a highly water-resistant glue may be used for concrete forms reusable 10 to 15 times.

Plastic coated plywood is called *High Density Overlaid (HDO).* This hard, impervious surface increases the usability of these plywood forms up to about 200 times. The smooth, laminated surface may be thermo setting resin of phenol or melamine.

Form plywoods may be specified as mill oiled, that is, the surfaces are impregnated with a coat of oil at the mill.

Generally, plywood is oriented with the face of the grain of the wood spanning across its principal supports.

HARDBOARD

Hardboard, if tempered, is a suitable forming surface. Plastic coatings have been applied to tempered hardboard that improve its ability to resist water penetration, and to prolong the forming life of the hardboard surface. Usually hardboard is about ¼ in. thick in 4 ft × 8 ft sheets. Hardboard is frequently used as a form liner when supported by solid wood forms. Various surface effects are obtained by patterned hardboards. The screen effect that is usually on the backside of the smooth face is frequently used for special architectural effects. Hardboard forms, when properly backed by framework, lend themselves to forming curved surfaces.

METALS

Steel has been used in various parts of forms for some time. Steel members, both cold rolled and hot rolled, have been used as framing members of the form panel, for support of the formwork frame, and for the form liner itself. Other metals such as magnesium and aluminum have been used for formwork. Because aluminum has a detrimental effect on the strength of the finished product, it should not be allowed direct contact with concrete. These lightweight metals do have the advantages of lighter shipping and handling and a rust-free, prolonged life.

PLASTICS

Glass-fiber reinforced plastic forms are used for the forming surface. This material is braced and framed with steel or wood framing materials. The plastic forming materials are glass-fiber reinforcement bound by a plastic polyester resin. The principal advantage of this forming material is its ability to take any designed shape and finish. Forms for architectural concrete in any finish or shape are obtainable by applying the plastic resin to a designed shape of plaster, wood, or other suitable forming. Plastic forms are seldom jobsite manufactured items; they are usually manufactured under controlled shop conditions.

FORM LINERS

Should a special finish be desired, it may be obtained by implementation of a designed surface called a form liner, which is attached to the forming surface that is to form the concrete surface. Plastic form liners made of various plastics, such as polyvinyl chloride and polystyrene, impart a design in the concrete surface. These forms are usually reusable for numerous pours. These patterned forms, more properly called moulds, give a variety of designs in high relief or low relief, which consist of depressed and raised surfaces. Designed surfaces may present problems of entrapped air on the face of the form liner. Vent holes and proper vibration can alleviate this problem.

Other special effects have been achieved by ingenious designers with the use of patterned neoprene form liners, sand castings (or more properly, sculptured sand surfaces), designed forms of foamed plastic, various insulation boards, and, of course, wood blocks.

If left in place, foamed polystyrene has the advantage of serving as an insulation material as well as a patterned form liner.

FIGURE 4.37 Prefabricated forms.

PREFABRICATED FORMS

Prefabricated forms of various types may be rented or purchased. They usually consist of welded light gage metal frames that feature a plywood panel (see Figure 4.37). These forms, which are designed for a high reuse factor, come in various sizes and are economical if reused to the optimum. Prefabricated forms are identified by two general classes according to usage. Ready-made forms are for general construction where forming consists of ordinary beams, columns, and walls. These forms are made in a modular dimension permitting some flexibility. Custom-made forms, as the name implies, are made for special designs and may be for a single job and for the more unusually formed concrete such as would be found in dams and tunnels. These forms may be used in forming the precast wall panels or for special curtain wall designs. Their pattern design is thus used only for the project at hand. Some of these forms may be made of heavy cardboard or treated paper.

Prefabricated forms may have a provision for an adequate number of form ties to eliminate the need for wales or walers.

Generally, prefabricated forms consist of a combination of light gage metal frames, wood frames, and plywood panels. All-metal panels with metal frames are also available.

FORM SURFACE PREPARATION

The interior surfaces of forms usually receive an application of a coating by brushing, spraying, rubbing, or dipping. These substances, which are frequently some type of oil, are intended to deter adhesion between the fresh concrete and the form surface, leaving an intended finish.

In any event, form liners should be of firm, rigid material that will not fold, crumble, or sag under the influence of the concrete. Otherwise, a misshapen surface finish is apt to result.

Well-oiled impervious form surfaces, even those of plywood, frequently produce a concrete surface that is riddled with minute holes, sometimes called bug holes, on the surface of the concrete. These slight imperfections, which can be eliminated by a coat of rich grout, are the result of air pockets that have adhered to the well-oiled surface and have not risen to the surface in spite of persistent vibration.

CONCRETE PLACEMENT

Various procedures produce suitable finishes on exposed surfaces of concrete walls. If a smooth finish with a minimum of form marks is desired, steel or plywood forms or forms lined with hardboard are used. The forms are oiled to protect them for reuse and to avoid adherence of mortar to

FIGURE 4.38 Cross section of slip form. (From *Formwork for Concrete,* Fourth Edition by M. K. Hurd. Copyright © 1979. Courtesy of American Concrete Institute.)

the form surface; however, excessive oil is likely to stain the concrete. Tight forms avoid mortar leakage and the consequent formation of surface defects. The same brand of cement and the same aggregates and proportions should reduce color variations. The consistency of the mix will insure complete filling of the forms, including corners and irregularities. Drier mixtures can be placed if concrete is vibrated properly. The concrete should be placed in one continuous operation between determined expansion joints, construction joints, or between other appropriate locations. The coarse aggregate should be worked well back from the forms with spades or other suitable tools, permitting the mortar to contact the forms and eliminating the formation of voids and aggregate pockets known as honeycomb.

With curing by water continuing, the forms must be removed as soon as feasible to permit any necessary surface repairs. Undesirable projections should be removed; and after wetting the surface, voids should be filled with grout matching the color of the concrete.

After defects have been repaired, the surface should be saturated and coated with cement grout and immediately scrubbed with a wood or cork float. Finally, after the grout has hardened sufficiently so that it will remain in the small air holes, the excess grout should be removed with a sponge-rubber float.

Various other methods are used for finishing concrete wall surfaces, including a rubbed finish which is formed by rubbing with carborundum stones. The concrete must have hardened sufficiently so that the aggregate will not be disturbed with or without the application of mortar while rubbing.

SLIP FORMS

Moving forms that shape the concrete as they slide over the fresh concrete are called *slip forms.* Horizontal slip forms shape the concrete for canals, tunnels, and highways. Vertical slip forms are used for forming concrete grain storage bins or silos, chimney stacks, and the central service core for buildings. These service cores usually house elevator shafts, ducts, pipe and conduit spaces, and stair wells. Some service cores of buildings that have been constructed by slip form methods act as the principal structural element — the floor is suspended from the central service core of the solid concrete walls serve as shear walls.

The principal components of a vertical slip form are a yoke, sheathing, wales, and a working deck. The yoke, usually made of steel, supports the formwork sheathing and a jacking assembly which raises the entire form and working deck assembly (see Figure 4.38).

The jacking system, either manually or hydraulically controlled, lifts the entire formwork assembly by jacking vertically upon steel rods that are embedded in the fresh concrete. In some systems, these rods are removable. Form

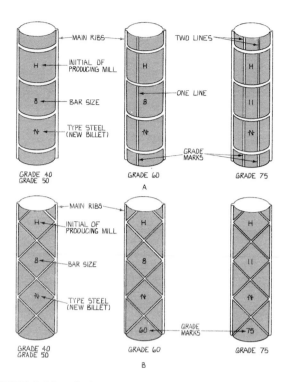

FIGURE 4.39 U.S. Standard bars — identification marks. *Manual of Standard Practice,* 1970 Edition. Published by the Concrete Reinforcing Steel Institute, Chicago, Illinois.

lifting operations proceed at increments of about 1 inch every 5 or 10 minutes, or about 6 to 12 inches an hour.

This type of construction requires a stiff concrete. Careful preconstruction planning is essential before concreting operations are undertaken. Usually slip form concreting procedures are a continuous, round-the-clock operation.

In the event that slip form construction operations are curtailed for any length of time, a cold joint will result. Such a concrete joint must be treated as a preplanned construction joint. Construction preplanning should anticipate such occurrences and provide for the resultant joint.

4.5 Concrete Accessories

REINFORCEMENT
Concrete has a low tensile strength and therefore is an ineffective material for members subjected to loads that tend to cause bending. Steel reinforcement, which has high tensile strength, is embedded in the concrete to resist these tensile stresses. In addition, vertical rods, commonly called longitudinal rods in columns, reduce the column size, or cross-sectional area, required to carry a given load because an area of steel is many times more effective in resisting compressive stresses than an identical area of concrete. The usual type of reinforcement is steel rods or bars.

Round reinforcement is classed as plain and deformed.

Plain bars are relatively smooth and are made in ¼ in. diameters only. Deformed bars have raised surfaces that facilitate an effective bond with concrete (see Figure 4.39). These deformations are spaced uniformly along the bars, following patterns that bond tests have proven most effective. Each steel mill rolls its own unique deformation pattern into the bars along with the mill identification mark. A numerical grade mark on each standard length identifies the tensile quality of the steel. The deformations are controlled by ASTM specifications. Most reinforcing bars are of this type, but deformed bars are not available with diameters less than ⅜ in.

Bars are classed as axle, rail, and billet. They are further graded as structural, intermediate, hard, regular, special, and high strength. Intermediate billet steel is the most commonly specified.

The available sizes of deformed bars have nominal diameters varying by ⅛ in. increments from ⅜ in. to about 1⅜ in. Each bar diameter is designated a number equal to the number of ⅛ in. increments included in the diameter. For example, a No. 7 bar is ⅞ in. in diameter. The standard mill lengths of bars are 40 and 60 ft. Two special size bars, 14 and 18 ft, are made in billet steel. They have 1.69 and 2.25 in. diameters, respectively (see Table 4.5).

Reinforcing is also available in the form of electric welded wire fabric with a rectangular or square mesh. The wire is of cold-drawn longitudinal or carrying wires and transverse wire with the two sets of wires welded at the intersections. The longitudinal wires are spaced from 2 in. to 6 in., and the transverse wires are spaced from 8 in. to 16 in. The fabric is identified by a letter W (wire) or D (deformed) followed by a number which is the nominal area of the wire in ¹⁄₁₀₀ sq in. For example, W30 identifies a wire of a cross-sectional area 0.30 sq. in. (see Table 4.6). They are also made in #4 bar grids. Various combinations of wire sizes and spacings are available. They are purchased in rolls 5 ft wide by 150 ft long, and 7 ft by 150 or 200 ft long.

FORMWORK HARDWARE
Connecting devices for formwork consist mainly of nails, bolts, or lag bolts of various sorts. Usually double-headed

Table 4.5 **Stock Size of Reinforcing Bars. All Bars are deformed except No. 2**

Bar Number	Nominal Diameter (in in.)	Bar Number	Nominal Diameter (in in.)[a]
2	¼	8	1
3	⅜	9	1.128 (1⅛)
4	½	10	1.270 (1¼)
5	⅝	11	1.410 (1⅜)
6	¾	14	1.69 (1⅝)
7	⅞	18	2.25 (2¼)

[a] Diameters in parentheses are approximate. Bar number equals number of whole ⅛ increments included in its nominal diameter.

Table 4.6 **Common Stock Styles of Welded Wire Fabric**

Steel Designation		Steel Area, sq in. per ft^c		Weight (approximate) lb per 100 sq ft^d
New Designation (by W-number)	Old Designation (by steel wire gage)	Longitudinal	Transverse	
Rolls				
6 × 6-W1.4 × W1.4	6 × 6-10 × 10	0.029	0.029	21
6 × 6-W2.0 × W2.0	6 × 6-8 × 8^a	0.041	0.041	30
6 × 6-W2.9 × W2.9	6 × 6-6 × 6	0.058	0.058	42
6 × 6-W4.0 × W4.0	6 × 6-4 × 4	0.080	0.080	58
4 × 4-W1.4 × W1.4	4 × 4-10 × 10	0.043	0.043	31
4 × 4-W2.0 × W2.0	4 × 4-8 × 8^a	0.062	0.062	44
4 × 4-W2.9 × W2.9	4 × 4-6 × 6	0.087	0.087	62
4 × 4-W4.0 × W4.0	4 × 4-4 × 4	0.120	0.120	85
Sheets				
6 × 6-W2.9 × W2.9	6 × 6-6 × 6	0.058	0.058	42
6 × 6-W4.0 × W4.0	6 × 6-4 × 4	0.080	0.080	58
6 × 6-W5.5 × W5.5	6 × 6-2 × 2^b	0.110	0.110	80
4 × 4-W4.0 × W4.0	4 × 4-4 × 4	0.120	0.120	85

^a Exact W-number size for 8 gage is W2.1.

^b Exact W-number size for 2 gage is W5.4.

^c 0.01 sq in/ft = 21.17 sq mm/m.

^d 1 lb/100 sq ft = 4.88 kgf/100 sq m.

From "Steel Reinforcement Properties and Availability" by ACI Committee 439. Courtesy American Concrete Institute.

common nails provide adequate holding ability. Withdrawal is not too difficult because of the double-headed feature. Box nails are often used for attaching the materials that contact the finished concrete because the smaller head leaves a less objectionable impression in the finished concrete surface.

The ability of nails to hold wood members together depends upon several factors, most of them variable — the diameter, length, nail and wood surface finish, wood quality, density and species, wood moisture content, edge or end distance, and the orientation of the wood grain to the axis of the load. Cement coated nails offer more resistance to withdrawal, at least initially. Other fastening devices are wood screws, lag bolts, and through bolts alone or in combinations with various metal connecting devices, such as split-ring and toothed ring connectors.

Concrete in the plastic state exerts lateral pressure in wall forms. To counteract this pressure, forms on each side of the wall are held in place by various form hardware devices called ties. There are generally two types with respect to designs: single member and internal disconnecting. Generally, the single member ties are equipped with form spreader devices that keep the forms from collapsing inward. These types usually feature a crimped or weakened breaking point that permits their separation and removal (Figure 4.40). The internal-disconnecting types are characterized by threaded male and female portions that can be separated by unscrewing. Some kinds, such as she-bolts, are similar to sex bolts and are reusable (Figure 4.41). Their application is usually for Class II forms.

If special architectural finishes are required, the specific form ties and formwork liners, if used, should be specified. The problem of patching or deliberately exposing tie holes depends upon the function of the structure or the desired aesthetic effect. Frequently, architects have required the bolt holes made by the form ties, especially she-bolt holes, to remain as a decorative feature. In such cases, these bolt holes should be spaced on a designed pattern.

FIGURE 4.40 Cone snap-ties.

FIGURE 4.41 She-bolt assembly.

(A) Steel strapping

(B) Light-gauge

FIGURE 4.42 Column clamps. (From *Formwork for Concrete,* Fourth Edition by M. K. Hurd. Copyright © 1979. Courtesy of American Concrete Institute.)

Square or rectangular column forms are held together by steel column clamps or steel strapping, or wood two-by members that are nailed together. Some column clamps have rigid angles at each corner; others have hinged or threaded devices to hold them together. Some are held together with wedge shaped pins or threaded devices (see Figure 4.42).

4.6 Precast Concrete

The term *precast concrete* applies to individual concrete members of various types cast in separate forms before placement. In contrast, the term cast-in-place or site-cast concrete refers to concrete members formed and cast in the positions they are to occupy in the finished structure.

Precast members cast at the building site or at a casting yard remote from the structure are transported by truck or by other means to the site of the structure and positioned by cranes. Concrete block, as described in Section 5.3, is the simplest form of precast unit, although it is not commonly given that designation.

To improve quality by using a low water-cement ratio and insuring that the forms are completely filled, the concrete is vibrated during placement, as described in Section 4.2. Lightweight concrete is often employed. In addition to the advantage of light weight, such concrete has a relatively high heat insulation value.

PRECAST AND TILT-UP CONSTRUCTION

Concrete walls and partitions are often made of precast units, rather than of cast-in-place concrete, and then positioned. Concrete wall slabs of considerable size are often cast at some distance from the building site and then placed into position. In tilt-up construction, they are rotated about their bottom edges from a horizontal position into their final positions.

TYPES OF MEMBERS

Although it may not always be advantageous, nearly every concrete member which can be cast in place can be precast. Included in these types are floor and roof slabs, wall panels, bearing walls and partitions, joists, beams, girders, columns, rigid frames, arches, domes, and piles. Trusses have been precast but not often advantageously constructed of concrete, either precast or cast-in-place. Precast piles are considered in Section 3.3.

BUILDING HEIGHTS

Except for lift-slab construction in which the floor and roof slabs are precast, most buildings whose main structural members are precast are one-, two-, or three-story buildings; however, buildings have been constructed of precast concrete to 16 stories. Precast beams, purlins, floor and roof panels, and curtain walls are used, however, irrespective of height.

PRESTRESSING

Precast concrete members may or may not be prestressed, as described in Section 4.7. In general, prestressing may be advantageous for members subjected to high flexural stresses, such as long-span or heavily loaded slabs, beams, and girders. A few examples of precast construction are illustrated in the following sections, but this type of construction is advantageous for a great variety of members and structures.

FRAMING

The superstructure of a building may be assembled in the following ways:

1. All the members precast.
2. Precast floor and roof decks supported by cast-in-place concrete of steel girders, columns, or rigid frames.

3. Cast-in-place floor and roof slabs supported directly by precast joists or purlins.

4. Precast wall panels supported by cast-in-place concrete or steel columns or rigid frames.

5. Heavy timber roof sheathing supported directly by precast purlins.

6. Precast arches supporting precast concrete purlins and cast-in-place concrete slabs or heavy timber sheathing.

7. Masonry exterior walls and various types of partitions with precast floor and roof decks.

CONNECTIONS

A common connection between precast members consists of anchoring steel plates in the precast members so that they will contact when the members are in position (Figure 4.43A). These are called matching plates. After the members have been positioned, the matching plates are welded together. Occasionally they are bolted, and sometimes angles are used instead of plates.

At the ends or edges of adjacent members, reinforcing bars may be extended so that they overlap (B). They may be joined by welding. The intervening space is then filled with concrete. Instead of welding, the connection may be established by the bond of the overlapping bars. This is called a wet joint.

Pipe sleeves or holes may be cast in members and so located that dowels or bolts cast in the supporting members (C), (D), and (E) can be inserted or threaded into the holes. Some form of anchorage is provided on the ends of the dowels which project beyond the end of the sleeve or hole, or the dowels are grouted into the sleeves.

Various methods are employed to connect beams to columns, one of which is shown in (D). A plate welded to the ends of embedded column reinforcing anchors a column base plate which in turn is bolted to its footing (G). In (H), a hollow column, positioned on its footing, is threaded over a looped anchor bar embedded in the top of the footing. An opening in the side of the column provides a temporary port through which concrete is poured, filling the hollow portion and surrounding the anchor bar protruding from the footing. A hollow end may be cast in a solid column for anchoring in this same manner. Wall panels are connected to columns as shown in (F).

Numerous other types of joints are used; some are explained in subsequent Sections.

ADVANTAGES

Precast concrete is more economical when many identical members are to be cast because the same forms can be used many times. In addition to economical formwork, precast concrete has other advantages over cast-in-place concrete:

FIGURE 4.43 Typical connection for precast members.

1. Concrete quality can be controlled more carefully.

2. Exposed surface control can be achieved, and plastering is not required to produce a finished surface.

3. Less jobsite storage space is required.

4. With suitable protection casting can proceed under all weather conditions.

5. Curing can be done more effectively.

6. Erection is less restricted by weather conditions.

7. Greater erection speed is possible.

8. Lower cost is possible under conditions favorable to precasting.

PRESTRESSED CONCRETE

Prestressed concrete is concrete subjected to compressive stresses by inducing tensile stresses in the reinforcement. The purpose of prestressing is to counteract tensile stresses in the concrete caused by external loads before the external loads are applied. The term conventional reinforced concrete applies to members that are not prestressed. To make prestressing feasible, both the concrete and the reinforcement must have much higher strengths than are required for conventional reinforced concrete members. As will be explained later, the reinforcement consists of high-strength steel wires or cables of high-strength alloy steel bars, all of which are called *tendons.*

The design procedures for prestressed concrete members are the same as those for conventional reinforced concrete members, except that they are extended to provide for the effects of prestressing.

Prestressed concrete is advantageous only under special conditions because of cost. Its use is confined largely but not exclusively to precast members, although only that use is considered in this chapter.

Basic Principle

To understand the structural action of prestressed concrete members, it is helpful to review this action in homogeneous beams, explained in Section 1.4 and illustrated in Figure 1.10E, and in conventional reinforced concrete beams, considered in Section 4.2. As explained in these sections, the lower position of a horizontal simple beam carrying downward vertical loads is subjected to tensile stresses. Because the tensile strength of concrete is low, a homogeneous concrete beam has very little flexural strength. To offset this deficiency, steel reinforcement provided near the bottom of simple beams carries the tensile stresses. The tensile strength of the concrete is neglected in the computations for the flexural strength of reinforced concrete beams.

By subjecting the tensile reinforcement of a beam to tensile stresses before the external loads are applied (described later), compressive stresses are induced in the concrete of the beam. Usually the tensile stresses in the concrete caused by the external load are nearly offset or absorbed by the compressive stresses in the concrete resulting from prestressing the reinforcement which, in turn, prestresses the concrete. The concrete, therefore, is effectively resisting tensile stresses produced by external loads rather than being neglected as it is in conventional design.

Flexural Stresses in Prestressed Concrete

The computed fiber stresses at the section A-A of a homogeneous simple beam with a symmetrical cross section for various designated conditions are shown in Figure 4.44A to E, and those in a prestressed beam in F.

Before the external forces F are applied, as shown in (A), the beam would normally be supported by forms throughout its entire length and there would be no flexural stresses. As soon as the forces F are applied, the beam deflects upward because of the uneven distribution of the compressive fiber stresses in the concrete (A), and it is supported only at the ends (B). In (B) and the remaining figures, the member acts as a simple beam.

It is not feasible to prestress the beam by applying equal and opposite external compressive forces F at the ends. Substantially the same effect is obtained simply by inserting tendons and anchoring them at the ends of the beam so that a force F is applied to these ends (A) and (E). This procedure is called posttensioning because the prestressing force is applied to the tendons after the concrete hardens.

A similar objective can be accomplished by prestressing the tendons in the forms before the concrete is poured.

FIGURE 4.44 Fiber stresses caused by various loading conditions.

After the concrete sets, it bonds to the tendons, which therefore retain most of the prestress after the prestressing force ceases to act. The member is then removed from the forms. This procedure is called pretensioning.

A significant portion of the initial prestress in the tendons is lost because various factors cause the concrete to shorten. Concrete shrinks as it dries. Concrete also shortens elastically as compressive forces are applied and shortens still further over a long period of time because of a phenomenon called creep, plastic flow, or time yield. The length of each tendon increases elastically while the prestress is applied. This does not reduce the prestress. Steel increases gradually in length, or creeps, at a decreasing rate when subjected to a constant unit stress. However, if the length remains constant, as in the tendons of prestressed concrete, the unit stress gradually decreases at a decreasing rate. This is called relaxation, and it is the significant factor in prestressed concrete design. Finally, there is a loss of prestress in posttensioning because of the friction between the tendons and the surrounding material. This is especially true if the tendons are curved or draped, as explained later. Appropriate allowances are made for these factors which decrease the initial prestress. This is also true for different external loads if the stresses do not exceed those caused by working loads.

The discussions in this Section refer to the flexural stresses in a prestressed simple beam. Similar procedures apply to prestressed continuous beams and to columns and piles if they are subjected to loads that would produce significant flexural stresses if they were not prestressed.

Types of Tendons

As stated, effective prestressing requires high-strength steel for tensile reinforcement. This is because the loss of prestress from shrinkage, elastic deformation, and creep in the concrete and the relaxation and frictional losses in the

FIGURE 4.45 Pretensioning beds and draping of tendons.

steel during prestressing offset most of the allowable stress in ordinary steel bars.

The individual units, or tendons, which comprise the total tensile reinforcement (corresponding to the bars used in conventional reinforced concrete) are usually two or more parallel wires about ¼ in. in diameter, or they are strands of such wires "spiraled" around a straight center wire. Seven-wire strands with diameters of ¼ to ½ in. are ordinarily used in pretensioned members. Large-diameter strands with 7, 19, 37, or more wires are used extensively in posttensioned members.

The wires of the desired diameter are formed by drawing steel rods, while cold, through dies of smaller diameter than the rods. This process of cold-drawing markedly increases the tensile strength of the steel. After drawing, the wires may be galvanized to resist corrosion.

High-strength alloy steel bars are also used for tendons. Their strength is further increased by heat-treating or cold-stretching. Diameters vary from ½ to 1⅛ in. They are used principally in posttensioned members.

Casting and Prestressing

Prestressing concrete members, usually precast, are divided into two classes, pretensioned or posttensioned, according to the sequence of casting and prestressing.

For pretensioned members, the tendons are prestressed in the forms before the concrete is poured. The long-line process is ordinarily used if several members of the same cross section and identical tendons are cast. The casting bed on which the forms are placed may be several hundred feet long and arranged as illustrated diagrammatically in Figure 4.45A.

The bed includes two end abutments. In the long-line process, tendons long enough to provide the tendons for several members to be cast in line are placed on the casting bed. They are anchored at one end to the abutment; at the other end, to hydraulic jacks operating against the other abutment. Various jacking arrangements have been devised. The tendons pass through a template provided at each end. Holes in each template hold the tendons in the desired positions. Bulkheads are positioned along the long-line form, subdividing it into forms for several individual members of the desired lengths. These bulkheads are notched so that they can straddle the tendons, or the tendons may be threaded through them. The long tendons are prestressed the desired amount by operating the jacks. The ends of the tendons are anchored and the jacks removed.

The concrete is then placed in the forms. When the concrete has gained its initial set, the forms are covered to retain moisture, or steam curing proceeds. After the concrete hardens sufficiently to carry the prestress, the bulkheads between the ends of the members are removed — a process requiring about 24 hours. The members are separated by cutting the exposed portions of the tendons with a welding torch or by some other method. The beams are removed from the forms by cranes and stored for shipment.

Stirrups or other steel embedded items to be cast in the members are, of course, placed in the forms before the concrete is poured.

Frequently, it is desirable to drape some of the tendons of each member so that they will anchor near the top at the supports and near the bottom in the central portion of a span. The long tendons to be draped are placed near the top of the members and prestressed. They are then pulled downward at the desired points and anchored as shown in Figure 4.45B and C. Care must be taken to avoid overstressing the tendons by this operation. Draping improves the distribution of the prestress in the concrete along cross sections near the support, and the inclined portions of the tendons help carry the shearing stresses.

Individual members can be pretensioned without using the long-line process.

For posttensioned members, the tendons are inserted in holes that are formed by removable cores cast in the concrete; or the tendons, placed in position before the concrete is poured, are surrounded with flexible metal tubes if they are to be bonded as described later. If the tendons are to remain unbonded, they are greased to reduce friction during prestressing and to protect against corrosion. They are then wrapped with mortar-tight sheathing, such as heavy waterproof paper or plastic films.

The tendons are anchored at one end with various devices. After the concrete hardens sufficiently and the forms have been removed, the tendons are prestressed by means of hydraulic jacks applied at the free end and the tendons anchored to maintain the prestress. The jacks are then removed.

The tendons of posttensioned members may be bonded or unbonded. If they are bonded, bond is established by forcing cement grout into the annular space surrounding the tendons after prestressing is completed.

Advantages and Disadvantages

As stated, most prestressed members are precast and have the advantages of this procedure as compared with cast-in-place construction. In addition, there are advantages gained by prestressing when conditions are favorable, such as:

1. Smaller dimensions of members for the same loading conditions, which may increase clearances or reduce story heights.
2. Smaller deflections.
3. Crack-free members.
4. Smaller loads on supporting members because of the smaller dimensions required.

Among the disadvantages are the following:

1. Higher unit cost of high-strength materials.
2. Cost of prestressing equipment.
3. Labor cost of prestressing.
4. Not advantageous for short spans with low concrete stresses.

PRECAST CONCRETE: FLOORS, ROOFS, AND WALLS

Floor and Roof Slabs

Several types of precast slabs or panels are used extensively for floor and roof decks. The most common are the channel and double-T in Figure 4.46.

Channel slabs vary in depth from 9 to 12 in. Spans of 50 ft or more have been used. The legs of the channels extend across the ends if desired, and the legs and top slab may be stiffened with cross ribs. The tensile reinforcement is mild steel bars if the channels are not prestressed, or high-strength steel tendons if they are prestressed. The top slab is reinforced with wire legs so that the joints between the slabs can be grouted to form keys between adjacent slabs. The long-line process is ordinarily employed.

Double-Ts vary in width from 4 to 6 ft and in depth from 9 to 16 in. Spans as long as 50 ft have been cast. The top slab varies from 1½ to 2 in. thick and is reinforced with wire mesh. Except for short spans, the slabs are prestressed, usually by pretensioning using the long-line process. The tendons can be draped as shown in Figure 4.45B and C.

Hollow or cored slabs or planks with various dimensions

are manufactured. For the longer spans or heavy loads, the bottom reinforcement may be prestressed high-strength tendons; the top reinforcement may be mild steel bars designed to withstand prestressing and handling stresses.

Hollow slabs of special forms of concrete are assembled in rows and reinforced with bars grouted in grooves provided in the lower surfaces of the block. The vertical contact surfaces are grouted or ground smooth to obtain good contact.

Solid slabs are sometimes used for roof decks when the low cost of the forms offsets the saving in material cost that would result from the use of structurally more efficient slabs.

Floor and roof slabs are ordinarily connected to the supporting members by welded matching plates.

Walls and Partitions

Bearing and nonbearing walls and partitions ordinarily are of panels precast in a horizontal position in a casting yard or on the floor of the building and placed in their vertical positions by cranes by the tilt-up procedure.

Usually, they are solid reinforced slabs from 5 to 8 in. thick, one or two stories high with lengths about equal to the clear distances between columns or other supporting members. Actual length depends upon the manner in which the slabs are fastened to the supporting members. Window and door openings are usually cast in the slabs. Steel window frames or pressed metal door frames are sometimes cast in exterior wall panels, but preferably openings are prepared for window and door frames. Extra reinforcement, both lateral and diagonal, should be provided around the openings.

The casting surface usually is a concrete floor slab with a smooth regular surface. Bond between this surface and the wall panels is prevented by coating the casting surface with some form of liquid bond breaker or covering with a plastic sheet material. The liquid bond breaker is more satisfactory. The upper surface of the panel may be finished in several ways such as troweling, floating, or brooming.

Precast channel and double-T panels, previously described, are used for exterior nonbearing walls. The ribs, placed vertically, are designed for adaptation to the different loading conditions. Prestressed double-T panels, with an intermediate support, have exceeded 60 ft in height.

Sandwich panels, used for exterior walls, provide additional heat insulation. The face slabs are tied together with wires, small rods, or in some other manner. Thicknesses vary from 5 to 8 in.

When precast concrete panels are used for curtain walls of multistory buildings, the panels are placed story by story. Wall panels are often connected to the building frame at their tops and bottoms and to each other by welded or bolted matching plates. Several other types of connections are used (Figure 4.43F). The joints between wall panels are

FIGURE 4.46 Channel and double-T decks.

made watertight by sealants on the outside and grouting on the inside.

Tilt-up construction is a construction procedure by which precast wall panels are rotated about their bottom edges to the vertical positions they are to occupy. The panels are designed to resist the lifting stresses. Small panels are sometimes hoisted by hand-operated cranes, but power equipment is usually employed. The simplest means of connecting the hoisting equipment to a panel consists of U-shaped bar loops cast in its top edge, which produce relatively high lifting stresses. A strongback made of steel I-beams or channels bolted to a panel reduces the lifting stresses, or a vacuum pad may be placed on the panel and held in position by creating a partial vacuum between the panel and the pad. This device is preferred to the strongback because the panel is not disfigured by bolt holes which are cast in the panel for attachment of a strong-back (see Figure 4.47).

Tilt-up construction is also used for placing rigid frames and arches.

PRECAST CONCRETE: JOISTS, BEAMS, GIRDERS AND COLUMNS

Joists and Purlins

Joists and purlins have T- or I-shaped cross sections (Figure 4.48A and B) and may be prestressed or of conventional design. Many manufacturers stock the common sizes for immediate delivery. Joists with inverted T-sections are available for composite construction where they support cast-in-place floor or roof slabs.

Beams and Girders

These terms are often synonymous; but when a distinction is made, those with the longer spans are called girders. They may be of conventional precast design or prestressed. The cross sections are usually I-shaped *(C)* except near the ends, where they are rectangular. T-shaped cross sections *(D)* are also used. The following discussion refers to prestressed members.

There are structural advantages in curving or inclining some of the tendons upward near the ends of a girder. In the earlier efforts of prestressing, it was considered necessary that pretensioned tendons be straight, as shown in Figure 4.48E. It has been found, however, that tendons can be draped *(F)* by anchoring them at two or more points before or after prestressing, as long as the tendons are not overstressed.

In posttensioning girders, tendons are usually curved *(G)*. Sloping tendons help carry shearing stresses. If additional shearing resistance is required, mild steel stirrups are used as in conventional reinforced concrete beams and as shown in *(C)* and *(D)*.

FIGURE 4.47 Precast tilt-up construction. Portland Cement Association.

FIGURE 4.48 Precast and prestressed beams and girders.

Girders with clear spans exceeding 100 ft may have nonrectangular profiles *(I)* and *(J)*. The profile in *(J)* raises the center of prestress at the ends, which is advantageous, without curving the tendons as in *(G)*.

The girders mentioned are simply supported; however, they may be continuous with single units or with several units, as shown in Figure 4.49*A*. Overhanging girders with a drop-in beam are illustrated in *(B)*. The ends of the drop-in beam rest on the ends of the overhangs and are stabilized by suitable anchors but do not develop continuity. These types may or may not be prestressed.

A prestressed cap cable develops continuity at a support of adjoining prestressed girders shown in *(C)*. After the girders are positioned, cables are inserted in ducts cast in the concrete, anchored at one end, and prestressed. If the girders support a cast-in-place slab, another means of developing continuity is preferable, as explained in the paragraph on composite construction.

Types of connections between girders and columns are illustrated in Figure 4.43. In the simplest *(A)*, matching plates are welded together after the members are in position. It develops no continuity. Others which develop partial or full continuity are shown in *(D)* and *(E)*. When full continuity is developed, the combination becomes a rigid frame. Such action must be considered in the design of the girders and columns.

Composite Construction

Composite construction consists of precast girders, beams, joists, or purlins on top of which a floor or roof slab is cast in place. The slab and precast units act together in resisting the weight of the slab and the applied loads, provided movement is prevented between the slab and the precast units and if the slab anchors to these units preventing vertical separation. Horizontal movement of the slab along the beam is prevented by notched keys with vertical sides on the tops of the precast members or by special preparation of the contact surface by sand blasting or other means that insure adequate bond. Vertical separation is prevented by casting vertical steel dowels in the tops of the precast units or by projecting the ends of vertical stirrups in these units.

Beams are made continuous over supports by including longitudinal reinforcement over the supports in the slab *(D)*. This procedure is preferable to using cable caps *(C)* if the slab is cast in place.

Columns

Precast concrete columns may be similar to cast-in-place columns, as described, or they may be hollow. Prestressing the longitudinal reinforcement is advantageous only for columns subjected to relatively large flexural stresses. When prestressed, the longitudinal reinforcement is of high-strength tendons rather than mild steel bars. The tendons

FIGURE 4.49 Overhanging girders and continuity connections.

may be pretensioned; the long-line process may be used if many identical columns are to be cast. The lateral reinforcement may be small diameter mild steel rods or wires. Columns are cast in a horizontal position and erected by cranes.

A simple type of column base (Figure 4.43*G*) is suitable for square solid or hollow columns. The type shown in *(H)* may be used for hollow columns. A looped rod cast in the column footing projects upward into the hollow core when the column is set. A temporary opening in the side of the column permits the lower portion of the core to be filled with grout. The embedded loop forms an effective anchor. The opening is then dry-packed with mortar. Various other types are used.

PRECAST CONCRETE: LIFT-SLAB CONSTRUCTION

The lift-slab method was conceived by Philip N. Youtz and Tom Slick about 1950 and is usually known as the Youtz-Slick Method.

In *lift-slab construction,* all above-ground floor and roof slabs for an entire building are cast in stacks on a previously prepared ground floor. Cast around the columns that are to support them, they are lifted into their final positions by simultaneously operating hydraulic jacks mounted temporarily on the tops of the columns. The slabs are connected by lift rods to steel lifting collars cast in and anchored to the slabs and surrounding the columns.

Because long columns tend to buckle when not supported laterally at intervals, not more than three or four stories are usually constructed at one stage.

Sequence of Lifting Operations

The sequence of operations for a six-story building, including a basement, which requires two lifting stages is illustrated in Figure 4.50. It will be noted in *(F)* that the columns are extended to their final height at the beginning of the second stage. Taller buildings require more stages. These are carried out by extending the two-stage procedure.

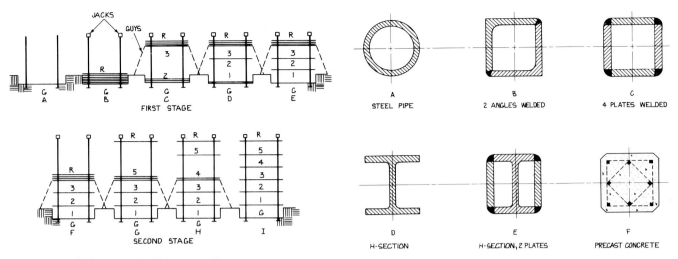

FIGURE 4.50 Sequence in lifting operations.

FIGURE 4.51 Types of columns.

Types of Columns

The columns, usually of steel (Figure 4.51*A* to *E*) vary in external lateral dimension from 8 to 12 in. For a given building, column dimensions are usually constant; however, the steel areas are varied by specifying columns of different flange and web thicknesses. One dimension is limited by the spacing of the lifting rod attachments on the jacks. Occasionally, columns are made of precast reinforced concrete with longitudinal and lateral bar reinforcement *(F)*. Prestressed columns with longitudinal wire tendons and mild steel lateral reinforcement are also used.

Columns are rigidly anchored to their foundations by built-up steel bases to stand vertically. In fire-resistive construction, steel columns are protected by concrete, metal lath and perlite plaster, or other appropriate noncombustible materials after the slabs are placed. Filling hollow steel columns with concrete improves their fire resistance.

Size of Slab

The hydraulic jacks, operated from a control console, must act in unison to avoid local overstressing. The usual number of jacks controlled in this manner is 12 or 18, although equipment does permit the number of jacks to be increased to 36. For this reason, large floor and roof decks are usually, but not always, divided into several slabs (Figure 4.52).

It is desirable, but not always possible, for a slab to cantilever out beyond the exterior rows of columns of a slab, as shown in the figure. The joints between adjacent slabs are located midway between rows of columns, as shown.

Closure Strip

In a space about 3 ft wide between adjacent slabs, bars project from the edges of adjacent slabs into this space and overlap to permit welding. A closure or pour strip of cast-in-

FIGURE 4.52 Sub-division of slabs.

place concrete fills the space and provides continuity. By providing wider spaces, stairways, elevator shafts, and other vertical shafts can be constructed. In addition, shear walls to provide lateral stability for the building can be built in these spaces as the construction proceeds.

Column Spacing and Slab Thickness and Types

Common column spacings vary from 25 to 30 ft or more and may differ in the two directions. The slabs, usually solid, vary from 5 to 10 in. thick. For the longer spans, waffle slabs, similar to the slabs shown in Figure 4.23, are used frequently. The areas adjacent to the columns must be solid. The top slabs are reinforced with wire mesh. Waffle slabs must be somewhat thicker than solid slabs of equal conditions.

Prestressing

The slabs are usually prestressed by posttensioning in both directions. Usually the tendons are inclined from the lower center portion of the slab to the upper portion at the columns and in the cantilevers to resist tensile stresses. Prestressing causes slabs to cant upward between columns. This is desirable because such slopes counteract most, if not all, of the deflection due to applied loads. In addition, prestressed slabs are crack-free, a quality which is always desirable.

Lifting Collars

Before each column is erected, the lifting collar required for each slab is placed on the column with approximately ¼ in. clearance between the collar and the column. Collars are made of cast steel or are built up of steel sections.

Slab Casting

Cast sequentially as they occupy the building from the ground up, the slabs are securely anchored to the lifting collars. These collars increase the resistance to shearing stresses near the columns which are caused by the vertical loads. To prevent bonding between slabs during casting, the top of each slab is coated with liquid wax or other liquid preparation or covered with a membrane of film before the next slab is cast.

Connecting Slabs to Columns

After a slab has been lifted to its final position, the lifting collars are welded to steel columns. Provision may be made for temporary support before the final welding takes place. If reinforced concrete columns are used, this connection may be made by welding embedded matching plates. Slabs lifted in two or more stages require temporary positioning of some of the slabs (Figure 4.50*E* and *F*). Several slabs may be lifted simultaneously, the lowest one of which, when fixed in its final position, temporarily supports the slabs above. Slabs may also be parked in any predetermined position by provisionally supporting them on shear pins passing through holes in the columns. The rate of lifting varies from 3 to 5 ft per hour.

Lateral Support

During construction, special lateral support may not be required for low buildings or for the first stage of erection of higher buildings. It may be wise, however, to provide at least temporary horizontal braces between the tops of the columns in both directions. Anchored guy wires provide a simple method for temporary lateral support (Figure 4.50). If space is unavailable for this arrangement, crossed guy wires within the structure in the closure spaces, or around the outside, may be used. Of course, such guy wires can be placed only where slabs are in final position.

Permanent reinforced concrete shear walls constructed as stairway or elevator shafts provide lateral support during construction and for the completed building. Masonry end walls supported laterally at the floor and roof levels may provide permanent lateral support.

The joints between slabs and columns should be designed to resist lateral loads. The provisions for lateral support depend upon the conditions which prevail. Wind loads (and sometimes earthquake shocks) must be considered during the erection procedure.

Exterior Walls and Partitions

Light exterior curtain walls may be located along the perimeters of the cantilever slabs. Projected slabs may effectively shade exterior enclosure walls located along the line of the exterior columns, although they are less effective on the east or west exposure. Interior partitions are constructed of the same materials as are used in other types of construction.

Advantages and Disadvantages

The primary objectives of lift-slab construction are to minimize form costs and to expedite erection. Some of the other advantages follow:

1. Partition locations are unaffected by beams because they are eliminated, as in conventional flat-plate construction.
2. The under surface of the slabs, as smooth as a well-troweled floor surface, does not require plastering to provide a finished ceiling.
3. Floor construction requires less vertical space than some other types, so that the story height is reduced.
4. If prestressed, deflections are minimal, and slabs are crack-free.
5. Utility lines can be incorporated in slabs at the ground level.
6. Slabs can be cast in cold weather within a minimum heated enclosure and can be lifted regardless of the weather.

Some of the disadvantages are the following:

1. It is a type of construction with which architects, engineers, and contractors are generally unfamiliar and costs may be affected adversely.
2. Column arrangement and other planning features must be favorable.
3. Lifting and prestressing costs are factors.

PRECAST CONCRETE: RIGID FRAMES

Rigid frames of various types are described in Section 1.4. Cast-in-place reinforced concrete rigid frames are considered in Section 4.2. Similar types can often be precast advantageously.

The joints between girders and columns and the

members themselves can develop full continuity. Although the units function as rigid frames, they are not usually so termed.

The units included in precast rigid frames are cast in a horizontal position, usually on the finished concrete floor of the building. Single-span frames, cast in one piece, reduce the weight to be hoisted at one time. Multiple-span frames are cast in several appropriate units. They are raised into their vertical positions by cranes and supported temporarily until they receive support from other parts of the building. The units of the rigid frame are rectangular in cross section, with uniform thicknesses and varying depths. They are usually solid, but occasionally they have hollow cores made by heavy cardboard tubes cast in the concrete.

The foundations of the outer vertical members, called legs, may carry the outward horizontal thrusts at the bottom of each leg if soil conditions permit. A tie beam, consisting of steel bars surrounded with concrete cast within or under the floor, ties the tops of the foundations together to resist lateral thrusts. Buildings subject to seismic shocks may require tie beams.

The hinges in rigid frames may have horizontal pins that offer only frictional resistance to rotation. Instead, they may include bars or dowels that tie the abutting ends of the units together so that the joints offer a negligible resistance to rotation.

Single-span, single-story frame buildings may have adequate longitudinal stability after the members that enclose the building are in place. However, multiple-span frames usually require precast or cast-in-place horizontal or diagonal longitudinal struts between the frames and at the tops of the vertical supporting members of adjacent frames and tied to them. These struts are also called tie beams, although they do not function as beams.

A building using precast rigid frames for the main supporting members may be enclosed by precast roof and wall panels, or the exterior walls may be constructed of masonry units, as described in Chapter 5. Precast wall and roof panels attached to the frames in various ways are explained at the beginning of this chapter. Occasionally, the roof construction spanning between widely spaced rigid frames consists of a series of precast folded plates or of thin shell arches as will be shown in Figure 4.58.

One or both of the exterior legs of precast frames can be T-shaped in profile to provide cantilevers to support an outside projection of the roof called a canopy. These may serve as shelters or sunshades.

Precast frames are sometimes prestressed, but usually they are not. Only frames which are not prestressed are considered in this discussion. They are designed as conventionally reinforced concrete members.

Single-Span Rigid Frames

Three types of precast single-span rigid frames are illustrated in Figure 4.53. The two-hinged frame in *(A)*, if cast in two pieces, reduces the weight to be hoisted at one time. A construction joint, called a wet joint, joins the frame at the center of the top member. A detail of this joint is shown. The two-hinged frame in *(B)* is cast in three pieces by providing two joints in the top member. A precast beam, hoisted in between the upper ends of the legs, is called a drop-in beam. A detail of the joints at the end of this beam is shown in the figure. A seat or notch provides temporary vertical support for the ends of the beam. To establish continuity at each joint, short projecting ends of the reinforcing bars are overlapped and welded. The open spaces then are dry-packed with cement mortar.

The three-hinged frame in *(C)* is cast in two pieces. A detailed hinge at the crown is shown. The tie beams are usually not required.

Multiple-Span Rigid Frames

Three types of multiple-span frames are shown in Figure 4.54. A three-span continuous frame with three drop-in beams and hollow members is illustrated in *(A)*. The joints at the ends of the drop-in beams are similar to those shown in Figure 4.53*B*. A longitudinal tie beam is provided between frames at the top of each support. This type of frame can be designed for any number of spans.

A three-span frame consisting of two L-shaped exterior units and two T-shaped interior units is shown in *(B)*. A joint functioning as a hinge is located at midspan of each top member. The frame functions as a series of three-hinged arches. This type of frame can be designed for any number of spans. Longitudinal tie beams extend between frames as shown.

A three-span frame, cast in two T-shaped pieces that are made continuous by a wet joint in the center of the top member, is shown in *(C)*. The outer ends of the frame extend to, but are not supported by, solid slab tilt-up enclosure walls. Longitudinal tie beams extend between frames as shown.

Multistory Rigid Frames

The two-story, two-span frame in Figure 4.55 is similar to the one-story frames in Figures 4.53*B* and 4.54*A*. The exterior and interior units include cantilever projections to receive the ends of the drop-in beams. Each of these two-story units is erected in one piece. The seated joints at the ends of the drop-in beams are similar to the type shown in detail in Figure 4.53*B*.

Multistory, single-span frames are sometimes constructed and erected in one piece.

Reinforcement

As mentioned in Section 1.4, rigid frames are subjected to relatively large bending and shearing stresses. As shown in the frames in Figure 4.53, longitudinal reinforcement is pro-

FIGURE 4.53 Single-span precast rigid frames. U.S. Navy.

vided near the outer and inner faces of the members. For clarity, layers of bars are shown to be more widely separated than they are actually separated. Reinforcement is provided normal to the members as required. This reinforcement corresponds to the stirrups used in beams. It is looped entirely around the longitudinal reinforcement. In addition to providing for shearing stresses, it retains reinforcement subjected to compressive stresses and thereby fulfills one of the functions of spirals or hoops in columns. It is essential in holding both tensile and compressive reinforcement in position in regions where the reinforcement is curved — for example, at the knees or haunches of the rigid frames.

Lifting Hooks
Appropriately located hooks cast in the members facilitate erection. Erection stresses produced by lifting must be provided for in the design of the members.

Acknowledgments
The various offices of the U.S. Navy have done much to develop precast construction as described in publications of the Portland Cement Association. The frame illustrated in Figure 4.55A was patterned after a frame designed for the U.S. Air Force. It was designed by Roberts and Schaefer Company and described in the April 1957 issue of *Civil Engineering*. The authors acknowledge the assistance from these sources in preparing this section.

PRECAST CONCRETE: ARCHES AND PRESTRESSED DOMES
The general types of arches, irrespective of their materials, were described in Section 1.4. Cast-in-place reinforced concrete arches were considered in Section 4.2.

Both rigid frames and arches involve so-called arch action, but they vary in the relative amounts of flexure. Because of differing forms of their profiles, rigid frames are subjected to relatively large flexural stresses, although for arches, the stresses are primarily compressive.

The horizontal thrusts on the foundations of both types of structures are comparable, and these thrusts are resisted by the foundations or abutments or by tie beams as described in the preceding Section.

Most precast arches are three-hinged, but occasionally no hinges are provided and they are called hingeless or fixed arches. Precast arch ribs are usually solid with rectangular cross sections constant in width and depth. Precast arches may be prestressed, but this practice is uncommon and is not considered here.

The floor area under an arch roof is limited by sidewalls, as shown in Figure 1.21A, with the ends of the arches exposed or enclosed within building space constructed along the sides, as shown by the dashed lines. With the

FIGURE 4.54 Three-span rigid frames. U.S. Navy.

FIGURE 4.55 A 50-ft span, two-story rigid frame with drop-in beams. Designed by Roberts and Schaefer for U. S. Air Force.

arches elevated, the side construction carries the arch thrusts as shown in Figure 1.21B.

Three-Hinged Ribbed Arch
A three-hinged arch precast in two sections included between the hinges supports the roof of the Citrus Union High

FIGURE 4.56 A 150-ft span, three-hinged arch. Architects: Austin, Field, and Fry. Structural Engineer: Ernest H. Lee.

FIGURE 4.57 A 115-ft span folded plate fixed arch. Architects: Toll and Milan. Consulting Engineer: Henry J. Boland.

School in Azusa, California, Figure 4.56. Various details are shown on the drawing. Heavy timber purlins and sheathing were used for economy; however, this decreased fire resistance.

Other types of deck are used for precast ribbed arches. Precast concrete purlins with dowel, matching plate, or bolted angle end connections to the arches anchor precast roof panels or a cast-in-place roof slab. The steep roof slope near the haunch of the arches makes cast-in-place concrete difficult. Precast concrete roof panels require secure anchorage to the purlins. These members are designed for the lateral load they carry. Securely anchored precast slabs can span between the arches and thereby eliminate the purlins.

Folded Plate Fixed Arch

The arched roof for the Holy Trinity High School Gymnasium at Trinidad, Colorado, shown in Figure 4.57, is made up of 13 folded plate arch ribs about 10 ft wide, as illustrated. Each rib consists of five identical segments about 31 ft long. The arch segments, hoisted by cranes attached to strongbacks bolted to the segments, were supported on falsework during erection. Open spaces provided between the ends and edges of adjacent segments had overlapping bars projected from the ends and edges of the segments into the open spaces. These bars were welded and then grouted in pneumatically to establish continuity. The roof was waterproofed with a spray-on plastic.

Thin-Shell Barrel Arches

A series of precast, thin-shell barrel roof arches supported by precast three-hinged rigid frames is shown in Figure 4.58.

FIGURE 4.58 Thin-sheet barrel arch roof deck. Architect: Mario Campi. Structural Engineer: Isadore Thompson.

Each arch unit was constructed of lightly reinforced, lightweight concrete 3½ in. thick, 15 ft wide, and 61 ft long, including an exterior cantilever projection of 9 ft. Spreading of the arches during erection was prevented by temporary bar ties located just above the springing lines.

The arches were anchored to the frames. Holes cast in the arches gloved over pipe dowels cast in the supports. After the arches were positioned, connections were welded to the tops of the dowels. The tie rods then were cut out. The arches spread slightly forming tight contacts. The edges of adjacent arches were tied together by welding matching plates. Built-up asphalt roofing covers the arches.

Thin-Shell Prestressed Concrete Domes

The common procedure for constructing thin-shell dome forms is by conventional means, which require no explanation. This paragraph is devoted to two procedures which make use of compacted earth fills or natural mounds, appropriately shaped, instead of forms. A pierced thin-shell reinforced concrete dome roof may be constructed in final position by using a compacted man-made mounded earth fill as a form. It need not be prestressed. Often the tension rings or ring girders of such domes are prestressed by posttensioning, as were those described in this paragraph.

A reinforced lightweight concrete thin-shell dome roof, constructed on a compacted earth fill and placed in final position by the lift-slab procedure, is illustrated in Figure 4.59. It has a diameter of 244 ft, a rise of 43 ft, and a uniform thickness of 4 in. The dome at the periphery is surrounded with a posttensioned concrete tension ring or ring girder 44 in. wide and 25 in. deep which is, in turn, surrounded with a cantilevered canopy 12 ft wide.

The ring girder is supported by 36 equally spaced steel columns 26 ft long, founded on spread footings and projecting 16 ft above the ground surface.

The construction procedure was as follows:

1. The concrete footings were constructed and the columns erected.

2. The steel lifting collars were placed around the columns and positioned to become anchored into the ring girder.

3. The ring girder or tension ring was formed and cast on the ground.

4. The earth was shaped in a mound of compacted earth and covered with plastic slabs 1 in. thick to provide the form for the thin shell.

5. The dome was reinforced on the mound.

6. The concrete dome was poured.

7. The tension ring was prestressed (after the concrete in the ring and the dome had set) by wrapping around its outside edge with three rings of ¼ in. steel wire. Each ring consisted of 43 wires that were prestressed while being placed.

8. A hydraulic lifting jack was placed on top of each column, connected to a single console for simultaneous con-

trol, and the lifting rods attached to the jacks and lifting collars.

9. The dome was jacked into position and secured by welding the lifting collars to the columns.

10. The canopy was constructed.

11. The earth fill was removed with the completion of the structure. The plastic slabs remaining on the underside of the dome serve as heat insulators.

This structure is the Warner Auditorium constructed in Anderson, Indiana, for the General Ministerial Assembly of the Church of God.

4.7 Concrete Shell Structures
by Milo S. Ketchum, Ketchum and Konkel, Consulting Engineers, Denver, Colorado.

FOLDED PLATES
The folded plate, shown in Figure 4.60, is the simplest of the shell structures. Its principal advantages are the ease of forming and its simple lines. The structure acts as a concrete slab across the short dimension. At the supports of the plates, it is necessary to provide a stiffener to pick up the reactions of the plates and deliver them to the columns. A horizontal tie is also necessary to hold the horizontal forces. At an edge, the arrangement of the plates must start with a short plate. A two-element plate with an edge member turned up at an angle is shown in (A). A three-element folded plate with a turned-down edge member is shown in (B). The advantage of this shape is that the width of individual plates may be less for the same column spacing. A three-element "Z" shell suitable for buildings having clerestory, north-light windows between the edges of adjacent units is shown in (C). A five-element folded plate that resembles a barrel shell is shown in (D).

The thickness of a folded plate depends primarily on the thickness necessary to carry the slab (short) span. This may range from 3 in. for a 5-ft width to 4½ in. for a 12-ft width. For structures greater than 12 ft, the slab should be haunched. The slope of the plates should not be greater than 45°, and the ratio of depth to span should be about 1 to 12 for simple spans and 1 to 15 for continuous spans.

BARREL SHELLS
Sketches of long-barrel shells are shown in Figure 3.34. In this type of cylindrical structure, the approximate ratio of span to width is assumed to be greater than 2 to 1. Short-barrel shells are described in the next paragraph.

The barrel shell acts as a beam in the long direction and as an arch in the short direction. The arch, however, is not

SYMMETRICAL ABOUT ₵

THICKNESS 4"

RADIUS 200'

43'

PRESTRESSED TENSION RING

COLUMNS

16'

FLOOR

122'

HALF CROSS SECTION

FIGURE 4.59 A 244-ft diameter prestressed concrete dome erected by the lift-slab method. Warner Auditorium, Anderson, Indiana. Architects and Engineers: Johnson, Ritchart, and Associates. General Contractor: Lewis Construction Company.

A

FIGURE 4.60 Folded plate roofs.

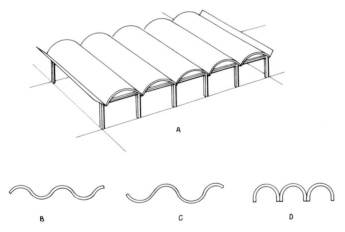

FIGURE 4.61 Long-barrel shell roof.

supported at its ends, as it is in the usual highway bridge arch, but is supported by the internal shears.

Several cross sections are shown. Figure 4.61A is a circular cylindrical barrel with a turned-up edge. The usual section is a circle, but other shapes are satisfactory. A continuous series of curves, as in a corrugated section, is shown in (B). Discontinuous units suitable for a north-light structure are shown in (C). Edge members at the junction of each barrel are shown in (D). The depth of the structure may be increased by this method and longer spans may be used.

The thickness of the barrel is dependent in most cases on the amount of cover over the reinforcing bars and varies from 3 to 4 inches. It is customary to thicken the shells slightly at the valley. The ratios of span to depth are about the same as for folded plates. However, the widths may be considerably greater for the same thickness.

SHORT SHELLS

The width of a short shell is large in comparison to the span as sketched in Figure 4.62A and B. The barrels are picked up by arches or frames that may be either above or below the shell. The arches may have many different forms, two of which are shown in (A) and (B). The short shell acts as an arch in the upper part of the curve and delivers its thrusts to a beam element at the lower end of the shell. This area must be braced by an upturned or downturned edge member. In (A), the shell is turned down. The thickness of short shells is usually a minimum, about 2.5 to 4 in., except at an edge which is not supported by an edge plate.

Short shells are often used for quite wide openings. A typical width is 250 ft with the arch elements spaced 25 to 35 ft. The arch is the predominant structural element.

DOMES OF REVOLUTION

A typical dome of revolution is shown in Figure 4.63A. This is a segment of a sphere. The shell acts as a membrane, and all stresses are direct compression or tension. There is very little bending in the shell except as a secondary stress near the tension ring at the lower edge. The ring holds the shell mainly in compression and may be prestressed by high-strength steel wires wrapped around the ring.

Many cross sections may be used for a dome of revolution, as shown in the figure. In *(D)*, a central column is used.

The thickness of domes is usually a minimum, and tanks with a diameter of 100 ft have been built with a roof thickness of 2 in.

The acoustical problems associated with domes may be very difficult to handle.

THE HYPERBOLIC PARABOLOID

The hyperbolic paraboloid is the name of a mathematical surface created by twisting a plane surface, and for that

FIGURE 4.62 Short-shell roofs.

FIGURE 4.63 Domes of revolution.

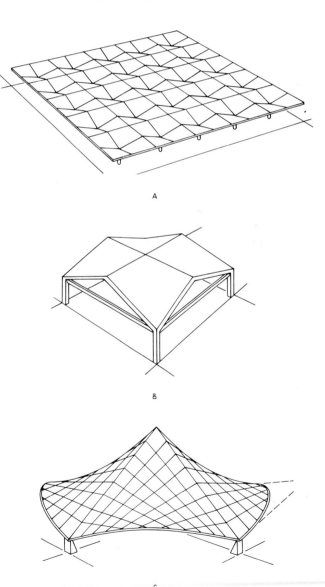

FIGURE 4.64 Hyberbolic paraboloid roofs.

reason these structures are often called twisted surfaces. The shell has a double curvature, convex in one direction and concave in the other.

If properly arranged, the stresses in a twisted surface are mostly membrane, that is, there is tension in one direction and compression in the other. Ribs are usually necessary at the exterior edges and at the junctions of the surfaces.

Several structures are shown in Figure 4.64A to C. A series of umbrella shells is shown in (A). The support is a column at the center of each square unit. The shell in (B) is a dome arranged with four square or rectangular surfaces supported by triangular tied arches. A circular dome with the corners clipped off is shown in (C). The thrusts from the shell are taken by curved arches. There are an infinite variety of shapes possible using the basic twisted surface.

The thickness of the shell may be a minimum. If two layers of ⅜-in. bars are used and ¾ in. of cover is required, the thickness should be 2¼ in.

INTERSECTION SHELL

The dome shown in Figure 4.65A is made by the intersection of cylindrical units. This structure acts essentially as a short shell, and the intersections form a rib to stiffen the dome. In (B), the axis of the barrels is reversed, and the shell must be supported by arch ribs at the edges.

FOLDED-PLATE DOME

A dome made with triangular folded plates is shown in Figure 4.66. The plates exert a thrust in the horizontal ring.

SHELL ARCH

An arch with the cross section of a folded plate is shown in Figure 4.67.

OTHER TYPES

The structures shown in this article are only a few of the many possible structures available for shell structures; this field requires the creative genius of the architect and the engineer.

FIGURE 4.65 Roofs formed by the intersection of cylindrical units.

FIGURE 4.66 Round folded-plate domed roof.

FIGURE 4.67 Arch with folded-plate cross section.

Summary

Concrete is indeed a versatile construction material. In its plastic state, it can be molded to any desired shape and finished to a smooth, hard surface. In its hardened state concrete is strong and durable. Concrete can be cast in place in the structure, it can be precast on the job site and later placed into the structure, or it can be precast at a remote site, transported to the job site, and then be positioned into the structure. It is used for walls, beams, girders, arches, shells, and columns in the building's structural framework. Concrete is often the specified material for site improvements including sidewalks, planters, curbs, and parking areas.

Concrete can be transported on the job site with a variety of readily available equipment. Wheelbarrows, power buggies, concrete buckets handled with cranes, conveyors, and concrete pumps. This equipment has a range of production capacities that will fit any situation — from 1½ cu yd/hr for the wheelbarrow to 300 cu yd/hr with belt conveyors. Concrete is molded with formwork that can be fabricated on the job, standardized by pre-engineered forming systems, and custom made systems designed specifically for a particular job application.

Care must be exercised in the production of concrete to ensure that the desirable properties of plastic and hardened concrete are obtained. Specified ingredients must be batched accurately and mixed thoroughly to produce a homogeneous mixture. Transportation equipment and handling methods are used that prevent segregation. After the concrete is consolidated in the forms, it is maintained at a uniform temperature with adequate moisture present to ensure complete hydration of the cement and strength gain of the concrete. This care will provide the owner with a material that is strong, durable, and meets the design requirements.

Key Terms

concrete	admixture	laitance	slip forms
portland cement	pozzolan	flat slab	precast concrete
aggregate	water-cement ratio	flat-plate construction	prestressed concrete
air-entrained concrete	slump test	slab-band construction	tendons
hydration	compressive unit strength	shear walls	tilt-up construction
fineness modulus	segregation	formwork	lift-slab construction
bulking	reinforced concrete	shores	

Review Questions

1. How are cement, water, and aggregates transformed into a hard, rocklike mass?

2. List the properties of both plastic and hardened concrete.

3. How does the water-cement ratio affect the properties of plastic and hardened concrete?

4. List four types of equipment used to transport concrete on the construction site and give an example of what type of placement they are best suited for.

5. What is the purpose of reinforced concrete?

6. List four common materials used in concrete formwork and state how they are used to mold and support plastic concrete.

7. Describe the function of three concrete structural elements commonly used in building construction.

CHAPTER 5
MASONRY

5.1 Brick Masonry
5.2 Stone Masonry
5.3 Unit Masonry

5.4 Masonry Accessories
5.5 Mortar

Masonry, an assembly of building units held together with mortar, is a class of construction that dates back to the beginning of recorded history. Four of the Seven Wonders of the Ancient World, including the pyramids of Egypt, were masonry structures. The materials and methods used have not changed appreciably since then. Essentially masonry consists of setting individual building units in a bed of mortar, one after another. A variety of shapes, patterns, and sizes can be incorporated into a single homogeneous structure. Common building units include brick, stone, concrete masonry units, and structural clay tile.

Brick are produced by molding clays and shale into desired shapes and sizes. The brick are then dried and burned in kilns. The hardness and durability of brick depends primarily upon the degree of burning. A great variety of colored brick is produced by selecting specific clays and introducing certain oxides into the mixture. Most common colors are red, brown, and gray. The face of the brick may be smooth or textured depending on the manufacturing process used.

Stone is nature's basic building material. It may be used as it is found in nature with very little shaping. Many farm homes were constructed with stones that were cleared from the fields after plowing. More uniform units of stone are obtained by milling quarried rock. A variety of finishes can be imparted to the exposed face. The finish can be as it appears in nature or it can be ground and polished to a high luster.

Concrete masonry units, also called concrete block, are formed of concrete in machines with steel molds that vibrate and compact the concrete mixture into desired shapes and sizes. After the molds are removed the units are cured and dried. They are used as a material for foundation walls, bearing walls, decorative screens, and as backing for brick or stone. The cores that are formed in the concrete masonry units reduce the weight and facilitate vertical reinforcing.

Masonry building units are joined together by mortar into a cohesive unified mass. Mortar is a mixture of well-graded aggregates, portland cement, and clean water. The overall strength of the unified mass depends on the strength of the masonry unit and mortar working together. Reinforcement is added to the unified mass when forces, which introduce tensile stresses in the masonry mass, are anticipated in the final structure. Masonry unit construction, as it has in the past, continues to play an important role in building construction.

Objectives

1. Understand the elements of masonry construction.
2. Become familiar with the three methods used in the manufacture of clay and shale brick.
3. Understand how headers and stretchers are used to establish different bonds.
4. Understand the process of bricklaying.

5. Become familiar with the different course arrangements used in stone masonry construction.
6. Become familiar with the four classifications of concrete masonry units.
7. Understand how the various masonry accessories are used.
8. Become familiar with the different ways mortar joints are finished.

5.1 Brick Masonry

Masonry construction is one of the traditional methods of building. Masonry structures from Egyptian through classical and medieval architecture to our present efforts are marked with a quality that is found only in masonry.

Masonry is essentially an assembly of building block units that has a distinctive architectural character and impact of its own — its massiveness, variety of patterns, rich texture, warmth of color, aging patina, and enviable agelessness. Masonry still provides an opportunity for individual craftsmanship in a mechanistic time.

Let us investigate some of the contemporary technical aspects of this historic system.

Prerequisite to the study of masonry construction, certain masonry terms common to all masonry construction must be defined. *Masonry* is an assembly or combination of small building units made of clay, shale, concrete, glass, gypsum, or stone that are set in mortar. Masonry consists entirely or partially of hollow or solid units laid contiguously in mortar. *Mortar* is a plastic mixture of cementatious materials with water and inert fine aggregates. Grout is mortar that is of pouring consistency; dry grout is used for dry packing, such as setting steel column base plates.

Brick masonry consists of brick walls, columns, arches, floors, and beams. Mortars used between the brick form the joints and hold the bricks together to act as a unit.

Kiln fired *brick* are made of clay or shale. They are used in all classes of construction, from private dwellings to the finest public building. Concrete or cement brick and sand-lime brick have limited use and are not burned. Adobe brick made of fired or sun-dried clay are now rarely used, except by the avant garde.

BRICK MANUFACTURE

Clay and shale brick are made by three different processes in which the bricks are molded, dried, and burned in kilns. The chief difference in the processes is in the method of molding. Brick are frequently specified by the method of manufacture.

In the soft-mud process, the clay is mixed with water and worked into a uniform plastic mass. Brick are shaped by pressing this material into molds by hand or by machinery. To keep the brick from sticking, the molds are watered or sanded. If the molds are wet, the method is slop molding, and the brick are called water-struck brick. If molds are sanded, the method is sand molding, and the brick are called sand-struck brick.

In the stiff-mud process, only enough water is mixed with the clay to produce a mixture which may be forced through a die, forming a ribbon with a cross section equal to the flat side, or to the end of a brick. The brick, cut from this ribbon by tightly stretched wires, are wire-cut brick. If the beds are cut, the brick are called side-cut; but if the ends are cut, they are called end-cut.

By the dry-pressed process, clay of dry consistency is pressed into gang molds by plungers that exert a heavy pressure. This process produces the most accurately formed brick.

Brick pressed in oversize molds, dried, and repressed to the correct size are called repressed brick. Such brick are accurately formed and strong. Stiff-mud brick are frequently repressed.

Concrete or cement brick are usually made by compressing a moistened mixture of portland cement and sand into gang molds. A dry mixture permits the molds to be removed immediately. The brick are then steam-cured or lightly sprayed with water. This brick should be called concrete brick rather than cement brick.

Although concrete brick is a dead cement color, different finishes are made by using aggregates or colored cements. Concrete brick are used where suitable clay is scarce.

Sand-lime brick are a mixture of sand and hydrated lime compressed in molds and steam-cured.

BRICK SIZES

Any attempt to remember brick sizes will surely lead to some confusion. The most cursory examination of the masonry literature convinces one that it is futile to memorize every brick size on the market (see Table 5.1).

Efforts have been made to standardize actual brick sizes and to eliminate the oddball sizes that plague designers. In some cases, there is more than one size assigned the same brick name. Brick sizes vary with locality or among manufacturers; moreover, brick made in the same size molds will differ because different clays vary in the amount of shrinkage in burning. Most brick manufacturers concentrate on producing certain sizes that are more marketable.

Table 5.1 Modular Brick Sizes[a]

Common Name	Height	Width	Length	Modular Coursing
Economy	4	4	8	
Utility	4	4	12	1C = 4 in.
6 Jumbo	4	6	12	
8 Jumbo	4	8	12	
Baby Roman	2	4	8	2C = 4 in.
Roman	2	4	12	
Modular	2⅔	4	8	
Norman	2⅔	4	12	3C = 8 in.
SCR	2⅔	6	12	
Double	5⅓	4	8	
Triple	5⅓	4	12	3C = 16 in.
Engineer	3⅕	4	8	
Norwegian	3⅕	4	12	5C = 16 in.
6 Norwegian	3⅕	6	12	

[a] Adapted from Ramsey and Sleeper, *Architectural Graphic Standards*, J. Wiley & Sons, 6 Edition, p. 148.

FIGURE 5.1 Brick positions and types.

The smallest nominal brick measures 4 in. wide, 2 in. high, and 8 in. long; it is called a baby Roman.

Modular bricks are intended to meet even coursing dimensions. Mortar joint thickness, which varies from ¼ in. to ½ in., in combination with the brick is designed to conform to even coursing dimensions. There are about five modular sizes that in combination with joints, meet standard course heights.

BRICK SHAPES

The six surfaces of a brick are the face, the side, the end, the cull, and two beds (Figure 5.1).

Brick are cut into various shapes; the more common are shown in Figure 5.1. They are known by the following names: half or bat, three-quarter, closer, king closer, queen closer, and split. They are used where the full brick will not fit. A *soap* is a brick that has been split to a dimension less than 2 in.

Special shapes are used for moldings or finishing an opening. They are not usually used for ordinary brickwork but are available in face brick and in the glazed and enameled clay brick described later. Other useful shapes are bull-nose and the double bull-nose, the external octagon, the internal octagon, the cove header, and the cove stretcher. Hollow brick used as face brick or backing brick reduce the weight of a wall and gain air space.

Cored brick have vertical cylindrical cores through the bed that reduce the weight. A brick may have a rectangular ⅜ in. deep recessed bed, called a frog. Neither a core nor a frog may come within ¾ in. of any edge. Deeper frogs are used, providing that a section through the net area of the frog is at least 75% of the gross area.

HARDNESS OF CLAY BRICK

The hardness and durability of clay and shale brick depend largely upon the degree of burning. Burned brick are sorted according to their hardness. The brick that immediately surround the fire are usually over-burns and are badly warped and discolored. These, known as arch or clinker brick, are suitable for foundations, or similar places, for they are very durable. Correctly burned hard or well-burned brick are for general use. Those remote from the fire that are underburned, known as soft brick, are weak and not resistant to weather; therefore, they are suitable only for backing brick, where moisture is minimal and where strength is not a major factor. The terms salmon, pale, and light are often applied to soft red brick.

COLOR OF CLAY BRICK

Common or building brick, used where appearance is not a factor, are usually made of clay which burns red, but sometimes common brick are white- or cream-colored. Very attractive walls are built of selected common brick, using well-tooled joints and the appropriate bond.

Face brick are used on exposed faces where appearance is a factor. By selecting mixing clays and introducing certain oxides, a great variety of colored face brick are produced—most commonly red, brown, and gray.

SURFACE FINISH OF CLAY BRICK

The exposed face of brick may be smooth or roughened by wire cutting or by combing, as in tapestry brick.

Salt-glazed brick are smooth-faced brick of special composition. A glaze forms on the face exposed to the furnace gases when common salt is thrown into the fires near the end of the burning. Salt glazes are gray, brown, and green. Salt-glazed brick are impervious, smooth, and easily cleaned. They are suitable for exteriors as well as interiors with wainscots or the entire surface glazed. Glazed and facing hollow clay tile are made for use with corresponding brick.

Vapors, which are produced by the action of heat on the salt, react chemically when they contact the brick or tile surfaces. This reaction forms a glaze.

The face of smooth unburned clay brick of special composition are sprayed with a coating and burned, resulting in an enameled or ceramic glazed face. The common glazes are white, green, and brown finished in bright, medium, or dull. Enameled brick possesses a more impervious, smooth, and easily cleaned surface than salt-glazed brick. Enameled brick are particularly desirable for swimming pools, commercial kitchens, hospitals, and other locations where their properties are required. Those called fire-flash or fire-mark brick have acquired a surface marking by exposure to the fires of a kiln.

BUILDING BRICK AND FACING BRICK

Brick is classified as building brick (ASTM C 62) and as facing brick (ASTM C 216). In this classification, facing brick is made especially for facing purposes by selecting the clays that produce the desired colors or surface textures that may be smooth, fine, combed, or coarse. Building brick, formerly known as common brick, is made from natural clay without regard to color or special surface treatment. Still, selected building brick with attractive fire marks are sometimes used as face brick. And, too, brick are called face brick and backing brick according to their position in the wall. Nevertheless, face brick requires a higher quality, greater durability, and better appearance, whereas facing brick that is overburned or underburned may be classified as inferior and be used as backing brick.

BRICK QUALITY

Brick quality is determined by its strength, durability, and appearance. ASTM Specifications C 216 distinguishes between three types of face brick made from clay or shale. These three types are *FBS, FBX,* and *FBA;* the type distinctions are based on color range, variation in size, texture, architectural effects, and mechanical perfection. Further classification of facing brick provides for two grades—*SW* and *NW*—which is an index of durability and weathering resistance (ASTM 12).

Based on durability to exposure, building brick is divided into three grades: *SW (Severe Weathering), MW (Moderate Weathering),* and *NW (Negligible Weathering).* This standard further provides for physical properties, appearance, strength, size, frogging, and visual inspection of building brick.

Figure 5.2 below is a map of the United States showing weathering indices of brick. The ASTM further states that:

Figure 5.2 indicates general areas of the United States in which brick masonry is subject to severe, moderate, and negligible weathering. The severe weathering region has a weathering index greater than 500. The moderate weathering region has a weathering index of 100 to 500. The negligible weathering region has a weathering index of less than 100.

The use of Grade MW brick in a wall area above grade is structurally adequate in the severe weathering region, but Grade SW would provide a higher and more uniform degree of resistance to frost action. The degree of durability called for by Grade SW is not necessary for use in wall areas above grade in the moderate weathering region. Grade MW brick performs satisfactorily in wall areas above grade in the no-weathering region, where the average compressive strength of the units is at least 200 psi. Grade SW brick should be used in any region when the units are in contact with the ground horizontal surfaces, or in any position where they are likely to be permeated with water.

The resistance to weathering by brick is indicated by the

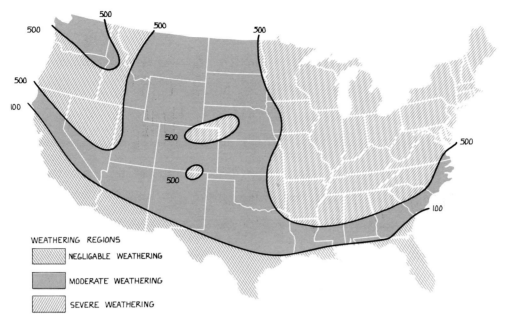

FIGURE 5.2 Weathering indices for masonry.

weathering index, a numerical value determined by multiplying the average number of freezing cycle days by the average annual winter rainfall in inches. In other words, the weathering index is a numerical value that approximates the number of freeze-thaw cycles.

HEADERS, STRETCHERS

Bricks are placed in a variety of positions in a wall. If they are laid on the bed with the end or cull exposed, they are called *headers;* but if they are laid with the face (long side) exposed, they are called **stretchers.** Half-brick are used as false headers giving the appearance of headers but not projecting into the backing. Brick placed on the side with the end exposed are called bull headers or rowlocks and are used for sills or for belt courses. Occasionally, they are laid on the side with the bed exposed forming bull stretchers or flatters. Belt courses and flat arches formed of brick set on end with the narrow side exposed are called soldiers; with the bed exposed, they are sailors. Quoins are brick placed at corners with one end and one face exposed. These positions and types of brick were illustrated in Figure 5.1C.

BONDS

The arrangement of brick tying units together in various ways is called the *bond.* A *course* is a bond of continuous horizontal layer forming part of a wall (see Figure 5.3.). Courses are measured vertically. A *wythe* is a tie or a course of masonry units measured horizontally through the wall (see Figure 5.4).

FIGURE 5.3 Brick bonds.

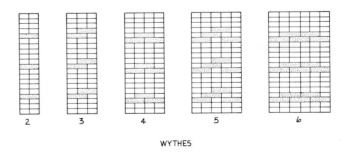

WYTHES

FIGURE 5.4 Methods of bonding brick walls.

HERRING - BONE   DIAGONAL   BASKET WEAVE

BRICK PATTERNS

FIGURE 5.5 Brick patterns.

In running or stretcher bond, the face brick are all stretchers as shown in Figure 5.3A. The face brick are tied to the backing by metal or reinforcing, or by using clipped or secret bond as described, or by setting a queen closer face brick at every sixth course so that a continuous row of headers may project halfway into the face course and into the backing.

In common or American bond, every sixth course of stretcher bond is usually made a header course, resulting in a much stronger wall than that secured with metal ties.

English bond consists of alternate courses of headers and stretchers. The vertical joints in the header courses aligning or breaking over each other, and the vertical joints in the stretcher courses are also in line while bisecting every other brick in the header course.

English cross bond, Dutch bond, or cross bond is similar to English bond, but the alternate courses of stretchers do

(A) Spreading the mortar

(B) Cutting excess mortar

(C) Forming the furrow

(D) Mortar voids

FIGURE 5.6 Bricklaying. TM5-742, *Concrete and Masonry,* Department of the Army, June, 1970.

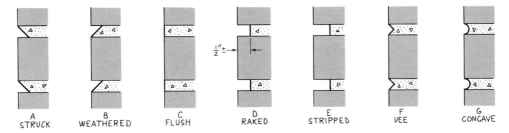

FIGURE 5.7 Joint illustrations.

not align. Built up of interlocking crosses, this wall consists of two headers and a stretcher, forming a cross. For illustrative purposes, the cross is emphasized.

In Flemish bond, each course has alternate headers and stretchers; the alternate headers of each course are centered over the stretcher.

A header bond is composed entirely of headers laid to break joints. An entire wall would not usually be laid in header bond, but certain areas of a wall may be in header bond for decorative effect (Figure 5.3F). Some of the headers may be false headers.

In clipped, or secret bond, face brick are laid in running bond, but the inside corners of the brick in every sixth course are clipped to permit a tie with the backing by headers laid diagonally. This bond offers little resistance to the separation of the face and backing, so it is desirable to add metal wall ties at every sixth course. These ties should be set on each brick of the course midway between the diagonal header courses. This construction gives a stronger wall if using wall ties only, but it is not as satisfactory as the other bonds.

Face brick, laid with the vertical as well as the horizontal joints continuous, is called stack bond. Brick may be laid with exposed faces or exposed headers. The objective is to secure an effect. Horizontal and vertical reinforcement is provided by including steel bars in the joints.

PATTERNS

Patterns are used primarily in brick floors, but can be laid in walls and fireplaces. A number of patterns may be created by arranging headers and stretchers in various ways. Emphasized headers may differ slightly in color from the stretchers. Other patterns are created by arranging face brick diagonally or vertically. The most common patterns are the herringbone, the diagonal, and the basketweave shown in Figure 5.5. Patterns should be bonded to the backing by using noncorrosive metal ties.

SKINTLED BRICKWORK

Skintled brickwork is the setting of face brick (as running bond) out of line with the face of the wall. The corners

project or recess from ⅛ in. to ¼ in. or more. The mortar which protrudes may be allowed to remain, forming a squeezed joint. This type of brickwork leaks and collects dirt.

BRICKLAYING

Brick masonry joints as thin as ⅛ in. are formed for enameled or glazed brick presenting an easily cleaned surface, while joints as thick as ¾ in. meet aesthetic requirements, although the most comon thickness is ¼ to ½ in., meeting modular requirements.

The joints are made with a trowel or jointer tool by the following:

1. Enough mortar is spread to form the horizontal joint for three or four bricks (see Figure 5.6A.)
2. The mortar that projects over the edge is cut off to keep it from running down over the face of the wall (see Figure 5.6B)
3. The brick is bedded by tapping with the trowel handle.
4. The mortar forced over the edge by the bedding process is cut off, the end to the brick is buttered to form the next vertical joint. This process forms a rough-cut joint.
5. The exposed surface of the joints is tooled in one of the various kinds of joints shown in Figure 5.7.

In spreading mortar, a shallow longitudinal furrow is formed in the mortar with the trowel. Such a furrow is necessary to position the brick accurately. If the furrow is made too deep, the joint will not be completely filled with mortar as is required for watertight construction (see Figures 5.6C and 5.6D).

Push or shove joints are formed by placing a brick on a heavy bed of mortar and pushing or shoving it into position against a brick already placed in the same course so that the vertical joint between the two is entirely filled with mortar. Walls constructed in this manner are stronger and more watertight than walls constructed in the usual way.

Buttered joints are formed by buttering mortar on the bottom around the four edges and on the vertical end that will contact the last brick laid. The brick is then placed and tapped into place with the handle of the trowel. Narrow joints in enameled or glazed brickwork are commonly formed this way. At one time, face brick were set with buttered joints ⅛ in. wide, but this practice has been practically discontinued. The mortar is around the edges of the brick for buttered joints but not under the central bed of the brick.

The brickwork for all party walls, fire walls, and bearing walls should be laid solid with all joints filled with mortar.

BOND REQUIRED

Every sixth course on each face of a wall should be a header course; however, walls laid in Flemish bond or English bond have full brick headers at every fourth course bonded into the backing. The remaining headers may be half-brick, called false headers. Running bond should be bonded by using clipped bond combined with metal wall ties, as described, or by using split stretchers.

In walls more than 12 in. thick, the inner joints of header courses should be covered with another header course which breaks joints with the course below.

Methods of bonding brick walls of various thicknesses and wythes are shown in Figure 5.4.

Although face brick should be laid at the same time as the backing, backing brick is sometimes laid ahead by apprentice masons, while the journeyman and master masons lay the face brick.

At intermittent work stoppage, such as at the end of the day, masonry should be stepped down. Toothing is accomplished by building the wall to full height and ending the work with a portion of the brick projecting at alternate courses. Toothing is usually prohibited, except as noted below.

ANCHORAGE AT WALL INTERSECTIONS

All intersecting walls should anchor and bond to each other. When such walls are not built at the same time, the perpendicular joint may be (with the architect's permission) toothed with 8 in. maximum offsets. Metal anchors 1½ by ½ in. by 2 ft long with bent-up ends or cross pins extend 12 in. on each side of the joint. They should not be spaced more than 4 ft apart vertically.

WETTING BRICK

Except in freezing weather, preferably 3 to 24 hours prior to setting, the brick should be wet down. This minimizes the absorption of water from the mortar. Immediate loss of water from the mortar results in a premature stiffening that lessens adhesion between brick and mortar. This is especially evident when the second brick follows. Moreover, prewetting washes accumulated jobsite dust away.

HOLLOW BRICK WALLS

Brick walls may be made hollow; the open space prevents rainwater from passing through. Water penetrating the outer wythe is conducted out again by flashing. At the lowest course of face brick, an oiled, ¼ in. cotton rope about 12 in. long is sometimes laid across the mortar bed at about 6-foot intervals. After the mortar has set, the ropes are pulled out, leaving a weep hole for the moisture to drain. There are three kinds of hollow wall: the rolock or rowlock wall, consisting of bull stretchers and bull headers, as shown in Figure 5.8A; the masonry-bonded hollow wall (B), in which the face brick wythe is separated from the backing by a 2 to 3 in. air space that is bridged by headers that bond the face brick to the backing; and the cavity wall (C), which bonds the facing with metal ties.

The hollow wall with headers is not as effectively bonded as is the solid wall with the same number of wythes. The headers in the rolock and masonry-bonded hollow walls may allow moisture penetration.

Other advantages of hollow walls are improved heat insulation, elimination of furring, and, as with the rolock wall, a saving in material. Hollow walls of brick are not widely used in this country, but the cavity wall is extensively used in Europe. They appear to have possibilities that deserve serious consideration because of their successful use abroad.

STUCCO ON BRICK

Brick walls are sometimes plastered with stucco. The brick should be rough, hard-burned brick set in portland-cement mortar with struck joints not less than ⅜ in. thick. This joint provides a better bond surface between the stucco and brick. The brick should be brushed free of all dust, dirt, or loose particles and wetted to prevent water absorption from the stucco.

FACE BRICK WITH BACKING

Face brick, backed with structural clay tile or concrete block, is either bonded to the backing with a row of headers every 16 in., or attached to the backing with embedded metal wall ties spaced not more than 1 ft apart vertically nor

FIGURE 5.8 Hollow walls of brick masonry.

A- ROW-LOCK ARCH

B- SEGMENTAL ARCH

C- BONDED ARCH

D-BONDING COURSES

F- FLAT ARCH

E- FLAT ARCH

G- THREE CENTERED ARCH

H- POINTED ARCH

LINTEL

I- RELIEVING ARCH

FIGURE 5.9 Brick arches.

BRICK ARCHES

Brick arches are used to span openings in brick walls. Various forms of arches were discussed in Chapter 1.

Brick arches are constructed of one or more wythes; they are soldier coursed with the end exposed (Figure 5.9A), or a rowlock arch is formed with one or more wythes of brick with the narrow side exposed (B), with the courses forming the arch ring bonded (C), or with bonding courses at intervals. (D).

The arch is formed by making wedge-shaped mortar joints or by beveling the brick to fit and forming joints of uniform thickness. Arches of shaped brick are termed gaged arches (Figure 5.9C, D, and G). Shaping is accomplished by laying the arch out on the floor and cutting and rubbing the brick to the proper shape before setting. Arches of other types than the rowlock are usually gaged.

Two forms of flat or jack arches are shown in (E) and (F). The flat arch is often supported on a concealed lintel; but, if so, it is not a true arch.

Brick arches, often constructed over lintels in the backing of brick or tone walls (I), take the load from the lintels and are called relieving or discharging arches.

REINFORCED BRICK MASONRY

Unreinforced brick masonry has considerable compressive strength but very little tensile or flexural strength. Embedded steel reinforcing bars in some of the horizontal bed joints provide horizontal tensile resistance. In addition, vertical reinforcing bars grouted in the vertical joints between wythes increase compressive strength, illustrated in Figure 5.10A, B, and C. By omitting the center wythe of brick at vertical intervals in a three-wythe wall, a grout-surrounded reinforcing bar is placed as shown in (D); thus, larger bars provide greater resistance. The head and bed joints in the outside wythes are made in the usual manner; care must be taken to keep the joints between wythes free from loose droppings. This type of construction is also called grouted masonry.

HIGH LIFT GROUTING SYSTEM

Because of its ability to increase resistance to shock and blast, reinforcement is used in brick masonry subject to blasts and earthquake shocks. Reinforcement is also desirable for parapet walls subject to temperature extremes which tend to induce tensile stresses resulting in cracks from longitudinal contraction.

Reinforced brick columns are constructed by pouring concrete columns in vertical openings formed within brick masonry walls, piers, or columns. The vertical reinforcement should have an area of not less than ½ nor more than 4% of the gross column area and should consist of not less than four ½-in. bars. Lateral reinforcement or ties or spirals should be provided.

more than 2 ft horizontally. If metal ties are employed, face brick veneer cannot be considered in determining the required wall thickness; but if brick headers are used, the face brick contributes to the required wall thickness.

Structural clay tile backing is sometimes placed when panel or curtain walls are supported by a steel or reinforced concrete frame. They increase the resistance to heat losses or reduce the cost when tile backing is more economical than lightweight concrete block.

Hollow brick in Jumbo brick size are used on the inside face of exterior walls; the air cells in the brick increase the resistance to heat loss or gain.

BRICK WALLS FACED WITH STONE

Brick is laid as backing for walls faced with stone masonry. Stonework veneer, not less than 4 in. thick, should be reasonably uniform in thickness, although not necessarily of the same thickness. Each stone should be bonded into the backing with noncorrosive metallic anchors.

FIGURE 5.10 Reinforced brick masonry walls.

Many other forms of reinforced brick masonry have been developed.

The following requirements are included in the *Building Code Requirements for Reinforced Masonry* approved by the American Standards Association as American Standard A41.2-1960, National Bureau of Standards Handbook 74, 1960.

All masonry units used in grouted masonry shall be laid plumb in full head and bed joints and all interior joints, cores, or spaces that are designed to receive grout shall be solidly filled. The grouted longitudinal joints shall not be less than ¾ in. wide. Mortar fins shall not protrude into spaces to be filled with grout. When the least clear dimension of the longitudinal vertical joint or core is less than 2 in., the maximum height of the grout pour shall be limited to 12 in. When the least clear dimension of the longitudinal vertical joint or core is 2 in. or more, the maximum height of the grout pour shall not exceed 48 times the lease clear dimension of the longitudinal vertical joint or core for pea gravel grout nor more than 64 for mortar grout but not to exceed 12 ft. Grout shall be agitated or puddled during placement to insure complete filling of the grout space. When grouting is stopped for 1 hr. or longer the grout pour shall be stopped 1½ in. below the top of a masonry unit. Masonry bonders (headers) shall not be used, but metal wall ties may be used to prevent spreading of the wythes and to maintain vertical alignment of the wall.

In reinforced grouted masonry, vertical reinforcement shall be accurately placed and held rigidly in position before the work is started. Horizontal reinforcement may be placed as the work progresses. . . . The thickness of grout or mortar between masonry units and reinforcement shall not be less than ¼ in. except ¼ in. bars may be laid in ½ in. horizontal mortar joints and No. 6 gage or smaller wires may be laid in ⅜ in. horizontal joints. Vertical joints containing both horizontal and vertical reinforcement shall be not less than ½ in. larger than the diameters of the horizontal and vertical reinforcement contained therein.

EFFLORESCENCE

The white soluble salt deposit that frequently appears on masonry wall surfaces is called *efflorescence.* It consists of calcium and magnesium sulfates in the masonry unit or in the mortars, leached out by water that penetrates the masonry surface.

Efflorescence, which is formed by the salt only in the presence of water, may be minimized or prevented by selecting materials free of the salts and by impeding water intrusion into the wall. The latter is accomplished by observing a number of good construction practices, namely, by using water-repellent mortar and solidly filled joints, by capping walls with tight jointed coppings sloped to drip free of the parapet wall onto the roof instead of toward the face of the wall, by effective flashing and calking, by providing a waterproof layer on top of foundation walls, and by protecing the walls during construction from rain and melting snow.

CLEANING

At the conclusion of masonry work, all surfaces of face brick should be thoroughly cleaned with a 5%–10% solution of muriatic acid (HCl) in water. A stiff wire brush is used to remove spots and stains and efflorescence. After cleaning, the surface is flushed with water to remove all traces of acid. This treatment is not desirable for soluble limestones or for polished surfaces on other stones.

TESTING

In masonry construction the strength of the composite (mortor and masonry unit) construction is the factor that dictates masonry design strength. Thus the "prism test" bears significance. While isolated brick tests and individual mortar tests are important, a test of these parts in assembled form as they will be constructed is significant. The numerical factor obtained from the prism test (f^1m) is the ultimate compressive strength at 28 days, which will be used in the design of masonry structures. This test may yield a maximum value of 6000 psi for solid clay units. If the test is not performed, the ultimate compressive strength value may be assumed as dictated by the code. This value ranges from 1350 psi for hollow CMUs to 5300 psi for the best solid clay units.

5.2 Stone Masonry

Geologists use the term rock to include the solid and unconsolidated material forming the earth's crust, the former designated as bed rock and the latter as mantle rock. In engineering, rock refers only to the solid or bedrock. The unconsolidated material is soil or earth. In agriculture, the term soil applies only to the few inches of surface or topsoil supporting vegetation; the underlying material is subsoil.

The terms *rock* and *stone* are often used synonymously, but generally rock relates to geologic formations, whereas smaller or quarried pieces of rock are called stone. However, this distinction is not always made.

Rock formations are of interest to the structural engineer and architect because rock formations are used to support the foundations of many structures. Stone is of interest because of its use in stone masonry, concrete aggregate, and as an ingredient in the manufacture of building materials.

Rocks are divided into three classes according to the method of formation. These classes are igneous, sedimentary, and metamorphic. Rocks are also divided into classes according to their chemical composition. The most abundant of these classes are argillaceous, siliceous, and calcareous. Argillaceous rocks are primarily alumina (Al_2O_3), the chief component of clay. Siliceous rocks are primarily silicon dioxide (SiO_2), the principal ingredient of quartz sand. Calcareous rocks are primarily calcium carbonate or lime ($CaCO_3$).

The earth's crust is composed chiefly of eight chemical elements. Nearly one-half is oxygen and more than one-quarter silicon. These elements in combination with silicon, aluminum, iron, calcium, sodium, potassium, and magnesium, form the materials mentioned as follows.

Nearly all rocks are of one or more minerals and have definite chemical compounds usually with crystalline structures, but some consist of natural glass or volcanic dust. The most common rock-making minerals are quartz (silicon dioxide), the feldspars (potassium, sodium, or calcium aluminum silicates), the micas (complex hydrous silicates of aluminum with potassium, magnesium, and iron), hornblend (primarily calcium magnesium silicate), kaolinite (hydrous aluminum silicate), calcite (calcium carbonate), and dolomite (magnesium carbonate).

IGNEOUS ROCKS
Igneous rocks are formed from the solidification of molten rock. If solidification occurs below the earth's surface, plu-

tonic or intrusive rock is formed; but if solidification occurs on the surface, the rock is volcanic or extrusive. Pyroclastic rocks are formed when molten rock is erupted violently into the air. The term lava is also applied to solidified extrusive rock. Molten rock forming igneous rocks is composed of a hot solution of feldspar, quartz, mica, water vapor, and carbon dioxide gases. The solidification of igneous rocks is due to a decrease in temperature and pressure. Igneous rock texture is determined greatly by the rate of cooling and by the volatile substances present. The texture may be coarse-grained if the cooling is very slow and fine-grained if the cooling is more rapid. If cooling is very rapid, glass is formed. The volatile substances facilitate crystallization. The entrapped gases in the solidfying mass form extrusive sheets with a vesicular or porous structure.

The most common igneous rocks are granite, felsite, basalt, and obsidian. Granite is usually a strong, durable, nonporous, and practically insoluble rock desirable as a foundation and building material. Felsite is a light-colored, fine-grained volcanic rock usually occurring as dykes or lava sheets. It is usually less porous than basalt. Basalt is dark-colored rock occurring chiefly in lava sheets or dykes. It is likely to be porous, cavernous, and badly fractured. Balsalt is practically insoluble; the caverns are caused by methods of formation and not due to the solvent action of water. Obsidian is a volcanic rock glass formed by rapid cooling of molten rock. Pyroclastic rocks include: volcanic ash, which are fine, glassy particles deposited at considerable distance from the volcano; lapilli, formed from the gravel-like particles deposited closer to the volcano; and braccias and tuffs, formed by consolidation of the coarser particles falling near the volcano. The volcanic material comparing in fineness to sand is known as puzzolana. Trap or trap rock is a commercial term confined to certain fine-grained, dense, durable igneous rocks, such as basalt. The difficulty in quarrying and finishing limits their suitability for building stone.

Granite
Most domestic granite is quarried in the states from Maine to Georgia, and in Minnesota and Wisconsin. Vermont produces the most granite. Granites are the hardest and most difficult to work but can be finished with highly polished surfaces. Colors include white, gray, pink, red, and green. Granite is used for curtain wall panels, steps, platforms, sills, trimstone, and as thin veneer over other masonry. It is also used in base courses and locations requiring an extremely durable stone.

SEDIMENTARY ROCKS
Sedimentary rocks are formed from the disintegrated products derived from igneous rocks or from other sedimentary rocks. This disintegration is brought about by weathering

factors: temperature changes, which produce cracking because of unequal coefficients of expansion of the minerals; temperature differentials, which result in disintegration because of unequal temperatures in different parts of a rock mass; alternate freezing and thawing, which produce a repeated disruptive action caused by the expansion of ice in the rock pores; abrasion, which results from moving glacial ice, running water, and wind, with the effectiveness accelerated by solid particles; and chemical action by atmospheric gases, by rain water that has absorbed such gases, or by ground water carrying chemicals in solution.

These products of rock disintegration may remain in place or be deposited as sediments by running water, by wind, or by glacial ice. The deposits may remain unconsolidated, as soil, or be solidified through pressure exerted by overlying material in consort with cementing materials included in the deposits or supplied subsequently by infiltration. Another formational factor in the geologic evolution of rocks is seashells, which are formed from calcium carbonate originally derived from rocks and carried in solution in sea water. These shells, which accumulate on the bottom as the organisms die, are ground by the shifting currents and become solidified by pressure and the cementing action of the calcium carbonate itself. Millennia are required for this continuous cycle of rock disintegration, transportation, deposition, and solidification to reform rock.

Characteristics of sedimentary rocks are their layers, or strata. The process of deposition is rarely uniform and continuous. Variations occur in water and wind velocity and, therefore, in the size and composition of the material carried in suspension or in solution. These variations have resulted in stratified layers. The dividing surfaces between these strata are called bedding planes or beds. Because of this division into strata, many sedimentary rocks are also termed stratified rocks, although some limestones show so little stratification that they are called freestones, their structure being uniform. The beds between strata may have weakened shear planes, particularly if they contain clay which becomes very slippery when wet. Movement may take place easily along these surfaces, sometimes called gliding planes. Sedimentary rocks are formed chiefly of the minerals quartz, kaolinite, calcite, and dolomite. The more common sedimentary rocks are sandstone, conglomerates, limestone, and shale.

Sandstones

Sandstones are formed by the consolidation of sand beds deposited by water carrying sand in suspension. The consolidation is due to pressure exerted by overlying material and to a cementing material, namely clay, calcium carbonate, iron oxide, or silica. The character of the cementing material has a pronounced effect on the properties of sandstone, silica being the strongest and most durable adhesive. Pure sandstone is silicon dioxide. Conglomerates are similar to sandstones but made of cemented gravel instead of cemented sand. Puddingstone is a conglomerate in which the pebbles are well-rounded, and in breccia they are angular. Sandstones of pure silicon dioxide are white, whereas iron oxide impurities produce various shades of yellow, brown, and red.

Sandstones are found in nearly every state, with Ohio producing the most sandstone. Sold chiefly in the Middle West, the stones from Ohio are blue, gray, and buff, with good working qualities and durability. Sandstones are used for the same applications as limestones. Bluestone and brownstone are sandstones named for their color. Bluestone is very strong and durable and splits readily into thin slabs. It is used for sidewalks, steps, flagging, and sills.

Limestones

Limestones are sedimentary rocks formed chiefly from the accumulation of shells on ancient sea bottoms which may now be many miles inland. Some limestones show fossils, but others show no trace of their origin because of the fine grinding imposed on the deposited shells. The cementing material is calcium carbonate, but magnesia, silica, alumina, and iron oxide are present in varying amounts.

Limestones are widely distributed with Indiana leading all states in production. Indiana, Bedford, or French Lick limestone, an oolitic limestone, is exported extensively. This stone varies from buff to gray; it is durable and can be sawn, planed, lathed, and carved easily, effectively, and economically. Low working costs permit Indiana limestone to compete with local stones in most parts of the country despite transportation costs. Limestone is used on interiors or exteriors for masonry veneer over other masonry, trimstone, steps, sills, coping, flagstones, and floor tiles.

Travertine is a limestone formed by the chemical precipitation of calcium carbonate from hot ground water. Characteristic of this stone are the small, irregularly shaped cavities. Travertine is used as floor tile and for limited ornamentation. Although this stone is imported from Italy, domestic travertine quarries are developing. Oolitic limestone contains many very small, rounded particles called oolites, which are concentric layers of calcium carbonate deposited around a nucleus. Most limestone is gray, but it may be buff or brown.

Shales are formed by the compacting or by the compacting and cementing of clays, muds, and silts. They may grade into sandstones if a large amount of siliceous material is present or grade into limestone if formed from silts containing an abundance of calcareous material. Shales have a finely stratified, impermeable structure. Those formed by compaction without cementation slack and disintegrate when acted upon by water after partial or complete drying. Such shales are unsatisfactory for supporting heavily loaded foundations because the shale gradually flows, a phenomenon known as plastic flow. Shales with grains cemented and compacted by pressure are not subject to plastic flow and do not disintegrate as do the shales which have been compacted only. For these reasons, nonplastic flowing shales are more suitable for foundation support. Shales do not possess the requisite durability for building stones.

METAMORPHIC ROCKS

Metamorphic rocks are either igneous or sedimentary rocks whose physical or chemical characteristics have been altered by pressure from the earth movements, temperature changes caused by intrusions of molten rock, or vapors or liquids permeating the rocks. The changes are in mineral composition, texture, and structure and include cementation by siliceous matter. The changes in mineral composition depend upon the chemical composition. Because all kinds of rocks are subjected to metamorphic action, there is a wide variation in the mineral composition of metamorphic rocks. Such rocks are highly crystalline in structure because of their origin. They are usually foliated or laminated similar to the stratified structure of sedimentary rocks and are known as schists. The common metamorphic rocks are gneiss, a laminated rock with a mineral composition similar to granite; schist, a laminated crystalline silicate rock that splits easily; slate, a fine-grained argillaceous rock that splits easily into slabs; quartzite, a hard durable crystalline quartz rock derived from sandstone; and marble, a crystalline rock that can be polished. Marble is derived from limestone and is therefore chiefly calcium carbonate. There is no definite demarcation between many of the metamorphic rocks. For example, schist may grade into gneiss, or into slate.

Marble

Marble deposits are rather widely distributed; about 90% is quarried in Tennessee, Vermont, and Georgia. Pure marble is white, but other substances and impurities produce a selection of beautiful colors and variations characteristic of marble. The color pattern, together with the ability to take a high polish, make marble a valuable medium for decorative uses. Marble is used as a curtain wall panel or as a veneer for monumental buildings. In general, it is used for exterior and interior decorative purposes, including wainscoting, panels, mantels, hearths, floor tile, and stairs.

ROCK STRUCTURE

The methods of formation of the various rocks have been considered. After rocks have been formed, their structures may be altered by movements of the earth's crust, resulting in bent and fractured formations, as shown in Figure 5.11A. The bends formed are called folds. Fractures are called joints if there is no displacement along the fracture, or faults if there is movement along the fracture, as shown in (B). The rock adjacent to a fault may be fragmented, as shown in (C), and cemented to form fault breccia, or the rock may become pulverized and referred to as gouge. Sedimentary rocks are usually deposited in horizontal layers or strata, but because of the folding activity, the beds may be sloped. The vertical angle that a bed makes with a horizontal plane is

FIGURE 5.11 Rock structure.

called a dip. The direction of a line parallel to the bed plane, perpendicular to the dip, with a horizontal plane is called the strike (D).

Because limestone is slightly soluble in water containing carbon dioxide, there is always the possibility that a limestone formation will be cavernous or contain solution channels caused by ground water. Such defects are particularly objectionable because they may induce failure of building foundations. If defects of this type are discovered before a structure is built, the cavities can usually be filled by pressure grouting or by cleaning out the openings and filling them with concrete.

Occasionally, large areas will be encountered in which rock formations have been broken up and crushed to great depths, though little surface evidence is apparent. Such areas are called shear zones.

PHYSICAL PROPERTIES

The physical properties of stone requisite to support foundations or for use in masonry structures are strength, durability, permeability, fire resistance, workability, solubility, color, and appearance. Some of these have already been considered.

Strength is mandatory for rocks serving as foundation support or as stone masonry. Sound bedrock is usually strong enough to support any imposed load transmitted by a concrete pier. Durable stone exposed to weathering is usually strong enough to support the subjected loads. The loads placed on rock formations and stone masonry are usually compressive, but flexural or bending loads are imposed on stone lintels and individual stones when resisting unequal settlement and improper bedding. Stone should not be used in a manner that will subject it to tensile stresses. The maximum compressive strengths of rock or stone may reach approximate values in excess of 5,000 lb per sq in. No specific values can be given. Stratified rocks have greater compressive strength normal to their bedding planes than parallel to them. Tests would be required if the strength of a given stone were in question. However, most rocks or stones considered for construction purposes are amply strong.

The durability of building stone is probably its most desirable property. Building stones (and rock formations) are acted upon by most of the weathering factors described previously. The resistance to weathering depends upon the composition, texture, and structure of the stone. The durability of sandstone depends largely upon the kind of cementing material that holds the grains together, silica being the most durable, cement and clay usually the least. Limestone and marble are slightly soluble in water containing carbon dioxide, but the dissolving rate is usually so slow that this action is negligible in building stones. However, this factor may receive consideration if a polished marble surface is maintained.

The best method for determining durability is by examining the rock outcropping or the parts of a quarry where the stone has been exposed for a long period. Similarly, examination of the same rock in older existing structures is a good index of the rock's weathering properties. Other properties that may indirectly indicate durability are its weight and its compressive strength, high values for these properties usually, but not always, being favorable indicators. Accelerated freezing and thawing laboratory test cycles are also valuable. Blocks of stone quarried may contain a considerable amount of water called quarry sap. Such stones are frequently broken by freezing; but if allowed to season, they will probably not break.

The porosity is the proportion of pore volume to the total volume and is often an indication of a rock's resistance to frost. It is not the amount of pore space available, but their uniform continuity measured by the permeability — the ability to permit water to pass through its pores. A stone may be very porous and still be quite impermeable because of lack of continuity in the pores. For this reason, it may not be seriously affected by alternate freezing and thawing. Moreover, an open free-draining texture is more resistant to frost action than a fine texture that retains capillary water.

The fire resistance of a stone is a structural consideration. Few building stones will withstand very high temperatures. This fact is particularly true when the heated stone is subjected to a stream of high pressure water. Because of low resistance to fire, the use of stone interior piers, caps, and bond stones is prohibited by some building codes, but this practice is probably too severe. Building stones may be arranged in order of their resistivity as follows: (1) fine-grained sandstone with silica binder, (2) fine-grained granite and oolitic limestone, (3) ordinary limestone, (4) coarse-grained granite, (5) marble. Limestone fails by calcination at a relatively low temperature.

Workability is an economic factor in the selection of building stones. Marbles and granites are durable, strong, and attractive but are expensive for building purposes because of the labor required to shape them. Some stones unsuitable for ashlar may be satisfactory for rubble or squared-stone masonry requiring relatively little labor in shaping. Stones soft enough to work readily, such as shales, are frequently not durable. Ornamental work, such as moldings and carvings, requires a stone with an even grain free from seams and other defects. Stones easily worked in any direction and free from stratification are called freestones. Stones are more easily worked when they are green than after they have seasoned and the quarry sap has drained and evaporated.

Abrasive resistance is desirable in stair treads, door saddles, and floor finishes.

The color of a stone may be a determining factor in its selection for a given building.

Stone masonry and cut-stone facings are used in exterior and interior walls where appearance is the deciding factor, and trimstone is set in exterior brick masonry walls. Stone is used on interiors for wainscoting, mantels, hearths, floor tile, steps, and stairways.

Many stones satisfactory for interiors are unsuitable for exterior climatic conditions, and some stones satisfactory for ordinary building purposes have low resistance to abrasion and are unsuitable for steps, door sills, and floors. Stones that are durable, strong, and attractive may be unsuitable because of excessive labor costs. Some stones not suitable for accurately shaped and carefully finished first-class masonry are satisfactory for cruder stone masonry. Stones soft enough to work readily frequently lack durability. Ornamental moldings and carvings require freestones with even grain, free from seams and other defects. Delicate carvings require a stone of considerable strength to withstand damage. Appearances may demand stone of a certain color.

QUARRYING

Quarrying separates rough blocks of stone from rock formations. In small quarries, hand tools may be used exclusively; but in larger quarries, special machinery is used. Because the use of explosives causes excessive waste, their use is confined chiefly to the removal of overburden to expose the solid stone.

The nature of the rock formation may determine the quarrying methods. The contact surfaces of adjacent layers or beds offer planes along which separation is easily accomplished. The beds may be so close that the stone is useful for flagging only, or the beds may be so far apart or so indistinct that they are of little assistance in quarrying; but the stones may be of greater value in spite of this fact, for the size of the stones is then not limited by the beds.

The unstratified rocks such as granite do not lie in separate layers but have a massive structure. Surfaces of separation have to be made by artificial means. Such rocks may split more easily in one direction than in another.

Both stratified and unstratified rock formations may be divided by seams running in any direction. Seams may be an advantage or a disadvantage because of the limitations of size and shape of the pieces. These seams may be very conspicuous and offer a distinct surface of separation; they may not be discovered until considerable work has been done on a stone; or they may even cause failure after work has been done in a structure. Streaks may occur in stone without necessarily reducing its strength.

If a formation is badly broken by beds and seams, the rock may be removed with crowbars, picks, and wedges, but the dimension stones are difficult to secure under these conditions except in small sizes.

Building stone is removed in rough blocks, which are later cut into the desired size. Rough blocks may be separated from the rock formation along a line by drilling a row of closely spaced holes and splitting the rock between the

FIGURE 5.12 Wedge and shims or plug and feathers.

holes by plug and feathers. The plug is a steel wedge, and the feathers are semicircular wedges that fit the hole; they are flat where the steel wedge is driven, as shown in Figure 5.12. Plug and feathers are placed in each hole, and each plug is gradually driven. By continuing this operation, sufficient force splits the rock. In stratified stone, the blocks are split along a cleavage plane parallel to the bed, which gives a natural surface of separation. In unstratified rocks, plug and feathers may be used along two planes at right angles to each other. Plug and feathers are also known as wedge and shims. The splitting is sometimes accomplished by wooden plugs driven in the holes and soaked with water, which causes the plugs to expand and split the rock.

Channeling machines, widely used for quarrying, cut narrow vertical channels along the face of the block, as deep as 10 or 15 ft. The blocks are separated from the quarry ledge at a bedding plane, or split along a horizontal plane by drilling holes and driving wedges.

The plug-and-feathers method, suitable on any kind of stone, is used in granite quarrying. The channeling method, not suitable for granite, is commonly used for quarrying sandstone, although the plug-and-feathers method is more suitable.

Fieldstones found loose in nature are used for building. They are used in their natural shape or they are split or shaped with a hammer. Cobblestones, defined as large pebbles, are used in the same way.

MILLING

Quarried blocks of stone are milled into the finished product. Milling includes sawing blocks into slabs of desired thickness with gang saws or circular saws; planing the surface finish or cutting moldings on their surfaces; turning columns, balusters, etc., in lathes; milling recesses, patterns, and lettering on the faces of stones by means of a milling machine; carving the stone into various forms with hand tools or with hand-operated pneumatic tools; and finishing the surface as described below.

Cut stone or dressed stone is the product of the stone mill. Stones of large size or special shape, or any stone with measurements specified in advance, other than finished cut stone, are called dimension stones.

SURFACE FINISH

There are various methods of finishing the exposed surface. The finish suitable for a given surface is governed by the kind of stone and its functional use and varies from the rough face formed in quarrying to the highly polished face often used on marbles and granites.

A quarry face is the face on a stone as it comes from the quarry. It may be scabbed by the quarrying operations, or by a natural seam called a seam face. Quarries producing seam-face stone are traversed in many directions by natural seams forming relatively small blocks of stone of irregular shape and size. Seam faces are often highly colored by deposits from mineral-laden waters which have penetrated the seams. A split face is formed by splitting a rock.

A sawed finish has visible saw marks. This may be similar to a shot ground or shot rubbed finish, which has arched markings left by drilled shot used in cutting. A smooth finish is produced by planers without handwork other than the removal of objectionable tool marks.

The 4 cut, 6 cut, and 8 cut are corrugated surfaces identified by the number of corrugations per inch.

A thermal finish, produced by heating a granite surface, causes certain crystals to expand and pop out and resembles a rough split face.

Rubbed and honed finishes are produced by machine grinding or hand rubbing a sawed or pointed surface. Small surfaces and moldings are usually hand finished. A coarse rubbed finish shows small scratches, but a honed finish gives a smooth dead surface practically free from scratches.

A polished finish is obtained by polishing honed surfaces. Granite and marble will hold a polish, but most other stones will not.

The margin or border of a stone may have one finish and the remaining area another. Stones finished with dual finishes are called drafted stones.

Sandblasting is used to cut lettering and designs into granite. In this operation, the polished surface is coated with a molten rubberlike substance called dope, which forms an elastic covering. The design is cut into this covering, exposing the stone surface. The exposed stone is then sandblasted, while the elastic coating protects the remaining stone.

SELECTING SURFACE FINISH

Appropriate finish depends upon the type of masonry, the kind of stone, its position and function in the building, the appearance desired, the atmospheric conditions, and the funds available.

The finish selection giving the desired results at least cost is usually chosen. Satisfactory results are often produced at low cost with quarry, seam, or split-face rubble masonry.

All the types of finish may be used on granite and marble;

and except for polishing, they may be used on sandstone and limestone. Limestone that can be polished is usually classed as marble. The hammered finishes are suitable only for the harder sandstones and limestones, for on the softer stones the ridges will not stand up but will break off leaving a bruised face. These finishes, often called hardstone finishes, are unsuitable for soft stone. The tooled finishes, similar to the hammered finishes, are more suitable for soft stones.

In general, rubble masonry is quarry face or pitched face; and ashlar or cut-stone masonry is a pointed or hammered face if granite and a sawed, smooth, or rubbed face if limestone or sandstone. Marble is usually rubbed or honed for exteriors and either honed or polished for interiors. A quarry face or pitch face may be used for ashlar.

Because of the ease in cleaning, polished surfaces are often the base courses for parts that might be soiled and for lower stories exposed to a smoky atmosphere. The fine finishes keep clean longer.

The sawed finish is the most economical finish for limestone and sandstone, except the harder grades.

The finer finishes are more suitable for interiors than the coarser finishes; but on the exterior the finer finishes fail to show if used above the first floor.

WASHES AND DRIPS

The exposed top surfaces of cornices, copings, belt courses, and sills, steps, platforms, and other stones should

FIGURE 5.13 Washes and drips.

be provided with sloping surfaces called *washes* (Figure 5.13A).

Projecting cornices, belt courses, and sills are provided with a groove or channel called a *drip* on the under surface near the outer edge. The drip causes water to drip from the lower edge of the stone rather than shedding along the wall. Drips should be at least ½ in. wide by ¼ in. deep *(A)*.

Stonework will usually streak or soil where washes pitch toward the face of the stonework. Thus, copings should pitch toward the roof and water drained off projecting stones.

Where other work is built on stones provided with a wash, it is usually necessary to cut raised seats and lugs at the jamb, forming level beds for the work built on them *(B)*.

CLASSIFICATION OF STONE MASONRY

Stone masonry is classed by the refinement in shaping the face stone arrangement and the surface finish of the stones.

There are no absolute classification standards; but in general, the crudest masonry, constructed of stones with little or no shaping, is called *rubble,* and the highest form, constructed of shaped stones, is *ashlar.* Between these two classes are degrees in shaping and various stone arrangements. The most common classification divides masonry into rubble, squared-stone masonry, and ashlar, according to the care in shaping the stones, and into range, broken range, and random, according to the arrangement of the stones in the wall. The latter classification does not apply to rubble. Rubble is classed as coursed or uncoursed. Ashlar is also called cut stone.

Lines of demarcation are undefined between ashlar, squared-stone masonry, and rubble. When stratified stone is used, the horizontal joints of rubble may be as narrow and as uniform as those of squared-stone masonry; the distinction between the two classes is the vertical joints. If only the sharp corners are knocked off loose rock, it is rubble; but if the stone is shaped to give a uniform vertical joint, it is squared-stone masonry. If the end joints are not vertical but are uniform in thickness, the class would be identical to squared-stoned masonry but could not logically be placed in that class because of the shape of the stone.

Sometimes the joints are as thin as ashlar joints, but the end joints are not vertical. Such masonry should probably be classed as ashlar. Polygonal masonry is made of irregular stones without parallel surfaces; these stones are shaped to fit the spaces they are to occupy, and the joints are neither vertical nor horizontal. Stones in polygonal masonry are sometimes accurately cut with joints as thin and uniform as ashlar. Often the stones are only roughly shaped, and the joints are nonuniform. This type of masonry is often called mosaic rubble or cobweb rubble. It is structurally questionable because it is difficult to reinforce.

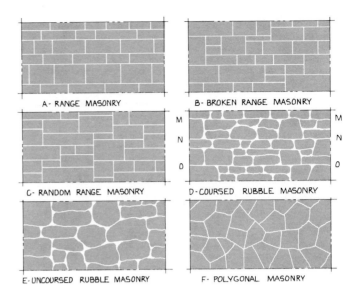

FIGURE 5.14 Classes of stone masonry.

ARRANGEMENT OF COURSES

In range masonry, the stones are laid in uniform courses throughout the length. All courses, however, are not the same thickness (Figure 5.14A).

In broken-range masonry, the stones are coursed, but for short distances only *(B)*.

In random masonry, no attempt is made to form courses *(C)*. The terms range, broken-range, and random are usually applied only to ashlar and squared-stone masonry; but where rubble masonry is constructed of stratified stones, the upper and lower surfaces may be parallel, resulting in random masonry, although rubble masonry is generally divided into coursed and uncoursed rubble.

In coursed rubble, the masonry is leveled at specified heights *(D)* or is laid in fairly regular courses marked *m-m, n-n, o-o* in the figure. Uncoursed rubble masonry is not leveled as in coursed rubble *(E)*.

BACKING

In rubble masonry, the face and backing are usually rubble, the better stones being selected for the face; however, concrete backing may be used.

The backing for squared-stone masonry and ashlar masonry may be rubble masonry, brick, structural clay tile, or concrete block. Rubble masonry is unsuitable for backing thin panel walls. If rough stone blocks are shaped at the building site, the stone shards are used in the rubble backing. Ashlar or squared-stone masonry is not used for backing.

Concrete backing should not be placed against limestone facing or against brickwork in contact with limestone without providing a waterproof layer between stone and concrete. If a waterproof layer is not provided, the stone may be discolored. Certain stones may not require waterproof backing, but it should not be omitted without a thorough investigation. Ashlar is often used as a veneer over concrete walls or other surfaces.

Facing stones used over brick or structural clay tile backing should intermesh with the backing, creating horizontal through-wall joints at intervals desired for bonding.

SETTING

Placing stone in position is called *setting.* Stones lifted by derricks are held with grab hooks, as shown in Figure 5.15*A,* or with lewises *(B),* or with pin lewises in inclined holes *(C).* If lewises are used, lewis holes must be provided 3 in. to 4 in. deep. The most common type of lewis is assembled in the hole, as shown in *(B).*

Stratified stone should be dressed to set with the natural quarry bed horizontally because, when so oriented, it has greater strength and greater resistance to weathering. Water enters more freely, and the stone weathers and scales off badly and more rapidly when the quarry bed is vertical.

The setting of Indiana limestone on its natural quarry bed requires little concern. The great majority of such ashlar is sawed with the grain parallel to the face of the wall, and monolithic columns are produced with the grain running vertical. However, most limestones are somewhat weaker when loaded parallel to the bedding than when loaded perpendicular to the bedding.

Door and window sill ends built into the masonry should be bedded only at the ends, the space between left entirely free from mortar except for the pointing mortar which is applied later. If this practice is not followed, the sills are quite certain to break when the ends are loaded. This type of sill is called a lug sill. Window sills called slip sills are made slightly shorter than the intended opening and are independent of the masonry, except the mortar bed. Exterior steps and sills are pitched to the front, permitting drainage.

Nonstaining mortar should be used in setting limestone facing and its backing. The application of waterproof cement mortar to the back of the facing masonry or the face of the backing material is called parging, pargeting, or back plastering. Parging increases the resistance of the wall to moisture penetration and prevents efflorescence. The use of nonstaining cement mortar, however, deters staining. It is preferred that the backing masonry be free from soluble salts.

The practice of back painting the sides or backs of facing stones with bituminous waterproofing to prevent efflorescence is objectionable because the stones may become discolored.

FIGURE 5.15 Methods of lifting stone blocks.

FIGURE 5.16 Bonding and anchoring stone masonry.

BONDSTONES AND ANCHORS

Longitudinal stone masonry bond is secured by breaking joints as in brick masonry, although in broken-range and random masonry a vertical joint may be three stones high.

Bond between the face and backing is secured by headers or bondstones by bond courses, by metal anchors, or by a combination of these materials.

The bond or anchorage required between the face and backing depends on whether the wall is a bearing wall or a nonbearing wall and if the required wall thickness includes the facing.

Headers extending entirely through the wall are shown in Figure 5.16A.

Bondstones projecting into the backing an amount equal to the thickness of the other facing stones are shown in (B), with one bed of every stone in contact with a bondstone. The arrangement shown in (C) makes every other course a bond course. Only 10% of the stones in a bond course are required to be bondstones; and in broken-range and random masonry, the bondstones are distributed at random throughout the wall, with each stone providing the tie for a given surface area. Noncorrosive metal anchors, usually stainless steel, tie the facing to the backing (D). Bond courses and anchors are usually used together. In (E), the anchors are supplemented by a bond course bearing on the spandrel beam of each story. The combination of bond courses and anchors is shown in (F). Every stone not a bondstone may be anchored to the backing, as shown in (G). The method of anchoring a cut-stone cornice is illustrated in (H). Special anchors should be provided for cornice and belt-course stones that have insufficient bearing on the wall. These anchors should be hooked into the stone at least 2 in. and spaced about 2 ft, with at least two anchors to a stone.

For further discussion of the bond requirements see Section 5.4.

JOGGLED, TABLED, AND REBATED JOINTS

The types of joints rarely used are the joggled joint shown in Figure 5.16P and the tabled joint or bed joggle joint shown in (S), designed to prevent movement along a joint. These joints are very expensive to form. A slate or metal joggle joint (Q) may be formed more economically. The joint is not usually continuous. A rebated joint shown in (R) is sometimes used for coping stones placed on a slope.

FACED AND VENEERED WALLS

Stone walls may be classed as faced walls and veneered walls according to the provision made for bonding the face to the backing. If the facing and backing are securely bonded and acting as a unit, the entire wall thickness may be considered in strength calculations and in satisfying requirements for minimum thickness. Such walls are called faced walls. If the facing is not attached and bonded to the backing to the extent that it forms an integral part of the wall, the wall is called a veneered wall, and only the backing may be considered in strength calculations and in satisfying the requirements for minimum thickness.

JOINTS AND POINTING

The mortar layers between stones are called *joints.* Horizontal joints are bed joints or simply beds; vertical joints are known as head joints or builds; and joints between wythes are called collar joints.

In rubble masonry, the joints are neither uniform in thickness nor constant in direction; they simply are the spaces between stones of irregular shapes. Large spaces in the backing may have small pieces of stone called spalls embedded in the mortar.

In squared-stone masonry, the joints are horizontal and vertical and are uniform in thickness, the stones having been roughly dressed to shape. In general, the joints in squared-stone masonry are ½ to 1 in. thick.

In ashlar or cut-stone masonry, the stones are accurately dressed to shape so that the joints do not exceed ½ in. in thickness. A very common thickness of joint for the ashlar facing of buildings is ¼ in. Joints ⅛ in. thick are sometimes used for interior stonework but are not desirable for exterior work.

The mortar in the horizontal and vertical joints of ashlar masonry is kept back from the face in setting the stone or is raked out to a depth of about ¾ in. In this space, a special mortar is placed to make a tighter and more attractive joint. This process is known as pointing. The various types of joints formed by pointing are shown in Figure 5.17. Pointing is done after the mortar in the joint has set and usually after all the stone has been placed and the wall has received its full load.

Squared-stone masonry may be pointed in the same manner as ashlar, or the joint may be finished at the time the stone is set.

The joints in rubble masonry are usually finished when the stones are set, and no pointing is done.

Often the joints of squared-stone masonry or rubble are made flush with the surface of the stones, and after the mortar has set, a narrow bead of colored mortar is run on the wide joints to give the effect of narrow joints (see Figure 5.17B). The wide joint is frequently made the same color as the stone, and the narrow joint is made a contrasting color.

The joints are often emphasized by forming rusticated or rebated joints (C). This joint is frequently used in the stonework on the lower stories, giving a massive appearance.

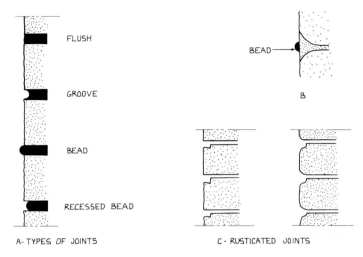

FIGURE 5.17 Joints for stone masonry.

TRIMSTONE

Cut stone is frequently used as a trim around window and door openings and for belt courses, copings, and cornices in walls constructed of brick or rubble masonry. Stone used in this manner is called trimstone.

5.3 Unit Masonry

CONCRETE BLOCK (CMU)

Concrete block, also known as *concrete masonry unit* (CMU), is made of a cement, aggregate, and water. The cement is usually standard portland cement or a blended cement. A pozzolan or Type S hydrated lime may be added. The aggregates are normal weight aggregate.

MANUFACTURE

Block are formed in machines with steel molds; the mix is consolidated by vibrating and compacting. This provides accurately formed block and permits the moist mixture. Thus, the molds can be removed immediately after impact. Commercial production is by a power-driven automated machine with gang molds that produce thousands of units each day.

The block are cured and dried. The tendency of the clock to crumble, shrink, and crack is deterred by curing. During the curing operation, the blocks are kept moist so that setting and hardening is gradual. During the drying operation, the moisture content is reduced to average air humidity, preventing the moisture of the block from being reduced by the surrounding air at the time of laying.

Curing and drying are accomplished in the open air with protection from the weather, by blowing heated air through stacked block, by high-temperature steam curing in sealed kilns, or by high-pressure steam curing in a pressure vessel called an autoclave that is filled with saturated steam at a temperature of about 370°F.

The open-air procedure requires from 2 to 4 weeks; the heated-air process is more rapid, although steam curing is accomplished in about 12 hours. Units stored, either at the plant or on the job site, should be protected against absorbing moisture from rain or snow.

Other added ingredients of CMUs may be air-entraining agents, water repellents or coloring agents. The water must be clean and free from deleterious substances, acids, or sugars. Generally, potable water is suitable. Water must be sufficient to produce a moist mixture that resembles damp, loose sand.

BLOCK CLASSIFICATION

Concrete masonry units fall into four general classifications: hollow, load-bearing (ASTM C 90), solid load-bearing (ASTM C 145), and as non-load-bearing block (ASTM C 129), which is either solid or hollow.

Classification of load-bearing units is divided into two grades, N and S, and two types, I and II. Grades are specified according to intended use; those blocks that qualify for the more severe exposure are designated Grade N. Block requiring protection from the weather are termed Grade S.

The distinction between solid CMUs and hollow CMUs is that solid units must be 75% solid material in any general cross section leaving a maximum of 25% of the gross area in cells or cores.

Non-load-bearing CMUs are generally used for interior partitions that carry no imposed loads. In favorable climates they may be used for exterior non-load-bearing walls.

BLOCK WEIGHT

Load-bearing block are classified by weight as normal weight, medium weight, and lightweight. Block weights are determined by the type of aggregate used. Ordinary aggregate such as gravel, crushed stone, and air-cooled slag produce heavier block. They weigh approximately 40 to 50 lb for a standard 8 by 8 by 16 stretcher block.

Lightweight aggregates are coal cinders, expanded shale, clay or slap, and natural lightweight materials, such as volcanic cinders, pumice, Haydite, and vermiculite. They are used extensively for lightweight block, which weighs approximately 50% of the block that is produced by heavyweight aggregates.

CMU DIMENSIONS AND SIZES

Concrete block is manufactured in standard or actual dimensions. These actual dimensions are ⅜ in. less that the nominal dimensions, or the difference between the actual dimensions and the nominal dimensions provides for a 3/8 in. mortar joint. The proper sequencing of a CMU dimension is to identify the width, height, and then length. Thus a CMU dimension that is nominally 8 in. wide by 4 in. high by 16 in. long is actually 7 5/8 in. by 3 5/8 in. by 15 5/8 in. or nominally billed 8 × 4 × 16. The nominal dimensions of CMUs are composed of nearly any combination of the following: widths are 4, 6, 8, 10 and 12 in. and lengths come in 6, 8, 12, 16, and 24 in. Generally a full block would be 16 in. long and a half block 8 in. long (see Figure 5.18).

Several special shapes are molded for specific locations. Single and double square, bullnose corner, sash or jambs, and header block receive the headers and serve as end block. Other special shapes are U-shaped lintel or beam block, sill block for openings, pilaster block, and column block for structural purposes.

Pilasters are usually 16 by 16 in. made of special pilaster block. Horizontal reinforcement passes through the pilaster and vertical reinforcement usually consists of about four No. 6 bars, which may have horizontal ties of No. 2 bars every 24 in. in height.

Specifications for concrete block include requirements for moisture content, absorption, and compressive strength.

SURFACE FINISH

The exposed surfaces are usually plain. The surface finish or texture may be fine, medium, or coarse, depending upon the grading of the aggregates.

Lightweight concrete block are glazed with an impervious surface 1/8 to 3/8 in. thick. This glaze is formed by mixing selected mineral aggregates, pigments, and a thermosetting plastic binder. The plastic binder is formed and then hardened at elevated temperatures using the high-pressure curing process. Block of the usual sizes are manufactured in nearly 50 colors. The surface of the shell face conforms to the requirements to form coves, returns, caps, and the other shapes necessary for a complete glazed masonry surface. This type of block has the distinct advantages of a glazed moisture-resistant surface in a single wythe unit, thus eliminating applied finishes with their attendant ties.

Some have surfaces with a molded face shell of various geometric designs.

PATTERNED BLOCK

Recent developments have produced patterned block that have face shells with a raised or recessed geometric design. These blocks can be used in various orientations that give more variety and emphasis when used in conjunction with the flat surface shell faces. Striking shadow effects are achieved with these blocks.

SCREEN BLOCK

Pierced grill block, called screen block, are frequently used as solar screens. These blocks, usually 12 in. square, may have designs similar to the patterned face shells of the solid block. These block require independent support by a structural frame.

WALL CONSTRUCTION

Concrete block walls and partitions are normally one block thick and laid with broken or staggered vertical joints. Concrete block are used as backing for exterior walls faced with brick or stone. (Figure 5.16). Special units are available for corners, jambs, and other purposes, as has been explained. Half-block units may also be obtained.

Cavity walls are constructed of two wythes of blocks, each at least 4 in. thick, separated by an air space of from 2 to 3 in. and tied together, as required, with noncorrosive metal ties.

The mortar in the bed joint usually covers only the face shells; but if strength is an important factor, the webs are also covered. The mortar covers only the shells in forming the head or vertical joints. The normal joint thickness is 3/8 in. The preferred joints are the Vee and concave joints, illustrated in Figure 5.7, which are made by exerting pressure while running a tool along full or flush partially set mortar joints. They are more watertight than other types of joints. Even then, exposed exterior wall surfaces should be treated.

SURFACE TREATMENTS

In regions subject to driving rains, exterior, above-grade concrete block walls are quite likely to leak because of water which penetrates the joints or the block. Such leakage can be prevented by the application of portland cement stucco or by coating with portland cement paint. Such paints are mixed with water and are available in an endless variety of colors.

The outside face of concrete block foundation walls should be parged.

Interior wall surfaces require no treatment except for decorative purposes. Neither exterior nor interior wall surfaces of glazed block, of course, require surface treatment, but extreme care should be used in laying exterior block to secure watertight joints.

FIRE-RESISTIVE CONSTRUCTION USING CMUs

Walls and partitions made of CMUs may qualify for the most restrictive fire ratings (4 hours) and for the most restrictive construction, Type I. However, the fire rating is dependent upon the type of aggregate used in the CMU and the face-

(Dimensions shown are actual unit sizes. A 7⅝″ x 7⅝″ x 15⅝″ unit is commonly known as an 8″ x 8″ x 16″ block.)

FIGURE 5.18 Typical sizes and shapes of concrete masonry units. TM5-742, *Concrete and Masonry,* Department of the Army, June, 1970.

to-face thickness of the unit. Blocks made of pumice provide the best protection; for example, a thickness of only 4.7 in. has a 4-hour rating. Practically speaking, this would require a 6-in.-wide block. Other CMUs with aggregates such as expanded clay or shale and limestone, cinders, or air-cooled slag, as well as calcareous or siliceous gravel have 4-hour ratings for units that are 8 in. wide.

CMU TESTING

A representative sample (6 per 10,000) of full-size units is tested for compression, absorption, and dimension according to ASTM C 140. In the compression test the block is capped and compressed to determine its ultimate strength. The compressive unit force is calculated and recorded in psi. The absorption test requires immersion in water for 24 hours and a like drying time. The units are weighed before, during, and after immersion and after drying. The moisture percentage absorbed and the moisture content of the CMU is calculated.

GLASS BLOCK

Glass block are hollow, translucent, masonry units formed by fusing, at high temperature, two sections that have been cast separately. A manufacturing process seals the block and produces a partial vacuum in an interior. The exposed faces are patterned or shaped. The interior or exterior surfaces of each face may be smooth, ribbed horizontally or vertically, or covered with a ceramic coat. If patterned on the interior, the exposed surfaces are smooth, which permits easy cleaning while assuring privacy and noise reduction. Their primary function is to transmit diffused light through walls. Suitable patterns direct the light to the ceilings from which it is reflected downward. They are more resistant to heat and sound transmission and condensation than ordinary glass.

Special block, more resistant to heat transmission, are more effective in brightness control—special properties are achieved by dividing the interior cavity with fibrous glass screens during manufacture. In some cases, the screen is a blue-green and imparts this color to the block.

Glass block are set in exterior walls and interior partitions but carry no load other than their own weight. Glass block are laid in stacked bond only.

Glass block were quite popular following their introduction in the 1930s. Their popularity waned, but renewed interest in this form is increasing; there are several innovative and tasteful variations of glass block units.

Sculptured glass modules measuring 12 by 12 by 4 in. wide have a shaped geometric design in the two exposed faces. Another type of unit features a design in gray ceramic that frames recessed antiqued clear glass while still another type is coated on the edges and has raised glass patterns on the block face.

Glass block are manufactured in numerous colors, as well as clear transparent glass.

CLASSES OF HOLLOW UNITS

Hollow units made of burned clay or shale, gypsum, and glass are less extensively used in the construction of walls and partitions. The terms tile and block represent a single unit or can be used collectively to represent a number of such units, as in the case of brick. The term *terra-cotta*, meaning "burned earth," is sometimes applied to structural clay tile, but this term is preferably reserved for ornamental building units of burned clay, usually classed as architectural terracotta. Hollow clay tile are usually called structural clay tile.

STRUCTURAL CLAY TILE

These units are manufactured by the stiff mud process, which consists of extruding or forcing a plastic clay through specially formed dies, cutting it to the desired dimensions, and burning it in kilns to various degrees of hardness, depending upon the grade being manufactured. The hollow spaces in the tile are called cells or cores. The outer walls are called shells, and the inner partitions between cells are called webs. The shells are ¾ in. or more thick and the webs ½ in. or more.

Many types of units are manufactured. Special shapes are for coves, corners, and jambs so that the ends of the cells will not be exposed if the cells are laid horizontally. Sills and headers receive the ends of brick headers so that cutting will not be required.

Specifications for structural clay tile include requirements for absorption and, for load-bearing units, compressive strength.

CLASSES OF STRUCTURAL CLAY TILE

Structural clay tile are divided into two classes according to the orientation of the axes of the cells when the units are placed in masonry. In side-construction tile, the cells are placed horizontally; and in end-construction tile, vertically (see Figure 5.19). Structural clay tile are divided into two classes according to loading condition: load-bearing (ASTM C 34) and non-load-bearing (ASTM C 56). Non-load-bearing tile are usually called partition tile because of their use in nonbearing partitions.

There are two grades of structural load-bearing tile. *LBX Grade* is used where exposure to weather is a factor, and *LB* is suitable in protected locations (ASTM C 34). Non-load-bearing tile has only one grade. *NB* (ASTM C 56).

2″ x 5″ SOAP

(A) Side construction   (B) End construction

FIGURE 5.19 Tile wall construction. TM5-742, *Concrete and Masonry*, Department of the Army, June, 1970.

Structural clay tile are divided into two broad groups according to their function in a multiple-unit wall: backing or back-up tile, which backs up various facing units such as brick and stone or serves as a base for stucco; and facing tile (ASTM C 212), which has a finished surface on the one or two exposed sides. Facing tile may have solid shells, double shells, or cored shells. Facing tile grading is based on mechanical perfection, absorption rate, stain resistance, ease of cleaning, color range, dimensional tolerances, surface texture, and suitability for exposure to weather. Type FTX is a better grade than Type FTS. Face tile is further classified as standard, which is for general use, and as special duty, which is used for areas requiring superior strength, resistance to impact, and better moisture impedance (ASTM C 212).

SIZES

Structural clay tile usually has a nominal length of 12 in., although some types are 16 in. The actual lengths are shy ½, ⅜, or ¼ in. The nominal dimensions allow for the mortar joints while still maintaining a 4-in. module.

Structural clay tile sizes identified by first stating the width, then the dimension perpendicular to the cells, and finally the dimension that is parallel to the long axis of the cells. The side-construction tile if called out as 8 by 5⅓ by 12, whereas the tile of the same dimensions in end-construction tile is identified as 8 by 12 by 5⅓ — a switch in the last two dimensions (see Figure 5.20).

SURFACE TEXTURE AND COLOR

The surface finish selected for structural clay is determined by the use to be made of the tile. The following finishes are available: natural or smooth, scored, combed, or roughened (by wire cutting or brushing), salt glaze, and ceramic glaze.

The natural or smooth finish is specified for exposed surfaces that are to be untreated or painted. The scored finish provides increased bond for plaster or stucco finishes, although investigations have shown that the unglazed, smooth finish provides an adequate plaster bond. The roughened finishes achieve a desired texture, but they may be used to receive plaster. The salt and ceramic glazes provide a desired appearance as well as low water absorption and easy cleaning.

Tile with natural or smooth and roughened finishes are produced in an assortment of colors, depending upon the composition of the clay and the degree of burning. Such colors include cream, gray, buff, brown, and various shades of red, purple, and black comparable to the colors of face brick.

Ceramic glazes or enamels are formed on surfaces of facing tile by spraying them with mineral glazing materials

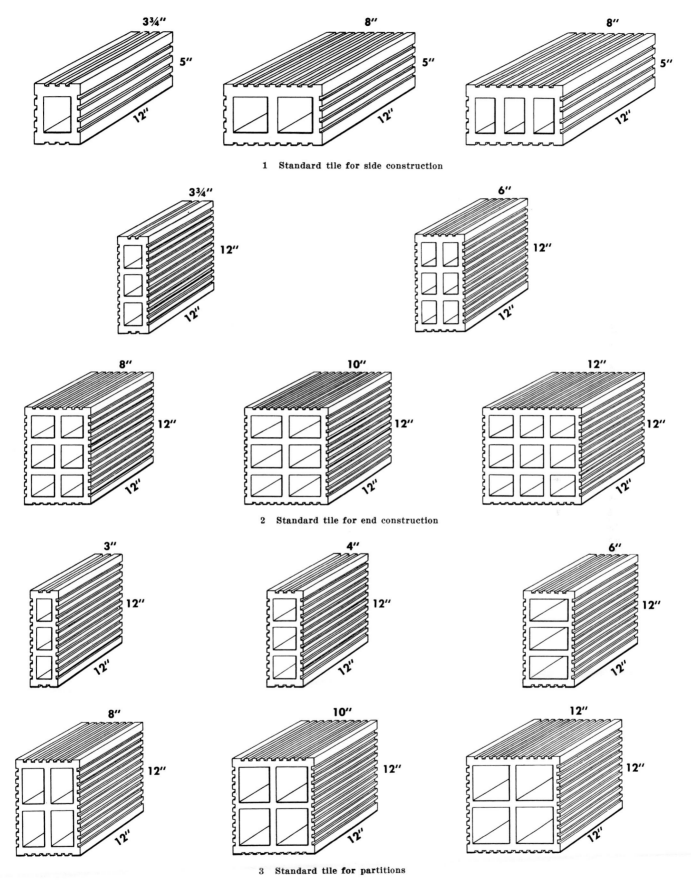

1   Standard tile for side construction

2   Standard tile for end construction

3   Standard tile for partitions

FIGURE 5.20 Types of structural clay tile. TM5-742, *Concrete and Masonry,* Department of the Army, June, 1970.

before burning. They are so constituted that they will fuse during burning and form a glass-like coating on the tile surface. They may form single or multicolor shades. Some of the single-color shades are white, light gray, ivory, yellow, coral, tan, blue, and green. Multicolor glazes include mottles of white, gray, cream, and green with a trim shade of black.

WALL CONSTRUCTION

Structural clay tile backing units are laid with facings of ceramic tile, concrete block, terra-cotta, brick, stone, and structural clay tile facing units. The backing units may be either end-construction or side-construction.

The tile are normally laid with the vertical joints staggered as in the stretcher bond of brick masonry (Figure 5.3), but they are altered to provide for bonders as required. Joints should have full mortar coverage of the ends and edges of the face shells.

Tile walls can be reinforced with horizontal reinforcing. Vertical reinforcing can be in-placed through grouted cells only in end-construction tile, whereas vertical reinforcing for side-construction tile must pass between wythes.

ARCHITECTURAL TERRA-COTTA

Architectural terra-cotta building units are hard-burned clay. They are glazed or unglazed, plain or ornamental, machine-extruded or hand-molded, and generally larger than brick or facing tile.

The units are hollow or ribbed and made in a great variety of surface finishes, textures, colors, and designs. Their function is decorative.

Ceramic veneer is architectural terra-cotta characterized by large face dimensions and thin sections. The thinner sections are held in place by adhesion to mortar between the terra-cotta and the backing; and the thicker sections, by grout and wire anchors connected to the backing.

Selection of terra-cotta for outside installation must consider a product that will not spall or crack and one whose exposed surface will not craze or flake off under weather conditions.

5.4 Masonry Accessories

There are a number of reinforcements and accessories that may be required for masonry construction. They include horizontal and vertical reinforcement, anchors, water stops, and inserts. These accessories are frequently made of plain and corrosion-resistant metal and plastics.

REINFORCEMENT

Prefabricated horizontal reinforcement is made of stainless steel, and cold drawn steel wire in brite (uncoated), in zinc coated, and in hot dipped galvanized finishes. These rods are drawn in 8, 9, and 11 gages and in 3/16 in. diameters. The rods are then fabricated using various rod size combinations and designs.

FIGURE 5.21 Masonry reinforcement.

Horizontal steel reinforcement may consist of an assembly of two, three, or four parallel side rods welded to cross ties or cross rods. The cross rods may run perpendicular to the side rods, forming a ladder assembly, or the cross rods may weave back and forth between the side rods, forming a trusslike shape. These zinc coated or galvanized reinforcement assemblies are made of 8, 9, 11, ga. or ³⁄₁₆ in. rods or various combinations of these sizes, the size being determined by structural considerations. The heavier combinations, ³⁄₁₆ horizontal rods and ties are required for resisting stronger lateral loads. These reinforcements are made especially for walls of one wythe from 3 to 16 in. wide and for faced walls or composite walls and for cavity walls. This type of reinforcement is usually 8 to 12 ft long. At outside or inside corners and at wall intersections special L-shaped and T-shaped fabrications are available that assure continuity in reinforcement. Usually, this prefabricated type of horizontal reinforcement is continuous with 12 in. laps at bar ends and generally placed in every other course (see Figure 5.21).

Galvanized woven wire mesh, similar in pattern to poultry wire, with two longitudinal rods, is also made. Regular reinforcement bars — usually No. 4 or No. 5 bars — set in grout-filled bond beam block are frequently used. Continuous bond beams are usually about 4 ft centers.

Vertical wall reinforcement invariably consists of reinforcement bars encased in the middle of the grout-filled cells. Rebar sizing is always dependent upon the structural requirements but usually consists of No. 5 bars spaced on about 24 in. centers. Bars usually extend out of the foundations at an optimum height of about 60 in., and the block are threaded over the reinforcement and set in place. Reinforcement continues to the full wall height with splices made as required, with laps measuring not less than 24 bar diameters.

Such reinforcement alleviates the stresses caused by block shrinkage or temperature change. The visible cracking on the surface that would otherwise result is thereby deterred. This action is similar to that of temperature and shrinkage reinforcement in reinforced concrete slabs. Reinforcement is also effective in reducing cracking caused by differential settlement or deflection over openings in the wall. By controlling cracking, increased resistance to water penetration is achieved. Lateral reinforcement ties the wythes of cavity walls together and laps or otherwise carries intersecting walls together around corners and anchors. In regions subject to seismic forces, lateral reinforcement is required to resist these shocks.

The cells of all blocks are usually filled with a grout mix.

METAL WALL TIES

Metal ties, if properly made, do not permit moisture penetration. Metal masonry ties should be corrosion resistant and crimped or twisted. This forms a drip so that moisture does not bridge across the tie. They are effective in separating two wythes, but a load applied to the inner wythes cannot be transmitted through the ties to the outer wythe.

ANCHORAGE

Anchors are usually placed in the horizontal joints and hooked into the tops of stones, but at times it is desirable to hook the anchors into the side of the vertical joints near the top and bottom of the stone, especially when structural clay tile backing is used. A typical form of anchor is shown in Figure 5.16 (I).

Anchors should not be placed in the mortar joint, but a sinkage or depression of ample width and of a depth slightly greater than the thickness of the anchor should be provided at the back of anchor holes (J). There are two reasons for providing sinkages. With the ¼-in. joints usually used in ashlar masonry, there would be difficulty in placing the anchors in the joints; the stones would tend to rest on the anchors rather than to secure uniform bearing on the mortar joint. This condition would tend to cause the stones to crack. The sinkages do not fit the anchor accurately but are usually larger than necessary and are crudely formed. Anchor holes should be kept about 2 in. from the outer surface of the stonework so that the anchor may be adequately protected. The anchors should be completely embedded in mortar or lead.

Rustproof anchors should be made of stainless steel or noncorrosive metal or steel that is galvanized after cutting and shaping. Rust may stain the stonework, split the stone by expansion while rusting, or finally destroy the anchor. Coating anchors with paint will not supplant galvanizing, but it is an additional precaution.

A dovetail anchor convenient for anchoring a stone facing to a concrete wall is shown in (K). Before the wall is poured, sheet-metal troughs are tacked vertically at proper intervals to the side of the form for the outer face. When the forms are stripped, the trough is exposed in the face of the wall. It is beveled on the sides to receive an anchor with a dovetailed end. The anchors are adjusted up and down to fit into the joints. This anchor is more convenient and effective than most types of anchors, which are cast in concrete walls and are bent out into the mortar joints of the facing.

LEWIS ANCHORS, CRAMPS, DOWELS

Anchors other than those described are sometimes required. When suspending the soffits of openings from steel work, lewis anchors, similar to the ordinary lewis, are used. Flat iron clamps or cramps keep coping stones and stair rails from falling apart. Cramps vary from 1¼ by ¼ in. for light work to 1½ by ½ in. for heavier pieces. These are turned down to 1½ or 2 in. at the ends and vary in length from 6 to

Table 5.2 **Mortar Proportions (parts by volume)**

Mortar Type	Minimum Compressive Strength at 28 Days (psi)	Portland Cement	Hydrated Limes or Lime Putty[a]		Masonry Cements	Damp Loose Aggregate
			Min.	*Max.*		
M	2500	1	—	¼	—	Not less than 2¼ and not more than 3 times the sum of the volumes of the cement and lime used
		1	—	—	1	
S	1800	1	¼	½	—	
		½	—	—	1	
N	750	1	½	1¼	—	
		—	—	—	1	
O	350	1	1¼	2½	—	

[a] When plastic or waterproof cement is used, hydrated lime or putty may be added but not in excess of one-tenth the volume of cement.

Reproduced from the 1976 edition of the *Uniform Building Code,* copyright 1976, with the permission of the publisher, the International Conference of Building Officials.

12 in. They may be set in sinkages in the tops of the stones, or they may be set under the stones with their ends turned upward into the stones. Cramps should be heavily galvanized after being bent to shape. On first-class work, they may be protected by pouring molten lead around them (Figure 5.16*L*), the holes being larger at the top in order to hold the lead and anchor in place. Cramps or keys of stone may be used in place of steel cramps *(M)*. The lead plug shown in *(O)* serves the same purpose but is rarely used. In forming the lead plug, molten lead is poured into the vertical channel and fills the dovetailed holes, which are sloped so that the lead can easily fill the holes. Brass or bronze dowels made of solid rods or of pipe are ordinarily used to hold the ends of balusters, window mullions, and similar pieces *(N)*. The ends of inclined copings may be doweled into the kneelers.

5.5 Mortar

Masonry units are bonded with mortar. It adheres to the units, joining them into a cohesive unified mass or bonding them to supporting structural members. Mortar strength is the critical factor in determining the design strength of masonry walls. Proportions are vital in obtaining desired strengths as indicated by Table 5.2.

Portland cements for mortars are usually Types I, II, or III (ASTM C 150). Air-entraining cements or admixtures are permitted but not recommended where high bond strengths are required. Specially manufactured masonry cement which is classified by Federal Specifications as

Type I is used in masonry above grade and not subject to frost. Type II masonry cement is more widely used for general masonry construction. If used, masonry cement should be the product of only one manufacturer because the properties vary among manufacturers and may produce undesirable results. Any unrevealed additives, whose bonding and durabilities may be questionable, should be avoided; and an architect or engineer would be exercising sound judgment in rejecting any material whose contents or results are unsubstantiated. Nonstaining cements should be used for marble, limestone, and terra-cotta masonry.

MORTAR FOR UNIT MASONRY

Mortar for unit masonry is a mixture of well-graded aggregates, portland cement, clean water, and — when required — hydrated lime. These materials are thoroughly mixed in a mechanical mixer for not less than 1½ minutes. The aggregates for unit masonry may be natural sand, sometimes called bank run sand, or "manufactured" sand, which consists of crushed stone, gravel, or air-cooled, iron blast furnace slag. The aggregate should conform to the grading limits specified by ASTM C 144. This requires grading by using the listed sieve sizes and the percentages passing that particular sieve.

The above gradation limitations provide for a well-graded and even distribution of different grain sizes. Excessive fines or material predominantly of one size is thus avoided. Proper gradation assures a more workable mix.

Mortar sands should be nonstaining and free from organic material. Sand is tested for organic impurities by placing a 3% solution of sodium hydroxide into a bottle containing a sample of sand. A discoloration appearing after 24 hours indicates the presence of organic matter. A standard color chart indicates the suitability of the sand for mortar use.

Lime putty is added to improve workability and water retentivity. Hydrated lime Type S, slaked not less than 24 hours before using, should be protected from the elements.

Water sufficient for a workable mix should be of the same quality required for concrete work, namely, clean, free from acids, sugars, and other impurities.

Mortar colors are produced by adding paste or powdered coloring agents to the mix. They are usually red, umber, or black. Other colors are available, but architects favor the earthen colors, which are more reliable. Colors should be finely ground and have high purity.

After all ingredients have been placed in a mechanical mixer, mortars should be mixed at least 3 minutes. Mortars that have lost water through evaporation may be retempered (water added) to maintain workability; however, mortars older than 2½ hours should be discarded.

TYPES OF MORTARS

Types of cement mortar for unit masonry are shown in Table 5.2. Type S and Type M are recommended for exterior structures at or below grade. Masonry load-bearing walls and parapets should be made of mortar with the qualifications of Types N or S. Non-load-bearing walls and partitions generally need only a mortar such as Type O.

GROUTS

The physical properties for aggregates to be used in grout are identical to those of mortar; however, the grading requirements are slightly different.

The grading requirements are identified as Size 1, Size 2, Size 8, and Size 89. Size 1 is the same grading that is used for the fine aggregate in concrete aggregate (ASTM C 33), and Size 2 is identical to the gradation for aggregates of masonry mortars. Size 8 and Size 89 are standard aggregate gradations that are used for highway construction.

The cement specifications for grouts are identical to those for mortars; however, the grout proportions are considerably different. Grout is mixed to a pouring consistency because it is most frequently placed by pumping.

MORTAR TESTING

Mortars are tested by the Compressive Strength Test. This test, ASTM C 91, requires casting three representative samples of mortar. Bronze molds form three 2-in. cubes. The mortar is placed in each cube and consolidated. The top is struck level with a straightedge and a damp cloth draped over the cubes. After 8 hours the cubes are removed from the molds and placed in a moist atmosphere or curing box. The cubes are tested to destruction on the

seventh and twenty-eighth days by a compression machine. Tests may be conducted on 3- or 14-day-old cubes.

COMPRESSIVE STRENGTH OF MOLDED MASONRY MORTAR CYLINDERS ASTM C 780

The cement mortar is spooned into the mold in three separate and equal volumes (Figure 5.22).

FIGURE 5.22 Preparing mortar cylinders.

FIGURE 5.23 Compressive testing of mortar.

After 48 hours the molds are opened carefully and the cylinders removed.

It is important that the top and bottom surfaces of the cylinders be parallel. After capping, the specimens are returned to the moist box and cured until tested. The capped cylinders are then carefully centered in a compression machine (Figure 5.23) and tested to destruction.

After each specimen has been broken, the compressive unit stress should be plotted on graph paper and, after the 28-day specimen has been plotted, a curve drawn.

TYPES OF MASONRY JOINTS

The exposed mortar joints are finished in one of several ways. Joint finishing, called tooling, is formed with a jointer tool at the time the masonry unit is laid and not afterwards, as in pointing stone work.

The struck joint, shown in Figure 5.7A, is the most commonly used finished joint. Suitable only for interior walls, it is likely to produce leaky exterior walls. It is used when masonry walls are to be plastered.

The weather joint (B), similar to the struck joint, slopes to shed water more effectively. More difficult to form than the struck, weathered joints are rarely used, although they are more watertight.

In the flush joint (C), the mortar is cut off flush with the face of the brick. A joint common for unexposed interiors, it is also used for face brick.

The raked joint (D) is formed by raking out the mortar to the depth of about ½ in. The stripped joint (E), similar to the raked joint, is sometimes formed by placing wood strips in the joints as the brick are laid. These strips, insuring a uniform joint, are removed as soon as the mortar has set. Raked and stripped joints, more suitable for the interior, are used on exterior walls to produce a desired shadow. They are relatively expensive and not too watertight. The Vee joint (F) and concave (G) are made with a special tool which is run along the joint. These joints in exterior walls, including the vertical joints and the interior joints, should be entirely filled with mortar to reduce moisture penetration. The outside face of the joints should be made smooth and dense by exerting considerable pressure on the jointer tool.

Summary

The durability of masonry unit construction is evidenced by structures all over the world that have been in use for hundreds of years. The appearance of a masonry unit structure connotes permanence. Brick, made from clay and shale, is available in a variety of shapes and colors and can be bonded to provide many attractive patterns. Stone is often used as it is found in nature or it is quarried and milled into desired shapes and sizes. The exposed face can be finished by grinding, honing, and rubbing to provide a surface that is easy to maintain and pleasing to the eye. Concrete masonry units are often hidden from view by the decorative brick and stone they are supporting. However, they can be molded to produce exposed faces with raised or geometric designs which deliver an architecturally pleasing appearance.

Anchors are used to secure facing masonry units to the backing support units. All of the masonry units are joined together by mortar to form a cohesive unified mass. This unified mass is reinforced when forces are anticipated that will produce tensile stresses in the final structure. Careful construction practices ensure that the owner will receive a facility having permanence and natural beauty.

Key Terms

masonry	bond	stone	ashlar
mortar	course	quarrying	setting
brick	wythe	washes	joints
header	efflorescence	drip	concrete masonry unit
stretcher	rock	rubble	

Review Questions

1. Define the elements of masonry construction.

2. Describe the three methods used in the manufacture of clay and shale brick.

3. Identify three bonds that illustrate how headers and stretchers are used to establish different bonds.

4. Describe the process of bricklaying.

5. Describe three different course arrangements used in stone masonry construction.

6. What are the four classifications of concrete masonry units?

7. Illustrate how the various masonry accessories are used.

8. List five different ways mortar joints are finished and indicate where they are commonly used.

CHAPTER 6
METALS

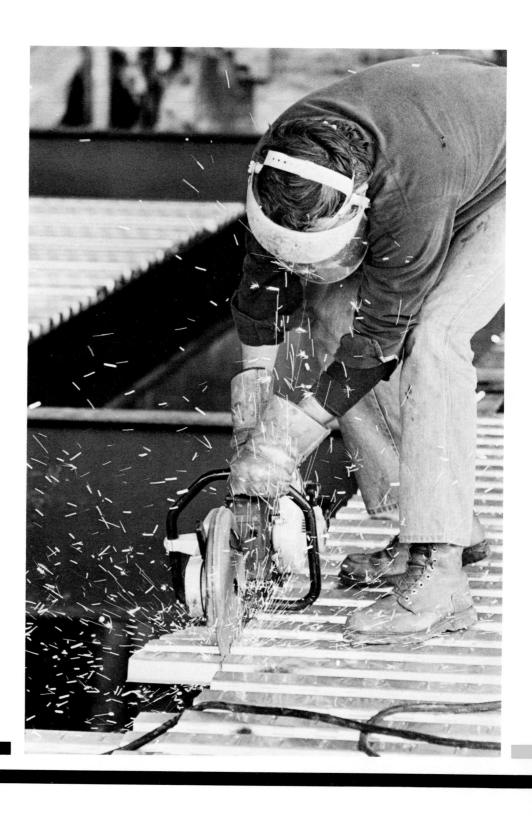

6.1 Steel Materials and Shapes
6.2 Structural Framing
6.3 Metal Building Systems
6.4 Lightgage Framing and Metal Joists

6.5 Metal Decking
6.6 Metal Fasteners
6.7 Metals and Alloys

Metals play important roles as basic materials for building construction. Almost any structure will have a variety of metals being used as building materials. Included are cast-iron gratings in the parking lot, structural steel shapes in the building framework, aluminum doors and windows, copper wiring and pipe, lead watertight pans under the showers and brass fixtures in the restrooms. Steel is by far the most used structural metal in building construction. The skeleton will be composed of steel beams, girders, and columns. Steel decking will support floors and roofing applications. Open-web bar joists will support the steel decking and other materials used for floor and roof construction. Lightgage steel framing will support interior partitions and exterior walls. It is hard to imagine any structure being constructed without utilizing steel in several of its many possible forms.

All of the metals are produced using raw materials that are found in the earth's crust. After mining, the ores containing the basic metals are processed to increase the metal content by removing much of the waste material. The processing will involve crushing, grinding, and screening. The ores are further processed by the addition of heat and fluxes that render the metal to its purest form. Most of the metals can improve their physical properties with the addition of other elements during the final processing of the metal. Examples include the addition of chromium to steel to make stainless steel, which is highly resistant to corrosion; and the addition of copper or magnesium to aluminum to increase its strength and hardness.

The following sections will describe the processes used to convert the raw materials found in the earth's crust into the metal products that are incorporated into today's structures.

Objectives

1. Understand how iron ore, coal, and limestone are transformed into steel.

2. Become familiar with the properties of carbon steel.

3. Understand what effects the elements of carbon, silicon, sulfur, and chromium have on steel.

4. Become familiar with the different methods of connecting steel.

5. Become familiar with the different structural shapes and where they are commonly used.

6. Become familiar with the nonferrous metals that are commonly used in building construction.

6.1 Steel Materials and Shapes

The primary object of the various steel manufacturing processes is to reduce the amount of carbon present in the pig iron and to control the amounts of phosphorus, sulfur, manganese, silicon, and other ingredients of steel manufacture.

Steel has more ductility and more malleability and less brittleness than pig iron and cast iron. It contrasts with malleable cast iron by having malleability without treatment after casting. Steel differs in chemical composition from pig iron, cast iron, and malleable iron principally by having a much lower percentage of carbon but also by the smaller amounts of manganese, silicon, and phosphorus present. Low-carbon steel and wrought iron have similar chemical composition; but in wrought iron, the iron itself contains a smaller percentage of impurities because a part of the impurities are in the slag, which is mechanically mixed with iron.

Low-carbon steel differs from wrought iron chiefly by the process of manufacture and structure, rather than any great difference in other physical properties.

EFFECT OF COMPOSITION ON PROPERTIES

Carbon has the most pronounced effect on the physical properties of steel. The amount of carbon present in steel may vary from almost 0 to about 1½%. Increasing the amount of carbon increases the strength, hardness, and brittleness of steel but decreases its ductility. Steel may be classified according to carbon content approximately as follows.

	Carbon Content, %
Low-carbon steel	0.06–0.30
Medium-carbon steel	0.30–0.50
High-carbon steel	0.50–0.80

No clear demarcation exists between the various grades, so these limits are subject to considerable variation.

Silicon, in the amounts usually found in steel, has little effect on its properties; but when present in amounts as high as 0.3 or 0.4%, it increases the strength without a sacrifice in ductility.

Sulfur has little effect on the strength or ductility of steel, but it makes steel brittle and likely to crack when worked in red heat. This property is called red shortness. The maximum amount of sulfur permitted by specifications for structural steel is about 0.05%.

Phosphorus is very objectionable because it causes brittleness at ordinary temperatures, or cold short. The maximum amount of phosphorus permitted by specifications for structural steel is about 0.06%.

Manganese in amounts ordinarily present is beneficial to steel, but its action is too complex to consider here.

EFFECT OF MECHANICAL WORKING

Hammering, pressing, and rolling steel while it is hot tends to eliminate flaws. If the working is continued while the metal is cooled past a certain critical temperature, the steel will be fine grained. This results from the breaking up of the crystals and deterring their reformation.

The cold-working of steel increases the strength and elastic limit but decreases the ductility.

EFFECT OF HEAT TREATMENT

Heating, annealing, and sudden cooling have very marked effects on the strength, ductility, and grain size of steel, but this subject is too complex for consideration here.

PROCESS OF MANUFACTURE

The steelmaking process starts with the bringing together of the three principle raw materials; iron ore, coal, and limestone. After mining, all of the raw materials are processed before being joined together in the blast furnace (see Figure 6.1).

The iron ore from the Lake Superior region dominates steel production. Most of the ore is taconite. Once the taconite is mined, it is processed by beneficiation, a treatment to improve the ore's iron content. Taconite, with a 25% iron content as it is mined, can be improved to 65% iron content by beneficiation. *Beneficiation* of the taconite consists of crushing, magnetic separation of ore particles, rolling into pellets, and baking to a hard dense consistency. The beneficiation is usually done near the mine sites to avoid transporting large quantities of non-iron-bearing minerals.

Coal is changed into coke, the basic fuel required in blast furnaces. Special grade bituminous coal, crushed and washed, is charged into ovens that are tightly sealed to keep out air so the coal will not burn. The coal is baked at an intense heat for about 18 hours. Gases and impurities are driven off during the baking and the white-hot material left in the ovens is pushed into special railroad cars and carried to a quenching tower. After quenching, the coke is ready for the blast furnace.

Limestone serves as a cleanser in both the iron and steelmaking processes. Acting as a flux that combines with impurities, it forms the slag that is separated from the molten iron and steel. The limestone is crushed, washed, and sized before being used in the iron and steelmaking processes.

Blast Furnace

The *blast furnace* is the meeting place of the raw materials —the charge of iron ore, coke, and limestone, from which *pig iron* is produced. The blast furnace is so named because of the continuous blast of air required to bring about the necessary heat and chemical reactions in the raw materials in the stack. As much as 4½ tons of air may be needed to make 1 ton of pig iron. Every 4 or 5 hours, the blast furnace is tapped by burning out a plug at the bottom of it. Fluid iron flows out through the hole and down a trough into a bottle car. The amount drawn off at one time, called a cast of iron, will range from 150 to 350 tons, depending on the size of the furnace.

The bottle car, which is insulated like a giant thermos bottle, is lined with refractory brick to resist and retain the heat of the molten iron which reaches it at temperatures near 2500°F. The bottle car keeps the iron at a high temperature so it will be ready for refining when it reaches the steelmaking furnaces.

Steelmaking Processes

The principle processes used in the manufacture of steel are the basic oxygen process (BOP), electric furnace process, and open-hearth process. All refine steel by applying high temperatures to a charge of molten iron and/or scrap metal. The basic oxygen process produces over half of the steel made in the United States. A single furnace can turn out 350 tons in less than an hour.

The basic oxygen process, which originated in Austria, employs oxygen of high purity. The oxygen is shot under extremely high pressure through a water-cooled, retractable lance that is lowered into the furnace to a position just above the molten metal. The impurities of the iron are burned off. This process is illustrated in Figure 6.2.

Open hearth furnaces, once predominant within the steel industry, are so named because limestone, scrap steel, and molten iron charged into the shallow steelmaking area are exposed to the sweep of flames across the top of the molten metal. In recent years, practically all open-hearth furnaces have been converted to the use of oxygen to speed up the melting process.

The electric furnace is equipped with three retractable electrodes which pass current through the solid scrap charge and melt it. This method of steel manufacture, which can be highly controlled, is used to produce steel that requires special alloys, such as stainless steel, surgical steel, spring steel, and other quality or specialty steels. For a descriptive illustration of this process, see Figure 6.3.

A vacuum melting and degassing process is used to produce steels that are exceptionally pure and of extremely high grade. They are produced by placing an electric furnace in a vacuum chamber. The gaseous impurities are removed by the vacuum, leaving a steel of exceptional physical qualities. This steel is used for the aerospace industry.

Steel Casting

No matter which steelmaking process is used, steel must solidify before it can be further processed. Traditionally, the first solid form of raw steel is the *ingot.* Ingot molds can be of various sizes, from 8 ft high and 3 ft across for high tonnage use or as small as 3 feet high and 6 in. across for specialty steels. Molten raw steel is teemed from the ladle into the ingot molds. The inside surface of the mold is coated to prevent splashing droplets of molten steel from sticking to the mold and marring the surface quality of the ingot. The coating also acts as releasing agent during the stripping

process. After the molds are removed, the ingots are taken to furnaces called "soaking pits" where they are soaked in heat until they are of uniform temperature throughout. The ingots are then carried to the rolling mill, where they are quickly and efficiently reduced into *blooms, slabs,* and *billets* — the semifinished shapes of steel.

Continuous casting is a newer method of handling raw steel which eliminates many traditional steps in the steelmaking process. The teeming, stripping, and soaking of the ingots is eliminated. In this method, molten steel is lifted by ladle to the top of a strand caster which produces slabs, blooms, or billets without rolling. As the steel flows into the water cooled, downcurving molds, sufficient skin forms to enable the steel to solidify as it travels downward. Rolling aprons guide the steel to a roller leveler, where it is leveled and cut into predetermined lengths by a traveling torch. Besides saving time and labor, this continuous caster reduces waste as well. The entire trip from the ladle to the semifinished form can take less than half an hour.

Once the semifinished shapes are formed, they continue through the rolling mill. Numerous passes through a rolling mill are required to change the heated semifinished shapes into the desired finished shapes such as bars, rods, plates, sheets, structural shapes, and rails.

PROPERTIES AND USES

As stated, the strength, ductility, and other properties of steel are affected by its composition, the mechanical treatment it receives when it is hot and cold during processing, and many other factors. In general, it may be classed as a relatively high-strength and low-cost metal. Its most significant defect is its lack of resistance to corrosion.

Steel is the most used structural metal in building construction. Its uses are so numerous and so well known that it seems unnecessary to mention them here, but many of them are considered in detail in subsequent sections.

ALLOY STEELS

Various alloying elements are introduced into steel to change the properties, such as increasing the strength and resistance to rust. Included in these elements are silicon, manganese, copper, nickel, chromium, tungsten, molybdenum, and vanadium. They may be introduced singly, or two or more may be used. Such steels are called alloy steels.

A common steel used for curtain walls, decorative purposes, sinks and counter tops, and other building purposes is stainless steel, which resists corrosion, takes a high polish, and is attractive. Some types are made by adding from 10 to 30% of chromium to steel. In others, from 5 to 15% of nickel also is included.

The melting points of various steels vary from 2600° to 2800°F. Their weight is 490 lb per cu ft. Small amounts of copper, ranging from 0.15 to 0.30%, introduced in steel increases its resistance to atmospheric corrosion without

PELLETS

IRON ORE

SINTER

LIMESTONE

CRUSHING

COAL

COKE OVENS

COKE OVEN BY-PRODUCTS

SLAG

CASTING PIG IRON

BLAST FURNACE

SCRAP OR PREREDUCED ORE

MOLTEN IRON TRANSFER CAR

MIXER

BASIC OXYGEN FURNACE

OPEN HEARTH FURNACE

ELECTRIC FURNACE

A FLOWLINE ON STEELMAKING

FIGURE 6.1 The steelmaking process. American Iron and Steel Institute.

having significant effect on its other properties. Copper-bearing steel is extensively used for sheet-metal products.

Structural Steels

Structural steels are identified by the ASTM designation number that specifies the steel. The most commonly used structural steel for buildings and general construction is designated A 36 steel.

ASTM A 36 (structural steel) is a weldable mild carbon steel and has a minimum yield of 36 ksi for all shapes.

This grade of steel is the most common steel in use today. ASTM A 529 (structural steel with a 42 ksi minimum yield) is a higher-strength carbon steel. When 0.02% copper is added, A529 has an atmospheric corrosion resistance twice that of structural carbon steel without copper. This steel is used in the relatively light structural members of standard steel buildings.

There are several steels that have greater structural abilities that are known as high-strength steels.

ASTM A 242 (high-strength low-alloy structural steel) has

FIGURE 6.1 *(continued)*

a minimum yield of 50 ksi and limits the addition of carbon and manganese for increased weldability. A242 is often specified when self-weathering steel is required. This steel has four times the atmospheric corrosion resistance of carbon steel without copper.

ASTM A 441 (high-strength low-alloy structural manganese vanadium steel) is a weldable steel with a yield of 42 ksi. It is a substitute for the phased out A440, which was intended primarily for bolting and riveting.

ASTM A 588 (high-strength low-alloy steel with a minimum yield point of 50 ksi) is intended primarily for use in welded bridges and buildings where decreased weight of steel, improved durability, and weather resistance are desired.

Weathering Steel

For years the corrosion deterrence of structural steel, especially at inaccessible places, has been a maintenance problem. This has been alleviated by the use of a bare, unprotected steel that acquires a protective oxide coat that deters rust and corrosion. This steel, called *weathering steel,* soon acquires a sepia-toned patina that eventually ripens

The principal material used in manufacturing steel by the basic oxygen process is molten iron. Therefore, most BOF facilities are built near blast furnaces. Some scrap steel is used in the process. Oxygen producing facilities are usually built in the same plant.

Molten pig iron accounts for between 65% and 80% of the charge and is poured from a ladle into the top of the tilted furnace.

The first step for making a heat of steel in a BOF is to tilt the furnace and charge it with scrap. The furnaces are mounted on trunnions and can be swung through a wide arc.

FIGURE 6.2 Basic oxygen process. American Iron and Steel Institute.

FLUX
CHARGE

During the oxygen
blow, lime is added as
a flux to help carry
off the oxidized im-
purities as a floating
layer of slag. Lime is
consumed at a rate
of about 150 pounds
per ton of raw steel
produced.

Oxygen combines with carbon
and other unwanted elements,
eliminating these impurities
from the molten charge and
converting it to steel.

The furnace is returned to
upright position. A water
cooled oxygen lance is lowered
into the furnace and high purity oxygen is blown onto the
top of the metal at supersonic
speed.

OXYGEN
LANCE

REFRACTORY
LINING

STEEL
SHELL

TAP HOLE

ALLOY
ADDITION

After steel has been refined, the furnace is tilted and molten
steel pours into a ladle. Alloy additions are made into the
ladle.

LADLE OF
MOLTEN STEEL

FIGURE 6.2 *(continued)*

ELECTROMAGNET

STEEL
SCRAP

STEEL SCRAP MAY VARY WIDELY
IN QUALITY. IT IS CAREFULLY SORTED
AND WEIGHED BEFORE IT GOES TO
THE ELECTRIC FURNACE.

WITH ITS CARBON ELECTRODES ATTACHED TO ELECTRICAL
CABLES, THIS ELECTRIC FURNACE IS SHOWN MOUNTED ON
"ROCKERS" SO THAT IT CAN BE TILTED TOWARD THE TAPPING
SPOUT, THROUGH WHICH MOLTEN STEEL EMERGES.

ELECTRODES

CHARGING
BASKET

THE ELECTRODES ARE LOWERED
THROUGH THE ROOF OF THE FURNACE
AND THE ELECTRIC POWER IS TURNED
ON. THE CURRENT IN AN ELECTRIC
FURNACE ARCS FROM ONE ELECTRODE TO
THE METALLIC CHARGE AND FROM THE
CHARGE TO THE NEXT ELECTRODE.

THE ENTIRE TOP OF AN ELECTRIC
FURNACE MAY SWING TO THE SIDE,
ELECTRODES AND ALL, SO THAT A
CHARGING BASKET OF STEEL SCRAP
MAY BE LOWERED INTO THE FURNACE.
THE BOTTOM OF THE BASKET IS
OPENED, THUS CHARGING THE FURNACE.

DOOR

TAPPING
SPOUT

FIGURE 6.3 Electric furnace process. American Iron and Steel Institute.

PURE OXYGEN MAY BE INJECTED TO SPEED UP CARBON REMOVAL FROM THE MOLTEN METAL.

CHARGING BOX

LIMESTONE AND FLUX ARE CHARGED ON TOP OF THE MOLTEN BATH. THROUGH A CHEMICAL INTERACTION, IMPURITIES IN THE STEEL RISE INTO THE MOLTEN SLAG, WHICH FLOATS ON TOP OF THE METAL. THE FURNACE IS TILTED SLIGHTLY AND THE SLAG IS RAKED OFF. ELECTRIC FURNACE STEEL CAN BE MADE EITHER WITH A SINGLE-SLAG OR A DOUBLE-SLAG PRACTICE. IN THE DOUBLE-SLAG METHOD, AN OXIDIZING SLAG IS FORMED, RAKED OFF, AND A REDUCING SLAG FORMED.

SLAG

ALLOYING ELEMENTS, WHICH COME FROM MANY PARTS OF THE WORLD, ARE USUALLY ADDED TO THE MOLTEN STEEL IN THE FORM OF FERROALLOYS. TYPICAL ELEMENTS INCLUDE CHROMIUM FROM THE PHILIPPINES, TUNGSTEN FROM BRAZIL, NICKEL FROM CANADA, AND COBALT FROM AFRICA.

WHEN THE CHEMICAL COMPOSITION OF THE STEEL MEETS SPECIFICATIONS, THE FURNACE TILTS FORWARD SO THAT MOLTEN METAL MAY POUR OUT THROUGH THE SPOUT. THE SLAG COMES AFTER THE STEEL AND SERVES AS AN INSULATING BLANKET DURING TAPPING.

LADLE

FIGURE 6.3 (continued)

into a deep brownish-mauve. During this aging, there is a small amount of the oxide residue that is carried off by rainwater and wind erosion. This residue deposits upon surfaces directly below the steel, leaving a stained coat upon those materials that are stainable, such as stucco and concrete. Weathering steel should not be used above permeable surfaces where appearances are important unless provision is made for protection and drainage of the runoff.

This steel is ideal for use in bridges, towers, and other structures where inaccessibility for maintenance is a factor. For the effect of its rich color, its maintenance-free quality, and its forthright honesty of structure, entire buildings of architectural character have been built using this steel exposed on both interior and exterior.

STEEL SHAPES

The standards of ASTM A 6 are applicable to most of the requirements and specifications of different structural shapes, plates, bars, and piling steels used for building construction. Although structural steels must be manufactured by either the open-hearth (OH) basic oxygen (BOF) or electric furnace (EF) process, they may be refined by the vacuum-arc-remelt (VAR) or the electroslag-remelt. Shapes or the flanged sections are classified into five groups according to their tensile properties. Group 1 contains the weakest members, and Group 5 the heaviest or strongest.

After the iron ore has been converted to molten steel, it is poured into molds. The ingots which are thus formed are placed in a soaking pit, then processed in the roughing mill into blooms, billets, and slabs. Blooms are members having an area exceeding 36 sq in. A billet is somewhat flatter, with a cross-sectional area between 16 and 36 sq in. The slab has a thickness not less than 1½ in. For a description of the process, see Figure 6.1.

After leaving the blooming mill, the steel is sent to the rolling mill, where the blooms are shaped into structural shapes; the billets, into rods, bars, and tubes; and the slabs are rolled into plates, sheets, and strips.

In the rolling mill, the blooms are run through a series of rollers that gradually shape the hot steel into its finished form. Figure 6.1 indicates the steps that would be required for shaping a wide-flange member.

Various rolled shapes or sections form columns, beams, girders, and other structural units that will be shown in Figure 6.4. The parts of these shapes are designated as flanges, webs, and stems.

The wide-flange, called W-shapes or sections, vary in depth from a maximum of 36 in. to a minimum of 4 in. and weigh from 7½ lb to 730 lb per linear foot. The inner faces of these flanges are parallel to the outer face, or the inner face may have a slope of 1 to 20, depending upon the manufacturer. There are two general forms of wide-flange shapes; those relatively deep and narrow (A) are more suitable for beams and girders, and those more nearly square (B) are desirable for column sections.

The American standard beams, called I-beams and identified as S-shapes (C), vary in depth and in weight per foot from a maximum of 24 in. and 120 lb to a minimum of 3 in. and 5.7 lb. The inner face of their flanges has a slope of 1 in 6.

The American standard channels and miscellaneous channels, called channels (D), vary in depth and in weight per foot from a maximum of 18 in. and 58 lb to a minimum of 3 in. and 4.1 lb. The inner face of the flanges of these sections has a slope of 1 in 6.

In addition to the wide-flange and standard shapes mentioned, light beams, joists, columns, and standard mill beams, called miscellaneous M-shapes, are used.

Angles are divided into those with equal legs and those with unequal legs (E). Equal-leg angles vary in size, thickness, and weight per foot from a maximum 8 × 8 × 1⅛ in. and 56.9 lb to 1 × 1 × ⅛ in. and 0.80 lb. Unequal-leg angles vary in size from 8 × 6 × 1 in. and 44.2 lb to 1¾ × 1¼ × ⅛ in. and 1.23 lb.

Tees (F) are commonly made by splitting the webs of wide-flange or American standard beam shapes, and thus are available in sizes which correspond to the sections from which they are cut. These are called structural tees, indicated as WT, and are ordinarily used in structural framing connections.

Square and rectangular tubular shapes are rolled in several sizes and wall thickness. Square tubes are available with 2 × 2 in. through 10 × 10 in. outside dimensions. The wall thicknesses vary from about 3/16 in. for the lightest 2 in. tube to ⅝ in. for the heaviest 10 in. tube. Rectangular tubes are 3 × 2 in. to 12 × 8 in. Their wall thicknesses vary from

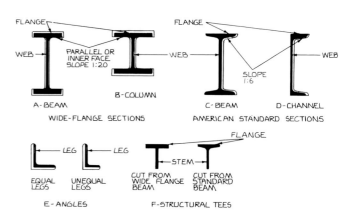

DARKENED SECTION REPRESENTS THE MINIMUM SECTION ROLLED WITH A GIVEN SET OF ROLLS. THE LIGHT AREA INDICATES THE METHOD OF INCREASING THE SECTION BY SPREADING THE ROLLS.

EDGES SHEARED OR FLAME CUT IN "SHEARED PLATES", OR ROLLED IN UNIVERSAL MILL PLATES.

G - PLATES   SHEET OR STRIP   H - SQUARE OR   I - ROUND
                                          RECTANG-   BARS
                                          ULAR BARS

FIGURE 6.4 Types of rolled steel sections.

Table 6.1ᵃ

Thickness (in.)	Width (in.)					
	To 3½ inclusive	Over 3½ to 6	Over 6 to 8	Over 8 to 12	Over 12 to 48	Over 48
0.2300 and thicker	Bar	Bar	Bar	Plate	Plate	Plate
0.2299 to 0.2031	Bar	Bar	Strip	Strip	Sheet	Plate
0.2030 to 0.1800	Strip	Strip	Strip	Strip	Sheet	Plate
0.1799 to 0.0449	Strip	Strip	Strip	Strip	Sheet	Sheet
0.0448 to 0.0344	Strip	Strip				
0.0343 to 0.0255	Strip	Hot-rolled sheet and strip not generally produced in these widths and thicknesses				
0.0254 and thinner						

ᵃ Courtesy of American Institute of Steel Construction, Inc.

about ³⁄₁₆ in. for the lightest to ½ in. for the heaviest tube. The large 10 in. square tubes and the larger rectangular tubes (12 × 8 in.) are not carried in stock as a "shelf" item. Structurally, these shapes have advantages over the wide-flange shapes when used as columns. Moreover, they fit into masonry walls and frame into partitions better than pipe and wide-flange columns. They do, however, present framing problems.

Plates, as illustrated in *(G)*, are one class of flat-rolled steel.

In general, flat, square, or rectangular steel of various thicknesses and widths are referred to as plate if thick and wide, as bar if thick and narrow, as sheet if thin and wide, and as strip if thin and narrow. There are, however, definite dimensions of these members which classify them. For structural steel, the classifications made by the AISC usually apply. See Table 6.1.

Plate is indicated by PL, and when billed or referred to on drawings, it is properly indicated by thickness × width × length, with all dimensions in inches—using fractions or decimals. If the width is 8 in. or less, they are usually classed as bars; if more than 8 in. they are plates. Plates which are more than 2 in. thick are called bearing plates because they are used to provide bearing areas for the ends of various members. Plates are available in thicknesses from ½ in. to 2 in., and widths from 8 in. to lengths of 15¼ ft. Bearing plates are available in sizes up to 56 in. and in thicknesses up to 10¼ in. For thicknesses up to 2 in., plates are sufficiently smooth and flat to use as bearing plates to receive accurately finished milled ends of columns, and plates up to 4 in. can be straightened in presses to the necessary flatness. The top surfaces of plates thicker than 4 in. should be planed over a sufficient area to receive milled-column sections if the plates are grouted on concrete foundations, but both faces should be planed if they rest on steel. Plates on which the edges are rolled when the plates are being rolled are called universal mill plates. Plates with sheared edges are called sheared plates.

Square and round bars *(H)* and *(I)* are used for ties, lateral bracing, sag rods, and hangers in structural-steel framing and as reinforcing in reinforced concrete structures. Many sizes are available.

The various weights available for the shapes (Figure 6.1) are obtained by spreading the rolls that produce the shapes. This process adds to the area of the shapes. The thickness of the flanges, as well as the depth of the wide-flange shapes, increases as the rolls are spread, but all the shapes in a given series are designated by a single nominal depth regardless of the actual depth. An increase in the flange thickness is desirable because a given amount of material added to the flanges increases the strength and rigidity of a member much more than the same amount of material added to the web. American standard beams and channel sections of a given depth are increased in weight and cross-sectional area by spreading the rolls in such a manner that all the additional material goes into the web, where it is not very effective in increasing the strength and rigidity of the section. The actual depth of all the shapes in a given depth series is the same and is equal to the depth by which the series of sections is designated. Spreading the rolls to increase the thickness of an angle also increases the lengths of the legs, but these increases are not taken into account in designating the size of the angle.

Structural-steel shapes are manufactured at steel mills. The operation of cutting the various shapes to the required size and fastening them together to form columns, girders, trusses, and other structural members is called *fabrication.* This work is done by fabricating plants. The individual units are shipped to the building site in sizes that can be transported and handled on the job, and are placed in position, or erected.

The individual sections are fastened together, in both fabrication and erection, by riveting, welding, or bolting, as described in Section 6.6.

Designation of Shapes

The standard designations for structural-steel shapes as adopted by the American Institute of Steel Construction are shown in Table 6.2.

Table 6.2 **Hot-Rolled Structural-Steel Shape Designation**[a]

New Designation	Type of Shape	Old Designation
W 24 × 76	W shape	24 WF 76
W 14 × 26		14 B 26
S 24 × 100	S shape	24 I 100
M 8 × 18.5	M shape	8 M 18.5
M 10 × 9		10 JR 9.0
M 8 × 34.3		8 × 8 M 34.3
C 12 × 20.7	American standard channel	12 20.7
MC 12 × 45	Miscellaneous channel	12 × 4 45.0
MC 12 × 10.6		12 JR 10.6
HP 14 × 73	HP shape	14 BP 73
L 6 × 6 × ¾	Equal-leg angle	∠ 6 × 6 × ¾
L 6 × 4 × ⅝	Unequal-leg angle	∠ 6 × 4 × ⅝
WT 12 × 38	Structural tee cut from W shape	ST 12 W 38
WT 7 × 13		ST 7 B 12
ST 12 × 50	Structural tee cut from S shape	ST 12 I 50
MT 4 × 9.25	Structural tee cut from M shape	ST 4 M 9.25
MT 5 × 4.5		ST 5 JR 4.5
MT 4 × 17.15		ST 4 M 17.15
PL ½ × 18	Plate	PL 18 × ½
Bar 1 □	Square bar	Bar 1 ⊡
Bar 1¼ o	Round bar	Bar 1¼ φ
Bar 2½ × ½	Flat bar	Bar 2½ × ½
Pipe 4 Std.	Pipe	Pipe 4 Std.
Pipe 4X — Strong		Pipe 4X — Strong
Pipe 4XX — Strong		Pipe 4XX — Strong
TS 4 × 4 × 0.375	Structural tubing: square	Tube 4 × 4 × 0.375
TS 5 × 3 × 0.375	Structural tubing: rectangular	Tube 5 × 3 × 0.375
TS 3 OD × 0.250	Structural tubing: circular	Tube 3 OD × 0.250

[a] Courtesy of American Institute of Steel Construction, Inc.

The number of pieces of a given type, size, and length is always shown by a numeral in front of these designations; and the length, by a dimension in feet and inches following the designation. For example, 2–L 3 × 3 × ¼ × 12 ft–6 in. would indicate 2 angles with 3 in. equal legs that are ¼ in. thick and a length of 12 ft–6 in. The symbols for inch and pound are not used in these standard designations except in lengths, but they are ordinarily used elsewhere.

Reference

The *Manual of Steel Construction,* Eighth Edition (American Institute of Steel Construction, Inc., New York, New York, 1980) gives complete information on all significant properties of all structural-steel shapes available and the companies which roll each shape; estimating and detailing; allowable loads on beams, columns, and their connections; standard specifications and codes; and many other pertinent subjects.

6.2 Structural Framing

The general term beam may include various flexural members such as beams, girders, joists, lintels, purlins, and rafters, (Section 1.4) which are given specific names because of their use.

TYPES OF BEAMS

The cross sections of various types of beams are shown in Figure 6.5. The wide-flange shape shown in *(A)* and the American standard S-beams shown in *(B)* are the most commonly used sections. They are available in a great variety of sizes. The channel shown in *(C)* is extensively used for roof purlins. The wide-flange shape or the S-beam may be provided with cover or flange plates (D). Beams may be built up of plates and angles *(E)* and *(F)* to obtain almost any size desired. The built-up sections shown in *(G)* and *(H)* are used occasionally.

SEPARATORS

In *(I)* and *(J),* two beams have been fastened together with separators to hold them in position and to make them act somewhat as a unit. The plate-and-angle separator in *(I)* is more effective in this respect than the pipe separator in *(J).* If the beams are not too far apart, two overlapping angles, with legs riveted together, can be used as an angle separator. Separators spaced 5 or 6 ft apart are usually required when beams are used in pairs.

FIGURE 6.5 Steel beams.

FIGURE 6.6 Welded plate girders.

LINTELS

The sections shown in (K) to (N) are lintels arranged to carry brick or stone masonry over openings and can be largely concealed. The single angle shown in (N) carries the outer layer of masonry; the remainder of the wall may be carried by a relieving arch, or another angle may be used.

PLATE GIRDERS

A built-up plate girder is illustrated in (O). The section consists of four flange angles, a web plate, and cover plates, as shown in (F). The web plate is usually made quite thin, a ratio of unsupported depth to thickness of 170 being permitted if web stiffeners are provided to keep the web plate from buckling. Since these stiffeners must project over the flanges, it is necessary to bend or crimp them around the vertical legs of the flange angles in order to place them against the web (P); or fill plates, equal in thickness to the flange angles, may be placed between the stiffeners and the web plate (Q). If the unsupported depth of the web does not exceed 70 times its thickness, intermediate stiffeners are not required; but end stiffeners are always required. Stiffeners are also required at all points where concentrated loads are supported. The spacing of stiffeners is determined by the shearing stresses. It is often required that the thickness of web plates be at least ¼ in.

A girder may be built up of two flange plates and a web plate welded together (Figure 6.6A) or of a wide-flange section split along the center of the web and separated to receive a narrow plate that increases the depth (B), the three parts being welded together. Stiffeners are provided by welding plates between the flanges and normal to the web (C) to (E). Welded girders are lighter than riveted girders with the same carrying capacity.

STEEL TRUSSES

Various types of trusses are described in Section 1.4 and illustrated in Figures 1.16 and 1.17. The most common types used for steel trusses for double-pitched roof supports are the Fink and Pratt trusses and, for floor and flat or gently sloping roof supports, the Pratt and Warren trusses. There is no reasonable limit to the span and loads for which steel trusses can be designed. They are always shop-fabricated and transported to the building site. Spans too long to be transported are made up of two or more sections and are spliced in the field.

Steel trusses are frequently used as a part of the interior framing of tall buildings to span auditoriums, lobbies, banquet halls, dance halls, and other rooms requiring large floor areas free from columns. Such floors are preferably located at the top or near the top of the building for purposes of economy in the structural framing, but other considerations may make it necessary to place these large floor areas in any part of a building. Very often they will be on the first floor with many stories above (Figure 6.7A). The depth of the truss may occupy one or more stories. It may not be possible to use one of the common types of trusses because of doors or hallways, for the floor or floors immediately above may have to pass through the truss and will determine its form. Such trusses have to be of very heavy construction. Some typical cross sections of truss members are given in Figure 6.7B.

Another common use for steel trusses is the support of theater balconies. Columns are, of course, objectionable and they are eliminated whenever possible. A common

208   METALS

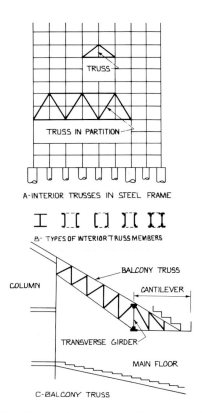

FIGURE 6.7 Trusses located in partitions and balcony truss.

A-INTERIOR TRUSSES IN STEEL FRAME

B- TYPES OF INTERIOR TRUSS MEMBERS

C-BALCONY TRUSS

form of construction consists of cantilever trusses overhanging a transverse supporting truss or girder (Figure 6.7C).

The various members of a truss are connected at the joints, or points where they meet, by bolting or welding, as described in the following paragraphs.

Bolted Trusses

The members meeting at a joint or panel point may be connected by attaching them to connection or gusset plates ¼ in. or more thick and large enough to provide for the number of bolts required by the stresses in the members, and, occasionally, by the stresses in the plates themselves. The bolts may be as small as ⅝ in. in diameter for light trusses but usually are ¾ in. and may be larger for long spans or heavy loads.

For trusses of ordinary spans, there is usually one gusset plate at each joint (Figures 6.8B and 6.9D). To avoid twisting action, the pieces of each principal member connected to a gusset plate should be symmetrically located with reference to the plate. To accomplish this objective, the principal members, such as the top and bottom chords, are made up of two units as illustrated by the two angles, placed back to back, of the top chord in Figure 6.8A and the two channels, placed back to back, for the bottom chord, shown in (B) and

in Figure 6.9C. These are spaced apart far enough to receive the connection or gusset plate between them (Figure 6.8B). Members carrying minor stresses may be composed of a single small angle which does not cause significant twisting action because of the low magnitude of the stresses.

If the top chord of a truss is subjected to bending stresses by members such as roof purlins or floor joists not located at the joints, it may be composed of two angles and a plate (Figure 6.9A), or two channels (C). Similarly, a bottom chord subjected to such stresses may be composed of two angles and a plate (B) of two channels (C). If the member includes a plate, that plate may also serve as a connection plate at the joints.

Truss members consisting of two angles or channels, without a plate, should be provided with stitch bolts at intermediate points between the connection plates (Figure 6.8B). The distance between the backs of the angles or channels is maintained by washers. Stitch bolts are provided to make the individual parts act together more nearly as a unit.

Wood or steel purlins may be fastened to the top chords of steel roof trusses by short lengths of steel angles, called clip angles (Figures 6.8B and 6.9D).

Heavy trusses are made up of large angles and many other types of members such as those shown in Figures 6.10A to D.

Welded Trusses

The connection of gusset plates in bolted or riveted trusses serve as indirect paths through which stresses are transferred from one member to another member connected to the same plate. A significant advantage of most welded trusses over bolted or riveted trusses is the direct transmission of stress from one member to another, which eliminates gusset plates. To accomplish this objective, appropriate types of members must be used.

The ends of members to be connected at a joint are so cut and so shaped, by slotting or otherwise, that they will provide suitable opportunities for welding. Most structural welding is done by the electric-arc welding process described earlier. The basic types of welds used are the groove weld by means of which abutting edges or ends of plates and shapes are joined (Figure 6.11B), and the fillet weld, formed along the junction of two surfaces which meet at an angle (Figure 6.11A and D).

The following comments concerning the structural shapes and arrangements of members at the joints are quoted, with permission and minor changes, from the eleventh edition of the *Procedure Handbook of Arc Welding Design and Practice,* published by the Lincoln Electric Company.

Arc-welded trusses may be designed in various ways using T-

FIGURE 6.8 Fink steel roof truss.

FIGURE 6.9 Simple steel roof truss details.

shapes, H-shapes, or U-shapes for chords. The web members are generally angles or channels. (Various types of arc-welded truss connections are illustrated in Figure 6.12.)

1. Perhaps the simplest type of truss connection is made of angle sections for web members (Figure 6.12A). This is easy to fabricate and weld because the sections lap each other and fillet welds are used.

2. For a heavier truss, the vertical member can be an I-beam or H-beam. The web of this member is slotted to fit over the stem of the T-section (B). The T-section is used for both the top and bottom chord members. The diagonal members are made of a double set of angles. (Fillet welds are used.)

3. Some trusses make use of T-sections for their diagonal members (C). The flanges of the diagonal members must be slotted to fit over the stem of the T-section used for the top chords as well as the bottom chords. The stem of the diagonals is also cut back and is butt-welded to the stem of the top and bottom chords. (Fillet welds are used elsewhere.)

4. Quite a few trusses are made completely of H-sections (D). Both top and bottom chords are made of H-sections, as are the web members. This allows loads to be placed anywhere along the top and bottom chords because of the high bending strength of the H-section. With the conventional truss design, loads must be placed only at points where diagonal or vertical members connect to the chord members. Almost all the welds are on flanges of the

ROLLED AND BUILT-UP STEEL COLUMNS

FIGURE 6.10 Steel columns.

top and bottom chords and, since they are flat surfaces, there is no unnecessary filling of the members to make these connections. (The welds are all fillet welds.)

5. In the connection shown in *(E)*, two T-sections are intermittently welded together at their flanges to form top and bottom chord members. The vertical member is an H-section set in between the stems of the T-sections. Each diagonal member is made of a set of angles. All the welding consists of fillet welds.

6. Sometimes the flanges are made of wide-flange beams and H-sections with the webs of the top and bottom chords placed horizontally *(F)*. The welding of these members consists mainly of butt-welding the flanges together. Under severe loading, gusset plates are added in between the flange connections in order to strengthen the joint and reduce the possibility of concentrated stresses.

The types of connections shown in Figure 6.12 can be adapted to many forms of truss, including the bowstring roof truss, for which the top chord can be cold-formed with the desired curvature.

The end panels of a heavy Warren roof truss with 12 panels and a span of 150 ft, connected to a column, are illustrated in Figure 6.13. Because of the large stresses involved, the types of connections in Figure 6.12 are not suitable and gusset plates are required. The edges of the gusset plates are curved between members, to improve the stress distribution within the welds. This also improves the appearance. They are also made straight.

Except at the top of the column, the structural section, of which each truss member is composed, ends at a gusset plate. At each end, its web is butt welded to the gusset plate. The flanges are butt welded to ends of the stiffener plates, which are welded normal to each side of the gusset plate.

Instead of ending the structural section of the gusset plate, as just described, the web of the section may be cut

off at this point and the projecting flanges slotted to form a forked end that fits closely over the gusset plate. The web is butt welded to the edge of the gusset plate, and the projecting flanges are fillet welded to the sides of this plate. No stiffening plates are required. The latter arrangement has the advantage of not breaking the continuity of the flange material, but it requires a longer main section and does not utilize the web material that is cut out in forming the slots.

The end top chord member that connects to the top of the column carries only the relatively small stresses due to lateral loads, such as the wind load. It is butt welded to the column. The gusset plate at the end of the bottom chord is fillet welded to the column. A suitable end connection can be devised for a truss, simply supported by a column, ending at the outer end of the lower chord; the end member of the top chord is omitted. The sizes of the gusset plates are determined by the stresses they must carry and by the lengths of the welds required to transmit the stresses from the members to the plates.

Types of Column Sections

Structural-steel columns may consist of a single piece, such as the wide-flange shape (Figure 6.10A), or they may be built up of various shapes *(B)* to *(N)*. The individual shapes are bolted or welded together to form the built-up sections.

Wide-Flange Columns

The most commonly used column section is the wide-flange column shown in Figure 6.10A, with nominal depths of 8 to 14 in. Various weights are available for each nominal depth, but it should be noted again that the spreading of the rolls to produce sections with several areas of the same nominal depth increases the actual depths of the sections. For example, the wide-flange shape which has a nominal depth of 14 in. and weighs 87 lb per ft has an actual depth of 14 in. and a flange thickness of 0.688 in.; whereas the maximum 14 in. section, which weighs 730 lb per ft, has an actual depth of 22.44 in. and a flange thickness of 4.910 in.

Cover-Plated Wide-Flange Columns

Column sections heavier than a maximum wide-flange shape can be obtained by riveting or welding cover or angle plates to such a shape (Figure 6.10B). There is a special 14 in. core shape weighing 320 lb per ft for this purpose. It has a relatively thick web, 1⅞ in., to support the thick flanges formed by cover plates. Cover plates, each with thicknesses of 1 in. or more, might be riveted or welded to each flange to give a total thickness 3 in. or more for each flange.

Other Types

The types of sections shown in Figure 6.10 *(E–K)* are seldom used to any extent. The angle sections *(L)* and *(M)* may

FIGURE 6.11 Types of welded joints.

FIGURE 6.12 Connections for simple welded trusses. Lincoln Electric Company.

FIGURE 6.13 Welded truss with gusset plates.

be used in very light corner columns or wherever their form is advantageous. These angle sections are extensively used, however, as members of trusses.

CONNECTORS

The preceding sections in this chapter have dealt with the structural-steel shapes, their use in constructing the various members used in the frames or framing of buildings, and

fastenings. Examples of gusset plates in forming the points of bolted and welded trusses and of welded joints without gusset plates have been given. This section is concerned with column, beam, and girder splices and connections and with lateral bracing for the frames of tier buildings and mill or industrial buildings.

A tall building with steel frame is often referred to as a skeleton construction building because its frame resembles a skeleton; it is called a tier building because its stories

FIGURE 6.14 Bolted splices in steel members.

The abutting ends of the columns at the splice are accurately milled so that the compressive stresses can be transferred directly from the upper column to the lower column by bearing. Splice plates are riveted to the flat sides of the columns and extend a short distance above and below the abutting ends. The functions of these plates are to hold the two sections in line, to resist bending stresses caused by wind and other causes, and to provide lateral rigidity. They are not relied upon to transfer any of the direct load from one section to the other, with the possible exception of columns carrying very light loads.

If the two sections are of the same width, the splice is simple *(D)*. If the widths are not the same, the difference in width is taken up by the fill plates *(E)*. If the difference in width is so great that the flanges of the upper columns do not bear on those of the lower column, a horizontal bearing plate is inserted between the abutting ends as shown in the figure.

constitute tiers and is known as a skyscraper because of its height. Buildings of any height that enclose undivided floor areas that can be subdivided to suit the tenants are often called loft buildings.

Bolted and Riveted Construction
Various details used in connections with bolts and rivets as fasteners are explained in the following paragraphs.

LAP AND BUTT JOINTS
Joints provided by bolting or riveting plates or parts of members that lap over each other (Figure 6.14*A*) are called lap joints. Those formed by butting the ends of two parts together and fastening them by bolts or rivets passing through a splice plate or connection plate *(B)* are called butt joints.

Column Splices
Steel column sections are usually made constant for two-story heights. Because of the change in the load on a column at each floor, it would be possible to save column material by reducing the column section in each story. This practice would be undesirable because the cost of the splices and the increase in erection costs would probably offset any saving in column section. In order that they will not interfere with the beam and girder connections, the splices are usually made about 2 ft above the floor line.

FIGURE 6.15 Bolted beam end connections and column bases.

Splices in Plate-Girder Webs

The size of plates available for webs of plate girders is limited, and it is often necessary to splice these web plates. Two forms of web splices are shown in (F).

Beam and Girder Connections

The usual method of connecting beams to girders is with framed connections, as illustrated in Figure 6.15A. The size of angles and the number of rivets to be used for each size of beam has been standardized to quite an extent, and such connections are called standard connections. Very often it is necessary to keep the top flanges of the beam and the girder at the same elevation. The beam flange must then be cut to clear the flange of the girder (B), and the beam is said to be blocked or coped. In many cases, the beam may rest on top of the girder, and the only connection required is bolts through the flanges (C) to hold them together. Channel purlins are usually supported on the sloping top chords of roof trusses by means of the clip-angle connection shown in (D). This connection may be bolted instead of riveted if desired.

Connection of Beams and Girders to Columns

There are two types of connections used between beams or girders and columns: the framed-connection type and the seated type.

The framed-connection type, illustrated in (E), consists of two angles riveted to the beam or girder in the shop, the rivets between the angles and the column being driven in the field. A shelf angle may be provided to support the beam or girder during erection. This is called an erection seat.

The seated type of connection shown in (F) consists of an angle at the bottom side of the beam which is shop-riveted to the column and an angle at the top which is field-riveted to the beam and column. For large reactions, it is necessary to provide one or two stiffener angles to support the outstanding leg of the bottom angle (G).

The shop work is simpler on the seated type, and fewer field rivets are required; but this type may project through the fireproofing if used in connecting to column flanges, and then the framed connection is used.

Wall Supports for Beams and Girders

Steel beams and girders may be built into masonry walls. Bearing plates are provided to distribute the reaction over a larger area, and anchors (H) tie the beam and wall together. Where beams and girders are not built into the wall, anchor bolts (I) are provided.

Column Bases

The load at the lower end of a column must be transferred to a concrete footing or pier which in turn transfers the load to the ground. If the end of the steel column were permitted to rest directly on the concrete, the concrete would be crushed where the two came in contact because the working stress in the steel is much greater than the strength of the concrete in bearing. It is therefore necessary to distribute the column load over a large area of the footing. This is done by means of the column base. Bases for steel columns may be divided into four classes.

1. Built-up bases made from structural sections (J).
2. Cast bases of steel or cast iron (K).
3. Rolled-steel slabs (L).
4. Steel grillages (M).

Built-up bases are suitable for light loads, but where it is necessary to distribute the column load over a considerable area, cast-iron or cast-steel bases may be used, cast steel being much stronger and more reliable than cast iron. These are rarely, if ever, used. Rolled-steel slabs have come into general use. They are more economical and reliable than the cast-iron bases and more economical than the cast-steel bases. The end of the column is milled and bears directly on the steel slab. A simple connection is made between the column end and the slab by means of two angles. Slabs are available up to 12 in. thick, but slabs over 6 in. thick are not usually economical.

Welded Construction

Typical details for welded beam, girder, and column connections are illustrated in Figure 6.16, together with the pertinent standard welding symbols.

Connections for Rods or Bars

The ends of round or square bars may be threaded to receive nuts to form an end connection. Several connections making use of nuts on threaded ends are shown in Figure 6.17A. When long bars are used, it is usually economical to enlarge the end of the bar so that the area of the section at the root of the threads is somewhat greater than the area in the body of the bar. A smaller bar can then be used, for the threads do not reduce the section area. These enlarged ends are called upset ends (B).

The clevis shown in (D) is a convenient form of end connection for round and square bars. Upset ends are usually provided. The pin in the clevis is a clevis pin, as shown, or an ordinary bolt and nut. The small split pin inserted in the larger pin is called a cotter pin or cotter key.

It is often desirable to make tension rods and bars adjustable so that they may be tightened. Two devices are used for this purpose: the turnbuckle (B) and the sleeve nut (C). In both devices, a right-hand thread is used at one end and a left-hand thread at the other so that the abutting ends of the bar may be drawn together or pushed apart by turning the turnbuckle or sleeve nut in the proper direction.

FIGURE 6.16 Typical welded connections.

A-END CONNECTIONS FOR THREADED RODS

B-TURNBUCKLE.   E-UPSET END

COTTER PIN

C-SLEEVE NUT   D- CLEVIS

FIGURE 6.17 Connections for rods and bars.

Tier Building Frame

The bolted frame of a tier building formed by assembling the various beams, girders, and columns is illustrated in Figure 6.18. In this frame, no special provision was required for wind bracing. The following points should be noted:

1. The outside wall, called a panel or enclosure wall, is supported at each story by the spandrel beams which transmit their load to the outside columns.

2. The panel walls shown are veneered with stone ashlar 3¾ in. thick, which is bonded to the backing by a bond course 7½ in. thick every third course and by galvanized anchors at the intermediate joints. The backing may be of brick or of structural clay tile. One bond course rests on the spandrel beam.

For certain occupancies such as offices, panel walls with large glass areas are used extensively. Such walls are usually called curtain walls or window walls.

3. The floor beams are placed at the third points of the girders where they cause the least moment. They are connected to the girders by framed connections.

4. The floor beams are attached to the columns by seated connections. Framed connections can be used if there is room for them.

5. Frame connections are used between the girders and columns. Seated connections can be used if the stiffener angles can be small enough so that they will not project through the fireproofing.

6. Wide-flange section columns are used. The columns are continuous through two stories, or sometimes continuous for three stories.

7. The column splices are located about 2 ft above the floor.

8. Reinforced concrete floor slabs supported by steel beams are shown.

9. The supports for the columns are not shown. The col-

umns would rest on slabs or grillages which would spread the column load over concrete footing or piers.

10. All steel members are made fire resistant.

Wind Bracing for Industrial Buildings and Arches

Buildings must be designed to resist the horizontal forces caused by wind as well as the vertical forces from the weight of the buildings and their contents. Provision must also be made for the lateral thrust of cranes and other equipment. Bracing provided to resist all lateral loads is usually called *wind bracing.*

A simple industrial or steel mill building frame with lateral bracing omitted is shown diagrammatically in Figure 6.19A. The steel frame for a building with three-hinged arches is shown in (B). The arches are braced in pairs, as shown by broken lines. Several types of steel industrial building frames are shown in (C). These are provided with lateral bracing as described in the following paragraphs. Three types of wind bracing are used in steel mill buildings. The simplest type makes use of knee braces to brace the columns rigidly to the trusses (Figure 6.20A), or trusses with considerable depth at the ends are rigidly fastened to the columns (B). This type of construction provides bracing to resist wind forces on the sides of the buildings, but wind forces against the ends of the buildings are resisted by cross bracing in the plane of the sides or by a rigid lattice girder just below the eaves.

Another method of bracing steel industrial buildings to resist wind forces consists of providing cross bracing in the plane of the bottom chord of the truss to make the building rigid from end to end in this plane. In addition to such bracing, the sides and ends are made rigid by diagonal bracing so that the whole structure acts like a rigid box (see Figure 6.21). It is not necessary to provide diagonal bracing in all the bays (spaces between columns) on the sides. Bracing is also provided in the plane of the top chord to hold the tops of the trusses in position, but this bracing is not essential to the wind bracing system, and, therefore, it is not shown in the figure. It is evident that this system might interfere seriously with the windows and doors.

A third system provides lattice girders in the sides and ends to make them rigid. The bracing in the plane of the bottom chord is the same as in the previous method (C). Various other arrangements are used.

Wind Bracing for Tier Buildings

In tall buildings of skeleton construction such as office buildings, providing adequate bracing to resist wind is an important feature of the design. If a frame, as illustrated in Figure 6.22A, is subjected to lateral forces such as wind forces, it would collapse by distorting as in (B). In low buildings of considerable width, the stiffening effect of the panel walls and partitions and the rigidity of the joints between the

FIGURE 6.18 Tier building construction without special wind bracing.

A - SIMPLE STEEL MILL BUILDING FRAME.

TRUSS
SAG RODS
COLUMN
PURLIN
GIRT
BRACING NOT SHOWN

LATERAL BRACING IN PLANE OF TOP CHORD SHOWN BY BROKEN LINES. SHOWN ON RIGHT HALF ONLY.

PURLINS

ALL PURLINS TRUSSED

B - STEEL FRAME WITH THREE-HINGED ARCHES

MONITOR
GLASS
GLASS
GLASS OR LOUVERS

C - TYPES OF STEEL MILL BUILDING FRAMES

FIGURE 6.19 Framing for steel industrial buildings.

KNEE BRACE

A

B

DASHED TRUSS PORTION NOT SHOWN

X-BRACING IN LOWER CHORD OF TRUSS

TRUSS

C

X-BRACING IN WALL IF REQUIRED

FIGURE 6.20 Wind bracing for steel industrial buildings.

girders and columns may be sufficient to provide satisfactory resistance to wind forces and earthquake shocks, but this is not true of tall buildings.

Code requirements for wind loads and earthquake shocks were considered in Section 1.2. Bracing methods employed to resist earthquake shock are similar but more extensive than those employed for wind bracing.

In designing the wind bracing for a building, the stresses in the structural frame must not exceed allowable values, and the deflections and vibrations of the building must be controlled to prevent damage to the structure. The maximum permissible lateral deflection at the top of a building is sometimes limited to $1/1000$ of the height.

Several types of wind bracings have been devised. The most direct type consists of diagonals crossing the vertical panels between the columns and the floor girders (Figure 6.21). It is evident, however, that this method is limited in its application because of its interference with the use of the building and with the locating of windows and doors, even though it is necessary to brace only a relatively small number of panels, as will be explained later.

If sufficiently rigid connections are provided between the girders and columns (Figure 6.22D), a skeleton frame will be able to resist the lateral forces. Obviously, there is a tendency to bend the columns and girders when this type of bracing is used, and, therefore, it is necessary to consider the bending stresses in the design of these members. This type of wind bracing can be arranged to interfere very little with the design and the use of a building.

The group of braced vertical panels in a single vertical plane designed to resist wind stresses is called a wind bent. It is not necessary to make all panels of a building rigid, although this may be desirable as it reduces the size of the bracing. Sometimes wind bents can be placed in the outside walls *(E)*. With this arrangement, the floors of a building tend to deform *(F)* under the action of wind forces. The floors used in modern building construction are usually rigid enough to carry the wind load to the wall bents; but if they are not, special bracing can be provided in the plane of the floors. It may be undesirable or impossible to place all the required wind bracing in the outside bents of a building; if so, some of the interior bents must be utilized. It is desirable but not necessary for these to be continuous across the

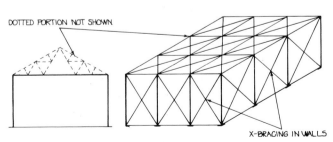

DOTTED PORTION NOT SHOWN

X-BRACING IN WALLS

FIGURE 6.21 Bracing for steel mill buildings.

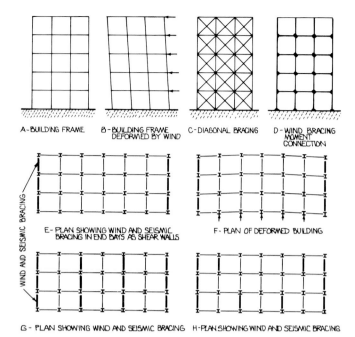

A-BUILDING FRAME.   B-BUILDING FRAME DEFORMED BY WIND   C-DIAGONAL BRACING   D-WIND BRACING MOMENT CONNECTION

E- PLAN SHOWING WIND AND SEISMIC BRACING IN END BAYS AS SHEAR WALLS   F- PLAN OF DEFORMED BUILDING

G- PLAN SHOWING WIND AND SEISMIC BRACING   H-PLAN SHOWING WIND AND SEISMIC BRACING

WIND AND SEISMIC BRACING

FIGURE 6.22 Wind and seismic bracing for steel office or tier building.

building (G), but wind bents each designed to carry its part of the wind load may be distributed throughout the building (H). They should be so placed that there is no twisting effect in the frame caused by greater rigidity on one side than on the other, and due consideration must be given to relative lateral deflections.

In buildings that diminish in size in the upper stories, wind bents located in the exterior walls may be continued down through the interior of the lower part of the building, or sometimes it may be desirable to transfer the wind loads to wall bents in the lower stories (Figure 6.23A). The horizontal effect of the wind on the upper section may be transferred to the wall bents or other bents in the lower stories by means of a heavy concrete floor slab where the building changes section, or by special bracing in the floor. The vertical reactions of the columns of the wind bents are transferred directly down through the corresponding columns in the lower section.

In buildings with towers projecting above a relatively low and broad main building, the towers are usually provided with wind bracing which is independent of the main structural frame (B). The tower bracing may be in the exterior bents only or in the interior bents also.

Buildings of irregular shape and buildings that change in section require special study. The system of bracing shown in (C) has been used on such buildings. No wind bracing is required for the upper floors. From sections 5–5, 6–6, and 7–7, it is seen that the wind bracing is placed entirely in the outside walls, but all outside walls do not contain wind bracing. The horizontal thrust on the portion of the building

above floor H is transmitted to the wind bents in the outside walls below floor H. In order to transmit this horizontal thrust, floor H must be specially designed. The vertical wind loads in the columns above floor H are transmitted directly down the same columns below floor H.

Walls enclosing elevator shafts and stairways or other walls without openings sometimes can include diagonal wind bracing, and sometimes vertical bents have been converted into vertical cantilever wind trusses. In addition, instead of using diagonal bracing or vertical trusses, reinforced-concrete walls may be installed in such locations. These are called shear walls. They are relatively rigid.

Wind-Connection Details

Various types of connections between wind girders and columns, using shop rivets and field rivets or high-strength bolts, are illustrated in Figure 6.24A-F. The simple connection in (A) may be used when the moment is small. It can be used on interior connections as well as on exterior connections, since it does not occupy any space. The knuckle connection (B) will develop considerable resisting moment and occupies very little space. The connecting members are structural tees cut from wide-flanged shapes. A framed connection can be used with this detail in place of the seated connection shown. The connection shown in (C) is sometimes used. The brackets are wide flange or S-beams which have been cut diagonally. A triangular plate and a pair of angles can be substituted for each wide flange or S-beam bracket, and a plate girder can be substituted for the wide flange or S-beam. The connection shown in (D) can be used to develop large resisting moments. A single plate is used to form both brackets and to replace a part of the web of the girder. This requires the use of splice plates as shown. The connection shown in (E) is similar to that in (D), except that stiffener angles are provided along the edges of the bracket, if necessary, to prevent buckling. The connections shown in (D) and (E) can be altered to have only a bottom bracket, and all three types may be changed so as to have top brackets instead of bottom brackets. The connections in (D) and (E) are called gusset-plate connections.

In tall slender buildings, the wind moment may place tension in some of the columns. These stresses must be provided for in the design of the column splices, in anchoring the columns to the foundations, and in the design of the foundations.

Many other types of riveted connections have been used, and connections which are suitable for welded construction have been developed.

Before 1950, all the taller skeleton construction buildings were field-riveted. Since that time, high-strength bolts have come into extensive use to replace rivets with no restriction on the building height. Shop and field welding is also being used for buildings of considerable height and its use will doubtless continue to expand.

FIGURE 6.23 Wind and seismic bracing for steel office or tier building.

Fire Protection of Structural Steel

The classification of buildings according to construction was considered in Chapter 1. The required fire ratings of the various parts of buildings in each class are given in Table 1.1, these ratings being based upon the behavior of materials in a standard fire test, which is explained. The ratings must be sufficient to withstand the hazard involved.

The capacity of structural steel to carry stresses is considerably reduced at the high temperatures that may be expected to prevail during a severe fire. For that reason, it is necessary to protect structural-steel members with fire-resistant materials.

Methods used in protecting structural steel against the action of fire are shown in Figure 6.25.

RIGID FRAMES

Rigid frames, as defined in Section 1.4, constructed of steel, are used for auditoriums, gymnasiums, armories, field houses, industrial plants, and buildings with many other classes of occupancy. Steel rigid frames normally are not advantageous for spans of 40 ft or less. They are widely used for spans up to 100 ft and have been constructed for spans exceeding 200 ft. For the longer spans, however, steel arches are usually used.

Rigid frames are constructed by connecting structural-steel shapes and plates either by bolting or welding them together. Welding is particularly well suited to this type of structure, however, and is usually employed.

The most common type of welded steel rigid frame is illustrated in Figure 6.26. The vertical legs or columns are provided with flat bases that bear on the tops of the foundations. Actual hinges are never provided at these points, and thus there is always some resistance to rotation. If the column bases are so anchored to the foundation that this resistance is nominal and is not considered in the foundation design, the connections are considered to be hinged in preparing the frame designs. If the bases are securely an-

FIGURE 6.24 Types of bolted wind connections.

chored to the foundations so as to resist the moment fully, and the foundations are designed accordingly, the connections are considered to be fixed. Between these two extremes, the condition of partial fixity is often considered.

Fixing the column bases increases the rigidity of the frame but may increase the cost of the foundations significantly. For that reason, rigid frames are usually designed on the assumption that the joints at these points are hinged. In most, if not all, frames, full fixity is provided at the crown. Therefore, the common type of single-span rigid frame is usually considered to be two-hinged for design purposes.

Advantages of Fixing to Foundations

The lateral wind loads on a high, narrow, rigid frame may cause it to deflect laterally enough to damage rigid enclos-

ing walls. In addition, a rigid frame whose columns support a traveling crane may have frequent and excessive lateral deflections caused by the operation of the crane. These might damage rigid enclosing walls and the frame itself and interfere with the operation of the crane. Since fixing the column bases reduces lateral deflections, fixed bases may be essential and fully justify the greater cost of the foundations.

Tie Between Foundations

The horizontal component of the thrust of each leg at the top of its foundation must be considered in the design of the foundation. The soil may be adequate to resist this component; but if not, the column bases at the two sides may be tied together by steel rods, embedded in concrete to resist corrosion, to form a tie beam located below the floor, as shown in the figure; or the tie rods may be embedded in a concrete floor. Turnbuckles (Figure 6.17B) are provided on the tie rods to adjust them accurately to the required length.

Basic Components of a Rigid Frame

The long-span frame (Figure 6.26) includes two knees and a crown with H-shaped cross sections, each made up of flange plates fillet welded to a web plate. The portions of the frame included between the ends of the crown and knees, often called rafters, may be wide-flange shapes or, to obtain greater depths, they may be built up of a web plate to which flange plates are fillet welded, as for the knees and crown. The various sections are groove welded together, as indicated by the heavy lines in the figure. The bottom of each leg is fillet welded to a heavy baseplate with holes to receive bolts that anchor the frame to the foundations.

Stiffeners

Stiffeners consisting of plates fitted between the flanges, normal to the webs, and fillet welded to the flanges and the web are used in various locations. They must be provided at all points where either of the flanges changes direction to prevent the flanges and the web from buckling. Such conditions exist at the groove welded joints between the various sections indicated by the heavy lines on the figure. They also exist at the center of each knee and the crown, as shown by the light solid lines in the figure. Stiffeners may be required at intermediate points along the length of each rafter and leg, as shown by the dashed lines. This condition may prevail if the web is relatively thin or if there are heavy roof purlin loads along the rafter.

Lateral Bracing

Effective lateral bracing is required between adjacent frames, at the ridge, and in the diagonal plane through the

A · CONCRETE FIREPROOFING

B · TERRA COTTA FIREPROOFING

C · GYPSUM FIREPROOFING

D · METAL LATH AND PLASTER FIREPROOFING

E · CONCRETE

F · HOLLOW CLAY TILE

G · GYPSUM

H · METAL LATH AND PLASTER

FIGURE 6.25 Fire protection for steel members.

knee where the stiffeners are located. The latter is called an eaves strut. Such bracing often consists of light trussed members.

Each frame and all its parts must be supported laterally to remain in its true position. Roof purlins, combined with diagonal cross bracing, consisting of angles in the plane of the top flange and located in alternate panels between frames, usually constitute the principal bracing for this part of the structure. In addition, lateral support must be provided for the legs.

Other Types

Many other types of knees and other parts may be used on rigid frames of the general type illustrated in Figure 6.27. The top member may be horizontal, steeply pitched, segmental, or curved, as shown in Figure 1.23.

Two-story buildings have been constructed, with a rigid frame for each story, and multiple-span frames (Figure 1.23) are rather common. For such frames, the knees of the interior columns are replaced by Y-shaped units. Rigid frames may be used to support sawtooth roofs (Figures 1.23 and 6.28).

Rigid frames are often used for craneways by supporting the crane girders on brackets welded to the legs. In addition, balconies may be cantilevered out from the legs of rigid frames (Figure 1.23).

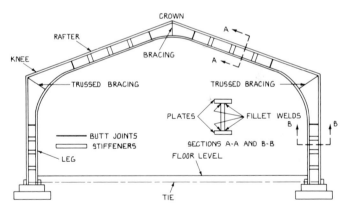

FIGURE 6.26 Steel rigid frame.

ARCHES
Use

Steel arches are used extensively to support roofs covering large unobstructed floor areas in structures such as hangars, field houses, and exhibition halls with spans that may exceed 300 ft. Often, rigid frames would be preferred for intermediate spans.

Classification according to Hinges

As explained in Section 1.4 and illustrated in Figure 1.20, arches may be three-hinged, two-hinged, one-hinged, and

FIGURE 6.27 Rigid frame in Field House at University of Colorado.

FIGURE 6.28 Sawtooth roof with welded steel rigid frames.

fixed or hingeless. The most common type is three-hinged. Hingeless arches are often used, two-hinged arches are occasionally used, and one-hinged arches are never used.

Comparisons of Classes

The stress computations for three-hinged arches are relatively simple, whereas those for two-hinged and fixed arches are more complex. The stresses in three-hinged arches are not affected significantly by minor movements of the abutments. Horizontal movements of the abutments can be prevented by tying the two abutments together with tie rods (Figure 6.29) if the soil supporting the foundations cannot provide adequate lateral support. The stresses in two-hinged arches are unaffected by minor vertical movements of the abutments if the span remains constant. The stresses in fixed arches are affected by vertical or horizontal movements or rotation of the abutments. In general, the three-hinged arch is usually preferred, except when significant savings in material can be achieved by the other types, especially the fixed arch. The latter requires favorable foundation conditions.

Types of Ribs

The arched members are ordinarily called ribs. Arches may be girder arches, whose ribs have solid H-shaped cross sections such as those of plate girders or wide-flange shapes, or they may be framed in a manner similar to trusses, in which case they are said to be trussed arches, as explained in Section 1.4 and illustrated in Figure 1.19.

Lateral Bracing

Since both chords or flanges of arch ribs are in compression, they must be braced laterally to prevent buckling in that direction. This is usually accomplished by using trussed purlins whose depth commonly is equal to that of the arch rib. If the spacing of the arches is relatively small, rolled sections shallower than the ribs are sometimes used for purlins, in which case the bottom chord or flange may be supported by knee braces located near the ends of the purlins. Other lateral bracing is required to give stability to the structure as a whole. This consists of diagonal bracing between the arches in the curved surface tangent to the top chord and sometimes the bottom chord also, a simple example of which is illustrated in Figure 6.19*B*.

Methods of Connecting

The various parts of an arch may be either riveted or welded together. The method used for this purpose determines, to a large extent, the structural shapes of which the members are composed.

Girder Arch Ribs

A riveted plate-girder arch rib is built up in a manner similar to a riveted plate girder (Figure 6.5*F*) with a web plate and two flanges, each consisting of two angles placed back to back and cover plates as required. A welded plate girder arch rib consists of a web plate to which top and bottom flange plates are welded, as for the welded plate girder section shown in Figure 6.6*A*.

Riveted or welded plate girder ribs may be made up of straight segments spliced together or they may be fabricated to conform to the curves of the ribs. The flange angles and flange plates for ribs of the latter type are cold-bent to the curve of the arch, and the webs are cut with this curvature. If wide-flange shapes are used for arch ribs, they may be made up of straight or cold-bent segments groove-welded together.

Trussed Arch Ribs

A determining factor in selecting the flange or chord sections of a trussed arch rib is the fact that provisions must be made for connecting the ends of the web members to the chords. In riveted trussed arches, these connections are usually made by gusset plates. Two angles placed back to back with gusset plates between them (Figure 6.29) is a common form. The cross section of the flange can be var-

FIGURE 6.29 Three-hinged trussed or framed steel arch with 2L chords and web members.

FIGURE 6.30 A 330-ft span, three-hinged plate girder rib, riveted arch. Hangar at Kennedy International Airport, Port Authority of New York. Arranged from *Engineering News-Record.*

ied, without changing the angles, by the use of appropriate cover plates. The web members used with chords of this type are usually composed of two angles placed back to back with the gusset plates between them.

The ends of members meeting at a joint of a trussed rib may be welded together in the same manner as truss members.

Welded Constant-Depth Hingeless Trussed Arch

A long-span welded constant-depth trussed arch without hinges is illustrated in Figure 6.30. The fixed ends are supported by reinforced concrete abutments. Each flange consists of a structural T-section, and each web member consists of two angles placed back to back and spaced far enough apart to fit over the stems of the flanges to which their ends are welded. The chord members are made up of segments straight for two panel lengths. The ends of adjacent segments are groove-welded together.

Since both chords are compression members and tend to buckle laterally under stress, they are braced effectively in this direction. The arches are spaced 25 ft apart. Purlin trusses located between the arches are framed into each radial arch truss member or post to provide lateral support. They are in the same planes as these members, are as deep as the arch ribs, and are welded trusses with T-section chords and angles for web members. Diagonal bracing, consisting of T-sections, is located in surfaces tangent to the top and bottom chords and between the chords of the trussed purlins.

For ease in erection, the chords of each arch are divided into five segments of about equal length and are spliced by field welding. The roof is wood sheathing spanning the distances between the trussed purlins.

Riveted Three-Hinged Girder Arch

A long-span, riveted three-hinged girder arch is shown in Figure 6.31. The ribs have I-shaped cross sections built up of four flange angles, a web plate, and cover plates riveted together as shown in the figure. Trussed purlins provide lateral support for the arch ribs as well as for the light-gage-steel roof deck. Other bracing is provided to increase the lateral support of the arch ribs and the structure as a whole. Each arch is erected in four sections, locating the field splices near the quarter points of the arch.

Welded Three-Hinged Girder Arch

The framing for the Field House at the University of Vermont, shown in Figure 6.32, consists of 28 welded three-hinged arches with a span of 153 ft covering a floor 486 ft long. The arch ribs consist of $26 \times \frac{3}{8}$ in. web plates and $15\frac{5}{8} \times \frac{5}{8}$ in. flange plates shaped to conform to the curvature of the arch and welded together.

The roof deck consists of tongue-and-groove planks 4 in. thick, spanning between arches. They are anchored to the arches by 4×10 in. wood nailing strips attached to the top flanges of the arches at the fabricating shop. The roof deck is covered with a built-up roofing.

CHORDS – STRUCTURAL T's
TOPS STEMS DOWN–BOTTOM STEMS UP

DIAGONALS AND POSTS – 2L MEMBERS
WELDED TO STEMS OF CHORDS

BUILT-UP WELDED BASE AT END OF
EACH FLANGE, ANCHOR BARS
WELDED TO BASE PLATE

ARCH

PURLIN TRUSS

ARCH

FLOOR

PURLIN TRUSS
AT EACH POST

BRACING IN PLANES
OF BOTTOM CHORDS
OF PURLIN TRUSSES

FIGURE 6.31 A 300-ft span, fixed arch with constant depth rib-welded trussed and structural T-chords. U.S. Navy hangar, Patuxent River, Maryland. Arranged from *Engineering News-Record.*

FIGURE 6.32 A 153-ft span welded three-hinge girder arch. University of Vermont Field House. Architect: Freeman-French-Freeman. Structural Engineers: Severud, Elstad and Krueger Associates. Steel fabricator and erector: Vermont Structural Steel Corporation. Structural steel furnished by Bethlehem Steel Corporation.

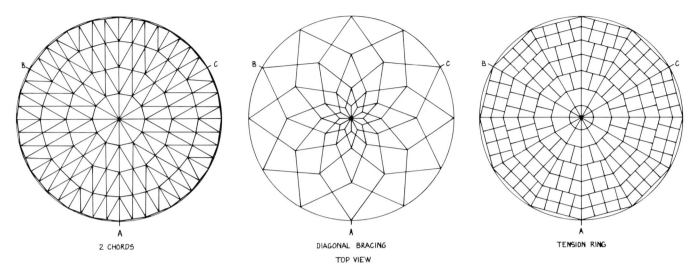

FIGURE 6.33 Patterns of dome framing.

Each arch was shipped to the site in four sections, assembled on the ground in two halves, and pin-connected to the foundations. The two halves were then raised into position by truck-mounted cranes and pinned at the crown. The two sections of each half arch rib were field-connected with high-strength bolts.

DOMES

Coliseums, field houses, exhibition halls, auditoriums, sports arenas, and other large floor areas are often roofed over with domes that have supporting members of steel. Such domes have been constructed with diameters of more than 400 ft.

A dome is an integral or self-contained unit. Its perimeter may be supported directly by the foundation, which carries the vertical and horizontal thrusts of the ribs. It is usually provided, however, with a steel tension ring that carries the outward thrusts of the ribs and is supported on steel or reinforced concrete columns located at the bottom ends of the ribs. They may be vertical or their tops may be tilted outward. They are braced together laterally to form a stable structure.

Patterns of Framing

Many arrangements or patterns of steel frames have been used for the support of domes. Most of them provide for a tension ring around the perimeter of the dome. Usually there are radial ribs, with bottom ends framing into the tension ring and top ends framing into a compression ring, with its center at the center of the dome.

Three types of patterns are illustrated in Figure 6.33. The tension and compression rings and the radial ribs are indicated by heavy lines. The rings are usually made up of straight segments. The number of radial ribs varies from 12

to 48, depending upon the diameter of the dome, the framing patterns, and other factors.

The tension ring is made up of straight segments between ribs. The rim of the compression ring is supported by radial members (shown by the dashed lines), which may be located at every second or third rib, causing the entire assembly to resemble a wheel.

For the pattern shown in the sector AB of the figure, the roof deck is supported directly by equally spaced straight purlins spanning from rib to rib. For the pattern in the sector AC of the figure, the roof deck is supported directly by rafters normal to straight purlins, which are in turn supported by the ribs. An interior view of framing with this pattern would resemble Figure 6.34. The pattern in the sector BC includes secondary framing members parallel to the main ribs, extending from the tension ring until they meet the ribs to form diamond-shaped patterns, as in the lamella pattern. The Houston, Texas, stadium has a 642 ft clear-span dome of this pattern with 12 trussed main ribs and secondary ribs dividing the tension ring into 72 segments all supported on 72 steel columns.

Types of Ribs

The ribs may be fabricated by welding or riveting. They may be of the girder or the trussed type, as described under arches. The ends of the ribs may be fixed or hinged at their junctions with the tension and compression rings.

Lateral Bracing

For all the patterns shown in Figure 6.33, the ribs receive lateral support from the purlins which frame into them. In the patterns in sectors AB and AC, additional lateral support is provided by diagonal cross bracing, as shown by the dashed lines. The pattern in sector BC is made up of dia-

FIGURE 6.34 Steel framed dome with wide-flange radial ribs. Field House, Syracuse University. Span 300 ft; 36 precast reinforced concrete columns. Seating capacity 2000. Architects: King and King. Structural Engineers: Eckerlin and Kleeper. General Contractor R.A. Culotti Construction Co.

mond-shaped panels which are subdivided into triangles by the circumferential members or purlins. Since triangles are stable units, each sector is stable against lateral forces.

As has been stated, a dome is usually supported on steel or reinforced concrete columns located at the bottom ends of the ribs. The dome itself, framed as described, is stable against lateral forces, but the lateral forces against the dome are transmitted to the tops of the columns. In addition, provisions must be made to resist the lateral forces on the portion of the structure below the perimeter of the dome. These may consist of rigid framing or of diagonal bracing in the panels between columns.

Dome with Wide-Flange Ribs
The roof framing for the Field House at Syracuse University (Figure 6.34) consists of a dome with thirty-six 18 in. wide-flange ribs spanning between a steel tension ring 300 ft in diameter and a steel compression ring 18 ft in diameter. It is supported on 36 tapered precast reinforced concrete columns 30 ft high. The domed roof is surrounded with an overhang which projects 18 ft beyond the exterior walls of the building.

The ribs consist of segmental sections groove-welded together. There are five intermediate circumferential rings of steel purlins, spanning between the ribs and bulb-tee rafters or subpurlins with a constant spacing of 2 ft 9 in. spanning between the purlins, as shown in the figure. These are shimmed to conform to the spherical roof surface. There are three sets of cross-rod bracing in each of the 36 segmental panels of the dome.

Between the tension and compression rings, the roof deck of the dome is made up of 3 in. wood-fiber-cement planks spanning between rafters. These are lightweight and noncombustible and contribute significantly to heat insulation and sound absorption. The planks are covered with a 1 in. rigid insulation, over which is a conventional 5-ply built-up roofing with a marble surface. A 7 in. slab of light-weight concrete 40 ft in diameter covers the opening within the compression ring and is elevated to provide ventilation. The 18 ft overhang is constructed of vermiculite concrete on a sheet-metal roof deck with an asbestos-cement board underside. The ventilator slab and the overhang are covered with a conventional 5-ply built-up roofing.

CABLE-SUPPORTED ROOFS
General Comments
As stated previously, cold-drawing of steel bars through dies to form wire markedly increases the strength of the steel. For this reason, cables made up of steel wires are efficient members for carrying loads that subject them to tension. Such action occurs in various forms of roofs that are supported by wire cables and are called cable-supported or cable-suspended roofs, the former designation

A-GALVANIZED BRIDGE STRAND

B-GALVANIZED BRIDGE ROPE

FIGURE 6.35 Wire strand and rope.

being less common but probably preferable because it is more general. Because of the flexibility of cables, special consideration must be given to the effects of unbalanced loads on deflections and the tendency of gusts of wind to cause vibration and flutter which, if excessive, may cause failure.

According to Roebling, a group of wires twisted together (Figure 6.35A) is called a strand and a group of strands twisted together, as shown in (B), is called a wire rope. Resistance to corrosion is markedly increased by using galvanized wire.

Bridge strand and rope are prestretched by the manufacturer to remove constructional looseness that is present when they come from the stranding or closing machines. The process is often called prestressing, but this term must not be confused with other meanings explained in Section 4.6.

Normally, the cables for cable-supported roofs consist of galvanized bridge strand. It is considered superior to galvanized bridge rope because it has higher strength for a given diameter and because it elongates less when subjected to a given unit tensile stress.

Galvanized bridge strand is available, from one manufacturer, in diameters varying from ½ in., made up of 7 or 14 wires, to 3⅝ in., made up of 223 wires. Galvanized bridge rope is available in diameters varying from ⅝ in., with 6 strands and 7 wires per strand, designated as 6 × 7, to 4 in., with 6 strands and 43 wires per strand, designated as 6 × 43. Other manufacturers have corresponding strands and wire ropes differing somewhat in available diameters and numbers of wires. Adjustable connections anchor the ends of cables.

Single-Layer Cable-Supported Roofs

The single-layer, cable-supported roof in Figure 6.36 (A) and (B) shows the basic structural features of a covered stadium, 310 ft in diameter, with cylindrical exterior walls 85 ft high, located in Montevideo, Uruguay. The rainfall in this area is very low, there is no snow, and earthquakes have not

occurred. Such favorable conditions rarely exist. The roof support consists of a reinforced concrete compression ring located on top of the 4 in. reinforced concrete wall surrounding the stadium, a steel tension ring at the center, and 256 galvanized wire cables radiating between the two rings. The cables are made of strands 0.6 in. in diameter. The roof deck consists of thin reinforced concrete slabs precast to the dimensions of the trapezoidal space each occupies in the completed roof. These slabs are anchored to the cables and to each other by means of projecting ends of the reinforcing rods.

After all the roof slabs were in place, the roof was temporarily loaded with brick to increase the stress in the cables. Loading increased their length and widened the joints between the slabs. The joints were then filled with cement mortar. After the mortar had hardened, the brick were removed and the cables tended to return to their previous length. Their action was resisted by the slabs and joints, which were compressed, and the joints remained tight. This procedure is known as prestressing. The prestressing also increased the stiffness of the roof.

Slabs were not placed in a circular area 65 ft in diameter at the center of the roof. This was covered with a ventilated skylight (Figure 6.36A). It was not necessary to provide for an unbalanced snow load.

The tops of the slabs were waterproofed. Rainwater that falls on the roof is collected in a trough around the central opening and conducted through four pipes, hung from the ceiling, to downspouts on the outside wall and into a storm sewer.

The single-layer type of cable-supported roof for the Chicago O'Hare International Airport Restaurant is illustrated in Figure 6.37. The reinforced concrete compression ring, whose diameter is 190 ft, is supported on 26 reinforced concrete columns 58 ft above the ground surface with diamond-shaped profiles. The tension ring is a wide-flange shape and has a diameter of 13 ft. The sag of the cables is 10 ft 6 in. There are 52 lengths of 2 in. prestretched galvanized bridge strand cables with their ends anchored to the compression and tension rings. The roof deck consists of precast reinforced concrete slabs 3½ in. thick which fit between the cables with projecting ends of the reinforcement hooking over the cables. The cables were prestressed in the manner described for the Montevideo Stadium, except that pig iron was used for the temporary load instead of brick.

A cable-supported roof similar to that of the Montevideo Stadium was constructed for the Assembly Building at San Antonio, Texas. The span is much smaller, only 132 ft. There are 200 cables attached to a welded built-up steel ring. This ring is designed to carry the compressive and flexural stresses to which it is subjected because it is supported by 20 vertical steel columns spaced about 20 ft apart around the perimeter. The inner ends of the cables are attached to a welded-steel tension ring 40 ft in diameter. Steel trusses radiating from a hub at the center of the roof to

FIGURE 6.36 Single-layer and double-layer cable-supported roofs.

the tension ring support the roof over the area surrounded by the tension ring.

The remainder of the roof consists of small trapezoidal shaped precast concrete slabs arranged in concentric rings, supported on the cables, with open joints which were filled with mortar after the cables had been prestressed by loading the roof with brick. All operations follow procedures similar to those used in building the Montevideo Stadium. This comment also applies to the drainage system.

Double-Layer Cable-Supported Roof

A roof supported by a double layer of cables is illustrated in Figure 6.36C and D. This roof covers the Memorial Auditorium at Utica, New York, a circular building 240 ft in diameter. The supporting system consists of two 72-cable layers. The outer ends of the cables in both layers are anchored to a reinforced concrete compression ring, with a section area of about 20 sq ft, supported on twenty-four 2-ft-square reinforced concrete columns equally spaced around the perim-

eter of the building and supported laterally. The two welded-steel tension rings are 18 ft apart vertically and are held apart by equally spaced steel pipes 5 in. in diameter. Vertical pipe struts are inserted at intervals of about 14 ft between each pair of cables in the same vertical plane and located on concentric circles.

The two tension rings were supported in contact on a temporary scaffold at the center of the building while the cables were being placed and anchored to these rings and to the compression ring. At this stage, the tension rings were at a predetermined elevation. Hydraulic jacks were inserted between the rings and gradually forced them apart. Downward movement of the lower ring was made possible by removing timber blocking that was provided on top of the scaffold. Jacking was continued until the two layers were 18 ft apart, vertically, at the center. Since the ends of the cables were anchored to the tension and compression rings, the vertical movement produced by the jacks subjected the cables to tension. The operations were so controlled that the stresses in the cables reached predeter-

FIGURE 6.37 Single-layer cable-supported roof. Chicago O'Hare International Airport Restaurant. Architects and Engineers: C. F. Murphy Associates. Roof Contractor: E. H. Marhoefer, Jr. Cables furnished by John A. Roebling's Sons Division, Colorado Fuel and Iron Corporation.

mined values. The jacks were replaced by permanent pipe separators. The tensions in the cables were then increased to desired values by inserting the vertical struts between the upper and lower cables, as shown in the figure. Diagonal cross bracing, consisting of rods, was placed in each panel between struts. This bracing distributed the effects of concentrated loads due to mechanical equipment and stiffened the roof. Final adjustments were made to ensure that the tension in the cables was in close agreement with the desired values.

Inducing tensile stresses in the cables before the loads to be carried are applied is called pretensioning or prestressing. Pretensioning controls the deflection of the roof and prevents objectionable vibrations which may develop in cable-supported structures. Both cables remain in tension under all conditions of loading.

The roof deck is constructed of light-gage steel supported directly on the upper cables except near the perimeter where intermediate channel purlins are required.

A cable-supported roof, which resembles the roof just described, was provided for the United States Pavilion at the Brussels Worlds Fair. The span is 302 ft. There are two layers of cables, but they are not prestressed.

Cable-Supported Cantilever Roofs

Cable-supported cantilevers are used to support the roofs of hangars. They may be of the single- or double-cantilever types. Portions of the structures other than the cables may be constructed of structural steel, reinforced concrete, or various combinations of these materials.

One example of a cable-supported, single-cantilever hangar is illustrated in Figure 6.38A. The principal roof support consists of a series of heavy wide-flange steel girders, each hinged at one end to a rigid side section of reinforced concrete and supported near the other end by a cable passing over a steel mast erected above the inner side of the side section and anchored to the outer side of that section. The roof deck consists of precast reinforced concrete channel slabs, as described in Section 4.7, supported on rolled-steel purlins spanning between the cantilever girders. The relative weights and dimensions of the cantilever and side sections and the anchorage provided must ensure stability.

A cable-supported, double-cantilever hangar is illustrated in Figure 6.38B. The steel cantilevers project outward from both sides of a center section. The inner ends of the cantilevers are hinged to the steel frame of the center section. Cables provide support near the outer two-thirds points of the cantilevers and extend inward over steel masts to anchorages on the center section.

Principal structural supports for the roof over the Sports Arena at Squaw Valley, California, are illustrated in Figure 6.38C. They consist of two independent cable-supported cantilevers with free ends meeting at the ridge of the roof. The inclined girders are tapered-steel box sections. The

A - SINGLE CABLE-SUPPORTED CANTILEVER HANGER

B - DOUBLE CABLE-SUPPORTED CANTILEVER HANGER

C - SPORTS ARENA ROOF WITH TWO CABLE-SUPPORTED CANTILEVERS

FIGURE 6.38 Cable-supported cantilever roofs.

columns or masts are tapered-steel four-flanged cross-shaped sections built up of plates welded together. The cantilever projection of each girder is supported at two points by cables that pass over the top of a column normal to the girder and are anchored to the lower end of the girder. The end is in turn anchored to a pier, the uplift at this point being resisted by the pile foundation. Each column is supported by a column pier. The entire system is arranged as shown in the figure.

The roof deck consists of cellular sheet-steel panels, 4½ in. deep, supported on heavy wide-flange steel purlins spaced about 12 ft apart and spanning the 32 ft between the cantilevers, all designed and connected so as to require no further lateral bracing in the plane of the roof. The top surface of the roof panels is arranged to serve as the finished roof surface to receive a plastic coating.

6.3 Metal Building Systems

SYSTEMS CONCEPT

The metal building systems industry has adopted a systems approach to the fabrication and erection of buildings. Frames, walls, roofs, as well as construction techniques, have been standardized in order to realize the advantages of mass production, resulting in less material, better quality control, and faster fabrication and erection (see Figure 6.39).

For the manufacturer, standardization of systems is accompanied by use of computer capabilities in design, drafting, and fabrication. In the plant, it means less unproductive time spent in retooling or equipment set-up, stockpiling certain components, and transferring expensive field labor into the plant where costs are lower and control is better. For the

FIGURE 6.39 Components of a metal building system. Metal Building Manufacturers Association, Cleveland, OH.

contractor, it means being able to estimate the cost of a building for a prospective owner in a relatively short period of time with a high degree of accuracy.

In the field, standardization of systems permits faster erection with a minimum of on-site labor, due to the familiarity of repetitive parts and practices. Less time spent in erection means that the owner can occupy the building, and begin realizing a return on his investment much sooner than would have been possible in other types of construction.

The net result of the systems approach, both in the factory and in the field, is a high quality building which is economical, and can be erected in a relatively short period of time.

STRUCTURAL SYSTEMS

The primary structural system of a metal building system is the frame that supports the roof, walls, and all externally applied loads. There are several different types of framing systems in use today. Putting aside minor individual differences between manufacturers, they can be categorized as follows:

1. Single span rigid frame, usually tapered.
2. Tapered beam with Type II connections at the columns.
3. Continuous beam frame, post-and-beam.
4. Single span and continuous trusses.
5. Lean-to.

Most manufacturers have the capability to produce several or all of these types. The selection of the appropriate type is determined by a combination of economics, function, and usage. For a given space requirement, a manufacturer will be able to recommend the most economical framing system, although function may dictate the use of a less economical system. For example, a prospective owner may require a wide, column-free interior which would suggest the use of a rigid frame, even though a continuous post-and-beam system might be more economical. A metal building systems contractor will be able to identify the needs of the owner and, with the help of the manufacturer, recommend the appropriate framing system.

The framing systems listed previously are usually welded up from plate and bar stock having a yield strength of 50 ksi. The member depths, and the plate thickness are determined by computer analysis in order to make the most efficient use of material. By tapering structural members, the most material can be used at those sections where the bending moments are highest. Standard hot-rolled sections are generally not used.

The frames are fabricated with prepunched splice plates for easy field bolting. There are two types of connections used: simple (hinged, pinned) and moment connections. A simple connection joins members but permits them to rotate relative to each other, and has only the capacity to transfer shear and axial force from one member to another.

This is referred to as an AISC Type II connection. A moment connection joins two members in such a way that bending moment can be transferred from one to the other.

Typically, all connections between members in a rigid frame are moment connections, made with end plates. Secondary members, which frame into the primary members at right angles, are generally joined with simple connections, as are columns to foundations. Simple connections require less bolts, thinner plates, and thus are less expensive than moment connections.

Single Span Rigid Frame

A rigid frame is used when interior columns cannot be tolerated. Standard spans up to 120 ft are available, but special requirements of up to 200 ft spans may be met with nonstandard designs. Columns are usually tapered and girders may be straight, singly tapered, or multiply tapered (see Figure 6.40).

Tapered Beams

A tapered beam may be used for moderate clear spans. The columns in this type of frame are straight and the girder tapers to a maximum depth at mid-span. The lower flange of the girder is thus kept horizontal, which is advantageous for certain applications, while the top flange provides the necessary roof slope for drainage. The column-to-girder connection is designed to resist moments due to wind loads, but provide enough flexibility under live load to be considered, effectively, a simple connection.

Continuous Beam Frames

The continuous beam frame, or post-and-beam, is used in applications where interior columns are not objectionable. The interior columns will cause the girder size to be reduced, which makes this frame more economical than a clear span rigid frame. Exterior columns are generally tapered and interior columns are straight in this system. The girders are normally tapered.

Single Span and Continuous Trusses

The single span truss and continuous truss are similar in application to the tapered beam and continuous beam. The only difference is that the roof support is a truss rather than a girder.

Lean-to

Lean-to systems are "add on" items. They normally are designed for vertical loads only, and rely on an adjacent structure for lateral support. Tapered beams and straight columns are usually used.

FIGURE 6.40 Rigid frame structural system. Metal Building Manufacturers Association, Cleveland, OH.

Most of the above structural systems are easily modified to accept cranes, monorails, or other materials-handling equipment. For guidelines on crane applications, the reader is referred to the *Crane Design Manual,* published by MBMA. Likewise, all structural systems can be designed for the addition of canopies and lean-tos, either as an extension of the roof line or at a level below the eave height.

WALL SYSTEMS

Wall systems usually consist of two components: the wall panel and the girt. The girts, cold formed "C" or "Z" sections, are attached to the columns of the primary frame, and support the wall panel against lateral loads. They may frame into the column webs, or be attached to the outer flange. Flush framing provides more usable building area. The panel and girt act in concert to resist pressure and suction on the system due to wind.

Wall systems are normally classified as either field assembled systems or as factory assembled systems.

Field Assembled Systems

Field assembled systems consist of an outer skin element, insulation, girts, and in some cases, an inner liner panel. The liner panel is used when it is desirable to protect the field installed insulation.

Specific advantages of field assembled wall panels include:

1. Rapid erection of panels.

2. Good cost competition with a large number of manufacturers and contractors being capable of erecting panels.

3. Panel replacement is quick and easy in the event of panel damage.

4. Openings for doors and windows can be created quickly and easily.

5. Panels are lightweight so that heavy equipment is not re-required for erection. Also large foundations and heavy spandrels are not required.

6. Acoustic surface treatment can be added easily to interior panel wall at reasonable cost.

Factory Assembled Panels

Factory assembled panels generally consist of interior liner panels, exterior metal panels, and insulation. Panels providing various insulating values are available from several manufacturers.

The particular advantages of these factory assembled panels are:

1. Panels are lightweight and require no heavy cranes for erection, no large foundations or heavy spandrels.

2. Panels have a hard surface interior liner.

3. Panel side lap fasteners are normally concealed producing a "clean" appearance.

4. Documented panel performance characteristics, determined by test, are usually available from reputable manufacturers.

Wall systems can be further classified as either "exposed fastener systems" or "concealed fastener systems," with the former usually being more economical.

Exposed Fastener Systems

Panels for exposed fastener systems vary in depth, and are available in widths of 2 to 4 ft, and thickness ranges from .0179 in. to .0478 in. in steel, and .024 in. to .050 in. in aluminum. The most common wall panel thickness is .0179 in. They are attached to "C" or "Z" girts with self-tapping screws, self-drilling screws, or expanded fasteners, and joined to each other at their sides and ends in lap joints.

There are several types of exposed fastener wall systems. The original wall system from the Quonset hut days is still available, and is called a "corrugated panel." This is clearly the most economical wall system available. It is ½ in. deep, and is available in standard width from 30 in. to 48 in.

Today, the common type of exposed fastener wall system is the "profiled panel." Profiled panels range in depth from 1 in. to 2 in., are available in widths from 28 in. to 40 in., and have intricate and varied patterns and colors — which are more architecturally appealing than the "industrial look" of corrugated panels. The edge details of these panels also provide a more weather-tight side lap than the corrugated panel.

"Deep ribbed panels" are used when extra strength is needed. These panels are 3 in. to 4½ in. deep and are most commonly available in 12 in. and 24 in. widths. The extra depth makes 20 ft spans between girts (with an applied 30 psf wind load) possible. Since these panels are stronger, they are manufactured in longer lengths which will reduce the number of pieces needed to construct a high wall.

Concealed Fastener Systems

Concealed fastener wall systems are designed with edge joints that conceal the fasteners. These panels are also available in many different profiles and finishes that provide a pleasing architectural appearance.

ROOF SYSTEMS

The roof system is made up of two components: purlins and roof panels. The purlins support the weight of the roof and any applied loads, and transfer these loads to the primary structural system. Two types of purlins in common use are cold formed steel "Z" or "C" sections and open web joists. The "Z" or "C" sections can have either a simple connection, or a moment connection where they meet and are attached to the frame, and can be used on spans of up to 30 ft. For spans greater than 30 ft, open web joists or deep "Z" or "C" sections may be used for purlins.

The roof panels are fabricated from light gauge steel, and fall into two general categories: lap seam roof and standing seam roof. The former has been used for a longer time period than the latter. The panels used for a lap seam roof are typically 1 in. to 2 in. deep and usually .020 in. or .024 in. (26 to 24 gauge) thick. They are connected to each other by lapping, as the name implies. A sealant is installed between the two panels at the side, and end laps and fasteners are used to secure them.

The selection of panel depth and thickness is affected by roof load, purlin spacing, and insurance considerations. The panel depth and thickness determine the strength of the panel. Given the roof loading and purlin spacing, the required panel strength can be calculated, and the appropriate panel can be selected. Often times insurance regulations, will require panel depth or thicknesses greater than the building codes will require.

The development of the standing seam roof was a major breakthrough in the design of metal roof systems. The system was first introduced in the late 60s, and today most manufacturers either offer it, or plan to provide it in the near future. The difference between the standing seam roof and lap seam roof lies in the manner in which two panels are joined to each other. The seam between two panels is made in the field with a tool that makes a cold formed weather-tight joint. (Note also that some panels can be seamed without special tools.) The joint is made at the top of the panel. The standing seam roof is also unique in the manner in which it is attached to the purlins. The attachment is made with a clip concealed inside the seam. This clip secures the panel to the purlin and may allow the panel to move when experiencing thermal expansion or contraction.

The special characteristics of the standing seam roof produce a roof that is superior to built-up or exposed roof systems. A continuous single skin membrane results after the seam is made since through-the-roof fasteners have been eliminated. The elevated seam and single skin member provide a watertight system. The ability of the roof to experience unrestrained thermal movement eliminates damage to insulation and structure (caused by temperature effects that built-up roofs commonly experience). Thermal spacer blocks are placed between the panels and purlins in order to ensure a consistent thermal barrier. Due to the superiority of the standing seam roof, most manufacturers are willing to offer considerably longer guarantees than those offered on lap seam roofs.

ACCESSORIES

In addition to frame, wall, and roof systems there are other components of a metal building system generally referred to as accessories. These include insulation, gutters, downspouts, roof ventilators, roof openings, interior liner panels, wall vents, wall openings, windows, pedestrian doors, overhead doors, canopies, skylights, fascia, and trim in general. Any number of these items are required to complete a metal building system. These individual components are also manufactured as integral units for the metal building system. When installed, they will be compatible in both design and appearance with the wall and roof systems that they penetrate.

SPECIAL SYSTEMS APPLICATIONS

The majority of metal building systems in existence today can be classified as being modular in layout and typically one story high. There are, however, numerous systems that are exceptions to this general description. Multistory buildings, circular buildings, heavy crane buildings, and airplane hangars are examples of projects that have used metal building systems successfully. The technology and experience to handle nonmodular building configurations exists, and provides a large market for metal building systems to enter in the future.

6.4 Lightgage Framing and Metal Joists

When the loads are rather heavy and joists are widely spaced, S-beams may prove economical, but special lightweight sections are available for light loads and closely spaced joists. One type of lightweight joist is the M-shape beam, a rolled section of the same form as the standard S-beam, but much lighter because the metal is rolled thinner. The sizes vary from a 6 in. depth weighing 4.4 lb per ft. to the 14 in. depth weighing 17.2 lb per ft. The web thickness of the smaller section is less than ⅛ in., and of the larger section about ³⁄₁₆ in. Other sections lighter than the American standard sections are available.

Another form of joist for light loads is the **open-web** or **trussed joist,** one type of which is illustrated diagrammatically in Figure 6.41(A). The flanges of joists of this type are made up either of two light angles, two bars, or a tee, with web members consisting of flat bars welded to the flanges, or of a continuous round bar bent back and forth to form the diagonals and welded to the flanges. Some types are called **bar joists** because they are made up largely of bars.

A-OPEN-WEB OR BAR JOIST

FIGURE 6.41 Open-web or trussed joist.

A-CONCRETE SLAB ON METAL LATH   B-WOOD FLOOR ON NAILING STRIPS   C-WOOD FLOOR ON NAILER JOISTS

FIGURE 6.42 Concrete and wood floors on open-web joists.

LIGHT STEEL JOISTS

Light steel joists and open-web joists (Figure 6.42) are spaced 12 to 24 in. apart. They may support a thin concrete or gypsum slab reinforced in both directions with small bars spaced about 12 in. or welded-wire fabric with ribbed expanded metal lath placed over, and fastened to, the tops of the joists, the metal lath or metal deck serving as the bottom form for the slab. Wood nailing strips running perpendicular to the joists and fastened to the joists (B) may be provided if wood finished flooring is to be used over a thin concrete slab. Instead of providing nailing strips in the concrete slab, nailable concrete may be used. If wood floors are to be used, nailer joists are available with a wood nailing strip anchored along the top flange of each joist to permit the nailing of the floor to the joists (C). Wood flooring may be fastened directly to the nailing strip shown in (B) and (C), or a diagonally laid wood subfloor may be used.

The light rolled-steel sections manufactured especially for use as floor and roof joists may be used in the same manner as the open-web joists, but nailer joists of this type are not available. The nailing strips are fastened to the joists on the job.

Horizontal or cross bridging is required for open-web joists to correspond to that used with wood joists. This bridging may consist of light steel rods or angles with their ends securely anchored to the flanges of the joists.

Ceilings may be provided on the underside of these types of floor construction by plastering over metal lath, or other plaster base, fastened to the underside of the joists. Such ceilings often improve the appearance and are usually required for that purpose as well as to increase the resistance to fire. A 4-hr rating may be attained by using metal lath and vermiculite gypsum plaster and a noncombustible subfloor.

6.5 Metal Decking

The floor decks of buildings with structural steel framing are often made of cellular panels consisting of light-gage galvanized or painted sheet steel with cross sections and interlocking edges, such as those illustrated in Figure 6.43A. These panels span the distance between floor beams, which may be 20 ft or more, and are covered with a poured lightweight concrete slab about 2 in. thick. No temporary intermediate supports are required. The panels are attached to the steel beams by welding.

The required fire resistance for the underside is provided by a suspended ceiling of metal lath and plaster. The thickness and composition of this ceiling is determined by the required fire-resistance rating. For example, a ceiling with ⅞ in. of vermiculite plaster on metal lath, suspended to provide at least 2¼ in. of air space between the underside of the panel and the back of the lath, gives the construction a 4-hr rating. If two coats of sanded gypsum plaster of specified mixes are applied on metal lath to give a total thickness of ¾ in. and no air space is provided, a 1½-hr rating is given.

This type of deck has light weight, provides a working platform before the concrete slab is placed, and makes possible the placing of present and future wiring in the open cells. It is suitable for use in office buildings, hotels, and apartment buildings because the floors do not carry heavy loads. Its use is permitted for fire-resistive buildings by many but not all building codes.

COMPOSITE STEEL AND CONCRETE DECKS

One type of light-gage galvanized or composite steel panel which is used in constructing short-span floor decks is illustrated in Figure 6.43B. It is provided with longitudinal ribs to give rigidity during construction and to provide reinforcement for the concrete floor slab for which it serves as a form. Only the ribs, which are embedded in concrete, are considered effective in providing reinforcement. When necessary, additional reinforcement in the form of bars is included between the ribs, as shown. Transverse temperature reinforcement is provided. If the slab is continuous over the supports, reinforcement is placed near the top of the slab in this region, as described elsewhere. The panels are anchored to the steel beams that support them, ordinarily by welding. Temporary supports usually will be necessary between the beams while the lightweight concrete is being placed and hardening.

The light-gage corrugated steel panel (B) is used in a manner similar to the ribbed panel. However, since the temperature reinforcement is welded to the tops of the corrugations, as shown, it anchors or bonds the corrugations to the concrete so effectively that the full cross-sectional area of the corrugated steel is available to resist flexural stresses.

6.6 Metal Fasteners

The various structural steel shapes and plates of which built-up members are composed are fastened together or fabricated in the shop by riveting, bolting, and welding. The pieces are cut to the required shapes and sizes and fastened together to form a completed member.

The members which are placed in position or erected in the field to form the structural frame are connected with field rivets, unfinished bolts, or high-strength bolts and by welding, as described in subsequent paragraphs. Field riveting is done with the riveting gun, and field welding is done with manually operated equipment.

DRIFT PINS

Before rivets or bolts are inserted, the holes in a connection are brought into matching positions by one or more *drift pins.* A drift pin is a tapered steel rod which is driven into a hole. Specifications prohibit enlarging mismatched holes by driving the drift pins. Such holes must be reamed to make them match, but inspectors reject poor connections with poorly matching holes.

TYPES OF BOLTS

The various types of fasteners used in shop or field connections are unfinished bolts, high-strength bolts, and welds. High-strength bolts have largely replaced turned bolts.

FIELD BOLTS

After the holes of a connection have been matched, an adequate number of temporary unfinished bolts hold the connected parts in position until the final fasteners are installed. The temporary bolts are removed when a sufficient number of the final fasteners are in place.

ASTM 502 steel structural *rivets* for structural steel are made in three grades. Grade 1, made of carbon steel, is used for general purpose construction. Grade 2, made of

A-CELLULAR STEEL AND CONCRETE   B-COMPOSITE STEEL AND CONCRETE ARRANGED FROM REFERENCE (1)

FIGURE 6.43 Types of lightweight steel and concrete decks.

FIGURE 6.44 Types of rivets.

A. UNFINISHED BOLTS

B. HIGH-STRENGTH BOLTS

C. HIGH-STRENGTH BODY BOLTS

FIGURE 6.45 Types of bolts.

carbon manganese steel, is used with high-strength carbon and high-strength low-alloy structural steels. Grade 3, similar to Grade 2, is corrosion resistant. Grade 1 rivets are not required to be grade marked.

Rivets are made in diameters from ½ to 1½ in.

Rivet sizes are identified by their shank diameter. Diameters range from ½ to 1½ in. in ⅛ in. increments. Lengths of rivets are from 1¼ in. to 8⅞ in.

Rivets are driven in holes ¹⁄₁₆ in. larger than the shank diameter. They usually consist of a buttonhead and a cylindrical shank long enough to provide material to form the other head (see Figure 6.44). A rivet with two buttonheads is shown in (B), with a flattened head in (C), and with a countersunk head and with a countersunk and chipped head in (D).

The buttonhead is the usual type. Countersunk and flattened heads may be required for clearance, and chipped countersunk heads are required on bearing surfaces.

The methods and equipment used in driving rivets are considered later. Rivets are heated to a cherry red before driving. As they cool, they contract and exert a clamping force on the included material. This action results in considerable friction between surfaces of the material connected, which augments the shearing and bearing resistance of the rivets. This clamping force is not considered in determining the number of rivets required.

The line passing through the centers of a row of rivets, in plan view, is called a gage line. The center-to-center spacing of rivets is called the pitch. The distance from the center of a rivet to the nearest edge is called the edge distance. The length of a rivet, determined by the total thickness of the material it penetrates, is called the grip.

UNFINISHED BOLTS

The threaded fasteners known as "unfinished" *bolts* (A307) are identified in two grades as Grade A for general application and Grade B for flanged joints in piping systems. These fasteners, frequently galvanized by a hot-dip zinc coat process, are made in diameters from ¼ in. up to 4 in. The tensile strength of these bolts is not less than 60,000 psi. Heads generally are not marked although they may be

marked with individual marks that identify the manufacturer. Unfinished bolts, or A307 bolts, are made of low-carbon steel and have rough unfinished shanks and square, unmarked heads and nuts (Figure 6.45A). They are used in holes ¹⁄₁₆ in. larger in diameter than the shank. The permissible carrying capacity is lower than that of rivets of the same diameter. They are relatively inexpensive. They may be tightened with hand wrenches; but when bolts are used, power wrenches may prove more economical and probably give more uniform results.

According to the American Institute of Steel Construction (AISC) Specifications, unfinished bolts may be used in tier building field connections providing they are not used for column splices on buildings more than 200 ft in height, nor for column splices on buildings with certain height-to-width ratios.

They are not permitted in roof truss splices and connections of trusses to columns, column splices, column bracing, knee braces, and crane supports in structures carrying cranes of more than 5-ton capacity.

They are permitted in column splices, with the limitations just given, because the abutting ends of column sections are milled and the splices so arranged that the compressive stresses are transmitted directly across the splice. Within the specified limits, unfinished bolts are considered satisfactory to resist the flexural stresses in the columns caused by lateral loads. Splice plates are required, regardless of flexural stresses, to hold the column section in alignment. Unfinished bolts are not permitted for connections of the members of structures that carry large cranes because the repeated action of the cranes tends to work the joints loose and permit the structure to rock back and forth with the movement of the crane.

A sufficient number of unfinished bolts are used temporarily in erecting members with riveted field connections to hold the members in true position while the field rivets are being driven.

HIGH-STRENGTH BOLTS

Some bolts that are used for connecting structural steel, especially high-strength structural steel, are identified as high-strength structural bolts. These bolts, which are identified by the ASTM number stamped on their heads, are designated as A325, and A490. Under Specification A325, there are three types of bolts. Type 1, which is of medium-carbon steel, is made in sizes from ½ in. to 1½ in. The heads of the bolts, in addition to the ASTM mark, are marked with three short radial lines 120° apart. Type 2 bolts are of low-carbon steel with diameters from ½ in. to 1 in. The heads of the bolts are marked with short radial lines 60° apart. ASTM A325 Type 3 bolts are made of weathering steel and are used to connect members that are of weathering steel. They may be identified by the underlined ASTM A325 on the head.

High-strength bolts A490 are made of alloy steel. A449 bolts are made of medium-carbon steel; two A449 bolts are illustrated in Figure 6.45B and C. The type shown in (B) is designated as the high-strength bolt, A325 or A490, and is inserted in a hole with a diameter ¹⁄₁₆ in. larger than that of the shank of the bolt. The type shown in (C) is designated as the high-strength bearing bolt or high-strength interference-body bolt. On the shank, it has a raised pattern consisting of straight or spiraled ribs or knurls. Since the outside diameter of the shank is greater than the diameter of the hole, the bolt must be driven into the hole with a maul or pulled in with the nut. This process causes the shank to bind in the hole, and the hole is more completely filled than it is when the plain high-strength bolt is used. This is referred to as an interference fit, which gives the bolt one of its names. It also gives better bearing between the bolt and the sides of the hole, which is recognized in the name bearing bolt.

According to the assembly specifications, the type of bolt, and the method of tightening, high-strength bolts may or may not require hardened washers under either the head or the nut or both. The head is kept from turning initially by gripping with a hand wrench. The high-strength bearing bolt binds in the hole and does not tend to turn when being tightened. The head is button-shaped, as shown in the figure. A hardened washer is generally required under the nut.

The nuts on both types of bolts are tightened with pneumatic impact wrenches. Because of the high strength of the bolts, they are generally tightened so that the clamping forces are sufficient to ensure, under most conditions, that the friction between the surfaces of the various parts connected is adequate to prevent any sliding movement due to the applied loads and to make sure that the nuts will not be loosened. In addition, the high tensile strength of the bolts and the initial tension to which they are subjected make them effective in resisting forces that subject them to tension. Under conditions where the tendency to slip is unusually high and where there are abnormal vibrations, bearing bolts are superior to bolts with plain shanks.

The allowable carrying capacities of high-strength bolts are equal to and, under ordinary conditions, greater than those of rivets of the same nominal diameter.

Both types of bolts are used for field connections under the same conditions as rivets. They have the advantage of being cheaper and quieter to install than rivets.

WELDING PROCESSES

Many processes are used to *weld* pieces of metal together. Those used in structural welding are divided into two main groups: pressure processes, in which the weld is completed by applying pressure after the pieces to be welded have been placed in contact where the weld is to be formed and have been heated to the required temperature; and the nonpressure or fusion process, which requires no pressure to complete the weld.

FIGURE 6.46 Types of welded joints.

Nonpressure or fusion processes used in structural welding are divided into arc welding and gas welding according to the source of heat.

In arc welding, the heat is provided by an electric arc formed between the work to be welded and an electrode held in the operator's hand with a suitable holder or in an automatic machine. The electrode may be a metallic rod, as in metal-arc welding, or a carbon rod, as in carbon-arc welding.

In gas welding, the heat is provided by a gas flame produced by burning a mixture of oxygen and a suitable combustible gas. The flame is formed at the tip of a blowpipe or torch, which is held in the operator's hand or in an automatic machine. The gas used in structural welding is acetylene, which gives this process the name of the oxyacetylene process.

In both the arc and gas processes, the pieces to be welded are placed in contact; the edges are melted so that metal from the two pieces flows together; and, when cooled, the pieces are joined by the weld. In order to make a satisfactory joint, additional metal must be supplied.

It is provided by the metallic rod used as the electrode in the metal arc process, but in the carbon-arc and gas processes a metal rod called a filler or welding rod is used. The end of this rod is melted off into the joint as the joint is being formed.

The only pressure-welding process used in structural work is the spot-welding process. In this process, a small area or spot on the surfaces to be joined is heated by placing electrodes against the outer surfaces of the pieces and passing an electric current through the pieces and across the contact surface. The heat required to raise the temperature of the pieces to a welding temperature at the spot where the weld is to be made is generated by the resistance offered by the metal between the electrodes to the flow of electric current. This is, therefore, a resistance process. Since the weld is consummated by exerting pressure across the spot, this is a pressure process. If spot welds are formed progressively in a continuous overlapping row, the process is known as seam welding. Disk electrodes are used to apply the pressure.

TYPES OF WELDED JOINTS

Various types of welded joints used in structural work, with the names applied to the parts of welds, are illustrated in Figure 6.46. The types of welds illustrated are the single- and double-fillet lap weld in *(A)*, the single- and double-vee groove weld in *(B)*, the groove weld with double-fillet welded backing strip in *(C)*, the double fillet T weld in *(D)*, and the plug or rivet weld in *(E)* — all of which are fusion welds — and the spot weld in *(F)*, which is a resistance-pressure weld. The electrodes are shown in this figure.

FABRICATING PROCEDURES

The following paragraphs on cutting, punching, drilling and reaming, riveting, milling and straightening, bending, and rolling are quoted, with permission, from *Structural Shop Drafting* published by the American Institute of Steel Construction.

These procedures apply specifically to riveted members, but the comments on cutting, milling and straightening, bending, and rolling apply also to welded members.

Cutting. There are several types of cutting operations, each of which is particularly adapted to the class of work involved. Plates are cut in a guillotine type machine, called a *shear*. Angles are cut on a machine with the shear blade shaped and set at an angle to cut both legs with one stroke. Beams, channels, and light columns are usually cut on high-speed saws. There are several types of saws for this purpose, the most common one being the *friction saw,* which cuts through steel as fast as a power crosscut saw passes through timber. Bars are cut by a shear of the guillotine type, the dies and shear blades of which are made in the shape of the material to prevent its distortion. Large bars are cut on a *power hack saw.*

Cutting of material which is over the capacity of the various machines and most cutting of curved and complex forms is done with the acetylene torch and is known as *flame-cutting* or *gas-cutting.* The cutting torch is the most useful and flexible means of cutting steel ever devised. [See *Explanatory Comments.*]

Punching, Drilling and Reaming. Punching is the most economical common method of making rivet and bolt holes in steel. Generally the material is punched rather than drilled, where the size of the hole and the thickness of the metal comes within the range of the machines and when punching is permitted by the specifications. Normally, mild carbon steel up to a thickness one-eighth of an inch greater than the diameter of the rivet can be punched without undue stress on the machine or excessive breakage of the punches.

Except in special cases, all holes are punched with a diameter $\frac{1}{16}$ of an inch larger than that of the rivet or bolt to be used. Some tolerance is required to provide for less than perfect matching of holes in adjacent parts when they are lined up for rivet driving.

Drilling of structural steel is largely confined to making holes in material thicker than the capacity of the punch machines and dies, as in slabs and the heavier wide flange beams and columns, or to meet specification requirements.

Specifications for bridge work and certain other specialized work require all holes to be punched at least one-eighth of an inch smaller than the final size. Then, after the piece has been assembled, it is placed under a battery of reamers operating like jibs or gantries, and the holes are reamed to the desired size. The procedure is usually referred to as *subpunch and ream.* Reaming produces a clean hole with all burrs and distorted metal removed. Reamed holes are also used for connections which will be field-bolted with close-fitting *turned* or *finished bolts.*

Riveting. Riveting machines of both the pressure and impact type are operated by compressed air at 80 to 100 lb per sq. in. pressure. The *pressure-type riveter,* frequently known as a *bull riveter,* has a C-shaped frame with a throat depth sufficient to permit a machine to reach halfway across an average girder. Small-size pressure riveters are hung from jib cranes while the larger machines are generally supported from a power-operated gantry or even from an overhead traveling crane. Pressure riveters complete the driving operation with one stroke, the larger machines exerting a pressure of 80 tons.

Impact riveters, generally referred to as *riveting guns,* are portable hand tools which can be connected to the end of a compressed air hose. A rapid succession of blows is delivered to the rivet by means of a plunger moving up and down in the gun barrel much as the piston in a reciprocating steam engine moves back and forth. These tools are also used by the fitter for driving tapered *drift pins* through holes to align the several parts of a member. The gun drives just as satisfactory a rivet as the pressure riveter but, being slower, its shop use is limited to driving rivets inaccessible to the larger machines and scattered rivets where the amount of driving does not warrant taking the work to the machines.

Standard-size rivets used in a structural shop are almost always heated before driving. The heating in most shops is done in either oil or gas-fired furnaces and then raised to a minimum temperature color of light cherry red. In some shops, electric rivet heaters are used. [See *Explanatory Comments.*]

Milling. The ends of columns, struts, and members in compression chords of trusses which are required to bear evenly against another or against supporting base plates are *milled* to a smooth even surface in a *milling machine.* The machine consists of one or more rotating cutting heads fitted with teeth or blades, and a bed on which to securely hold the work in proper alignment during the milling operation.

Column base plates over 4 in. in thickness must be milled over the area in contact with the column shaft. This milling is usually done on a *planing machine.*

Straightening, Bending, and Rolling. All material which is bent or distorted during shipping, handling, or in the punching operation must be straightened before further fabrication is attempted. The machine generally used for straightening beams, channels, angles, and heavy bars is commonly known as a *bulldozer.* This machine has a heavy cast steel frame with a horizontal plunger or ram centered between two lugs about 2 ft apart set on an anvil or head. With the piece to be straightened placed against the two lugs, pressure is applied by the ram at points along the length of the bent member until it is in alignment once more.

The bulldozer also is used to make long-radius curved beams, channels and angles and to make minor angle bends in heavy pieces and to make other bends within its capacity. Short-radius curves, where material must be heated, are handled by the blacksmith. [See *Explanatory Comments.*]

Long plates which are slightly curved or cambered out of alignment in the direction of their longitudinal center line are usually straightened by cold rolling. By passing these plates between a pair of rolls bearing against their top and bottom faces, with more pressure exerted along the shorter or concave side than along the convex side, the thickness of the plates on the concave side is reduced ever so slightly. The metal thus displaced by the rolls increases the length of this side enough to bring the plate back into true longitudinal alignment."

EXPLANATORY COMMENTS

Certain explanations of the procedures in the foregoing paragraphs seem desirable.

In driving buttonheaded rivets with the pressure riveter, the heated rivet is placed in the hole provided for it. The member is then moved into position between the jaws of the C-frame. A depression is provided to receive the formed head. The end of the plunger is provided with a depression in which the other buttonhead is formed as the pressure is applied to the projecting end of the rivet. If a rivet is driven with a riveting gun, the formed head is supported in a heavy dolly. The other head is formed by several blows from the

plunger of the gun, the impact of the plunger being resisted by the dolly, which acts as an anvil. Rivets with one head flattened or countersunk are formed in a similar manner.

Flame cutting or gas cutting is also known as oxygen cutting. It includes a group of processes in which the cutting is accomplished by the chemical reaction of oxygen with the base metal at elevated temperatures. These temperatures are attained by means of gas flames resulting from the combustion of oxygen and one of several kinds of gas, the most commonly used gas being acetylene, as in oxyacetylene cutting. Steel is also cut by arc cutting, a group of processes in which metals are cut by melting them with the heat of an electric arc between an electrode and the base metal. Accurate cuts can be made by these procedures regardless of the thickness of the metal.

At least one plant, the Commercial Shearing and Stamping Company, Youngstown, Ohio, is equipped to cold-bend S, W, or wide-flange shapes, with depths as great as 30 in., in the plane of the web. Bends in the plane perpendicular to the plane of web are made more easily. The minimum radius of curvature for bending in the plane of the depth is about fourteen times the depth. A single piece can be bent to various radii along its length. The maximum length of piece which can be handled is 30 ft.

WELDING

The following comments on welding procedures are quoted, with permission, from *Structural Shop Drafting,* published by the American Institute of Steel Construction:

The process most commonly used in the welding of structural steel is known as *metal-arc welding.* In this process energy is supplied by an electric arc established between the *base* or *parent* metal (the parts being joined) and a metal *electrode.* The instant the arc is formed tremendous heat is concentrated at the point of welding, which is located at the junction formed by the two parts to be welded together. The parent metal melts in a small pool; additional metal supplied by the electrode is transferred through the arc in the form of tiny globules and deposited in the pool. As the electrode (and hence the arc) is moved along the joint, either manually or automatically, the molten metal left behind solidifies as a uniform deposit or *weld,* which joins the parts solidly, thus forming the desired connection.

Electrodes may be either *bare* or *coated,* although most welding is done today with coated electrodes. Bare manually operated electrodes produce welds which are not as reliable as those made with electrodes that are heavily coated. In the case of the coated electrode, the heat from the arc produces from the coating a gaseous and slag flux shield, as shown in Figure 6.47, which completely envelops the arc and the molten metal, thus preventing contact with the oxygen and nitrogen of the air, contamination from which tends to produce brittle welds. The slag coating which is formed floats on the molten pool thus protecting it from the atmospheric elements. This slag is easily removed after the weld has cooled.

In *manual welding,* the welding operator manipulates the electrode by hand. An insulated gripping device connected by a flexi-

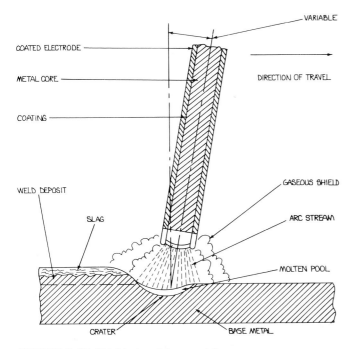

FIGURE 6.47 Shielded metal-arc welding process.

ble cable to the source of current is used to hold the electrode. The operator wears proper covering and a helmet which affords protection against *weld spatter* (globules of metal thrown off during welding), heat, the blinding light so characteristic of the process and harmful rays emanating from the arc.

Note: Welds in any accessible position can be made by manual welding because the globules of metal from the electrode are forced across the arc almost independently of the action of gravity.

When a weld is terminated abruptly, a *crater* is formed in the base metal by the blast of the arc. It is required that this crater be filled with weld metal so that the finished appearance and the cross section of the weld are uniform.

In *submerged-arc automatic welding,* the electrode is fed by a machine which has a reel for carrying a coiled supply of uncoated wire. With this method, the arc is shielded by a granular flux automatically deposited on the joint ahead of the arc. The welding wire pushes through the flux; the arc is established; part of the flux melts to form a slag flux shield; and the customary slag floats on the molten pool. Unfused flux is recovered for re-use.

6.7 Metals and Alloys

There are several metal alloys that are used extensively in building construction. Most are expensive and used sparingly. They usually are applied as specialties or where a

particular property is required, such as resistance to corrosion.

MALLEABLE CAST IRON

Castings made of white cast iron may be made malleable and ductile by subjecting them to an annealing process which converts the combined carbon into free carbon in a very finely divided state. The annealing may be accomplished by packing the castings in some inert material, such as sand or clay, and heating to a red heat which is maintained for several days, after which the castings are slowly cooled.

Better results may be secured by packing the castings in an oxidizing material such as iron oxide. The oxide draws the carbon from the castings to a depth of 1/16 in. or more, forming a skin of soft iron on the castings in addition to converting the combined carbon in the body of the castings into free carbon.

White cast iron is used so that all the free carbon will be in the form of very minute particles evenly distributed throughout the castings and not in the form of large flakes which have such a weakening effect on gray cast iron.

Malleable castings are used for small articles such as builders' hardware. Malleable iron washers are extensively used in timber construction.

STAINLESS STEEL

Stainless steel, sometimes referred to as an architectural metal, is used where corrosive conditions make maintenance costly and where appearance may be a factor. It is ideal for roofing parts that require a metal, such as spires, gutters, facias, downspouts, flashing, expanson joints, and flagpoles. Stainless steel is widely used on interiors such as lobbies, elevators, entrances, stairways, and doorways — nearly any location where a material may be subjected to abuse.

Because it has a greater strength than most other metals that are used for architectural finishes, it is more resistant to wear and tear. Stainless steel has a nonstaining character which permits its use in conjunction with other nonstaining materials without the danger of deterioration through galvanic action with dissimilar metals.

Like most other sheet metals, stainless steel is most frequently designated by gage numbers. As manufactured, it is referred to as plate if more than 3/16 in. thick and in widths greater than 10 in.; sheet if less than 3/16 in. thick and 24 in. or more in width; and strip if less than 3/16 in. in thickness and less than 24 in. in width.

Grades

There are three basic groups of stainless steel (USS Stainless Steel, Architectural Design Details, United States Steel Corporation, San Francisco):

Austenitic grades contain both chromium and nickel and possess the highest corrosion resistance. They are not hardenable by heat treatment and are nonmagnetic in their annealed state, although some types become magnetic with cold working.

Ferritic grades generally contain 14% or more of chromium. They are not hardenable by heat treatment, are hardened only moderately by cold working, and are always magnetic.

Martensitic grades generally contain a maximum of 14% chromium, and are of lower corrosion resistance than austenitic or ferritic grades. They are hardenable by heat treatment and are magnetic. Because of their lower corrosion resistance, they find limited application in architectural uses.

Types

There are more than 40 types of stainless steel; however, only five concern building construction. Types have been established according to a numbered system by the American Iron and Steel Institute. The types listed below are of interest to the building industry, especially Type 302, which is probably the most useful.

AISI Type 302

This, a United States Steel 18-8 grade stainless steel, is the most commonly used in architecture and is virtually the all-purpose grade in either interior or exterior applications. It is readily formed and welded and may be specified for such exterior uses as column covers, doors and door frames, facias, exposed or concealed flashing, gutters and rain-carrying equipment, mullions, panels, and soffits.

AISI Type 304

This stainless steel is sometimes recommended in lieu of Type 302 and differs from it only in having a lower carbon content. For architectural purposes, it is interchangeable with Type 302 both functionally and economically.

AISI Type 301

This, a United States Steel 17-7 grade, is a stainless steel which contains slightly smaller amounts of chromium and nickel and has somewhat higher work-hardening characteristics. Otherwise, it retains essentially the same characteristics and properties as Type 302. In strip widths (less than 24 in.) with cold-rolled finishes (not including No. 4 finish), it is slightly less expensive than Type 302. In applications that must perform structurally, the use of Type 301 may be advantageous since high strengths can be achieved by cold rolling and with greater facility than with Type 302.

AISI Type 316

This is a modified United States Steel 18-8 grade to which molybdenum has been added to increase resistance to attack in highly corrosive atmospheres. While this grade is somewhat higher in cost than Type 302, it is the preferred material in marine and harsh industrial-chemical environments, and similar areas where the other chromium-nickel grades might not be adequate.

AISI Type 430

This United States Steel 17 grade stainless steel contains 16–18% chromium and no nickel. It has satisfactory resistance to weathering and atmospheric corrosion in the average urban environment but is not quite as good as Type 302 in resistance to many atmospheres. It costs less than Type 302 and is commonly used for interior applications, trim, and hardware items.

Finishes

Stainless steel is finished and marketed in several standard mill finishes and in special textured finishes. The standard mill finishes are referred to as unpolished and polished finishes. When stainless steel is specified, the desired finish should be indicated.

Unpolished finishes (USS Stainless Steel, Architectural Design Details, United States Steel Corp., San Francisco):

No. *2D Special.* A frosty, matte finish produced on either hand sheet mills or continuous mills by cold rolling to the specified thickness, annealing, and descaling. The dull finish may result from the descaling or pickling operation or from a final light temper pass on dull rolls. The comparable strip finish is referred to as 'No. 1 Strip Finish.'

No. *2B.* A dense, bright, cold-rolled finish of higher reflectivity. It is produced in the same way as No. 2D finish except that the annealed and descaled sheet receives a final pass on polished rolls. Should polishing be required after fabrication, this finish is the easiest to polish. The comparable strip finish is referred to as 'No. 2 Strip Finish.'

No. *4.* A bright, but not highly reflective finish, having a fine-grained linear appearance. It is the most frequently used architectural finish and is achieved by coarse grinding followed by polishing with 120–150 grit abrasives. This finish has a distinct advantage in that weld areas may be easily and inconspicuously blended into it.

No. *6.* A soft satin finish having lower reflectivity than No. 4 finish. It is produced by Tampico brushing the No. 4 finish in a medium of abrasive and oil.

No. *7.* A highly reflective finish produced by buffing a surface which has first been finely ground with abrasive of approximately 240–280 grit. The grit lines are not removed by the buffing.

Textured finishes are most useful where the stainless steel is to be subjected to abuse or where a particular richness is desired. An *engine turned* finish, which is a pattern of several concentric circles, is particularly attractive for door push plates.

Shapes

Stainless steel can be made into a variety of shapes, including sheet, strip and bars, solid rounds and tubes which are round, rectangular, square, or oval. Stainless steel members such as channels and angles are cold-rolled as well as hot-rolled. (See Figure 6.48.)

Joining

This material may be joined by welding, brazing, soldering, mechanically formed lap or batten seams, and by mechanical fasteners, such as screws and bolts. Mechanical fasteners should be of the same type of stainless steel.

NONFERROUS METALS AND ALLOYS
Concentrating

The first step in the production of most nonferrous metals from their ores consists of increasing the proportion of metal present by removing much of the waste material. This process is called concentrating. It includes various mechanical treatments, such as crushing, grinding, and screening, which do not involve heat and cause no chemical changes.

ALUMINUM
Ores

Aluminum occurs abundantly in nature in combination with oxygen, sodium, fluorine, and silicon. The chief source of aluminum is bauxite, which is hydrated oxide of aluminum and iron with some silicon. The most extensive occurrence of aluminum is as the oxide alumina (Al_2O_3), the principal constituent of clay. No process has yet been devised to obtain aluminum from clay in commercial quantities.

Extraction

The stages in the extraction of aluminum from bauxite are:

1. Roasting bauxite to drive off the water.
2. Grinding roasted bauxite and heating under pressure with a solution of sodium hydrate forming sodium aluminate.
3. Precipitating aluminum hydroxide by heating sodium aluminate solution with aluminum hydroxide or with carbon dioxide.
4. Separating aluminum hydroxide with filtering and dehydrating by heating to form alumina (Al_2O_3).
5. Extracting aluminum from alumina by the electrolytic decomposition of alumina in a molten bath of cryolite which is the fluoride of alumina and sodium.

In the last-named process, the containing vessel is lined with carbon in the form of graphite or coke, which forms the cathode. Carbon rods suspended in the bath form the anode, to which the oxygen goes. The cryolite is melted by the heat generated by the passage of the electric current

A-ANGLE   B-CHANNEL

FIGURE 6.48 Cold-rolled members.

across a gap which exists between the anodes and the cathodes. When the cryolite bath becomes molten, alumina is thrown on the bath; as it melts, it is broken up into molten aluminum, which settles on the cathode, and oxygen, which goes to the anode with which it combines, forming carbon monoxide which escapes as a gas. The molten aluminum is tapped off as it accumulates. The heat for the process is supplied by the electric current.

Properties and Uses

Aluminum is formed by forging, casting, drawing, rolling, and extruding. The latter two methods of forming are of particular interest to building construction. In the extrusion process, heated aluminum is squeezed through a die by a hydraulic actuated press. The extruded aluminum is formed into the cross-sectional shape of the die, which can be of almost any design. Thus, aluminum can be economically shaped into most any section desired. This accounts for an abundance of various aluminum mouldings, edgings, window and curtain wall mullions, and sections. Generally, these aluminum members are referred to as extrusions.

Aluminum has a low electrical resistance which makes it valuable for transmission lines and other electrical uses. It is a good heat conductor and is noncorrosive. Because of its lightness, it has many special uses; its weight is only about one-third that of iron. It is very malleable, quite ductile, noncorrosive, and strong in proportion to its weight.

Aluminum Alloys

Because aluminum in its refined state is soft and of low strength, it is of limited use in the building industry. Fortunately, this material forms numerous alloys. Manganese, copper, zinc, silicon, and magnesium are alloyed with aluminum to improve its properties. Most of these alloying elements improve both the strength and the hardness of aluminum.

Wrought alloy types of aluminum are classified by a series code number in a system established by the Aluminum Association. In the 2000 Series, copper is the principal alloying material. The tensile strength is improved, and materials of this alloy are suitable for building structures and bolts. The 3000 Series has manganese as the principal alloy material. The result is a strong workable alloy that is used for corrugated and stamped roofing, siding, and other sheet-metal work. Silicon produces an alloy that is numbered in the 4000 Series. This alloy is used for castings and forgings. This material may be finished with a fine anodized finish. Magnesium alloy, the 5000 Series, is used for architectural trim and nails. The magnesium silicon alloys are indicated in the 6000 Series and are used for structural members, nails, railings, windows, doors, and extrusions.

Other symbols that are a part of the series code number indicate temper: annealed or strain hardened.

COPPER
Ores
Copper is found in the native or pure state and in a great variety of ores, of which sulfides are the most common.

Extraction
The stages in the extraction of copper from concentrated sulfide ores are as follows.

1. Roasting the sulfide ore by heating it in an oxidizing atmosphere where a part of the iron sulfide ore is converted into the oxide by the burning out of the sulfide. The temperature is not high enough to melt the ore. The roasted ore contains chiefly copper sulfide, iron oxide, and siliceous gangue, although some copper oxide may be present.

2. Smelting in a blast furnace with coke as a fuel or in a reverberatory furnace. Copper sulfide and iron sulfide settle to the bottom forming a matte, and the slag, containing the gangue or earthly materials and iron oxide, forms on top where it may be drawn off.

3. Converting the molten matte, containing the sulfides of copper and iron, in a converter similar to that used in the manufacture of Bessemer steel. Air is blown through the molten matte and provides oxygen, which combines with the iron sulfide to form a slag of iron oxide on top of the remaining copper sulfide. By continuing the process, the sulfur is burned out of the sulfides, forming sulfur dioxide which passes off as a gas and leaving an impure form of copper known as blister copper.

4. Refining the blister copper either in a reverberatory furnace or electrolytically. In furnace or fire refining, the blister copper is melted in a reverberatory furnace; the slag which is formed is skimmed off; and air is blown over the molten bath and oxidizes the impurities which either pass off as gas or form slag on top of the molten metal. Some of the copper is oxidized and must be reduced by adding charcoal and stirring with a green wood pole. Steam formed by the water in the green pole agitates the bath, and the carbon from the charcoal combines with the oxygen of the copper oxide, forming carbon monoxide which passes off as a gas, thus leaving fairly pure copper which is cast into ingots.

In the electrolytic process, anodes of blister copper or fire-refined copper and cathodes of pure copper are placed in a copper sulfate bath. An electric current is passed through the bath and causes pure copper to be transferred from the blister copper anode to the pure copper cathode. The impurities, which often include the precious metals, are not soluble in copper sulfate, and being of higher specific gravity, they fall to the bottom of the bath and are removed.

Fire-refined copper is not as pure as that obtained by the electrolytic process. The former is used for wires, tubes, and plates, and for making brasses and bronzes. The latter is used primarily for electrical purposes which require the purer form.

Properties and Uses
The most important properties of copper are its electrical conductivity and its resistance to corrosion. Its strength and ductility are greatly affected by the mechanical and heat treatment it receives. If heated to a red heat and cooled slowly it is brittle; but if cooled quickly, it is malleable and ductile. It may be cast and welded and may be rolled or drawn when hot or cold. Cold working increases its strength but decreases its ductility. When exposed to moist air, as when used for a roofing material, a thin coating of the green basic carbonate is formed. This protects the copper so that no further treatment is required.

Copper is used primarily for electrical purposes, but it is also used extensively as a constituent of brasses and bronzes and for sheet-metal roofing and shingles, gutters, rain conductors, flashing, and pipe for plumbing. Copper wire is formed by drawing through dies. If it is cold-drawn, it produces what is called hard-drawn wire, which is springy.

The alloys of copper, like those of aluminum, are classified by a number series code. The copper that is used mostly for building construction in the form of sheet, roll, and strip is known as alloy copper 110. This alloy is further known as electrolytic tough pitch copper and is produced in flat form as cold-rolled and soft-rolled sheets, cold-rolled strip, and soft-rolled rolls. These forms of copper are specified by the number of ounces of the material in a square foot. Sheet is available from 16 oz to 32 oz, while strip and roll is available only in 16 oz weights.

This copper alloy may be joined by mechanical bending in seams of various types, or by soldering and brazing. Generally, welding is not recommended.

Copper, a soft metal, takes several mechanical finishes. It may be brushed, burnished, polished, sandblasted, or buffed. However, the natural turquoise patina called verdigris that it acquires is its most outstanding finish on exterior applications.

ZINC
Ores

The ores of zinc are the sulfide (ZnS), the carbonate ($ZNCO_3$), the silicates ($Zn_2SiO_4H_2O$) and (Zn_2SiO_4), and franklinite, which is composed of the oxides of zinc, manganese, and iron. The most common source of zinc is the sulfide zinc blende.

Extraction

The stages in the extraction of zinc from its ores are as follows.

1. Roasting the ore to drive off the sulfur from sulfides and the carbon dioxide from the carbonates to form zinc oxide.

2. Mixing the oxide with a nearly equal amount of finely ground anthracite coal and placing it in fire-clay retorts.

3. Heating retorts to a white heat so that the coal will form carbon monoxide which will combine with the oxygen of the zinc oxide to form carbon dioxide and zinc vapor.

4. Condensing the zinc vapor at a temperature above the melting point of zinc to form molten zinc, which is poured into molds and allowed to cool, forming zinc spelter, the form commonly used. If the temperature at which the condensation is carried on is too low, zinc dust is formed. This cannot be melted to form a solid mass and has limited use in the powdered form.

Properties and Uses

Zinc has a fairly high resistance to corrosion. For this reason, it is used as a roofing material in the form of sheet zinc. Exposure to the weather causes dull-gray zinc carbonate to form on the surface and protect the remainder of the metal.

If zinc is cooled suddenly from the molten state, it is malleable, but if cooled slowly, it is hard and brittle. Commercial zinc is quite brittle, but if heated to about 250°F it becomes malleable and ductile. It may then be drawn into wire or rolled into sheets which are ductile and malleable when cool. Molten zinc shrinks very little in solidifying and casts well.

Zinc is extensively used as a protective coating for steel in the galvanizing and sherardizing processes. It is also used as one of the constituents in brass, nickel, silver, and other alloys and in making electric batteries.

LEAD
Ores

The only important ore of lead is galena, the sulfide (PbS) mixed with gangue.

Extraction

There are two stages in the extraction of lead from its ores.

1. Roasting by charging crushed ore into a reverberatory furnace where it is heated at a low temperature in an oxidizing atmosphere. Part of the sulfur in the sulfide is oxidized forming lead oxide and sulfur dioxide gas, and some lead sulfate is formed:

$$PbS + 3 O = PbO + SO_2$$
$$PbS + 4 O = PbSO_4$$

2. Smelting the lead oxide, the lead sulfate, and the remaining lead sulfide in a blast furnace with limestone, coke, and some other materials to form lead and sulfur dioxide:

$$PbS + 2 PbO = 3 Pb + SO_2$$
$$PbS + PbSO_4 = 2 Pb + 2 SO_2$$

The molten lead thus formed is drawn off and cast into ingots. This lead must usually be purified before it is ready for the market.

Properties and Uses

The important physical properties of lead are its resistance to corrosion, its plasticity, and its malleability.

Lead sheets are used to a considerable extent for watertight pans under the floors of shower baths and in similar positions. They are used to a limited extent for roofing, particularly for curved or irregular surfaces to which lead can be easily fitted by stretching and working. Lead has a high coefficient of expansion and is difficult to hold in place, particularly on pitched roofs.

A roofing known as hard lead is composed of lead and antimony. It is stronger and has a lower coefficient of expansion than ordinary lead and can be used on any slope.

Lead pipes are used in plumbing but not as much as they were in former years. The pipe is formed by forming the metal through dies by means of hydraulic presses. The term plumber is derived from the Latin word for lead, plumbum.

Solder is an alloy of lead and tin.

TIN
Ores

The principal source of tin is the black oxide (SnO_2), known as cassiterite or tinstone. Tin is the only important metal not found in the U.S.

Extraction

The stages in the extraction of tin from its concentrated ores are as follows.

1. Roasting in a reverberatory furnace to oxidize the sulfur and arsenic which exist as impurities. These oxides pass off as gases.

2. Smelting in reverberatory or blast furnaces. The oxygen

of the tin oxide combines with carbon to form carbon dioxide, the carbon being mixed directly with the ore in the furnace, or the oxygen combines with carbon monoxide derived from the partial combustion of coal used as a source of heat. The molten tin accumulates and is drawn off. This crude or raw tin contains copper, iron, arsenic, sulfur, and other impurities.

3. Refining by liquidation and boiling. The ingots of crude tin are placed in a reverberatory furnace, and as the temperature is gradually increased, the tin melts and is removed, leaving the unfused impurities. The molten tin thus obtained is still further purified by boiling while bundles of green twigs are held submerged in the molten tin. The steam given off by the green twigs develops violent boiling which causes the impurities to become oxidized by coming in contact with the air. These oxides form a scum on the surface. This scum is removed and the tin is cast into ingots. Some of the impurities are heavier than the tin and do not pass into the scum but settle toward the bottom. For this reason, the tin that comes from the top of the vessel is purer than the tin that comes from the bottom. The former is called refined tin and the latter common tin. The common tin is often liquefied and boiled again.

Properties and Uses

Tin is extremely malleable and may be rolled into very thin sheets called tinfoil. It is very resistant to corrosion. Its principal use is in coating sheet iron or steel for use as a roof covering. Tin plate used for roofing does not have a coating of pure tin but of an alloy of 25% tin and 75% lead. This is known as terne plate and is much less expensive than bright tin plate, which is coated with pure tin.

Tin is used in making bronzes and other alloys.

ALLOYS
The Brasses

The brasses are alloys of copper and zinc. The most useful brass alloys range in composition from 60% copper and 40% zinc to 90% copper and 10% zinc. Standard brass contains two parts of copper to one part of zinc and is the most commonly used of all the brasses. Those carrying a large amount of copper are copper red in color, and those with a small amount of copper are a silvery white.

Brass may be shaped by casting, hammering, stamping, rolling into sheets, or drawing into wire or tubes.

Muntz metal contains 60% copper and 40% zinc.

The addition of even small amounts of tin to brass greatly increases its resistance to corrosion.

The Bronzes

The bronzes are alloys of copper and tin ranging in composition from 95% copper and 5% tin to 75% copper and 25% tin. The chief effect of tin on copper is to increase its hardness.

Gun metal contains 90% copper and 10% tin. It is the strongest of the bronzes. Bell metal contains 80% copper and 20% tin. It is hard and is used for making bells. Speculum metal contains two parts copper and one part tin. It is a hard white metal which will take a polish and is used for making mirrors.

Phosphor bronze is a copper-tin alloy to which a small amount of phosphorus has been added as a deoxidizer to eliminate copper oxide. This results in a very marked improvement in the strength and quality of the bronze. It is highly resistant to corrosion.

Manganese bronze is really a brass, for it contains a large amount of zinc and little or no tin. The manganese acts as a deoxidizer and does not appear in the resultant alloy since it has been oxidized and removed in the flux. The addition of manganese greatly improves the strength of the alloy. Manganese bronze is an excellent material for castings and is very resistant to corrosion.

Monel Metal

An important alloy of nickel and copper is Monel metal, which is about two-thirds nickel, somewhat less than one-third copper, and has small amounts of iron, manganese, carbon, and silicon. It is resistant to corrosion, takes an attractive finish, and is easily worked. Monel metal is used for counter tops, sinks, and other purposes in buildings.

Summary

Using the metal ores found in the earth's crust and processing these ores into the usable metals and metal alloys that contribute to the strength and beauty of today's buildings is an example of how technology continues to work for the improvement of our everyday environment.

Steel, used more than any other metal, is produced from iron ore, limestone and coal. It has strength, ductility, weldability, and versatility. Because steel can be shaped into a variety of configurations, it is used for the manufacture of countless industrial and consumer products. Products include sheet used in the manufacture of automobiles and household appliances, plate used for shipbuilding and construction, and bars, rails, and structural shapes.

Four basic methods are used to produce the many shapes and sizes of the metals and their alloys; rolling, forging, extruding, and casting. All these methods are used to produce metal products that are utilized as materials in building construction. It is hard to imagine any building without metal products.

Key Terms

steel	*blooms*	*wind bracing*	*rivets*
beneficiation	*slabs*	*open-web (trussed) joists*	*bolts*
blast furnace	*billets*	*bar joists*	*weld*
pig iron	*weathering steel*	*drift pins*	*stainless steel*
ingot	*fabrication*		

Review Questions

1. Describe how iron ore, coal, and limestone are transformed into steel.

2. Identify the desirable properties of carbon steel.

3. What effects do the elements of carbon, silicon, sulfur, and chromium have on steel?

4. What are the most common methods for making steel connections?

5. List four structural shapes and state where they are commonly used.

6. List four nonferrous metals that are commonly used in building construction and state how they are used.

CHAPTER 7
WOOD AND PLASTICS

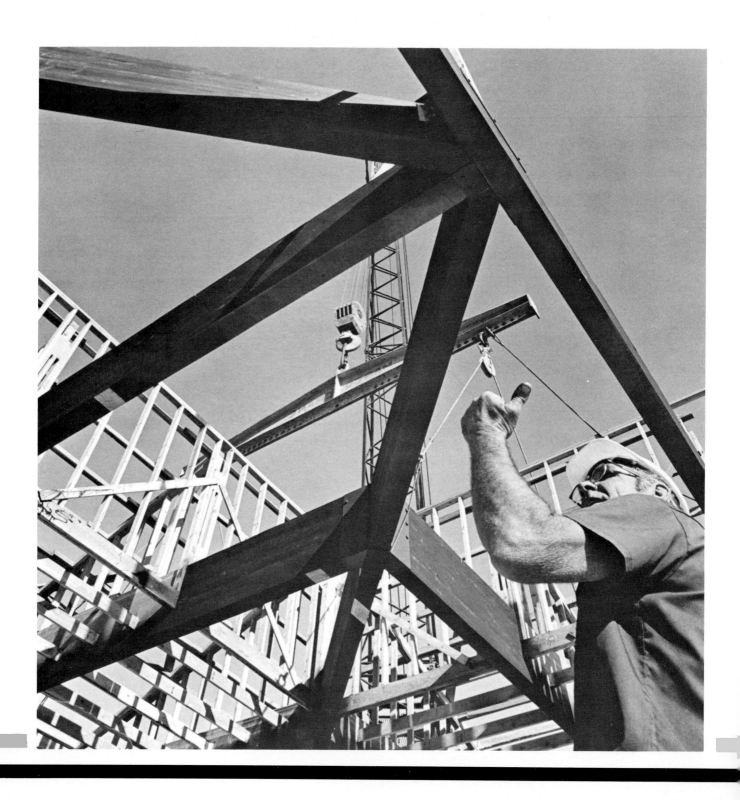

7.1 Lumber and Wood Terminology
7.2 Wood Framing
7.3 Structural Plywood
7.4 Prefabricated Structural Wood

7.5 Wood Treatment
7.6 Connectors
7.7 Plastics

Products made from the wood of hardwood and soft-wood trees are used extensively in building construction. The wood is logged and processed into lumber before it is ready for most applications. Processing includes sawing into rough sizes, seasoning by drying, surfacing into dressed dimensions by planing, and grading for appearance and strength. Unlike steel and concrete, which are processed to meet specific strength and appearance requirements, wood is processed and then graded to determine what strength and appearance standards it has met. In this chapter, wood will be considered for its structural uses. Other wood products will be discussed in later chapters.

Wood structural elements include dimensional lumber that is nominally 2 to 4 in. thick and 4 to 12 in. wide, used in wood frame construction, and timber over 5 in. thick and over 5 in. wide, used in heavy timber construction. Also included are glued laminated beams and girders. They are factory produced and have been made in lengths exceeding 100 ft and depths of up to 8 ft. Glulams, short for glued laminated structural members, can be manufactured for use as rigid frames, arches, lamella arches, and domes.

When wood is used where moisture is present, it should be treated to prevent decay. The substances commonly used for this purpose are called wood preservatives. Wood preservatives are chemicals that are impregnated into the wood. Common preservatives are creosote, pentachlorophenol, and chromated copper arsenate.

Various materials are used to fasten wood members of a structure together. Known as connectors, they are an important part of the structure. Many failures in building construction can be traced to the improper use of connectors. Nails, screws, bolts, sheet metal assemblies, and engineered metal connectors will be discussed.

The use of plastics is becoming more prevalent in building construction. Some of the most common are acrylics, used for windows and skylights; polyethylene, used as vapor barriers and temporary enclosures; vinyls used for floor and wall tiles; melamines, used for decorative laminates and counter tops; and polyesters, used for window glazing and skylights. The advantages are formability, strength, light weight, and corrosion resistance.

Objectives

1. Become familiar with the two classes of trees and how they are used in construction.
2. Understand the difference between plain-sawed lumber and quarter-sawed lumber.
3. Become familiar with how lumber is seasoned and why it is done.
4. Understand how the water content of lumber can affect its mechanical and physical properties.
5. Understand the rules of lumber grading.
6. Become familiar with the three classes of buildings that make extensive use of wood structural members.
7. Become familiar with the different prefabricated wood structural members.
8. Become familiar with the various materials that fasten the wood parts of a building together.

7.1 Lumber and Wood Terminology

This chapter is concerned with building construction primarily of wood. Various terms such as lumber, wood, wooden, frame, and timber are applied to parts of a building constructed of wood. The basic material is always wood, just as steel and concrete are basic materials. In general, the term timber designates heavy wood construction. There is a tendency to use the term wood in place of the term timber; therefore, it is difficult and probably not worthwhile to be entirely consistent in the use of these terms.

The terms wood, lumber, and timber, often used interchangeably, do have distinct meanings. *Wood* is the hard fibrous substance forming the trunk, the major stems, and the branches of trees. *Lumber* is the product of the saw or planing mill, not processed beyond sawing, resawing, or lengthwise planing, crosscutting to length, and working. *Timber* is lumber 5 in. or larger.

The term *millwork* applies to the wood building materials manufactured in planing mills and millwork plants and includes doors, window frames, shutters, porch work, interior trim, stairways, mantels, panel work, and moldings but not flooring, ceiling, and siding.

CLASSIFICATION OF TREES

Timber is furnished by two classes of trees. The needle-leaved conifers such as pines, firs, and spruces are classed as softwood. The broad-leaved trees are classed as hardwoods, for example, maple, oak, and sycamore. Basswood, which is classified as a hardwood, is softer in texture than most softwoods; some of the softwoods are nearly as hard as the hardest hardwoods.

Softwood is invariably used in structural applications that include the framing, sheathing, and blocking of buildings. Seldom is hardwood used for these applications. Hardwood is used mostly in flooring, wall and ceiling paneling, decorative moldings, and for furniture. Softwood is used for these purposes too; however, hardwood usually offers better choice of colors, quality, and workmanship.

GROWTH AND STRUCTURE

Trees grow by adding a layer of wood to all parts of the tree each year. This layer shows in the cross section as a new annual ring surrounding the old wood. The cross section of a tree consists of an exterior bark over annual growth rings surrounding a pith at the center that varies in diameter from $\frac{1}{20}$ in. to nearly $\frac{1}{4}$ in.

The annular rings near the outside form the sapwood and are lighter than those near the center, which form the heartwood.

PLAIN- AND QUARTER-SAWED LUMBER

Boards sawed tangent to the annual rings are called plain-sawed, slash-grained, or flat-sawed, whereas those sawed in a perpendicular direction are called quarter-sawed or edge-grain.

If the annual rings are neither tangent nor perpendicular to the sides, they are classed as quarter-sawed if the grain makes an angle greater than 45° with the side of the board. If this angle is less than 45°, the boards are classed as plain-sawed. Quarter-sawed lumber shrinks and warps less than plain-sawed lumber. The exposed grains of quarter-sawed wood are different from those of wood that is plain-sawed. In some woods, such as straight grained woods — the spruces, Port Orford Cedar, and vertical grained redwood — more attractive effects are secured in quarter-sawed boards. In other woods, such as knotty pines, the plain-sawed boards with attractive knots and burls may be desirable. Because quarter-sawed lumber yield is less, it is more expensive than plain-sawed lumber.

UNITS OF MEASURE

The *board foot* is the unit of measure for lumber. It is the quantity of lumber contained in a piece of rough green lumber 1 in. thick, 12 in. wide, and 1 ft long, or its equivalent in thicker, wider, narrower, or longer lumber. Lumber less than 1 in. thick is considered 1 in. thick.

In referring to commercial lots of lumber, this method of measurement is called board measure and is abbreviated b.m. The common unit is 1000 board feet, designated as M. For example, a lot of lumber that contains 25,000 board feet is designated as 25 M.b.m.

Moldings are measured by the lineal foot and shingles by the number of pieces of a specified length.

SIZE STANDARDS

Lumber usually is designated by its rough, green, or nominal size, not its actual size. Rough lumber is larger than surfaced lumber by the amount necessary for surfacing. Because shrinkage and dressing reduce softwood yard lumber, sizes designated as 1 in. thick are reduced to $\frac{25}{32}$ in. thick after surfacing; and 2-in. material is planed to $1\frac{9}{16}$ in. thick and seasoned to $1\frac{1}{2}$ in. thick. Corresponding allowances varying from $\frac{3}{8}$ in. to $\frac{3}{4}$ in. are made in the widths; the amount depends upon the width and the species of the material. A smaller allowance is made for a 4 in. nominal width, while those with a nominal width of 12 in. have larger allowances.

Hardwood lumber is cut oversize so that it will be full size when dry. When it is surfaced on one side *(S1S)*, the thickness is $\frac{1}{8}$ in. less than the rough size; when surfaced on two sides *(S2S)*, it is $\frac{3}{16}$ in. less than rough size.

The standard lengths for softwood lumber vary by 2-ft increments from 4 ft up; the most common lengths are 12, 14, and 16 ft. A few odd lengths as 9, 11, 15, and 17 ft are considered standard for specified sizes.

The standard lengths of hardwood lumber vary by increments of 1 ft from 4 to 16 ft, but grading rules permit not more than 15% of the odd lengths.

SEASONING

Wood that is prepared for construction requires more preparation than simply shaking out the squirrels. It requires a cured product. Timber that is seasoned by natural drying by exposure to the air is called *Air Dried* (AD). This drying may be accelerated by subjecting the timber to high temperatures in a kiln, a process called kiln drying. The lumber is referred to as *Kiln Dried* (KD). The principal effects of seasoning are reduced moisture content; decreased shrinking, warping, and checking; and an increase in strength and resistance to decay.

Proper seasoning of lumber requires that lumber be stacked in a manner that will allow the free circulation of air upward through the stack. Improperly stacked lumber will prolong drying time. This could result in development of decay in the seasoning lumber. Air drying requires from 2 to 6 months for properly seasoned lumber — time depending upon the location, natural humidity, and the species and size of the lumber.

Kiln drying, which is accelerated drying, is more controlled and satisfactory seasoning. Excessively high temperatures will result in an increase in splits, checks, and warp of the lumber. This is the result of the internal stresses that develop in the wood. These stresses are caused by the differences in the moisture content of the dry surface and the moist interior. On the other hand, if drying is too slow, there is the likely danger of fungus and stain.

Chemicals may serve as an aid in seasoning. Spread over the surface of the lumber, urea salts extract moisture.

MOISTURE CONTENT

The Moisture Content (MC) of wood is a variable that affects several important mechanical and physical properties of wood. The moisture includes water or sap. The moisture is contained as free water in the wood cell cavities and intercellular interstices and as absorbed water in the capillaries of the fibers of the walls and ray cells. In seasoning, the free water moisture is first removed, thereby reducing the moisture content to a state referred to as the fiber saturation point. Below this point, a further reduction in the moisture content results in shrinkage of the wood. In most species, the fiber saturation point is reached at about 30% moisture content. Thus, shrinkage does not take place until there is a loss of absorbed water.

The shrinkage of lumber is directly related to the moisture content. In general, hardwoods shrink more than softwoods, and the heavier woods shrink more than the lighter woods, although there are notable exceptions.

A reduction of the moisture content by seasoning increases resistance to fungi attack and improves structural ability. The moisture content, which is expressed in terms of a percentage, is the weight of the moisture in a given representative sample of wood divided by the oven dry weight of the sample. As recommended by ASTM D 2016, the testing for moisture content is by four methods — ovendrying method, electric moisture meter method, distillation method, and hydrometric method. The required moisture content of lumber is specified by the various grading rules for lumber.

LUMBER CHARACTERISTICS

After lumber has been sawed, planed, and shaped in the mill, it is visually graded — its quality and intended use are established based upon lumber characteristics. In order that grading quality be reasonably uniform, terms have been defined that identify both natural characteristics and manufactured imperfections. These listed characteristics, frequently referred to as "defects," are most frequently cited in grading literature and in construction specifications.

Natural characteristics are those defects or deviations in the wood grain that have resulted from natural causes. They are usually the more frequent, although their severity or extensiveness in the finished product may not be serious. These defects may be cut out or, if left, the wood may be assigned a suitable usage that will not be impaired by the defect. Conversely, some of these characteristics, such as knots or burl, may be desired in paneling or furniture.

Below are listed some of the more frequent natural characteristics as defined by PS 20-70.

Check — Lengthwise grain separation, usually occurring through the growth rings as a result of seasoning.

Cross break — Separation of the wood across the width.

Gum pocket — Opening between growth rings which usually contains or has contained resin or bark, or both.

Gum seam — Check or shake filled with gum.

Gum spot — Accumulation of gumlike substance occurring as a small patch. May occur in conjunction with a bird-peck or other injury to the growing wood.

Gum streak — Well-defined accumulation of gum in more or less regular streak. Classified in the same manner as pitch streaks.

Peck — Channeled or pitted areas or pockets as sometimes found in cedar and cypress.

Pitch — Accumulation of resin in the wood cells in a more or less irregular patch.

Pitch pocket — Opening between growth rings which usually contains or has contained resin or bark, or both.

Pitch seam — Shake or check filled with pitch.

Pitch streak — Well-defined accumulation of pitch in a more or less regular streak.

Shake — Lengthwise grain separation between or through

the growth rings; may be further classified as ring shake or pith shake.

Split—Lengthwise separation of the wood extending from one surface through the piece to the opposite surface or to an adjoining surface.

Stain—Discoloration on or in lumber other than its natural color.

Wane—This is bark or lack of wood from any cause on the edge or corner of a piece.

Warp—Any variation from a true or plane surface, includes bow, crook, cup, or any combination thereof.

> *Bow*—Deviation flatwise from a straight line from end to end of a piece, measured at the point of greatest distance from the straight line.
>
> *Crook*—Deviation edgewise from a straight line from end to end of a piece, measured at the point of greatest distance from the straight line; and classified as slight, small, medium, and large. Based on a piece 4 in. wide and 16 ft long, the distance for each degree of crook shall be: slight crook, 1 in.; small crook, 1½ in.; medium crook, 3 in.; and large crook, over 3 in. For wider pieces it shall be ⅛ in. less for each additional 2 in. of width. Shorter or longer pieces may have the same curvature.

KNOTS

Knots are perhaps the most frequently cited defect in grading rules. Their frequency, size, shape, location, and occurrence are important factors in determining lumber grades. This is especially true for lumber that is intended for structural applications. Knots may be desirable for aesthetic purposes as in paneling. PS 20-70 defines knots as follows:

Knot—Branch or limb embedded in the tree and cut through in the process of lumber manufacture; classified according to size, quality, and occurrence. To determine the size of a knot, average the maximum length and maximum width, unless otherwise specified.

> *Pin knot*—Not over ½ in. in diameter.
>
> *Small knot*—Over ½ in., but not over ¾ in. in diameter.
>
> *Medium knot*—Over ¾ in., but not over 1½ in. in diameter.
>
> *Large knot*—Over 1½ in. in diameter.

Knot Quality:

> *Decayed knot*—Softer than the surrounding wood and containing advanced decay.
>
> *Encased knot*—Its rings of annual growth are not intergrown with those of the surrounding wood.
>
> *Hollow knot*—Apparently sound except that it contains a hole over ¼ in. in diameter.
>
> *Intergrown knot*—A knot partially or completely intergrown on one or two faces with the growth rings of the surrounding wood.
>
> *Loose knot*—Not held tightly in place by growth or position, and cannot be relied upon to remain in place.
>
> *Fixed knot*—Will hold its place in a dry piece under ordinary conditions; can be moved under pressure, though not easily pushed out.
>
> *Sound knot*—Solid across its face, as hard as the surrounding wood, shows no indication of decay, and may vary in color from the natural color of the wood to reddish brown or black.
>
> *Star-checked knot*—Having radial checks.
>
> *Tight knot*—So fixed by growth or position as to retain its place.
>
> *Firm knot*—Solid across its face, but containing incipient decay.
>
> *Water-tight knot*—Its rings of annual growth are completely intergrown with those of the surrounding wood on one surface of the piece, and it is sound on that surface.

Knot Occurrence:

> *Branch knots*—Two or more divergent knots sawed lengthwise and tapering toward the pith at a common point.
>
> *Corner knot*—Located at the intersection of adjacent faces.
>
> *Knot cluster*—Two or more knots grouped together, the fibers of the wood being deflected around the entire unit. A group of single knots is not a knot cluster.
>
> *Single knot*—Occurs by itself, the fibers of the wood being deflected around it.
>
> *Spike knot*—A knot sawed in a lengthwise direction.

DECAY

Timber decay is caused by fungi, which feed on the cell walls. To develop, these fungi require warmth, air, and moisture. At low temperatures, the fungi lie dormant; however, they are killed by elevated temperatures. Timber that remains under water will last indefinitely because the air that fungi require is absent—pieces of timber that have been totally immersed in water have lasted for centuries. If moisture is not present, wood exposed to air will not decay. In dry rot, moisture is present. The development of dry rot fungi may be promoted by sealing a partially seasoned surface with paint or by embedding the timber in masonry so that the moisture present in the timber cannot escape.

Wood in the early stages of decay is usually characterized by slight discoloration that is called incipient decay. Although this type of decay has not usually progressed to the point of impairing soundness or strength, architects frequently specify that wood with incipient decay be rejected.

Decay is defined by PS 20-70 as follows:

Decay — Disintegration of wood substance due to action of wood-destroying fungi. Also known as dote and rot.

Advanced (or typical) decay — Older stage of decay in which disintegration is readily recognized because the wood has become punky, soft, spongy, stringy, shaky, pitted, or crumbly. Decided discoloration or bleaching of the wood.

Pocket rot — Typical decay which appears in the form of a hole, pocket, or area of soft rot, usually surrounded by apparently sound wood.

Water soak or *stain* — Water-soaked area in heartwood, usually interpreted as the incipient stage of certain wood rots.

INSECT DAMAGE

Various boring insects attack timber and cause considerable damage. Among these are bark beetles, which damage wood by tunneling under the bark; ambrosia beetles; roundhead beetles, which get into freshly cut timber; powderpost beetles, which attack freshly cut and seasoned hardwood by burrowing holes about 1/16 in. in diameter through the wood; and termites or white ants, which are the most destructive of all and will be given further consideration. Most insect damage in wood construction is caused by termites, which are light-colored, resemble ants in appearance, live in colonies (like ants), and thus are commonly called white ants.

Two types of termites, the subterranean and the drywood, are found in the United States. The subterranean termites live in the soil but leave it in order to attack trees and wood structures. To live, they must have access to moisture from the ground. Therefore, they build shelter tubes from the ground to the areas where they are active. They bore holes along the grain while devouring interior wood, leaving only an intact exterior shell. A member appearing to be in prime condition may actually be on the verge of failure. The most effective control prevents the passage of the termites from the soil to the wood. By using concrete foundations reinforced to prevent cracks, or by using cement mortar to fill all the joints solidly in brick and stone masonry, termites cannot work their way through the joints. Termite shields of noncorrosive metal placed between the top of the foundations walls and the wood plates or sills (Figure 7.1) should extend 2 in. over the wall and bend down 45°. This projection prevents the termites from building shelter tubes from the foundation walls to the wood plates or sills. All scraps of lumber should be removed from the building site. Wood treated with preservative by a process that penetrates the interior will resist termites; however, termites attack timber from the interior, making surface coatings and sprays ineffective. Subterranean termites are prevalent in nearly all parts of the United States.

Drywood termites attack wood directly and do not main-

FIGURE 7.1 Termite shields.

tain contact with the ground. They are confined to the warmer climates and are not such a serious menace as the subterranean termites. All structures in this country constructed wholly or partially of wood, except those of temporary character, should be protected against termites.

MARINE BORERS

Wood in salt water, such as timber piles for marine structures, may be attacked by marine wood borers, such as the teredo or shipworm and the limnoria or wood louse. Various methods of protecting wood against these borers have been devised, including impregnating the wood with creosote.

MANUFACTURED CHARACTERISTICS

Manufactured characteristics are blemishes that may be imposed on the wood at some stage in its processing into salable lumber. The general classification of these blemishes, known as mismanufacture, may occur at any time between initial cutting and final shipment. PS 20-70 identifies several of the more common mismanufacture characteristics as:

Chipped grain — Area where the surface is chipped or broken out in very short particles below the line of cut. Not classed as torn grain and, as usually found, is not considered unless in excess of 25% of the surface involved.

Hit-and-miss — Series of surfaced areas with skips not over 1/16 in. deep between them.

Hit-or-miss — To skip or surface a piece for a part or the whole of its length, provided it is nowhere more than 1/16 in. scant.

Loosened grain — Small portion of the wood loosened but not displaced.

Machine burn — Darkening or charring due to overheating by machine knives.

Machine gouge — Groove due to the machine cutting below the desired line of cut.

Mismatched lumber — Worked lumber that does not fit tightly at all points of contact between adjoining pieces or in which the surfaces of adjoining pieces are not in the same plane.

Raised grain—Roughened condition of the surface of dressed lumber in which the hard summerwood is raised above the softer springwood but not torn loose from it.

Skip—Area on a piece that failed to surface.

Torn grain—Part of the wood torn out in dressing.

Variation in sawing—Deviation from the line of cut.

GRADING

It is appropriate to forewarn the student that grading may be a slippery field. An understanding of the art of lumber grading requires study, experience, and that rarest of qualities, common sense. The confusion that is certain to greet the tyro is in part due to the multiple definitions of some terms —that is, dimension and boards. "Grade" as it applies to lumber may relate to manufacture, usage, sizes, and qualities.

Wood, being a product of nature, is varied in its properties—strength, appearance, size, and physical characteristics such as grain pattern. In order to establish reasonable uniformity for commercial use, lumber must be graded. The multiple uses of lumber, as in timber structures, require lumber of known specific qualities.

The process of evaluating the quality and use of wood that has been sawn, planed, and seasoned is called *grading.* The assigned designation is the grade. This grade marked lumber is usually stamped with a grade mark symbol that may designate quality, species, use, strength, and grading authority, or symbols denoting other wood properties.

Grading is a visual process based upon established lumber-grading rules. These rules, usually established by a lumber inspection bureau, are generally applicable to only a single species or to several similar species.

Grading attempts to assign to lumber some defined value, called the grade, based upon criteria that evaluate characteristics both natural and manufactured. The absence or the frequency of defects, the degree of severity, location, and the intended construction use are factors that determine grade.

Some of the most common defects that are visually graded are knots, stain, warp, splits, bark, and undesirable grain configurations.

Property variations may exist between sapwood and heartwood. These variations might have marked implications on the color (if color is a factor), the structural ability, and the resistance to decay. The cuts of wood determine the exposed grain pattern of grain configuration, which in turn affect the wearing quality and the natural beauty of the finished product.

SOFTWOOD GRADING

Guidelines for softwood lumber have been established by the National Bureau of Standards. Voluntary product Standard 20-70 provides voluntary guidelines for standardized grading, inspections, and sizes of softwood lumber. PS 20-70 classifies softwood lumber according to size, use, and manufacturing.

Three size classifications, based upon nominal sizes, are identified as boards, dimensions, and timbers. *Boards,* according to size, are less than 2 in. in thickness and 1 in. or more in width (see Figure 7.2). Boards that are less than 6 in. in width are called strips. Lumber that is 2 in. but less than 5 in. thick, and 2 or more in. wide is called *dimension lumber.* Lumber that is 5 in. or more in width or thickness is timber.

Use classification is divided into structural lumber, factory-and-shop lumber, and yard lumber. Structural lumber includes dimension lumber and timbers that are used where stress-graded material is required. Factory-and-shop lumber is for industrial and remanufacturing, or in other words, for wood products—boxes, etc. Yard lumber is for general building construction purposes. It is further classified as select and common, which are appearance grades. Common is broken down into four grades of descending quality.

Three classifications based upon the extent of manufacture are rough lumber, dressed (surfaced) lumber, and worked lumber. Rough lumber is that which has rough saw marks visible on the lumber surfaces. Lumber that has been run through a planing machine and brought to a smooth finish is called dressed lumber or surfaced lumber. This material is machined to a uniform size. If surfaced on one side, it is identified as S1S; surfaced on two sides is S2S; and S4S is surfaced four sides. Another surfaced lumber is S1S1E, which is surfaced one side and one edge. Other examples of lumber abbreviations will be found in Table 7.3. Worked lumber is first dressed and then is matched, shiplapped, or patterned. Lumber that has been tongued and grooved is referred to as matched lumber. Shiplapped is material that has been rabetted on one or both edges. Patterned lumber may be shiplapped or matched and shaped to a determined pattern (see Figure 7.3).

THE NATIONAL GRADING RULE

The National Grading Rule for Dimension Lumber, which

FIGURE 7.2 Lumber classification.

FIGURE 7.3 Types of wood siding and ceiling.

Table 7.1

Width Category	Use Category	Grade
Dimension up to 4 in. wide	Structural Light Framing	Select Structural No. 1 No. 2 No. 3
	Light Framing	Construction Standard Utility
	Stud	Stud
Dimension 6 in. and wider	Structural Joists & Planks	Select Structural No. 1 No. 2 No. 3
	Appearance Framing	Appearance A

was developed by a committee established by PS 20-70, clarifies, simplifies, and unifies softwood dimension lumber sizes and grades. The National Grading Rule classifies dimension lumber into two width categories and five use categories.

The two width categories are dimension up to 4 in., and dimension that is 6 in. and wider. These broad classifications are further classified into the use categories and subclassified into grades as shown in Table 7.1.

SOFTWOOD STANDARD SIZES

The sizes of dimension lumber, as standardized by the PS 20-70, are based upon an established moisture content of the lumber. If the moisture content of the lumber exceeds 19%, it is classified as green or *green lumber.* Lumber which is at 19% moisture content or less may be classified as S-Dry, or *dry lumber.* Lumber which has been air dried or kiln dried to a moisture content of 15% may be designated MC 15; however, if the lumber has been kiln dried to 15% moisture content, then the lumber may be stamped KD. Table 7.2 is from Table 3, PS 20-70.

SOFTWOOD GRADING RULES

Following the guidelines of the National Grading Rules, several associations or agencies have established grading and inspection services that conform to these standards. The grading rules usually apply to several species, although they may apply to only one species.

The Southern Pine Inspection Bureau classifies, grades, and inspects southern pines — namely slash pine, shortleaf pine, longleaf pine, loblolly pine, and several others that are of lesser commercial importance.

Two grading associations primarily serve the grading and inspection of the western lumbers — that is, the firs, spruces, and pines. The Western Wood Products Associa-

tion (WWPA) and the West Coast Lumber Inspection Bureau (WCLIB) serve the lumber industry for Douglas fir, Sitka spruce, western hemlock, western red cedar, and several other pines, spruces, firs, and cedars.

In certain species, special aspects or properties of the lumber may require grading terms that are peculiar only to that species. For example, redwood, which is graded by the Redwood Inspection Service (RIS), is graded in a manner that makes a marked distinction between lumber that is all heart redwood and that which contains sapwood.

Some trees are distinguished by their rate of growth. The rate of growth determines the spacing of their annual rings in the wood. If the rate of growth is relatively slow, the annual rings are usually closely spaced. This results in a lumber that is termed dense. Dense lumber is more likely to have better structural qualities than wood which is not so dense. Thus, a special grading usually denotes lumber that qualifies for a dense classification. Other terms that relate to density of the lumber are close grain, medium grain, open grain, and coarse grain.

HARDWOOD GRADING

Hardwood is graded and inspected by several associations, most of which are concerned with two or three species and their applications. However, the National Hardwood Lumber Association has extensive rules that apply to a great variety of hardwoods, especially domestic hardwoods, that are commercially important. Comments below are based upon these rules.

Standard hardwood grades are based upon the number and size of cuttings that can be obtained from a board or, restated, the amount of clear usable lumber in a piece. Except in certain cases, standard grade is determined from the poorer side of the boards. In certain grades, such as No. 1 Common Face, grade determination is made from the

Table 7.2 **Nominal and Minimum-Dressed Sizes of Boards, Dimension, and Timbers (the thicknesses apply to all widths and all widths to all thicknesses)**

Item	Thicknesses			Face Widths		
	Nominal	Minimum Dressed		Nominal	Minimum Dressed	
		Dry	Green		Dry	Green
		Inches	*Inches*		*Inches*	*Inches*
Boards				2	1½	1⁹⁄₁₆
				3	2½	2⁹⁄₁₆
				4	3½	3⁹⁄₁₆
				5	4½	4⅝
	1	¾	²⁵⁄₃₂	6	5½	5⅝
				7	6½	6⅝
	1¼	1	1¹⁄₃₂	8	7¼	7½
				9	8¼	8½
	1½	1¼	1⁹⁄₃₂	10	9¼	9½
				11	10¼	10½
				12	11¼	11½
				14	13¼	13½
				16	15¼	15½
Dimension				2	1½	1⁹⁄₁₆
				3	2½	2⁹⁄₁₆
				4	3½	3⁹⁄₁₆
	2	1½	1⁹⁄₁₆	5	4½	4⅝
	2½	2	2¹⁄₁₆	6	5½	5⅝
	3	2½	2⁹⁄₁₆	8	7¼	7½
	3½	3	3¹⁄₁₆	10	9¼	9½
				12	11¼	11½
				14	13¼	13½
				16	15¼	15½
Dimension				2	1½	1⁹⁄₁₆
				2	1½	2⁹⁄₁₆
				4	3½	3⁹⁄₁₆
				5	4½	4⅝
	4	3½	3⁹⁄₁₆	6	5½	5⅝
	4½	4	4¹⁄₁₆	8	7¼	7½
				10	9¼	9½
				12	11¼	11½
				14		13½
				16		15½
Timbers	5 & Thicker		½ Off	5 & Wider		½ Off

better face of the board. There are eight standard grades of hardwood and several combination grades. The standard grades are Firsts, Seconds, Selects, Sound Wormy, No. 1 Common, No. 2 Common, No. 3A Common, and No. 3B Common. The standard grades are frequently formed into combination grades, such as Firsts and Seconds (FAS), which contains a specified amount of Firsts. Another is Selects and No. 1, which may combine as one grade except in mahogany, walnut, and cherry. A combination grade made up of No. 3A Common and No. 3B Common is known as No. 3. Other combination grades are No. 1 and Better, No. 2 and Better, and No. 3B and Better. The term "Better" means that no material of inferior grade is permitted below the stated standard grade.

Sound Wormy, a standard grade, may have defects such as worm holes, bird pecks, stain, or sound knots ¾ in. or less in diameter. Sound Wormy and the more restrictive standard grades may form a combination such as Firsts and Seconds Sound Wormy, or No. 1 Common and Better Sound Wormy. However, either in combination or as a standard grade, Sound Wormy must not grade less than No. 1 Common.

The extremes in quality may be illustrated by the difference between Firsts and No. 2 Common. The former must have a minimum width of 6 in., and 91⅔% of the surface measure of a piece must be able to be cut into clear face material. The number of pieces into which a piece can be cut to give the required percentage of clear material depends upon the grade and upon the size of the piece. For example, a piece with 14 sq ft of surface measure can be cut into only 2 pieces, with a minimum size of 4 in. by 5 ft or 3 in. by 7 ft if the piece is to be classified as Firsts; but a piece of No. 2 Common of this size can be cut into 7 pieces with a minimum size of 3 in. by 2 ft. There are other requirements which are not mentioned here.

HARDWOOD SIZES
Dressed hardwood lumber of less than 8 in. in nominal widths is cut ⅜ in. scant; lumber 8 in. or more is cut ½ in.

scant of their nominal width. Hardwoods are cut in lengths from 4 ft to 16 ft in one foot increments. These are known as standard lengths. The thickness of hardwood lumber is based upon both a rough lumber and a lumber surface on two sides (S2S). Frequently, hardwood lumber is expressed in terms of the number of quarter-inches in the nominal thickness. Thus, 1½ in. thick rough will be expressed as 6/4. Rough thicknesses from ⅜ in. to 1½ in. are surfaced down to a thickness 3/16 in. less than their rough measurement, and thicknesses of 1¾ in. up to 6 in. are surfaced to a thickness ¼ in. less than the rough thickness.

LUMBER ABBREVIATIONS
Lumber terms are most frequently abbreviated in commercial usage, grading literature, and in construction specifications and drawings. Table 7.3 lists some of the most frequently abbreviated terms that should be committed to memory.

Table 7.3 Lumber Abbreviations

AD—air dried
B1S—beaded one side
B2S—beaded two sides
B&B or B & Btr.—B and better
B&S—beams and stringers
Bd.—board
Bd. ft.—board foot
Bdl.—bundle
Bdl. bk. s.—bundle bark strips
B/L—bill of lading
Bm.—board measure
CB1S—center bead one side
CB2S—center bead two sides
CG2E—center groove two edges
Clr.—clear
CM—center matched
Com.—common
Csg.—casing
CV1S—center V one side
CV2S—center V two sides
DB. Clg.—double-beaded ceiling (E&CB1S)
DB. Part—double-beaded partition (E&CB2S)
DET—double and trimmed
D&CM—dressed (1 or 2 sides) and center matched
D&H—dressed and headed
D&M—dressed and matched
D&SM—dressed (1 or 2 sides) and standard matched
D2S&CM—dressed two sides and center matched
D2S&M—dressed two sides and (center or standard) matched

D2S&SM—dressed two sides and standard matched
Dim.—dimension
Dkg.—decking
D.S., D/S or D Sdg.—drop siding
DT&G—double tongued and grooved
E—edge
EB1S—edge bead one side
EB2S—edge bead two sides
E&CB1S—edge and center bead 1 side; surfaced 1 or 2 sides and with a longitudinal edge and center bead on a surfaced face
E&CB2S—edge and center bead 2 sides; all 4 sides surfaced and with a longitudinal edge and center bead on the 2 faces
ECM—ends center matched
E&CV1S—edge and center V 1 side; surfaced 1 or 2 sides and with a longitudinal edge and center V-shaped groove on a surfaced face
E&CV2S—edge and center V two sides
EG—edge (vertical) grain
EE—eased edges
EM—end matched, either center or standard
ESM—ends standard matched
EV1S—edge V one side
EV2S—edge V two sides
FAS—First and Seconds
FBM—foot or feet board measure
Fcty.—factory (lumber)
FG—flat (slash) grain
Flg.—flooring

Table 7.3 **(Continued)**

FOHC—free of heart center or centers	S2E—surfaced two edges
F.o.k.—free of knots	S1S—surfaced one side
Frm.—framing	S2S—surfaced two sides
GM—grade marked	S1S1E—surfaced 1 side and 1 edge
G/R or G/Rfg.—grooved roofing	S2S1E—surfaced 2 sides and 1 edge
Hdwd.—hardwood	S1S2E—surfaced 1 side and 2 edges
H&M—hit and miss	S4S—surfaced four sides
H or M—hit or miss	S4S&CS—surfaced four sides with a
Hrt.—heart	calking seam on each edge
Hrtwd.—heartwood	S&M—surfaced and matched; that is,
J&P—joists and planks	surfaced 1 or 2 sides and tongued and
KD—kiln-dried	grooved on the edges; the match may
K.d.—knocked down	be center or standard
Lbr.—lumber	S2S&SM—surfaced two sides and
Lr. MCO—long run, mill culls out	standard matched
Lth.—lath	S2S&CM—surfaced two sides and center
M—thousand	matched
MBM—thousand (feet) board measure	S2S&M—surfaced two sides and center
MC—moisture content	or standard matched
MCO—mill culls out	S2S&S/L—surfaced two sides and ship-
Merch.—merchantable	lapped
M.G.—mixed grain	Sap.—sapwood
Mldg.—molding	SB—standard bead
MR—mill run	Sd.—seasoned
M.s.m.—thousand (feet) surface measure	Sdg.—siding
MSR—machine stress rated	Sel.—select
M.w.—mixed widths	SESdg.—square-edge siding
N1E—nosed one edge	SE&S—Square edge and sound
N2E—nosed two edges	Sftwd.—softwood
Og.—ogee	SG, S/L, SL—slash (flat) grain
PE—plain end	Ship.—shiplap
PET—precision end trimmed	S.M.—surface measure
Pln.—plain, as plainsawed	SM—standard matched
P&T—post and timbers	Snd.—sound
Qtd.—quartered—when referring to	SR—stress rated
hardwoods	Std.—standard
R/S, Res.—resawed	SW—sound wormy
Rfg.—roofing	T&G—tongued and grooved
Rfrs.—roofers	TB&S—top, bottom, and sides
Rgh.—rough	Tbrs.—timbers
R/L—random lengths	V/S—V 1 side; that is, a longitudinal
Rnd.—round	V-shaped groove on 1 side face of a piece
R. Sdg.—rustic siding	of lumber
R/W—random widths	V2S—V on 2 sides; that is, a longitudinal
R/W&L—random widths and lengths	V-shaped groove on 2 faces of a piece
S&E—surfaced 1 side and 1 edge	of lumber
S1E—surfaced one edge	VG—vertical grain

WOOD IDENTIFICATION AND USE

There are several woods that are known by more than one common or commercial name. This variation may be caused to some extent by the wide geographical distribution of the species. Clarity in construction requires specific terms. Although woods are frequently spoken of by their commercial, or common, name, they should be identified by their botanical name when written in construction specifications.

Table 7.4, which is adapted from ASTM D 1165, lists the more useful domestic woods and some of their construction applications.

Table 7.4 **Standard Nomenclature of Domestic Hardwoods and Softwoods from ASTM D 1165**

Commercial Names for Lumber	Official Common Tree Names	Botanical Names	Usual Uses
		Hardwoods	
Red alder	Red alder	*Alnus rubra*	Interior finishes, sash, doors
Black ash (Brown ash)	Black ash	*Fraxinus nigra*	
Oregon ash	Oregon ash	*F. latifolia*	
Pumpkin ash	Pumpkin ash	*F. profunda*	Plywood, interior finishes
White ash	Blue ash	*F. quadrangulata*	
	Green ash	*F. pennsylvanica*	
	White ash	*F. americana*	
Aspen (Popple)	Bigtooth aspen	*Populus grandidentata*	Plywood
	Quaking aspen	*P. tremuloides*	
Basswood	American basswood	*Tilia americana*	Door frames, finishes, patterns core stock for veneer
	White basswood	*T. heterophylla*	Architect models
Beech	American beech	*Fagus grandifolia*	Flooring, cabinets
Birch	Gray birch	*Betula populifolia*	
designated as	Paper birch	*B. papyrifera*	Plywood, doors, interior finishes
Red Birch,	River birch	*B. nigra*	
Sap (White)	Sweet birch	*B. lenta*	
Birch or Birch	Yellow birch	*B. alleghaniensis*	Above, and flooring
Butternut	Butternut	*Juglans cinerea*	Plywood, interior finishes
Cherry	Black cherry	*Prunus serotina*	Plywood, flooring, interior finishes
Chestnut	American chestnut	*Castanea dentata*	Core stock, plywood, interior finishes, poles, posts
Gum (may be designated Red or Sweetgum)	Sweetgum	*Liquidambar styraciflua*	Plywood, trim, interior finishes
Hickory	Mockernut hickory	*Carya tomentosa*	Plywood, flooring
	Pignut hickory	*C. glabra*	
	Shagbark hickory	*C. ovata*	
	Shellbark hickory	*C. laciniosa*	
Pecan	Bitternut hickory	*C. cordiformis*	Plywood, flooring
	Nutmeg hickory	*C. myristicaeformis*	
	Water hickory	*C. aquatica*	
	Pecan	*C. illinoensis*	
Holly	American holly	*Ilex opaca*	Plywood
Hard Maple (If specified as white, requires sapwood.)	Black maple	*Acer nigrum*	Special floors (i.e., bowling alleys and dance halls, interior finishes)
	Sugar maple	*A. saccharum*	
Oregon Maple	Bigleaf maple	*A. macrophyllum*	Flooring, interior finishes
Soft Maple (If specified as white, requires sapwood.)	Red maple	*A. rubrum*	Flooring, interior finishes
	Silver maple	*A. saccharinum*	
Red Oak	Black oak	*Quercus velutina*	
	Blackjack oak	*Q. marilandica*	
	California black oak	*Q. kelloggii*	
	Cherrybark oak	*Q. falcata var. pagodaefolia*	
	Laurel oak	*Q. laurifolia*	Subflooring

Table 7.4 **(Continued)**

Commercial Names for Lumber	Official Common Tree Names	Botanical Names	Usual Uses
	Hardwoods		
	Northern pin oak	*Q. ellipsoidalis*	Flooring
	Northern red oak	*Q. rubra*	Interior finishes
	Nuttall oak	*Q. nuttallii*	
	Pin oak	*Q. palustris*	
	Scarlet oak	*Q. coccinea*	
	Shumard oak	*Q. shumardii*	
	Southern red oak	*Q. falcata*	
	Turkey oak	*Q. laevis*	
	Willow oak	*Q. phellos*	
White Oak	Arizona white oak	*Q. arizonica*	Subflooring, flooring,
	Blue oak	*Q. douglasii*	trestles, paneling,
	Bur oak	*Q. macrocarpa*	exterior doors,
	California white oak	*Q. lobata*	thresholds, frames,
	Chestnut oak	*Q. prinus*	interior finishes
	Chinkapin oak	*Q. muehlenbergii*	
	Emory Oak	*Q. emoryi*	
	Gambel oak	*Q. gambelii*	
	Mexican blue oak	*Q. oblongifolia*	
	Live oak	*Q. virginiana*	
	Oregon white oak	*Q. garryana*	
	Overcup oak	*Q. lyrata*	
	Post oak	*Q. stellata*	
	Swamp chestnut oak	*Q. michauxii*	
	Swamp white oak	*Q. bicolor*	
	White oak	*Q. alba*	
Persimmon	Common persimmon	*Diospyros virginiana*	Plywood
Poplar	Yellow-poplar	*Liriodendron tulipifera*	Plywood, siding, weatherboard, interior finishes (painted or stained), frames, sashes
Sycamore	American sycamore	*Platanus occidentalis*	Flooring
Walnut	Black walnut	*Juglans nigra*	Parquet flooring, interior finishes, cabinet work, plywood
	Softwoods		
Alaska Cedar	Alaska-cedar	*Chamaecyparis nootkatensis*	Interior finishes, cabinets
Incense Cedar	Incense-cedar	*Libocedrus decurrens*	Split shingles, foundation sills
Eastern Red Cedar	Eastern red cedar	*Juniperus virginiana*	
	Southern red cedar	*J. silicicola*	Plywood, closet linings
Western Red Cedar	Western red cedar	*Thuja plicata*	Plywood, shingles, interior finishes, frames, siding
Northern White Cedar	Northern white cedar	*T. occidentalis*	Construction framing
Southern White Cedar	Atlantic white cedar	*Chamaecyparis thyoides*	Construction
Cypress (Red White, or Yellow)	Baldcypress	*Taxodium distichum*	Gutters, shingles, siding, millwork, framing, plywood, exterior trim

Table 7.4 **(Continued)**

Commercial Names for Lumber	Official Common Tree Names	Botanical Names	Usual Uses
Softwoods			
	Pondcypress	*T. distichum var. nutans*	Plywood
Douglas Fir May be specified as Coast Region or Inland Region	Douglas fir	*Pseudotsuga menziesii*	General construction, plywood, framing, sheathing
White Fir	Subalpine fir California red fir Grand fir Noble fir Pacific silver fir White fir	*Abies lasiocarpa* *A. magnifica* *A. grandis* *A. procera* *A. amabilis* *A. concolor*	Plywood, general construction, sash, doors
Eastern Hemlock	Carolina hemlock Eastern hemlock	*Tsuga caroliniana* *T. canadensis*	Framing, subflooring, sheathing
Mountain Hemlock	Mountain hemlock	*T. mertensiana*	Framing, subflooring, sheathing
West Coast Hemlock	Western hemlock	*T. heterophylla*	Framing, subflooring, sheathing, floors, siding, joists, planks
Western Larch	Western larch	*Larix occidentalis*	Rough dimension, flooring, sash, doors, planks, poles, small timbers
Jack Pine	Jack Pine	*Pinus banksiana*	Post, poles
Lodgepole Pine	Lodgepole pine	*P. contorta*	General construction, poles, siding, flooring
Norway Pine	Red pine	*P. resinosa*	General construction, piles
Ponderosa Pine	Ponderosa pine	*P. ponderosa*	Piles, posts, doors, panels, trim, general construction
Sugar Pine	Sugar pine	*P. lambertiana*	Sash, doors, frames, general construction
Idaho White Pine	Western white pine	*P. monticola*	General construction, paneling, siding, exterior doors, patterned wood construction, trim, frames
Northern White Pine	Eastern white pine	*P. strobus*	Exterior doors, trim, frames, panels, patterned siding
Southern Yellow Pine	Loblolly pine	*P. taeda*	Kraft paper and below listed uses of other Southern Yellow Pines
	Longleaf pine Shortleaf pine Slash pine	*P. palustris* *P. echinata* *P. eliottii*	general construction, siding, timbers, flooring
Redwood	Redwood	*Sequoia sempervirens*	Shingles, plywood, foundations, siding, general construction
Eastern Spruce	Black spruce	*Picea mariana*	Framing, general

Table 7.4 **(Continued)**

Commercial Names for Lumber	Official Common Tree Names	Botanical Names	Usual Uses
	Softwoods		
	Red spruce	*P. rubens*	millwork
	White spruce	*P. glauca*	
Engelmann	Blue spruce	*P. pungens*	Flooring, sheathing,
Spruce	Engelmann spruce	*P. engelmannii*	siding, studs, dimension stock
Sitka Spruce	Sitka spruce	*P. sitchensis*	Doors, millwork
Tamarack	Tamarack	*Larix laricina*	Framing

7.2 Wood Framing

The structural elements of many buildings are made of wood. According to the classification based on the types of construction given in Section 1.2, there are three classes of buildings which make extensive use of wood structural members: wood frame construction, ordinary construction, and heavy timber construction. Consideration will be given to each of these types.

WOOD FRAME CONSTRUCTION

Wood frame construction, frequently called frame construction, is defined in Section 1.2 and is used extensively in dwellings. It is that type of construction in which the walls, partitions, floors, and roof are wholly or partly of wood or other combustible material. Our discussion is confined to buildings of this type. The height is usually limited to two habitable floors above the grade line, not including a finished attic or a basement. Wood frame construction is not permitted within certain fire zones.

The structural frame is lumber, most of which has a nominal thickness of 2 in. The center-to-center spacing of the various structural members is a module of 48 in. that is usually 16 in., but occasionally they are spaced at 12 in. and 24 in. Unless this spacing is constant, framing difficulties ensue. The depths of joists and rafters are determined by the loading conditions, span, allowable stresses, and required rigidity. Most studs and plates are 2 × 4s. Types of wood frame construction are illustrated in Figures 7.4 and 7.5.

The exterior wall framing is usually covered with sheathing which is, in turn, covered with finished surfaces of siding or a masonry veneer, as later described. The roof framing is covered with a deck of sheathing or other material to receive roofing. The floor framing is covered with a subfloor on which a finish is laid. The wall and roof sheathing are factors in insulation and, together with the subfloors, provide essential lateral rigidity.

Before the frame is started, termite shields (Section 7.1) should be installed on top of all foundation walls. Two by or three by *mud sills* or plates are then placed on top of the foundation walls and anchored by bolts previously installed. These sills, which may be 4 or 6 in. wide, are the first members of the frame.

If there are unexcavated spaces below the first floor, there should be a crawl space with a clearance of at least 18 in. between the bottoms of the joists and the ground. This space provides for ventilation (to avoid decay) and access for inspection and repairs. If the soil is of a type, such as clay, which conducts moisture upward by capillary action, the surface of the unexcavated soil could be covered

FIGURE 7.4 Platform frame. Adapted from *Manual for House Framing,* National Lumber Manufacturers Association, Washington, D.C.

with a layer of heavy polyethylene film to serve as a vapor barrier and assist in humidity control.

There are two types of wood frames commonly used for dwellings. These are the *platform frame* (Figure 7.4) and the *balloon frame* (Figure 7.5). These can be adapted to one-story frames, special conditions, or individual preferences. Although the illustrations are for frames of two-story dwellings, the changes are required to adapt them to other types of sloping roofs are obvious. Changes required for one-story frames are considered later.

Platform Frame

This type of frame, sometimes called western framing, is illustrated in Figure 7.4. The drawing indicates that the framing and subfloor for the first-floor construction can be completed to form a platform before the first-story exterior walls and the partition framing are started.

Subfloors are most frequently made of plywood sheets of a thickness that is structurally adequate. Plywood thickness, which depends upon the spacing of the supports, is from ½ in. to 1¼ in. The face grain of the plywood is laid perpendicular to the supporting joist and nailed at all boundaries and at all intermediate supports with 8d or 10d common nails. Nailing at intermediate supports is called field nailing. Glue for plywood that is used for subfloor application need only be interior type glue; however, if moisture conditions are anticipated, an exterior type plywood with exterior glue should be specified. The grade of plywood that is usually specified is called standard.

Strip board subfloors, laid diagonally, permit a tongue-and-grooved or matched, finished wood floor to be laid

FIGURE 7.5 Balloon frame. Adapted from *Manual for House Framing,* National Lumber Manufacturers Association, Washington, D.C.

either perpendicular or parallel to the joists. The former is preferred, with the flooring nailed to the joists. In addition, a subfloor laid diagonally adds significantly to the rigidity of the frame.

Rows of *bridging* are provided at the joist midspan or on rows that are not more than 8 ft apart. One function of bridging is to distribute the concentrated loads over several joists, thereby increasing the strength and rigidity of the floor, preventing torsion or twisting of the floor joists, and increasing resistance to lateral loads. There are two types of bridging — cross-bridging and solid blocking. The preferred form of bridging is solid blocking, which consists of short pieces of the same depth and width of the joists fitted between the joists at right angles to them and offset to permit end nailing. Cross-bridging, also called X-bracing, which is usually of 1 by 2's, is nailed in at the top and bottom. Solid blocking may be preferred to X-bracing because it may serve as a solid support and nailer for the side edges of plywood subflooring; it transmits lateral loads and may form a solid support for partitions.

Framing the first-story walls and partitions is started by nailing the sole plates to the subfloor. The first-story studs are then erected, diagonally braced, fire-blocked, and capped with doubled top plates. The frame is now ready to receive the second-floor joists, bridging, and subfloor to complete the second-floor platform.

The framing for the second-story walls and partitions can now be completed, the ceiling joists placed, and the attic subfloor laid if there is to be one.

Double joists must be provided under partitions which are parallel with the joists. If these are bearing partitions unsupported by walls, partitions, or girders, the partition should be trussed by one or more diagonal braces. The 1 × 4 in. or 1 × 6 in. diagonal brace is nailed on temporarily; a power saw is run along the brace, cutting the studs to the depth and width of the brace. The wood is chipped out and the diagonal brace is nailed in flush to the studs, forming a let-in brace. Properly installed, let-in braces should extend from the top plate to the sill plate. Bracing arrangements are necessary to avoid partition openings, such as doors and ducts.

Finally, the rafters are erected. They are notched, a birds-mouth, to provide bearing on the top plate of the exterior wall studs. The upper ends of full-length rafters are cut to fit against the vertical sides of the ridge board to which they are nailed. To strengthen the roof, horizontal members, called collar beams, are often nailed to every third pair of rafters at approximately their upper third points.

The frame is now ready to receive the exterior sheathing. Because wall sheathing, including horizontal wood sheathing, does not provide adequate lateral stability, the frame must be braced laterally by corner bracing (Figure 7.4). Such bracing, similar to that described above, consists of 1 × 4 in. boards let-in to notches cut in the outer faces of the studs so that the outer faces of the braces are flush with the outer edges of the studs to which they are nailed.

Often the framing for various portions of the walls and partitions is assembled in a horizontal position on the platform, tilted into the vertical position, and secured, facilitating constuction operations.

The frame for a two-story dwelling is identical with the portion of the one-story frame above the foundation sill. This is the usual type of frame for one-story dwellings that do not have masonry veneers or stucco finishes.

Balloon Frame

The basic difference between the balloon frame and the platform frame is that the balloon frame exterior wall studs extend as one piece from the foundation sill passing through the two floors. The interior partition studs are interrupted only by a single top plate. No header is provided at the exterior ends of the first-floor joists. They are simply nailed to the studs.

The two-story exterior wall studs and their double top plates are erected with the lower ends at the studs bearing on the sill. The ends of the second-floor joists (first-floor ceiling) are supported on a flat 2 × 4 block resting on a 1 × 4 in. ledger board let-in to the inside of the notched studs. This board is called a ribbon or rib-band. The joists are placed in contact and nailed to the studs. If there are interior foundation walls under the first-story partitions, the first-story studs are extended to plates on these walls; otherwise, they are supported on girders. The second-story joists are lapped at their interior, which is a single 2 × 4 top plate of the first-story bearing partitions. The relative positions of the first- and second-story bearing partition studs and the second-story joists are shown in Figure 7.5.

The lower portion of the frame for a one-story dwelling is identical to the lower portion of the frame for a two-story dwelling. A double wall plate placed along the tops of the one-story studs supports the ceiling joists and the roof rafters.

The bridging, roof framing, double joists, and corner bracing required for platform framing apply also to the balloon frame. Horizontal sheathing requires that the frame be corner braced, but diagonal sheathing or plywood sheathing does not.

The Merits of Platform and Balloon Frames

The primary advantage of the platform frame over the balloon frame is its relative ease of construction. The primary advantage of the balloon frame is its relatively smaller vertical shrinkage.

The easier erection of the platform frame results primarily from utilizing the platform in each story for wall and partition frame presassembly.

The small vertical shrinkage of the balloon frame results from the continuity of the exterior wall studs extending through the two stories and the approximate continuity of the bearing partition studs. This takes advantage of the negligible longitudinal shrinkage of wood.

The relatively large vertical shrinkage of the platform frame is due to the inclusion of considerable cross-grain wood along the lines of vertical support. The shrinkage of wood in cross-grain is relatively large because the shrinkage of the wood cells in their cross-sectional dimension is large when there is a reduction in moisture content.

The vertical shrinkage produces unequal vertical movements at different points. This causes plaster and glass to crack, joints to open up, openings to be out of plumb and distorted, and doors and windows to bind. Such movements can be minimized in both types of frame by equalizing the total vertical thickness of cross-grain wood along all lines of vertical supports.

Difficulties due to vertical shrinkage cannot be avoided by the platform frame if the building is faced with a masonry veneer. Masonry veneers do not shrink with reduction in moisture content, but the supporting frame does shrink. The relative downward movement of the frame causes stresses which are difficult to avoid even if foreseen, especially at openings. They are, of course, more pronounced in two-floor than in single-floor dwellings. Exterior finishes such as shingles and wood sidings can adjust themselves to vertical shrinkage of the supporting frame, but stucco finishes cannot unless expansion joints are included.

Considering vertical shrinkage in the platform frame, horizontal sheathing is preferable to diagonal sheathing. Diagonal sheathing would restrict the vertical movement of the first- and second-floor construction and preclude the equal vertical settlement of the structure, which is an objective of the platform frame.

If lumber were seasoned to the ultimate in-use moisture content, shrinkage problems would be minimized. This is unfeasible for many reasons, including the seasonal variations in the moisture content of the framing. The most objectionable shrinkage occurs after the finished wall surfaces have been completed.

Framed Openings

Typical framings around window and door openings are illustrated in Figure 7.6A to (C). In general, the jambs at these openings are doubled. The heads consist of two pieces proportioned according to the span and load and supported by the double jambs, as shown in (A), (B) and (C). Short studs above and below openings (A) and (B) are called *cripple studs*. A double jamb may be separated (A) if blocks are securely nailed between the two studs. Wide door and window openings may be trussed (C), or deep headers may be used. The framing must support the subjected loads without exceeding permissible stresses and deflections. The framing around an opening in a floor is illustrated in (D), where a header, trimmers, and tail beams are shown.

FIGURE 7.6 Framing around openings.

Fire-stopping

Concealed spaces between studs, joists, and rafters, in the clearance space required between masonry chimneys and wood framing, and in other locations permitting air currents to circulate should be sealed by barriers to impede the spread of fire. Usually 2 in. thick wood members are used for fire-stopping, although noncombustible materials, such as cement asbestos, are permitted. Examples of fire-stopping given in Figure 7.7 are similar to joists supported on steel girders or masonry walls.

Nailed Connections

Nailing is the most common means for joining the 1 in. and 2 in. lumber used in wood frame construction. Nails are driven in various ways with reference to the pieces they connect. In balloon frames, the faces of the joists and studs are placed in contact (Figure 7.5) and nailed together.

The types of nailing (Figure 7.8) are face nailing, end nailing, toe nailing, and blind nailing. In face nailing, the nails are driven through the face of one piece into the face or edge of another (A).

In end nailing, the nails are driven through the face (perpendicular to grain) of one piece and into the end (parallel to grain) of another piece (B). In toe nailing, the nails are driven at about a 30° angle through the face of one end and into the face of another (C). Usually toe nails are driven into both faces of the first members; but sometimes, as in cross-bridging, only one face is accessible. Blind-nailing is used for nailing matched flooring to the subfloor. The nails are driven at about a 45° angle at the top of the tongue and into subfloor and joists, as shown in (D). Finishing is not consid-

FIGURE 7.7 Fire-stopping.

FIGURE 7.8 Types of nailing. Timber Engineering Company.

ered a part of the framing. Two-inch matched subflooring is secured by both face and blind nailing to the supporting members.

The type of nailing is determined partially by the accessibility of the nailhead. Nailed joints are strongest when nails driven perpendicular to the grain are subjected to shearing stresses (Table 7.5). They are weakest when the withdrawing forces act parallel with the length of the nail. This is especially true for end nailing, in which the nails are driven parallel to the grain in the supporting member.

The usual minimum recommended nail penetration into the supporting member is one-half the thickness of the attached member.

A nailing schedule giving the types of nailing and the sizes of nails suitable for various connections in light wood framing is given in Table 7.6.

Plank and Beam Construction

A type of framing for dwellings uses 2 in. thick planks for subfloors and roof sheathing, supported by beams and rafters spaced from 6 to 8 ft apart, which in turn are supported by posts or by trussing the rafters. The planks are perpendicular to the beams. The frames resemble platform frames.

The plank subfloors and the roof sheathing are usually exposed on their lower sides, frequently presenting attractive surfaces. Because of the wide spacing of the beams, tongue-and-grooved planks or planks with grooves on both edges to receive wood strips, called loose tongues or splines, are used to diminish differential deflection between members and to distribute the floor loads. The finished wood flooring is nailed at right angles to the subfloor planks.

The beams, designed to satisfy structural requirements, may be solid sections, planks placed on edge and spiked together, or planks separated by blocks. To improve appearance, a single piece of wood can cover built-up beams. Utility lines can be located in separated beams.

Columns or posts are spaced to correspond to the beam spacing. Columns must be large enough to carry their loads and to provide adequate seating or bearing for the beams. The minimum post size is 4 × 4 in. When the beams abut

Table 7.5 **Safe Lateral Strength and Required Penetration of Box and Common Wire Nails Driven Perpendicular to Grain of Wood**

Size of Nail	Standard Length (in.)	Wire Gauge	Penetration Required (in.)	Loads (lb)[a,b]	
				Douglas Fir Larch or Southern Pine	Other Species
Box Nails					
6d	2	12½	1¼	47	See
8d	2½	11½	1½	59	U.B.C.
10d	3	10½	1⅝	71	Standard
12d	3¼	10½	1⅝	71	No.
16d	3½	10	1¾	80	25-17[c]
20d	4	9	2⅛	104	
30d	4½	9	2¼	116	
40d	5	8	2½	132	
Common Nails					
6d	2	11½	1¼	63	See
8d	2½	10¼	1½	78	U.B.C.
10d	3	9	1⅝	94	Standard
12d	3¼	9	1⅝	94	No.
16d	3½	8	1¾	107	25-17
20d	4	6	2⅛	139	
30d	4½	5	2¼	154	
40d	5	4	2½	176	
50d	5½	3	2¾	202	
60d	6	2	2⅞	223	

[a] The safe lateral strength values may be increased 25% where metal side plates are used.

[b] For wood diaphragm calculations, these values may be increased 30%. (See U.B.C. Standard No. 25-17.)

[c] For other species, the lateral strength values of box wire nails shall not exceed 75% of the values listed in the Standard.

Reproduced from the 1976 edition of the *Uniform Building Code* copyright 1976, with permission of the publisher, the International Conference of Building Officials.

Table 7.6 **Nailing Schedule**

Connection	Nailing[a]
Joist to sill or girder, toe nail	3-8d
Bridging to joist, toe nail each end	2-8d
1″ × 6″ subfloor or less to each joist, face nail	2-8d
Wider than 1″ × 6″ subfloor to each joist, face nail	3-8d
2″ subfloor to joist or girder, blind and face nail	2-16d
Sole plate to joist or blocking, face nail	16d at 16″ o.c.
Top plate to stud, end nail	2-16d
Stud to sole plate, toe nail	4-8d
Doubled studs, face nail	16d at 24″ o.c.
Doubled top plates, face nail	16d at 16″ o.c.
Top plates, laps and intersections, face nail	2-16d
Continuous header, two pieces	16d at 16″ o.c. along each edge
Ceiling joists to plate, toe nail	3-8d
Continuous header to stud, toe nail	4-8d
Ceiling joists, laps over partitions, face nail	3-16d
Ceiling joists to parallel rafters, face nail	3-16d
Rafter to plate, toe nail	3-8d
1″ brace to each stud and plate, face nail	2-8d
1″ × 8″ sheathing or less to each bearing, face nail	2-8d
Wider than 1″ × 8″ sheathing to each bearing, face nail	3-8d

Table 7.6 **(Continued)**

Connection	Nailing[a]
Build-up corner studs	16d at 24″ o.c.
Built-up girder and beams	20d at 32″ o.c. at top and bottom and staggered 2- 20d at ends and at each splice
2″ planks	2-16d at each bearing
Particleboard:[e]	
Wall Sheathing (to framing):	
⅜″-½″	6d[c]
⅝″-¾″	8d[c]
Plywood:[e]	
Subfloor, roof, and wall sheathing (to framing):	
½″ and less	6d[b]
⅝″-¾″	8d[c] or 6d[c]
⅞″-1″	8d[b]
1⅛″-1¼″	10d[c] or 8d[d]
Combination Subfloor-underlayment (to framing):	
¾″ and less	6d[d]
⅞″-1″	8d[d]
1⅛″-1¼″	10d[c] or 8d[d]
Panel Siding (to framing)	
½″ or less	6d[f]
⅝″	8d[f]
Fiberboard Sheathing:[g]	
½″	No. 11 ga.[h]
	6d[c]
	No. 16 ga.[i]
25/32″	No. 11 ga.[h]
	8d[c]
	No. 16 ga.[i]

[a] Common or box nails may be used except where otherwise stated.

[b] Common or deformed shank.

[c] Common.

[d] Deformed shank.

[e] Nails spaced at 6 in. on center at edges, 12 in. at intermediate supports (10 in. at intermediate supports for floors), except 6 in. at all supports where spans are 48 in. or more. For nailing of plywood diaphragms and shear walls refer to Section 2514(c). Nails for wall sheathing may be common, box, or casing.

[f] Corrosion-resistant siding and casing nails.

[g] Fasteners spaced 3 in. on center at exterior edges and 6 in. on center at intermediate supports.

[h] Galvanized roofing nails with 7/16-in. diameter head and 1½-in. length for ½-in. sheathing and 1¾ in. for 25/32-in. sheathing.

[i] Galvanized staple with 7/16-in. crown and 1⅛-in. length for ½-in. sheathing and 1½-in. length for 25/32-in. sheathing.

Reproduced from the 1976 edition of the *Uniform Building Code* copyright 1976, with permission of the publisher, the International Conference of Building Officials.

over a post, the column size should be not less than 4 × 6 in.

Special framing is provided under bearing partitions and heavy concentrated loads. Lateral bracing is provided by solid wall panels with diagonal wood or rigid plywood sheathing or by diagonal corner bracing. Abutting ends of beams should be tied together, preferably with nailed metal straps. The longitudinal joints between the planks of exposed ceilings may be beveled or attractively finished in various other ways.

ORDINARY CONSTRUCTION

Ordinary construction is defined in some model codes. Although other codes may not identify and specify a category as ordinary construction, there are types of construction described that meet many of the criteria of ordinary construction.

As defined in the first chapter, ordinary construction requires noncombustible walls, such as masonry or concrete of equivalent structural stability under fire conditions, and a

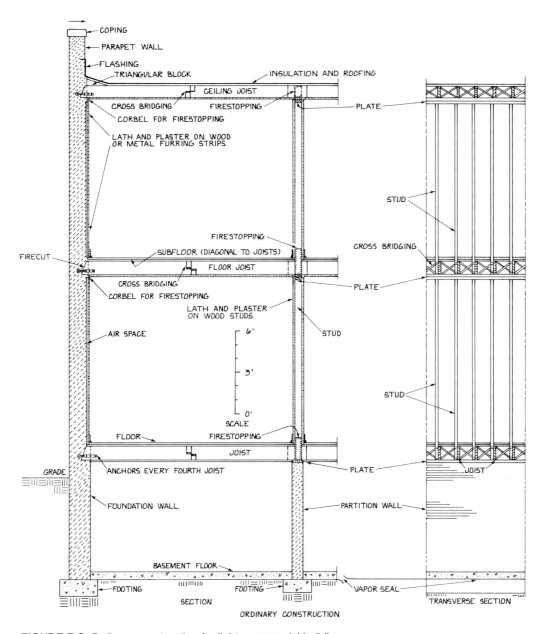

FIGURE 7.9 Ordinary construction for light commercial building.

fire resistance rating of not less than 2 hours. The interior assemblies are entirely or partially of wood with sizes less than those required for heavy timber construction. The interior is wood frame as described above in wood frame construction; however, wood trusses and steel beams, girders, and trusses without fireproofing are often used. This class of construction is used extensively for most occupancies when it is not prohibited by fire district regulations.

A cross section of a typical two-story building of ordinary construction with brick or concrete exterior walls is illustrated in Figure 7.9. Some of the features that identify it as representative of ordinary construction are:

1. The exterior masonry walls conform to the minimum thickness-to-height ratio specified by the codes.

2. The parapet wall satisfies requirements for fire protection where required.

3. The joists bearing on the masonry wall are end cut on an acute angle so that their top edges are free of the masonry, while their bottom edges bear 4 in. into the masonry. This is called a fire cut. In the event of collapse caused by fire, it permits the joists to rotate out of the wall without tending to pull over the wall.

4. Wood joists, beams, and girders supported by exterior masonry walls should have not less than 4 in. of masonry between the ends of the beams and the outside face of the wall.

5. The exterior ends of the ceiling joists rest on 2 in. thick plates anchored to the top of the masonry wall.

6.   The interior framing is wood frame construction corresponding to the balloon frame illustrated in Figure 7.5. This type of construction, preferable to the platform frame construction, minimizes vertical shrinkage.

7.   Interior joists require a minimum of 3 in. bearing.

8.   The wood columns bear directly on the columns below with the loads transferred through suitable connections.

9.   Wood subflooring and finished flooring should not be less than 2 in.

10.   Interior assemblies should be of not less than 1 hour rating.

Not illustrated by the figures is the requirement that the floor and roof joists that run parallel to the exterior wall should be anchored to the exterior wall by metal ties.

HEAVY TIMBER CONSTRUCTION

As previously stated, heavy timber construction requires exterior walls of noncombustible materials, such as masonry or concrete with a fire resistance rating of at least 2 hours. Moreover, the interior structural members including columns, beams, and girders must be solid or laminated timber. Floors and roofs must be heavy plank or laminated wood or a material providing equivalent fire resistance and structural properties. Noncombustible structural members, if used in lieu of heavy timber, must provide a fire resistance rating of not less than ¾ hour. Heavy timber is sometimes called slow-burning construction or mill construction.

Code Requirements

The requirements for heavy timber construction are illus-

HEAVY TIMBER CONSTRUCTION

FIGURE 7.10 Building with heavy timber construction.

trated by the partial vertical cross section and the details of a building with heavy timber shown in Figure 7.10.

The foundation walls are poured concrete walls on spread foundations.

A given building would, of course, make use of only one type of construction. The member sizes are not indicated but would be determined by the building dimensions and the structural requirements. The minimum permissible sizes stated by the code are that timber columns must be at least 8 in. × 8 in. nominal and that beams and girders supporting floors must be at least 6 in. wide and not less than 10 in. deep. The various framings and other details must satisfy the code requirements.

The first floor framing consists of longitudinal girders (Figure 7.10). The exterior ends of the outer girders project into recesses in the walls and are supported by bearing plates with anchor lugs to tie them to the walls (Figure 7.11A), leaving adequate ventilation to prevent dry rot. The end of each girder is fire-cut. If a girder burns through, the embed-

ded end rotates off the anchor lug and the girder falls free, preventing a collapse of the masonry wall.

The interior ends of girders are supported by wood columns with beveled or chamfered corners, which increase their fire resistance. The girder ends are supported on the brackets of steel post caps (Figure 7.11B), thus permitting second-story columns to bear directly on the post caps. The adjacent ends of the two girders which rest on a single post cap are tied together by lateral ties and lag screws through the cap. The bottom of each column bears on a metal base (Figure 7.11C), which is supported by, and anchored to, a concrete footing.

The outer panels of the first floor deck are constructed of splined or tongued-and-grooved planks of a 3 in. minimum thickness between girders. A clearance of ½ in. left between the edge of the deck and the wall surface provides for expansion. This open space is covered by moldings fastened to the wall, or the bottom is covered by a 3 × timber ledger that is bolted to the masonry wall, or the masonry wall

FIGURE 7.11 Details for heavy timber construction.

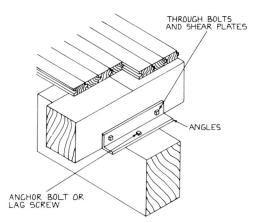

A. Beams supported on top of girder.

B. Metal column cap supporting roof girders.

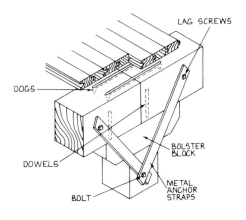

C. Wood bolster block supporting roof girders.

D. Wall beam.

FIGURE 7.12 Details for heavy timber construction.

is corbeled to support the deck. This ledger or corbel also serves to deter deflection of this one unsplined deck member that may deflect and tear away from the base molding (Figure 7.12D).

The second-floor framing of longitudinal girders supported by the wall and the interior columns is similar to the first-floor framing. Transverse beams spanning between girders (Figure 7.10) are supported by metal hangers such as those shown in Figure 7.11D. A tongued-and-grooved or a laminated deck may span between beams. Although beams do frame directly into columns, in the figure, the beams frame into the girders rather than directly into the columns (Figure 7.12A). This results in simpler column connections. Beams that frame into a column from several directions are usually employed in steel and concrete construction, where such connections are less complicated.

The roof framing members must be at least 6 × 8s, and a roof deck must be not less than 2 in. thick, either splined or tongued-and-grooved. Types of post caps to support roof

girders are illustrated in Figure 7.12B and C. The latter includes a wood bolster block. Such blocks are not permitted in floor framing. Waterproof paper or 15 lb felt is placed between the deck and the finished floor.

Where parapet walls are provided (Figure 7.10), scuppers should be placed in the outside walls to discharge rainwater. The invert of the scuppers should not be flush with the deck unless a gravel stop is provided. In no event should the invert of the scuppers be placed more than 1 in. above the low point of the roof deck.

7.3 Structural Plywood

Floor construction for wood frame and ordinary construction buildings consists of a matched-wood finished floor that is supported by wood joists. Preferably a layer of building paper of 15 lb felt is laid between the subfloor and the finished floor as shown in Figure 7.13A. This insulates and helps to alleviate squeaking. Other finished floor materials may be used in place of matched flooring, with appropriate construction made to receive the various finishing materials.

Joists are usually 2 in. wide and from 6 to 14 in. deep. For heavy loads, the joists may be 3 or 4 in. wide. Heavy timber construction, mentioned elsewhere, requires joists not less than 6 in. wide. Usual joist spacings are 12 and 16 in.; 24 in. spacing is too great for lath that is to support plaster. Light metal lath may span up to 12 in., but heavy rib lath permits greater joist spacing. In some cases, 1 × 2 in. furring strips, properly spaced for lath, are nailed at right angles to the underside of the joists. The spacing of joists is therefore independent of the lath. However, the airspace below the joists may enable rapid spread of fire. Another objection to wood furring strips nailed to the underside of wood joists is that the nails loosen their grip as the joists dry out.

A convenient function of the subfloor is to serve as a platform during the early stages of construction. A subfloor makes the floor system more substantial, more fire-resistant, and decreases sound and heat transmission. When a subfloor is used, there is a tendency to nail the finished floor to the subfloor rather than to the joists. This practice is objectionable because the finished floor does not remain in place as well. Another objectionable practice is to lay the finished floor parallel with the joists.

Plywood Subfloor

The thicker ⅝ in. to 1¼ in. *plywood* panels are used for floor sheathing. The sheets are laid with the face grain perpendicular to the supporting joists. They are placed so that the joints formed by the ends that are on supports are staggered. These plywood panels are usually secured with 8d or 10d common nails. The nails at the panel perimeters, which are spaced about 6 in. apart, are called boundary nails. The nails that are in the central portion of the panel are called field nails. These are usually spaced farther apart but nailed to each intermediate support.

The joint (the long side of the abutting plywood panels) that spans between joists should have solid blocking beneath. This will prohibit differential deflection between adjoining plywood panels. This problem is sometimes alleviated by the use of a metal, H-shaped clip placed between adjacent panels.

The sheathing grades are frequently used for this application. They are stamped with a number, in inches, that is the recommended spacing of the supporting members.

Underlayment

Frequently, in order to attain a smooth finished floor surface, a second layer of thinner plywood is placed over the thicker supporting plywood sheathing. This thinner plywood is called an underlayment. This underlayment ply is nailed to the supporting panel. All joints of the underlayment are staggered so as not to align with the joints of the supporting panel. The purpose of this underlayment is to provide a smooth, deflection-free surface that will in turn support some finished floor covering. This type of construction is used for underlaying carpets and various resilient floor tile installations. Subfloors may be of ordinary sheathing, matched boards, shiplap, or plywood sheathing. Sometimes the subfloor is omitted entirely to decrease the cost, and if so, the finished floor would probably have to be laid before plastering, during which operation it must be protected from dirt and water. It will absorb moisture given off by the plaster. This will cause swelling, followed by shrinking and opening of the joints.

Some form of layer between the subfloor and the finished floor should always be used. Asphaltic felt, asbestos paper, or gypsum board increase fire-resistance and sound-deadening and warrant the additional expenditure, although kraft building paper is more economical and is insulating.

The joists are bridged as shown in Figure 7.13A.

If a wood subfloor is laid before the building is enclosed from the elements, provisions should be made for the swelling of the subfloor, or the exterior walls may be cracked and pushed out. To prevent this, spaces ¼ × ½ in. may be left

FIGURE 7.13 Wood floor construction.

between the boards, or every tenth or twelfth board may be omitted at first and placed after the building is under cover.

If a tile floor is supported by wood joist construction, the joists may be designed to carry a reinforced-concrete slab (Figure 7.13B), which is a base for the tile. The construction shown in (C) is also used but is more likely to produce cracks than the construction in (B). A thin-setting bed for ceramic floor tile does not require special construction.

This type of floor construction is used in residences and other buildings of wood frame and ordinary construction and may be used in buildings with steel frames. Inexpensive and light, it is sufficiently strong for heavy loads but very combustible unless protected on the underside by plaster or metal lath.

Heavy Wood Subfloor on Wood or Steel Beams

Wood subfloors vary in thickness from 3 to 10 in., depending upon the loaded span. They are supported directly by girders running between columns, or by beams which are supported by the girders, as shown in Figure 7.11. In the first arrangement, the lateral spacing of columns commonly is not over 10 or 12 ft because of the heavy subfloors required for longer spans. In the second arrangement, the beams are spaced 4 ft or more apart, and the column spacing is not restricted by the length of the subfloor.

Heavy wood subfloors are either matched (Figure 7.13F), loose-tongue (G), or laminated (H). The matched floor is used for thickness of 3 or 4 in. However, greater thicknesses produce excessive waste in matching; therefore, the hardwood loose-tongue may be more economical. This loose-tongue is also called a slip tongue or spline.

Laminated floors 4 in. or more in thickness are constructed by laying 2 in. lumber on edge and nailing the adjacent pieces together with spikes spaced about 18 in., 2×4s are used for a 4 in. floor, 2×6s for a 6 in. floor, and so on. A laminated floor is easier to lay than a heavy loose-tongue floor. The pieces are smaller, more easily handled and drawn together; however, more feet, board measure, are required because 2 in. material is only 1½ in. thick. The cost of the loose-tongue is saved in the laminated floor.

7.4 Prefabricated Structural Wood

COLUMNS AND STUDS

Wood columns, as ordinarily used, are square timbers rarely smaller than 4×4 in., and usually not larger than 12×12 in., although larger timber columns can be obtained. Columns built up of small timbers fastened for unified action of the timbers under load are not as effective as glued or solid columns. One type of built-up compression member is the spaced column (Figure 7.14A), which has a load-carrying capacity much greater than that of the individual vertical members when not connected by a spacer block.

Several planks may be spiked together (B) to form a column, but the arrangement shown in (C) results in a more unified action and is more effective. Columns are glued in several laminations as described in the paragraph on *glued laminated beams,* rather than by spiking (B). Glued laminated columns have the same advantages as beams of this type.

SOLID BEAMS AND GIRDERS

Several specific types of flexural members are included under the general designation of beams and girders. Among these are floor and ceiling joists, rafters of sloping roofs, roof purlins, and beams and girders in various locations.

In wood frame construction, the closely spaced joists and rafters usually have a thickness of 2 in. and a common depth of from 4 to 8 in. for rafters and 6 to 12 or 14 in. for joists, depending upon the span and loading. Consideration must also be given to the rigidity, as determined by the deflection under load. Often rigidity rather than the allowable stress determines the size. Beams may have a solid section of the required size; but in this type of construction, the required size is often achieved by spiking together 2 in. planks set on edge. Such pieces are readily available and easily assembled, or fabricated, on the job.

In heavy timber construction, the minimum thickness permitted for floor joists, beams, girders, and other members of this general type is 6 in., and the minimum depth is 10 in. This size may not be determined by structural criteria, but it is a fire resistive requirement.

GLUED LAMINATED BEAMS AND GIRDERS

If several pieces of laminations of uniform section laid flat on each other form a beam supported at the ends, their load-carrying capacity and vertical rigidity is relatively low. When loaded, they deflect, slide on each other along the surfaces of contact, and act as individual units. If sliding or relative movement can be prevented, the several pieces will act as a composite or solid unit, and the load-carrying capacity and rigidity will be markedly increased. Various devices have been used satisfactorily, but the most effective procedure is gluing and clamping wood laminations together under pressure. These beams are called glued laminated beams and are widely known as *glulams* (Figure 7.15A). The usual thickness of laminations is 1½ in., or nominal 2 in., although ¾ in. laminations are used for attaining small radius curves. The minimum number of laminations is 2, which produces a 3 in. member, whereas the larger members may have as many as 60 laminations. Glued laminated members are produced in several standardized widths. The usual widths expressed in inches are 2¼, 3⅛, 5⅛, 6¾, 8¾, 10¾, 12¼, and 14¼.

Adhesives, which are known as water-resistive glue or dry-use adhesives, are used for interior glued laminated

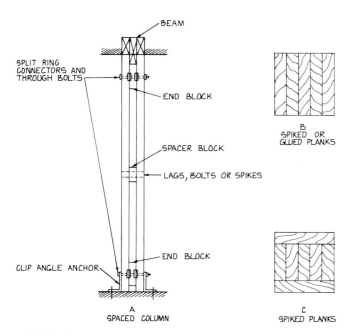

FIGURE 7.14 Built-up wood columns.

members. These glues which are the casein type, are used on laminated members intended for interior applications where the moisture content of the wood is not expected to exceed 16%. Members that are intended for exterior use, or where interior use will be subjected to extreme moisture conditions (showers, commercial laundries) require a waterproof glue known also as wet-use adhesive. The waterproof glues are resorcinol, phenolresorcinol, phenol, and melamine.

Although it is not always practical to apply both types of adhesives on the same member, some structural engineers may require dry-use adhesive and wet-use adhesive on a long beam. Dry-use adhesives are less expensive; hence, the portion of the beam that spans a wide interior is specified with dry-use adhesive, and that portion extending out to the exterior may be specified with a wet-use adhesive.

To obtain the desired lengths, laminations are spliced with inclined scarf joints made by pregluing overlapping ends with opposite bevels with slopes of about 1 in 10. After a lamination is spliced, it is surfaced to uniform thickness and width throughout its length and is then assembled into the glued beam. Each lamination is usually as wide as the beam, although two laminations may be placed side by side to make up the beam width. The longitudinal vertical joints between adjacent laminations in successive layers must be staggered. Full width top and bottom laminations should be used.

Glued laminated beams and girders are factory produced. They may have a constant cross section, a tapered top, the maximum cross sections at the center or elsewhere, chambering or other profiles. Girders with spans exceeding 100 ft have been constructed, and girders with 2 in. laminations have been made as deep as 8½ ft.

Glued laminated construction has advantages compared with solid members because small sizes can be utilized, larger members can be constructed, defects can be eliminated; and because the moisture content may be reduced, there is better opportunity for seasoning. It is sometimes called glulam construction.

GLUED LAMINATED APPEARANCE GRADES

There are three grades that refer to the appearance of the glued laminated members. They are industrial, architectural, and premium. These appearance grades refer to the lumber characteristics and surfacing and to the structural qualities of the members. Industrial appearance grade is surfaced on only two sides and has visible sound knots. This grade is used in applications where appearance is not a prime consideration. Architectural appearance grade is used where appearance of the member is a consideration. These members have only slight imperfections. They are surfaced on the exposed sides. Premium appearance grade, which is used where appearance is paramount, consists of lumber

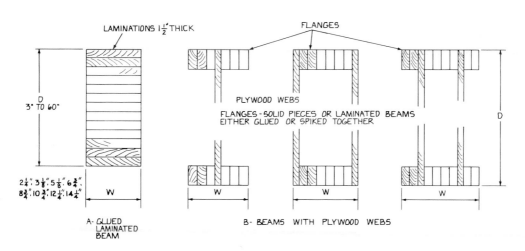

FIGURE 7.15 Glued laminated beams and beams with plywood webs.

that is clear with matching grain characteristics. The finished laminated surface is smoothed on the exposed faces.

Because premium grade is the most expensive, architects most frequently specify that the member will be architectural grade, with the last or bottom exposed member of premium grade.

PLYWOOD BEAMS

Beams and girders are sometimes constructed with plywood webs and with built-up flanges (Figures 7.15*B*). The possible depth is limited by the width of the plywood because horizontal splicing is not feasible. Because the maximum length of plywood is limited, vertical web splices are required for spans exceeding 12 ft. The flanges may be made up of vertical laminations or solid sections. If shop-fabricated, the member may be pressure-glued, but if field fabricated, the members are nailed or bolted with or without glue between them. This type of construction is rarely used but does have advantages.

TRUSSED BEAMS

Beams, trussed (Figure 7.16) to increase their load-carrying capacity, are used occasionally.

WOOD TRUSSES
Types of Trusses

The various types of trusses are considered earlier and illustrated in Figures 1.16 and 1.17. The most common types of wood trusses for symmetrical roofs are the Howe (Figure 1.16*I*), the Pratt *(J),* the Fink *(M),* and the Belgian.

Flat or gently sloping roofs may be supported by the Howe truss, the Pratt truss, or the Warren truss *(P)* to *(S).* These types frequently support column-free floor areas.

Timber Connectors

Timber connectors have made it possible to use wood members with small cross-sectional areas. These connectors are readily available, require little labor to assemble, and result in only small reductions in the effective cross-sectional area of the timber. One of the most efficient connectors for wood to wood connections in trusses for buildings is the split ring connector (Figure 7.29 and Figure 7.30). With this type of connector, the only function of the bolts is to hold the adjacent wood surfaces in contact with one bolt passing through several connectors.

The stress that a single connector will resist depends upon the size of the connector and the properties of the wood in which it is embedded. The number and size of the connectors required is determined by the total tendency to slide along the contact surfaces.

Another connector is the shear plate (Figure 7.30*D*). It also makes field connections between two wood members

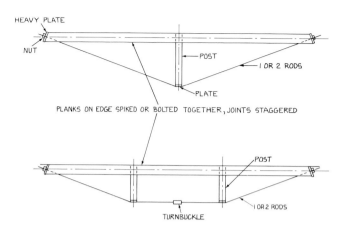

FIGURE 7.16 Elevation of trussed beams.

FIGURE 7.17 Joint details of wood Pratt truss using connectors.

with plates embedded in each member as shown in Figure 7.31A. In such arrangements, the bolts are subjected to the entire shearing stress between the two pieces connected.

If the lumber in a truss is not seasoned to its ultimate expected moisture content, the bolts should be tightened at intervals. However, lock washers should be used on all bolts to alleviate this problem, as the spring action of the lock washers will allow expansion and contraction.

General Requirements

All members, joints, and trusses should be symmetrical to avoid twisting due to asymmetry. The connectors which transmit the stresses should be centered at middepth of the pieces; or if there is more than one row of connectors, they should be symmetrically arranged about the center line. These requirements are illustrated in the examples referred to below. In addition, the trusses must be suitably anchored to their supports and properly braced to hold them in position to resist the subjected loads. The roof deck usually provides adequate lateral support for the top chord, but other bracing is usually required.

A Pratt roof truss and a Fink roof truss with sloping top chords and split ring connector are illustrated in Figure 7.17 and 7.18, respectively. Note that the ends of the Fink truss are attached to wood columns and that knee braces are provided by continuing certain truss chords until they con-

nect to the columns. The truss and columns form a transverse bent capable of resisting lateral or transverse loads on the roofs and sidewalls. A Fink truss supported by walls is similar to the one illustrated; but the knee braces are omitted, and the stresses in the truss members are changed.

A bowstring roof truss with a two-piece glued laminated top chord and split ring connectors at all joints except the heel joints is shown in Figure 7.19. An enlarged cross section of the top chord and an enlarged detail of the heel joint are shown. The web members fit in between the divided chords and are fastened with split ring connectors. Six pairs of shear plates, illustrated in Figure 7.30D, and 7.31A, are required at each joint.

A typical bowstring roof truss with single-piece glued laminated chords is illustrated in Figure 7.20. Both chords and all web members have the same width so that the web members can be joined to chords by bolted steel-strap end connections. Shear plates are used with the bolts when the stresses require them. Each chord is spliced at midspan by steel splice plates attached with bolts and passing through shear plates embedded in the members. A detail of the end connection is shown in the figure. This connection is assembled by welding a heavy inclined thrust plate between two side plates at the required angle to receive the end of the top chord, which is cut normal to the axis of the member. A steel bearing plate is welded to the side plates and projects beyond them far enough on each side to provide

FIGURE 7.18 Wood transverse bent with Fink truss using connectors.

FIGURE 7.19 Bowstring truss with two-piece glued laminated top chord. Adapted from Timber Engineering Co. design.

for the anchor bolt holes. Trusses of this type are factory-produced with spans up to 150 ft, and trusses with longer spans can be obtained. Trusses with spans of 250 ft have been constructed. Because each chord consists of one unit rather than two units, this type of truss is sometimes called a monochord bowstring truss.

As explained previously, there is no clear distinction between rigid frames and arches. The evaluation made in that Section 1.4 will be followed in this discussion, although many authorities would not make such a distinction. The classification based on the number of hinges, as has been explained, is always followed.

Glued laminated construction is used extensively in con-

structing wood rigid frames and arches. The frames are factory-produced and transported to the site. Because it is not feasible to transport completed frames of the usual sizes, they are assembled and connected by field joints or splices.

For rigid frames, which include portions with relatively small radii of curvature, it is necessary to use laminations which are thinner than the 1½ in. thickness ordinarily used for beams. For example, the minimum permissible radius for 1½ in. laminations varies from 30 to 40 ft; and for ¾ in. laminations, from 7 to 12 ft, depending upon the species of wood.

Rigid Frames

Typical forms of glued three-hinged laminated rigid frames are illustrated in Figure 7.21A, for which the slopes of the top members are relatively small, in (B), where the slopes are steep, and in (C), in which the top member is curved. A more detailed illustration of the frame in (A) is shown in (D). In all of these, outer surfaces of the legs are vertical, but the inner surfaces may be vertical instead. Frames may be curved at the eaves, as shown by the dashed line on the left side of (D), rather than angular. Various types of connections are made at the bottom of each leg and at the crown, some of which are shown in Figure 7.21E to H. Even though the joints at the footings and the crown are considered to be hinged, the usual types of connection develop some resistance to rotation.

The two units of the frame are usually raised to position separately, and the leg and crown joints are then secured.

In the crown connections shown in Figure 7.21F and G, a steel dowel passing through shear plates embedded in adjacent ends of the two pieces are provided to resist the shear caused by unbalanced loading. To hold the ends together horizontally, splice plates are bolted to the sides of the member and across the joint in (F) and on the top and bottom surfaces in (G). These plates are not provided to develop resistance to rotation. Shear plates are not required around these bolts. In the crown connection shown in (H), a bolt with countersunk ends may be used instead of a dowel because of the acuteness of the angle. Therefore, splice plates are not required to hold the ends together horizontally.

A simple connection of a leg to a footing is illustrated in Figure 7.21E. If the soil has inadequate resistance to carry the horizontal components of the end thrust of the frames, a steel rod may be provided to tie appropriately designed bases of the two legs together and thus to resist the equal and opposite horizontal components. This tie is placed below the floor level and is embedded in concrete to protect the rod from corrosion. This member is called a tie beam.

A two-hinged glued laminated rigid frame is illustrated in Figure 7.22. It is similar in construction to the three-hinged frame in Figure 7.21A and D, but it is constructed in three

FIGURE 7.20 Glued laminated monochord bowstring truss.

FIGURE 7.21 Three-hinged glued laminated rigid frames. Partially from Unit Structures, Inc.

sections, as shown in the figure. These are spliced together on the job. The splices are located at points where bending moments have minimum values. However, since various combinations of dead load, unbalanced snow load, and wind loads from any direction must be provided for, a splice in any location must always be designed to resist bending moments of considerable magnitude.

One effective form of splice is shown in Figure 7.22. The bent plate is nailed to the leg at the factory. Top and bottom splice plates receive the lag screws which attach these plates. Shear plates are embedded in the members, and holes are bored to receive the screws. These operations are accomplished at the factory. The shearing resistance of the

splice may be increased by means of dowels and shear plates (Figure 7.21G). The three sections may be assembled flat on the floor, or they may be placed in position separately. If the latter procedure is used, the legs are erected first. After they are in position, the center beam is hoisted and lowered into place on the projecting legs of the bent plates. It is called a drop-in beam. It is supported while the lag screws in the splice plates are driven and the splice is secured.

The roof decks are usually constructed of heavy matched planks spanning the distance between frames or between purlins supported by the frames. The underside of the deck is usually exposed and is appropriately finished.

FIGURE 7.22 Detail of splice. Unit Structures, Inc.

Glued laminated rigid frames are attractive in appearance. They are used for many kinds of buildings such as gymnasiums, churches, and auditoriums where unobstructed floor areas are required and the clearances provided at the sides by the vertical legs are desired. They are used for spans as short as 30 ft or less and have been constructed with spans approaching 150 ft. The type shown in Figure 7.21B is often used for churches.

Arches

In contrast to rigid frames, arches are so proportioned that the stresses produced by the loads are primarily compressive and the shears and flexural stresses are relatively small. Flexural stresses must be considered, however, in the design of the arch section, splices, and supports. The arch ring commonly has a constant radius and constant cross section, although rings with parabolic profiles and variable cross sections are sometimes used. Glued laminations are usually ¾ or 1½ in., the actual thickness depending upon the species of lumber used and the curvature. The arches may be fixed, two-hinged, or occasionally three-hinged for the longer spans.

A glued laminated arch supported on piers is diagrammed in Figure 7.23A. Vertical sidewalls may be provided as shown by the inner dashed lines. If such sidewalls are constructed, the projecting ends of the arches may be

exposed and treated to resist the weather, or they may be incorporated in building space. An arch may be elevated (B) and supported on rigid reinforced-concrete buttresses or on walls or columns with the horizontal thrusts at the ends carried by steel tie rods (C). Sagging of the rods is prevented by vertical sag rods, or straps. The arches shown in (A) and (B) may have fixed or hinged ends, but the ends of the tied arch in (C) are always considered to be hinged.

An enlarged drawing of half the arch shown in Figure 7.23A or B, with fixed end supports, is illustrated in (D), and a detail of the support is shown in (E). A hinged end support for these arches is illustrated in the half-arch in (F) and the detail in (G). They are usually built up of steel plates welded together. If these arches are three-hinged, there is a hinge at the crown as shown in (F) and the detail in (H). An end support for the tied arch in (C) is illustrated in (I). This would be attached to a column or bearing wall with appropriate provision made for stability. The horizontal components of the end thrusts are carried by the tie rods. To prevent them from sagging under their own weight, sag rods may be used as shown in (C). Tied arches may also be used if the end supports are very near the ground level. Such an arrangement would only be used if the foundation soil were incapable of carrying the horizontal components of the end thrusts.

It may be necessary to fabricate an arch in two or more sections to facilitate transportation or for other reasons.

FIGURE 7.23 Glued laminated timber arches.

Joints are made normal to the arch axis, and provisions are made at the factory for splicing the adjacent sections together in the field. A type of splice suitable for a heavy long-span arch is illustrated in *(J)*. The shear plates are embedded in the timbers at the factory, and the necessary holes for bolts or lag screws are bored. For light arches, only the top and bottom plates, or only the side plates, held in position by bolts or lag screws, may be adequate. The designer, of course, determines the make-up of the splice appropriate for a given situation.

The types of decks used are those described for rigid frames.

Glued laminated arches are used to support the roofs over unobstructed floor areas for many buildings such as auditoriums, churches, recreation buildings, gymnasiums, garages, and warehouses. Spans exceeding 240 ft have been constructed. They are fabricated at factories.

Light glued laminated arched rafters, spaced as close as 2 ft, are sometimes used for small buildings such as barns. They are covered with 1 in. sheathing.

Lamella Arches

A special form of arched roof known as the *lamella roof* is constructed of short pieces of wood varying in size from 2 × 8 in. to 3 × 16 in., in lengths from 8 to 14 ft, as illustrated in Figure 7.24. The short pieces, called lamellas, are bolted together in diamond-shaped patterns *(A)* to form a complete roof structure, as shown by the roof plan and longitudinal sections of a simple form in *(B)* and *(C)*. The diamond-shaped panels are all the same size and shape. The apparent curvature and distortion of the panels in *(C)* is caused by the changing slope of the arched roof. The thrust of lamella roofs may be taken by tie rods or by buttressed walls (Figures 7.23*B,* and C). Roofs of this type have been used for spans from 25 ft to 150 ft on many gymnasiums, dance pavilions, exhibition halls, auditoriums, churches, garages, warehouses, and sheds.

Domes

Glued laminated construction is used for the frames of domes covering circular floor areas. For the building illustrated in Figure 7.25, the structural supports for the walls and roof consist of 16 half three-hinged, glued laminated timber rigid frames with their legs supported on footings equally spaced around a complete circle, their crowns meeting on a thrust block at the center of the roof. The wedge-shaped roof areas between frames are spanned by equally spaced timber purlins of varying lengths with their ends supported on the frame by steep strap hangers. These purlins support a timber roof deck.

An outstanding example of another type of heavy timber circular domed roof has arched radial ribs (Figure 7.26). The

A- DETAILS AND ARRANGEMENT OF LAMELLA

TO FIT CURVE OF ROOF

LAMELLA
SPECIAL NAIL
MACHINE BOLT
LAMELLA WASHER
CARRIAGE BOLT

B - LONGITUDINAL SECTION

TIE RODS   SHEATHING

C- ROOF PLAN

FIGURE 7.24 Wood lamella arch roof.

dome has a span of 300 ft and a rise of 51 ft above the springing line. There are 36 glued laminated ribs with the same radius and cross section. Each rib was factory-fabricated in three equal sections to facilitate transportation and erection and field-spliced with top and bottom steel plates, shear plates, bolts, and dowels. The outward rib thrusts at the springing line are carried by steel base shoes anchored to the top surfaces of reinforced concrete wall columns, to which the adjacent ends of the 36 straight segments of a built-up steel tension ring are welded. The inward rib thrusts at the crown are carried by a built-up steel compression ring supported radially by 18 steel struts framed together at the center in such a manner that the unit resembles a wheel 18 ft in diameter. Equally spaced glued laminated straight purlins frame into the sides of the ribs. Light, closely spaced, solid wood subpurlins are attached to the tops of the purlins and are normal to them. These support 3 in. wood-fiber concrete roof deck panels. Each of the 36 sectors between ribs has sets of diagonal steel-strap cross bracing, with one system located immediately above and one immediately below the subpurlins. The ends of the sets of cross bracing in adjacent segments and in each layer are welded together to form

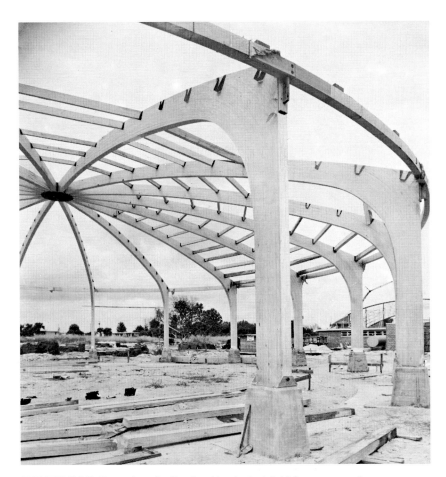

FIGURE 7.25 Domed roof with glued laminated rigid frame supports.

FIGURE 7.26 A 300-ft diameter dome with 36 glued laminated wood
(7 × 16 ¼ in.) ribs.

FIGURE 7.27 A 140-ft diameter wood lamella dome roof.

steel nets enveloping the entire dome. The 36 columns are connected by horizontal reinforced concrete girts, and brick panel walls are constructed between columns to provide lateral support to the columns and the structure as a whole.

A dome with wood lamella construction is illustrated in Figure 7.27. The outside diameter is 142 ft, and the rise is 18½ ft. A reinforced concrete tension ring is located around the perimeter of the dome and on top of reinforced columns spaced about 12 ft apart. Alternate panels between columns are filled with masonry walls. A crown block is located at the center of the dome to carry the thrusts of the lamellas that frame into it. The lamellas vary in cross section from 4 by 16 in. for those framing into the tension ring to 2 by 12 in. at the crown. The lamellas are connected in the same manner shown for the arch roof in Figure 7.28. The roof deck is matched sheathing varying in thickness from 2 in. for the lower portion of the dome to 1 in. for the portion surrounding the crown.

The pattern of the lamellas in Figure 7.27 is shown in Figure 7.28B. In this pattern, the number of lamellas for each concentric passing through the lamella intersections remains constant. The lamellas terminate into collective radial ribs at the crown.

Another pattern is shown in (A). For this pattern, the 360° angle at the crown is divided into from 4 to 12 units, permitting all the lamellas and ring purlins to have the same radius and cross section.

7.5 Wood Treatment

Proper seasoning of timber is the simplest way to prevent decay but, when timber is used where moisture is present, seasoning naturally loses its effectiveness. Under these conditions, the best method for checking decay is to introduce substances into the timber that will poison the fungi. The substances commonly used for this purpose are called wood preservatives.

Wood preservatives are chemicals that are impregnated or applied to wood for the purpose of thwarting the activity of various decay-producing fungi and destructive insects. The preservatives, applied by the methods mentioned below, are usually induced by some vehicle that leaves the preservative impregnated in the wood. These wood preservatives are creosote and creosote solutions, oil-borne solutions, water-borne solutions, and gas-borne solutions.

Creosote is applied directly and is also applied as a creosote-coal tar solution and a creosote-petroleum solution. Creosote is widely used as a preservative for timber piles, railroad ties, and other rough wood construction intended for direct contact with the soil.

Creosote may be brushed or sprayed, but these methods are ineffective because the coating is thin and does not penetrate or fill all the cracks. The advantage of this method

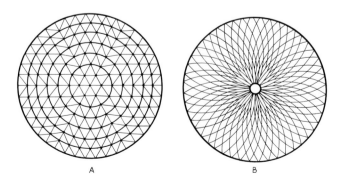

FIGURE 7.28 Lamella dome patterns. Lamella Roof Associates.

is the low cost. Another method, dipping the timber in a tank of hot creosote, is more effective than brushing or spraying, but only a slight penetration into the wood is realized.

In the open-tank process, the timber is first placed into a tank of hot creosote and then into a tank of cooler creosote. In the first tank, the air contained in the timber expands, and some air is forced out. When the timber is placed in the second tank, the entrapped air contracts, drawing the creosote into the wood; thus, a deeper penetration is obtained than by dipping into hot creosote only.

Various processes secure a deeper penetration of the preservative into the timber by pressure. These processes require extensive equipment and are expensive, but their use is justified where the most effective treatment is required, as in piling. These processes use cylinders as large as 8 ft in diameter and 150 ft long. The material is loaded on cars and run into a cylinder; the ends are then sealed.

In the full cell process, the first step is to pump air from the cylinder, thus drawing the air and moisture from the timber. Creosote, introduced into the tank, is forced into the wood cells by pressure. The treatment is completed by drawing off the creosote and removing the timber after the excess creosote drips off. This process leaves the cells, to the depth of penetration, full of creosote.

In the empty cell process, the creosote is first forced into the timber by pressure and then the creosote, which is in the cells, is removed by creating a vacuum. Only the creosote in the cell walls remains. The empty cell process is therefore less expensive than the full cell process.

When zinc chloride is used as a preservative, the full cell process is adopted.

Pentachlorophenol may be either gas-borne or oil-borne. By using a gas-borne solution, the wood is left in a condition which permits finish application or a surface that may be glued. Pentachlorophenol impregnated with an oil-borne solution leaves an oil film on the wood. This may restrict the usage of the wood.

Water-borne salt preservatives, which are frequently identified in specifications by their initials, are Acid Copper Chromate (ACC), Ammoniacal Copper Arsenite (ACA), Chromated Copper Arsenate (CCA), Chromated Zinc Chloride (CZC), and Fluor Chrome Arsenate Phenol (FCAP). These preservatives are generally used on wood that is intended for protected areas. The preservative is likely to leach out of the wood if used in locations exposed to moisture. Some water-borne solutions will result in discolorations to the wood, which may limit their use to wood that is covered or unsuitable for finished appearance.

7.6 Connectors

This section considers various materials that fasten the wood parts of a building together. All the devices considered are not only used in framing a structure; many are used on such parts as interior finish. For instance, large nails and spikes are used in framing, whereas finish nails are not. However, it is convenient to consider finish nails in this article.

Connectors are of the utmost importance in building construction. Many failures in building construction can be traced to poor connector use.

NAILS

Steel-wire nails are ordinarily used in building construction. They are formed from steel wire of the same diameter as the nails. Nails are also made of copper, stainless steel, and aluminum. The usual forms of nails are shown in Figure 7.29.

A nail has a shank, tip, and head. Nail lengths are usually denoted by the shank length. Shank designs may be plain or deformed. Deformed shanks have barbs or annularly threaded, or helically threaded spirals. The threaded shank nails are usually called drive screws. Nails that have a grooved shank are called fluted nails or rolled grooved nails. The nails that have deformed shanks with ridges are called

FIGURE 7.29 Nails, screws, bolts, washers, and dowels.

barbed nails. These nails have greater resistance to withdrawal than plain shank nails.

Tips are diamond shaped, chiseled, or flat tipped. The process of bending over the tips of the nails that have been fully driven is called clinching. Some nails have tips specially designed to facilitate clinching. These nails are referred to as clinched nails.

Heads of nails are usually flat, although cylindrically shaped heads are used for finish work. (See Figure 7.29.) Double headed nails have two heads that are separated about ⅜ in. to facilitate removal. These nails are also known as duplex head or dual head nails. They are used for securing temporary work such as formwork, batterboards, and the necessary temporary construction incidental to the project.

Nails that have a natural finish or a polished surface are referred to as bright finished nails. If the nail is heated, the surface attains a deep prussian blue cast, and the nails are called blued nails. Nails that are called cement coated nails have a resinous coating that is applied by a dipped or tumbled process. This resinous coating, intended to improve bond between the nail and the surrounding wood, provides only a temporarily improved bond when driven into less dense woods. Cement coated nails driven into dense or hardwoods do not realize lasting or appreciably improved withdrawal resistance. Nails that have a roughened surface, such as sand blasted or chemically etched shank, have increased withdrawal resistance. Zinc coated nails have increased resistance to nail corrosion and stain of the wood; the zinc coating does not contribute to increased withdrawal resistance.

Several factors determine the ability of nails to support their implied loads. The loads may be of short duration, extended, repetitive, or vibratory. Other factors that affect nail holding ability are the physical properties of the wood, the nail, and the manner of driving. The physical properties that affect withdrawal resistance are the configuration of the shank, length, diameter, point design, and surface coating. Wood characteristics that influence withdrawal are the moisture content, density, and the grain configuration. Another factor affecting withdrawal is the grain pattern with respect to the orientation of the nail. Nails driven perpendicular to grain have greater holding ability than nails driven parallel to grain or into the end grain. Generally, nails that have sharp points have greater resistance to withdrawal than those with blunt points. The sharper point does not destroy the fibers of the wood immediately adjacent to the nail. Likewise, nails driven into predrilled holes, called pilot holes, have greater holding ability.

Deterioration of nails and the staining of wood is inhibited by the use of nails made of corrosion resistant materials, such as aluminum alloys, copper alloys, and stainless steel. These materials will inhibit the "bleeding" or staining that may disfigure a finished wall surface. Steel nails that are to be used for exterior applications should be galvanized or zinc coated.

Nail size is designated by penny and is symbolized by the lowercase d; thus, 2d is called 2-penny, a nail that is 1 in. long. Historically, the penny designation originated with the cost for 100 nails. Nails are sold in smaller quantities by the pound, but in construction they are sold by the keg, which contains 100 lb of nails.

Probably the most frequently used nail in general wood construction is the common nail. Common nails are used in wood construction framing when there is no objection to the exposed head and where the wide head is desirable. They are used in sheathing, subflooring, and for securing joists, studs, and other wood rough framing members. Common nails may be bright or cement coated. They vary in size from 2d to 60d, the latter being 6 in. long.

Similar to the common nail is the box nail, which has a more slender shank for a given length or size. They are available in sizes up to 16d. They are sometimes called slim nails. These nails cause less splitting than common nails when driven near the end of a board; however, they have less holding ability. To avoid splitting by nails, predrilled holes somewhat smaller than the nail diameter may be drilled.

Casing nails are used principally with matched flooring, ceiling, and drop siding. Finish nails are used with interior and exterior finish applications. Finish nails sizes range from 2d to 20d, which have a length of 4 in. The nail heads, countersunk below the surface with a nail set, form a hole that is filled with putty or plastic wood filler. A barbed flooring nail is illustrated in Figure 7.29D. Shingle and lath nails are small nails of the same general shape as common nails. Wire spikes are also of the same general shape, but they may have diamond or chisel points and flat or convex heads. Their size is designated by the length in inches and varies from 6 to 12 in. Wire nails, plain or galvanized, with large heads, are used with prepared roofing; galvanized and zinc-coated nails are used where resistance to corrosion is required. Various other types of wire nails are on the market, and galvanized common nails are available in various sizes.

Cut nails and spikes (Figure 7.29E) are stamped from steel plates of the same thickness as the nail. Various sizes and shapes are manufactured to correspond with wire nails and spikes.

The initial holding power of cut nails is greater than that of wire nails, but due to their pyramidal shape, the holding power when they are partly withdrawn is less. Wire nails are more easily driven than cut nails. Cut nails have a longer life when exposed than the more widely used wire nails.

Boat spikes, which are used in heavy timber framing, are made of square bars of steel or wrought iron. They have a wedge-shaped point and a head (F). The size of boat spikes varies from ½ in. square by 3 in. long to ⅝ in. square by 12 in. long.

The various types of nailed joints used in light wood framing and the number and sizes of nails are shown in Figure 7.8 and Table 7.6.

SCREWS

Screws are divided into two general classes, finish wood screws and lag or coach screws.

Wood screws are made of steel, brass, or bronze. Steel wood screws may have the natural steel finish called bright, or they may be blued, chromium- or nickel-plated, bronzed, lacquered, galvanized, or anodized. Various forms of wood screws are shown in Figure 7.29G to K. Slotted-head screws can be driven with a common screwdriver. The Phillips-head recess screw has a cross-shaped depression that requires a screwdriver with this shape.

With the exception of the drivescrew, screws have gimlet points. Drivescrews have diamond-shaped points and steep-pitched threads so that they may be driven with a hammer. Wood screws are identified by their head shape. Only a few of the head shapes are used in wood construction.

Flathead screws (G) are the most common. Oval-head screws are used for a better class of finish woodwork. They, like the flathead, are countersunk into the wood surface. Roundhead wood screws are most suitable for connecting light-gage metals to wood members. They are not countersunk.

The size of wood screws is designated by the gage, length in inches, and head shape, for example: #10 × 1″ O.H.W.S. (oval-head wood screw). Several gages are available in each length. These lengths vary from ¼ in. to 6 in. Their length is determined by that portion which is embedded in the wood.

Lag screws have a conical point and a square head. Coach screws have a gimlet point and a square or hexagonal head, as shown in (L), but both forms are usually called lag screws. The size of lag and coach screws is designated by the diameter and length of the shank in inches. The lengths, measuring from the bottom of the head to the tip, vary from 1 in. to 12 in. and the diameters from ¼ in. to 1¼ in. They are used for heavy timber framing.

Screw holes should be prebored to prevent wood from splitting, to make driving easier, and to improve withdrawal resistance. This pilot hole, smaller than the root diameter, is approximately ¾ the root diameter of the thread. However, this hole diameter depends upon the species of wood penetrated.

BOLTS

Bolts used in wood construction may be divided into carriage bolts, machine bolts, and drift bolts.

Carriage bolts have a round head shaped as shown in (M) and a square nut. To prevent the bolt from rotating while the nut is turned, the portion of the shank immediately under the head is square, and the remainder of the shank is round. Bolt size is designated by the length of shank and the diameter in inches. Carriage bolts may be obtained in sizes from ¼ in. to 1 in. They are used in bolting steel, cast-iron members, and timber connectors.

A drift bolt is a piece of round or square steel rod, with or without head or point, driven as a spike. Drift bolts are used in heavy framing. Before driving, a pilot hole must be bored.

Expansion bolts have many different forms, but in all forms, a special nut or shield is used which is so designed that, after insertion in a hole, the process of turning the bolt will so enlarge or expand the shield that it cannot be withdrawn. One form is illustrated in (O). Expansion shields shown in (P) are often used with lag screws. Lead expansion shields are available for use with ordinary screws. Expansion bolts are used to fasten wood to masonry or concrete which is already in place.

A toggle bolt is so arranged that, after the bolt has been inserted head first into a hole on the other side of the piece, it will rotate or open up in such a manner that it cannot be pulled back through the hole. Two forms of toggle bolt are illustrated in (Q). Toggle bolts are used where bolts cannot be inserted in the usual way because one face is inaccessible.

WASHERS

Washers used under the head and below the nut of a bolt provide a larger bearing area and prevent crushing of the wood fibers. Washers are of five types and various sizes to suit the various sizes of bolts. These types are circular cut washers (R), cast-iron O.G. washers (S), whose name is derived from the Ogee curve; cast-iron ribbed washers (T), malleable-iron washers (U), and steel-plate washers (V), which are specially made.

DOWELS

Dowels are steel drift bolts or wooden pins extending into and connecting, but usually not through, two members of a structure. A tree-nail, similar to a wood dowel, has one or both ends exposed. Wood dowels are usually glued.

TIMBER CONNECTORS

Various types of metal connectors designed to connect individual pieces of wood are called *timber connectors* and consist of metal rings, plates, and disks embedded in the surfaces of two members (Figure 7.30A to E). The embedding prevents sliding; thereby stress is transmitting stress from member to member. Joints with these connectors are much more effective than simple bolted joints. Metal connectors have greatly extended the possibilities of timber construction for trusses and arches.

Many kinds of connectors have been devised, but only a few are used to any extent. The more common types are illustrated in Figure 7.30. Many require bolts passing through the centers of the connectors to hold the timbers in contact; with some connectors, the bolts force the connectors into the timbers. Special tools groove the timbers to receive the connectors when connectors require such preparation.

WOOD IS GROOVED TO RECEIVE CONNECTOR

SHOWING POSITION OF RINGS AND BOLTS

A-SPLIT RING JOINT

$2\frac{1}{2}''$
$4''$

B-SPLIT RING

WITH HUB

WITHOUT HUB

C-TOOTHED RING   D-SHEAR PLATES   E-CLAW PLATES

FIGURE 7.30 Modern timber connectors.

The split ring in *(A)* and *(B)* fits into precut grooves in the timber faces and is used in heavy construction. The toothed ring in *(C)* is placed between the surfaces of two timbers without previous preparation and is forced into the timbers by pressure to produce joints in light construction. The shear plates in *(D)* are used in pairs, with each unit let into a prepared depression or dap in the timber face until its back is flush with the surface of the timber; or else one unit is inserted into a timber member so that a metal member can be bolted to it (Figure 7.31). In either case, the stress is transmitted between members by shear in the bolt. The claw plates shown in Figure 7.30*E* are used in the same manner as shear plates, but the dap is not made deep enough to receive the teeth, which are forced into wood below the depth of the dap. These units are used singly or in pairs. One has a flush back, whereas the other has a projection that fits into the hole of the other so that stress can be transferred across the joint by the units themselves without producing shear in the bolt. Either unit can be used to connect a metal member to a timber member. It is desirable to relieve the bolt from the shearing stress; the hole in the metal member is made large enough to receive the projection on the back of the claw.

Each type of connector is available in several sizes and capacities. The number of connectors required in any joint is determined by the stresses in the members and the properties of the wood. When they first came into use many years ago, timber connectors were called modern connectors, a designation now rarely used.

SHEET METAL CONNECTORS

Zinc-coated and galvanized sheet steel connectors of various types are manufactured to replace the usual nailed joint in light wood framing (Figure 7.32). They are attached to the members with special half-length nails designed for driving into prepunched holes provided in the connectors.

Some connectors have several "toothed nails," which are formed when they are stamped out and bent at right angles from the rectangular piece of sheet metal. The connectors are pressed into an assembled wood truss. These lightweight trusses, usually 2 by 4s or 2 by 6s, are used for framing roofs of relatively short span. The connectors usually receive several common nails that are installed for erection and handling stresses.

STEEL PLATE

BOLT

CONNECTION WITH BOLT

PLATE

LAG SCREW

CONNECTION WITH LAG SCREW

FIGURE 7.31 Use of shear plate connectors.

One of the most widely used sheet metal connectors is the sheet metal *joist hanger* or beam connector. These connectors, made of various gages and sizes, accommodate all sizes of wood members and facilitate wood framing. They are usually held in place by half-length nails. There are several designs. Some are simply nailed into the side of the supporting wood members; others hang from the supporting beam. Most have a pocket that receives the member that it is supporting.

Small wood posts may be anchored at top or bottom with galvanized metal framing bases. The bases are anchored into supporting concrete by anchor bolts.

Lightweight gage metal tie-down anchors are used to stabilize a structure against lateral and uplift forces. These tie-downs may consist of an assembly of an embedded anchor bolt that is threaded through a steel angle that is nailed to a post or stud. Specially fabricated sheet-metal tie-downs are embedded into concrete. They are nailed through prepunched holes to a wood post, column, or stud. These connectors are used at each end of wood stud shear walls that resist seismic and wind loads.

FIGURE 7.32 Sheet metal connectors. Timber Engineering Company.

POWDER DRIVEN STUDS

Metal studs that are driven through wood, metal, or concrete by controlled explosive shot are called powder driven studs. These devices are designed to anchor wood and metals to metals or concrete. For wood construction, powder driven studs are frequently used to anchor wood sill plates to concrete slabs or to a steel anchorage. These studs, which are made of heat treated steel, are from ¼ in. to ½ in. in diameter and from ¾ in. to 6 in. in length.

The drive studs are loaded into a "gunlike" device that is actuated by a powder charge. The size of the powder charge (or "shell") is determined by the material that is to be penetrated as well as by the material into which the drive stud will be embedded. Excessive loads will tend to split wood plates or penetrate entirely through the member. Charges that are too light will not embed the stud properly into the anchorage material. Heavy charges are capable of penetrating up to ½ in. of steel.

These studs have an assortment of head designs that permit a choice of anchorages. Drive pins have a flat or button head; others that have an "eye" or hole through the head permit metal hangers or wire to be threaded through them. Threaded studs permit nut fasteners on the stud.

These types of fastening devices have the distinct advantage of providing economical and quickly assembled anchorages requiring field assembly. This is especially true where intended embedded concrete anchorages have been omitted, where engineered revisions require field changes, or where embedded anchorages may be awkward or time consuming if set at the time of the concrete placement.

7.7 Plastics

Many materials used in building construction are plastic, that is, they will continue to deform under a constant load, for varying conditions of temperature and stress intensity, and with duration of stress. The large and ever-increasing group of materials known as plastics, however, includes certain common characteristics. A plastic may be defined as follows.

A *plastic* is a material that contains as an essential ingredient an organic substance of high molecular weight which, although solid in the finished state, is soft enough at some stage of its manufacture to be formed into various shapes, usually through the application, either singly or together, of heat and pressure.

ESSENTIAL INGREDIENTS

All organic substances contain carbon. The ones that are involved in the manufacture of plastics are complex substances called resins. These may be natural resins, but they are usually synthetic resins built up by chemical processes from such materials as coal, petroleum, natural gas, water, salt, and air. The chemical elements whose atoms form the molecules of plastic resins are principally carbon, hydrogen, oxygen, and nitrogen.

Many kinds of resins are used, with other materials, in the manufacture of plastics to form products with a great variety of physical and chemical properties. The other materials included in plastics are called plasticizers, fillers, and colorants. These are considered in a subsequent paragraph.

FORMATION OF LARGE MOLECULES

The large size of the molecules in a plastic resin is an important factor in determining its properties and those of the plastic of which it is the essential ingredient. In forming synthetic resins, long chainlike molecules are built up by linking small molecules together by processes involving various combinations of heat, pressure, or chemical action. In some plastics, the long molecular chains become attached to each other by cross links, when heated, forming netlike structures.

BROAD CLASSIFICATION OF PLASTICS

All plastics include tangled masses of long resin molecules. They are divided into two classes according to their behavior when heated and cooled during manufacture.

Thermoplastics are softened by heat during the manufacturing process and regain their original properties as they solidify during cooling to form the finished products. No chemical changes occur, and the process can be repeated.

The resin molecules of thermoplastics are chainlike with few if any cross links between molecules. They form a tangled mass, but they can slide over each other when the plastic is stressed. If the stress is not too large, they will slowly recover their original relative positions when the stress is removed, and the deformation caused by the stress will disappear.

Thermosetting plastics change chemically when heated during manufacture, solidify while still hot, and assume the form of the finished products. The process cannot be repeated.

Cross links form between the chainlike molecules of the resin and bind them together into a netlike structure that is retained on cooling. The cross links restrict the relative movement of the molecules when the plastic is stressed so it tends to become rigid. Plasticity decreases as the number of cross links increases.

OTHER INGREDIENTS

As has been stated, the essential ingredient of all plastics is some type of resin. However, nonresinous ingredients are included in plastics to achieve certain desired properties, facilitate processing, or reduce the cost. These are classified as plasticizers, fillers, and colorants.

Plasticizers are materials that may be included in plastics to make them more plastic or flexible at ordinary temperatures and during the manufacturing process. They are usually organic compounds. Their primary, but not exclusive, use is in thermoplastics. Plasticizers are usually liquids that have high boiling points and act as solvents for the resins.

Fillers are materials included in plastics to provide or improve certain properties and lower their cost. They may be powders or fibrous materials. Powdered quartz or slate may be added for hardness; mica, clay, and asbestos fiber for heat resistance; wood flour for bulk and malleability; and glass and cotton fiber for tensile strength and flexibility. By the addition of appropriate fillers, plastics with widely varying properties can be made from the same kind of resin. A considerable portion of the volume of a plastic may be due to the filler. Fillers are extensively used in thermostating plastics.

Colorants are responsible for one desirable feature of plastics. This is the great variety of colors in which they are available. These are obtained by the addition of coloring materials that include organic dyes and pigments, and inorganic pigments that are usually metallic oxides.

SOLVENTS

Plastics are used in liquid form as one of the ingredients of some surface-coating materials. Among such materials are various kinds of paint, varnish, enamel, and lacquers. Most of the resins suitable for use in such products are hard and brittle. To convert them to liquids, as required in the manufacture and application of these products, appropriate organic solvents are used. The resin hardens as the solvent evaporates after a coating is applied. Solvents are also used to liquefy the granular or powdered compounds as required in some manufacturing processes.

SHAPING OR PROCESSING PLASTICS

Plastic products can be manufactured in a great variety of forms by selecting the appropriate kinds of resin and other materials and using suitable equipment and processing procedures. The compounds to be converted into manufactured products are supplied in granular or powdered forms, both commonly called molding powder, or in liquid form. The molding powders are heated to form viscous liquids during processing.

The temperatures required to make plastics sufficiently fluid for processing are relatively low compared with those required for most metals. Plastics cannot withstand high temperatures.

In the molding processes, the liquid is forced by pressure into molds to produce the desired shape. There it solidifies either by cooling, as with thermoplastics, or by the cross linking of the molecules of thermosetting plastics.

In the usual extrusion process, a viscous liquid thermoplastic is forced through an orifice or die shaped to yield a product of the desired cross section. After passing through the die, the extruded plastic is deposited on a moving belt or other device. The extruded material may be cooled in various ways. The processes are usually continuous. Simple dies can be shaped to form solid rods and sheets. Special devices are used to form tubes and to coat wires with plastic. Instead of using long shallow dies or orifices for extruding films or sheets, such forms are more commonly produced by splitting large extruded tubes longitudinally and spreading them out to flatten.

In the calendering process, molding powder warmed to a doughlike consistency is fed between the first pair of a series of heated horizontal rolls and emerges from the last pair of heated rolls as a flat plastic film or sheet whose thickness is determined by the gap between the rolls. It is then cooled by a chill roll and may be stored for further processing on a takeoff roll. This process is extensively used for producing thermoplastic film or sheeting.

In the casting process, liquid plastics are poured into molds, where they harden slowly. The plastic may be supplied in liquid form or in granular or powdered form which may be liquefied by heat or adding solvents. Both thermoplastics or thermosetting plastics are used. The former will solidify at room or relatively low temperatures, but the latter require heating. No pressure is involved for either.

Laminates are usually formed by impregnating sheets of cloth, paper, asbestos, or woven glass fibers with liquid thermosetting resins; stacking them in layers; and curing by heat and pressure to form solid sheets. If low pressures are used, they are called low-pressure laminates or, more commonly, reinforced laminates. The latter designation is used especially if the impregnated sheets are woven glass fabric. Reinforced laminates differ from molded plastics in which the fibrous materials are not in layers but are included to increase their flexural strength. If high pressures are used, the products are called high-pressures laminates.

Plastic foams may be made by introducing air or some other gas into liquid thermosetting resin and solidifying by heating and curing. The foam may be formed mechanically by whipping air into the liquid resin, by dissolving a gas in the resin under pressure and then lowering the pressure to permit the gas to expand, or by producing gas in the liquid resin by chemical action of materials introduced into the resin. Such foams may be rigid or flexible. They are effective as heat insulation and are very lightweight.

In sandwich constructions, two thin, dense, strong, and hard facing layers of plastic, metal, or wood are bonded with adhesives to a core of lightweight material to form a panel. For the panel to function effectively, the core and adhesive must be strong enough to resist the shearing and compressive stresses due to normal loads and impacts. Plastics used for cores are either foamed or honeycombed, the former having superior heat-insulating properties.

COMMON PROPERTIES

The physical and chemical properties of plastics vary depending upon the type of resin, the kinds and proportions of fillers and plasticizers, the type of reinforcing fabrics, and the temperatures, pressures, and equipment used in the manufacturing processes. The following comments summarize the properties of plastics used in building construction.

They are formable into a great variety of shapes and available in a range of colors.

Most plastics have strengths comparable with those of wood or concrete, but those of some laminates and reinforced plastics are very high.

Stiffness is relatively low.

They have relatively light weight as compared with most building materials except wood and lightweight concrete.

They have a high coefficient of expansion, a low thermal conductivity, and the range of temperature resistance, from low to high, is relatively limited.

They will burn but not support combustion although they may emit lethal gases.

They are noncorrosive for conditions encountered in buildings.

Deformation due to creep tends to disappear when load is removed.

When considering many other properties, distinction should be made between thermoplastics and thermosetting plastics.

Thermosetting plastics are superior to thermoplastics in resistance to heat.

Thermoplastics are usually tough but may be soft, flexible, and tough or hard, rigid, and brittle, depending upon composition.

Although usually rigid, thermosetting plastics are elastic for the stresses to which they are usually subjected.

All plastics are subject to creep under load, but this tendency is much greater for thermoplastics than for thermosetting plastics.

Thermoplastics are soluble in some solvents, but thermosetting plastics are mostly insoluble.

Some thermoplastics have excellent light-transmitting qualities.

NAMES OF PLASTICS

A plastic may be designated by the chemical type of resin used as its essential ingredient or by a trade name given by the manufacturer.

SPECIFIC PROPERTIES, FORMS, AND USES

The pertinent properties, forms, and uses of various plastics employed in building construction are summarized in Table 7.7.

PLASTIC SHEETS

Perhaps the widest application of acrylic sheets is in glazing windows and flat, curved, or domed skylights. This plastic, a thermoplastic material, is usually ⅛ to ¼ in. thick for glazing,

Table 7.7 Properties, Forms, and Uses of Plastics

Chemical Type	Properties	Forms	Uses
		Thermoplastics	
Acrylics	Transparent, hard, weather-resistant, shatter-resistant, easily scratched	Cast sheets	Window and skylight glazing
Polyethylene	Flexible, tough, translucent, low cost, easily scratched	Film and sheet	Vapor barriers, temporary glazing and building enclosing, protection and materials stored outdoors
		Open mesh	Window screen
Polystyrene	Hard, clear, brittle, water- and chemical-resistant, low cost	Tile and sheet	Wall covering and tile
Vinyls	Tough, wear- and stain-resistant	Tile and Sheet	Floor and wall tile, and sheet covering
		Coated glass fiber	Window screen
Polyamides (Nylon)	Tough, hard, wear-resistant, expensive	Cast	Rollers and bearings
		Thermosetting Plastics	
Alkyds	Weather-resistant, tough, good adhesive properties	Liquid and solid	Surface coatings such as paints, enamels, etc., molded products
Melamines	Hard, durable, abrasion-resistant, chemical- and heat-resistant	Sheets	Decorative laminates, high-pressure laminates, counter tops
Polyesters	Weather- and chemical-resistant, stiff, hard	Corrugated and flat translucent laminates, woven glass reinforced	Window glazing and skylights

although it may be as thick as 4 in. Sheets are made as large as 10 ft × 14 ft. Although it is somewhat soft compared to glass and is subject to scratching, acrylic is highly resistant to shattering and breaking. This plastic is transparent in several colors, colorless or white in translucent sheets, and in several colors in opaque sheets. The latter are used for facias and as curtain wall panels. Translucent acrylics are used for diffusers in luminous ceilings and light fixtures (luminaires) and as glazing where privacy is required.

Acrylic sheets may be coated with a plastic that produces an abrasion resistance that approaches the scratch resistance of plate glass.

The surfaces of these plastics are usually smooth for transparent glazing, although they may have pebbled or orange-peel surfaces for translucent and opaque sheets. This material is flexible, colorful, durable, and is made into attractive colored mosaic windows. Decorative sheets are also made by embedding materials. Designs vary — burlap, leaves, colored paper, etc. In glazing, these sheets require frames, glazing, or fastenings that allow them to seat upon the frame in a manner that permits thermal expansion and contraction in the frame without rupturing the seal or mechanical fastening.

Acrylic plastic is marketed under several trade names such as Acrylite and Plexiglas.

The reason that thermoplastic plastics have not been permitted more extensive use in construction is that they are soft and melt or deform under heat.

A polycarbonate plastic sheet, which is used for glazing windows and skylights, has exceptional resistance to impact and breakage. It is colorless or may be of various colors, including a glare-reducing bronze or gray in different intensities. It is known by proprietary names such as Tuffex and Lexan.

Modified acrylic plastic with glass fibered reinforcement is formed into flat, corrugated, or ribbed panels. These translucent panels in several colors measure from 26 in. to 50 in. in width and from 8 ft to 14 ft in length. They have exceptional strength, especially the corrugated panels. These sheets are used primarily for siding and roofing of industrial buildings; however, they are used for a variety of other building applications such as fences and visual barriers.

PLASTIC FILMS
Polyethylene film is made in several thicknesses measured in mils. The material, sold in rolls with widths of 10 ft or more, is used as a vapor barrier under floors, in walls, as drop cloths for painting, and temporarily encloses buildings under construction for protection against weather and heat loss. It is colorless or black.

CELLULAR PLASTICS
Thermosetting rigid foam plastic, mentioned above, is also known as cellular plastic. Polyurethane and polystyrene are cellular plastics used in the building industry. Although a cellular plastic is usually applied in its processed solid form, the ingredients may be purchased and the cellular plastic cast, foamed, or sprayed in place. These plastics, which are snow white, have extraordinary thermal insulating value, are

lightweight, and are resistant to moisture and decay. As stated above, they are used as an insulating core in sandwich panels that have a structural and finished surface, such as plywood, sheet metal, or cement asbestos. Although it is not a structural material itself, cellular plastic can support limited imposed loads such as thin sections of concrete. They are used with masonry construction as an insulating wythe in a cavity wall or applied to the interior surface with mechanical fasteners or adhesives. Foamed plastics are used on roofs, walls, ceilings, and under floors. This material will not support combustion, although it will sublimate into a gas when exposed to a flame or intense heat. Styrofoam is a trade name of a well-known polystyrene.

EPOXY RESINS OR EPOXIES
Introduction
Epoxy resins, often called epoxies, are thermosetting plastics introduced into building construction in about 1954. Epoxies have remarkable bonding properties. Architects and engineers have not yet made full use of them, largely because they are cautious in the use of materials whose value has not been demonstrated by experience, and few workers are skilled in their use. As time goes on and experience demonstrates the wide field of usefulness of epoxies in building constructions, they seem destined to assume an important role in this field.

Definitions
The term epoxy refers to a three-member ring structure containing two hydrogen atoms and one oxygen atom. Materials containing an average of more than one epoxy group per molecule are considered as epoxy resins.

Epoxy resins alone are chemically stable and may be stored indefinitely, but they are useless. By adding a curing agent or hardener to the resin in its liquid state, infusible and insoluble solids are formed. The length of time that an epoxy mixture is usable after the curing agent is added is called the pot life.

Substances added to epoxy resins during the manufacturing process to alter the properties of the cured resins are called modifiers.

Manufacture
The basic resins, together with the modifiers, are cooked under pressure by the manufacturer.

For resins used in construction, the cooking is terminated when the resins are honey-colored liquids having viscosities about the same as those of a 20-to-30-weight motor oil.

The characteristics of the manufactured product depend upon such factors as the ingredients, the temperature, the pressure, and the cooking time during manufacture. Each manufacturer produces a variety of resins suitable for various uses.

Modifiers
The basic resins without modifications are useless. The modifiers added during the manufacturing process to provide the desired properties are classified as flexibilizers, fillers, pigments and dyes, and diluents.

Flexibilizers or plasticizers are always required to increase the flexibility. Ordinarily they are mixed with the curing agent by the manufacturer. Among the materials used are a synthetic rubber in liquid form and various coal tar products.

Fillers are added to provide certain desired properties or to reduce the cost. They extend the pot life, lower shrinkage while curing, and reduce the coefficient of expansion. Materials used as fillers are coal tar products, which react chemically with epoxy resins, and inert materials such as clay, asbestos or glass fibers, powdered metals, aluminum oxide, silica, mica, powdered glass, fine sand, or marble dust, which merely occupy space. Inert minerals are the most commonly used fillers for epoxies used in construction. Powdered metals and aluminum oxide are used in coatings and paints.

Pigments and Dyes. The color of many epoxy formulations is satisfactory for most uses but may be modified as desired by using appropriate pigments or dyes.

Diluents are added to improve workability, permit the application of thinner coats, reduce viscosity, or increase penetration. There are few applications except in paints and other coatings.

Curing Agent or Hardener. The curing agent or hardener may be reactive and become a part of the molecules in which case it imparts to the molecules some of its own characteristics. It may also act as a catalyst to facilitate the reaction but not become a part of the molecules.

The pot life may be controlled to a few minutes or a few hours, depending upon the ingredients and the temperature created by the chemical changes which take place or by heat applied externally, both of which are affected by the size of the batch. On construction work, only the former is used, but factory production may utilize the latter for some products. The curing agent completes the chemical changes which were interrupted when the manufacturing process was terminated.

Properties
Epoxies cannot be classed together as materials with specified properties.

An epoxy can be as brittle as glass or as resilient as rubber. It can be a high molecular weight solid of great density, or a low molecular weight liquid of such low viscosity that it will leak out of containers capable of holding water. And it can be anywhere between these two extremes (*Those Wonderful Epoxies,* Engineering News-Record, July 12, 1962, p. 28).

The properties of cured resins may be varied within wide limits with the proper choice of curing agents, modifiers, and diluents.

Some of the more significant properties that can be achieved are the following (*Application of Synthetic Resins and Adhesives to Wood Bridges and Trestles,* American Railway Engineering Association Bulletin 562, February 1961, p. 526).

1. The liquid resin is convenient to use in many different types of applications.

2. The curing time may be controlled by selecting the curing agent from the variety of those available.

3. The properties of cured resins may be varied within wide limits with the appropriate choice of modifiers and curing agents.

4. The overall strength properties such as tensile, compressive, and flexural strength are excellent. In general, their strength is greater than that of most of the materials they are used on.

5. The shrinkage during curing is small.

6. Hardness, toughness, and resistance to abrasion are outstanding.

7. The resistance to corrosion, salts, acids, petroleum products, solvents, and other chemicals of many kinds is exceptionally good.

8. Adhesion to the surfaces of most materials is excellent. Their ability to bond similar or dissimilar materials is exceeded by no other organic compounds.

9. The color is satisfactory for most purposes. Epoxies can be formulated to be almost any color.

10. Modification of resins to improve one property usually results in a sacrifice in one or more of the other properties.

Application

Cured epoxy compounds may be applied by brush, spraying equipment, trowel, squeegee, or other means appropriate for the characteristics of the material being applied and the type of operation.

The curing agent is added to the modified resin immediately before application. The operations must be completed during the pot life of the mixture.

Before applying, the materials must be properly mixed. Careful preparation of the surfaces to be joined, repaired, or protected is required. Any dust, loose material, oil, or grease must be removed from any surfaces involved and rust, surface coatings, and mill scale must be removed from steel.

Epoxies should not be applied when the air temperatures are below 60° or above 95° unless special precautions are taken to protect them from the effects of lower or higher temperatures. Workers experienced with the use of epoxies are required.

As stated, in *Application of Synthetic Resins and Adhesives to Wood Bridges and Trestles.*

Prolonged or frequent skin contact of materials used in epoxy resin systems may cause dermatitis for some individuals. The reactive diluents used in epoxy resins are found to be sources of skin irritations. . . . Most persons can work with these materials for some time without taking any precautions to avoid skin irritation. A few persons under these conditions may suddenly break out with skin irritations which will disappear when transferred to other types of work.

Among the precautions suggested in the references, the following are included.

1. Care in preventing skin contact.

2. Regular washing of hands, arms and face with warm soapy water. Solvents should not be used.

3. Use of plastic or rubber gloves and protective clothing that have not been contaminated by prior use.

4. Complete protection of the body by clothing including a hat when spraying epoxies. Exposed body surfaces should be coated with protective cream, and a respirator should be used.

Uses

As previously stated, epoxy compounds have many remarkable properties and seem destined to assume an important role in building construction.

In general, they are used as bonding materials to join most similar and dissimilar materials, as bonding agents for aggregates, as watertight crack and joint sealers, and as protective coatings including paints. They are expensive, but where their special characteristics are important they can be extremely economical. An epoxy compound must be specially suitable for the purpose for which it is to be used. Some of the uses that have been made or suggested are given in the following paragraphs.

Terrazzo floor surfaces are installed with epoxies as the matrix rather than portland cement. The required thickness is only ½ in. instead of the usual thicknesses of 1 or 2 in., with the resultant saving in dead load.

Concrete overlays can be bonded to eroded or worn concrete surfaces.

Corners that have broken off concrete slabs and pieces that have been broken off concrete members can be replaced by coating the broken edges with epoxies or by replacing the broken parts with new concrete sealed with epoxies to the remaining parts.

Bonding the components in composite steel and concrete construction.

"Cold-welding" structural steel components instead of welding, bolting, or riveting under certain conditions.

Repair of cracked or checked timber members.

Adhesive for laminated timber and other timber parts, and for bonding precast or cast-in-place concrete slabs to timber or steel girders.

Waterproofing concrete surfaces by brush or spray coatings.

Corrosion-resistant coatings for steel.

The full uses of epoxies will provide many entirely new methods of construction.

Summary

Wood products and plastics play important roles as materials used for building construction. Wood processed into dimension lumber is the basic material used in the wood frame construction of residences and light commercial facilities. Processed as timber, wood provides a slow burning interior structural frame for warehouse and mill construction. Prefabricated into glued laminated rigid frames and arches, wood provides a column-free interior space suitable for large assembly halls and sports arenas. Wood is a renewable natural resource that will continue to maintain its position as one of the basic building materials.

Plastics, made of synthetic resins built up by chemical processes from such materials as coal, petroleum, natural gas, water, salt, and air, provide us with products that are strong, light in weight, formable, and resistant to corrosion. Products include acrylic sheets for window glazing, polyethylene film vapor barriers, vinyl floor tile, and melamine laminated counter tops.

Key Terms

wood	grading	balloon frame	creosote
lumber	boards	bridging	joist hanger
timber	dimension lumber	plywood	plastic
millwork	green lumber	glued laminated beam	plasticizers
board foot	dry lumber	glulam	fillers
air dried	mud sill	lamella roof	epoxy resin
kiln dried	platform frame		

Review Questions

1. What are the two classes of trees and how are they used in construction?

2. Explain the difference between plain-sawed lumber and quarter-sawed lumber.

3. How is lumber seasoned and why is it done?

4. What affect does the water content of lumber have on its mechanical and physical properties?

5. Why is lumber grading important to the users of wood products?

6. What are the three classes of buildings that make extensive use of wood structural members?

7. List the various prefabricated wood structural members commonly used in construction.

8. List four connectors that are commonly used to fasten the wood parts of a building together and explain how they work.

CHAPTER 8
THERMAL, ACOUSTICAL, AND MOISTURE PROTECTION

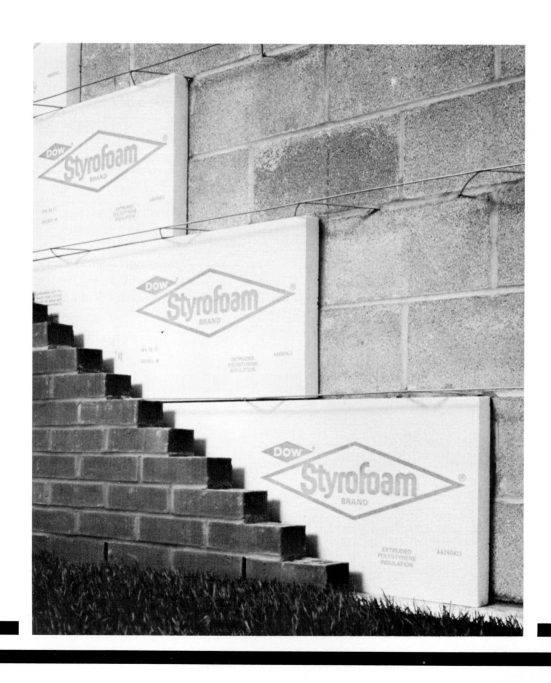

The protection of the interior spaces of a building from unwanted moisture, temperature, and sound is a function of the building's envelope. Probably no other element of building construction causes the owner more grief and headaches than the building's envelope. Whether the interior space is used for working, living, or playing, a breakdown in the protection against unwanted moisture, temperature, and sound will disrupt the activities within this space. When the roof leaks, or cold air infiltrates through windows and doors, or noise from outside or inside the building intrudes on the individuals inside, we know the protection has failed.

To ensure the integrity of the building's envelope, the proper methods and materials must be selected, and the specified installation procedures followed. The proper selection of a roofing material will depend on the type of roof, roof deck construction, and climate conditions. Each roofing material has specific installation instructions that must be followed to ensure the material will perform as specified. An understanding of how heat is transmitted is necessary before the appropriate insulation, sealants, and gaskets can be selected. And it is important to know the nature of sound before a decision can be made about controlling sound, both wanted sound and unwanted sound, in a particular environment.

Objectives

1. Become familiar with the different types of roofs and roof decks.

2. Become familiar with the different roofing materials and the conditions under which they are used.

3. Understand how sealants and gaskets are used in building construction.

4. Understand how heat is transmitted through walls and roof of a building.

5. Become familiar with the different types of insulation.

6. Understand how sound is transmitted throughout a building.

7. Become familiar with the methods used to control unwanted sound in an enclosed environment.

FIGURE 8.1 Types of roofs.

FIGURE 8.2 Types of dormers.

FIGURE 8.3 Types of roofs.

8.1 Roof Types and Roof Decks

Roofs of buildings are divided into various types, depending upon the shape.

Flat roofs (Figure 8.1 *A*) are extensively used on all kinds of buildings. They are sloped from ⅛ in. to 2 in. vertical to 12 in. horizontal to ensure proper drainage, although some roofs are designed without any slope whatever. Even though watertight roofs can be secure without any slope, a dead-level roof is not recommended.

Roofs which slope in one direction only *(B)* are called shed roofs. This type of roof is used on entire buildings or in connection with other types shown in *(C)* to form a lean-to. A butterfly roof slopes in two directions: two shed roofs meet at their low *eaves (G)*. Gable roofs also slope in two directions *(D)*; two shed roofs meet to form a ridge. This type of roof, widely used on residences, slopes often as low as 4 in. vertical to 12 in. horizontal and is occasionally as steep as 20 in. vertical to 12 in. horizontal. The most common slopes are between 4 in. vertical to 12 in. horizontal and 12 in. vertical to 12 in. horizontal.

Hip roofs slope in four directions *(E)*. This widely used roof has the same slopes as a gable roof.

Gambrel roofs slope in two directions, but there is a break

in the slope on each side *(F)*. The gambrel roof is used for residences because the space under the roof can be used efficiently, especially when a long shed dormer (Figure 8.2*A*) is used. Mansard roofs slope in four directions but have a deck at the top (Figure 8.1*H*).

The various types of roof dormers are shown in Figure 8.2*A*.

The saw-tooth roofs shown in Figure 8.3*B* and *C* are used extensively on industrial buildings because of the opportunities they offer in light and ventilation. The steep face of *(B)* and the vertical face of *(C)* are mostly glass and usually face north. Northern light (in the Northern Hemisphere) is more constant throughout the day than light from other directions, and the glare and radiant heat of direct sunlight is avoided. The type shown in *(C)* does not have as large an area of glass as that shown in *(B)*, but it is more easily made watertight in the valley. At least a part of the windows, usually the upper half, are open for ventilation.

The parts of a roof such as ridge, hip, valley, gable, rake, cricket, and eaves are indicated in Figure 8.1. Monitors (Figure 8.3*D* and *E*) provide better light and ventilation. Their vertical face is called the clerestory. If only ventilation is desired, louvres may be used for ventilation in the clerestory *(D)*.

Thin-shell roofs are described and illustrated in Section 4.7.

The *roof deck* is that portion of the roof construction to which the roof covering or roofing is applied and through which the loads on the roof are transmitted to the principal supporting members. Roof decks include sheathing, roof planks or slabs, rafters, purlins, subpurlins, and joists. The principal supporting members include girders, trusses, rigid frames, and the ribs of arches and domes, all of which are described elsewhere. Sometimes, as in shell roofs, the decks also serve as principal supporting members. In others, the roof covering and deck are one and the same — for example, the various forms of corrugated roofing which span between purlins.

The deviation of the surface of a roof deck from the horizontal is measured in terms of the ratio of its vertical projection to its horizontal projection and is expressed in inches of vertical projection per foot of horizontal projection. This ratio is called the *slope* or *incline.* It is also called the *pitch,* but the other terms are preferable because the ratio of the *rise,* or center height, to the span of a symmetrical roof truss with inclined top chords or a framed roof is also called its pitch. Such a truss with a rise of 10 ft and span of 40 ft is said to have a $^{10}\!/_{40}$ or quarter pitch; the roof slope, however, is $^{10}\!/_{20}$ or 6 in. per foot.

The surface area of a roof deck and its covering is expressed in squares; a square is 100 sq ft.

FLAT ROOF DECKS

If the roof of a multistory building is flat, it usually will be constructed according to the same system as that used for the floors. When all of the factors involved are considered, such a procedure is usually cheaper and more satisfactory than any other system of equal quality. Various types of floor construction are discussed in Section 10.11. Some systems will result in level decks. Roof decks that do not slope to the drains are objectionable because shallow pools of water, called *bird-baths,* remain in slight depressions and deflections of the deck surface. A further objection to dead-level roof decks is that standing water will cause early deterioration of the roofing surface. However, slopes of at least ⅛ in. to the foot are provided by using shaped wood members or, more often, fills of lean, lightweight concrete placed on top of a flat concrete deck.

For single-story buildings, flat roof systems may be of the same types as some of the floor systems described in Section 7.4. Types that are especially suitable for heavy loads, such as the flat-slab, would not be appropriate for such buildings because roof loads are relatively light.

Decking especially designed for roofs include precast gypsum and concrete planks and wood-fiber cement planks in various forms installed on steel rafters or purlins. Gypsum is nailable; and by using appropriate aggregates, concrete can be made nailable. Cast-in-place or poured gypsum slabs are also used for roof decks but are not extensively used in floor constructions. Lightweight, non-combustible termite-proof wood-fiber-cement planks 2, 2½, and 3 in. thick, made of a compressed chemically treated wood fiber and portland cement, are manufactured for roof decking. The standard width is 32 in., with lengths up to 9 ft. Usually supported on bulb-tee subpurlins spaced 2 ft 9 in., the edges are rabbeted to fit under the bulb projection so as to be anchored when joints are filled with mortar. These planks have good heat-insulation and sound-absorbing properties.

Also designed especially for roof decks are light gage steel-ribbed panels of various types similar to the floor panels illustrated in Figure 6.43 but installed with the flat surface on top and without concrete. The flat surface permits a rigid insulation or roofing with less chance of a surface rupture.

The only types of roofing suitable for flat or gently sloping roofs are the build-up roof and the sheet-metal roof with flat soldered seams. The built-up roofs can be used on all types of flat decks, but sheet-metal roofing involves nailing and therefore cannot be used directly on nonnailable concrete.

SLOPING ROOFS

Three sloping roof decks and their parts are shown in Figure 8.4. The principal supporting members shown in *(B)* and *(C)* are trusses, but the same arrangements can be used with other types. A typical wood frame construction is shown in *(A)*. Usually there are no main supports for the rafters between the plate and the hip. In *(B)*, timber or steel purlins support the rafters, with 1 in. wood sheathing, on light wood

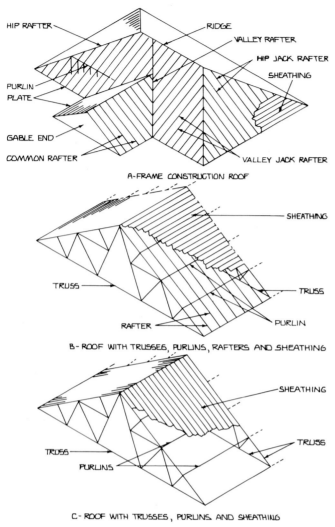

FIGURE 8.4 Roof framing.

rafters. The assembly in *(C)* does not include rafters, but the sheathing spans between purlins. The construction might consist of wood sheathing, usually 2 in. thick, and timber or steel purlins; precast gypsum; wood-fiber cement or nailable concrete planks and steel or precast concrete purlins; or some form of corrugated sheets spanning between timber or steel purlins while serving as a roof covering. The methods shown in *(B)* and *(C)* are suitable for a flat roof, although corrugated sheets would not serve as a roof covering.

The coverings for sloping roofs must be fastened to the decks with mechanical fasteners, usually nails if the deck is continuous. For this reason, a type of nailable deck must be selected or wood nailing strips can be installed which will have adequate nail holding ability. Included in such decks are those constructed of wood, gypsum, and nailable concrete. The gypsum and nailable concrete are usually in various forms of precast planks because this procedure is more economical and the installation is faster than casting-in-place.

Cast-in-place decks of ordinary concrete are not nailable; thus, for this form of deck, provision must be made for fastening the roofing to the deck. This is accomplished by providing wood nailing strips, called *sleepers* or nailers, that are treated with preservatives. For built-up roofs, these nailers are embedded in the concrete at intervals of 3 ft, running parallel with the slope and with their top surfaces flush with the top surface of the concrete. If rigid insulation with a thickness at least equal to that of 1 in. nominal thickness lumber is used, the nailing strips are placed between the sheets of insulation with their tops flush. The usual method for fastening built-up roofing to poured concrete decks with slopes of less than 1 in. per foot is to cement the roofing to the deck with roofing pitch, but this procedure is not suitable for greater slopes because of the tendency of the roofing to creep down the slope.

HEAT INSULATION

The roof or the ceiling of the top story of buildings should be insulated. This reduces the heat losses and condensation on the ceilings and reduces temperatures. Various insulating materials are described in Section 8.11.

ROOF DRAINAGE

Roofs may range from flat with no slope whatever to roofs with a considerable slope. Few engineers and architects advocate the absolutely flat or dead-level roof despite its simplicity of construction, maintaining that standing water for short periods on a roof has harmful effects on the roofing materials. Standing water contributes to increased deflection of the roof framing and the consequent accumulation of more water, leading to the collapse of the entire roof. Flat roofs are often sloped by using tapered roof insulation or fill material.

8.2 Membrane Roofing

Built-up roofings consist of several overlapping layers of bituminous-saturated roofing felt cemented together with bituminous roofing cement, also known as bitumen usually applied so that in no place does felt touch felt. The bituminous material may be tar or asphalt. Tar is a by-product driven off in the process of converting coal to coke and is called coal tar pitch. Asphalt is a by-product driven off in the process of refining petroleum. Roofing felt is made from organic or asbestos fibers and is furnished in rolls 3 ft wide. The organic fibers are primarily graded rags, and for that reason, the felts from which they are made are called rag felts, but other organic fibrous materials are used along with rag fibers. Asbestos felt is composed of at least 85% asbestos fibers, with other materials used to provide desirable properties.

Both asphalt and coal-tar roofing bitumens are solid at ordinary temperatures. Before applying, they are heated until they become liquid. Tar has a lower melting point than asphalt, a quality which is desirable because it tends to be self-healing if punctured or ruptured but undesirable because tar is less stable on sloping roofs when it is heated by the sun. Tar is also less affected by standing water than asphalts. Asphalt roofing cement is used with asphalt-saturated felts and coal-tar roofing pitch with felts saturated with coal tar. Asphalt is usually preferred for sloping roofs and coal tar for flat or nearly flat roofs.

In addition to the roofing felts and bitumens, built-up roofs include various surfacing materials, which are embedded in the top layer of bitumen to protect them from the action of the elements. These are usually fine gravel and crushed slap, but felts with smooth top surfaces designed to be exposed are available. Flat roofs that serve as promenades carrying foot traffic may be covered with built-up roofs surfaced with floor tile or flagstones bedded in a 1 in. layer of portland-cement mortar.

Built-up roofs are adaptable to the various types of nailable roof decks, such as those of wood, poured or precast gypsum, precast nailable concrete, and other less common materials, and to those which are nonnailable, such as cast-in-place concrete. They are also adaptable to flat and sloping roofs. They can be applied over decks that are not insulated and to decks covered with rigid insulation. A bituminous vapor seal is applied to the deck before the insulation is installed. The seal prevents the accumulation of moisture from the air on the interior of the building in the insulation. The top surface of the insulation is mopped with roofing cement before the first ply of felt is applied. Sheet-steel decks must always be insulated. Wherever insulation is used, it must be adequately secured to the deck.

The simplest form of the best type of built-up roof usually installed is illustrated in Figure 8.5, in which the roof deck is made of cast-in-place concrete and its slope does not exceed 1 in. per foot. The plies are lapped the distance required to produce a cover whose thickness at every point is equal to the number of plies desired. The roof in the illustration is a 4-ply roof. The plies are laid with their lengths perpendicular to the slope. The laps are made in the direction required to shed water, the direction of flow in the illustration being downward.

The surface of the deck is first covered with a mopping of hot roofing cement, the portion of the surface of each ply which is to be overlapped is similarly covered before placing the next ply, so that in no place does felt touch felt; and, finally, a uniform coating of hoot roofing cement is mopped or poured over the top surface of the top ply, and in this coating, clean fine gravel or crushed slag is embedded.

For nonnailable decks with slopes greater than 1 in. to the foot, nailing strips are required, to which each ply can be nailed in a specified manner using tin-plate disks 1 in. in diameter under the nailheads. The nailing strips are made of wood which is creosoted to preserve it. They are usually placed 3 ft apart, parallel with the slope, with their top surface flush with the surface of the deck and with sides beveled for anchorage or anchored in some other manner.

If a wood or other nailable deck is used, a layer of sheathing paper or unsaturated felt is nailed to the deck. The top surface of this layer is mopped with hot roofing cement, and then the desired number of plies of saturated felt are placed and surfaced as for the concrete deck illustrated in Figure 8.5. A 5-ply roofing on a nailable deck, placed as described, is considered equivalent to a 4-ply roofing on a concrete deck, also placed as described.

Various manufacturers' specifications for laying built-up roofing differ in some respects. They are essentially in accord with the descriptions already given but are more detailed.

Built-up roofs are widely used and durable. Roofs such as those described are guaranteed for 20 years against repair and maintenance expense by the manufacturers if their

FIGURE 8.5 Four-ply built-up roofing on concrete deck.

specifications are followed, but the expected life is much longer. If the number of plies is reduced by one, the guarantee period is reduced 5 years.

Built-up roofs are sometimes placed by cold processes; in one process, the bituminous cementing material is thinned with kerosine to produce what is called a cutback. The cementing action occurs as the solvent evaporates. The cold process is used primarily for maintenance rather than new construction.

ROLL ROOFING

Roofing consisting of sheets composed of a felt base impregnated and coated with asphalt is furnished in rolls and therefore is called *roll roofing.* Because it is prepared ready for application, it is called prepared or ready roofing; it is also called composition roofing. To prevent sticking when rolled, both surfaces are dusted with mineral matter, such as mica, talc, or fine sand, or the top surface is coated with crushed slate, quartz, burned clay, or other minerals with or without coloring agents embedded in the asphalt coating.

Roofings with smooth surface coatings are lowest in cost, but they are less desirable because coarse mineral surfacing gives considerable protection from the weather and increases the fire resistance. The surfacing also makes possible the manufacture of roofing in a variety of colors.

Roll roofing, available in various weights or thicknesses, is usually furnished in rolls 3 ft wide and 36 ft long. It is also furnished in rolled sheets 18 in. wide and 76 ft long. The most extensive use of roll roofing is over wood decks to which it is nailed with galvanized roofing nails which have large heads. In addition, it is cemented in various ways, using roofing cement which can be applied cold and which hardens as the thinner evaporates.

One type of roof covering composed of roll roofing, when laid on a wood deck, is placed over a layer of lightweight roofing felt laid dry. The roofing is 18 in. wide and is laid with 8 in. exposed, leaving an unexposed selvage of 10 in. It is cemented to the ply below over the selvage area. A row of nails is driven along the upper edge of each ply and another above the lower edge of the selvage where it will be covered by the next ply. This arrangement provides 2 plies of protection.

A similar type of construction makes use of roll roofing 36 in. wide, laid with an 11½ in. exposure and a 24½ in. selvage. This arrangement provides 3 plies of protection.

The least expensive and shortest-lived roof covering composed of roll roofing on a wood deck makes use of 36 in. roofing with all its surface except about 2 in. exposed to the weather. This 2 in. edge is side- and end-lapped, cemented, and nailed with the heads of the nails exposed. Because of the distance between rows of nails and its light weight, this type of installation can be blown off by air currents filtering through the deck during windstorms and, being only 1 ply thick, is easily punctured by hail. It is suitable only for temporary structures.

Roll roofing can be used for slopes as flat as 2 in. to the foot.

SINGLE PLY MEMBRANE ROOFING

Single ply membrane roofing systems consist of a single membrane laid in sheets over the roof deck. The membrane is sealed at the joints to act as a total barrier to rain, or standing water. The most common material used for the membrane is an *elastomeric,* EPDM (Ethylene Propylene Diene Monomer), a synthetic rubber material. Other materials include PVC (polyvinyl chloride) and CPE (chlorinated polyethylene). The membranes come in sheets that are 10 or 20 ft wide and up to 200 ft long. Most of the membranes are available in two thicknesses, 45 and 60 mil. The membranes are formulated to provide strength to resist tears, impacts, and punctures. The membrane can be stretched to 300% of its original size to accommodate structural movement without splitting or cracking. It can withstand extreme temperature fluctuations without loss to seam or surface integrity, and remain watertight in sub-zero temperatures. It is resistant to ultra-violet light and ozone. The single membrane can be applied to new roof decks of concrete, steel, or wood and directly over old roofs in reroofing situations.

Installation is performed by one of three accepted methods: ballasted, fully adhered, and mechanically fastened. In the ballasted method, the membrane (45 mil) is loosely laid over an approved roof deck and mechanically secured only around the perimeter and at penetrations. Adjoining membrane sheets are overlapped a minimum of 3 in. to allow for bonding. The seams are bonded and then the membrane is covered with round river stone to keep it in place. Since the membrane is not attached to the roof deck, it can accommodate extreme building movement without splitting or cracking. This method is most suitable for dead flat roofs or roofs not exceeding a 2 in. : 12 in. slope. The roof deck must be capable of withstanding the additional weight of the ballast, 10.5 lb/sq ft. This method is the least expensive of the three discussed.

For those roofs that cannot support the weight of the ballast or have severe slopes, the fully adhered method is used. Installation begins by loosely laying the membrane (60 mil) over an approved roof deck, allowing for a 3 in. overlap in the adjoining sheets. The sheets are folded in half and adhesive is applied to both the underside of the membrane and roof deck, avoiding the seam area. The membrane is then bonded to the roof deck and the procedure is repeated for the other half of the sheet. Once adjacent sheets have been bonded to the roof deck, the seams are sealed. The completed roof system weighs an average of 0.5 lb/sq ft.

The most expensive method is the mechanically fastened method. This method combines the advantages of both the loosely laid ballasted and fully adhered methods. It is light weight, no ballast required, accommodates extreme building movement, and has no slope limitations. The membrane (60 mil) is loosely laid allowing for 3 in. of overlap on adjoining sheets. The seams are bonded and the membrane is fastened to the roof deck using metal battens and fasteners in a pattern around and across the roof. The pattern used will depend on building conditions and installation recommendations from the membrane manufacturer. The battens and fasteners are then covered with a 6 in. width of membrane which is bonded to the underlying membrane. This roof system weighs 1.5 lb/sq ft.

PLASTIC COATINGS

During recent years, several liquid coatings that can be sprayed or rolled on thin-shell concrete roof decks to make them waterproof have been developed. One of them is polyethylene rubber in combination with pigments and fillers. It is resistant to the temperatures to which a roof may be subjected and to atmospheric gases and weathering. The coating forms a membrane that expands and contracts with the base to which it is applied and maintains a continuous covering over hairline cracks that may develop in concrete surfaces. It will not fill visible surface imperfections. The membrane should be reinforced over cracks other than hairline cracks. The coating is available in several colors.

After the surface to be coated has been prepared and cleaned, a prime coat is applied and permitted to dry for a few hours. A minimum of four topcoats is then applied. The coats may be applied in alternating colors to ensure that each coat covers the entire surface. This plastic coating is suitable for application to plywood and metallic surfaces as well as to concrete.

A relatively new product, this plastic coating has been successfully used on many thin-shell roofs, and accelerated weathering tests indicate that it will have a life of at least 15 or possibly 20 years.

two sheets and run between two standing seams for two flat seams. Flat seams are soldered, but standing seams are not. The sheet metal is fastened by metal cleats nailed 8 to 12 in. apart on the deck and locked into the seams.

If possible, the nails should be of the same material as the roofing to avoid galvanic action between dissimilar metals; tinned nails with terne plate roofs, copper nails with copper roofs, galvanized nails with galvanized iron or steel and zinc roofs, and aluminum nails with aluminum roofs. Nails should not be driven through the sheets. Batten or ribbed roofs are formed by using wood battens or ribs. Special extruded aluminum battens are available for aluminum roofs. Sheet-metal troughs are fitted between these battens, and caps are placed over the battens (Figure 8.6C).

Before sheet metal is placed over matched wood sheathing, gypsum, or nailable concrete slabs, a layer of roofing felt is placed between metal and the deck. An important function of this felt is to prevent quick ignition of the wooden decking when the roof is exposed to burning brands or radiated heat. It should be at least $1/16$ in. thick. Tar paper should not be used under tin or terne roofing on account of its possible deleterious effect on the metal, but a rosin-sized paper is satisfactory.

Longitudinal crimps, shaped like an inverted V, formed in sheet-metal roofing (Figure 8.6D) increase its stiffness. Such crimps may be only at the edges, but a crimp may also be in the middle, as shown in the figure. For further stiffness, double crimps are formed along the edges and the middle. Triangular wood strips are provided under the outside crimps for nailing. Such roofing is unsuitable for flat roofs.

GALVANIC ACTION
As reported by the Bureau of Standards.

Galvanic action or *electrolysis* is defined as the deterioration by corrosion of one metal while protecting a dissimilar metal in metallic contact with it. This action will occur only when metals occupy-

8.3 Metal Roofing

Sheet-metal roofing of galvanized iron or steel, terne plate, copper, zinc, aluminum, or lead is widely used. To prevent leaks, it is necessary in the installation of sheet-metal roofs to provide for the large amount of thermal expansion that takes place. The expansion of various metals in inches per 10 ft of length for a temperature rise of 100°F is as follows: steel and iron, 0.08; copper, 0.11; aluminum, 0.16; lead, 0.19; and zinc, 0.21. Expansion is the chief factor controlling the design of the seams and the methods used in fastening the sheet metal to the roof. Laid with a flat seam (Figure 8.6A) or with a standing seam (B), seams on steeper slopes run parallel or perpendicular with the slope of the roof. The seams are clinched tight; the separation shown in the figures is shown for clarity. Cross seams, always flat, connect

FIGURE 8.6 Sheet-metal roofing.

ing different positions in the electropotential series (aluminum, zinc, iron and steel, tin, lead, and copper, arranged in order) are in intimate metallic contact in the presence of a suitable electrolyte, such as moisture.

TERNE PLATE

Tin plates are made by dipping plates of sheet-metal or iron in a molten bath of tin to form bright tin plates. If dipped in a molten bath of tin and lead, they form terne plates. When taken from the molten bath, the plates are usually passed through rolls; the pressure on the rolls determine the thickness of the plate. Bright tin plates are superior to terne plates but are so expensive that terne plates are used for roofing. The common sizes of sheets are 14 × 20 in. Several sheets may be assembled at the factory by jointing their ends together to form long sheets that are shipped in rolls, but sheets 50 ft long can be seamless.

The sheets are usually painted on both sides at the factory; but if they are not, the bottom side must be painted before laying. Terne plate roofs will last for many years if kept properly painted.

A recent development is terne-coated stainless steel. This roofing sheet is a superior terne plate that provides a maintenance-free and durable sheet-metal roof.

TITANIUM, COPPER, AND ZINC ALLOY

Sheets made of copper, zinc, and titanium alloy are used for a durable, lightweight roofing. Noncorrosive, these sheets weather to an attractive blue-gray patina. They may be easily installed using batten seams or standing seams supplemented with soldering if desired. This alloy sheet may be used in combination with several other metallic materials without fear of galvanic action. These sheets may be used with galvanized steel, aluminum, lead, or tin. If used in contact with other more electrolytically active materials, they must be protected with a coat of asphaltum paint. Like several other sheet-metal roofing materials, this alloy is used widely for flashing, facias, gutters, and other roofing accessories.

LEAD

Lead sheets are used for roofing to a limited extent. Lead is particularly suitable for curved or irregular surfaces, for it can be stretched easily and worked to fit such surfaces without cutting. It has a high coefficient of expansion and is difficult to hold in place, particularly on pitched roofs. It has a long life and need not be painted.

A roofing known as hard lead is composed chiefly of lead, but 4% to 6% of antimony is added to increase the elastic limit and decrease the coefficient of expansion. This material has the advantages of ordinary lead without its disadvantages. It may be used on any slope.

Lead is also used for flashing difficult places and as a waterproof barrier for garden roofs that are to be finished with a tile wearing surface.

COPPER

Sheets of soft copper make an excellent roof covering that has a high initial cost but is durable and requires no painting. Exposure to the weather causes a green copper carbonate to form on the surface. It protects the remainder of the metal and is attractive. Sheet copper is available in sheets 24, 30, and 36 in. wide and up to 10 ft long.

Copper roofs are made in batten seams, standing seams, or flat seams. The joints of these seams are frequently accentuated. Heavy shadow lines created by the seams emphasize either a horizontal, diagonal, or vertical design. A chevron or horizontal pattern which is sometimes called a Bermuda roof is quite popular.

Copper sheets lend themselves to application of nearly all parts of a roof covering and the necessary accessories. Flashing, reglets, facias, gutters, and downspouts are some of the parts of roofs that are made of copper.

GALVANIZED IRON AND STEEL

Iron and steel sheets are galvanized by dipping clean sheets in a bath of molten zinc. The zinc protects the sheet from corrosion in proportion to the thickness of the coating. Sheets which are to be sharply bent in forming the joints or for other reasons are given thinner coats to decrease their tendency to flake while being bent. For use in laying galvanized sheet roofing with standing seams, several sheets are assembled at the factory to form continuous sheets, usually 50 ft long, which can be rolled for shipping. The ends of the sheets are joined by double cross-seam locks. Other forming necessary for the standing seams is done on the job. U-shaped caps are placed over the standing seam with the sides squeezed together with tongs to form roll and cap roofing. V-crimp roofing (Figure 8.6) and sheets with U-shaped edges, which are overlapped and squeezed to form standing seams, are also available. Galvanized sheet roofing is used extensively, is relatively low in cost, and lasts for many years if kept painted.

STAINLESS STEEL

Stainless steel sheets are occasionally used for roofing if the importance of long life, because of inaccessibility or for other reasons, justifies their high cost. They are highly resistant to corrosion and do not require painting.

ALUMINUM

Aluminum sheets are available for laying on sloping roofs with standing or batten seams to provide for the relatively high coefficient of expansion. The battens may be of wood or specially designed extruded aluminum. Aluminum is highly resistant to corrosion and has a relatively long life as a roofing material. It does not require painting.

Aluminum sheets are finished in various colors. The colors are processed permanently by a baked enamel process, by an electrochemical process that is identified as a duranodic finish, and by fluorocarbon finish.

CORRUGATED STEEL

Corrugated steel sheets are widely used for roofing as well as siding of industrial buildings. Sheeting, which is a relatively thin material, forms the outside surface of exterior walls and roofs to exclude weather. In many respects, the siding and roofing materials are similar and often identical, or the same types of materials are used for both purposes. Siding seldom serves a structural purpose, although siding may be anchored and able to serve as a shear wall to resist horizontal forces.

The size of corrugated sheets is indicated by their corrugations, thickness, and sheet size. The nominal size of the corrugations of sheets is measured from crown to crown of the corrugation. This measurement is called the pitch, whereas the measurement of the height from crown to valley is the depth. Corrugation sizes range from 1¼ in. to 3 in. pitch and have depths from ¼ in. to 1 in. The most widely used sheet is the normal 2½ × ½ corrugation. The actual pitch of the sheet is 2⅔ in. The thickness of sheets is indicated by the gage, which ranges from 29 gage, the thinnest, to 12 gage, the thickest. The usual width of sheets is 26 in. for siding sheets and 27½ in. for roofing sheets. Lengths are up to 10 ft.

Steel sheet siding and roofing is further identified as uncoated, galvanized, painted, ceramic coated, asbestos protected, or black.

Corrugated sheets may be nailed to wood sheathing or may be supported directly by wood or steel purlins spaced 2 to 9 ft with spacing dependent upon the gage of the corrugated sheets, which depends upon the imposed loads. The sheets are lapped 1½ to 2 corrugations on the sides and 6 or 8 in. on the ends, depending on the slope of the roof. On slopes as flat as 2 in. vertical to 12 in. horizontal, standing seams should be used instead of side laps.

Where steel purlins are used, the corrugated steel may be fastened to nailing strips (Figure 8.7B), or the sheets may be held in place by straps passing around the purlins and riveted to the corrugated steel on each of the purlins (Figure 8.7C). Long malleable nails called clinch nails or J-bolts may be driven through the corrugated steel and clinched around the purlins (Figure 8.7D). The side laps are held together by galvanized-iron rivets spaced about a foot apart. All rivets and nails should be driven in the crown or peak of the corrugations to prevent leakage. The fasteners should be heavily zinc coated. Lead or neoprene washers are used under the heads of all fasteners.

Unfinished sheets must be protected against corrosion

A—COMMON TYPES OF CORRUGATED STEEL

B—NAILING STRIP   C—STRAP   D—CLINCH NAIL

METHODS OF FASTENING CORRUGATED STEEL TO PURLINS

FIGURE 8.7 Corrugated steel roofing.

by frequent painting. Some sheets are coated with colored plastics.

Because galvanized sheets are not subjected to severe bending when forming the corrugations, they may have a heavy coating of zinc. Because of their relatively low cost and fair length of life, they are extensively used on industrial buildings. They are not suitable where appearance is paramount.

Thicknesses range from 16 to 18 gage, painted or galvanized. Cleats fasten the sheets to wood or steel purlins without the use of rivets or nails. The use of this roofing is the same as that of ordinary corrugated steel.

8.4 Roofing Specialties

GUTTERS AND DOWNSPOUTS

The slopes required for various types of roofing are discussed in this chapter. The rainwater that falls on a roof may run off and drip from projecting eaves, but usually it is necessary or desirable to collect the water in *gutters* placed along the lower eaves. The water is carried in the gutters to vertical pipes called *downspouts,* conductors, or leaders. Flat roofs or other roofs not having projecting eaves are drained by downspouts or conductors placed at joints where the water is carried by the slight slope provided in the roof. The size of the gutters and conductors is determined by the contributing area and by the intensity of rainfall.

Several types of gutters for sloping roofs are shown in Figure 8.8. The hanging gutter is the simplest form, although not as attractive as the crown-mold gutter or the wood gutter, which fit into the design of the cornice. An O.G. gutter has an exposed side shaped like an Ogee curve.

Gutters made of metal, copper, aluminum, or galvanized steel are rust resistant. Redwood is used for constructing gutters which have a simple Ogee curve face.

FIGURE 8.8 Roof drainage.

The standing gutter is inconspicuous and easily constructed, but the concealed is quite expensive. Gutters are sometimes called eave troughs.

Conductors or downspouts should be provided with strainers at their upper ends (Figure 8.8) so that debris cannot clog them. Conductor or leader heads are installed as shown in Figure 8.8. It may be desirable to enclose conductors on the interior of a building rather than to expose them on the outside walls because the heat of the building keeps the pipes from freezing. They may be placed in chases on the inside of exterior walls, along columns, or in partitions. If placed on the outside of exterior walls, it is desirable to keep them off north walls if at all possible. Steam outlets are sometimes provided in exposed conductors so that, by discharging steam into them, they can be kept from freezing. Cleanouts should be provided so that clogged conductors and the connecting drains can be easily cleaned. Exposed conductors are commonly made of copper and galvanized steel. Copper, cast-iron, and steel pipe are used for concealed or interior conductors or where appearance is not a factor.

SCUPPERS

Frequently, flat roofs that have a parapet wall have a sheet metal spillway or channel which penetrates through the parapet wall. Known as *scuppers,* these devices are designed to conduct rainwater runoff from the roof through the parapet and discharge into a gutter, a leader, or directly in a free fall. Scuppers should be made of noncorrodible (cop-

per or galvanized) metal of leak-proof construction. Scuppers should be located at the low points of the roof slopes with bottom or invert of the scupper at the low point of the roof line. Usually they have a 1 in. vertical projection called a *gravel stop.* All roofs that are equipped with scuppers and roof drains should have overflow drains that are located remote from the scuppers and drains. Because scuppers and drains are subject to clogging by leaves and other debris, overflows should be located with their inverts slightly above the inverts of the scuppers to deter the clogging of the overflows.

8.5 Preformed Wall and Roof Panels

Ribbed or crimped sheets of steel, aluminum, and stainless steel are used for roofing and siding. There are various patterns or profiles of these sheets which suit jobsite functions and designs. There are those identified as 3-V-Crimp and 5-V-Crimp. The sheets, 24 in. wide, are made in various trapezoidal patterns. These are used for siding and for roofing on both sloping and flat roof decks.

Many of these materials have porcelain baked enamel coatings, vinyl plastic coatings, and asbestos protected finishes in various colors. These are frequently made into *sandwich panels* that have a rigid heat insulation core between the metal sheets.

These materials are attached to a rigid structural frame of wood or timber, concrete, or structural steel. They are

FIGURE 8.9 Corrugated and V-beam aluminum roofing.

usually attached with neoprene washered, sheet metal screws.

At the eaves and the sills of these structures where the metal corrugated and ribbed sheets terminate, a filler strip of neoprene material serves as a gasket or filler strip between the sheet metal and the supporting frame. These filler strips, which are identical in profile to the sheet metal, serve to close the gap from the weather.

ALUMINUM

Corrugated aluminum sheets are illustrated in Figure 8.9, and one form of ribbed sheet in (B). Sheets are 35 and 48 in. wide, 0.024 and 0.032 in. thick, and up to 12 ft long. Their use is similar to the use of corrugated steel. Aluminum should not be used in direct contact with steel, however, because of possible galvanic action. Therefore, asphaltum paint or felt strips should be placed between aluminum sheets and steel purlins; aluminum fasteners, such as nails, should be used.

Uncoated aluminum sheets are usually employed, but sheets coated with porcelain or baked enamel provide a variety of colors. In addition, several colors are obtained by anodizing, which consists of applying a natural oxide and inorganic dye to the surface by an electrochemical process.

STAINLESS STEEL

Corrugated stainless-steel sheets are specified for roofs subjected to the highly corrosive effects of some industrial atmospheres, where their superior resistance to corrosion justifies their higher initial cost.

ASBESTOS-PROTECTED METAL

Asbestos-protected metal consists of sheet steel covered first with a layer of asphalt, then a layer of asbestos, and finally a heavy waterproof coating. It may be obtained in flat sheets or corrugated sheets of the same size and shape as the plain corrugated sheets just described. The method of application is the same as for plain corrugated steel sheets, but it does not require painting for it is well protected from corrosion. It is a poor conductor of heat and therefore may be used in places where the uncoated sheets are not suitable.

Because of the relatively lightweight and fairly good insulating properties, corrugated sheets are extensively used on long-span roofs, such as those of hangars and field houses. They are fastened directly to the purlins. The development of plastic coatings has made it possible to obtain sheets of many colors.

ASBESTOS-CEMENT BOARD

Corrugated sheets made of asbestos fiber and portland cement under pressure are used in the same manner as corrugated steel. This material is a good nonconductor of heat, and no trouble is experienced with condensation. It is durable and does not require painting. Sheets are also made with plastic coatings in a great variety of colors.

WIRE GLASS

Corrugated wire-glass sheets similar to corrugated steel sheets can be used alone or in connection with corrugated roofing to assist in lighting the interior of buildings. These sheets are ¼ in. thick and have wire netting embedded in the glass to strengthen it and to hold it in place when a break occurs. The glass sheets are not laid with side laps, but the joint is covered with metal caps held in place by bolts passing between the sheets. The sheets are held to steel purlins by clips bolted to the metal cap covering the joint between sheets. Strips of asphaltic felt are placed over the purlins to cushion the glass.

Where a fire resistance rating is required, codes usually require wire-glass where glass is permitted.

ASBESTOS-CEMENT MATERIALS

Asbestos-cement shingles as described in Section 8.7 and plain or corrugated sheets are manufactured in many colors and used for siding materials. Sandwich panels with a core of heat-insulating material and outer surfaces of asbestos-cement boards are manufactured.

ASPHALT MATERIALS

Asphalt materials are used for siding in two forms. They may be either in the form of shingles as described in Section 8.7 or in rolls as described in Section 8.2. Roll sidings, applied over wood siding, are made to resemble brick or stone masonry.

PLASTICS

Transparent and translucent acrylic plastic sheets are used for roofing, siding, or skylight installations. These flat sheets, which resemble glass materials, are usually ⅛ or ¼ in. thick and are either clear, bronzed, or gray. Several colors are available and are used where effects are desirable. Thinner acrylic sheets that have a fiberglass reinforcement are manufactured in profiles, usually corrugated or flat, that are identical to many of the metal roofing and siding sheets. These plastic sheets are used in roofing and siding installations which require light as well as weather protection, such as in greenhouses and warehouses.

The fire resistivity or flamespread resistivity of most plastics is somewhat limited; therefore, most codes do not permit more than a specified area on a roof.

8.6 Cladding and Siding

Wood in the sizes required for wood frame and ordinary construction is used extensively in constructing walls and partitions. The most common application is the supporting wood stud. These studs are vertical members, usually 2 × 4 in. nominally, but occasionally 2 × 6 in. studs are fastened in various ways, as described in Chapter 7.

SHEATHING

To increase the rigidity, lateral stability, and heat-insulating properties of the exterior walls and to form the base for a finish, sheathing is nailed to the studs. This sheathing may be plywood ⅜, ½, or ⅝ in. thick, wood boards with a nominal thickness of 1 in., fiberboard ½ and ²⁵⁄₃₂ in. thick, or gypsum board at least ½ in. thick.

One of the most widely used forms of wood is plywood. Plywood is an assembly of thin wood sheets, forming a panel that is glued and pressed together. The grains of the plys run alternately at right angles, with an odd number of plys required for a panel. This arrangement equalizes surface tension between plys and deters warping, shrinking, and splitting.

The exposed panel surface is called the face veneer; the hidden side is the back veneer. The interior plys are referred to as the core or inner ply. Normally, the face and the back grain run parallel to the long side of the panel; otherwise, the panel is referred to as crossband plywood.

The quality, the use, and the structural properties of the plywood are determined by the species of wood, the type of glue, the veneer grades, the use grades, and the thickness of the panels. (Table 8.1)

Plywood is broadly classed according to application into exterior plywood and interior plywood. For exterior plywood, the better grades of veneer are used with a glue that has high resistance to water penetration and delamination. (Table 8.2)

For structural considerations, about 47 softwood species and 8 hardwood species are classified according to their stiffness into the groups listed in Table 8.1. These species are applied as face and back veneers.

The face and back of plywood sheets, which are called the veneers, are further classified according to the wood quality and grading characteristics. Splits, knots, and other imperfections according to frequency and severity determine veneer grade. Table 8.2 clarifies.

Interior type grade plywood is usually glued with protein type glue that is moisture resistant. Intermediate glue, used for interior grade, is more resistant to moisture, bacteria, and mold. Where interior plywood is expected to be subjected to excessive moisture, an interior plywood that is assembled with exterior glue may be used. Glues used for exterior grade must be capable of resisting water penetration and repeated wet and dry cycles.

Plywood standard widths are 3, 4, and 5 ft; and lengths starting at 5 ft increase by 1 ft increments up to 12 ft. By far, 4 ft by 8 ft is the most common size.

The nominal size of plywood is determined by the number of plys. The face or veneer plys are usually thinner than the interior or core plys. Plywood is usually manufactured in an odd number of plys: 3, 5, or 7. Plys are usually ⅛ in. thick, although they may be as thin as ¹⁄₁₆ in. The thinnest plywood is nominally ¼ in. and the thickest is nominally standard 1¼ in. Thickness of plywood is usually increased in ⅛ in. increments.

Veneers to be used on exterior plywood must be classed at least "C" by the criteria listed in Table 8.2.

PLYWOOD SHEATHING GRADES

Plywood is classified according to sheathing grades. Based upon the species group (Table 8.1) and the veneer classification, there are three sheathing grades. Listed in descending order:

Structural I is composed of woods only from Species Group 1. Structural II is made from the woods that are listed in Groups 1, 2, and 3. These two grades are used for structurally engineered applications, such as sheathing diaphragms, shear walls, gusset plates, box-beams, folded plates, stress skin panels, and other places requiring a quality structural plywood. Standard (C-D) sheathing grade is used for general sheathing applications. The C and D indicate the veneer quality. The D veneer grade indicates that such sheathing would be for interior application only. Should standard grade be used for exterior application, both faces must be C veneer grade, and the sheathing grade would be Standard (C-C). These three sheathing grades are stamped with a notation that indicates the recommended spacing of the supports for the sheathing. The plywood is stamped with a number that indicates the recommended span of the plywood with the face grain of the plywood perpendicular to the supports. The indication, for example, may be ³²⁄₂₄; this means that the recommended spacing for supports when the plywood is used for roof sheathing is 32 in. and that

Table 8.1 **Classification of Species**

Group 1	Group 2	Group 3	Group 4	Group 5
Birch	Cedar, Port Orford	Alder, Red	Aspen, Quaking	Fir, Balsam
Yellow	Douglas Fir 2[b]	Cedar	Birch, Paper	Poplar, Balsam
Sweet	Fir	Alaska	Cedar	
Douglas Fir 1[a]	California Red	Pine	Incense	
Larch, Western	Grand	Jack	Western Red	
Maple, Sugar	Noble	Lodgepole	Fir, Subalpine	
Pine, Southern	Pacific Silver	Ponderosa	Hemlock, Eastern	
Loblolly	White	Redwood	Pine	
Longleaf	Hemlock, Western	Spruce	Sugar	
Shortleaf	Lauan	Black	Eastern White	
Slash	Red	Red	Popular, Western[c]	
Tanoak	Tangile	White	Spruce, Engelmann	
	White			
	Almond			
	Bagtikan			
	Maple, Black			
	Meranti			
	Mengkulang			
	Pine			
	Pond			
	Red			
	Western White			
	Spruce, Sitka			
	Sweetgum			
	Tamarack			

[a] Douglas Fir 1 — Washington, Oregon, California, Idaho, Montana, Wyoming, British Columbia, Alberta.

[b] Douglas Fir 2 — Nevada, Utah, Colorado, Arizona, New Mexico.

[c] Also known as Black Cottonwood.

Courtesy American Plywood Association, Tacoma, Washington.

Table 8.2 **Veneer Grades Used in Plywood**

N	Special order "natural finish" veneer. Select all heartwood or all sapwood. Free of open defects. Allows some repairs.
A	Smooth and paintable. Neatly made repairs permissible. Also used for natural finish in less demanding applications.
B	Solid surface veneer. Circular repair plugs and tight knots permitted.
C	Knotholes to 1″. Occasional knotholes ½″ larger permitted providing total width of all knots and knotholes within a specified section does not exceed certain limits. Limited splits permitted. Minimum veneer permitted in Exterior-type plywood.
C	Improved C veneer with splits limited to ⅛″ in width and knotholes and borer holes limited to ¼″ by ½″.
D	Permits knots and knotholes to 2½″ in width and ½″ larger under certain specified limits. Limited splits permitted.

supports should not exceed 24 in. when the plywood is used as floor sheathing.

OTHER SHEATHING MATERIALS

Wood sheathing boards plain, matched, or shiplapped, with a nominal width of at least 6 in. or 8 in., should be nailed to each stud with not less than two 8d common nails. Sheathing may be installed horizontally or diagonally. Horizontal sheathing is more economical than diagonal sheathing but lacks rigidity; therefore, the frame must be diagonally braced at the corners by preferably continuous 1 × 4 in. pieces let-in to the studs in a continuous line. Ducts or window openings may complicate bracing.

Fiberboard is made of cane fiber, straw, or similar fibrous materials pressed into sheets 2 and 4 ft wide and usually 8 ft long. The 4 ft wide sheets, placed with the length parallel or perpendicular to the studs, are nailed with galvanized large-head roofing nails 1½ to 1¾ in. long. Field nailing (nails in the central surface) is spaced 6 in., and edge or boundary nailing is spaced 3 in. apart. The 2 ft wide sheets are edge matched and are placed with the length horizontal. A special board impregnated or coated with bituminous material is available, which should not be vapor-proofed.

EXTERIOR SURFACES

The exterior walls may be covered with horizontal or vertical siding and nailed to the studs with or without an intervening layer of sheathing. Noncorrosive nails, such as zinc-coated steelwire nails or aluminum nails, are used to avoid rust spots. A heavy, specially treated paper, such as kraft building paper, or sheathing paper placed under the siding, minimizes air infiltration and weatherproofs the sheathing.

Wood products that are called patterned, worked, or worked to pattern are machined to a configuration or a designed profile. This includes various shaped sidings and moldings.

There are two general types of wood siding: bevel siding, sometimes called weatherboarding, which is tapered and laid so that the thinner upper edge laps over the lower edge, and drop or novelty siding, which has a tongue-and-groove joint or a rebated or shiplap joint (Figure 7.3B to H) and is installed flush against the sheathing. Some forms of the latter siding give the same effect as bevel siding. Redwood bevel siding is graded Clear All Heart, VG (Vertical Grain), Clear All Heart, Clear VG, and Clear. Moldings are made from Clear grade, either heart or sapwood.

Siding materials worked to pattern are shiplapped, Centermatched (CM), Dressed and Matched (D & M), and Tongue and Groove (T & G).

Many other designs, such as rustic sidings and colonial sidings, are special forms of drop sidings. The common siding widths are 6 in. to 8 in. (nominal), and the thicknesses are 9/16 and ¾ in. (actual); but other widths and thicknesses are manufactured.

Siding is made of Douglas fir, white and yellow pine, spruce, hemlock, redwood, cedar, and cypress.

Figure 7.3 shows representative redwood patterned sidings.

Clapboards, once widely used as siding, are now seldom used.

The use of siding without sheathing, illustrated in Figure 8.10A is an inferior grade of construction.

WOOD SHINGLES

Wood *shingles,* applied to solid wood or plywood *(C),* may be placed with more shingle exposure than on roof applications. Shingles with a scored face, called *shakes,* although longer, are laid in the same manner with a considerable length to the weather. Asbestos-cement or asphalt shingles are also used in a similar manner.

FIGURE 8.10 Types of frame walls.

SIDING

Square-edge boards attached vertically to horizontal girts, with the joints covered with battens, may be used for siding (Figure 8.10J). Tongued-and-grooved boards, without battens, may be used in the same manner. In a better type of construction, vertical siding is nailed to 1 in. wood sheathing. Air infiltration is minimized by nailing kraft paper between the siding and the sheathing.

VENEER

Sheathed exterior stud walls may be veneered with brick *(H)* or with other masonry. The veneer resting directly on the masonry foundation should be tied to the frame at intervals not to exceed 16 in. vertically and horizontally.

The weakest point in veneer construction is the tie between the face brick and the backing. The usual method of typing is illustrated in Figure 8.11A. The masonry is brought up to the elevation at which a corrugated galvanized-steel tie, sharply bent into an L, is placed in the position shown in

FIGURE 8.11 Tying face brick to wood frame.

(1) and attached by a nail driven into a stud. The bend should be placed at the height of the joint, and the nail should be driven into the bend. This practice is not usually followed because it is possible for the veneer to pull away from the frame. This can be avoided by the procedure illustrated in *(B)*. The masonry is stopped one course below the elevation of the tie (1); the tie is placed flat along the stud and nailed to the stud (2); another course of brick is laid (3); and the tie is bent sharply over the head of the nail and into the joint (4). If this procedure is followed, the tie cannot yield. Minimum nail size required for anchors is an 8d common galvanized or aluminum nail driven slightly inclined into a stud.

A 1 in. air space between the brick and the sheathing, which is covered by a layer of nonvapor-resistant sheathing paper, increases the insulating properties of the wall. Openings should be carefully flashed to prevent moisture penetration behind the facing. The frame construction should not extend below the first-floor joints. By using the balloon frame, shrinkage in the timber will be minimized, especially where the window and door frames penetrate the masonry veneer.

Veneered construction resists exposure to exterior fires far better than frame construction. Its resistance to interior fires is about the same as that of frame construction; but if not properly firestopped, it may be difficult to extinguish fires behind the brick facing.

8.7 Shingles and Tiles

The best wood shingles are sawn or hand-split cypress, red cedar, or redwood. Standard lengths are 16, 18, 24, and 32 in. Shingles are tapered in thickness; the thickness at the butt or thick end is expressed in terms of the number of shingles required to produce a total butt thickness of a designated number of inches. Sixteen inch shingles are usually 5 butts in 2 in.; 18 in. shingles, 5 butts in 2¼ in.; and 24 in. shingles, 4 butts in 2 in.; they are called 5/2, 5/2¼, and 4/2, respectively. Although regular shingles are variable in width, they must be uniform in their measurements; the maximum width permitted by grading rules is 14 in., and the minimum width 3 in. for 16 and 18 in. shingles, and 4 in. for 24 in. shingles. Shingles are termed random shingles if the widths in a bundle vary or dimension shingles if their widths are cut to specified uniform widths.

Not more than one-third of the length of a shingle should be exposed to the weather on roofs, nor more than one-half on side walls. Heartwood is more decay-resistant than sapwood; edge-grain shingles are less likely to warp or cup than flat-grain shingles. Thick shingles warp less than thin shingles, and narrow shingles warp less than wide shingles. Shingles should be clear, entirely heartwood, and entirely edgegrain. It is not economical to use any but the best grade of shingle except for temporary construction.

Thick heavy shingles are called shakes. They are usually hand-split, and sometimes they are then sawn. They are called resawn shakes. In their manufacture, a mallet is used to strike a sharp bladed steel cleaving tool called a froe. This tool is placed on the end of a block of wood parallel to the grain of the wood. Hand-split shingles, used when their rough-textured surface is desired, are nonuniform and considerably thicker than sawn shingles.

REDWOOD SHINGLES AND SHAKES
Redwood shingle sizes are indicated as 18 in. 5/2¼ in. random shingles; 16 in. 5/2 in. random shingles; 16 in. × 4 in. — 5/2 Dimension Shingles; 16 in. × 5 in. — 5/2 Dimension Shingles; and 16 in. × 6 in. — 5/2 Dimension Shingles. These shingles are graded as No. 1 Grade, No. 2 Vertical (VG) Grade, and No. 2 Mixed Grain (MG). Redwood shingles are not less than 5 butts to 2 inches.

There are five redwood shake types; all are made from clear heartwood. They are: Handsplit-and-Resawn Shakes that have split faces and sawn backs, Taper-Sawn Redwood Shakes that have split or rough edges, Machine-Grooved Shakes which are the same as Handsplit-and-Resawn except that they may contain flat grain material, and Tapersplit Shakes and Straight-Split Shakes, which are handmade. Redwood shakes are not less than ¾ in. thickness or less than 4 in. wide. Lengths are 18, 24, and 32 in.

WESTERN RED CEDAR SHINGLES AND SHAKES

These widely used shingles are made in five distinct grades. The finest grade is No. 1 (Blue Label), which is made of clear, edge-grain, all heartwood. Grade No. 2 (Red Label), a flat grain, contains some sapwood. Where economy is a factor, No. 3 (Black Label) is used. Grade No. 4 (Under Coursing) is used as the under course in side wall applications. Another grade, No. 1 or No. 2 Rebutted-Rejointed, consists of material that conforms to the above grades, although they are machined to assure parallel sides and right angle butts.

Western red cedar shakes are made in three grades: No. 1 Handsplit and Resawn, No. 1 Tapersplit, and No. 1 Straight Split. Cedar shakes are 18 and 24 in. in length. The thickness of the butts is up to 1¼ in.

Machine grooved sidewall shakes are made in No. 1 grade (blue label). These shakes have a combed or striated face and parallel edges. They are made in the standard shingle sizes.

FANCY-BUTT SHINGLES

A type of shingle that has specially shaped butts is called a fancy-butt shingle. These specially designed shingles (Figure 8.12) are used where decorative effects are desired. Their use is especially effective where used in limited applications on side walls as accents to contrast with the standard butt shingles. These shingles, cut to order, are made in lengths of 16 and 18 in. and 5 in. wide. They are usually laid with a 6 in. weather exposure.

SHINGLE ROOF APPLICATIONS

Wood shingles are nailed to wood sheathing or slats; each row of shingles is lapped over the row below to give an exposed surface varying from 4 to 7 in; the smaller exposure to the weather is for short shingles on flat slopes, and the greater exposure is for long shingles on steep slopes. Shingles are laid in courses.

Shingles should be fastened with two aluminum or two steel hot-dipped, zinc-coated, steel-wire nails, 3d or 4d, depending on the thickness of the shingle.

The sheathing may be square edged (Figure 8.13A), matched (B), or shiplapped (C). The use of wood slats, or strips, illustrated in (D), is sometimes called open or spaced sheathing. If spaced sheathing is used, the open space should not exceed the width of the sheathing board or exceed 4 in. The portion of the shingle that is exposed is referred to as the weather exposure. Weather exposure varies from 3¾ in. to 13 in., depending upon the type of shake, the location (wall or roof), and the length of the shake.

When the sheathing is not spaced, or when matched sheathing or shiplap is used, a layer of waterproof paper is sometimes "shingled" between the sheathing and the shingles. This paper makes the roof more air- and watertight; but where there is heavy rainfall, it may reduce the life of the shingles by making it difficult for them to dry out from the underside, thus causing cupping and rotting.

Shingle roofs with a slope less than 4 in. vertical to 12 in. horizontal are not recommended; a 6 in. to 12 in. minimum slope is preferred. The chief use of wood shingles is in residence construction.

An ever-present danger attendant to wood shingles or shakes may be their propensity of fire; however, this may be alleviated by treating shingles with a proprietary fire-retardant chemical.

WALL APPLICATIONS

Shingles are frequently applied to walls as well as roofs. Wall application is referred to as sidewall application. They are usually applied with greater weather exposure than in roofing. Sidewall shingles are made by two methods of application, single course and double course. Single coursing is similar to roof applications, whereas double coursing has an underlayment of shingles. This underlayment, made of inferior grade under course shingles, permits an increased weather exposure and dramatic deep shadow lines at the course lines.

Sidewall applications are frequently accented with fancy-butt shingles mentioned above.

ASPHALT SHINGLES

Asphalt shingles, also called composition shingles, are made of heavy felt composed of rag, paper, or wool fiber, saturated and coated with asphalt. Crushed slate or other aggregate embedded in the top surface coat forms a weather-resistant and colored exposed surface. They are made in various shapes, sizes, and colors. A common shape is a strip 12 × 36 in. with the exposed surface cut to resemble three 9 × 12 in. shingles. These are called *strip shingles.* To resist the tendency of winds to raise the exposed butts, some of the types are tapered, provided with mechanical fasteners or tabs, and made in interlocking shapes. Some are provided with a bank or area of self-sealing adhesive along the underside of the lower edge of the butts.

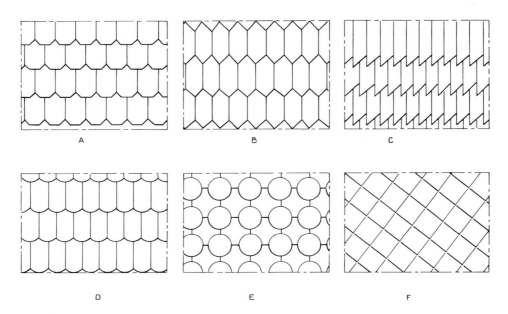

FIGURE 8.12 Fancy-butt shingles.

Asphalt shingles are laid over a layer of roofer's felt and nailed to solid wood sheathing, as described in the discussion on wood shingles, with hot-dipped, zinc-coated steel nails. The exposure varies with the dimensions of the shingles and will usually give a lap of 2 or 3 in. over the upper end of the second shingle underneath. This is called the head lap. The minimum slope that should be used depends upon the characteristics of the shingle; usually the minimum is 4 in. per foot.

FIGURE 8.13 Types of sheathing for wood shingles.

ASBESTOS-CEMENT SHINGLES

Asbestos-cement shingles, composed of asbestos fiber and portland cement under pressure, are made in various shapes, sizes, and colors in a thickness of about 5/32 in. and ¼ in. They are laid on a wood deck over a layer of roofer's felt, with a head lap of 2 in., using copper or hot-dipped, zinc-coated steel nails, on a minimum slope of 4 in. per ft.

Asbestos shingles are much stiffer, more fire-resistive, and more durable than asphalt shingles. They are cheaper than clay tile and slate and more expensive than asphalt shingles.

CLAY TILE

Clay tile, made by shaping moist clay in molds and burning in kilns, are made in several patterns, colors, and textures. The most common shapes are French, Spanish, English, Greek, Roman, and mission or pan tile (Figure 8.14A-D). Shingle tile are rectangular slabs about ½ in. thick in widths up to 9 in. and lengths up to 14 in. Tile of constant width are always used. They are laid in rows to break joints with the length exposed not more than one-half the length of the tile, minus 2 in. The rows may be regular or irregular.

FIGURE 8.14 Clay roofing tile.

All forms of tile may be nailed to wood sheathing. Clay tiles may be nailed, through prepared holes, to wood nailers or solid blocking. They are laid over a layer of asphalt-saturated rag felt, gypsum, or nailable concrete. Nails should preferably be copper, but hot-dipped galvanized steel nails are often used. Some forms of tile may be wired to closely spaced steelangle subpurlins or special anchorage devices. They may be wired (through prepared holes) with annealed wire that is attached to a strip of noncorrodible metal. The metal strips, which have perforations or hooks to receive the wire, saddle across the ridge and run down the slope of the roof. These strips are nailed securely to the roof.

Special tile are made for the ridges and hips. Preferably, valleys should be made with sheet copper, but in most localities galvanized steel is satisfactory. One or two layers of roofers' felt placed under the tile serves as a cushion, keeps air currents from lifting the tile from beneath, and sheds water while damages or defects are remedied. This is an underlayment.

The usual forms of clay roofing tile should not be used on slopes less than 4 in. vertical to 12 in. horizontal. A special form of tiles called pavers' or promenade tile, laid on a waterproof base, forms the floor of a roof an inch thick. A waterproof base is constructed in the same manner as a built-up roof; but the surfacing is omitted and the tile are bedded in a 1 in. layer of cement mortar.

Clay tile are fireproof, durable, and attractive, but they are expensive and require strong supporting roof members.

SLATE

Slate roofing is quarried and split from the natural rock by shaping it into rectangular pieces of the desired dimensions. Roofing slate should be hard, tough, and have a bright metallic luster when freshly split. It should ring clear when supported horizontally on three fingers and snapped with the thumb of the other hand.

Slate has a great variety of colors such as gray, green, dark blue, purple, and red. Furnished in almost any size from 6 to 14 in. wide, 12 to 24 in. long, and ⅛ to 2 in. thick, the most common sizes are 12 × 16 in. and 14 × 20 in., 3/16 and ¼ in. thick.

Roofs may be made of pieces of uniform size, thickness, and color, but random sizes, thicknesses, and colors are also used.

Slate may be laid like shingles, each course lapping 3 in. over the second course below, or they may be laid at random as long as care is taken to give sufficient sidelap. They are nailed through prepunched holes to matched wood sheathing, nailable concrete, or gypsum slabs. A layer of underlayment of number 30 asphalt-saturated felt is used between the slate and the deck. The nails should preferably be copper or yellow-metal slater's nails, although redipped galvanized nails and copper-coated nails are often used.

Slate is joined at the ridges by a saddle ridge or a combed

ridge. Hips of slate roofs are built by one of four methods: a saddle hip, Boston hip, mitered hip, or fantail hip.

In dryer regions, slate may be nailed to properly spaced wood strips without an underlay of felt. They are sometimes supported directly on steel subpurlins to which they are wired. Slate roofs should not be used on slopes less than 4 in. vertical to 12 in. horizontal.

Slate flagging is used for roof gardens by omitting the surfacing on the ordinary built-up roof and by bedding the slate in a 1 in. layer of cement mortar.

Slate roofs are fireproof, durable, and attractive. All the slate used in the United States is quarried in the eastern states, mostly in Vermont and Pennsylvania. Its cost increases in relation to the distance from these sources. The first or initial costs of slate roofs are relatively high. The first cost may eventually be offset by slate's exceptional durability—100 years of more.

CEMENT TILE

Roofing tile made of portland cement and a fine aggregate are known as concrete tile or cement tile. These tile are flat and resemble various clay tiles, such as English tile or French tile. These tile are manufactured in several colors and in various sizes that compare to the clay tiles that they imitate. They are supplied with various trim pieces that are designed for rake closure, ridges, and hips. Their installation is similar to that of the clay tiles that they resemble. Their physical properties include a high resistance to fire and deterioration by weather.

MISCELLANEOUS SHINGLE MATERIALS

Several other materials have been processed into roofing and siding materials. Porcelainized aluminum and mineral based materials have been shaped into shingle material. These materials are usually shaped or pressed into forms that are intended to resemble other materials, such as wood shakes or shingles.

8.8 Roofing Accessories

Incidental parts built onto the roof are smoke or heat vents, scuttles, and skylights.

Smoke and heat vents are required on disparate types of buildings, such as theaters and office buildings. Smoke vents must be located where smoke would likely accumulate, for instance, at high points of the roof. Usually smoke vents have mechanically operating doors that open automatically when a spring device is actuated. Normally the spring is held by a fusible link that separates when heated, and the doors fly open.

In a fire, these vents allow excessive heat and smoke to

escape in order that smoke damage may be minimized and the chance of smoke inhalation by personnel is diminished.

Smoke vents are usually made of sheet metal, either steel or aluminum. Their releasing devices must remain rust free and capable of operating hatch doors that may be bound by dirt, snow, or ice. Moreover, they must be resistant to vandalism and burglary.

Scuttles are horizontal doors or hatches that provide access through the roof by penetrating the roof itself. Like smoke vents, they should be raised above the roof surface by a curb and be watertight. Generally they are made of sheet metal or wood and need only be large enough to accommodate people or equipment.

Skylights permit direct natural light to reach the interiors of buildings and provide a concept of space to architectural design. Although codes may impose limits, the sizes of skylights range from 2 ft by 2 ft to expanses that include solariums, covered walkways, and spacious glass-roofed lobbies of hotels and megastructures. The designs of skylights may represent an integral part of a structure or be a simple unit which is square, rectangular, circular, domed, pyramidal, vaulted, hemispherical, or bulbous.

Skylights are framed in stainless steel, wood, concrete or in aluminum of various finishes. The glazing of skylights may be of laminated safety glass, tempered glass, wire glass, fiberglass, reinforced plastic, or acrylic plastic. Glazing materials are usually clear and transparent; however, translucent, patterned, and low-intensity materials may be used.

The accumulation of condensate on the underside of skylights may be a problem that may be solved by installing condensate gutters and weep holes or double glazing.

8.9 Flashing

Flashing and calking (or caulking) are important factors in reducing rainwater penetration and damage of walls. Water penetrating the outer face of finish layers may continue until it finds an outlet over a door, window, or other opening. This condition is critical over oriel or bay windows or where an exterior wall becomes an interior wall because of an extension of the building in the lower stories. Subsidence or alleviating of water penetration by proper material selection and good workmanship has been mentioned previously. Flashing and calking are used as additional precautions at critical locations, such as the junction of dissimilar roofing materials or under the copings on parapet walls and chimney tops, under window sills, and over and under projecting belt courses.

The function of calking is to exclude water, while flashing may have the additional function of conducting water outward to lessen its harmful effects. This is particularly true over wall openings. Typical uses of flashing and calking are illustrated in Figure 8.8.

Flashing materials are sheets of copper, lead, zinc, aluminum, galvanized steel and terne plate; bituminous roofing paper; plastics; and copper-backed paper. While appropriate material selected will reflect quality of construction, it is much more expensive to replace defective flashing than to install high-quality flashing initially.

Where a roof surface meets a vertical wall, it is necessary to provide flashing to make the joint watertight. Made L-shaped to fit over the joint (Figure 8.8), one leg of the flashing runs up the wall and the other along the roof. Rainwater driven against the vertical face of the wall is kept from running down behind the vertical leg of the flashing by counterflashing or cap flashing, also made in the form of an L. In counterflashing, the L is inverted; the horizontal leg is built or fitted into a joint of reglet (Figure 8.8), and the vertical leg fits over the flashing. A reglet is a continuous formed joint in masonry or concrete. Reglets may be formed of sheet metal and filled with caulking. Counterflashing inserted in the reglet is secured by friction. Counterflashing allows expansion of the metal or differential settlement and movement of the structure without rupturing the flashing from its anchorage. Built-up roofing is often flashed, as shown in Figure 8.8, without the use of sheet metal. To avoid the sharp corner between the wall and the roof, cant strips or boards or concrete cants are often used. Flashing block, as shown in the figure, are frequently used. The acute angle between the back side chimney or other projection and a sloping roof is protected with a saddle or cricket, which is two sloping surfaces meeting in a horizontal ridge perpendicular to the chimney. The valleys on sloping roofs are made watertight by sheet-metal strips, preferably of copper, bent to fit the two intersecting roof surfaces. Roll roofing is used for valley flashing on asphalt-shingle roofs, but it is short-lived.

8.10 Sealants and Gaskets

Sealants and *gaskets* are elastomeric polymers used for weatherproofing joints in building construction. Sealants, of paste consistency, are applied by pressure and cure to a rubberlike solid. Gaskets are formed elastomeric prismatic strips that are placed as seals in construction joints.

The most widely used sealants are polysulfides, polyurethane, and silicone. There are two classes of sealants with respect to their application: self-leveling for horizontal surfaces, and nonsag for vertical surfaces. The latter may be used for either application. Some polysulfides are one-part types, which can be applied directly from a cartridge or a bulk container. The two-component systems, which require the addition of an accelerator, have greater bonding capability.

Desirable properties expected of sealants are flexibility, weather resistance, tenacious adhesion to all construction,

FIGURE 8.15 Gaskets.

cohesion to prevent cracking, and the elastomeric ability to expand or contract.

Sealants are used extensively for sealing joints that must be leakproof, waterproof, and weatherproof while remaining expansible. The use of sealants in curtain wall joints and as a glazing compound is extensive. These polysulfides have also been used to seal swimming pools.

Sealants are more expensive than caulking and should be used only where their superior qualities are required and where caulking will not suffice. For optimum results surfaces to which sealants are to be applied should be clean, free from loose material, and applied when temperatures are moderate.

Gaskets are usually made of an elastomeric such as neoprene or butadine rubber. The profiles or cross sections of the gaskets range from single rectangles such as tapes to complex designs intended for joints in concrete, masonry or wood construction (Figure 8.15). Gaskets serve as fillers in thermal or seismic joints in masonry and concrete construction.

Gaskets that have a "dumbbell" profile or variations of this design are used extensively between joints in cast-in-place concrete construction, and are known as waterstops.

8.11 Building Insulation

There has been an increasing interest in making the air in occupied buildings more comfortable and healthful and in conditioning the air in manufacturing buildings to suit the manufacturing processes. There is also interest in reducing the operating costs and fuel consumption involved in such improvements. Two important factors in bringing about these conditions are the temperature and the humidity of the air in the buildings. Both factors are closely associated with the construction of the building. In winter, the problem is largely one of providing additional heat and additional humidity, whereas in summer these may be present in ex-

cessive amounts. There is a considerable operating cost involved in increasing or decreasing the temperature of the inside air. Usually the savings in this cost which can be brought about by proper design and construction, including insulation, will more than justify the additional expenditure involved. The direct cost of increasing humidity is not large, but humidities of 35 to 40% and more, which are often maintained, may cause condensation in the outside walls and the roof or ceiling of the top story, which can only be avoided by appropriate types of construction. Decreasing the humidity, as may be desirable in many parts of the country during the summer, is not as easily and cheaply accomplished as increasing the humidity, but this does not require any special consideration as far as the construction of buildings is concerned, except where unusually low humidities or temperature are employed.

HEAT TRANSMISSION

Heat is transmitted from one side of the walls and roof of a building to the other in the following ways.

1. By air infiltration, or leakage through cracks and other open spaces. The volume of air entering a building is offset by an equal volume leaving the building. Since the temperature of the two volumes would normally be different, there is a transfer of heat with the air change.

2. By transmission through the walls, windows, doors, and roofs.

Air infiltration is minimized by good construction, which reduces or eliminates cracks and other openings through the walls, around cornices, along the sills on foundation walls, and through the roof construction; by the proper design, construction, and installation of doors and window sash and their frames; by calking between frames and surrounding masonry; by covering the sheathing of frame walls with a good quality of building paper or polyethylene plastic with tight joints; and by plaster surfaces on masonry walls. Air infiltration through an unplastered brick wall is considerably lessened through the same wall after plastering. The effectiveness of storm sash depends upon how tightly they fit and is relatively high on windows that are not weather-stripped.

Because of the "chimney effect" in tall buildings, the tendency for air infiltration at the lower stories, and for a corresponding outward movement in the upper stories, is large enough to require special provisions to be made to reduce this effect. These provisions consist of closing, with doors or by other means, all openings from floor to floor, such as stairways and elevator shafts. This is also a necessary fire-protection measure. Heat losses by air infiltration increase rapidly as the wind velocity increases and may exceed the losses due to the difference in temperatures inside and outside a building.

Heat is transmitted through walls and roofs in three ways.

1. By conduction from molecule to molecule of the wall material and, to a certain extent, from molecule to molecule of the air in open spaces in the wall.

2. By convection by air currents, which circulate in open spaces within the wall or roof construction and which absorb heat as they pass upward over a warm boundary surface of the air space and release heat as they pass downward over a cold boundary surface of that space. The circulation is produced by the decrease in density of air, which accompanies increase in temperature.

3. By radiation, the process by which energy, called radiant energy, is transmitted from one body or surface to another body or surface by electromagnetic waves.

Heat passes through a solid wall entirely by conduction; but if there is an air space inside the wall, it will cross this space by radiation, convection, and conduction. The resistance that a given homogeneous material offers to the passage of heat varies directly with its thickness and inversely with its density, and decreases with increases in the moisture content of the material. The resistance of an air space, such as a stud space in a frame wall or a cell space in a hollow tile wall, to the passage of heat by radiation is independent of the width of the space but is greatly affected by the nature of the boundary surfaces, being low for the surfaces of ordinary building materials but very high for bright metallic surfaces. The resistance by an air space to the passage of heat by convection is practically independent of the width of this space if it exceeds ¾ in., but it decreases very rapidly as the width decreases below ¾ in. More than half of the heat transmitted through an air space over ¾ in. wide bounded by ordinary materials is radiant heat.

SOLAR HEAT

Solar heat, or radiant heat from the sun's rays, which is transmitted through windows, is an important factor in heating the air in a building. During the winter months, this effect is usually desirable, but in many parts of the country it increases the inside temperatures above the comfort range unless excess heat is removed by air conditioning, which significantly increases the initial and operating costs of a building.

There are several ways for reducing the solar heat gain through windows. These include shading windows from the sun's rays, double glazing, and the use of heat-absorbing glass as described in Section 9.9.

Canvas awnings, which were extensively used in the past, and the more modern types made of aluminum or plastics are very effective, especially if they are so designed as to permit the heated air beneath them to escape.

A detailed discussion of window shading is included in a paper by Donald J. Vild, which has been helpful in preparing

Table 8.3 Relative Value of Solar Heat Transfer for Various Fenestrations[a]

Type of Fenestration	Relative Value
Regular window glass	100[b]
Heat-absorbing glass	69
Double glass — heat-absorbing glass outside, regular plate inside	52
Regular window glass, inside venetian blinds	58
Glass block panel	50

[a] Arranged from paper by Donald J. Vild.

[b] 100 equals heat transfer of 183 Btu per sq. ft per hour. Regular window glass considered as 100.

Conditions: typical clear afternoon in midsummer at 40° north latitude with fenestration facing southwest.

Table 8.4 Relative Merits of Heat Gain Reducing Methods through Glass[a]

Type of Area	Sunlit	Not Sunlit
Single glass	100	33
Double glazing	73	22
Heat-absorbing glass	68	24
Double-glazed heat-absorbing glass	51	17
Sunscreen on single glazing	35	17
Sunscreen on double glazing	26	12
Sunscreen on heat-absorbing glass	24	12
Sunscreen on double-glazed heat absorbing glass	18	9

[a] As given by G. R. Munge.

these comments and Table 8.3. The table gives the relative values of solar heat transfer for various fenestrations under the conditions stipulated in the table.

The relative values in Table 8.4 will be of interest in comparing results achieved by several methods for reducing heat gain from all sources, including solar heat, through various types of glazing with the heat gain through ordinary glass which is considered 100 for comparative purposes. Values for sunlit surfaces, with and without sunscreens, are given in the first column, and those for surfaces that are not sunlit are given in the second column. It will be noted that the values for sunlit areas with sunscreens are approximately the same as those for corresponding areas that are not sunlit. Some of the areas listed as sunlit would be sunlit if sunscreens were not provided.

Heat loss by residential buildings during the winter months is often reduced by replacing window screens with storm sash. Heat gain by such buildings during the summer is sometimes reduced by attic fans, which ventilate the attic and replace air heated by solar heat transmitted through the roof with cooler outdoor air. Hot attic air, of course, transmits heat to the rooms beneath. An insect screen is available with horizontal wires replaced by thin flat metal strips and vertical wires about ½ in. apart to form venetian blinds with miniature slats. Because they are located outside, they act as sunscreens and are quite effective for windows with south exposure but less effective for those with east or west exposure.

RADIANT HEAT AND COMFORT

Air temperatures which are considered desirable for comfort depend upon various factors, but normally they are within the range of 70° to 75°F. The effects of the temperatures of the surfaces of the walls, ceilings, and floors which surround a person are not, however, always understood. If any such surfaces are cooler than the desired air temperatures, a person will feel too cool even though the temperature of the intervening air is within the desirable range. Conversely, if any of the surrounding surfaces are warmer than the desirable range in air temperature, the person will feel uncomfortably warm. These conditions are due to the loss or gain of heat by the body caused by the radiation of heat between the body and the surrounding surfaces. Therefore, it is important that the temperatures of these surfaces be maintained to a reasonable extent within the comfort range. This factor is significant in selecting insulation.

CONDENSATION

The amount of water vapor that air can contain increases with the temperature of the air. The ratio of the amount actually present to the maximum amount that can be present at that temperature is called the *relative humidity* or simply the humidity. It is expressed in percentage. As the temperature of air containing a given amount of water vapor falls, the relative humidity rises until the saturation or *dewpoint temperature* is reached and some of the vapor is condensed. This *condensation* may occur on cold interior wall surfaces and be apparent; but the water vapor tends to pass through the walls and, since the interior of a wall becomes progressively colder toward the outside, a temperature may be reached at which the vapor will condense within the wall. The conditions favorable for this action are an inside humidity of 35 or 40% and higher and a long-continued cold outside temperature. The amount of water that condenses gradually increases and, if the temperature where the water collects is below freezing, ice will form. If porous insulation is present, it will accumulate water as ice and largely lose its effectiveness. The ice will melt when the outside temperature rises sufficiently. Condensation may also occur in insulation over the ceiling of the top story or on the underside of the roof sheathing, particularly around the points of protruding roofing nails. The condensation that forms in the walls, ceiling, or roof construction may come through the finished wall and ceiling surfaces and spoil the decorations, disintegrate the plaster, cause any wood

present to swell with resultant cracking, cause paint on exterior wood surfaces to peel off, and damage a building in other ways. These effects are sometimes wrongly attributed to leaking walls and roofs. In wood construction, the wall may be so tightly sealed with sheathing paper that evaporation occurs very slowly, causing the studs and sheathing to decay. Insulation may make conditions worse by causing the outer portions of a wall to be colder, and porous insulation accumulates the water. Some of the higher grades of sheathing paper used on stud walls retard or prevent the escape of water vapor from the walls and increase the condensation effect.

The following procedures prevent condensation of this type; avoiding high humidities during long periods of low temperatures; placing a vapor barrier or seal under the lath in stud walls and on the bottoms of ceiling joists of the top story and using a sheathing paper which is sufficiently airtight but not an effective vapor barrier; placing a vapor seal under the lath on furred masonry walls; placing a vapor seal under the insulation on wood or concrete roof decks, if insulation is used; and ventilating attic spaces. A glossy-surfaced tar paper or a polyethylene film are good vapor seals for use under lath. They must be lapped and tightly fastened at all joints. The longitudinal joints should be over the studs or joists, and the paper should extend from the floor to the ceiling without end joints in the paper. Slaters' felt is considered a satisfactory sheathing paper. On roof decks, a 2-ply seal should be made of saturated felt applied by mopping with hot asphalt or roofing pitch. The vapor seal should always be on the inside.

Some of the rigid insulating materials are coated with bituminous material or encased in bituminous paper to exclude water vapor; many insulating quilts have so-called vaporproof paper coverings; and mineral wool batts are available with vaporproof backs which are placed next to the lath in wood stud walls. These are not regarded as high types of vapor barriers.

TYPES OF INSULATING MATERIAL

Insulating materials may be divided into two general classes according to the way they function. In the first group may be included all the low-density, porous, or fibrous materials with low conductivity or high resistance to the passage of heat, whose effectiveness is due to the minute air spaces of which they are largely composed. This group includes three general types of insulating materials as follows: rigid or board and slab insulation, flexible or quilt, blanket, and batt insulation, and fill insulation. As stated in *Fundamentals of Building Insulation,*

Still air is the best heat insulator we know. But air is seldom still. The slightest change in temperature will make air expand or contract; the warmer air becomes lighter and floats above the cooler, heavier air. So the job is to keep still air still.

Insulating materials confine the air that they contain, and upon which their effectiveness depends, in cells, voids, or other spaces, some or all of whose dimensions are so small that there can be little if any movement of the air within their boundaries.

The second group of insulation materials includes those of the reflective type which is used to form boundaries of air spaces and whose insulating value lies in their effectiveness in reflecting radiant energy.

The rigid, flexible, and fill insulators consist of wood, cane, and other vegetable fibers, mineral wool, cork, hair felt, expanded mica, foamed glass or plastics, or light granular materials. They owe their insulating properties to the minute air spaces they contain. The insulating value per inch of thickness is about the same for all these materials. It is approximately equal to the insulating value of 3 in. of wood, 17 in. of glass, 31 in. of brickwork, and 40 in. of concrete.

Reflective insulation consists of some form of sheet metal, metal foil, or a metallic coating which is made very thin because its effectiveness is practically independent of the thickness. The most effective insulation of this type will reflect about 95% of the radiant energy that strikes its surface. Since a large proportion of the heat which passes through an insulated wall is produced by radiant energy, reflective insulation can be very effective.

Rigid Insulation

Fiberboards are used for insulating purposes. To be effective, the fibers are not highly compressed as in the hardboards. Moisture and water vapor are partially excluded from some of the fiberboards if the boards are coated with asphalt or encased in a bituminous waterproof paper. For increased insulating value, fiberboards and gypsum boards are available with aluminum foil coating on one surface to serve as reflective insulation. Another form of rigid insulation is corkboard made of pressed cork in thicknesses up to 6 in. Some forms of rigid insulation serve the dual purposes of insulation and sheathing or insulation and lath. The common thickness for sheathing is 1 in., but any desired thickness may be obtained.

Flexible Insulation

This type of insulation may be in the form of quilts or blankets and batts, often spelled bats. The quilts and blanket consist of a fibrous material such as treated wood fiber, hair felt, flax fiber, eel grass, or shredded paper stitched between sheets of waterproof paper to form a flexible material available in various thicknesses up to 1 in.

Another form of flexible insulation is made from mineral or rock wool, formed by blowing molten rock into fibrous form by steam under pressure. This producds a fluffy, noncombustible product weighing about 6 lbs per cu ft. It is usually furnished in batts 15 × 24 or 48 in., to fit between studs and ceiling joists spaced 16 in. center to center. The thickness is ordinarily about 4 in. to fill the space completely between 2 × 4 in. studs, but batts 2 in. thick are available. Batts are furnished plain or with a waterproof paper cemented to the back and projecting about 2 in. on each side to provide nailing flanges, which lap over the studs or joists to which they are nailed or stapled and form a seal. This paper is supposed to serve as a vapor barrier or seal, but if it is to be effective the end joints must be tight. It is better practice to provide an additional vapor barrier, as previously described, over the batt insulation after it is in place, and under the lath. Mineral-wool insulation is also furnished in roll form and as fill insulation, as described in the next paragraph. Glass wool is a fibrous glass insulating material similar to mineral wool. It is available in batt, blanket, and fill form.

Fill Insulation

This material consists of granulated rock wool in the forms of nodules or pellets, granulated cork, expanded mica, and other material which is blown through large tubes or dumped into open spaces in the walls and ceilings of buildings, such as the stud space in frame walls and the ceiling joist space. Fibrous mineral wool and glass wool are also furnished in loose form for packing by hand into open spaces.

Reflective Insulation

Reflective insulation is placed in air spaces and functions by reflecting a large percentage of the radiant energy which strikes it. The materials used for reflective insulation are very thin tin plate, copper or aluminum sheets, or aluminum foil on the surface of rigid fiberboards or gypsum boards. A common form of reflective insulation is aluminum foil mounted on asphalt-impregnated kraft paper, the strength of which may be increased by the use of jute netting. This material is used for lining air spaces or for curtains to increase the number of air spaces in a given overall space. To be effective, the edges of such curtains must be tightly sealed.

Methods of Installation

Rigid insulation can be used as sheathing on the outside of wood studs (Figure 8.16A); as building board without plaster on the inside of wood studs (B); and on the lower side of ceiling joists or rafters. It may also be used as lath to receive plaster on the inside of wood studs (C) and on the lower side of ceiling joists. When used with masonry walls, it is nailed to furring strips (D). It may be exposed; it may serve as a plaster base (E); or it may be covered with lath and plaster,

FIGURE 8.16 Installation of insulation.

with furring strips between the insulation and the lath and on top of the other furring strips or at right angles to them *(F)*.

Rigid insulation may be used on wood and concrete roof decks under built-up roofing *(G)* and *(H)*. Wood decks are first covered with one or two layers of rosin-sized building paper, lapped at the joints and securely tacked down. This paper keeps asphalt from running through the cracks between the roofing boards. Over this paper or directly on concrete roofs, a layer of asphalt-saturated felt is mopped with hot asphalt or roofing pitch. This layer serves as a temporary roofing. If there is to be considerable vapor in the room below, another layer of asphalt-saturated felt is applied by mopping with hot asphalt or roofing pitch to improve the vapor seal. The insulation is applied by coating the surface of the felt with hot asphalt or roofing pitch just before placing the insulation. Each board is bedded in the hot asphalt or roofing pitch. As many layers of insulation as

desired are placed in this way. Finally, with staggered joints, a built-up roofing is applied by mopping the first ply to the top of the top layer of insulation. Slate and tile wearing surfaces can be placed on top of the built-up roofing if desired.

In placing the insulation, precautions must be taken to protect the insulation from rain or other moisture by placing, at one time, only such an area as can be covered in a short period and never leaving the insulation unprotected over night. It is also good practice to localize the effect of any leakage that may occur and to provide a place where work can be stopped, by dividing the roof into about 30-ft squares with water cutoffs. These are made by inserting a 16-in. strip of asphalt-saturated felt at joints (Figure 8.16*I*), the strip being tightly cemented to the surface below the insulation and to the insulation itself. Other cutoffs should be located parallel to the parapet walls and about 2 ft from them. All interruptions in work should occur at waterstops, and the insulation that has been placed should be protected temporarily with at least one ply of the built-up roofing extending to waterstops on all sides. Insulation laid on wood decks sloping more than 3 in. to the foot should be nailed to the deck. Insulation applied in this manner should not be used on concrete decks with such slopes.

Flexible insulation is installed in open spaces in the wall, ceiling, or roof construction where it will not be subjected to loads, for it is easily compressible. Quilts or blankets are installed between the studs and ceiling joists in frame construction or between furring strips on masonry walls *(J)*, *(K)*, and *(L)*. More than one layer of quilt, together or separated, can be used if desired. Quilt insulation divides the space it occupies into two or more air spaces. To be efficient, the insulation should be so fastened at the sides and ends that there will be no air leakage between spaces. Batts are inserted between studs *(O)*. If they are provided with vaporproof back and with nailing flanges, they are lapped over the studs, as shown. If the studs, joists, or rafters are deeper than the thickness of the batts, the nailing flanges are nailed to the sides of these members *(N)*. Ceilings are insulated *(O)*, or the batts may be inserted from below *(N)*, before the lath are placed.

Fill insulation is installed by pouring the loose granulated or nodulated form into open spaces between the studs of stud walls and between ceiling joists, or it is installed by blowing this material into place through large flexible tubes using low air pressure. Fibrous mineral wool and glass wool are available in bulk form. They are packed by hand into the space between studs and joists. Great care is necessary to ensure the complete filling of stud spaces.

Reflective insulation is applied between studs, joists, or rafters (Figure 8.16*P*). Nailing strips may be used to hold it more tightly. Some forms may be installed by lapping over the studs *(Q)*, or by inserting between furring strips on masonry walls *(R)*. This insulation divides the space into two or more air spaces. For the most effective results the insulation must be fastened at the sides, top, and bottom, and at all laps, so that there will be no circulation of air between the two spaces.

8.12 Selection of Roof Coverings

FACTORS TO BE CONSIDERED
Many factors enter into the selection of a roofing material for a given building. Some are quite definite, but others vary with local conditions, the class of occupancy, and the preferences of the architect and owner.

The most pertinent factors (not listed in order of their importance) are: slope of roof deck, type of roof deck, weight of roofing, climatic conditions, fire exposure, durability, cost, appearance, and maintenance.

Slope of Roof
All forms of shingles, tile, and slate are suitable for use on roofs with a slope of 6 in. or more to the foot and are often used with slopes of 4 in. to the foot. The flatter the slope, the greater the tendency for driving rains to cause leaks. The various kinds of corrugated roofs require a slope of 4 in. to the foot. Special attention should be given to the tightness of the end laps. Sheet-metal roofs can be used on any slope from flat to steep by employing appropriate joints or seams. Built-up roofings and single membrane roofing can be used on any slope from flat to steep. Roll roofings require a slope of at least 2 in. to the foot.

Type of Roof Deck
The methods of fastening the various types of roof coverings to various types of roof decks have been explained. Because of these relationships, it is seen that the type of roof covering and the type of deck should be selected concurrently.

Weight of Roofing
The weight of the roofing affects the design, weight, and cost of the roof deck and the supporting members. The weight of a given roofing depends upon the specifications being used and range as shown in Table 8.5.

Climatic Conditions
The durability of roofing materials is affected by the climatic conditions to which they are subjected. Strong winds may damage slate, tile, and asbestos-cement shingles, and asphalt shingles and roll roofing are especially vulnerable unless special provisions are made. Hail punctures asphalt shingles and roll roofing and may break tile and slate, the thicker types being less vulnerable than the thinner.

The expansion and contraction of sheet-metal roofs from extreme temperature changes may cause the sheets to crack and the joints to leak if adequate provision is not made for this action. Asphalt shingles and roll roofing are also adversely affected by extreme temperatures, especially high temperatures, and sunlight. Those with mineral surface coatings are more resistant to these actions than smooth surfaces.

Fog, salt air, smoke, and other gases in industrial areas tend to corrode metal roofings. Copper, lead, aluminum, and zinc are highly resistant to atmospheric corrosion and do not require protection by painting. Terne plate is resistant to corrosion if protected by paint. Although zinc is resistant to atmospheric corrosion, galvanized steel and iron may corrode because of defects in the zinc coating. Corrugated sheets can be more heavily coated than sheets which are bent sharply to form seams and can be therefore more durable. Galvanized sheet metal should be painted to prolong its life.

Clay tile, slate, asbestos-cement, and built-up roofings are unaffected by the composition of the atmosphere.

Durability
Durability of a given roofing material is affected by its quality, its suitability for the purpose used, climatic conditions, quality of workmanship in laying, effectiveness of maintenance, and many other factors. Thus, no definite comparisons of different materials may be made.

Considering the best quality of each type, proper installation, and appropriate maintenance, roofing materials may be arranged in groups in decreasing order of length of life, somewhat as follows.

Table 8.5 **Weights of Roofing Materials in Place**

Material	Weight[a]	Material	Weight[a]
Terne plate	60–75	Built-up roofing	400–675
Copper	80–120	Roll roofing	130–325
Corrugated galvanized steel	120–220	Shingles, wood	200–300
Clay tile	850–1800	asphalt	130–325
Slate	550–1000	asbestos-cement	275–600

[a] Values in pounds per square of 100 sq ft.

1. Sheet copper, lead, stainless steel, aluminum, clay tile, slate, concrete tile, asbestos-protected metal.

2. Terne plate, galvanized iron, asbestos-cement tile, built-up roofing, and single membrane roofing.

3. Wood shingles

4. Asphalt shingles.

5. Roll roofing.

Cost

The cost of roof coverings in place, exclusive of the cost of the deck, vary with some exceptions in about the same order listed under durability. Special comment should be made about slate because of the transportation costs involved in shipping from the limited sources of supply.

Appearance

Appearance is an important factor in selecting a roof covering for some buildings and is of little consequence in other cases, such as many industrial buildings. Furthermore, some roof coverings are installed on flat or nearly flat roofs where they will usually not be seen. The architectural style of a building and the class of occupancy may be determining factors.

Clay tile, slate, concrete tile, and wood shingles are considered to be attractive roof coverings. Asphalt shingles are surfaced with granular material in a great variety of colors to suit individual preferences. Unless thick butt shingles are used, such coverings have a flat appearance. Copper weathers to a pleasing soft blue-green color. Aluminum weathers to a dull gray. Terne plate and galvanized sheets are painted to protect them from corrosion, and any color can be applied. Corrugated sheets of various materials are extensively used but are not considered to be attractive unless colored sheets are used.

Maintenance

The initial costs of roof coverings are naturally considered in selecting a roof covering, but the cost of maintenance must also be given consideration.

Copper, aluminum, lead, and stainless-steel roof coverings are noncorrosive and do not require painting. Built-up roofs require very little maintenance. Terne plate and galvanized sheet steel require periodic painting because of the tendency of the base metal to corrode when defects develop in the coatings. Asbestos-protected metal requires little maintenance.

Individual state, clay tile, concrete tile and asbestos-cement tile may be broken by large hailstones or other objects and require replacement; asphalt shingles and roll roofing may be damaged by hail or wind and require repairs.

The life of wood shingles can be prolonged by coating

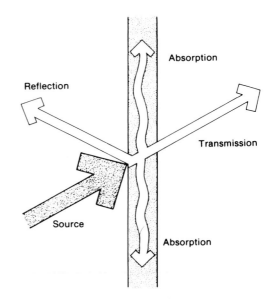

FIGURE 8.17 Reflection, absorption, and transmission. *Building Control Systems,* Vaughn Bradshaw. Copyright © 1985, John Wiley & Sons, Inc. Reprinted by permission of John Wiley & Sons, Inc.

them occasionally with creosote and, less effectively, with shingle stain. Oil paint should not be used because it causes them to warp and curl.

The life of smooth-surfaced asphalt roll roofings can be prolonged by frequent recoating with asphalt roof coatings.

Fire Exposure

Building code requirements for roof coverings are based upon their resistance to fire. The classification of roof coverings included in most codes is based on the classifications by the Underwriters Laboratories. They arrange the coverings into three classes, A, B, and C.

Classes, A, B, and C include roof coverings which are effective against severe, moderate, and light fire exposures, respectively, and which are resistant to flying brands. The *National Building Code* of the National Board of Fire Underwriters requires class A or B coverings on all buildings, although class C coverings are accepted on dwellings, buildings of wood frame construction, and buildings outside the fire limits which, on the basis of height and area, could be of wood frame construction.

8.13 Acoustical Control

Acoustical control encompasses two types of sound control — control of the sounds within a room, and isolating the room from unwanted sound, called *noise,* that is generated in other spaces within the building or from sources outside the building. Recent legislation requires that sound be controlled in the work place. Excessive noise can cause permanent hearing loss, and sound from other sources can distract workers from their appointed tasks, students from learning, and music listeners from their listening enjoyment. This section will discuss the nature of sound, control of sound within the space, and isolation of sound.

NATURE OF SOUND

Sound is a rapid fluctuation of air pressure. Vibrations from a source of sound set the surrounding air molecules into motion. The result is a series of pressure pulses moving outward from the source. These vibrations can be transmitted through air or any other "elastic" medium, including most building construction materials. In a vacuum, where there is no medium, sound cannot be transmitted.

In free space, the intensity of sound will diminish in proportion to the square of the distance from the source. In an enclosed space, the sound intensity will be maintained because of the sound being reflected by the enclosure surfaces. When sound strikes a boundary or any sizable surface, part of its energy is absorbed, part is reflected, and part is transmitted through the construction (see Figure 8.17). The proportion falling into each category will depend on the physical properties of the material and of the impinging sound.

Hard surfaces such as concrete reflect nearly all of the incident sound energy, while soft, porous materials such as wood and fabrics absorb a large part of the energy striking them. When sound is absorbed, part of the energy is dissipated as friction by the air movement in the pores of the material, but a large portion is also transmitted through the material. A material may reduce the sound energy level in a room but not prevent transmission to adjacent spaces. The *absorption coefficient* of a material is the ratio of the sound energy absorbed to the sound energy impinging upon the material surface. An absorption coefficient (α) of 1 represents total absorption. Sound insulative qualities of a material are measured by *transmission loss* (TL), which represents the difference in sound pressure level between the incident side and the opposite side of the construction. The values of transmission loss are measured in decibels.

A *decibel* (dB) is the ratio of sound pressure to a base level chosen at the threshold of hearing. Values on the dB scale range from zero (the threshold of hearing) to 130 (painful sound). An increase of 6 dB at any point on the scale represents a doubling of pressure, and a decrease of

FIGURE 8.18 Structure-borne sound. *Building Control Systems,* Vaughn Bradshaw. Copyright © 1985, John Wiley & Sons, Inc. Reprinted by permission of John Wiley & Sons, Inc.

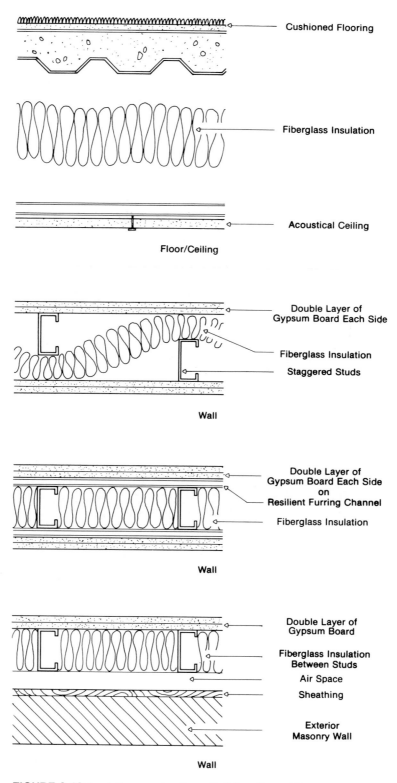

FIGURE 8.19 Insulative constructions. *Building Control Systems,* Vaughn Bradshaw. Copyright © 1985, John Wiley & Sons, Inc. Reprinted by permission of John Wiley & Sons, Inc.

6 dB represents a halving of pressure. The decibel scale also represents the energy of sound. A doubling of sound energy is expressed as an increase of 3 dB. Decibel levels for common sounds include: jet plane — 120 dB; thunder — 100 dB, rock and roll music — 90 dB, noisy office — 70 dB, average conversation — 50 dB, empty theater — 30 dB, and a whisper — 10 dB.

The decibel scale is also used to describe the sound reduction achieved by an insulative construction element. The sound insulating value of a wall will depend on the wall construction. The method used to rate sound insulating performance is the Sound Transmission Class (STC). A 2 by 4 wood stud wall covered on both sides with ½ in. drywall has a STC rating of 32. This is a TL of 32 through the wall. Normal conversation from an adjacent room would be heard, but would be difficult to understand.

ROOM ACOUSTICS

Room *acoustics* is concerned primarily with the behavior of sound in enclosed spaces, where sound is acted upon by the room boundaries and any obstructions within the room. The shape of the room and the placement of reflective and absorptive surfaces determine the distribution of sound in the room. How we control the distribution will affect the functions or activities taking place in the space, such as excessive noise in a factory or the enhancement of music in a church.

The control of sound within a room can be done in one of three ways; masking the sound, controlling the reflective sound, and sound absorption. Electronic *sound masking* systems are used to create a windlike "white noise" in order to unobtrusively raise the background noise level. This provides acoustical privacy and makes undesirable sounds, such as neighbor's conversation, less comprehensible and, therefore, less distracting. The shape of the room will determine how the sound will be reflected and this concept is commonly used to provide a room shape that is conducive to the satisfactory distribution of sound in auditoriums. Most building materials are hard and highly reflective. This reflection causes the sound to build up to a high level and die out slowly. Acoustical materials are designed to absorb most of the sound striking them and reflect less than 50% back into the room.

Absorption coefficients are assigned to materials and measure the percentage of incident sound energy absorbed by the material. If a material has an absorption coefficient of 0.5, it means the material will absorb 50% of the sound that strikes it and will reflect 50% back into the room. Absorption coefficients for some typical construction materials are listed below:

Unglazed brick	0.03
Porous concrete block	0.31
Smooth plaster on lath	0.04
Carpet on foam rubber pad	0.57
Plywood paneling, ⅜ in.	0.17
Drywall, ½ in., nailed to 2 by 4	0.05
Acoustical tile	0.35 to 0.95

SOUND ISOLATION

Sound isolation deals with the design of building construc-

FIGURE 8.20 Isolation of sound and vibration from mechanical and electrical equipment. *Building Control Systems,* Vaughn Bradshaw. Copyright © 1985, John Wiley & Sons, Inc. Reprinted by permission of John Wiley & Sons, Inc.

tions to control noise transmission through walls, floors, and ceilings. Sound is transmitted through the construction when the walls, floors, and ceiling surfaces vibrate. The surface may be set into vibration by either the alternating air pressure of incident sound waves, called airborne transmission or by direct mechanical contact or impact caused by vibrating equipment, a footstep, or an object dropped on a floor. Transmission as a result of direct mechanical impact or contact is called structure-borne sound transmission. The possible paths of transmission are through the air or through the solid parts of building construction and equipment. Noises originating within a room are generally airborne, while those intruding from elsewhere may be transmitted both through the air and through solid structure. All possible transmission paths must be considered, because when sound has a choice of paths, it will take the path of least resistance (see Figure 8.18).

Discontinuity in construction is an effective means of improving sound insulation against both airborne noise and structure-borne vibration. To achieve this, a wall is divided into two separate skins, and consequently vibrations are not easily transmitted from one to the other. If a wall consists of two walls with an air space between them, both walls must be set in motion in order to transmit sound across the construction. In general, two walls will decrease sound transmission more than a single wall equal to their combined thickness (see Figure 8.19).

Mechanical equipment should be isolated from the structure of the building so that vibrations are not transmitted. Separate equipment foundations, that rest on the ground and are independent of the building structure, are an excellent solution to noisy equipment. When the equipment is on upper floors, vibration isolators should be used (see Figure 8.20).

Summary

The types of roof, roof deck construction, and the roofing material must be compatible in order to ensure the desired performance. These elements, correctly chosen and constructed according to the specifications, will contribute to an environment that is free from unwanted moisture. The proper selection and installation of insulation, sealants, and gaskets will provide interior spaces that are free of drafts, cold exterior walls, and high energy costs. The control of sound within enclosed spaces can enhance one's work, enjoyment, and health. Isolating equipment noises will decrease the noise transmitted throughout a building. Using sound absorbing materials in an enclosed space prevents the build up of sound intensity within the space and the use of discontinuity in wall construction prevents the sound from intruding on adjacent spaces. Care in the selection and installation of the above elements will ensure an environment in which people will be productive in their work or relaxed at home.

Key Terms

roof deck
slope
pitch
rise
birdbaths
sleepers
built-up roofing
roll roofing

single ply membrane roofing
elastomeric
gutters
downspout
scuppers
sandwich panel
shingles

shakes
strip shingle
scuttles
skylights
flashing
sealants
gaskets
relative humidity

dew-point temperature
condensation
sound
noise
absorption coefficient
transmission loss
decibel
acoustics
sound masking

Review Questions

1. List six different types of roofs and three different types of roof decks.

2. List four different roofing materials and state under what conditions they are used.

3. How are sealants and gaskets used in building construction?

4. How is heat transmitted through the walls and roof of a building?

5. List four different types of insulation and state how they are used in building construction.

6. How is sound transmitted throughout a building?

7. Describe three methods used to control unwanted sound in an enclosed environment.

CHAPTER 9
DOORS AND WINDOWS

Entrances, curtain walls, and windows are an integral part of the building's envelope. They have to be compatible with the other elements of the envelope to maintain the integrity of the interior spaces. The entrance to a building gives the prospective client or visitor his first impression of what he can expect on the inside. It is important to the owner that the entrance is inviting and accessible and not a barrier to future relations.

Doors are the operating part of the entrance that allow access to and egress from the building. Their classification and number are determined by the use of the building and the building codes that are in force for the location of the building. Doors serve as part of the building's envelope by preventing the intrusion of unwanted weather, noise, and unauthorized personnel. Doors are designed to permit the passage of people, including the handicapped or equipment and supplies or both. The primary materials used in the construction of doors are metals, wood, glass, and combinations of two or all three.

A curtain wall is an exterior building wall that carries no roof or floor loads. It is usually constructed of metal in combination with glass, plastics, and other surfacing materials and is attached to the structural frame of the building. The primary functions of a curtain wall are to withstand the actions of the natural environment, prevent access by intruders, and control the infiltration of air and sound. It should be aesthetically appropriate and have permanence consistent with the design life of the building enclosed.

A window is an opening in a wall to provide natural light, natural ventilation, and vision for the occupants of the enclosed spaces. A window also has to provide protection against weather, sound, and entry by intruders. To be satisfactory, windows must be durable, weathertight, easily cleaned, and attractive in appearance. Windows are available in a variety of types that meet both design requirements and individual preferences. They are made of glass or plastic, framed with metal or wood construction.

Objectives

1. Understand how the various classes of doors operate.
2. Become familiar with the common door sizes.
3. Understand how the various door types are constructed.
4. Become familiar with the basic types of curtain walls commonly used in building construction.
5. Become familiar with the different types of windows and how they operate.
6. Become familiar with the factors to be considered in the selection of a window type for a specific use.
7. Become familiar with the different types of glass and how they are manufactured.
8. Become familiar with the various door hardware assemblies.

9.1 Entrances

A *doorway* is an opening through a building wall or partition, providing passage for persons or vehicles. The opening may be closed by a movable barrier, a *door,* held in position by a *door frame,* the members of which are the sides or jambs and top or head of the opening. A doorway is often considered to be the clear opening within the frame. Saddles or thresholds are provided at the bottom or sill of exterior doorways.

CLASSES OF DOORS

Ordinary doors, whose primary function is to permit the passage of persons, are classed as exterior and interior doors. Interior doors between rooms are known as communicating doors. Doors at the principal entrances are commonly called entrance doors. Light screen doors, much of whose area is covered with insect screen, are mounted on the outside of the frames of exterior doors. During the winter months screen doors are often replaced with storm doors which have glass panels. Doors with interchangeable screened and glazed panels that can be changed seasonally are called combination doors. Doors designed to resist the passage of fire are called fire doors. A wicket door is a small door within a large door, provided to permit passage without opening the large door.

In addition to the classes of doors mentioned in the preceding paragraph, many others, such as elevator doors, garage doors, hangar doors, industrial doors, and scuttle doors, are given little, if any, consideration herein.

OPERATION OF DOORS

Doors usually open by swinging about a vertical axis or by sliding horizontally, but sometimes they may swing about a horizontal axis or slide vertically. These axes are provided by means of *hinges* or pivots fastened to the door and the door frame. Horizontal sliding doors are suspended from hangers containing wheels which operate on tracks placed at the top of the door openings. Vertical sliding doors move between guides provided at the sides and are operated by cables or chains passing over pulleys in much the same way that double-hung windows are operated. They may be either counterweighted or counterbalanced, as will be explained later.

The most common type of door is the swinging door shown in Figure 9.1A.

Two doors hinged at opposite sides of an opening *(B)* are referred to as double doors or a pair of doors. Such doors are used at the entrances of buildings, of large rooms, and even of small rooms in residences to give a more spacious effect and to provide more clear passageway.

The double-acting door *(C)* is provided with special hinges that keep the door closed when it is not held open. The door can easily be pushed open in either direction.

FIGURE 9.1 Operation of doors.

The folding or accordion doors shown in *(D)* and *(E)* are used singly or as folding partitions so that two rooms may be used as a single room or separately. They are made for very wide openings. Doors are also hinged together *(E),* forming a folding partition.

The *sliding doors* shown in *(F)* and *(G)* were once used extensively in residences. Swinging doors or cased openings without doors have replaced them. The slide-into pockets provided in the partitions are concealed when not in use. Sliding doors are used in many other locations, particularly residential closets.

Doors sliding on one side of a wall or partition *(H)* and *(I)* are extensively used for fire doors which normally stand open, but they close (released by a fusible link) in case of fire. They may be made self-closing by sloping the tracks from which they are suspended or by properly arranging weights and pulleys.

Sliding doors *(I)* and *(J)* are often used for elevator doors. They are so arranged that they will all open when one is pulled back. The inner doors in *(J)* are arranged to move

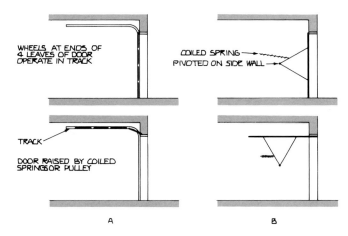

FIGURE 9.2 Vertical-opening garage doors.

may be locked when desired. The doors are allowable but highly restricted by codes.

Two forms of garage doors which move vertically to open are illustrated in Figure 9.2. The door in *(A)* consists of four leaves that are hinged together as shown. Wheels in the sides of the doors move in guides so that the door takes the position shown in the figure when it is open. A coiled spring balances the weight of the door so that it is easily operated. It may be operated electrically and is often called an overhead door. The door shown in *(B)* consists of a single leaf, which is pivoted on each side as shown. It is opened by lifting vertically and rotating around the pivots. A spring is arranged to assist in opening the door and to hold the door open. This door requires a wall or other support close to each side of the opening to which the pivots can be attached.

faster than the other two so that they will all be completely open at the same time. Two doors opening to the same side are more extensively used than the four-door unit shown.

The right-angle door *(K)* is used to a limited extent on garages. The doors are suspended from an overhead track.

Vertical sliding doors in *(L)* and *(M)* are counterweighted and may be operated electrically. They are pulled up by cables or chains that are placed at each side of the opening and that operate over pulleys in the same manner as for double-hung window sash. Such doors are used for large openings in industrial buildings, particularly for freight elevator doors.

Where conditions permit their use, the counterbalanced vertical sliding doors shown in *(N)* are convenient. Used for freight elevator doors, they are easily operated by hand. When one panel moves up, the other panel moves down an equal distance.

The canopy door shown in *(O)* is used for large openings in industrial buildings. The door is counterweighted and may be electrically operated. If desired, it may open outward to form a canopy over the opening.

The *rolling door* shown in *(P)* operates in the same manner as a window shade. The roller on which the door rolls is operated by hand or electrically or by a spring that counterbalances the weight of the door. The door is made flexible by using interlocking slats of wood or sheet metal. The ends of the slats are held behind guides at the sides of the doors. Wood rolling doors are used to form movable partitions in the same manner as accordion doors and folding partitions shown in *(D)* and *(E)*. Steel rolling doors are used extensively for large exterior doors of industrial buildings and for fire shutters which will close automatically in case of fire.

The *revolving door* shown in *(Q)* is used at the entrances of certain buildings, such as banks and stores. It does not permit much cold air to enter from outside when it is in use. During mild or warm weather when it is not in use the revolving part may be moved out of the way as shown. The door

DOOR MATERIALS

Wood, aluminum, carbon steel, and glass are the materials most extensively used in the manufacture of doors, but stainless steel, bronze, and copper are also used, as are facing materials such as hardboard, fiberboard, asbestos, and plastics.

DOOR SIZES

The sizes of ordinary stock doors whose primary function is to permit the passage of persons vary with the types and the materials used in their construction.

The common widths of single wood doors are 2 ft 6 in., 2 ft 8 in., and 3 ft for interiors, and 2 ft 8 in., 3 ft, and 3 ft 4 in. for exterior doors. Heights are 6 ft 6 in., 6 ft 8 in., and 7 ft for exterior doors. Thicknesses are 1⅜ in. and 1¾ in. for interior and exterior doors, but doors 3 ft 4 in. wide are a minimum thickness of 1¾ in. Exterior doors with a thickness of 2¼ in. are not unusual, and such doors with heights of 7 ft 6 in. and 8 ft are sometimes used.

When double doors are used (Figure 9.1*B*), each door may be somewhat narrower than a single door. Storm doors, screen doors, and combination doors are usually 1⅛ in. thick.

The stock sizes of metal doors are more limited than those for wood doors but correspond quite closely with the sizes mentioned.

PANEL AND FLUSH DOORS

The most common type of door is the *panel* or framed *door*, usually consisting of vertical and horizontal members which frame rectangular areas in which opaque panels of panes of glass or louvers are located. Such doors with glass panels are called sash doors.

Another common type of door is the *flush door*, which usually consists of flat, relatively thin, face panels the full height and width of the door; the door is rigidly bonded or otherwise attached to a solid or hollow core with finished edges. Openings may be provided in flush doors for the insertion of glass vision panels or of louvers for ventilation. A vision panel is a small glazed panel at eye level enabling a person approaching a door to see a person approaching the door from the opposite side. Doors with panels that are of approximately the same thickness as the stiles and rails are called flush panel doors.

Panel and flush doors of various materials correspond in appearance with the wood doors illustrated in Figure 9.3. A great variety of other types with standard sizes are manufactured and carried in stock as stock doors. Other sizes and types are manufactured on order to the architect's specifications.

PARTS OF PANEL DOORS

The parts of panel doors, regardless of the material of which they are constructed, have the same designations as those of wood doors illustrated in Figure 9.3. These parts may be defined as follows:

Stiles. Vertical members at each side of the door which extend its full height. For doors swinging about a vertical axis located on one edge, the stile to which the hinge or pivots are attached is called the hinge or hanging stile. The edge of the hinge stile is called the butt. The stile to which the lock, latch, push, or pull is attached is called the closing or lock stile.

Rails. Horizontal members extending the full width between stiles and framing into them. The rails at the top and bottom of the doors are called the top rail and the bottom rail. Rails located between these two rails are called intermediate or crossrails. The crossrail at lock height is called the lock rail.

Mullions. Relatively heavy vertical members which subdivide the areas between stiles and rails. Muntins are light vertical or horizontal members corresponding in position to mullions and crossrails.

Panels. Members which fill the areas between, and which are surrounded by, the stiles, rails, mullions, and muntins. Wood panels may be flat panels of plywood or raised panels with a border thinner than the remainder of the panel. One or more panels of a door may be replaced by glass to form a sash door for vision, light, or architectural effect or by louvers for ventilation.

PARTS OF FLUSH DOORS

Flush doors vary widely in their construction, but all types include face panels, which form the faces; a core, which is the construction between the face panels to which they are attached, which gives them support, and which may be solid or hollow; and edge strips, which surround the rim of the core to provide finished edges to match the material in the face panels. Hollow cores may include vertical or horizontal ribs, rectangular grids, or small cells. Some cores include stiles and rails. Cores usually include special provisions such as solid blocking for attachment of locks and other hardware. Openings may be provided through flush doors for the insertion of panes of glass for light or vision or of louvers for ventilation.

ASTRAGALS

An *astragal* is an overlapping strip of material usually on the exterior surface of a door. The strips are made of metal, wood, neoprene, felt, or rubber. They may be attached or an integral part of the door. Astragals are located on the lock stile of the active leaf of a pair of swing doors. They lap over to engage the inactive leaf, thus covering the space between the closed doors. The function of an astragal is to protect the building interior against driving rain and tampering with locks. Astragals may also be used to cover the crack created by the meeting of sliding doors. Pivoted hinge entrance doors that do not have latch sets may have rubber astragals that act as closure strips to keep out rain and cold.

LEDGED AND BRACED   FLUSH   ONE PANEL   TWO PANELS   FOUR PANELS

FIVE PANELS   SIX PANELS   LOUVERED   FRENCH   DUTCH

A-TYPES OF DOORS

SOLID DOOR WITH RAISED PANELS   SOLID DOOR WITH RAISED PANELS, FLUSH MOLDING   FRENCH DOOR GLASS SET WITH STOPS

GLASS BEAD

RAISED PANEL   FLAT PANEL

VENEERED DOORS

B-TYPES OF DOOR CONSTRUCTION

FIGURE 9.3 Types and construction of wood doors.

LABELED DOORS

Building codes require that doors provide not only safe egress but also restrict the spread of fires. Doors that meet these conditions are known as *fire doors.* Fire doors are labeled and known also as labeled doors, or rated doors. A labeled door is classified according to its ability to resist penetration or destruction by fire. This rating is established by conducting standard fire tests, which simulate actual fire conditions, against doors and door assemblies. These tests indicate the ability of certain doors to resist fire and destruction by a fire hose. Accordingly, the doors of a specified construction are fire rated as capable of resisting fire for a specified time in certain locations.

Fire ratings are identified according to time in hours. Hourly ratings are 3, 1½, and ¾ hours. A letter designation of A, B, C, D, or E, following the hourly rating, designates the class location for which the door is intended. The actual label is an embossed metal plate attached to the butt side of the door.

Fire doors are produced under the factory inspection and label service program of the Underwriters Laboratory and are identified by a label designating hourly rating, class location letter, and the UL stamp. Factory Mutual Research Corporation also rates doors. Their approval is indicated by the initials FM within a diamond.

Most importantly, fire doors should be installed only in frames, walls, and assemblies that are equal to the fire door rating. Therefore, walls that require fire resistivity, such as fire towers, division walls, and corridors, should have door assemblies that are compatible with the wall construction.

Other factors that determine door ratings are the location, usage, the minimum door thickness which is 1¾ in., the maximum glass size if permitted, the door opening dimensions, and hardware requirements.

DOOR FRAMES

Door frames retain the door, anchor door hardware, and present a finished appearance by forming a transition between the door and the wall. Commonly used frame materials are wood, solid steel sections, hollow aluminum, stainless steel, and hollow cold-rolled pressed steel.

The side members of a door frame are called the jambs; and the top member, the head. Door stops are projections or strips on the faces of the jambs and head against which one-way swinging doors close (Figure 9.4). The term is also applied to projections or strips between which doors slide. A small sash, called a transom, which may be fixed or operated for ventilation, may be located above the door and included in the same frame. A horizontal bar, called a transom bar, is used to separate the door and the transom. Although operable transoms were once very common, they are rarely used in contemporary buildings. Fixed transoms of material identical to the door are now quite popular. These do not have a transom bar.

Door frames intended for a pair of doors frequently have a framed member called a mullion. This vertical member, which has the same profile as the door frame, is located in the middle of the double door frame. It serves as a lock base and door stop. These mullions are sometimes removable, permitting the full double opening to be used as a wide open passage.

Frames have various profiles. Some have a simple lip and plaster stop, whereas others have fluted moldings. Profiles or plaster keys intended to meet plaster and wall board are sometimes called plaster stops or backbends. Frame profiles usually have a ½ in. protrusion that stops the closed door. To dampen noise, these stops may have a rubber lining or rubber mutes set in predrilled holes.

To eliminate dust pockets, stops are sometimes cut off about 6 inches above the floor line with a beveled or square cut. These cuts are called cut-off stops, sometimes hospital

FIGURE 9.4 Parts and details of a framed wood panel door.

FIGURE 9.5 Metal and metal-covered doors and frames.

stops or sanitary stops. This cut permits the base material to wrap around the door frame or a stainless steel spat to be installed (Figure 9.4). Frames frequently have a subframe, rough buck, or subbuck. The subframe provides the heavy anchorage that the door requires, whereas the door frame is a casing or finished frame.

The members ordinarily used to provide a finish around door openings are called the trim. Trim consists primarily of vertical side members called casings and a horizontal top member called a head casing which, as used for a wood door in a wood stud partition, are illustrated in Figure 9.4. Metal frames and casings are often included in a single unit (Figure 9.5C). A metal-covered frame is illustrated in Figure 9.5D.

Door frames may be set in masonry walls at the time the walls are constructed; and if so, they are anchored to the walls by metal Tee-anchors fastened to the frames and built into the walls. Wood blocks may be built into masonry walls to form an anchorage for frames that are set after the walls are built. Door frame openings are provided in walls and partitions with wood studs by doubling the wood members forming the jambs and heads. These members may be

called the subbuck or subframe. Masonry partitions are provided with door bucks, which are rough frames (Figure 9.4) set at the time the partitions are built and anchored to the masonry by metal anchors, such as bolts, lag screws, and nails. The openings provided are larger than the outside dimension of the finished door frames, thus permitting the finished frames to be plumbed and trued.

An exterior doorway is also provided with a sill located across the bottom of the opening. A threshold, sometimes called a saddle, is a relatively thin member with beveled or rounded top edges. It is located below the bottom of an exterior door and on top of the sill. It raises the bottom of a swinging door to provide clearance so that it will swing free above the floor or floor covering but will be reasonably weathertight when closed. It also provides a finished appearance for the floor material at the door. Hardwood thresholds are used with wood doors and metal thresholds with wood and metal doors. Thresholds are used with exterior doors of various materials. Thresholds are sometimes used with interior doors in order to provide a finish for two dissimilar materials when the flooring on two sides of a door are different.

Frames may be factory preassembled or shipped "knock-down" (KD).

Frames should be mitered for appearance as well as for construction.

9.2 Metal Doors and Frames

METAL DOORS

The metals most commonly used in the manufacture of doors are aluminum and carbon steel; but bronze, stainless steel, and copper are also used.

The metal members for door construction are usually hollow, with or without some form of nonmetallic filling; and therefore such doors might be classed as hollow metal doors. The usual practice, however, is to class aluminum and bronze doors separately and restrict the use of the term *hollow metal doors* to doors constructed of hollow members of steel with fillings or core materials other than wood, except plywood cores in the panels. In addition, doors with metal facings fitting tightly over wood cores are called metal-covered doors. Finally, crudely formed solid-wood fire doors covered with terne plate, although covered with metal, are called tin-clad doors. There are many other special types.

Aluminum Doors

Both panel and flush doors are constructed of aluminum. The most common type is the panel door with tubular extruded aluminum stiles and rails approximately rectangular in cross section (Figure 9.5A), with a minimum thickness of 1/8 in. The members are joined by electric-arc welding with the joints located and finished to be invisible. The frames are constructed of the same material and are also tubular and rectangular in cross section. The doors are usually 1¾ in. thick, with stiles and top rails varying in width from 2⅛ to 5 in. and bottom rails, from 4 to 10 in. The frames vary in cross section upward from a minimum width of 1¾ in. and a depth of 4 in. The finish of the doors and frames is usually a special polished or satin finish but may be of various architectural colors.

For entrance doors, the space between the stiles and rails is usually occupied by a tempered glass panel but may be divided by a narrow aluminum center cross panel. The glass, which must be tempered, is held in position by continuous aluminum glass stops with vinyl glazing beads, or in other ways to make putty unnecessary.

Instead of using two glass panels, the lower panel is often faced with aluminum sheets. It is of sandwich construction with a core ¾ in. thick of resin-impregnated honeycomb, with ¾ in. hexagonal cells, on each face of which is bonded a hardboard layer 1/8 in. thick, to each of which is bonded an outer layer of sheet aluminum about 1/32 in. thick. The bonds are formed under heat and pressure.

Aluminum flush doors have face panels of fine vertical-ribbed or fluted aluminum sheets. For one type of door (Figure 9.5B), these sheets are about 1/32 in. thick and are bonded to 1/8 in. hardboard which are in turn bonded, under heat and pressure, to a resin-impregnated honeycomb core with ¾ in. hexagonal cells. The edges of the door may be extruded aluminum sections to which the surface sheets are securely attached. Various types of flush doors are available. They may be pierced for one or more lights of glass or for louvers.

Another form of flush door consists of a framework with extruded aluminum stiles, a top and a bottom rail, and intermediate rails, with the space between rails filled with a solid fibrous core and faced with aluminum sheets.

The flush panel door has a stile and rail frame with panels of about the same thickness as that of the stiles and rails.

Hollow Metal Doors

Hollow metal doors are either the panel or flush types. They are usually 1¾ in. thick. They are constructed primarily of cold-rolled sheet steel especially processed to give smooth flat surfaces. They ordinarily have a factory finish consisting of one or more coats of baked enamel.

The panel doors resemble in appearance the wood panel doors of various designs (Figure 9.3). The stiles and rails are made of sheets about 1/20 in. thick and are accurately formed as shown in Figure 9.5C, with the joints welded and ground smooth. The edges of the doors are usually reinforced internally with channels welded in position. Reinforcement is provided where hardware is to be attached. The stiles and rails are filled with mineral wool, asbestos, or other material for sound deadening so that the doors will not have a metalic sound when closing.

The panels are of sandwich construction with sheet-metal faces about 1/20 in. thick and cores of asbestos, composition board, sheetrock, hardboard, or other material.

Flush doors (Figure 9.5D) consist of sheet-metal face panels about 1/20 in. thick and the full size of the door. They are separated by vertical sheet-metal ribs of various forms, spaced 6 or 8 in., to which they are spot-welded at frequent intervals.

The rim of the door is closed and strengthened, usually by channels, and the face panels are firmly secured to the rim. Sound-deadening material may be bonded between the stiffening ribs on the inside of the face panels or the entire space between ribs may be filled with asbestos or mineral wool insulation or other sound-deadening material. Provisions are made for the attachment of hardware.

The frames for hollow metal doors are made with various profiles which are break-pressed from steel sheets welded and ground smooth at the corners (Figure 9.5C).

Metal-Covered Doors

Doors of this general type, which are commonly called kalamein doors, consist of sheet-metal facings securely bonded or attached to nonresinous kiln-dried wood interior construction. All joints in the metal covering are recessed locked joints finished with solder and ground smooth. The metal is usually galvanized steel or furniture steel, which is a sheet steel specially processed to give a smooth flat surface. Copper, bronze, aluminum, and stainless steel are also used. The usual thickness is 1¾ in.

Kalamein doors are obsolete, having been largely replaced by the flush, solid-core, fire-rated doors.

Panel doors are constructed of doweled or mortised and tenoned stile and rail frames with wood cores and sheet-metal coverings tightly filled by drawing through dies. The panels consist of cores of asbestos board, for the maximum fire resistance, or of composition, plywood, or other board to which metal facings are glued under heat and pressure. The types of panel doors available are similar to those for wood panel doors, some of which are shown in Figure 9.3.

A common type of flush door consists of a wood core with a horizontal and a vertical ply, which may have a thin covering of sheet asbestos glued to one or both sides, both sides covered with sheet metal without seams pressure-glued to the core. The edges are reinforced with wood strips covered with sheet metal. The frames and trim may be sheet metal break-pressed to the desired profile, or wood with metal-covered exposed surfaces.

Tin-Clad Doors

Tin-clad doors consist of a wood core covered with terne plate. The cores are made of either two or three layers of 1 in. boards, preferably tongued-and-grooved, and not more than 8 in. wide. If two layers are used, one is vertical and the other horizontal. If three layers are used, the outer layers are vertical and the inner layer horizontal. The layers are securely fastened together by clinched nails or in some other manner to give smooth surfaces. The covering of terne plate is made of 14 × 20 in. sheets, preferably with double-lock joints. Solder, if used, must serve only to improve the appearance. The terne plate is held flat against the core by nails.

The 3-ply doors are required where the most effective resistance is desired, and the 2-ply where only a moderate degree of protection is necessary.

Steel-Plate Doors

Steel-plate doors consist of steel plates fastened to one side of an angle-iron frame or both sides of a channel frame, the frames being braced by intermediate members.

Corrugated-Steel Doors

This type of door is constructed of heavy corrugated-steel sheets supported by a structural steel frame. The better

doors consist of two thicknesses of corrugated sheets, one with corrugations vertical and the other with corrugations horizontal, with an asbestos lining between the sheets. This lining is from ⅛ in. to 1 in. thick. Sometimes the structural steel frame is covered with a ⅛ in. layer of asbestos. A cheaper and less fire-resistant door is made of one thickness of corrugated steel with corrugations vertical, riveted to an angle-iron frame, intermediate braces being provided where necessary.

Steel Rolling Doors

This type of door consists of a curtain of interlocking corrugated-steel slats which rolls up on a roller or drum in much the same way as a window shade (Figure 9.1P). The edges of the curtain operate in vertical guides, and the roller is housed in a steel hood. The curtain may be counterbalanced by springs so that it can be easily raised or lowered by hand; it may be operated by an endless chain with sprocket and gear, by a crank, or by electric motor. Devices for closing the door automatically in case of fire are available.

Pressed Metal Frames

Pressed metal cold-rolled steel frames are made in 12, 14, 16, or 18 gages. They are used in most wall type construction. Pressed metal frames provide a variety of profiles in single rabbeted or double rabbeted shapes. Hinge points are predrilled and mortised and reinforced for the reception of mortised, template butt hinges. The strike plate is likewise reinforced.

Frames set in cast-in-place concrete walls are frequently set and plumbed in place in the formwork. The concrete is then poured with the frames integral with the wall. Obviously, no other anchorage is needed. Frames anchored to precast concrete are secured by installing flat head machine screws into a steel expansion shield. The screw is threaded through a pipe sleeve that prevents frame collapse or rupture. Each frame should have a minimum of three anchors for each jamb; heavier doors and doors wider than 3 feet should have at least four anchors for each jamb, otherwise cracking or frame tear-out from the wall is likely to happen. Masonry anchors are loose tees, galvanized. They may be corrugated and are adjustable so that they may be placed in a mortar joint. Pressed metal frames in masonry walls or precast concrete are usually grout filled to obtain added strength or for noise dampening. In stud walls, these frames are secured with adjustable sheet-metal anchors that are nailed to a wood subframe. Floor knees or clip angles provide anchorage to floors. Hollow frames in stud walls are usually filled with insulation for noise abatement.

Frequently, it is necessary to have a pressed metal subframe. These subframes, called cabinet frames, are installed in the rough door opening, and the finished pressed metal casing is screwed to the cabinet frame.

Pressed metal frames may be treated by a Phosteem process, consisting of an iron phosphatizing coat which increases the resistance to rust. Steel frames should then be primed with red oxide-zinc chromate primer and baked.

Aluminum Frames

Aluminum frame extrusions, usually rectangular in profile, are used extensively as door frame assemblies for glass entrance doors. They usually have the anodized aluminum finish.

Aluminum frames that are used where high winds prevail may have steel subframes. Precautions must be taken to prevent electrolysis by coating them with asphaltic paint at their points of contact.

Steel Frames

Steel channels and angle sections are used for door frames on sliding and roll-up type industrial doors. Some sliding fire-resistant doors require steel channel frames approximately 4 to 8 in. deep. Steel bar or channel stops of approximately ¾ in. are welded to the channel jamb and head.

Labeled Frames

A labeled frame has met the requirements of thickness and construction specified for fire rated door frames. They must be at least 14 gage steel for a 3 hour (A) rating and of 16 gage steel for a lesser rating. These ratings are established by the Fire Underwriters Laboratories (UL) or the Factory Mutual Research Corporation (FM). Special frames of bronze or stainless steel, labeled or nonlabeled, are for special purposes, such as matching a door design.

9.3 Wood Doors and Frames

WOOD DOORS

The most commonly used wood for door construction is ponderosa pine. A considerable portion of the wood resembles white pine in appearance and texture and is usually accepted when specifications call for white pine unless true white pine is specified. It is used for constructing panel doors, as the base to which veneers are applied, and sometimes for the construction of cores for flush doors. Among the other woods used for constructing panel doors are Douglas fir, western red cedar, and sitka spruce.

Veneers of various decorative woods are used for facing panel and flush doors. These include ponderosa and white pine, red and white oak, walnut, hard maple, gum, red and white birch, and African and Philippine mahogany. These face veneers are bonded directly to the solid cores of the stiles and rails of panel doors. They are also used for ex-

posed outer plys called face veneers, for plywood used for the panels of panel doors, and for the face panels of flush doors. For a description of plywood, see Section 8.6. The required width of face veneers is obtained by assembling separate strips matched for grain and color. The selection of the species of wood for face veneers is based on the appearance and suitability to receive the surface coating to be applied. The cross bands of plywood used for face panels of flush doors are usually hardwood.

The face veneers of flush doors are often made of thermosetting laminated plastics. Such veneers are available in a great variety of colors, are not painted or surface treated in any way, and are durable and easily cleaned. Patterns can be obtained if desired. The veneer thickness is usually ¹⁄₁₆ in. Edge strips that match the face veneer are used.

Manufacture of Veneer

Veneers are thin sheets of wood. They are made by three processes: the sawing process, the slicing process, and the rotary-cut process. In the sawing process, the thin sheets of wood are cut from large blocks of wood by a circular saw. This process is wasteful because of the wood consumed in the saw-kerf, but it produces the best grade of veneer because it injures the wood less than the other processes. In the slicing process, the thin sheets of wood are cut from large blocks with a cutting knife. The wood is softened by steaming to make possible cutting without splitting. In the rotary-cut process, a log that has been softened by steaming or boiling is placed in a lathe and revolved against a wide stationary blade that gradually moves toward the center of the log and cuts off a continuous slice. The entire log cannot be cut up in this manner; there remains a core which cannot be cut for veneer.

Before the explosed surface is finished by sanding, sawed veneers are from ⅛ to ¼ in. thick. They are more natural in appearance and more durable than the veneers produced by the slicing and rotary-cut processes. Rotary-cut veneers are from ¹⁄₂₈ to ¹⁄₁₆ in. thick and sliced veneer ¹⁄₂₀ in. and less thick.

Panel Doors

Many designs and layouts are used for wood panel doors, some of which are illustrated in Figure 9.3. The French door shown is also called a casement door. The ends of the rails are usually fastened to the edges of the stiles, against which they abut by wood dowels held in position by hidden water-resistant joints. Panels are fastened to the stiles and rails in grooves provided in these members (Figure 9.3); or a separate continuous mold, called sticking, may be used, usually on one side only.

The panels of doors with solid stiles and rails may be solid raised panels not less than ⁷⁄₁₆ in. thick or flat plywood with a minimum thickness of ¼ in. but they may be raised.

The stiles and rails of veneered doors have cores built up of low-density wood blocks not more than 2½ in. wide (Figure 9.3B) and of varying lengths with end joints in adjacent rows staggered. These core blocks are bonded with water-resistant adhesive. Side edge strips of the same species of wood as the veneer are provided. Top and bottom edge strips may be of any suitable species of wood. The face veneers of stiles and rails should be not less than ⅛ in. thick before sanding.

The panes of glass in sash doors are held in position by glass beads of the same species of wood as a solid door or as the veneer of a veneered door. The panes of outside doors are bedded in putty for watertightness.

Flush Doors

Various types of flush doors are illustrated in Figure 9.6. Any of these may have openings to provide for panes of glass or louvers. Stile and rail frames may be used with or without intermediate rails. The rails are connected to the stiles by glued dowels.

There are two general types of flush doors: the solid-core door and the hollow-core door (Figure 9.6). The cores of both types are usually made entirely of low-density kiln-dried wood, such as ponderosa pine, but other materials are used, especially in special-purpose doors.

The face panels are usually constructed of plywood, which may have 1, 2, or 3 plys. The face panels should include at least 1 ply whose grain runs in the direction normal to the predominant direction of the grain of the units that make up the core. The face panels are bonded to the core under pressure with water-resistant adhesives and surfaced by machine sanding. The exposed edges of the core are covered with matching edge strips about ¾ in. thick, of the same species of wood as the face veneer. The face veneer is always placed with the grain of the wood vertical. Face panels are also made of laminated plastic. They are especially suitable for exterior doors that have hard usage.

The core of the most common types of solid-core door is built up of vertical strips made of wood blocks about 2 in. wide and several inches long, with the ends of blocks in adjacent strips staggered (Figure 9.6A). The strips are glued together to form a solid panel. No frame is required, but matching edge strips are provided. Each face panel is plywood with 2 plys for a 5-ply door and 3 plys for a 7-ply door, the core being counted as 1 ply. Particle board is used for solid cores also. These doors have solid wood stiles and rails and a 3-ply plywood veneer finish. Particleboard is an ideal core that resists warping.

The solid-core door shown in (B) consists of a doweled stile and rail frame with one or more intermediate rails and horizontal blocks glued together and assembled in the frame. Each face panel usually consists of 1 ply of sawed veneer ¼ in. thick for doors 1¾ in. thick and 1 ply ⅛ in. thick for 1⅜ in. doors. Matching edge strips are provided.

FIGURE 9.6 Wood flush doors.

The solid-core shown in (C) is made up of a doweled stile and rail frame with one or more intermediate rails and horizontal blocks or strips interspaced between the rails. Since these blocks are not glued together, the core is called a floating core. The entire core is bonded to the face panels, however. Matching edge strips are provided. The doors may be 5-ply or 7-ply.

Fire-resistive solid-core doors of the type shown in (D) are constructed with noncombustible mineral or asbestos-type cores or impregnated wood chip cores, plywood face panels, each with 2 or 3 plys, and impregnated matching edge strips.

A solid-core door similar in construction to the door in (A) has the core, cross bands, and edge strips chemically impregnated to improve its fire resistance.

Solid-core doors that serve specialized functions may have an interior shield. Doors that house X-ray equipment or other sources of radiation require shielded doors containing a sheet of lead. The sheet of lead, which may be from 1/16 in. to ½ in. thick, is located on the interior and covered with a veneer of finished material — usually wood. Doors to areas that house sensitive electronic equipment usually require shielding. These shielded doors have an interior sheet or mesh of copper. The shield is provided with grounding wires, which must be grounded at the job site.

Several general types of hollow cores are used in the

construction of flush doors. Various kinds of spacers are located between the face panels to which they are glued and assembled within stile and rail frames with matching edge strips. The bond to the face panels holds the spacers in position, and the spacers provide lateral support for the panels. A door with a ladder core which includes closely spaced horizontal fiberboard strips is shown in Figure 9.6. One with wood of fiberboard strips placed vertically is shown in (F).

Another type (G) includes thin vertical and horizontal wood strips located and interlocked to form a mesh, lattice, or grid, with cells or spaces between the strips. A core that includes closely spaced fiber rings is shown in (H).

To provide for the face attachment or mortising of locks and other hardware to hollow-core doors, lock blocks are provided on each stile, as shown in the figures, so that the door can be hung at either edge.

Solid-core doors are heavier, more fire-resistant, and better insulated against the transmission of heat and sound than wood panel and wood hollow-core doors. They are more suitable for curved heads than either of these types and can be more easily adapted to receive glassed and louvered openings than hollow-core doors.

Wood Frames

Wood frames of various species complement the door design and materials with finishes to match or to contrast. The hidden side of the casing or frame is kerfed full length with shallow saw cuts that prevent warping. Wood exterior frames should be treated to resist termites and decay. They are finished or painted in accordance with wood painting and stains.

Wood frames are usually anchored with nails in stud walls or with anchor bolts in masonry and concrete walls. These members may also be rabbeted or rebated to provide the stops, or the stops may be ploughed or plowed in.

9.4 Glass Doors

This section is concerned with the common type of tempered-plate-glass single- or double-acting swinging door, and sliding door.

In the tempering process, plate glass is heated to a high temperature and then cooled suddenly. The sudden cooling has an immediate effect close to the surfaces only. As the interior of the glass slowly cools to a normal temperature, it contracts. This action causes compressive stresses to develop near the surface and balancing tensile stresses to develop in the interior, an equilibrium which remains permanently.

Tempered plate glass is much more resistant to pressure and impact than normal plate glass and is more flexible. It cannot be cut, drilled, or altered in any way after tempering. The glass thicknesses used are ½ and ¾ in. The surfaces of the glass are usually smooth and polished, but rough-textured glass is available when it is desired to obscure vision. The edges of the glass are finished smooth.

Fittings are attached to the door and cemented in position to the glass at the factory in order to receive aluminum, bronze, or stainless steel hardware. Top and bottom pivots are used rather than hinges to provide for the swing of the doors. Pivot door checks or closers are recessed in the floor. Push bars and plates, door pulls, and other hardware required are adapted when necessary for use on this type of door, with appropriate connections to the door.

Cross sections of one type of glass door, with its frame and metal fittings designed to receive the glass and to provide for hardware connections at the top and bottom of a door are illustrated in Figure 9.7A and B. They may extend entirely across a door or may be located in any of the positions near the edges shown in (C), or in others as required. Holes to receive bolts for attaching certain hardware may be drilled in the glass before tempering but not after.

The frames for glass doors are tubular metal approximately rectangular in cross section, reinforced with steel channels, with the rods located inside the members (Figure 9.7A and B). The metals used in their construction are extruded aluminum or bronze; or stainless-steel sheets pressed into shapes similar to the extended shapes.

The steel channel that reinforces the finished aluminum frame should be coated to prevent electrolysis.

FIGURE 9.7 Tempered-glass doors and their frames.

9.5 Curtain Walls

by W. S. Kinne, Jr., Director, University Facilities Research Center, Madison, Wisconsin

A *metal curtain wall* is an exterior building wall that carries no roof or floor loads; it is fastened to the structural frame and acts solely as an enclosing envelope. It usually consists of metals in combination with glass, plastics, and other surfacing materials, supported on metal unit frameworks. There are three basic types of curtain walls now in general use. Custom walls are designed specifically for one major project, using parts and details made specially for this purpose. Commercial walls are made up principally of parts, components, and details standardized by a manufacturer and assembled either in the fabricator's stock patterns or in accord with the architect's general design. Industrial walls are those in which ribbed, fluted, or otherwise performed metal sheets in stock sizes are used for major surface coverage, along with standard metal windows, as the principal elements. The commercial and industrial types are sometimes referred to as window walls.

Custom curtain walls are most often used for high-rise buildings or multibuilding complexes — office buildings; large-scale housing and apartment developments; corporate building programs; large municipal service expansions such as airport terminals; and major new campus expansions of high school, junior college, college, and university organizations. Commercial curtain walls have had their most frequent use for local educational buildings at the primary, elementary, and secondary school levels, for commercial and industrial office accommodations, and for semispeculative buildings built primarily for rentals to other than the original owners. Industrial curtain walls have been used for large-scale, essentially low-cost wall enclosures for factory and loft types of occupancies, as well as for low-budget applications sometimes considered to be adequately serviced by the commercial curtain wall types.

In metal curtain walls, major emphasis is placed on repetitive factory parts production and prefabricated assembly of reasonably thin, large-area wall surface units, with the objective of keeping assembly and erection labor on the building site at a minimum.

The chief functions of a metal curtain wall are to withstand the actions of the natural environment — wind, rain, snow, hail, sleet, and sunlight; to prevent access by intruders; the absorption or retention of water vapor, and damage by fire; and to control the flow of heat and the passage of air, light, and sound. It must be aesthetically appropriate and have permanence consistent with the design life expectancy of the building enclosed by the wall. The possibility of curtain wall replacement, or substitution, within the useful life of the basic structural frame is always present.

The principal elements of a metal curtain wall are the supporting curtain wall frameworks, usually vertical but sometimes horizontal mullions; the glazing units, operating windows (see Section 9.6) or fixed glass panels; the opaque enclosing panels; the anchors for the attachment of the curtain wall system units to the structural frame of the building and the joints and sealants at the junctions between wall units, which compensate for movements within the curtain wall caused by external forces of nature, by movements of the building frame, and by thermal changes. Solar screens are often made an integral part of the curtain wall to be a means of controlling the thermal effect of sunlight both on the wall itself and on the internal building spaces enclosed by the wall.

The mullions are usually manufactured to a structurally stable profile made from extruded aluminum or aluminum sheet and solid stock, often protected with electrochemical anodic coatings; or they are made of rolled stainless or carbon steel or extruded bronze. Color can be applied to the mullions as part of the basic manufacturing process by the use of coatings of porcelain, baked enamel, vinyl, and other plastics or specialized anodic treatments. Vertical mullions usually extend through one or two stories of the building's height, with slip joints to provide watertight junctions while allowing linear expansion movement.

Sash frames for glazing units are usually attached to, or are an integral part of, the mullion system. Operating window sash are often chosen primarily for the ease of washing glass surfaces, since many buildings of the kind that use metal curtain wall have year-round air conditioning, and window ventilation is not an important factor except in between the seasons. Where fixed glass is used, exterior glass washing is often accomplished by power-driven vertical stagings suspended from the roof and restrained from side sway by movable attachments to the mullion system portions of the curtain wall.

Panels are usually composite fabrications of two or more materials into a single assembly. Two principal types are produced, classified by the method of assembly. Mechanical panels are held together by screws, rivets, or other mechanical fasteners, and laminated panels are held together with adhesives. Panels are designed to provide adequate strength, dimensional stability, thermal insulation, resistance to weather and corrosion, control of condensation, sufficient sound isolation, the necessary degrees of fire resistance, and desired appearance. Structural glass is sometimes used as a panel, backed up with an air space and a secondary panel to provide the desired physical qualities. Composite panels are covered with a wide variety of exterior facings in a wide variety of colors and texture ranges. Porcelain on steel sheet or aluminum sheet, thin-set ceramic tile, thin precast concrete or terrazzo, preformed chemically treated metal sheet, and plastic-coated inorganic sheets are frequently employed. Among the more common core materials for laminated panels are treated paper expanded honey comb, foamed closed-cell insulation units, and compressed glass fiber insulation boards. Vapor barriers on the warm side of the assembly are advisable for all conditions needing condensation control.

Several notable custom curtain wall systems have been designed with the idea of having a preformed metal panel of large size become the entire curtain wall unit assembly. Here the large single-sheet metal units have the structural capability of acting as substructural mullions, present an arrangement possible for the introduction of glazing elements within their unit area, and make possible logical jointing and sealing junctures with adjacent similar units. These units can be laminated to, or backed up with, other materials to make overall physical performance acceptable.

Anchors which provide for the support of curtain wall units at the point of contact with the building frame are usually factory-fabricated from structural steel shapes which are protectively coated by being galvanized or bonderized for corrosion resistance; these frequently employ stainless steel bolts and point-of-contact fasteners. Anchor assemblies must be designed to allow rather sizable dimensional tolerances, in the range of ½ in. to ¾ in. plus or minus, adjustable during the field erection process in three directions: (1) vertical; (2) horizontal, parallel to the curtain wall surface; and (3) horizontal, perpendicular to the wall.

Curtain wall units and assemblies are manufactured and fabricated to closely predictable sizes, but the basic building structural elements to which the wall will be attached are much less precisely dimensioned at the erection site. Thus, flexibility of anchorages is very important in assuring a logical and sure junction of wall and structure.

Joints and sealants for metal curtain walls are perhaps more critical to the satisfactory performance of the wall than they have been to conventional stone and brick masonry exterior walls. For the metal curtain wall, materials are essentially nonabsorbing. Infiltrated water or internal condensation in an essentially metal assembly will normally collect in substantial quantities. Then it may be forced through the wall as a leak or remain entrapped, causing most undesirable effects on insulation materials and metal fittings subject to corrosion. In contrast, moisture in more absorbent masonry and its joints can be evicted by flashings and removed by slow evaporation without serious local effects.

Metal curtain walls are essentially multimaterial assemblies. The variety of materials used have varying coefficients of thermal expansion, as shown in Table 9.1.

Thus, it may be seen that large metal curtain wall units or their components will grow and shrink in different magnitudes within ranges of temperature encountered on the exterior of a building. The joints between the units, and within them, are designed to provide for these movements mechanically. Then they are sealed to control air and water migrations within the wall, with the idea of repelling and expelling water to the outside while preventing inward or outward air movements which might be disturbing to control of interior air conditioning and ventilation. The sealants or gaskets must have qualities of long life, adequate elongation without failure, and good adhesion. They may be considered to be of two types, liquid sealants and preformed gaskets, both manufactured as synthetic plastics. The usual sealants are polysulfide polymers, known as Thiokol (a trade name). These are applied in liquid form, but at room temperature they convert to flexible synthetic rubber. The preformed gaskets are factory-made as extrusions in profiles appropriate for their use. They are most often polyvinyl chloride plastics or synthetic neoprene rubbers, chemically designed to provide desirable properties of hardness, durability, elongation, and adhesion.

Solar screens should be considered an integral part of metal curtain walls or as a potential adjunct. The idea of controlling the effect of solar energy on the interior of a building has long been understood; but the metal curtain wall assembly, using materials with relatively high coefficients of heat transmission and relatively large glass areas, emphasizes the desirability of diverting or reflecting solar heat before it touches the wall surface. This solar energy can then be dissipated in the atmosphere before it enters the interior of the building envelope.

Glass normally covers a rather substantial surface area of metal curtain walls ranging from less than 20% to about 80% of the total exposed surface of the wall. The general subject of glass is covered in Section 9.9. It might be well to describe here the variations of heat transmission expected from the kinds of glass that are usually employed in metal curtain wall assemblies.

Heat transmission, sunlight through glass:

¼-in. plate glass—88% heat transmitted through.

¼-in. heat-absorbing glass—66% heat transmitted through.

¼-in. heat-absorbing glass, air space, ¼-in. plate glass —50% heat transmitted through.

These data represent the sum of reradiation and transmission.

There are three types of exterior solar controls now in general use: horizontal overhangs, canopies, or eyebrows. These may be solid or louvered and are usually fixed but sometimes movable. They are most effective for southern exposures in the Northern Hemisphere but can be quite effective on northern exposures in the tropics. Perforated vertical screens, or preassembled grid systems placed parallel to the wall and window system, can be effective for all orientations. They are usually fixed installations and often

Table 9.1 Dimensional Change, in Inches, Caused by 100°F Temperature Difference for 10 Lineal Feet of Material

Material	Value	Material	Value
Aluminum	0.156	Glass	0.060
Stainless steel	0.115	Concrete	0.096
Porcelain on steel	0.084	Stone	0.048
Bronze	0.113	Reinforced plastic	0.194
Carbon steel	0.084		

become a rather dominant aesthetic factor, for they are literally a screen wall outside of the curtain wall. Outside vertical fins or louvers are most effective for eastern and western exposures in the middle and high latitudes of the Northern Hemisphere, especially when the fins are movable to compensate for varying early-morning and late-afternoon sun angles through the year.

Interior solar screens, although somewhat less effective than the exterior type because the diverted solar energy is trapped within the building, are still important components of metal curtain walls with large glass areas. With their use, trapped heat can be isolated on the inside of glazed areas and diverted by air-conditioning installations designed for the purpose. Horizontal or vertical retractable venetian blinds placed in pockets or tracks built into the curtain wall system, often in conjunction with heating or cooling elements of mechanical systems, are common. One prime advantage of the interior solar screen idea is that it allows greater flexibility of use under the direct control of the individual building occupant—dictated by considerations of sun position, cloud cover, and glare implications.

CONCRETE CURTAIN WALLS

Precast concrete curtain walls are considered in Section 4.6. They are appropriate for use when windows occupy a relatively small portion of the wall area. The following discussion is concerned with such walls when appearance is an important factor. It is based on a bulletin entitled *Concrete Curtain Walls* published by the Portland Cement Association.

Concrete curtain walls are made up of precast reinforced concrete slabs whose size and shape can be selected to meet specific requirements. A common size of slab is 8 by 14 ft. The thicknesses range from 4 to 6 in., depending upon code requirements and upon the degree of fire-resistance and heat insulation required.

Composition

The slabs are constructed of lightweight concrete not only to reduce their weight but also to improve their heat insulation properties. They may be of the same composition throughout, or a layer about 1 in. thick, adjacent to the exposed face, may have a special composition for decorative effect.

Color

Various colors are provided for the facing layer by selecting appropriate aggregates or mixtures of aggregates or mortars. Some of the aggregates used are quartz, marble, granite, gravel, tile and ceramic, and other vitreous materials. Each of these is available in a wide range of colors. The ceramic and vitreous materials are manufactured and thus can be produced to match samples submitted by the architect. Ceramic facing tile are available in a great variety of colors and patterns. The tile are laid in cement mortar applied to the face of the concrete slab and are usually laid in regular rows which occupy up to 90% of the exposed surface. They are often 1 in. square or 1 by 1½ in. rectangular tile.

The mortar or matrix in which the aggregate is embedded has a marked effect on the color. Curtain walls whose color depends primarily on the color of the matrix can be made. White portland cement is usually employed in the facing mix to ensure purity of color even for the darker shades. The matrix is colored by using mineral oxide pigments. Practically all colors can be obtained in this manner.

Texture

The textures of the exposed surfaces of curtain walls are important factors in their appearance. They vary from glossy to rough or rugged textures, depending upon the kind of surfaces against which they are cast, upon the treatment the surfaces receive after removal from the forms, and upon the size and shape of the aggregates. An exposed aggregate finish is often used. It is produced by using various techniques in casting and finally brushing the surface to expose the aggregate. Exposed aggregate facings may be ground smooth to resemble terrazzo. Desired effects are sometimes secured by mechanical means such as bush-hammering, tooling, and sandblasting. Finally, the characteristics of the surface against which the facing is cast largely determines its texture unless the surface is treated after removal from forms.

Patterns

Patterns of various designs are created on the exposed faces of panels by high and low relief in adjacent areas, by differences in the aggregate colors, and by contrasting textures. In addition, any desired form can be produced on the exposed face by casting against an appropriate mold.

Panel Shapes

Panels of almost any desired shape can be manufactured. The most common shapes are rectangular and square, but diamond-shaped panels have been used.

Panels are cast with open grillwork over a part or all of their surface to serve as a solar screen on the outside of glazed areas. The same effect is achieved by building a wall of small perforated units located just outside the wall containing the windows.

Erection

The procedures followed in placing panels in position and

Table 9.2

| Horizontal Separation | Exterior Bearing Walls | | Exterior Nonbearing Walls | |
	Minimum Fire-Resistance Rating (hours)	Maximum Window-to-Wall Area (%)	Minimum Fire-Resistance Rating (hours)	Maximum Window-to-Wall Area (%)
0–3 ft	4	0	3	0
Over 3–20 ft	4	20	2	30
Over 20–30 ft	4	30	1	40
Over 30 ft	4	40	None required	No limit

anchoring them in place correspond to those described in Section 4.6.

Heat Insulation

The effectiveness of lightweight concrete aggregate curtain walls can be increased by plastering the inside surfaces with perlite or vermiculite plaster. Sandwich panels, described in Section 4.6, are also used to achieve a high degree of insulation.

Fire Resistance

Concrete curtain walls can be constructed with the thickness and quality of concrete necessary to conform to any building code requirements.

OTHER MATERIALS

Curtain walls are also constructed of brick masonry, stone masonry, structural clay tile, concrete block, and glass block.

FIRE-RESISTANCE REQUIREMENTS

Curtain walls as an important feature in the architectural treatment of buildings have developed markedly in recent years. Few building codes have been modernized to recognize this development adequately. There are also major differences in those that have been modernized. As one example, the requirements of the National Building Code for the highest-quality fire-resistive building are quoted in part. The requirements for lower types of buildings are less severe. According to this code, with minor editorial changes:

Horizontal separation means a permanent open space between the building wall under consideration and the lot line or the center line of a facing street, alley, or publicway. Where two or more buildings are on a lot, the horizontal separation of the wall under consideration shall be measured from an imaginary line drawn at a distance from the facing wall equal to the horizontal separation applicable for that wall.

1. Bearing and nonbearing walls shall be of approved noncombustible material. Interior bearing walls shall have a fire-resistance rating of not less than 4 hours. The fire-resistance rating of each exterior wall and the maximum allowable percentage of windows to wall area in any story, except in the first story facing a street or public place, shall be as shown in Table 9.2 for the horizontal separations indicated.

2. Where there are two or more buildings on the same lot and the total area of the buildings does not exceed 1½ times the allowable area of any one of the buildings, no fire-resistance rating is required for the nonbearing portions of exterior walls of these buildings that face each other.

3. Openings in exterior walls shall be protected and vertical separation between openings in exterior walls shall be provided.

4. Lintels over openings in walls shall have a fire-resistance rating not less than required by this section for the wall in which the lintel is placed; however, no fire-resistance rating shall be required when the opening is spanned by a masonry arch designed to carry all imposed loads, or the opening is spanned by a beam above the lintel that has a fire-resistance rating not less than required by this section for the wall in which the beam is placed, or the span does not exceed 4 ft. Stone lintels shall not be used unless supplemented with steel lintels, reinforced concrete or masonry arches designed to support the imposed loads.

Except as listed below, every opening in an exterior wall of a building shall be protected by an approved fire window, fire door or other approved opening protection when such opening: Faces on a street and is less than 30 ft from the opposite building line; is less than 30 ft distant in a direct unobstructed line from an opening in another building or from a wood frame building; is above and less than 30 ft from any part of a neighboring roof of combustible materials or any roof having openings within this distance; faces on and is located less than 15 ft from an adjacent lot line.

Except as listed as follows, the exterior openings located vertically above one another shall have not less than 3 ft vertical separation provided by an assembly of noncombustible material having a fire-resistance rating of not less than 2 hours between the top of one opening and the bottom of the one next above, or the exterior openings shall be separated by such an assembly extending outwardly from the building wall a horizontal distance of not less than 3 ft. No vertical separation is required between exterior openings under certain specified conditions.

9.6 Window Types

In general, a *window* is an opening in a wall of a building to provide any or all of the following: natural light, natural ventilation, and vision. The term also refers to the construction installed in the opening to provide protection against entry and the weather. To be satisfactory, windows must be durable, weathertight, reasonable in cost, readily installed, and, for many uses, attractive in appearance. Windows are also used to a limited extent in partitions for vision from room to room, or for borrowed light.

Only exterior windows are considered in this chapter. In addition to the glass, they are made of wood, steel, aluminum, stainless steel, and bronze. They are available in a great variety of types to suit many requirements and individual preferences.

Much has been done by the associations representing the manufacturers of windows of each material to standardize the types, sizes, and construction details of their windows. Lower costs and prompter deliveries are possible if stock, rather than custom-made, windows can be used.

PARTS OF A WINDOW
A window frame includes the members that form the perimeters of a window; it is fixed to the surrounding wall or other supports. The horizontal top member of a frame is the head; the vertical side members, the jambs; and the horizontal bottom member, the sill. A vertical member that subdivides a frame or a vertical member placed between and attached to adjacent frames is called a mullion. Similar horizontal members are also called mullions.

A sash is a framed unit that may be included within a window frame and may be fixed in position or arranged to open for natural ventilation or cleaning. The top member of a sash is the top rail; the bottom member, the bottom rail; and the side members, the stiles. If one sash is placed above another, the adjacent rails are called meeting or check rails. If one sash is placed beside another, the adjacent stiles are called meeting stiles. If a separate member is placed between adjacent sash, as described, it is called a meeting rail or meeting stile.

The units of glass included within a window frame or sash area are called panes or lights. If more than one light is included in this area, the vertical and horizontal members between panes and those that directly support them are called muntins. The panes of glass are held in position by putty, glazing compounds, metal clips, wood or metal moldings, or beads. The last one mentioned is called a glass bead or stop. Placing the glass in position is called glazing. Windows may be designed for glazing from the outside or the inside.

Narrow strips of sheet material in various forms made of metal, felt, rubber, or plastic, called weatherstrips or weatherstripping, may be placed around the edges of operating sash to exclude moisture and air.

A screen consists of wire mesh surrounded by a rigid frame that is placed in a window or sash opening to exclude insects. A storm window or sash is an additional glazed unit placed in a window opening to reduce the heat loss during winter. It is usually placed on the outside of the sash but may be inside. It is often interchangeable with a screen. A shutter is a panel provided to cover a window to exclude light, obscure vision, or to provide protection or decoration. Usually one edge is hinged to a jamb and shutters are usually provided in pairs. They are rarely used, and then only for decorative purposes, on residences, in which case they are often fixed in the open position. They are also called blinds. A fire shutter, also called a fire window, is fire resistant and provides protection against outside exposure fires. It usually operates automatically.

WINDOW TYPES
The usual types of windows, regardless of the materials of which they are constructed, are shown diagrammatically in Figure 9.8. The glass areas in these examples may be subdivided in various ways. Some windows may include only a single pane of glass. Subdivisions may be made to permit the inclusion of ventilating units, for convenience in cleaning, to limit glass size for safety, for architectural effect, or for other reasons. Various types of windows or sash are often combined in a single window opening.

A fixed window is illustrated in *(A)*. It makes no provision for natural ventilation.

A double-hung window is shown in *(B)*. Both sash slide vertically, with the weight of each counterbalanced by sash weights, spiral spring balances, or tape spring balances similar to clock springs; the sash is easily operated and edge friction will hold it in any set position. For a single-hung window, only the lower sash operates. Some types are arranged so that the sash can be removed from the inside.

A horizontal sliding window is shown in *(C)*. One or both sash may be arranged to slide. Some types are arranged so that the sash may be removed from the inside. Heavy sash are often provided with nylon rollers for ease in operation. Sash are sometimes suspended from rollers operating on overhead tracks.

In general, any hinged window is a casement window. It may swing out or in and may be hinged at either side, the top, or the bottom, but the term is usually applied only to side-hinged windows. An outswinging casement window

FIGURE 9.8 Window types—outside views for open positions.

monitor and are operated in unison from the floor by a mechanical operator.

A vertical pivoted sash is shown in *(H)*. Such sash are often arranged to swing in a full circle.

Sash may be top-hinged and swing out *(I)* or top-hinged and swing in *(J)*. They may also be bottom-hinged and swing in *(K)*.

Windows with ventilator sash that operate like those in *(L)* are called projected windows. The ends of the arms are pivoted to the stile of the sash and to the frame. Shoes are attached to the top rail of the sash and move vertically along the stiles. They are guided by tracks attached to the vertical members at the sides of the opening. The window shown in *(L)* is an outward-projecting window, and that shown in *(M)* is an inward-projecting window. If the latter is located at or near the bottom of a window *(N)*, it is called a hopper ventilator. If several outward-projecting ventilators are located vertically adjacent to each other *(O)* and are arranged to be operated simultaneously by a single operator, the window is called an awning window. Fixed meeting rails sometimes are provided between adjacent sash. The downward movement of the top rail of projected sash provides an opening through which the outside of outward-projecting sash can be cleaned.

A jalousie window is shown in *(P)*. It is similar to an awning window except the ventilating units are heavy glass slats from 3 to 8 in. wide with metal end supports to which the operator is attached. Adjacent edges of the slats overlap ½ in. or more to exclude rain and reduce air infiltration. There is considerable air leakage when closed, and they are usually used only for enclosed porches or where air leakage is not objectionable.

A wicket panel is a small sliding or hinged panel in an inside screen provided so the operating mechanism of an outswing sash can be reached from inside.

DESIGNATIONS

A procedure for indicating the type of rotating operating units included in a window is illustrated in Figure 9.9*A*. The meeting point or intersection of the two diagonal lines on a ventilator is located on the axis about which the ventilator rotates. The procedure does not indicate whether the movement is outward or inward. There is no distinction between ventilators rotating about horizontal or vertical axes through their centers, but the axis is usually horizontal.

A system has been devised for designating windows according to the arrangement of lights and ventilators. This designation consists of digits arranged in the following order: Lights wide; lights high; number of ventilators; lights in lower, or only, ventilator; lights in upper ventilator, if any; lights between lower or only ventilator and bottom; lights between upper ventilator, if any, and bottom. Items not present are omitted in designation. The legend was devised for steel windows and is used occasionally for aluminum windows.

with two sash is shown in *(D)*. Each sash swings on extension hinges attached to the hanging stile of the sash and the jamb of the frame. The extension provides an open space between the hanging stile and the jamb to facilitate cleaning the outside. An inswinging casement window is shown in *(E)*. Extension hinges are used to make the sash swing clear of the inside surface of the wall. One or more casements of either type may be included in a single opening. For example, three sash could be included by providing a mullion between a single sash and a pair of sash. Outswinging casements are much more widely used than inswinging. The folding window is illustrated in *(F)*. It is a form of outswinging casement window with the two sash hinged together on their meeting stiles rather than each to its outside stile. Projection arms, which are shown in the figure, are so arranged that the sash operate symmetrically.

A horizontal pivoted sash, pivoted at the center, is shown in *(G)*. Such sash are often arranged in a row to form a continuous or ribbon window located in a sawtooth roof or

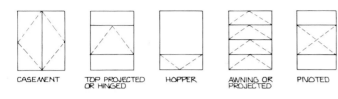

DESIGNATION OF VENTILATOR TYPES

FIGURE 9.9 Designation of ventilators.

FACTORS IN SELECTION OF TYPE

Several of the factors considered in the selection of the type of window for a specific use are given in the following paragraphs.

Ventilation

The following comments refer primarily to buildings that are not air-conditioned but depend on natural ventilation. A vertical or horizontal sliding sash has little effect on the direction of flow of outside air into a room. A rotating ventilator tends to guide the flow in the direction at which the sash is set. For this reason, projected hopper, awning, jalousie, and horizontal pivoted sash, as usually arranged, direct the inflowing air upward toward the ceiling, an effect which is usually, but not always, desirable. Similar but horizontal effects result from the directions at which casement and vertical pivoted sash are set. Outswinging casements can be set to direct air currents flowing parallel to the wall surface into a room. Outward projecting sash, awning windows, or jalousie windows serve as canopies in deflecting rain while the sash are open for ventilation. Folding windows are said to have a chimney effect which tends to draw air out of a room. Ribbon or continuous horizontal pivoted or projected ventilators operated mechanically in groups and located high up on the walls of industrial buildings or in roof monitors or sawteeth are especially effective in ventilating industrial buidings.

Screening

Any operating unit can be screened, but sometimes screening is difficult. The screen wire mesh is installed in frames and is renewable. The wire mesh may be painted or galvanized steel, plastic-coated glass fiber, aluminum, or copper, the last two being the most durable. Screens are arranged to be installed from the inside.

Double-hung, single-hung, horizontal sliding, inswinging casements, and ventilators which open inward (Figure 9.8) may be provided with outside screens. Ventilators which open out, also shown in this figure, may be provided with inside screens. The inside screens for outswinging casement, awning, and jalousie windows do not interfere with the operators, but special provision must be made for oper-

ating outward-projecting ventilators. Horizontal and vertical centrally pivoted ventilators are difficult to screen.

A special type of screen is available which keeps all or part of the direct sunlight from entering a window, depending upon the exposure. Instead of horizontal wires, the screen has flat miniature metal slats corresponding to the slats of a venetian blind. The slats are set at the angle for greatest effectiveness. The vertical wires are more widely spaced than the usual screen wires. This type of screen, if placed outside, is quite effective in reducing temperatures during the summer, especially for rooms with south exposure.

Cleaning and Repairing

The possibilities for cleaning, replacing broken lights, or eliminating water leakage are important factors to consider in selecting the type and location of windows. Double-hung, single-hung, and horizontal sliding sash are often removable for cleaning or repair from the inside. Outswinging casements are fitted with extension hinges which provide an open arm space between the hanging stile and the jamb. Sometimes the entire outside surface of a window can be reached from the inside for cleaning by adjusting the position of the ventilator. In others, the ventilator or movable sash provides for access to the outside for the window cleaner. Except for windows close to the ground or an adjacent roof surface, anchors for the safety belts of window cleaners are often attached to the jambs of windows. Various types of installations have been devised to provide for window washing to be done entirely from the outside even if all the windows are fixed.

Vertical pivoted sash that can rotate through a full circle and top-hinged inswinging sash are designed especially for use in air-conditioned buildings where the sash are only opened while their outsides are being cleaned. Off-season and emergency ventilation may be provided by including a hopper ventilator in the window with one of the types of sash mentioned.

The suitability of the various types of windows for cleaning can be judged by examining Figure 8.8. If the windows are screened, it will be necessary to remove the screens on some types.

Other Factors

Many other factors must be considered in selecting the type of window, regardless of the material of which it is constructed. A ventilator that projects inward may interfere with the use of space adjacent to a window and with the operation of shading equipment such as window shades and venetian blinds; vertical and especially horizontal members in a window may interfere with desired vision through a window; large glass areas may result in personal injury from glass breakage when someone falls against a window;

need for access to the controls of operating units may restrict the placing of furniture or equipment against walls; and the type of occupancy and the appearance may have a significant effect on the selection. Such factors as durability and cost are more closely related to the designs and the materials used in construction than to the type of window.

MINIMUM AREA

Building codes usually require that every habitable room, that is every room arranged for living, eating, or sleeping purposes, must be provided with natural light and ventilation by one or more windows opening on a street, alley, or court. The total glass area in the windows is usually not less than 1/10 of the floor area, with a minimum total glass area of 10 sq ft, except in bathrooms where the minimum is 3 sq ft.

Windows or other openings required for ventilation must have a total openable area of at least 50% of the glazed area required for lighting.

This requirement does not apply to rooms provided with artificial ventilation or air conditioning. Windowless rooms are common, and even windowless buildings are frequently constructed because of the better control they afford for illumination, ventilation, temperature, and humidity than is possible with windows.

Special requirements are included that apply to other types of occupancy and to artificial lighting and ventilation.

9.7 Metal Windows

Metals used for window construction are aluminum, steel, bronze, and stainless steel (arranged in order of the quantity used). Steel windows were introduced in the United States early in the twentieth century. The use of aluminum windows on a commercial scale started about 1930.

ALUMINUM WINDOWS

All types of aluminum windows are made from sections or shapes made by extruding an aluminum alloy through dies which produce cross sections of the desired size and shape. The thickness of the metal used for windows in residences and low-cost housing projects varies from about 1/16 to 1/8 in.; and for those in industrial, commercial, and monumental buildings such as stores, factories, schools, and office buildings, the thickness varies from about 1/16 to 3/16 in. All the window types illustrated in Figure 9.8 may be made of aluminum. The most widely used type is probably the projected window.

Aluminum windows will not corrode, except under extreme conditions, and thus do not require painting. The usual types of finish are the mill or natural finish; the satin finish produced by etching, belt polishing, or rubbing with abrasives; the bright finish produced by buffing; and the anodized finish, which is an electrolytic finish that provides a much thicker and more protective oxide coating than the one that forms naturally. The anodized finish or coating can be given any one of the three finishes first mentioned. Aluminum windows should always be coated with a special temporary clear lacquer applied by the manufacturer to protect against the action of mortar and plaster during construction.

Any possible galvanic action between aluminum and other metals should be avoided. This possibility should be considered in the selection of hardware and weatherstripping. The preferable nonaluminum metals for use with aluminum are nonmagnetic stainless steel, heavily galvanized steel, and zinc. Copper and nickel alloys should be avoided. Since moisture must be present for galvanic action to occur, watertightness and drainage are important precautions, as are protective coatings, suitable gaskets, and seam compounds. The drainage of salts from nonaluminum metals over aluminum windows should also be avoided. Window details which require one aluminum surface to slide over another such surface should not be used because of the excessive wear which may occur.

STEEL WINDOWS

Steel windows are constructed of hot-rolled solid sections and of cold-roll-formed strip steel. The solid sections are used for nearly all industrial types of window and for the casement and projected types for nonindustrial buildings. Cold-formed strip steel is used principally for double-hung windows in nonindustrial buildings. It has not proved to be economically feasible to shape steel for window construction by extrusion through dies. Almost any form, type, or size of steel window can be manufactured if the cost can be disregarded. Because of the high cost of equipment used for forming solid sections or cold-formed sections and for assembling the shapes into windows, the shapes of sections and types and sizes of windows have been standardized to a considerable extent, but substantial savings could be made by further standardization. All the types of windows illustrated in Figure 9.8 are manufactured of steel.

Solid hot-rolled section steel windows are classified according to the kinds of building for which they are best suited: Architectural for buildings in which appearance and quality are of major importance, such as residences, apartments, hotels, office buildings, school buildings, and hospitals; and commercial and industrial for which a plain substantial design is suitable, such as stores, factories, warehouses, storage buildings, and power houses.

Windows made of hot-rolled sections are usually protected against corrosion by a special factory treatment of the surface, called bonderizing, to improve the adhesion of paint, and then by painting periodically as required. Windows made of hot-rolled steel sections are sometimes galvanized by hot-dipping the completed window, but this practice is not common.

The use of steel windows has been somewhat curtailed by the use of aluminum windows. Steel windows are now used mostly in security installations such as psychiatric hospitals and prison works. There is, however, a plastic-covered steel window that is used for public buildings.

BRONZE AND STAINLESS STEEL

Bronze and stainless steel are attractive materials that do not corrode and are highly weather-resistant. The shapes used in constructing bronze windows are extruded in the same manner as those for aluminum windows. For this reason, any of the window types available in aluminum can also be constructed of bronze.

Stainless-steel windows are made from cold-roll-formed strip metal following details similar to those used for double-hung steel windows. The vertical pivoted type is also manufactured using similar details.

Windows constructed of these materials are expensive and therefore are used only on the highest type of buildings. Because of the small demand, they are custom-made.

9.8 Wood Windows

Wood windows are used extensively in many types of buildings when not excluded by the fire-resistive requirements of building codes.

Wood windows have been used for centuries. The large-scale production of such windows by machines in factories started about 1840. They are used mostly for residences. The most widely used type was the double-hung window, as illustrated in Figure 9.8B, although now the outswinging casement in (D) is quite common, and horizontal sliding in (C), the outward projecting in (L), the hopper in (N), the awning in (O), and the jalousie in (P) are also used.

CASEMENT WINDOWS

An outswinging casement window with two sash for a masonry wall is illustrated in Figure 9.10A; and an inswinging casement window, in (B). The principal parts of each window are the frame, the sash, and the trim. Many of the parts of these windows have corresponding parts in the double-hung window. They are illustrated in the figures. A part peculiar to this type of window is the astragal, which may be provided to cover the joint between meeting stiles and make it more weathertight.

Casement windows may include one or more sash, the two-sash casement being the most common. All types can be controlled by operators located on the inside.

SPECIES OF WOOD

The wood used for the exposed parts of wood windows should be highly weather-resistant and should not warp or shrink. The most commonly used wood is ponderosa pine, but white pine, sugar pine, fir, redwood, cypress, and cedar are also used extensively, the selection being governed largely by relative availability at a given location. The jambs of double-hung windows are subjected to considerable wear, and therefore they should be made of some relatively hard wood or durable softwood such as yellow pine. They are sometimes protected with aluminum. The parts which are exposed only on the inside are made of the same wood as the interior trim.

Frames and sash should be treated with water-repellent wood preservative. All exposed exterior surfaces of wood windows should be protected by periodic painting and interior surfaces by appropriate finishes, except the contact surfaces of double-hung and sliding windows, which should be protected by oiling. Some are made with a plastic coating that protects the wood.

THICKNESS OF SASH

The actual thickness of sash most often used is 1⅜ in., but 1¾ in. material is used for the better class of construction and 2¼ in. for the best large windows. Small basement sash may be 1⅛ in. thick. Screens are normally ¾ or 1⅛ in. thick and storm sash 1⅛ in. thick.

9.9 Glazing

Glass is composed of about six parts white sand, one part lime, and one part soda, with small amounts of alumina and other materials.

DEFINITIONS AND MANUFACTURE

The definitions and brief statements of the methods of manufacture of the various kinds of glass, as given by Specification 123 of the Federal Specification Board, are as follows.

Plate glass. Transparent, flat, relatively thin glass having plane polished surfaces and showing no distortion of vision when viewing objects through it at any angle. Plate glass is made at present by casting and rolling large sheets periodically or by rolling a continuous sheet. The sheets are then ground and polished.

Clear window glass. Transparent, relatively thin, flat glass having glossy, fire finished, apparently plane and smooth surfaces, but having a characteristic waviness of surface which is visible when viewed at an acute angle or in reflected light. Clear window glass is made at present by hand blowing or by machine blowing and drawing into cylinders and flattening, or by drawing directly into a sheet, the surface finish being that obtained during the drawing process.

FIGURE 9.10 Details of wood casement windows.

Processed glass. There are three kinds of processed glass either in plate or window glass, viz., ground glass, chipped one process, and chipped two processes. The ground glass is made by either sandblasting or acid etching one surface. The chipped glass is made by applying either one or two coatings of glue to the ground surface. The glue is applied hot and in cooling and drying shrinks and pulls small chips off the surface of the glass.

Rolled figured glass. A flat glass in which the vision is more or less obscured either by the roughened surface produced in rolling or by the impression of a large variety of decorative designs in one surface of the sheet.

Wire glass. Rolled flat glass having a layer of meshed wire incorporated approximately in the center of the sheet. This glass is produced with polished or figured surfaces.

Ornamental plate. A figured plate glass made by rolling or rolling and pressing and having the plane surface ground and polished.

Prism glass. A flat glass having prism-shaped parallel ribs designed for deflecting light. This is made as a rolled plate or as a pressed plate, of which one side may be ground and polished, or as a pressed tile.

THICKNESSES AND GRADES
The most common thickness of polished plate glass is ¼ to ⁵⁄₁₆ in., but ⅛ in. and ³⁄₁₆ in. glass is fairly common. Other thicknesses up to 1¼ in. are obtainable by special order. Second silvering quality is used where the highest quality is desired, but most of the glass used is known as glazing quality.

The most common thicknesses of clear window glass are single strength, varying in thickness from ¹⁄₁₂ to ¹⁄₁₀ in., and double strength, varying in thickness from ⅛ to ⅛ in. Other thicknesses up to ⅕ in. are obtainable. All clear window glass should be relatively flat, but a slight irregular curvature is not objectionable if it does not exceed 0.5% of the length of the sheet. Glass with a reverse curve or which is crooked should be rejected. A small amount of A A quality window glass is sometimes selected for special purposes and may be obtained at a high price. The grade most often used in windows where appearance is an important factor is A quality, but B quality is used quite extensively. Two grades inferior to B quality are on the market. They are Fourth quality and C quality. Fourth quality glass contains many defects and distorts the objects viewed through it. It should never be used where vision is important. C quality is too poor for use in buildings.

Rolled figured sheet glass is made in thicknesses from ⅛ to ⅜ in. It is made in a great variety of surface finishes which obscure the vision, diffuse the light, and give decorative effects.

Wire glass is made in thicknesses from ⅛ to ¾ in., the standard thickness being ¼ in. Only one quality is manufactured for glazing purposes. It is made with polished surfaces and with a great variety of surface finishes which obscure the vision, diffuse the light, and give decorative effects. The wire is in the form of a wire mesh, the standard size of mesh being 1¼ by ⅞ in. and the weight of wire No. 24 B & S gage.

The wire is placed in the glass by any of three methods: (1) by rolling a sheet of glass, placing the mesh on it while the glass is still plastic, pressing the mesh into the glass, and finishing the surface; (2) by rolling a thin sheet of glass, placing the mesh, and rolling another sheet of glass on the first sheet; (3) by placing the wire on the casting table and holding it in position while the glass is poured around it. Polished wire glass is not of the same quality as polished plate glass.

SAFETY AND BULLETPROOF GLASS
Laminated glass, built up of layers of glass between which are cemented layers of colorless transparent plastic resembling celluloid, is called shatterproof or *safety glass.* The chief use of a glass of this type is in automobiles, but it is also used for skylights and in the windows of asylums. Bulletproof glass or bullet-resisting glass is a thick safety glass used in banks. Ordinary safety glass is ⅛ to ¼ in. thick, but bulletproof glass has several laminations built up to thicknesses of ½ to 2 in. The thickness most commonly used is 1⅛ in. This glass will not be penetrated by bullets from most firearms, although 2 in. glass is recommended to resist shots from a 30-30 rifle. These types of glass will crack under impact, but the plastic layers hold the various pieces of glass together so that it does not shatter.

TEMPERED GLASS
Tempered glass is used where safety precautions are required. Store fronts, residences and other public areas should be glazed with tempered glass. Glazing installation may be from ¼ in. to 1¼ in. in thickness. Tempered glass may frequently be identified by two tong marks on one edge of the glass, although these tong marks are usually covered by glazing materials. Tempered glass is obtainable without tong marks.

HEAT-ABSORBING GLASS
Heat-absorbing or actinic glass is a kind of glass which, because of its special composition, excludes a high percentage of the ultraviolet rays to which it is exposed, transmits less solar heat into a building than other kinds of glass, and has less bleaching effect on colored fabrics.

This type of glass has the advantage of reducing air-conditioning loads and costs. It should not be set in frames where the glass will be partially shaded. For if a portion of the glass is shaded and a portion is in direct sunlight, a differential in expansion and contraction will likely result. If differential expansion does result, cracking of the glass is likely.

Quartz glass transmits a larger percentage of ultraviolet rays than ordinary window glass. Since these rays are beneficial to the health, this kind of glass may be used where this quality is desired.

MULTIGLAZING
Windows are often glazed with factory-produced panes consisting of two or three parallel sheets of glass separated by a thin dehydrated air space maintained by an airtight glass seal between the sheets and located around their edges. Because of the seal and the dehydrated air, there is no condensation or accumulation of dirt within the air space. The heat transmission through the window is substantially reduced during the winter, and the heat gain during the summer is correspondingly reduced, especially if the outer sheet is heat-absorbing glass. Various other combinations, which may include tempered, are used. Multiglazing also reduces sound transmission. This type of insulation is called *insulating glass.*

REFLECTIVE GLASS

A glass that is of laminated construction with a reflective film in the middle is called reflective glass. This glass behaves as a mirror reflecting heat and glare. Thus, it is also used as a heat absorbing glass.

LOW-TRANSMISSION GLASS

Tinted or coated glass is designed to reduce light transmission. Called low-transmission glass, it is made in several shades of gray and bronze. These glasses are identified by their transmission capabilities, which are expressed as a percentage of the light that passes through.

PSYCHIATRIC GLASS

This glass, which features a mirror on one side and on the other side appears are transparent glass, is called psychiatric glass. It is popularly known as one way glass. To function properly, the side of the glass that is viewed as transparent must be on the side in which the light intensity is less than the side that appears as a mirror. This glass is used for security installations or where private controlled observations are desired.

SELECTION OF GLASS

Polished plate and float glass is used for exposed windows in the better grades of buildings. It is much superior to window glass in appearance and in the clearness of vision through it but is much more expensive. Large windows such as show windows are always made of polished plate or float glass.

Clear window glass is extensively used in all classes of buildings.

Chipped and ground glass are used to a limited extent where light is to be admitted but vision is to be obscured. Chipped glass is more attractive than ground glass and is used in interior partitions. Rolled figured glass serves the same purposes as chipped and ground glass, is usually cheaper, and is available in more attractive designs.

Rolled figured glass is extensively used on the exterior and interior of buildings to obscure the vision or diffuse the light. Many attractive designs are available, and the cost is less than that for clear window glass.

Wire glass may be used in outside windows and fire rated partitions because of its resistance to fire. When heated and drenched with water it will crack, but, owing to the action of the wire mesh, it will remain in position and protect the interior of a building from fires originating outside except when exposed to extremely high temperatures. Wire glass is also used in doors and in other positions where breakage is likely to occur. It will continue to give service even though badly fractured.

Prism glass is used to light areas remote from a window. Light striking the glass is deflected so that it is effective for a considerable distance away from the glass. A common use for prism glass is in the upper part of store windows where the stores are deep and windows are in the front only.

It is desirable to use some type of figured glass in basement windows below grade because such windows cannot be kept clean and dirt is conspicuous on clear glass. The diffusing effect of figured glass is also usually desirable.

9.10 Glazing Accessories

The process of placing glass in windows is called *glazing*. Rebates or rabbets are provided in the edges of the members that support the panes of glass. They must be deep enough to receive the glass and provide the space required by the medium which holds the glass in place. This medium may be putty, glazing compounds, and wood or metal moldings called glass beads or stops. Before putty is placed in wood sash, the surfaces should be spar varnished and allowed to dry. The panes of glass in wood sash are held in place by small triangular or diamond-shaped pieces of zinc called glazier's points, driven into the rabbet. For metal windows, glass is held in a similar manner, before the glazing compound is placed, by spring wire glazing clips or other devices.

Wood windows are usually glazed from the outside. Some types of metal windows are glazed on the outside and others on the inside. If a pane of glass is set in position and the putty applied with a putty knife or by other means as shown in Figure 9.11A, the operation is called face puttying. Back puttying consists of forcing putty into any spaces that

A - FACE PUTTYING   B - BEDDING IN PUTTY

C - WOOD GLASS BEAD   D - CONTINUOUS GLAZING ANGLE

FIGURE 9.11 Methods of glazing.

may be left between the edges of the sash and the back of the glass. Before the glass is placed in position, a layer of putty may be spread on the surfaces of the sash to receive the glass. This operation, called bedding the glass in putty, is illustrated in (B), where the final step consists of face puttying. In (C), a pane which is bedded in putty in a wood frame is held in position by a wood glass bead. In (D), a similar pane in a steel frame is held in position by a steel glazing angle. Such continuous metal moldings are required on industrial windows. The objectives of bedding are to provide a cushion for uniform support of the glass in order to avoid cracking and to make a water- and airtight seal. Other means are used for holding panes of glass in position.

STRUCTURAL GLAZING GASKETS

Neoprene gaskets that are designed to receive and hold glass are called structural glazing gaskets. These gaskets, placed in a structural supporting frame, are capable of holding large and thick sheets of glass. The glass is placed in the gasket and a neoprene strip insert is placed in a prepared slot. The gasket then firmly holds the glass in place.

9.11 Door Hardware

Basically, door hardware requirements are fulfilled with the installation of a hinge set and a latch system. Specialized devices such as automatic closers and miscellaneous hardware items meet specific needs. Code requirements may demand a panic device.

Traditionally and by definition, hardware is metallic, although ceramics and plastics are now used. In general, function decides the most appropriate material. Stainless steel is best suited for the corrosive atmospheres of marine and industrial areas. Wrought iron and steel are used where heavy industry demands ruggedness. The softer materials (brass, bronze, and aluminum) in either cast or wrought forms may be more aesthetically appealing for commercial, public, and residential uses.

HANDING OF DOORS

The standard procedure for indicating door swings is called handing or handing of the door. Many hardware items must be oriented or handed to the door swing.

Handing is determined as follows:

1. For exterior doors, handing is from the outside.
2. For interior doors with locksets, handing is from the key side.
3. For communicating doors without locksets, handing is determined from the side from which the hinges are not visible.

FIGURE 9.12 Handing of doors.

4. For closet and cabinet doors, the handing is from the room side.

With hinges on the left, doors are left hand (LH); hinges on the right are right hand doors (RH); strike bolt bevels that face the observer are regular bevel; strike bolts with the bevel facing away are reverse bevel (RB). Figure 9.12 will clarify handing.

HINGES

Through usage, the term butt has become synonymous with hinge, a usage that refers to the part of the door where hinges are frequently applied—the butt edge. The term butt hinge refers to hinges applied to the door surface as well as those mortised into the butt edge. Usually the hinge is comprised of three basic parts: a male leaf with an even number of knuckles and normally attached to the door; a female leaf with an odd number of knuckles designed to receive the male leaf, and a pin inserted into the cylindrical hole formed by the joined knuckles which compose the barrel.

PINS

On exterior doors where the barrel is exposed, unauthorized pin removal is deterred by using nonrising loose pins, sometimes called nonlifting pins. They are retained by an inaccessible set screw on the inner top knuckle and are adjustable only when the hinge is fully open. Loose or removable pins are used on interiors where pin removal may be desired. Fast pins or rivet pins, which may have both ends machine-spun, are oval shaped and factory sealed. They are nonremovable and are intended for industrial and institutional buildings. Hospital hinges require a type of nonremovable pin. Friction pins on friction hinges are special pins with an

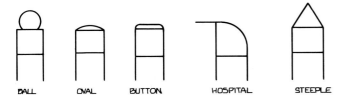

FIGURE 9.13 Hinge tip designs.

adjustment enabling the pin to operate as a hold-open device or to close the door gently. Stainless steel pins are used to bronze, aluminum, and stainless steel butt hinges.

TIPS

The most common tip design is the convex top button tip, replacing the once very popular ball tips. Oval head or oval tips form an integral surface with the barrel and are used where simplicity is desired. Hospital tips have a curved tip formed as a part of the top knuckle. The bottom knuckle may be shaped like the top. They improve sanitary conditions; but more importantly, these tips do not provide a surface or catch to which cords or clothing may be attached. Steeple tips are cone shaped and are used where appearance is paramount. The bottom tips of certain mortise hinges have a small hole used to facilitate the removal of the loose pin. These holes are called plugs. Flat tips are flush with the top and bottom knuckles of the barrel. Spun tips have a convex profile and are used on fast pins. Figure 9.13 illustrates several tip designs.

HINGE CLASSIFICATION

There are four general types of butt hinge classifications with respect to application. Full mortise hinges (Figure 9.14A) have both leaves embedded flush with the door and door frame. Conversely, full surface hinges (B) have leaves applied to both the door surface and the front face of the door frame. Hinges that have one leaf mounted on the front face of the door frame and the other leaf mortised into the door butt edge are half-mortise hinges (C). Half-surface hinges (D) are those that have one leaf surface mounted on the door and the other mortised to the frame. The exposed faces of surface hinges are usually beveled. See Figure 9.14.

Hinges are further classified by the screw hole pattern and by function. Those having a standardized screw hole size and pattern are template hinges. Their primary use is for metal doors and pressed metal frames. The countersunk screw holes are in several template patterns. Nontemplate hinges are used principally on wood doors and wood frames; their screw hole pattern is usually staggered. Blank face, also called plain hinges (E) have no predrilled holes. Their chief use is on welded full surface or mortise installations as needed for industries and institutions having maxi-

mum security requirements. Also, where field-drilled holes are desired for bolted construction, blank face hinges are used.

Several hinge types are identified by function. Clear swing hinges (F), (G) feature an offset pivot located to allow the door to swing free of the passageway, permitting full use of the opening. Such hinges are used in hospitals or other institutions where the frequent movement of wide furniture and equipment requires the extra space. These may be installed by any of the four methods of application. Mortise butts called wide throw hinges are used where a wall reveal or return or applied trim would interfere with the door swing. These hinges have extra wide leaves, permitting the pivot point to extend well beyond the door face. Anchor hinges are a special full mortise hinge featuring an extension of one or both leaves bent at a right angle and mortised into the top and bottom edges of the door. They are handed. Pivot hinges (H), usually used on exterior doors, may be applied full mortise. The double knuckle features an extended pivot located beyond the face of the door which swings fully open. Olive knuckle types (H), so named because of their shape, are a pivot hinge or paumelle type usually full mortise. These handed hinges meet aesthetic criteria. Slip-in hinges are designed to slip into a slot in doors and frames. The screw holes are not countersunk.

HINGE SELECTION

Proper hinge selection in respect to application is determined by the door or door frame materials. All wood doors and wood frames should have mortised butt hinges. Mortised applications are mandatory for hollow metal doors and pressed metal frames. These various combinations of door and door frame materials will determine if a surface or mortise application is appropriate.

The choice of butt hinge bearing types is determined by traffic loads and door weight. Butt hinges feature three general types of bearings:

1. Plain bearing hinges (I) of standard weight are used on doors with light traffic loads or on lightweight doors of expected low frequency use, such as doors to church confessionals. Plain bearing hinges are made of wrought bronze and wrought steel in polished and unpolished finishes. They are not made of aluminum.

2. Ball bearings hinges (J) are used on doors having moderate weight and moderate use and are recommended for all doors using automatic closing devices. Communicating doors on public institutional and commercial buildings have moderate use requirements, making the use of ball bearing hinges imperative. They generally have five knuckles with two ball bearing raceways and beveled leaves. For a smooth operation that will result in longevity to hinges, the ball bearings of polished hardened steel are enclosed in a

FIGURE 9.14 Types of hinges.

bearing raceway containing a nonfluid lubricant. These hinges are made of wrought bronze and wrought steel.

3. Extra-heavyweight ball bearings hinges *(D)* are employed on heavy doors of high frequency use, such as entrance doors and restroom doors on buildings accessible to the general public. The barrels have four ball bearing raceways.

HINGE SIZING

The principal factors that determine the hinge dimensions are the door height, width, and thickness and the necessary clearances. When sizing butt hinges, the length, which is the length of the barrel, is stated first. The width, if indicated at all, is stated secondly and is the measurement of the unfolded hinge. The hinge length is determined by the width of the door specified. The width of the hinge is determined by the thickness of the door plus the offset necessary to assure a clear swing of the jamb and the trim. Table 9.3 will clarify the requirements for sizing.

The minimum number of hinges recommended for passage doors is three; however, doors 90 in. or more in height should have a minimum of four butts. Doors 60 in. or less require two hinges, although doors of this size seldom occupy the entire door frame opening, that is, toilet stall doors. Hinges are billed in pairs; most applications require 1½ pair.

SWAGING

Swaging is the bending of the hinge leaf intended to bring the leaves into closer contour with the barrel. Fully swaged hinges have parallel leaves when closed or folded. All full-mortised hinges should be swaged. Hinges may be swaged flat on one leaf. Template hinges intended for application to metal doors and metal frames must be swaged to produce equal width leaves. Nonswaged hinges called flat back hinges are used for full-surface applications such as blank face hinges. On quality hinges, the leaves (in addition to swaging) have beveled joints, which means the leaves are bent near the barrel, improving appearance.

SURFACE CLOSERS AND DOOR CHECKS

Door closers and surface closers are mechanical devices designed for closing and controlling hinges on pivoted doors. The closer, while permitting an easy opening, protects against door damage. The closing is the checking action, thus closers are called checks, door checks, or checking floor hinges (see Figure 9.15). The checking action should be smooth throughout the closing. Floor checks and surface closers have two closing speeds. The main closing speed, or sweep speed, is the closing speed up to the last five degrees of closure. The final closing speed, a deceleration, is called the latch speed and may be adjusted independently, bringing the door to a gentle, soft closing.

An adjustment made on closers to stop the opening swing action at a determined point is called the back-checking and protects the door, the closer, and the surrounding construction from damage. All doors should have stationary door stops that will assure positive stopping, notwithstanding back-checking. Adjustments and control on accessible regulating valves of the closers and checks are made by special key operated plugs that deter tampering. Casings are made from cast iron, aluminum alloy, or cast bronze. They are of one-piece construction to prevent excessive leakage of the hydraulic fluids, which should be a glycerine-based mixture, such as glycerine alcohol, petroleum lubrication oil, or a silicone fluid capable of operating in freezing weather.

SURFACE CLOSERS

Surface closers may be mounted on either side of the door and concealed by mortising into the door or by encasement within the transom bar. The three general types of surface closers are the rack and pinion type (Figure 9.16A), the crank shaft type *(B),* and the rotary vane *(C).* Closers may be handed or nonhanded to permit interchangeability.

ARMS

The arms forming the link between the door and the closing mechanism are made of steel, cast iron, or malleable iron. There are two operating type arms: regular arms perpendicular to the door and parallel arm types with arms parallel to the face of the door and mounted to the side opposite the hinges. Various special features are associated with arm design. A hold-open feature allows the door to be held open, able to be released with only a slight push or pull. Hospital hold-open arms are adjustable to hold the door in any of several positions. Fusible links installed on hold-open arms are set to hold a door open. These links are a small piece of low melting-point (eutectic) metal. They are used on fire doors kept open for normal use but which may be closed when excessive heat fuses the link. Delayed action may be incorporated into the arm, permitting cart and service trucking through an open door that will close of its own accord.

BRACKETS

Brackets hold the exposed surface closer in proper position, permitting it to function efficiently. They are made of malleable iron, cast iron, or steel suitable for mounting on the door frame. Corner brackets (Figure 9.17A), when properly located, provide leverage to the closer, enabling it to operate more efficiently. Soffit brackets *(B)* are used where no other adequate mounting surface is available or where space allowances are insufficient. Adjustable brackets *(E)* are for rounded or arched in-swinging doors.

Table 9.3 **Rules for Sizing Hinges**

Door Thickness (in in.)	Door Width (in in.)		Height of Hinges (in in.)
Cabinet doors	To	24	2½
Screen doors or combination doors	To	36	3
Doors 1⅜ in. thick	To	32	3½
	Over	32	4
	To	36	4½
		36 to 48	5
Doors 1¾ in. thick	Over	48	6
Doors, 2, 2¼, 2½, in. thick	To	42	5 extra heavy
	Over	42	6 extra heavy

FIGURE 9.15 Checking floor hinges.

FIGURE 9.16 Door closers.

FLOOR CHECKS

Floor checking devices, which are set flush with the floor, may be single acting or double acting. Some types have an adjustment enabling conversion from one action to the other. They may be centrally pivoted with pivots integral with the checking device. Otherwise, the checking device is independent of the hinge action as with butt hinge installations and offset pivots. Helical springs with a preset or adjustable tension are used on helical torsion and helical compression types of checks. The closing force is adjusted by the spring tension on the check or by positioning the check on its mounting plate. Floor plates are usually used for covering the embedded floor checking types. Hydraulic-electric actuated door checks are used on more expensive public buildings where a high frequency use warrants the added cost for installation.

CLOSER SELECTION

A number of factors determine door closer choice. The choice of surface applied closer or concealed closer depends upon maintenance, weather conditions, frequency of use, appearance considerations, and, most importantly, the type of closer that would function with the selected door. Surface closers may be unsightly but present fewer maintenance problems than concealed floor checks. Checking floor closers are subject to water damage and dust penetration. On the other hand, concealed overhead closers, located in the transom bar of the door frame, are more accessible for maintenance though initial cost may be higher. Exterior doors are subject to more traffic, weather conditions, drafts, and severe winds that would require a closer meeting these conditions. The door swing will be a factor if center-hung by pivots, or by offset pivots, or if hung by butt hinges. Most closers handle a variety of closing conditions; however, certain concealed closers are designed for specified hanging methods. Surface closers may be mounted on the frame or on a bracket that is mounted on the frame, or the closer may be mounted on the door itself. Bracket mounted closers are located on the interior side of the door, providing weather protection in addition to improving the appearance of an otherwise cluttered exterior elevation.

LOCKING DEVICES

The latch system should have smoothly coordinated durable moving parts devoid of looseness. The use of plastics is confined to nonmoving parts not subject to excessive wear.

There are four types of lock sets with respect to installation:

Rim locks are mounted on the interior surface of the door and have square or rectangular boxes with matching strikes. They are little used now except where traditional residential doors complement the architecture. They frequently have lever type handles.

Cylinder locks provide better lock concealment. They are installed by inserting the lock into a hole at the lock stile. The lock is located laterally by measuring from the beveled edge of the stile to the keyhole center line, a distance called the backset. A door or a wall return makes a standard backset awkward; therefore, an extended backset positions the lock a few inches toward the middle of the door. This is used in conjunction with wide throw hinges mentioned above. The core is replaceable when rekeying.

Mortise locks are set flush to the lock stile edge. The locking portion may be similar to the cylinder lock or rim lock in other respects.

Unit locks are applied to the door surface and seated into a square cut made into the locking stile. These one-piece units are installed quickly and efficiently, requiring little adjustment.

LOCK FRONTS AND FACE PLATES

Lock fronts and face plates are used on the lock stile edge. They are a part of the lock assembly acting as a guide sleeve to the latch bolt while sealing the lock. Their shape conforms to the door edge — flat where required, or beveled ⅛ in. per inch on beveled edges. Rounded lock fronts with a 4 in. radius are used on double acting doors.

PANIC HARDWARE

Building codes usually require that exit doors on public buildings shall have hardware easily openable. The code specifies that *panic hardware* shall have a push bar to release the locking mechanism and, moreover, that the bar must extend across at least three-fourths of the door width. Push bars may be adjusted, or dogged, in an open and down position that will effect a quick release. There are three types of push bar panic devices:

1. Rim types (Figure 9.18A) have the locking mechanism mounted directly on the interior surface of the door. A strike plate is required for the inactive leaf. When paired doors are used, the inactive leaf must employ a vertical rod type, protected by an overlapping astragal. Rim devices may be used singly or in pairs; but if paired, they require a fixed mullion between them to hold the strike box. They are handed.

FIGURE 9.17 Brackets.

RIM TYPE

MORTISE TYPE

VERTICAL ROD TYPE

FIGURE 9.18 Types of panic hardware.

FIGURE 9.19 Door coordinator, for double doors with overlapping astragals or with rabbeted stiles.

2. Mortise type devices *(B)* have the concealed lock mortised into the door edge. They are used singly; if used in pairs, they must have a mullion between the leaves. Mortised locks may be used in combination with the vertical rod type when the mortised device is the active leaf.

3. Vertical rod types *(C)* are surface mounted with a surface mounted top and bottom vertical rod threaded through several guides mounted on the locking stile. The vertical strike bolts enter a soffit mounted strike box and a sill strike mortised flush into the threshold. For appearances, a variation has concealed rods within the lock stile. These installations have mortised strike plates in the head and sill. They are installed singly or in pairs or as the inactive leaf in pairs combined with other types. The vertical rod devices may be used on both leaves of the doors providing a split or meeting astragal is used. Where an overlapping astragal is used on the active door, the inactive leaf may be a vertical rod type; however, the active leaf must be a rim type or mortise type. Restated, vertical rods cannot be used in pairs on double doors with an overlapping astragal.

MISCELLANEOUS HARDWARE

A coordinator is used on double doors that have a rabbeted face or an astragal on the active leaf. This device, designed to coordinate the closing sequence of the doors, is centrally mounted on the top of the door frame (see Figure 9.19).

STRIKE PLATES

Flat strike plates mortised into the jamb are slightly curved and are designed to engage smoothly and hold the beveled strike bolt. Extended lip strike plates are used on wide jambs or deepset reveals. Box strikes, with the interior side of the strike box deleted, allow independent door operation on double doors. They are located on the inactive leaf. Dust-proof strikes are floor mounted and mortised. When not engaged, they present a flush surface that will prevent clogging.

STOPS AND HOLDERS

Stops and holders protect and retain the door in an open position. Plunger stops and lever stops suited for interiors have rubber tipped arms mounted on the door. Two-piece holders for exterior doors have a friction roller mounted on the door that engages a wall or floor mounted catch. Automatic smoke detector hold-open devices connected to a fire detection system hold the door open for normal routine but release it when energized.

PLATES

Flat plates of various sizes protect the door from damage. They are made from stainless steel, wrought brass, bronze, aluminum, or plastic. Surface mounted plates are usually beveled; if flush mounted, they are square edged. Kick plates are installed on doors with a high frequency use. Mop plates are similar but smaller. Full width stretcher plates with wraparound edges protect doors where service carts are used. Armor plates cover the entire lower portion of a door. Push plates are simple, flat, light material installed on the lock stile. They may be made of plastic.

Escutcheons are plates that cover the entire locking mechanism, including keyhole and knob spindle. Simple or elaborate and decorative, escutcheons may portray some motif. Roses are similar to escutcheons but smaller.

FINISHES

Economic factors aside, hardware finishes are selected for appearances and the ability to withstand corrosion and exposure. Brushed and sprayed finishes are applied to aluminum, stainless steel, and brass. Dull bronze, gold, statuary bronze, and jappaned are examples of sprayed surface applied finishes; whereas chrome, galvanized, and anodized finishes are plated. Bonderized and lacquered finishes serve as priming for painting.

When specified, the finish is applied to hardware on both sides of the door. However, if the sides require different finishes, a split finish is stated — the exterior is named first, the interior second.

Surface finishes have been standardized by the United States Department of Commerce (see Table 9.4).

Table 9.4 **Hardware Symbols and Finishes**

Symbol	Finish
USP	Primed for painting
US 3	Bright brass
US 4	Dull brass
US 10	Dull bronze
US 10B	Dull bronze, oxidized and oil rubbed
US 14	Nickel plated, bright
US 26	Chromium plated, bright
US 26D	Chromium plated, dull
US 27	Satin aluminum, lacquered
US 28	Satin aluminum, anodized
US 32	Stainless steel, polished
US 32D	Stainless steel, dull

Finishes noted are federally approved with samples on file (except US 10 B — no sample). For other finishes, consult manufacturers.

Summary

As a part of the building's envelope, doors, curtain walls, and windows are designed to withstand the effects of weather, prevent the intrusion of sound, deny access by unauthorized personnel, and be aesthetically appropriate. They are constructed of various combinations of wood, metals, plastics, glass, and other surfacing materials.

Doors also provide access and egress for people and equipment essential for the activities taking place in the interior spaces. Building codes usually specify the classification and number of doors needed to meet the occupancy requirements of the building. Windows provide natural light, natural ventilation, and vision for the occupants of the enclosed spaces. Associations of door and window manufacturers have standardized the types, sizes, and construction details of their products. This permits mass production of the more commonly used products and provides a lower cost and greater availability to the consumer. Curtain walls often contain windows, may provide doorways, and always meet the requirements of a nonload-bearing exterior wall.

Key Terms

doorway

door

door frame

hinges

sliding door

rolling door

revolving door

panel door

flush door

astragal

fire door

hollow metal door

veneer

metal curtain wall

window

plate glass

clear window glass

processed glass

safety glass

tempered glass

insulating glass

glazing

door closers

panic hardware

Review Questions

1. Explain the operation of the following classes of doors: swinging; rolling; revolving

2. List three common door sizes.

3. Explain how panel, flush, and hollow metal doors are constructed.

4. List the three basic types of curtain walls commonly used in building construction.

5. Explain how awning, casement, and jalousie windows operate.

6. List the factors to be considered in the selection of a window type for a specific use.

7. How are plate glass, clear window glass, and wire glass manufactured?

8. Explain the operation of panic door hardware assemblies.

CHAPTER 10
FINISHES

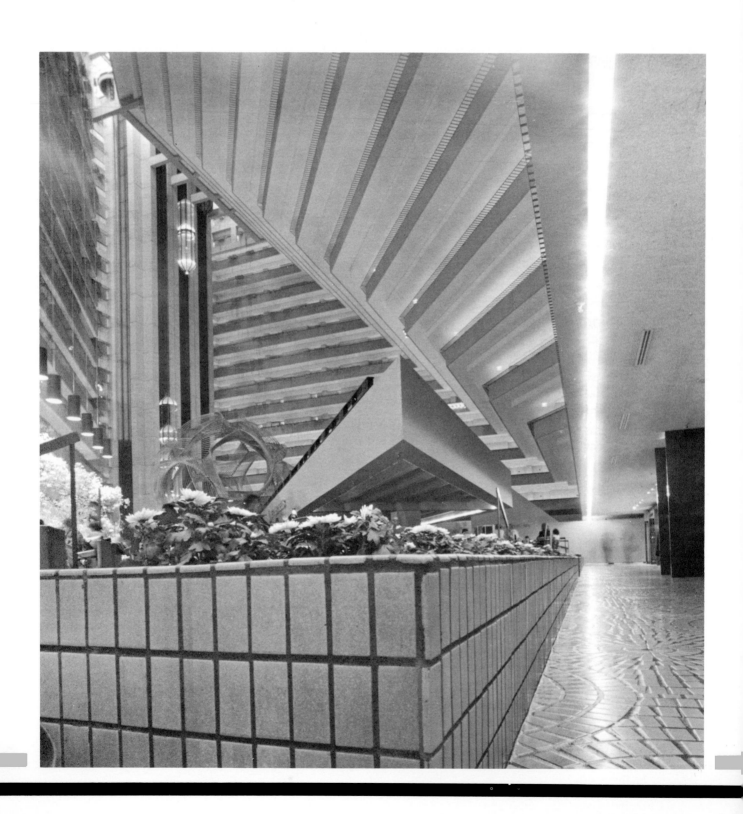

The selection of the interior finishes that will be used in a building is one of the most important and, at the same time, one of the most difficult decisions that has to be made in the building construction process. The appearance, usefulness, and cost of maintenance and cleaning are greatly affected by the type of interior finishes that are installed. Initial cost, cost of upkeep, expected life, building codes, availability of material, personal preference, availability of skilled workers, and suitability for the intended use are all factors that have to be considered in the selection of finish materials for installation in the building.

For most interior finishes, there are a variety of materials that could be used, but not all of them would be right for a specific use. In a simple wall partition, for example, a 2 in. by 4 in. frame with particleboard installed on each side and painted would offer physical separation of the spaces. However, sound generated in one of the spaces would intrude on the other space, and a fire in one of the spaces would quickly spread to the other space. This may not meet building code requirements or provide a space that is free of sound intrusion. A three coat plaster application on metal lath would offer fire protection and decrease the sound transmission, however, this construction would be more expensive and require skilled workers to accomplish the installation. Or, ½-inch gypsum wallboard laminated to ¼-inch gypsum sound deadening wallboard on each side would further reduce the sound transmission and offer about the same fire protection for one half the cost of the plaster installation. This scenario could be repeated for most interior finishes.

The selection of interior finishes requires that all of the alternatives be given consideration to ensure the materials specified will meet the needs of the space, satisfy building code requirements, be cost effective, and be aesthetically appropriate. The discussions that follow will describe various materials available for consideration as interior finishes.

Objectives

1. Become familiar with the basic raw materials used in plaster construction.

2. Become familiar with the various support systems used in plaster construction.

3. Understand the application process for plaster construction.

4. Become familiar with the various types of gypsum wallboard.

5. Understand the application process for drywall construction.

6. Become familiar with the various materials used for finish floor applications.

7. Become familiar with the factors involved in the selection of a floor system.

8. Become familiar with the factors involved in the selection of finish flooring.

10.1 Plastering Materials

The ceiling and wall surfaces of many buildings are finished by covering them with two or three coats of a mixture that consists of a cementing material, an inert fine aggregate, and water. This mixture, known as *plaster,* is mixed to a plastic state and troweled on.

The cementing material for interior surfaces is usually gypsum plaster or hydrated lime, but surfaces which are to be subjected to extreme moisture conditions or hard usage are plastered with portland cement. For exterior surfaces, mixtures of portland cement and hydrated lime are used. When used on the exterior, this mixture is frequently called stucco.

Usually the terms plaster or stucco are used irrespective of their composition but denote only their use and locations. The term mortar, however, frequently implies a plastic mixture of a cementing material, fine aggregates, and water regardless of its use.

QUICKLIME

Quicklime is frequently called lime. Commercial quicklime, which is pulverized, contains varying amounts of magnesium oxide (MgO) resulting from the presence of magnesium carbonate ($MgCO_3$) in the raw material. Silica, alumina, iron, and other impurities are always present.

Lime comes from the kiln in lumps or in unpulverized form called lump lime — it is not sold in this form.

MANUFACTURE OF QUICKLIME

Quicklime is the product derived from the burning of pure limestone ($CaCO_3$) at a temperature sufficiently high to drive off the carbon dioxide, leaving calcium oxide (CaO), a pure quicklime. Calcium oxide (CaO) is a white solid, and carbon dioxide (CO_2) is a gas.

CLASSIFICATION AND GRADES

Quicklime is divided into four classes depending on the relative amounts of calcium oxide and magnesium oxide present: high-calcium contains 95% of calcium oxide; magnesian has between 25 and 40% of magnesium oxide; high-magnesian or dolomitic contains a high percentage of magnesium oxide. However, common practice recognizes the division of quicklime into only two classes — calcium limes and magnesian limes.

Quicklime is divided into two grades: selected, a well-burned lime free from ashes, core, clinker, and other foreign material; and run-of-kiln, a well-burned lime without selection.

Hydrated lime is the dry product produced by treating quicklime with water in sufficient quantity to complete its hydration. Hydrated lime is furnished in two classes according to plasticity. Masons' hydrated lime, of lower plasticity

than finishing hydrated lime, is used for mortar and for the scratch and brown coats of plaster. It is further classified as Type N (Normal) and S (Special) according to its ability to develop high early plasticity [ASTM C 207]. Finishing hydrated lime, with higher plasticity, is used for the finish coat of plaster as well as the uses made of masons' hydrated. It, too, is further defined as *Type S* [ASTM C 206].

SLAKING

In preparing lime mortar, quicklime is mixed with water, forming calcium hydroxide, $Ca(OH)_2$. This is a fine white powder, but an excess of water is always used, forming a paste called lime paste or lime putty. The form of lime known as hydrated lime is simply the hydroxide formed by adding water to quicklime at the manufacturing plant rather than at the job site. During slaking, considerable heat is generated, and a marked increase in volume occurs.

The calcium limes slake more rapidly than the magnesium limes and give off a greater amount of heat. Quick-slaking limes begin slaking in less than 5 minutes, while medium-slaking limes start to react in 5 to 30 minutes. Limes that do not start slaking for about one half hour are termed slow-slaking limes. For quick-slaking limes, Type S (Special) [ASTM C 206], the lime should be added to the water; and when steam appears, the lime should be hoed and enough water added to reduce the steaming. For medium-slaking and slow-slaking limes, Type N (Normal) [ASTM C 6], water is added to the lime. To avoid slow-slaking lime in cold weather, it may be necessary to heat the water. There is little danger that too much water will be added to quick-slaking lime, but an excess of water may cause magnesium lime to be "drowned." If too little water is added to either calcium or magnesium limes, they may be "burned." In either burning or drowning, a part of the lime is spoiled, for it will not harden, and the paste will not be as viscous and plastic as it should be.

Slaked lime should age 2 weeks before it is used for plastering, but 24 hours is sufficient if the lime is for masons' mortar.

In making putty or paste from hydrated lime, the lime is sifted slowly into the water and the mixture stirred constantly. The putty is aged or soaked for at least 24 hours. The aging process increases the workability and sand-carrying capacity of the putty. Because hydrated lime has been slaked before shipping, the increased volume of the putty is small. A sack of hydrated lime which weighs 50 lb and contains 1 cu ft will make about 1.1 cu ft of lime putty.

SETTING

In setting, the excess water evaporates and the calcium hydroxide combines with carbon dioxide from the air, forming calcium carbonate, as shown by the formula

$$Ca(OH)_2 + CO_2 = CaCO_3 + H_2O$$

A corresponding reaction occurs when magnesium hydroxide is present. The absorption of carbon dioxide occurs very slowly, and in heavy masonry walls the setting may never occur.

The term air-slaked is often applied to quicklime that has become slaked by absorbing moisture from the atmosphere; but the process does not stop when this change has occurred, for the hydroxide thus formed absorbs carbon dioxide to form calcium carbonate, which has lost its cementing properties.

Besides plastering, quicklime is used in a variety of manufacturing processes and in several construction procedures. In road building and foundations, it is used for the treatment of soils having a high content of expansive clay. As previously mentioned, slaked lime is used in masonry mortars. Lime is used in the manufacturing processes of paper, bleaches, brick, and steel.

GYPSUM

The basic material in all gypsum plaster, the mineral *gypsum,* occurs in three forms: gypsum rock, gypsum sand, and gypsum earth or gypsite. Gypsum rarely is found in a pure state but contains clay, limestone, iron oxide, and other impurities. Pure gypsum is a soft, white mineral, a form of which is alabaster.

Manufacture of Gypsum

Heated to a temperature between 212°F and 400°F, gypsum loses three-fourths of its combined water, that is, some of the water is driven off as steam. The remaining product is calcined gypsum, or plaster of paris if pure gypsum is processed. Plaster of paris and cement plaster are made by calcining or burning gypsum in large kettles or in rotary kilns. If kettles are used, the gypsum is finely ground before burning; but in rotary kilns, the gypsum is crushed to a size of about 1 in. The final pulverizing is accomplished after burning.

Cement or hard-wall plaster results if certain impurities are present or are added in the manufacturing. These impurities cause the product to set more slowly than the rapid setting plaster of paris. If gypsum is heated to about 1400°F, practically all the combined water is driven off, forming a dead-burned, or anhydrous, plaster. If certain substances such as alum or borax are added, hard-finish plaster is produced.

The time of set of hard-wall plasters is regulated to the convenience of the artisans. Ordinarily the setting time must be delayed; therefore, a retarder such as glue, sawdust, or blood is added. The working quality and sand-carrying capacity of plasters are improved by adding clay or hydrated lime by the manufacturers; and the cohesiveness is increased by the addition of cattle hair, wood fiber, or glass fiber. In localities where good sand is not available, plaster may be purchased with the proper amount of sand premixed.

Generally, gypsum plaster is grouped into two classifications — base plasters and finish plaster. Base plasters are troweled on a suitable firm base and followed with a finish plaster, which forms the finished surface.

BASE PLASTERS

ASTM C 28 identifies four types of basecoat plasters. Gypsum ready-mixed plaster is a calcined gypsum plaster that has a mineral aggregate added to the plaster during milling. This type of plaster may be mixed with a vermiculite, perlite, or sand aggregate. This plaster, which serves as a basecoat plaster, requires only the addition of mixing water at the job site to prepare it for application. These plasters may have setting times ranging from 1½ hours to 8 hours.

Another calcined gypsum plaster is gypsum neat plaster, which is premixed with materials that control setting time and working quality. This plaster permits an extended setting time ranging from 2 to 16 hours. Sold in unfibered, fibered, or extra fibered form, this plaster is intended for job site mixing that requires the addition of water and aggregates. The term neat means that the plaster (though it may be fibered) is sold without aggregates.

Similar is gypsum neat plaster, type R, which is intended for mixing with sand only. It has a shorter setting time of not more than 3 hours.

Gypsum wood-fibered plaster requires the addition of a sand aggregate. This material, which serves as an excellent basecoat plaster, has a normal setting time of 1½ to 8 hours. The nonstaining, mill-mixed, shredded wood fibers give this plaster superior binding qualities. Glass-fibered plaster is also available and exhibits excellent binding qualities.

Gypsum bond plaster contains mill-mixed ingredients that permit a bond to untreated concrete and masonry surfaces. This plaster serves as a base coat under finished gypsum plaster surfaces. It has normal setting times.

FINISH PLASTERS

There are several plasters classed as finishing plasters. Gypsum ready-mixed finish plaster is a mill-mixed neat finish material that requires only the addition of water for job site mixing.

Gypsum gauging plaster, a finely ground gypsum finishing plaster, is mixed with slaked lime putty for improved workability. This material, which is troweled on in a coat about 3/32 in. thick, results in a hard, smooth, white finished surface. It is provided in slow set or quick set. When setting time is not retarded, it should set up in about 20 to 40 minutes. Otherwise, slow set requires 40 minutes or more.

The most common and best known form of hard finish plaster is Keene's cement plaster [ASTM C 61], first processed in 1838 by R. W. Keene of England. This material forms by calcining lump gypsum, immersing it in a 10% alum solution, recalcining it, and finally pulverizing it. This gypsum plaster, which is referred to as "dead burnt" or "hard burnt," offers a hard, blanched, impervious finish. It is characterized by high resistance to abrasion and water penetration. It is ideally suited for kitchens, bathrooms, and other locations requiring a finished wall material that will not absorb water. It is available in quick setting or standard setting — 20 minutes to 6 hours.

Gypsum molding plaster, a very white gypsum plaster, is employed primarily for molding cornices, column capitals, seals, and other decorative features. It is used to form a suitable mold for precast concrete where special forming demands a design of unusual requirements.

Plaster of paris is used for ornamental castings, but the rapidity with which it sets makes it unsuitable as a wall plaster or for mortar.

Portland cement is used in portland cement plaster, which is both a finish plaster and base plaster. Type I, Type II, and Type III portland cements are used; and where the advantages of air entrainment are required, Type IA, Type IIA, and Type IIIA are used. Portland cement plaster is applied where exposure to moisture is a problem — especially at exterior applications.

Portland cement-lime plaster, which contains Type S finishing hydrated lime, is applied in similar locations as portland cement plaster. The lime serves as a plasticizing agent, resulting in better workability.

Plastic cement is a portland cement, Type I or Type II, containing a mill-mixed plasticizing agent — usually a quantity not in excess of 12% by weight. Plastic cement improves workability, increases water retentivity, and reduces shrinkage in the drying plaster. The addition of plasticizing agents is prohibited during mixing.

BONDING AGENTS

A *bonding agent* is a liquid resinous water emulsion applied to base surfaces requiring adhesion between a base surface and a base plaster. The colored liquid is evenly sprayed, rolled, or brushed. The water soluble, dried bonding agent is re-emulsified by the water in the plaster. As the plaster dries, the bond film dries again, thus forming a bond between the plaster and the base material.

Bonding agents are effective between most plasters (gypsum, cement) and several backing materials, namely: concrete, cinder block, brick, ceramic tile, gypsum lath, gypsum wallboard, glass blocks, gypsum block, wood, and steel. Backing materials may be new or used, unfinished or painted with an oil base, rubber base, or vinyl base paint. Bonding agents should not be used over water soluble paints, glues, or wallpaper.

AGGREGATES

Plaster aggregates are identified as sand aggregates and lightweight aggregates. Aggregates should be well graded,

clean, inert material, free from excessive amounts of organic impurities and water-soluble impurities. Sieve gradations should conform to standard grading criteria as defined by the American Society for Testing and Materials.

SAND

Sand is classified as natural or as manufactured sand by ASTM C 35. This standard defines natural sand as "the fine granular material resulting from the natural disintegration of rock or from the crushing of friable sandstone"; and manufactured sand as "the fine material resulting from the crushing and classification by screening, or otherwise, of rock, gravel, or blast furnace slag." Sand for gypsum base plaster, gypsum-lime plaster, and portland cement plaster must pass a No. 4 sieve, with 90 to 100% retained on a No. 100 sieve. Up to 5% of the sand should be retained on the No. 8 sieve, while proportional amounts of graded sand must be retained on the No. 16, No. 30, and No. 50 sieves.

LIGHTWEIGHT AGGREGATES

Perlite or vermiculite aggregates improve the plaster's fire-resistive and heat-insulating properties.

Natural *perlite* is a siliceous rock of volcanic origin ranging from light gray to glossy black. When heated, its volume increases up to twenty-fold resulting in a snow-white product. Heated above 1600°F, combined water and occluded gases in the crude crushed perlite explode, forming numerous minute glassy air bubbles. This cellular structure gives the processed perlite its extraordinary insulating properties, unusual light weight, and exceptional fire resistivity.

Perlite, a form of natural glass, is chemically inert; thus, it does not combine chemically with plasters or cements. This inert aggregate does not accelerate or retard the plaster setting.

In addition to its high insulation qualities, perlite or vermiculite as an ingredient of plaster results in a plaster with marked acoustic absorptive ability. As an aggregate for plaster, these lightweight materials must meet grading requirements — that is, all perlite particles must pass a No. 8 sieve with only 5% of the aggregate retained thereon. At least 88% of the perlite must pass the No. 100 sieve [ASTM C 35].

High insulating values and a low unit weight of about 7½ to 15 lb per cu ft make perlite ideally suited as an aggregate for plasters that are used for fire protection.

Vermiculite which is a micaceous mineral, is greatly exploded into a fan-shaped aggregate when subjected to temperatures of about 2400°F.

Vermiculite, which weighs from 6 to 10 lb per cu ft, exhibits the same above mentioned physical properties of perlite. Grading requirements are similar, although slightly coarser grading is permitted.

WATER

Although potable water is usually satisfactory, mixing water should not contain oils, acids, minerals, or organic substances in amounts sufficient to accelerate or retard plaster setting. Moreover, water in which equipment has been cleaned should not be used for mixing.

10.2 Lathing Materials

Plaster is applied to properly prepared bases such as masonry, monolithic concrete, or lath bases. The masonry bases include brick, stone, hollow clay tile, concrete block, and gypsum block. The lath bases which are designed to receive plaster include metal lath and gypsum lath. Gypsum plaster can be applied to any of these, but lime or portland cement plaster should not be applied to untreated gypsum block or gypsum lath.

MASONRY

A base coat on masonry is held in place by bond. To ensure adequate bond, the surface of the masonry must be rough and free from glaze, oil, dirt, efflorescence, or any other foreign material that would prevent the development of a strong bond. Wire brushing or chipping may be necessary to roughen monolithic concrete surfaces because dressed lumber, metal, or plywood oiled forms and well-vibrated concrete tend to produce smooth surfaces that inhibit adequate bond.

The first coat of gypsum plaster applied to untreated monolithic concrete or concrete block should consist of gypsum bond plaster. If a gypsum bond plaster is not used, a liquid bonding agent should be employed. Several proprietary solutions are available that will prepare the monolithic concrete or concrete block surface. Lime plaster or stucco should not be applied to untreated monolithic concrete or concrete block.

Except in arid climates, plaster should not be applied directly to the interior surfaces of exterior masonry walls but should be furred as described below.

METAL LATH

Metal lath is an expanded or perforated sheet metal material into which a base coat of plaster is "keyed." Metal lath, which is attached to a supporting structure of solid material or a frame of studs, is primarily intended for interior plaster applications free from excessive moisture. Various types of metal lath are manufactured from zinc alloy or galvanized strip steel or from copper bearing strip steel that has been coated with a rust-inhibiting paint after fabrication. The basic types ordinarily used in plastering are diamond mesh (small) or flat expanded metal lath, ⅛ in. flat rib lath, ⅜ in. rib lath, and ¾ in. rib lath, sheet lath, and large diamond mesh. Metal lath sheets are generally 27 in. wide and 8 ft long, with the ribs, if any, running longitudinally; however, ¾ in. rib lath is made in 24 and 29 in. widths and in 8, 10, and 12 ft lengths.

In manufacturing expanded metal lath types, 8 in. wide steel strip is cut with sized and spaced longitudinal slits. The strip is then expanded laterally by pulling, thus forming sheets 27 in. wide. Sheet lath is stamped and perforated as full-sized sheets.

Expanded lath is either flat or self-furring. Rib lath does not require a furring system. Self-furring expanded lath has spaced depressions or crimps that resemble a dimple. This presents raised points on the lath side that is placed adjacent to the supporting surface. This results in an airspace or furred space of about ¼ in.

Metal lath is usually packaged in bundles of 10 sheets to each package.

WIRE LATH

Wire lath is a fabrication of wire woven or electrically welded into a fabric, screen, or mesh. Wire lath generally backs exterior plaster or interior applications exposed to excessive moisture. Usually the wire is copper-bearing, cold drawn steel that has been galvanized or painted with a rust-inhibiting paint. Wire lath is made flat or self-furring; or it may be unbacked or backed with a water absorbent kraft building paper. If paperbacked, wire lath is usually self-furring.

Woven wire fabric lath is a galvanized, woven, hexagonal mesh. It resembles "chicken wire," and is sometimes so called. It is produced in 1 in. hexagonals with 18 gage wire, 1½ in. hexagonal holes of 17 gage wire, and in 2¼ in. hexagonals of 16 gage wire. It is marketed in rolls of 36, 48, and 60 in. widths. This wire lath is frequently used as a stucco mesh.

Electrically welded wire fabric (plain), which is composed of galvanized wire of not less than 16 gage, is made in rectangular or square mesh of not less than 2 in. All wires of this mesh must be welded at each intersection. This lath may be flat or self-furring.

Paperbacked welded wire fabric lath, an excellent stucco lath, is a self-furring type similar to plain welded wire fabric. However, the paper backing is sandwiched between the vertical wires and the horizontal strands. Horizontal slots in the paper permit the vertical wires to be welded to the horizontal wire. Frequently, additional horizontal reinforcement rods give added support and rigidity. The paper backing, a waterproof, absorbent kraft paper, is held securely in this arrangement. This type of lath is made into sheets 28 in. wide and 50 and 98 in. long.

Wire cloth lath consists of a mesh of about ⅜ in. square made of not less than 19 gage wire and galvanized or finished with a rust-inhibiting paint.

METAL LATH INSTALLATION

The maximum permissible spacings of vertical and horizontal supports for metal lath and wire lath vary from 12 to 24 in., depending upon the type and weight of the lath. For wire fabric, this spacing is always 16 in.

The various types of metal plaster bases are anchored to wood supports with roofing nails, common nails, or staples —the choice of fastener varying with the type and the direction of the supports. They are fastened by wire, not smaller than 18 gage, to open-web steel joists, to steel studs, and to concrete ceilings with wires partially embedded. The anchors should be not more than 6 in. apart and side laps not less than 1 in. between supports for metal lath, wire lath, or wire fabric. They are stitch-wired together at intervals not more than 9 in. The long dimension of metal lath sheets is oriented perpendicular to the supports; however, wire lath and fabric may be placed with the long dimension parallel to supports.

Metal lath are commonly nailed to both sides of wood studs to form partitions (Figure 10.1A). Special prefabricated metal studs 2 to 6 in. deep are used in a similar manner for nonbearing partitions from 4 to 7½ in. thick (Figure 10.1B). Lath are wired to the studs that are firmly attached to steel *runners,* which in turn are anchored to the floor and ceiling or end-anchored. The studs, spaced from 16 to 24 in. as determined by the type and weight, can be used for partitions 26 ft high or more. Two ¾-in. channels braced together may be used instead of a prefabricated stud as shown in Figure 10.1B.

Nonbearing solid plaster partitions are constructed by anchoring light hot- or cold-rolled steel studs to the floor and ceiling, placing wiring metal lath to one side of the studs, and plastering both sides of the metal lath to embed completely the studs by backplastering. The studs vary in depth from ¾ to 1½ in., depending upon the partition height; and spacing varies from 12 to 24 in., depending upon the type and weight of lath used. The thicknesses vary from 2 to 3 in., depending upon the height and the ratio of the height to the unsupported length of the wall. For heights exceeding 20 ft, horizontal channel or ¼ in. rod stiffeners, spaced not more than 6 ft vertically, are wired to the channel side of the lath.

Solid studless nonbearing partitions are constructed of diamond mesh or of ⅜-in. rib metal lath with the long dimension vertical. They are secured at the ends to anchored floor and ceiling horizontal channels called runners. The sheets are edge-lapped 1 in. and wired together at least every 9 in. of height. Temporary bracing is required until the scratch and brown coats are applied to the unbraced side. The total thickness is usually 2 in., the optimum height 8½ ft or less, and the maximum permissible height 10 ft.

Furred and suspended ceilings are constructed with metal lath, supported so that the permissible spacing of supports is not exceeded for a given type and weight of lath. If available structural members are not spaced to exceed

FIGURE 10.1 Types of metal lath partitions. Metal Lath Manufacturers Association.

the permissible spacing or permissible span of the lath, no further furring is required.

Sometimes cross furring with the appropriate spacing is provided perpendicular to its supports. Rods ¼ to ¾ in. or 1½-in. channels are used; the choice depends upon the distance between supports. When the cross furring is supported directly by attaching to the underside of the structural members, such as joists, the ceiling is a furred ceiling.

When the supports described are unfeasible, when a flat ceiling surface is desired, or when this method of support would not provide such a surface, a suspended ceiling may be used. For a suspended ceiling, the cross furring is attached to main runners, which are usually ¾ in. or 1½ in. cold-rolled steel channels, the size depending upon the spacing of their support. The main runners are perpendicular to the furring and suspended from the floor system above by heavy galvanized wires, light steel rods, or light strap iron hangers. The sizes and spacings of the hangers depend upon the ceiling area each supports. All attachments for metal lath, metal furring, and metal runners are made with annealed galvanized steel wire or special metal clips.

Furred or suspended ceilings conceal the structural members and provide flat unobstructed ceilings, or they are used to increase the fire resistance of floor and ceiling construction. For the latter purpose, plaster with vermiculite or perlite aggregate is more effective than plaster with sand aggregate.

A stucco surface reinforced with expanded metal, sheet-metal lath, or wire fabric and applied over waterproof building paper or felt serves as a thin concrete slab. This is especially the case when stucco cannot be bonded adequately to masonry, when the walls are wood sheathed, or when the structure is of steel frame. The paper serves as a backing against which the stucco is forced to provide full embedment of the metal reinforcement. Supports to which the metal reinforcement is attached must not be spaced more than 16 in. The reinforcement is furred out from the backing at least ¼ in. by a spacing device so that the lath will be completely surrounded with stucco.

GYPSUM LATH

Gypsum lath, sometimes referred to as gyplath or plasterboard, consists of a sheet of gypsum plaster with the surfaces covered with heavy paper. This is called plain gypsum lath. The sheets are ⅜ in. or ½ in. thick, 16 or 24 in. wide, and 48 in. long, although sheets are made as long as 12 ft and are so identified as long gypsum lath.

Similar to plain gypsum lath is perforated gypsum lath, which has holes at least ¾ in. in diameter and spaced about 4 in. apart both ways. Plain gypsum lath that has a sheet of aluminum foil on the back is called insulating gypsum lath. This foil serves as a vapor barrier and as a reflective heat insulator. Gypsum lath that is classified as fire retardant by ASTM C 37 is identified as Type "X" gypsum lath.

In combination, an assembly of ½ in. finish plaster over Type "X" gypsum lath will have a fire rating. The plaster is held to the gypsum lath by adhesive bond, and supplemented by keys if perforated lath is used.

Generally, gypsum lath is attached to supports spaced not more than 16 in.; however, ½ in. plain lath may be used on supports spaced at 24 in. centers. The long dimension is usually placed horizontally. Usually the vertical joints are staggered, but they may be continuous if covered with 3 in. strips of expanded metal lath. They are fastened to horizontal or vertical metal supports with special metal clips.

Gypsum lath is used for hollow partitions with metal studs and for solid partitions with or without metal studs for constructing nonbearing partitions similar to those constructed with meta lath. It is also used for furred and suspended ceilings in a method similar to that described for metal lath.

For solid studless partitions, ½ in. thick gypsum lath 16 to 24 in. wide, with a length equal to the ceiling height, is placed vertically. Fastened top and bottom similar to the manner described for the corresponding metal lath partition, it is braced until the brown coat has been applied to one side. The usual finished thickness is 2 in.

GROUNDS AND OTHER ACCESSORIES

The required uniform thickness of a plaster coat is of paramount importance in attaining first-class workmanship. The thickness is controlled by installing various guides called grounds, corner beads, and casing beads on the perimeters of openings and at the tops, corners, and bases of walls (Figure 10.2). Cornices and baseboards conceal grounds at the top and bottom. The accessories are usually made from solid sheet metal that has been stamped and formed, from expanded metal, or from welded or woven wire. Several of the beads or screeds that are made from sheet metal have attached reinforcement strips of expanded diamond mesh. These reinforcements are called expanded flanges or expanded wings. Accessories are galvanized or painted with a rust-inhibiting finish.

In locations where guides cannot be installed, narrow strips of plaster are accurately built up to a thickness that will be flush with the brown coat. These plaster screeds become integral with the brown coat. The screeds, which are often placed horizontally across walls and across and around ceilings, assist in forming true surfaces for the brown coat.

Grounds, screeds, and other accessories can be set to provide a minimum thickness of ⅝ in. over metal lath, wire lath, and masonry and concrete walls; ¼ in. over gypsum lath; and from ⅛ to ⅜ in. over monolithic concrete ceilings.

Stucco with metal reinforcement should be at least ⅞ in. thick measured from the face of the reinforcement. Stucco on unit masonry should not be less than ¾ in. thick.

Walls that are backed with gypsum lath require reinforcement for the plaster at all vertical and horizontal interior corners and on perimeters of openings. Ell-shaped reinforcement used at interior corners is known as cornerite. There are two types — a smooth-edge, expanded diamond mesh and a woven, or welded wire fabric.

Strip reinforcing, which is nailed to the perimeters of

FIGURE 10.2 Plaster grounds and corner beads.

openings, is a flat, smooth-edged, expanded diamond mesh 4 or 6 in. wide.

At projecting (exterior) corners, plaster is reinforced and protected with corner beads. The two types which also serve as plastering guides are small nose corner beads and bull nose corner beads. Both types are made of solid sheet metal or of solid sheet metal with attached expanded flanges.

At doors and other edges where the plaster is terminated, grounds or metal plaster stops that are also called casing beads are installed. They are sheet metal, or sheet metal with expanded flanges. Several profiles are made — square, ¼ round, and beveled.

Metal plaster stops that are called base screeds serve as dividers between plaster and a dissimilar material such as stucco or terrazzo.

Drip screeds are used at plaster eaves or rakes or at water tables. They provide an even termination of the plaster with provisions for a water drip.

There are several other sheet metal plastering accessories such as picture moldings, partition terminals, and control expansion joints that minimize plaster cracking.

FURRING

In general, *furring* is a light, nonstructural framework of strips or metal channels that is applied to supporting surfaces such as walls, studs, columns, ceilings, joists, or beams. Wood furring of 1 in. and 2 in. size is usually nailed to the supporting surface. Cold rolled steel channels, ¾, 1½, and 2 in. deep, are supplied in 16 and 20 ft lengths.

Furring must provide a true, level, and even horizontal and plumb surface. It enables closer, appropriately spaced supports for lath that will not span between widely spaced structural supports and encloses areas called furred down spaces that form a ceiling to cover unsightly pipes, conduits, or duct work. Furring provides a nonstructural frame necessary for framing various built-up shapes such as arcades, vaults, domes, and decorative features. It also creates a dead air space between the structural support and the base plaster. The air space formed by the wall furring has four functions:

1. It intercepts moisture that penetrates an exterior wall.

2. It acts as an insulator and prevents condensation from forming on a cold interior wall surface.

3. It reduces heat transmission through the wall. The insulating properties of the air space realize a conservation of fuel in cold weather and keep the building cooler in hot weather.

4. It permits a space for the base plaster to penetrate a perforated or expanded lath. This results in a more positive bond or "keying."

There are several methods of furring. One consists of a direct application of furring strips vertically to a wall surface

or to the bottom of beams and joists. Another employs specially designed blocks of structural clay or gypsum tile that are veneered to the masonry wall. They are held to the masonry walls by any one of a variety of masonry ties, or by hooking the tiles over heads of nails that have been driven into the mortar joints. The blocks are pointed with mortar, then coated with a bonding agent if necessary, then plastered. Still another method of furring is used for ceilings. The furring strips may be suspended by soft, annealed wires that are called hangers or tie wires.

10.3 Plaster Mixing and Application

Plaster and stucco applications are classified, according to the number of coats, into two-coat work and three-coat work.

The last or final coat is called the *finish coat*. The coat, or combination of coats, applied before the finish coat is termed the base coat. The coat directly beneath the finish is known as the *brown coat*. In two-coat work, the brown coat is also the base coat and is applied directly to the plaster base. In three-coat work, a *scratch coat* is applied to the plaster base before the brown coat is applied. Its outer surface is scratched to improve the bond to the coat that follows. This operation gives the coat its name. Three-coat work is required over metal lath.

In two-coat work, the base coat may consist of a scratch coat, which is not scratched, and a brown coat placed before the scratch coat has set. This is called the double-up method or double-up work, and is widely used in applying plaster to unit masonry and gypsum lath. It is also called laid-off and laid-on work.

APPLICATION

Plaster is applied by hand or machine. If applied by hand, the mortar is dumped on a mortarboard. The hand tools used by the plasterer are shown in Figure 10.3. Mortar is shoved from the board onto the wood or metal hawk with a metal trowel, transferred from the hawk to the wall, and spread with the trowel.

In applying the scratch coat, exerted pressure forces some of the mortar through the open spaces of the lath, forming keys which clinch the mortar to the lath. The hair or vegetable fiber included in the scratch coat permits only enough mortar to enmesh onto the lath surface, forming good keys. Fiber also adds strength to the key during the early stages of setting. This coat is about ¼ in. thick and is not accurately finished. Its surface is scratched with appropriate tools while it is still soft to provide a better bond for the coats that follow.

Machine application is by pneumatic plastering machines, which blow the plaster into position.

The brown coat is applied directly to bases of unit masonry or gypsum lath or to a scratch coat over metal lath after the scratch coat has set firm and hard. It is troweled on and brought to a true surface with a darby or rod (Figure 10.3), the ends of which bear on grounds, screed, or other guides. Given a partial rotary motion, the tools leave the brown coat surface rough enough to receive the finish coat.

Gypsum lath are not wet down. Unit masonry surfaces on which suction must be reduced before applying the brown coat directly to them should be properly wet down. Irregularities in stone walls should be filled with mortar before applying the brown coat. It is unthinkable that one would find it necessary or be so insensitive to plaster over stonework that has an architectural quality; but if it must be done, that is the way to do it. The finish coat is applied to a partially dry brown coat or to a thoroughly dry one which has been evenly but not excessively wetted by brushing or spraying.

For a gypsum-lime putty or white-coat trowel finish on plaster, the finish mortar is allowed to draw for a few minutes and then, with ample watering, is well troweled to a smooth finish free from all defects. The Keene's cement finish is applied in the same manner. Sand float finishes are obtained by applying the mortar with a trowel and finishing by floating with a wood float (Figure 10.3) or with such a float with its surface covered by carpet, cork, or other material, forming a plaster surface free from slick spots or other blemishes.

The finish coat of stucco is textured by manipulating trowels and tools of various shapes, using floats with wood, cork, or carpet surfaces, brushing with fiber or wire brushes, dashing small quantities of mortar on the surface, or finishing in colors.

BACKPLASTER

In another form of exterior wall construction, using metal lath, the sheathing and waterproof paper are omitted. The scratch coat and brown coat are applied to the exterior. Then a backing coat ⅝ in. to ¾ in. thick is applied from the inside to the interior surface of the exterior metal lath bonding to the scratch coat, which was placed from the outside. This process is called backplastering. The face of this backing coat should be about ¼ in. back of the face of the studs; in other words, the studs should be embedded in the plaster about ¼ in. To retard decay, it is desirable to paint the face of the studs. This procedure is known as back-plastered construction. This type of construction, using metal lath, will be sufficiently rigid if the corners of each wall are braced diagonally by 1 by 4 in. boards let-in to the studs on the inner side and securely nailed.

ORNAMENTAL PLASTERING

Ornamental interior plastering includes moldings, cornices, panels, decorative ceilings, or rosettes made of plaster or similar material.

FIGURE 10.3 Plasters' tools.

The base for moldings or small projections is built up solid with the same material as the brown coat into approximately the finished shape, assuring that there is adequate clearance for the finish coat. The finish coat, which is composed of lime putty and gauging plaster, is applied to this base and is cut to the desired profile by means of a sheet metal template operating as a guide. The finish coat cannot be cut with sharp outlines in one operation but must be gone over several times. The low places are filled in with mortar. For larger moldings, the base is built up of metal lath and braced.

Moldings and similar ornamental plastering are placed before the finish coat on the remainder of the walls and ceiling because the guides cannot be placed on the finish coat without marring. Parts of moldings, such as internal and external miters that cannot be run with templates, are hand-formed or cast and placed in position before the moldings are run. Dentils and brackets may be cast separately and placed after moldings are run. Ornaments that cannot be run are cast in gelatin molds, or they may be purchased from firms that specialize in this kind of work.

ACOUSTIC PLASTER

Acoustic plasters are special plasters with porous aggregates troweled on as a final coat to improve the sound-absorbing properties of walls and ceilings (see Section 10.1).

FIREPROOFING

Fire-resistive plaster applied on metal lath over structural steel members to prolong their resistance to high temperatures is made with perlite or vermiculite instead of sand.

PROPORTIONS

Usually, the proportions for plaster materials are measured by parts of volume—the cubic foot. However, fiber, if added, is measured by weight. For the base coats of gyp-

Table 10.1 **Proportions for Plaster**

	Sand, lb Damp, Loose	Vermiculite or Perlite, cu ft
Two-coat work (double-up method)		
Over gypsum lath	150	2½
Over unit masonry	300	3
Three-coat work		
Scratch coat over lath	200	2
Over masonry	300	3
All brown coats	300	3

sum plaster, the proportions of sand, vermiculite, or perlite to a 100-lb bag of gypsum neat plaster should not exceed those given in Table 10.1.

Fibered plaster is sometimes used for the scratch coat over metal lath. The proportions for lime-cement stucco on metal lath are:

Scratch coat. Stiff lime putty 1 part, portland cement 1 part, aggregate 6 parts, with 6 lb of fiber per cu yd.

Brown coat. Stiff lime putty 2 parts, portland cement 1 part, aggregate 9 parts, with 3 lb of hair per cu yd.

The proportions for lime-cement stucco on unit masonry except gypsum block which do not provide a suitable base for stucco are: base coat of two-coat double-up work, stiff lime putty 2 parts, portland cement 1 part, aggregate 9 parts, with 6 lb of fiber per cu yd.

For portland cement plaster and stucco, each coat should consist of 1 part of portland cement to not less than 3 but not more than 5 parts of damp, loose aggregate.

Lime and finely divided clays are added to increase the workability of portland cement plaster and stucco. White portland cement is used in the finish coat for white and the lighter-colored stucco. Colors are obtained by using mineral pigment.

Gypsum ready-mixed plaster is furnished with the sand aggregate added at the mill. No further additions, except water, are made on the job. Gypsum bond plaster is applied as the first coat over monolithic concrete surfaces without the addition of aggregate on the job. Gypsum wood-fibered plaster, also used in this same manner, is applied over all types of lath. When applied to unit masonry, equal parts by weight of damp sand and wood-fibered plaster may be used.

The proportions of lime plaster are as follows:

1. For the scratch coat required only on metal lath—1 cu ft lime putty, 2 cu ft sand, and 7½ lb hair or vegetable fiber per cu yd of mortar.

2. For all brown coats—1 cu ft lime putty to 3 cu ft sand and 3½ lb hair or fiber per cu yd of mortar.

FINISH COATS

The final or finish coat of plaster is extremely important. It must be attractive, the desired texture, hard, and durable. Many types of finish can be used; the most common is known as the white-coat finish. The sand float or sand finish is also widely used, and the lime-Keene's cement finish provides an especially hard surface that is impervious to water. The proportions for these finishes follow:

1. For application over either a gypsum or lime plaster brown coat, a white-coat finish of 1 volume of gypsum gauging plaster, which is calcined gypsum, is mixed with not more than 3 volumes of lime putty.

2. Gypsum-sand float finish—1 part gypsum neat, unfibered plaster to not more than 2 parts of fine sand by weight.

3. Lime-sand float finish—3 parts lime putty, 3 parts fine sand, and 1 part gauging plaster by weight.

4. Keene's cement finish—one 100 lb bag of Keene's cement to 1½ cu ft of lime putty, for medium hard finish, or ⅝ cu ft of lime putty for hard finish.

5. Lime-cement stucco—the proportions for a smooth trowel finish are: stiff putty 5 cu ft and portland cement 1 cu ft; for sand finish—stiff lime putty 5 cu ft, portland cement 1 cu ft, and silica plastering sand or marble dust 500 lb.

PREPARED FINISHES

Several finishes are prepared at the mill and made ready for use on the job by adding water.

WATER PROPORTIONS

Water is added to the specified mixtures in the amounts required to make them workable. Too little water makes the plaster or stucco difficult to spread. If too much water is added, the mixture slides off the trowel or off the wall surface. If mixtures are over-sanded and the excess water is added to make them workable, the strength, hardness, and durability are reduced; and the service they will render is impaired. By avoiding oversanding, the need to add excess water is eliminated.

MIXING

The ingredients of which the mortar for plaster and stucco is made are mixed in batches, or batched, by a mortar mixer. For lime plaster, hydrated lime, which is a dry powder, is usually used. Water is mixed with the lime on the job to form lime putty. The manufacturer's instructions should be followed in preparing this putty. Sometimes it may be used immediately, and sometimes a soaking period of approximately 24 hours is required.

When gypsum is present in the mortar, all tools and equipment should be thoroughly cleaned after the mixing of each batch. Cleaning is important because the presence of partially set gypsum may cause plaster to set too rapidly.

10.4 Drywall Construction

Gypsum wallboard construction for ceilings is commonly called drywall construction because little or no moisture is required for construction. Although plywood, hardboard, and fiberboard are also called "drywall," the term generally refers to gypsum wallboard. Plywood, hardboard, and fiberboard will be discussed in Section 10.5. Gypsum wallboard products are flat panels which have a fire-resistant core between surfaces of paper or other sheet material. The major difference between gypsum wallboard and the other "drywall" boards is that the gypsum products are noncombustible and fire resistant.

TYPES OF GYPSUM WALLBOARDS

Gypsum wallboard is manufactured in a variety of types and sizes depending on the intended use. Standard thicknesses are ⅜ in., ½ in., and ⅝ in. The standard width is 4 ft and lengths are available from 6 ft to 16 ft.

Regular gypsum wallboard has gray liner paper on the back and a smooth special paper on the face. It comes with tapered edges to permit smooth joint treatment. The surface takes any decoration including paint, wall paper, and other surface treatments.

Insulating gypsum board has a sheet of aluminum foil bonded to the grey liner paper on the back. The foil surface provides an effective vapor barrier and when accompanied by an air space it also serves as a reflective heat insulator.

Water resistant gypsum backing board has a water resistant gypsum core and water repellent face paper. It serves as a base for application of wall tile in baths, showers, and other wet areas. The board is tapered on the edges so joints above the area to be tiled can be treated in the usual way.

Type "X" gypsum wallboard has a specially formulated core to give increased fire-resistance ratings when used in recommended systems.

Prefinished gypsum wallboard has a decorative vinyl or paper sheet bonded to the exposed surface which does not require further decorative treatment. They are fire resistant and usually have a scrubbable finish.

The standard edges on gypsum wallboard are beveled, tapered, or square (see Figure 10.4).

APPLICATION OF GYPSUM WALLBOARD

Gypsum wallboard can be applied over any firm, flat base such as wood or metal framing or furring supported by underlying construction. Gypsum wall board can also be applied directly to masonry or concrete, but usually furring is required to separate the wallboard from possible dampness

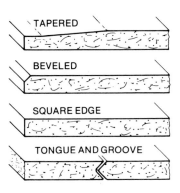

FIGURE 10.4 Standard edges for gypsum wallboard. *Using Gypsum Board for Walls and Ceilings,* Gypsum Association.

in masonry walls. Self-supporting, solid walls or partitions can be built. These are constructed by laminating three or more boards together and attaching them to the floor and ceiling with runners.

Gypsum wallboard can be applied in a single layer or in multiple layers (see Figure 10.5). The single layer construction is common in residential and light commercial construction. The multiple layered construction provides increased sound isolation and fire resistance. It also provides better surface quality as the face layers are laminated and have fewer fasteners on the exposed face. Multiple layered construction is usually specified for commercial installations.

The wallboard can be installed either perpendicular or parallel to the support framing (see Figure 10.6). The framing is usually spaced 16 or 24 in. on center depending on the thickness of the wallboard and code requirements. Gypsum wallboard is attached to wood framing with special nails, special screws, or adhesives supplemented with mechanical fasteners, Special screws are used to attach the wallboard to metal framing and adhesives are used for attachment to masonry walls.

Two nailing methods are used, the single nailing or the double nailing method. In general, space between nails is determined by the requirements for fire resistance and for firmness of board to stud contact necessary to reduce surface defects. Single nails should be spaced a maximum of 7 in. on ceilings and 8 in. on walls (see Figure 10.7). Double nailing can provide tighter board to stud contact and fewer loose boards. In double nailing, a first set of nails is driven 12 in. o.c. in the middle of the panel, and then a second set is driven 2 in. from each of the nails first applied see Figure 10.8. After the second nail is driven, the board is held tighter than before, and the first nails driven should be given an extra blow to reseat them firmly. Nails should be driven with a crown headed hammer which forms a uniform depression about ¹⁄₃₂ in. deep around the nail. This facilitates application of topping compound to cover the nails and produce a smooth surface on the finish face.

(a) Single Ply Application

(b) Double Ply Application

FIGURE 10.5 Single layer and multiple layer drywall construction. *Using Gypsum Board for Walls and Ceilings,* Gypsum Association.

TAPING AND FINISHING

After the gypsum wallboard is erected, it is necessary to make the joints and fasteners inconspicuous to give the wall or ceiling a desirable appearance. Panel joints in the same plane and interior corners are usually covered with paper tape and compound. Exterior corners and exposed edges require metal trim for protection and appearance.

At least three coats of joint compound are recommended for all taped joints. The first is an embedding coat to bond the tape and two finishing or topping coats over the tape (see Figure 10.9). Each coat must be allowed to dry before the next coat is applied to complete its maximum shrinkage before it is covered. After each coat dries, it is sanded to smooth out any rough spots and the next coat is applied.

When done skillfully, the joints and fasteners will be hidden and a smooth, even surface will result.

10.5 Plywood and Wall Board

Wallboards of various materials are usually manufactured in sheets 4 by 8 ft. They are used mainly for interior wall surfaces attached to a supporting framework. These frameworks most frequently consist of wood studs (2 by 4 or 2 by 6), a framework of pressed, stamped metal, or cold rolled steel channels. These studs are commonly spaced at 12, 16, or 24 in. centers — spacing depending upon the height

FIGURE 10.6 Perpendicular and parallel applications for drywall construction. *Using Gypsum Board for Walls and Ceilings,* Gypsum Association.

of the stud wall and its function as either a nonbearing or load-bearing partition.

The space between studs is most often braced with a horizontal member located at midheight which acts as fire blocking and an insulation serving thermal and sound deadening purposes. The finished sheet materials are then placed on the studs and secured with nails, staples, screws, or special clips.

PLYWOOD

Plywood pertaining to structural framing and formwork has been discussed in Chapters 3 and 8. Our discussion here concerns plywood manufacture and plywood used as a finished surface for walls and ceilings. Generally, this type of construction is called paneling; and the plywood sheets, panels.

Plywood consists of thin layers or plys of wood glued or pressed together. The plys are arranged with the grain direction of adjacent plys at right angles to each other. Plywood ranges in thickness from ⅛ in. to 1 in., the actual thickness depending upon the number of plys and the core material. The most commonly used thickness for interior paneling is ¼ in. or ⅜ in. Widths are usually 4 ft and lengths are usually 8 ft, although they may be as long as 16 ft in certain species. The number of plys, always an odd number to prevent warping, is 3, 5, or 7. The outside plys are called the faces or face and back. The intermediate plys with grain

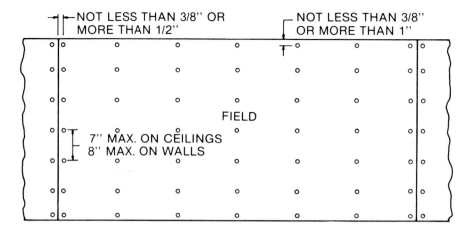

FIGURE 10.7 Single nailing method. *Using Gypsum Board for Walls and Ceilings,* Gypsum Association.

FIGURE 10.8 Double nailing method. *Using Gypsum Board for Walls and Ceilings,* Gypsum Association.

perpendicular to the face grain are called crossbands, while those in the middle are called the core. The core of plywood may be another ply, solid strips of wood, or a sheet of particleboard.

On the face that is to be exposed, panels may have a special finish, texture, or design. Plywood panels that have a hardwood veneer have the finished hardwood surface on one side only. The core and the back side are made of less expensive wood.

The grain configuration of plywood panels is determined by the manner of cutting the veneer ply from the log as well as the species of wood. The wood ply that is cut from the log is called a flitch. Plywood panels, as they are designed for paneling a room, may be arranged in several ways for layout patterns. Layout patterns are based upon the grain configuration of the panels. If panels are to follow a determined order continuously, such as bookmatched pattern, they are referred to as bookmatched in sequence.

The texture of plywood panels may be smooth or sanded;

rough sawn, which shows saw marks; or weathered. The panels are sometimes grooved in several widths — even or random. Panels are also made to give the appearance that the panel is made up of several individual boards.

Plywood panels are made with finished surfaces in more than 20 hardwoods and in about 5 softwoods. Among the hardwood veneers are black walnut, birch, red oak, white oak, ash, pecan, and cherry. The plywoods that have an attractive softwood finish are redwood, several of the pines, and Engelmann spruce.

PARTICLEBOARD

A panel that consists of compressed wood chips, slivers, sawdust, and shavings combined with an adhesive is called *particleboard*. As stated by ASTM D 1554, particleboard is compressed by two methods. In the flat-platen pressed method, the sheets are formed by compressing perpendicular to the faces; whereas by the extruded method, the

TAPERED EDGES
OF GYPSUM BOARD

TAPE

FINISHING
(THIRD) COAT

FINISHING
(SECOND) COAT

EMBEDDING
(FIRST) COAT

FIGURE 10.9 Three coat application for joint treatment. *Using Gypsum Board for Walls and Ceilings,* Gypsum Association.

binder and wood materials are extruded through a heated die, and the pressure is applied parallel to the face of the sheet and in the direction of the extruding. This is known as extruded particleboard. Particleboards are further classified by their density as low density of less than 37 lb per sq ft; medium density between 37 and 50 lb per sq ft; and high density or more than 50 lbs per sq ft. Particleboard is made in sheets 4 ft wide and 8 ft long in thicknesses from ⅜ in. to 1¾ in. The surface finish of these panels may be smooth or grooved.

These panels are dimensionally stable and nonwarping due to their lack of grain. They are ideally suited as an underlayment or core for hardwood veneer and as a backing for the laminated plastics mentioned below. Particleboard is also used in doors and cabinet work, as backing panel to receive fabric wall surfaces, and directly as a finished wall surface to receive paint.

10.6 Wall Covering

LAMINATED PLASTIC VENEERS

Laminated plastic consists of sheets of plastic-impregnated papers. Sometimes called melamine sheets, these high pressure laminates are made by assembling several sheets of phenolic-impregnated kraft paper into which are impressed a melamine-impregnated printed pattern sheet and a translucent melamine overlay. These materials are assembled and compressed at pressures of about 1400 lb per sq in. at temperatures exceeding 300°F. The sheets are marketed in several widths: 2, 2½, 3, 4, and 5 ft, with lengths of 6, 7, 8, 10, and 12 ft.

Three grades are commonly made with respect to use and the thickness of the finished sheet. General purpose grade is 1/16 (0.062) in. thick and is used primarily for horizontal applications, and for some vertical applications. This grade is the most durable and is intended for the most severe use. Postforming grade is made with stretchable papers and a thermosetting laminate that will soften upon reheating and reset when cooled. It is used mostly for kitchen counter tops and splashbacks where a small radius curved surface of coves and bullnoses must be formed. This grade, 0.050 in. thick, is thick enough for self-edging. Self-edging means that the laminate is beveled or chamfered at the square edges. The durability of this grade compares to that of the general purpose grade. Vertical grade is thinner, about 1/32 (0.035) in. thick. It is used for veneering vertical surfaces that take little abuse. It is made in a postforming or a nonpostforming material that may be self-edged.

Laminated plastics are impervious, hard, nonbreakable,

durable, fire-resistant, and attractive. They are cemented as veneers to a backing of plywood, hardwood, particleboard, or asbestos cement. A great variety of plain colors and wood and marble imitations are available. This easily cleaned veneer is very resistant to acids, alkalies, and alcohol. They are used for table and counter tops and as finish wall panels. Panels with laminated plastic veneers are fastened by special nails, clips, or adhesives.

High pressure laminates are frequently identified by their trade names: Formica, Nevamar, and Texolite.

FABRIC WALL COVERING

A plastic covered, fabric backed wall covering that is applied to a wall surface is called fabric wall covering. These vinyl coated coverings are made in rolls 48 in. to 54 in. wide and in lengths up to 36 yd. They may be installed over almost any surface that is smooth, dry, clean, and free of loose material. They should not be applied over surfaces that have been covered with oil base paints or stain.

Wall fabrics are frequently made in colors and patterns intended to resemble other materials such as brick, wood, linen, and burlap. The fabric is generally attached with a wheat paste.

Fabric covered wall surfaces are easily cleaned and are resistant to most agents that soil walls.

10.7 Ceramic Tile and Quarry Tile

Hard materials of various kinds, including ceramic tile, brick, stone, and glass, are used in tile or slab form for wall surfaces and, with the exception of glass, for floor surfaces also.

Ceramic tile of various shapes, sizes, thicknesses, colors, and surface finishes are manufactured for use as a surfacing material for interior and exterior floors and walls where a quality surface is desired.

Structural clay facing tile, as described in Section 5.3, are manufactured for use as structural units in constructing partitions and interior and exterior wall surfaces. They are manufactured with dull and glazed exposed surfaces to provide a finished wall surface. Extruded wall ashlar, which is similar to structural clay facing tile but is more accurately finished, is available for use as a combined structural and facing wall material and for use as a surfacing material only.

Clay brick, as described in Section 5.3, and special paving brick are used for floor surfaces under conditions of heavy wear. Facing brick and brick with glazed and enamel exposed surfaces are used as facing material as well as a structural material for interior and exterior surfaces of brick walls and partitions.

CERAMIC TILE

Ceramic tile are usually set in portland cement mortar when used on the interior of buildings. Quarry tile and promenade tile are set in cement mortar over membrane waterproofing on roof gardens or in similar positions where a watertight floor is required. Floor tile are usually set on a concrete slab foundation or base; so wood floors must be specially constructed to receive this base, as illustrated in Figure 7.13B. Wall tile are set in a bed of portland cement mortar applied to masonry walls or over portland cement plaster on metal lath if applied to walls or partitions with wood studs. A thinsetting bed for floor tile has also been developed. It consists of emulsified asphalt and portland cement and is designed for use over wood, steel, and concrete surfaces. Its small thickness of $1/16$ to $3/8$ in. makes possible the use of tile floors in locations which formerly would not have been suitable.

Ceramic tile are divided into many classes depending upon the processes of manufacture, the degrees of vitreousness, and other properties. These classes are considered more in detail in subsequent paragraphs. The Tile Manufacturers Association divides tile into exterior and interior tile, according to their exposure, and into wall and floor tile, according to their position. Trimmers are available for angles, corners, recesses, and special uses.

Ceramic tile are made by burning special clays or mixtures of clays which have been pressed into the desired shape. Two processes are used: the plastic process and the dust-pressed process.

In the plastic process, the clays are mixed with water and run through pugging machines until a uniform plastic consistency is secured. They are then pressed by hand or machine in dies or molds and, after drying, are burned in kilns. The plastic nature of the materials has a tendency to produce tiles which are slightly irregular in shape.

In the dust-pressed process, the clays, after being finely ground and mixed with water, are passed into filter presses where the excess water is pressed out. The resulting mass is dried, pulverized, pressed into shape in metal dies, and burned in kilns.

The production of special sizes and shapes in the dust-pressed process involves special dies and handling and is a deviation from the regular routine of manufacture. In the plastic process, special sizes and shapes may be produced without distinct departure from the methods of production common to the regular tile.

Ceramic tile may be glazed or unglazed. For use in residences, all types of floor glazes are sufficiently durable for floors; but for public buildings subjected to severe traffic, a special high-fire type of glaze is available.

The colors in unglazed tiles are produced either by the selection of clays which will burn to the desired colors or by the addition of certain materials, such as the oxides of cobalt and chromium. Some clays and color ingredients can be fired to complete vitrification, producing vitreous tile, while others will not stand this high temperature and produce semivitreous tile. A great variety of colors and textures are available.

Unless otherwise noted, the various types of vitreous tile

are obtainable in the following colors: white, celadon, silver gray, green, blue-green, light blue, dark blue, pink, cream, and granites of these colors. The semivitreous tiles are available in buff, salmon, light gray, dark gray, red, chocolate, black, and the granites of these colors. The term granite means a mottled color resembling granite.

The most common shapes of tile are square, rectangular, hexagonal, octagonal, triangular, or round; the sizes vary from ½ in. to 12 in., and the thickness from ¼ to 1½ in. Trim tile are available for use as wall base or to meet any other decorative or utilitarian demands.

Various names are given to the tiles of different sizes and shapes. The more common types used for floor surfaces are the following. Ceramic mosaic include unglazed dust-pressed tile ¼ in. thick with an area of less than 2¼ sq in. They are vitreous or semivitreous, depending on the color, and may be square, oblong, hexagonal, or round. These tile usually are mounted with exposed face stuck to paper in sheets about 2 ft by 1 ft, the paper being removed after the tile are set. If desired, the tile can be obtained loose.

Plastic mosaic include the same size and shape tile as ceramic mosaic, mounted or loose, but these tile are made by the plastic process, and the colors are those that result from the firings of natural clays.

Cut mosaic floors are made from unglazed, dust-pressed, vitreous or semivitreous strips, ¼ in. thick and ½ and ⅝ in. wide, which are cut into the irregular pieces necessary in the production of ungeometric designs and pictorial work. These tile are furnished in loose strips or are assembled in designs mounted with exposed face on paper which is removed after the tile are set.

Vitreous tile and semivitreous tile are names applied to unglazed, dust-pressed tile ½ in. thick. These tile are vitreous or semivitreous, depending on the color. They are furnished in the same shapes as ceramic mosaic, except round, but are larger, having an area of 2¼ sq in. or greater, the largest vitreous tile being 3 in. square; and the largest semivitreous tile, 6 in. square.

Paving tile are unglazed, dust-pressed tile ¾ in. thick. Flint tile are vitreous paving tile, and the semivitreous are called hydraulic tile. These tile may be square, oblong, hexagonal, or octagonal. With the exception of the oblong tile, the smallest size is 4¼ in. and the largest 6 in. Oblong tile vary in size from 6 in. by 3 in. to 10 in. by 5 in.

Corrugated paving tile are semivitreous, unglazed, dust-pressed paving tile ¹³⁄₁₆ in. thick, and 6 in. square with corrugated face.

Rough red paving tile are semivitreous, unglazed, dust-pressed tile, ½ in. or ⅝ in. thick, depending on the size, and 6 in. or 9 in. square with the corresponding oblong half-tile.

Inlaid or encaustic tile are unglazed dust-pressed decorative tile, ½ in. thick, produced by inlaying a figure or ornament of one or more colors into a body of a contrasting or harmonizing color before firing. They are vitreous or semivitreous according to colors.

Quarry tile are machine-made unglazed tile, ¾ in. to 1½ in. thick, made from common clays. They are always square, the usual sizes being 6 in., 9 in., and 12 in. The colors may be various shades, plain red, or the following granites: red, light gray, dark gray, black, chocolate, light brown, dark brown, or green.

Promenade tile are machine-made, unglazed tile 1 in. thick, made from common clays. The size is always 6 in. × 9 in., and the color some shade of red.

Plastic tile are unglazed tile made by the plastic process from natural clays. Any size or shape can be obtained. The thickness is ½ in. or more, depending upon the size.

Ceramic tile is probably the most frequently used wall tile, although several other materials are used. For all tile — copper, stainless steel, aluminum, or plastic — installation and construction criteria are similar. Ceramic wall tile is installed similarly to floor tile. Differences, if any, are in the backing materials, the method of set, adhesive, and the use of more sculptured tile in wall installations. Sculptured tile or tile with a patterned relief are seldom used for floors. Masonry, a common wall backing material, is not used as a backing surface for floor tile work, although application to masonry walls is similar to a concrete surface.

When wall tile are set, foreign matter, loose material, and oiled or soiled material are removed. Each of the two setting methods, cement mortar setting bed or thin set method, has advantages. The traditional mortar setting bed method permits a wall backing surface to be horizontally evened and plumbed before installation commences. Thin set methods permit little correcting of a backing surface.

When wall tile are to be set, the lateral center of the wall surface is established and marked. This center line will be a joint line, or the center of a tile will be placed on this line. The number of full size and fractional part tile for half the lateral distance of the wall are then determined. The desired result is to have each end tile the same size, either a full tile or a fractional part tile preferably larger than one-half tile.

Adhesives and mortars are spread on the back up surface with a serrated trowel. This saw toothed or notched edge trowel assures an even depth of spread of the mortar or adhesive.

MORTARS AND ADHESIVES

There are several adhesives that are used to secure ceramic tile. The use of traditional mortar cement is suitable for most backing surfaces. The thin-set methods are newer methods and are suitable for many applications.

Cement mortar methods for wall installations require a mixture of portland cement, sand, and hydrated lime, their proportions varying with job conditions and backing materials. The cement mortar scratch coat is troweled onto a supporting or backing surface in a thickness of approximately ¾ in. A leveling coat of about ¼ in. to ½ in. removes the imperfections that may exist from an uneven supporting surface. The tile may then be placed on a neat cement skim coat, or cement adhesive may be buttered to the back of larger individual tiles before placing. Tile intended for mortar beds should be presoaked with water to prevent their drawing water from the cement mortar. The cement mortar method provides a more water-resistant and durable installation and is recommended where water penetration may be a problem, such as in showers or where severe exposure is to be encountered. This method is exceptionally well suited where masonry or concrete backing is the wall material. It may, however, be used with wood framed structures; moistureproof kraft paper as well as reinforcing with metal lath or mesh on solid wood sheathing should be used.

There are several mortars referred to as thin-set mortars because the actual thickness of the mortar or adhesive bed ranges from 1/16 in. to 1/4 in. One of these, dry-set mortar, is a premixed mortar to which a small quantity of water is added. Some include sand; others are unsanded. Suitable for most surfaces, this adhesive has excellent holding qualities.

Closely resembling dry-set mortar is latex-portland cement mortar, a mixture of portland cement, sand, and a latex solution. Types of tile adhesives called two-part mortars or adhesives are epoxy mortar, epoxy adhesive, and furan mortar. These materials are used in thin-set methods. The epoxy is mixed with a catalyst which causes a rapid set of the epoxy resin. Furan is likewise mixed with a catalyst. The two-part adhesives are made for application to a solid surface that requires excellent bonding. Another thin-set adhesive is called organic adhesive. This material, which is like a mastic, requires no catalyst and is ready for immediate use. Its adhering qualities are not as reliable as those of other thin-set adhesives.

After tile are set, the joints are grouted. Various types of grout, similar to the adhesives, should be water-resistant and compatible.

10.8 Terrazzo and Concrete Flooring

Terrazzo wearing surfaces are constructed in a manner similar to concrete wearing surfaces, but a special aggregate of marble chips or other decorative material is always used, and this aggregate is exposed by grinding the surface.

The mortar-base course should be at least 1 1/4 in. thick and should be composed of 1 part portland cement and 4 parts sand with only enough water to produce a mortar of the stiffest consistency that can be struck off accurately with a straightedge.

The mortar base can be placed directly on the concrete slab and bonded to it by first cleaning this slab, thoroughly wetting it, and applying a thin coat of neat cement broomed into the surface for a short distance ahead of placing the mortar base; or the surface of the slab can first be covered with a thin smooth layer of fine dry sand about 1/4 in. thick, on which is placed a layer of waterproof paper with end and side laps of at least 1 in., on which the mortar base is placed.

The mortar base is struck off at least 3/4 in. below the finished floor level. Metal or plastic dividing strips are inserted in the mortar base before it hardens, in positions which will control the cracking and conform to the design or pattern desired. The tops of dividing strips should extend at least 1/32 in. above the finished floor level so that they can be ground down flush with the floor surface when the terrazzo is being ground.

The terrazzo mixture should consist of 1 part of gray, white, or colored portland cement, according to the decorative effect desired, to not more than 2 parts by weight of marble chips, other decorative aggregate or abrasive aggregate, or such a mixture of any of these as is desired. Use just enough water to produce a workable plastic mix. Wet mixtures do not produce good results. Any special coloring agents should be mineral pigments.

After the mortar base has hardened enough to stand rolling, the terrazzo mixture should be placed to the level of the tops of the dividing strips and struck off. It should then be rolled in both directions to secure a thorough compacting. Additional aggregates of the desired color should be spread over the surface during the rolling process until at least 70% of the finished surface is composed of aggregate. As soon as the rolling is completed, the surface should be floated and troweled once without attempting to remove trowel marks.

After the terrazzo has hardened sufficiently to hold the aggregate firmly, it should be ground by hand or with a grinding machine, the floor being kept wet during the process. The material ground off should be removed by flushing with water. Any air holes or other defects should be filled with thin cement paste spread over the surface and worked in. After the paste has hardened for at least 72 hours, the floor surface should receive its final grinding. It should be kept continuously wet for at least 10 days, scrubbed clean with warm water and soft soap, and mopped dry.

This type of floor is more expensive than concrete and less expensive than tile or marble. Attractive and durable, terrazzo is inelastic and cold. The greatest objection to terrazzo floors is their tendency to crack. Dividing strips greatly reduce this objection.

Terrazzo is not used directly over a wood subfloor. If placed over wooden construction it should have a base similar to that used for tile floors, as shown in Figure 7.13B.

A terrazzo wall base is commonly used with terrazzo floors. It is usually made in the form of a sanitary cove base, the angle between the floor and the wall having a fillet to facilitate cleaning. A terrazzo base will not adhere to lime plaster, hardwall plaster, gypsum block, or plasterboard. The backing should be brick, stone, concrete, hollow clay tile, or metal lath.

CONCRETE
Concrete wearing surfaces are used very widely where the structural part of the floor is of concrete. The wearing surface may be an integral part of the construction beneath, or

it may be added as a separate layer. If the wearing surface is placed before the base has set, a thickness of ¾ in. to 1 in. is satisfactory; but if it is placed after the base has set, the thickness should be 1 in. to 1½ in., and the surface of the base should be roughened, thoroughly cleaned, and coated with cement grout just before the wearing surface is placed. This is done to secure a bond between the wearing surface and the base, but the results are uncertain.

The wearing surface which is an integral part of the floor may be considered as contributing to the strength of the structure; whereas a wearing surface that is added cannot be so considered and its weight increases the dead load that must be carried by all the beams, columns, and foundations. In spite of this disadvantage, a separate wearing surface may be cheaper than the integral wearing surface, for it is placed after the rough work on the building has been completed and does not need to be protected as carefully as the integral surface. The conditions that exist while the structural part of the floor is being placed may be such that the accuracy required of a finished floor is difficult and expensive to secure.

A truer surface can be secured with the separate wearing surface as the deflection due to the weight of the floor and the yielding of the forms has occurred before the surface is placed, and any discrepancies can be taken up in the wearing surface. The separate wearing surface is sometimes made thick enough to permit the placing of electrical conduits on top of the structural slab.

The coarse aggregate is excluded from the wearing surface, and a richer mixture than that used in the structural parts is used. The aggregate grains and not the cement resist the wear, and therefore the grains should have a high resistance to abrasion. Beyond a certain limit, an increase in the amount of cement reduces the wearing qualities of a surface and increases the tendency to crack. Usually the mixture or topping for the wearing surface consists of 1 part cement to not less than 2 or more than 3 parts fine aggregate.

For surfaces subjected to severe wear, the mixture should be 1 part cement, not more than 1 part fine aggregate, and not more than 2 parts coarse aggregate with a maximum size of ½ in. Various admixtures, or hardeners, are available for use in the topping to improve its wearing properties.

Concrete wearing surfaces or topping must be carefully laid using a minimum amount of water, troweling as little as possible, and protecting against drying out for at least 10 days. Excessive troweling brings excess water and laitance to the surface, causing hair cracks to form and the floor to give off objectionable dust. This process is called dusting. Topping applied to a hardened base should be struck off and compacted by rolling or with tampers or vibrators and finished with a steel trowel. The use of dry cement or cement and fine aggregate sprinkled on the surface to stiffen the mix or absorb excess moisture is objectionable because it may cause hair-cracking, scaling, or dusting. Dust-

ing may be prevented or remedied somewhat by the use of floor hardeners and other preparations, or by painting.

Painted surfaces are satisfactory if the amount of wear is small; but if subjected to severe use, the surfaces must be frequently repainted. Special paints are manufactured for use on cement floors. A cement-colored paint, of course, shows the wear less than paint of any other color. Paint should not be applied until after the floor has been in place 3 or 4 months. Before painting, the surface should be thoroughly scrubbed with a 10% solution of muriatic acid and washed so that the acid is completely removed. The floor should then be allowed to dry before the paint is applied. Paint for the first coat is thinned. Three coats are usually required.

Concrete wearing surfaces are sometimes colored and marked off to imitate tile. Colored concrete floors finished with wax may be attractive in appearance.

If artificial coloring matter is used, only those mineral colors should be employed which will not appreciably impair the strength of the concrete.

Mineral coloring material is preferred to organic coloring material because the latter fades more and may seriously reduce the strength of concrete. Mineral coloring may reduce the strength of concrete somewhat, but where the quantities used are less than 5%, this is not serious. The use of colored aggregates is preferable in obtaining color effects, the surface of the floor being brushed or ground to expose the aggregate.

Concrete floors are inelastic and cold and tiresome to work on, but they are durable if well constructed, are easily cleaned, and are relatively inexpensive. Concrete wearing surfaces should not be used over wood subfloors without taking special precautions to prevent cracking. The construction should be similar to that used for tile floors (Figure 7.13B).

A cement wall base is often used with concrete floors. If a separate wearing surface is used, the wall base may be placed at the same time as the wearing surface with a curving fillet at the junction. This facilitates cleaning. A cement base will not adhere to lime plaster, hard wall plaster, gypsum block, Keene's cement, or plasterboard. The backing should be brick, stone, hollow tile, concrete, or metal lath.

A concrete floor is sometimes called upon to serve the double purpose of a floor and a roof. Under these conditions, a built-up roofing, as described in Section 8.2, is placed on the structural slab. A wearing surface, consisting of a concrete slab about 3 in. thick, is placed over this roofing and is divided into sections not over 16 ft square by expansion joints about ¾ in. wide with a bituminous filler.

10.9 Wood Flooring

Wood flooring is available in the following forms:

1. Strip flooring, consisting of long narrow pieces or strips

with tongued-and-grooved joints along the sides and often along the ends also for hardwoods. Generally called matched flooring or simply flooring.

2. Plank flooring, consisting of wider boards than strip flooring with tongued-and-grooved joints along the sides and ends.

3. Parquet flooring, consisting of short narrow boards cut to form patterns or mosaics.

4. Industrial wood block flooring, consisting of heavy pieces cut in lengths of from 2 in. to 4 in. forming blocks which are set with the ends of the grain exposed to wear.

5. Fabricated wood block flooring, consisting of small square or rectangular blocks formed by fastening short pieces of strip flooring together, tongued-and-grooved joints being provided on all sides.

METHODS OF FASTENING

Wood flooring may be nailed to wood joists through a wood subfloor. Nailing strips are often provided on concrete floor slabs and other types of supporting floors. These strips may be beveled (Figure 10.10A) and embedded in concrete, which holds them in place. Nails may be driven into the sides of the strips to grip the concrete. Expansion bolts or screws may be used as anchors. Special clips to receive the strips may be embedded in the top of the slab when the slab is poured, or the strips may be nailed to other strips at right angles to them, the whole grid being embedded in concrete (B).

Nailable concrete, described in Section 4.1, may be used, with more or less satisfactory results, instead of nailing strips. These concretes are of special composition that permits nails to penetrate. They are usually applied in a layer 2 in. thick with the top surface struck very accurately to receive the finished floor.

Industrial and fabricated wood blocks are usually cemented, and parquet, plank, and short pieces of strip flooring are often cemented to concrete floors, or to a concrete fill, with an asphalt mastic. These mastics are of two types, the hot mastic, which is made fluid by heating, and the cold mastic, which is made fluid by a solvent. The hot mastic is applied to the slab, and the flooring is bedded in it before it cools. The cold mastic gradually solidifies by the evaporation of the solvent after the flooring is placed. The layer of asphalt mastic is called an underlayment.

Flooring which is provided with tongue and groove is blind-nailed to joists or nailing strips (D) so that the nail does not show on the surface. To avoid injuring the floor by the last blow of the hammer which drives the nail home, a square bar, or the square end of a nail set, may be placed in the corner and against the nail head to receive the hammer blow and protect the flooring. Special flooring nails with small heads are used in blind nailing. The ends of plank flooring are commonly screwed to the subfloor, the heads of the screws being sunk in holes bored part way in the wood. These holes then are filled with wood plugs that are specially

FIGURE 10.10 Wood floor surfaces.

manufactured for that purpose. The plugs are quite visible, but this is the effect desired. To provide for expansion, plank flooring should be laid with temporary metal spacers 1/32 in. thick placed in the cracks between the planks. Parquet floors are fastened to wood subfloors with brads driven through the face, the brads being set by driving their heads below the surface with a nail set. The holes above the heads are filled with putty.

KINDS OF WOOD

Strip flooring, plank flooring, parquet flooring, and fabricated wood blocks are available in the hardwoods: white and red oak, maple, beech, birch, and walnut. The oaks may be plain-sawed or quarter-sawed, often called vertical-grain or edge-grain. Strip flooring is also available in the softwoods: fir, yellow pine, white pine, cypress, and many others. Only the quarter-sawed or vertical-grain softwoods should be used, except in the cheapest construction or for attics or other floors which are little used. Industrial wood blocks are usually made of yellow pine, oak, gum, or Douglas fir.

SIZE, GRADES, ETC.

Strip flooring, which is called flooring or matched flooring, is usually 25/32 in. thick. The most common widths of hardwood flooring are 2¼, 3, and 4 in., which have exposed faces of 1½, 2¼, and 3¼ in.; and the common widths of softwood flooring are 3 and 4 in., with exposed faces of 2⅜ and 3¼ in. Oak flooring ⅜ in. and ½ in. thick and maple flooring ⅜ in., 1 in., and 1¼ in. thick are available. Thicker maple flooring may be obtained on special order. The thinner flooring is for use over old floors and is not usually satisfactory for new buildings because it is likely to squeak. Thick maple flooring is suitable for severe usage such as in warehouses, factories, and gymnasiums. Heavy trucking may break off the tongues or lower part of the grooves of ordinary strip flooring. Maple, beech, and birch flooring is furnished in three grades depending upon the quality, i.e., first, second, and third. Oak flooring is available in five grades, i.e., clear, sap clear, select, No. 1 common, and No. 2 common.

Plank flooring is usually $^{13}/_{16}$ in. thick and from 3 to 8 in. wide. It is commonly used in random widths and is known as colonial plank flooring. The exposed edges may be slightly beveled to form V joints.

Parquet flooring is usually $^{5}/_{16}$ in. thick and 1, 1½, or 2 in. wide with square edges, but $^{13}/_{16}$ in. flooring, 2¼ in. wide, which is side- and end-matched is also available.

Industrial wood blocks vary in thickness from 2 to 4 in., depending upon the severity of the service. The width is from 2¼ to 4 in. and the length from 4 to 9 in. The blocks are often provided with wood or metal splines and may be assembled in strips, up to 8 ft in length, whose width equals the length of a single block, as shown in Figure 9.4F. The joints between the blocks are filled with bituminous filler. Expansion spaces about 1 in. wide should be provided against all walls and around all columns, thresholds, and permanent fixtures.

Fabricated wood blocks are made of flooring usually $^{13}/_{16}$ in. thick, but ½ in. and 1 in. thick blocks are also available. The squares vary in size from 6¾ in. to 11¼ in., and the rectangles are about 6 in. by 12 in. The number of strips to a block may be 4, 5, or 6. Expansion spaces should be allowed around all walls, columns, thresholds, and permanent fixtures, the width being about $^{1}/_{16}$ in. for each foot of width or length. These spaces may be partly filled with asphalt mastic, may be completely filled with cork strips, or may contain springs to hold the edge blocks in place. If a room is much longer than it is wide, square blocks should be laid diagonally. The blocks are often sanded, filled, waxed, and polished at the factory.

USES

Wood floors are warm and elastic and therefore are not tiresome to work on. They are clean and, if proper selection is made and they receive proper care, they are durable. They may be made attractive in appearance and are suitable, from that point of view, for the highest type of use. Wood floors supported by fire-resistive construction are used in many buildings classed as fire-resistive because they burn very slowly in case of fire. However, they are not used in the highest type of fire-resistive buildings. They are one of the most satisfactory floors for residences and are usually the cheapest.

Wood floors should not be placed until after all concrete work and plastering have been completed and the building has had a chance to dry out. The flooring should not be stored in the house during this period. The cracks in wood floors which are permitted to absorb moisture before they are laid will open up as the wood dries out. Special care should be used in wood floors laid over concrete to make sure that the concrete has dried out. An asphalt mastic dampproofing layer should preferably be placed over the concrete.

10.10 Resilient Flooring

Elastic or resilient materials of various kinds, including vinyl asbestos, cork, rubber, and vinyl plastic, are used for floor and wall surfaces and are called *resilient flooring.* These materials are usually cemented to wood, concrete, or plaster surfaces with special cements.

VINYL PLASTIC

Vinyl plastic floor coverings have thermoplastic binders, as described in Section 7.7, together with plasticizers and granular mineral fillers and pigments selected and proportioned to give the desired properties and colors. They are manufactured in sheets 6 to 12 ft wide and in tile of many sizes. The thicknesses available are $^{1}/_{16}$, $^{3}/_{32}$, and $^{1}/_{8}$ in. in tile and 0.090 in. and other thicknesses in sheet material. A large assortment of solid colors, as well as marbelized and other patterns, are available. It may be unbacked or backed with various materials.

Vinyl plastics are wear- and indentation-resistant, impervious, resistant to oil and grease, resilient, easily maintained, and attractive.

Vinyl asbestos tile may include asbestos fibers in their composition. They are less flexible than the other types, are less resistant to indentation, and are available only in tiles 9 in. and 12 in. square. Sheet vinyl flooring is also made with foam cushion backing.

SEAMLESS FLOORING

A flooring material that features a unified and unjointed surface is called *seamless flooring.* These types of flooring are frequently applied integrally, forming a wall base; sometimes the material is extended up the wall, forming a wainscot. Both risers and treads of stairways may be surfaced with this material. Most seamless flooring materials may be classified as plastics. Some have a polyester binder, or vinyl resin base, or a two-component epoxy resin base; some have a urethane finish coat. Most seamless flooring systems offer a decorative floor surface in a variety of colors, with embedded marble chips. These chips, cast in the unset base material, are intended to give the appearance of traditional terrazzo. The finish texture of seamless floors is frequently a pebbled or "orange peel" surface.

Depending upon the manufacturer, seamless floors are applied by brush, roller, or trowel in thicknesses that are measured in fractions of an inch — about $^{1}/_{8}$ to ½. These floor surfaces have a combination of features offered by few other resilient floor finishes. Seamless floors are resistant to most common chemicals. They are a resilient, comfortable, easy-to-maintain, water-resistant, nonslip, and durable surface. Some are sparkproof and are most suitable for hospital operating rooms and other areas where spark resistance and sanitation are mandatory. These floors are used in public, institutional, and commercial buildings.

Cork tile are made from pure cork shavings compressed in molds to a thickness of ½ in. and baked. They are used over wood or concrete floors, to which they are cemented. Cork tile are elastic, noiseless, fairly durable, and quite absorbent. They are available in various shades of brown. The rosin in the cork liquefies during the baking process and cements the shavings together when the tile cools. The brown color of cork tile is largely caused by the baking it receives, the darker browns having been baked longer than the lighter browns. Cork tile are used for wall coverings as well as for flooring.

RUBBER

Rubber flooring is made of synthetic rubber combined at high temperatures with fillers, such as cotton fiber, various minerals, and with the desired color pigments. It is made in form of sheet rubber and rubber tile. The thickness varies from ⅛ to ¼ in. Many colors and patterns are available. Rubber flooring is cemented to concrete or wood. It is attractive in appearance, elastic, noiseless, durable, easily cleaned, but quite expensive. Rubber floors are not resistant to oil, grease, and gasoline and should not be used on floors in contact with the ground. Rubber is used as a wall covering, stair treads, and cove bases as well as a flooring material.

10.11 Selection of Floor System

FACTORS INVOLVED
Some of the factors involved in selecting the type of floor construction for a building are:

(a) general type of construction used in the building
(b) plan of the building
(c) floor loads
(d) lateral resistance
(e) floor thickness
(f) resistance to fire
(g) sound transmission
(h) weight
(i) ceiling, flat or exposed beams
(j) wearing surface
(k) position of floor, ground floor or above ground
(l) installation of utilities
(m) use of building
(n) cost

These factors overlap in many cases, and their relative importance varies with different classes of buildings. Local conditions such as prevailing types of construction, availability of labor and materials, weather conditions, time available for construction, and other factors enter into the selection.

Unless precast concrete is specifically mentioned, the comments in this article refer to cast-in-place concrete construction. Special consideration is given to the use of precast concrete construction in Section 4.6.

GENERAL TYPE OF CONSTRUCTION
The floor system and the structural frame are so interrelated that selections of basic materials and types of construction are made for the building as a whole. For a given building, several alternatives may be investigated, the advantages and disadvantages of each being considered. The local building code requirements must always be satisfied. There are marked differences in the requirements of such codes.

Wood stud walls and partitions would naturally be associated with light wood joists and subfloors. Such floor systems might also be used with wood columns, beams, and girders; or a heavy timber floor system might be used.

If a steel frame is used, the floor system might be one of several types of reinforced concrete plain or ribbed floor systems, except the flat-slab, flat-plate, or slab-band. This type of frame is also suitable for use with thin concrete slabs on light steel or open-web joists or on light-gage steel cellular, ribbed, or corrugated panels. If the framing can be arranged so that there are many identical panels, some form of precast reinforced concrete or gypsum panel may prove advantageous.

If the beams and girders are to be of reinforced concrete, the floor system will be plain or ribbed reinforced concrete slabs and the columns usually will be reinforced concrete. Such columns will also be used with flat-slab, flat-plate, and slab-band floor systems. Precast concrete or gypsum panels may be advantageous for the same conditions given in the preceding paragraph.

Various types of floor systems can be used with masonry bearing walls, including light wood joist and subfloors, heavy timber floor systems, wood or concrete floors supported on steel I-beams or light steel or open-web joists, reinforced concrete beams and slabs, reinforced concrete ribbed slabs, and precast concrete or gypsum slabs supported on steel joists.

PLAN OF BUILDING
If the floor is divided into panels which are square or very nearly square, reinforced concrete flat-slab or flat-plate construction may be desirable, or the two-way plain or ribbed reinforced concrete slab with beams on the four sides of each panel may be seriously considered. If the spans are short, the plain slab might be used, whereas for long spans the ribbed slabs will be more satisfactory. If the building is to be divided into rooms, flat-plate or slab-band construction may prove desirable, but flat-slab construction is not as

satisfactory as it is for undivided areas because of the interference of the column capitals and drop panels with the partitions. Concrete ribbed slabs are particularly suitable for long spans.

The adaptability of a floor system to changes in the locations of partitions to suit changing occupancy is of importance in office and some other types of buildings.

FLOOR LOADS

Reinforced concrete flat-plate floors, light and open-web steel joists, and cellular, ribbed, and corrugated light-gage steel panels all with thin poured concrete slabs are suitable for light and medium floor loads, such as those of apartment houses, office buildings, hotels, and schools.

Reinforced concrete slabs supported on reinforced concrete or steel beams, girders, and columns, reinforced concrete flat-slab construction, and heavy timber matched or laminated decks supported on heavy timber or steel beams, girders, and columns are appropriate floor systems for heavy loads.

Even though the distributed floor load may not be heavy, consideration must be given to the possibility that a floor may be subjected to a heavy concentrated load. Such a load may be the determining factor in the thickness of the top slab in ribbed floors or floors with closely spaced joists.

LATERAL RESISTANCE

Low tier buildings or even relatively high tier buildings with a low ratio of height to width will usually not require that special provisions be made to resist the lateral forces produced by wind. Girders framing into columns, either steel or concrete, offer the maximum opportunity for providing lateral resistance without the use of shear walls or other special arrangements. Reinforced concrete flat-plate floors and columns are not effective in this respect. Comments might be made on other systems, but these serve as extreme examples. In addition, if shear walls or wind bents are used, the floor system will be required to transfer the lateral load horizontally to the bents. This factor sometimes requires consideration.

FLOOR THICKNESS

The minimum height of building for a given number of stories and clear ceiling height is obtained with flat-plate, slab-band, or flat-slab construction.

Thin concrete slabs supported on light-gage cellular steel panels, wood subfloors, or thin concrete slabs supported on open-web steel joists, ribbed concrete slabs, and hollow precast panels form relatively thin floor systems if the girders that support them are located over partitions. Concrete slabs or wood decks supported on beams and girders take up the most room.

Any increase in height means an increase in the cost of walls, columns, elevators, stairways, and many other items, individually small, which may reach a total worth considering. By using thin floor systems, it may also be possible to construct one or more additional stories within a height limitation in a code.

RESISTANCE TO FIRE

When a building must be cheaply constructed and resistance to fire is not a decisive factor, ordinary wood joist construction with wood subfloor may be used. These conditions prevail in residence construction more than in any other class of building.

In warehouses and many types of industrial buildings, heavy timber construction may offer sufficient resistance to fire and provide a building at a lower cost than that of a more fire-resistive building, if automatic sprinkler systems are installed.

In the congested downtown districts of many cities, building ordinances require fire-resistive construction, and therefore wood joist construction and heavy timber construction cannot be used. Floors constructed of open-web steel joists and concrete slabs protected with suspended ceilings of metal lath and vermiculite or perlite gypsum plaster are approved by some, but not all, cities as fire-resistive construction. It is always necessary to consult the local building code to determine the acceptability of the fire resistance of a floor system. The cost of fire insurance is an important factor entering into the choice of floor construction; the rates depend upon the fire resistance of the construction as well as the nature of the building contents, the location, and many other factors. The rate is lowered in many classes of buildings by the installation of automatic sprinkler systems which come into action in any part of a building when fire raises the temperature in that part.

SOUND TRANSMISSION

The various types of floor systems differ quite markedly in their effectiveness in resisting the transmission of sound. For some types of occupancy, such as warehouses, this factor is of minor importance, while for other types, such as hotels, schools, and apartment houses, it must be given serious consideration. Sound transmission of impact noises is influenced by the type of wearing surface as well as by the floor system. This subject is considered in Section 10.12.

WEIGHT

The weight of a floor system to carry a given load is an important factor because it affects the weight and cost of the supporting members and the foundations. Wood construction is advantageous where its use is permissible. Systems with closely spaced joists that permit the use of thin lightweight slabs are lighter than those that require thicker slabs of reinforced concrete and may satisfy code requirements. Considerable weight reduction can be achieved by using lightweight aggregate in concrete.

CEILING

Ordinary wood joist construction, flat-plate construction, slab-band construction, and ribbed concrete slabs provide flat ceilings, but plain concrete slabs supported by beams and girders and some other types of construction require *suspended ceilings* if flat ceilings are desired. Girders running between columns interfere with flat ceilings whenever they are present. In addition to their better appearance, flat ceilings do not interfere with the locations of partitions. Partitions are often located under girders in which case girders are not objectionable.

Plastered ceilings are provided by applying two coats of plaster directly to the underside of ribbed slabs with clay, concrete, or gypsum tile fillers, flat slabs, or plain slabs supported by concrete or fireproofed steel beams. The ribbed slabs and the flat slabs provide a flat ceiling, but the slabs supported by beams necessitate breaks in the ceiling, and the cost of plastering is greater because of the increased area and the additional labor required in finishing around the edges of the beams. Wood joists, heavy timber construction, metal joists, and ribbed slabs with steel forms require lath and preferably three coats of plaster or plasterboard and two coats of plaster on the underside to provide a plastered ceiling. The ceiling supported by wood joists, ribbed slabs with steel forms, and metal joists will be flat, whereas the ceiling supported by heavy timber construction will probably follow around the beams. The cost of the lath and the additional cost of plaster should be considered in selecting the floor construction if plastered ceilings are required. Monolithic concrete ceiling surfaces are often finished by painting directly rather than on plaster.

WEARING SURFACE

The type of *wearing surface,* as considered in the following sections, is a factor in selecting the type of floor system, or the reverse may be true.

If wood flooring is to be used for the wearing surface, light wood joist and heavy timber construction have an advantage in cost over other forms of floor construction where nailing strips with concrete fill between have to be provided. To avoid nailing strips, the builder may cover the closely spaced light steel joists with nailable concrete slabs or nailing strips may be anchored to the tops of the joists with a light concrete slab between nailing strips. Some forms of wood floors may be cemented directly to carefully finished concrete surfaces with bituminous cement.

If the wearing surface is to be cork, concrete, asphalt tile, vinyl tile, carpet, rubber, or ceramic tile, any of the forms of floor construction that provide a concrete top surface are suitable, but the additional cost of providing a finished surface on the concrete must be considered.

With wood joist or heavy timber construction, a concrete surface required as a base for some wearing surfaces would add to the cost. Resilient flooring requires a matched floor or plywood.

Ceramic tile, marble, slate, and terrazzo usually require a concrete foundation, and thus the various forms of floor construction which provide a concrete top surface are suitable for the installation of these materials without further expenditure, but wood subfloors require a 2 in. or 3 in. slab, which increases the cost considerably. The thin-setting bed for ceramic tile may, however, suffice.

For many purposes, a smooth troweled finish on a concrete slab may be satisfactory. It may be colored or, if subjected only to light traffic, a painted surface may wear sufficiently. Such a finish can be provided readily by several floor systems.

POSITION OF FLOOR

Floors placed on the ground will normally be concrete slabs, and, if not subject to hydrostatic pressure, will have light wire fabric or no reinforcing.

INSTALLATION OF UTILITIES

Although the utilities installed in a building are not considered in this book, the provisions that often must be made in floor systems to provide for conduits and pipes, wiring, plumbing, and heating, and ducts for ventilating and air conditioning require consideration. Open-web steel joists provide space through which pipes and conduits can be run to any position in a floor and ducts can be placed between joists. Light-gage cellular steel panels afford similar but more restricted opportunities for wiring conduits. The space above suspended ceilings is used extensively for such purposes. Wiring conduits are ordinarily located in concrete floor slabs or in concrete fills placed on top of the structural slabs, but water pipes should not be embedded in this manner because of the cost of repairing leaks. Wood joist floors have the same advantages as open-web steel joists but require that holes be bored for pipes and conduits running perpendicular to the joists.

USE OF BUILDING

The function of a building enters into the choice of the type of construction. It is a determining factor paramount in the selection of a particular type of construction.

COST

Of course, one of the most important factors to be considered in selecting a specific floor system and wearing surface from several that satisfy all of the basic requirements is the cost. The total cost may be divided into the direct cost, the indirect cost, and the continuing annual cost.

The direct cost is the cost of the floor system, including the wearing surface, the supporting beams, and ceiling surfaces, directly applied or suspended. The indirect costs are the costs of the girders, the columns, and their foundations. The relative effects of floor systems on the total height of a building may also be considered because differences in cost caused by this factor may be of some significance. Differences in height are reflected in differences in the costs of exterior walls, columns, elevators, stairways, vertical pipes, conduits, ducts, and other items. The different continuing annual costs include differences in costs of care and maintenance of the various wearing surfaces.

Finally, the selection of a floor system should take into account the differences in annual cost of fire insurance. For many classes of occupancy and types of construction, the installation of automatic sprinkler systems may markedly reduce the annual cost or make possible changes in the type of construction that reduce the overall cost.

Because of the many factors involved, including the effects of local customs and the relative availability and costs of different kinds of labor and materials, no specific comparisons can be made. When cost is an important factor in the selection of the floor system, and it usually is, comparative estimates are made of the costs of the types that warrant consideration after all other factors are considered.

10.12 Selection of Finish Flooring

The selection of a proper floor surface is one of the most important and, at the same time, one of the most difficult problems in the construction of a building. The appearance, usefulness, and cost of upkeep of a building are greatly affected by the type of floor installed. Considering the importance of the subject, it is unfortunate that it is not possible to devise a more satisfactory basis of selection.

The report of a Committee on Floors of the American Hospital Association has been of considerable value in preparing this section. The definitions of the properties of floor surfaces follow those of the committee quite closely.

The following discussion of the relative merits of the various floor surfaces is limited because of the great variations in the materials and workmanship and in the kind of usage and care a floor will receive.

Floors that are manufactured complete and ready for installation, such as vinyl tile or rubber, will show less variation in quality than such floors as terrazzo, concrete, and seamless that are manufactured on the job, and are not subject to as rigid control as factory-made products. Natural flooring materials such as marble and slate are also quite variable in quality.

Each property of a wearing surface will be discussed, and an attempt will be made to classify roughly the various materials according to the degree to which they possess that quality.

APPEARANCE

Appearance is the attractiveness of the material, its color range, texture, and its decorative value in an architectural sense.

There are many floor surfaces that are attractive when suitably used, such as hardwood when properly finished, terrazzo, ceramic tile, marble, and, to a somewhat less degree, vinyl plastic, rubber tile, cork tile, linoleum tile, asphalt tile, linoleum, cork carpet, sheet rubber, slate, and magnesite composition. Concrete without special treatment and industrial wood blocks are not suitable for use where appearance is a factor. Concrete floors may be painted or waxed and are not unattractive as long as the surface is maintained, but this is difficult to do where the traffic is at all heavy.

DURABILITY

Durability may be defined as the resistance to wear, temperature, humidity changes, decay, and disintegration as well as the adhesion of a material to its base.

The most durable floor surfaces for foot traffic are ceramic tile, terrazzo, slate, and concrete, but terrazzo floors are likely to crack if not divided into blocks by dividing strips or laid in the form of tile. Marble is widely used in floors subject to severe wear, but it does not stand as well as the materials just mentioned. Some marbles are much more resistant to wear than others. Concrete surfaces to be durable must have durable aggregates.

Hardwood, vinyl plastic, and rubber tile give very satisfactory service, whereas cork tile and asphalt tile are fairly satisfactory.

With the exception of concrete, none of the materials mentioned so far is suitable or satisfactory for heavy traffic, such as trucking. Brick and wood block may be used under these conditions. Heavy maple flooring may also be satisfactory.

COMFORT AND SAFETY

Comfort and safety under foot is determined by the shock-absorbing qualities, sure-footedness, evenness of surface, and conductivity. A floor which is a good heat conductor will always feel cold.

The most comfortable floors to work on are carpet, cork tile, cushioned vinyl, and rubber. Wood, vinyl plastic, and asphalt tile, are satisfactory; but concrete, terrazzo, ceramic tile, marble, slate, and brick are tiresome and cold.

NOISELESSNESS

Cork tile, carpet and rubber are practically noiseless; wood, vinyl plastic, and asphalt tile are slightly less satisfactory but still acceptable; but concrete, ceramic tile, marble, slate, and brick are the noisiest of flooring materials.

FIRE RESISTANCE
Materials may be noncombustible but still suffer severely in case of fire. Concrete, ceramic tile, and brick are probably the most fire-resistant floor surfaces, but terrazzo, marble, and slate are very satisfactory. Asphalt tile will not burn but may suffer seriously in a fire. Rubber, vinyl plastic, carpet, and wood are combustible; but if laid on a fire-resistant base, they are not considered a serious defect in a fire-resistant building.

SANITATION
To be sanitary, a floor surface must be nonabsorbent and easily cleaned. Joints that are not watertight are an unsanitary feature.

The most sanitary floor surfaces are terrazzo, ceramic tile, marble, and slate. Asphalt tile, rubber, and vinyl plastic are quite satisfactory. Concrete is difficult to clean, and so is wood because of its porosity and the presence of open joints.

ACID AND ALKALI RESISTANCE
The factors that should be considered under this heading are immunity from damage by occasional spillings of strong acid solutions and resistance to the continuous use of soap, lye, cleaning and scouring compounds, and disinfectants.

Ceramic tile is the most satisfactory floor surface in this respect; asphalt tile and vinyl plastic are quite resistant; rubber, terrazzo, marble, and concrete are sufficiently resistant for ordinary purposes; but cork tile should not be subjected to the action of acids and alkalies.

GREASE AND OIL RESISTANCE
Grease and oil are not absorbed by ceramic tile and by vinyl coverings and do not affect these materials. Grease and oil are absorbed by wood, brick, concrete, terrazzo, and cork tile and therefore detract from their appearance, but do not seriously affect their durability. Asphalt and rubber floors, except greaseproof asphalt tile, are seriously affected by grease, oil, and gasoline.

DAMPNESS
Ceramic tile, brick, concrete, terrazzo, and asphalt tile are not affected by dampness and are suitable for use on ground floors, such as basement floors; but wood, rubber, carpet, and cork tile are unsuitable for such locations.

INDENTATION
The hard flooring materials, such as ceramic tile, concrete,

terrazzo, and brick, do not suffer indentation from chair legs, heels of shoes, and other objects. Maple and oak flooring yield very little and do not retain imprints. Other materials such as rubber and vinyl sheet yield considerably under such loads but recover quite well when the load is removed. Asphalt and vinyl asbestos tile may become permanently indented.

TRUCKING
Three factors are pertinent when considering the suitability of a floor for trucking. It must stand the abrasive action of the truck wheels, the tractive effort required to pull the truck must not be excessive, and the flooring must have structural resistance sufficient to carry the load transmitted to it by the truck wheels. Concrete, heavy maple flooring, and industrial wood blocks are satisfactory in all three respects if the materials are of high quality and if the trucking is parallel to the length of the maple flooring rather than crosswise. The maple flooring must be heavy enough so that the weight of the trucks will not break the tongued-and-grooved joint. The aggregate in the concrete may have to be specially selected with regard to high resistance to abrasion. Rubber-tired wheels are much easier on all types of flooring than wheels which are steel-tired.

MAINTENANCE
This heading includes such items as the ease with which a flooring is cleaned, the necessity for care and surface treatment, such as waxing and painting, the necessity for repairs, and the cost of such operations.

Ceramic tile, marble, terrazzo, slate, vinyl plastic, and rubber tile floors are easily cleaned and require very little care. Asphalt tile and carpet are easily cleaned but should receive surface treatment occasionally. Cork is not easy to clean and requires surface treatment. Hardwood floors are fairly easy to clean if in good condition, but require frequent surface treatment. Concrete is not as easy to clean as ceramic tile if it is not painted or waxed. Painting makes cleaning easier but requires frequent renewal.

The monolithic floors such as terrazzo and concrete are difficult to repair satisfactorily. Floors composed of separate units of tile, slate, or marble are more easily repaired, but require skilled mechanics. Cork tile and carpet may be easily repaired by replacing the damaged parts.

The maintenance costs of wood block, heavy asphalt mastic, brick, and concrete are relatively low except under extremely severe traffic. With the exception of concrete, these materials are easily repaired. They receive no surface treatment.

INITIAL COST
One of the first factors in selecting a floor surface is the initial cost, but even the most expensive materials do not possess all the desirable features.

Flooring materials may be roughly divided into classes according to their cost in place. In the following list, the most expensive materials are given first.

1. Ceramic tile, marble, and rubber tile.
2. Terrazzo, cork tile, and hardwood.
3. Vinyl tile and asphalt tile, carpet.
4. Concrete.

This list assumes that a concrete base is available to receive the wearing surface. Brick and wood block floors are not included in these lists, for they are used for a different class of traffic from that to which the materials included, except concrete, are subjected, and a comparison would be of no value.

WEIGHT

The heavier floor surfaces add indirectly to the cost by requiring stronger floor construction, beams, girders, columns, and foundations. Ceramic tile, marble, and slate are bedded on 1½ in. of cement mortar that has no structural value; terrazzo requires 1¼ in. of material that is simply a dead weight; and hardwood flooring usually requires about 2 in. of filling between the nailing strips if placed over concrete. Rubber tile, cork tile, carpet, and concrete do not require this additional material. This additional weight exists when the structural floor is some form of concrete slab.

Summary

Various materials available for use as interior finishes have been described. Some of the factors considered in selecting finish material for a particular interior space are appearance, conformance to building codes, durability, fire resistance, sound control qualities, resistance to moisture, ease of cleaning, cost of maintenance, availability of skilled installers, and the initial cost. For most of our interior finishing needs, we have a variety of materials and installations available. It is the responsibility of the designer and contractor to provide the most appropriate material to meet the requirements of the owner.

Of all the elements of the building process, interior finishes probably cause more headaches for the contractor than any other single element. Usually, different subcontractors are used for each of the separate materials and coordinating their activities on the job is a monumental task. Also, the interior finishes are the most visible to the owner and his representatives and therefore the most susceptible to rejection or rework orders. Attention to details is the key to ensuring final acceptance of the project.

Key Terms

plaster
gypsum
bonding agent
perlite
vermiculite
metal lath

wire lath
runners
gypsum lath
furring
finish coat
brown coat

scratch coat
gypsum wallboard
particleboard
terrazzo
concrete wearing
    surface

resilient flooring
seamless flooring
suspended ceiling
wearing surface

Review Questions

1. List the basic raw materials used in plaster construction and describe their function.
2. List the various prepared bases to which plaster is applied and explain how each holds plaster in place.
3. Describe the application process for a two-coat plaster installation on gypsum lath.
4. List and describe four types of gypsum wallboard.
5. Describe the application process for a single layer drywall installation on a wood framing system.
6. List four common materials used for finish floor applications and the advantages for each material listed.
7. List the factors to be considered in the selection of a floor system.
8. Become familiar with the factors involved in the selection of finish flooring.

CHAPTER 11
COMPOSITE MATERIALS

11.1 Composite Materials
11.2 Applications

The construction industry is the second largest end user of conventional reinforced plastic composites. The majority of these products are composed of conventional composites and used in non-load-bearing applications. Tub showers and chopped strand corrugated sheet paneling constitute about 65% of these applications. The purpose of this chapter is to present case studies of load-bearing applications of composites or advanced composites in this industry.

Objectives

1. Become familiar with composites as materials in the construction industry.
2. Understand how composite building elements are manufactured.
3. Become familiar with various applications for composite materials in the construction industry.

By **Andy Green,** President, and **Tanongsak Bisarnsin,** Composite Technology, Inc., Fort Worth, TX

11.1 Composite Materials

A *composite* is defined as an assembly of dissimilar constituents intended to do a job that none of the individual materials can do alone. Chopped strand and woven roving laminates as used in shower stalls and corrugated sheeting and paneling are examples of a conventional reinforced plastic. An *advanced composite* is one in which the reinforcing is advantageously placed within the section to enhance its superior features and, furthermore, is installed to optimize the design and mechanical properties of the member for predictable short- and long-term performance. It can consist of a blending of various forms of reinforcing to overcome internal stress, with the overall end result of minimum deflection and high unit strength. It further consists of selecting binders that have substantial elongation (greater than the fiber reinforcement) to enhance the ability to obtain average stress levels. Thus we may say that an advanced composite is one which is composed of the same raw materials as its conventional composite counterpart but, by judicious placement of the reinforcing, develops substantial increase in performance. An advanced composite purlin or girt of equivalent performance to a steel purlin or girt is an example.

11.2 Applications

These applications are only of fiberglass reinforced composites because they have the highest strength and stiffness per dollar; good dimensional stability, electrical properties, and corrosion resistance; ease of handling in fabrication; and reliable mechanical properties for predictable performance of the composite. The cost of employing aramid, carbon, or boron fibers as reinforcing materials is too prohibitive for building and construction applications at this time. They are employed where high strength and stiffness-to-weight ratios are critical, such as in aerospace applications.

WALKWAY BRIDGES

Advanced composite walkway bridges are used at wastewater treatment facilities in chemical plants. They are used by personnel for access to aeration equipment at the center of the pond. Their steel counterparts require frequent inspection, sand blasting, and painting and replacement in 3 to 6 years, because of the highly corrosive atmosphere of these plants.

Advanced composite bridges weigh one-third as much as their steel counterparts and can be prefabricated in one piece by *hand lay-up.* The FRP bridge can span 90 feet without any visible settlement during its service period. This is possible because of the selection of structural and continuous reinforcing fibers which act similarly to steel rebars in concrete structures (see Figure 11.1).

FIGURE 11.1 Seventy-foot clear span personnel bridges over wastewater treatment facility. Composite Technology, Inc., Fort Worth, Texas.

FIGURE 11.2 Beam design. Composite Technology, Inc., Fort Worth, Texas.

FIGURE 11.3 Composite structural beams. Composite Technology, Inc., Forth Worth, Texas.

FIGURE 11.4 Advanced composite roof and ridge vents. Composite Technology, Inc., Fort Worth, Texas.

FIGURE 11.5 Sixty-foot side wall panels. Composite Technology, Inc., Fort Worth, Texas.

BEAMS

Composite beams are used to support panels and decks in industrial buildings exposed to chemical environments. They are designed to replace conventional steel shapes. To overcome the low modulus of electricity, composite beams are deeper than their steel counterparts but taper on the ends to maintain a typical building profile (see Figure 11.2).

The box section is laterally stable to overcome lateral stability limitations of flanged structural sections. Continuous glass rovings are employed as the major load-carrying element in the way steel rebars are used in reinforced concrete beams. The results are advanced composite beams with a load-carrying capacity of rolled steel sections that are more than twice as heavy.

These beams are primarily bending elements comparable to bar joists but without the lateral buckling problem and bracing requirements (see Figure 11.3).

These beams can be manufactured by either hand lay-up or the *pultrusion* process.

PANELS FOR BUILDING CLADDING

Profiled structural panels have been used to replace mental or cement asbestos siding and roofing in the highly corrosive environments of numerous industrial plants, such as cogeneration, mining operations, and chemical process plants (see Figures 11.4, 11.5, and 11.6).

DECKING

Roof decks employing continuous glass reinforcement are used as a structural part of a built-up roof system for sustained dead load and live load. The decks are designed and manufactured to meet the same criteria used for metal decks in regard to deflection limits and strengths.

The applications of advanced composite decks are similar to those of panels. They have been used in chemical bulk storage and caustic chlorine facilities.

FIGURE 11.6 Translucent panels transmit natural lighting. Composite Technology, Inc., Fort Worth, Texas.

Both panels and decks are manufactured by a continuous laminating process; heavy decks are made by pultrusion (see Figure 11.7).

COOLING TOWERS

Cooling towers are required to resist wind loads, earthquake tremors, and load from the tower fill under corrosion induced conditions at elevated temperatures. This system consists of structural walls for cladding and supporting the fan, fan deck and stack, and beams to support the ceramic fill. The wall system has internal columns which transfer the total load to the concrete foundation.

The beams of the cooling tower demonstrate the long-term integrity of advanced composite structural components under sustained load. The beams, after years of operation, exhibit no visible settlement or signs of deterioration.

Advanced composite cooling towers offer lightweight

FIGURE 11.7 Composite roof deck used to support built-up roof. Composite Technology, Inc., Fort Worth, Texas.

FIGURE 11.8 Advanced composite cooling towers. All components are advanced composites: stressed skin, columns, and beams. Composite Technology, Inc., Fort Worth, Texas.

FIGURE 11.9 Composite cooling water pipes. Composite Technology, Inc., Fort Worth, Texas.

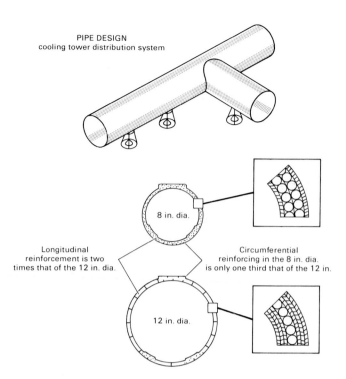

PIPE DESIGN
cooling tower distribution system

8 in. dia.

12 in. dia.

Longitudinal reinforcement is two times that of the 12 in. dia.

Circumferential reinforcing in the 8 in. dia. is only one third that of the 12 in.

FIGURE 11.10 Pipe design for cooling tower water distribution. Composite Technology, Inc., Fort Worth, Texas.

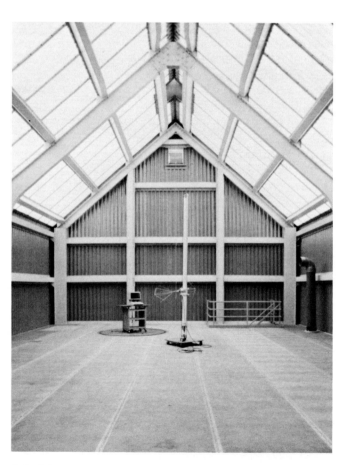

FIGURE 11.11 End wall for pre-engineered building. Composite Technology, Inc., Fort Worth, Texas.

modular units which are convenient to transport and assemble. They are maintenance free, corrosion resistant, and fire retardant (see Figure 11.8).

The towers are manufactured by hand lay-up processes and pultrusion.

PIPES FOR COOLING TOWER WATER

Circulating water in cooling towers is pumped to the top of the tower and sprayed over ceramic tiles to remove heat. These pipes must be able to resist the corrosive elements in water; however, they do not have to withstand high pressures. Holes must be cut in the bottom side of the pipe to permit the attachment of spray nozzles. The top of the pipe is flat to support the mist eliminators (see Figure 11.9).

A unique cross-sectional design allows the pipe to be made of advanced composites, keeping weight to a minimum while meeting all of the other requirements (see Figure 11.10).

This pipe is a typical example of the considerations made and used in placement of reinforcement. The two sections weigh approximately the same, but longitudinal reinforcement in the 8 inch diameter pipe is two times that of the 12 inch, while circumferential reinforcing in the 8 inch diameter is only one-third that of the 12 inch.

PRE-ENGINEERED BUILDINGS

Industrial buildings used as testing facilities for computer

FIGURE 11.12 All composite pre-engineered building. Composite Technology, Inc., Fort Worth, Texas.

and electronics products are required to be made of non-metal materials for electromagnetic interference-free environments. Structural components are designed as stressed-skin structures using torsion box configurations as in aircraft design. Sidesway deflections are kept within limits by using fixed end supports.

Pre-engineered buildings are fabricated using hand lay-up rigid frame bents and the components described earlier, then assembled with composite mechanical fasteners and bonding (see Figures 11.11 and 11.12).

Summary

These applications of advanced composites for a niche market were successful because they provided lower life-cycle costs or offered a service unavailable with conventional materials. The potential for growth should be good because the market has been here for many years but has not been serviced. Taking an approach that utilizes the unique characteristics of the material, rather than forcing the material into patterns derived directly from conventional structural building materials, will increase the market because end user cost will be reduced.

Key Terms

composite   advanced composite   hand lay-up   pultrusion

Review Questions

1. Define composite and advanced composite.
2. Explain two methods of manufacture for composite building materials.
3. List four applications of composite materials in construction and why they are used in that application.

GLOSSARY

Absorption coefficient   The ratio of the sound energy absorbed to the sound energy impinging upon the material surface. An absorption coefficient of 1 represents total absorption.

Acoustics   The branch of physics dealing with phenomena and laws of sound. The qualities of an enclosed space with respect to the transmission of sounds.

Admixture   Material added to cement or the concrete mix to increase workability, strength, or imperviousness; to lower freezing point; to prevent scaling; or otherwise to affect the concrete. Accelerators, plasticizers, and air-entraining agents are admixtures.

Advanced composite   Defined as one in which the reinforcing is advantageously placed within the section to enhance its superior features.

Aggregate   Inert materials which when bound together into a conglomerated mass by a matrix form concrete mastic, mortar or plaster; crushed rock or gravel screened to size for use in road surfaces, concrete or bituminous mixes; any of several hard materials such as sand, gravel, stone, slag, cinders or other inert materials used for mixing with a cementing material to form concrete.

Air dried   Said of lumber which is seasoned by drying in the air instead of a kiln or oven.

Air-entrained concrete   A concrete which has air incorporated in the form of minute bubbles. The entrained air increases the workability of the concrete and its resistance to frost.

Allowable bearing pressure   The maximum bearing pressure allowed by the governing building code or recommended by appropriate agencies.

Alluvial soil   Soil, sand, or gravel deposited by flowing water, especially during times of floods.

Arch   A curved structural member used to span an opening or recesses; also built flat. Structurally, an arch is a piece, or assemblage of pieces, so arranged over an opening that the supported load is resolved into pressures on the side supports, and practically normal to their faces.

Ashlar   Squared and dressed stones used for facing a masonry wall.

Astragal   An overlapping strip of material usually on the exterior surface of a door.

Balloon framing   A system of framing wooden buildings in which the corner posts and studs are continuous in one piece from sill to roof plate, the intermediate joist being carried by girts spiked to, or let into, the studs, the pieces being secured only by nailing, without the use of mortises and tenons or the like.

Bar joists   A truss form of steel top and bottom members, of plates, channels, or T-sections, with heavy wire or rod web lacing; used for floor and roof supports.

Beam   A term generally applied to the principal horizontal members of a building so installed as to support the load of the structure. Beams may be made of wood, steel, or other materials; also called girders. There are three types, simple, continuous, and cantilever.

Bearing capacity   The maximum unit presssure which a soil or other material will withstand without failure or without settlement to an amount detrimental to the integrity or the function of the structure.

Bearing piles   A pile which carries weight, as distinguished from a sheet pile which takes earth pressure or a raker which takes thrust. It may be a friction pile or an end-bearing pile.

Bearing pressure   The load on a bearing surface divided by its area.

Bedrock   Solid rock which underlies any superficial formation; hence a firm foundation on which to erect a building, especially a heavy structure.

Beneficiation   Improvement of the chemical or physical properties of a raw material or intermediate product by the removal of undesirable components or impurities.

Berm   An artificial ridge of earth, generally side slopes of a roadbed and commonly called the shoulder. The space between the toe of a slope and excavation made for intercepting ditches or borrow pits. Berms are built to hold water on land that is to be flood irrigated.

Billet   A semifinished shape of steel with a cross-sectional area between 16 and 35 sq in. Used for finished bar and rod shapes.

Birdbath   A concavity in a pavement or roofing surface which holds water after a shower or rain.

Blast furnace   A tall, cylindrical masonry structure lined with refractory materials, used to smelt iron ores in combination with fluxes, coke and air into pig iron.

Bloom   A semifinished shape of steel with a cross-sectional area greater than 36 sq in. Used for finished structural shapes and rails.

Board   A flat piece of wood having a nominal thickness of 1 inch or less and a width of 4 inches or more; for hardwood, the term is interchangeable with plank.

Board foot   A unit of measure represented by a board 1 foot long, 1 foot wide and 1 inch thick, or 144 cubic inches; (1 in. by 12 in. by 12 in.).

Bolt   A cylindrical bar which is threaded at one end for a nut and forged with a square or hexagonal head at the other end. One of the oldest and commonest methods of fixing metal parts together.

Bond   Adhesion and grip of concrete or mortar to reinforcement or to other surfaces against which it is placed, including friction due to shrinkage and longitudinal shear in the concrete engaged by the bar deformations; the adhesion of cement paste to aggregate; adherence between plaster coats or between plaster and a substrate produced by adhesive or cohesive properties of plaster or supplemental material.

Bonding agent   A liquid resinous water emulsion applied to base surfaces requiring adhesion between the base surface and plaster application.

Brick   A structural unit of kiln-burned clay; its shape is generally that of a rectangular parallelepiped. The standard size of a brick is 8 in. by 3¾ in. by 2¼ in. or 2 in. by 4 in. by 8 in.

Bridging   Bracing floor joists by fixing lateral members between the joists.

Brown coat   The coat of plaster directly below the finish coat in a plaster application.

Building codes   The legal requirements set up by various governing agencies covering the minimum requirements for all types of construction.

Building process   The entire process which embraces every step from the conception to the total satisfaction of all building requirements.

Built-up roofing   Two or more layers of roofing material, covering the same roof area, which are cemented together, built-up, on the job; roll roofing produced especially for the use of built-up roofs.

Bulking   Increase in the bulk volume of a quantity of sand in a moist condition over the volume of the same quantity dry or completely inundated.

Caisson   A wood, steel, concrete or reinforced concrete, air-and-water-tight chamber in which it is possible for men to work under air pressure greater than atmospheric pressure, to excavate material below water level.

Cantilever   A beam supported only at one end.

Capillary rise   The height above groundwater level that water is elevated by capillary action.

Chicago method   A method, originated in Chicago, using vertical sheeting to retain earth in open well excavations.

Churn drilling   The use of a machine that drills holes by dropping and raising a bit and drill string hung by a cable.

Clear window glass   A transparent, relatively thin, flat glass having glossy, fire finished, apparently plane and smooth surfaces, but having a characteristic waviness of surface which is visible when viewed at an acute angle or in reflected light.

Coarse-grained soils   Soil in which the large grain sizes, such as sand and gravel, predominates.

Cofferdam   A watertight enclosure usually built of piles or clay, within which excavation is done for foundations.

Column   A compression member, vertical or nearly vertical, the width of which does not exceed four times its thickness and the height of which exceeds four times its least lateral dimension.

Column footings   Concrete footings, reinforced with steel rods, used as supports for columns which in turn carry the load of T-beams which serve as supports for the superstructure of a building.

Combined footing   A structural unit or assembly of units supporting more than one column load.

Compaction   The process of inducing a closer packing of the solid particles in freshly mixed concrete or mortar during placement by the reduction of the volume of voids, usually by vibration, centrifugation, tamping, or some combination of these actions; also applicable to similar manipulation of other cementitious mixtures, soils, aggregate, or the like.

Composite   Defined as an assembly of dissimilar constituents intended to do a job that none of the individual materials can do alone.

Composite pile   A pile made up of different materials, usually concrete and wood or steel fastened together end to end, to form a single pile.

Compressibility   The degree to which a soil will compress under external loading.

Compressive unit strength   The measured maximum resistance of a concrete or mortar specimen to axial loading; expressed as force per unit cross-sectional area; or the specified resistance used in design calculations; in United States expressed in pounds per square inch (psi), and designated fc.

Concrete   A composite material which consists essentially of a binding medium within which are embedded particles or fragments of aggregate; in portland cement concrete, the binder is a mixture of Portland cement and water. When set it attains hardness and strength not unlike stone.

Concrete masonry unit   A solid or hollow masonry unit made from water, portland cement, and suitable aggregates such as sand, gravel, crushed stone, bituminous or anthracite cinders, expanded clay or shale, pumice, volcanic scoria, air-cooled or expanded blast furnace slag, with or without other materials and molded into various shapes.

Concrete wearing surface   The top layer of a concrete floor system. It may be placed separately or integrally with the floor system. Various admixtures, or hardeners, are available for use in the top layer to improve its wearing properties.

Condensation The conversion of moisture in air to water, as on the warm-room side of a cold wall; the forming of water on a surface can usually be prevented by insulating the inner wall so that its surface is kept warmer.

Consolidation The compaction of a soil due to a decrease in the void-ratio caused by external forces.

Construction-management (CM) A project delivery system that differs from the traditional design-bid-build system by utilizing the services of a construction manager who becomes a member of the team of owner-architect-construction manager. The manager's role is to coordinate and communicate the entire project process utilizing his skill and knowledge of construction to clarify cost and time consequences of design decisions as well as their construction feasibility; and to manage the bidding, award, and construction phases of the project. When utilizing construction management, the project owner minimizes time and cost while maintaining quality, function and aesthetics.

Course In masonry, a horizontal range of units the length and thickness of the wall.

Creosote Oil distilled from coal tar, used as a timber preservative.

Cross-lot bracing Bracing that extends in both directions across the excavation.

Dampproofing Treatment of concrete or mortar to retard the passage or absorption of water, or water vapor, either by application of a suitable coating to exposed surfaces, or by use of a suitable admixture or treated cement.

Decibel A unit of loudness of sound derived from the vocabulary of communication engineering. It is the equivalent of the loss in power in one mile of standard cable at 860 cycles.

Design-bid-construct A construction project delivery system that includes design by an architect/engineer, competitive bidding by contractors, and construction performed by the lowest bidder.

Design-build A single contract to provide both design and construction services.

Dew-point temperature The temperature at which air becomes over-saturated with moisture and the moisture condenses.

Diamond drilling The use of a light rotary drill most often used for exploratory work and blast holes.

Differential settlement Uneven sinking of different parts of a building.

Dimension lumber Material pre-cut to specified standardized sizes.

Dome An inverted cup on a building, as a cupola, especially on a large building; the vaulted roof of a rotunda, so constructed as to exert equal, oblique thrust stresses in all directions.

Door A hinged, pivoted, or sliding member, permitting passage through a wall.

Door closers A mechanical device designed for closing and controlling hinges on pivoted doors.

Door frame The surrounding case into and out of which the door shuts and opens. It consists primarily of two upright pieces, called a jamb and a head.

Doorway An opening for passage through a wall.

Downspout A pipe for carrying rain water from roof gutters to the ground or the storm sewer system.

Drift pin A tapered pin used during erection to align holes in steel members to be connected by bolting or riveting.

Drip A cutout in the underside of a projecting piece of wood, stone, or concrete to prevent water from working its way back to the wall.

Dry lumber Lumber with a moisture content of 19% or less.

Efflorescence A deposit of soluble salts, usually white in color, appearing on the surface of concrete and masonry construction. Also called whiskering and saltpetering.

Elastomeric A synthetic rubber material.

End-bearing pile Pile acting like a column; the point has a solid bearing in rock or other dense material.

Epoxy resin Chemical bonding systems used in the preparation of special coatings or adhesives.

Fabrication In steel construction, the operation of cutting the various shapes to the required size and fastening them together to form columns, girders, trusses, and other structural members.

Factor of safety The ratio of the ultimate strength, or yield point, of a material to the working stress assumed in design, stress factor of safety; or the ratio of the ultimate load, moment or shear of a structural member to the working load, moment, or shear, respectively, assumed in design; load factor or safety.

Filler Finely divided inert material such as pulverized limestone, silica or colloidal substances sometimes added to epoxy resigns or other materials to reduce shrinkage, improve workability, or act as an extender.

Fine-grained soils Soil in which the smaller grain sizes predominate, such as fine sand, silt, and clay.

Fineness modulus An abstract number used to compare different particles or graduations of aggregate. The fineness modulus is computed by adding the cumulative percentages retained on the six standard screens (#4, #8, #16, #30, #50, and #100) and dividing the sum by 100.

Finish coat The last and final coat of plaster in a plaster application.

Fire door A metal sheathed door that will resist fire.

Fire limits A boundary line establishing an area in which there exists, or is likely to exist, a fire hazard requiring special fire protection.

Fire resistance The ability of a material or assembly to withstand fire or give protection from it; the ability to confine a fire or to continue to perform a given structural function, or both.

Flashing Sheet metal, copper, lead, or tin used to cover open joints of exterior construction such as roof-valley joints or roof-parapet joints to make them waterproof.

Flat-plate construction A flat slab without column capitals or drop panels.

Flat slab A concrete slab reinforced in two or more directions, generally without beams or girders to transfer the loads to supporting members.

Floating foundation In building construction, a special type of foundation made to carry the weight of a superstructure which is to be erected on swampy land or on unstable soil.

Flush door A door having two flat surfaces. The surfaces are bonded to a solid or hollow core.

Footing drain A perforated or open joint conduit placed around the exterior foundation to carry surface and ground water away from basement walls.

Formwork The total system of support for freshly placed concrete, including the mold or sheathing which contacts the concrete as well as all supporting members, hardware, and necessary bracing.

Framing The primary and secondary members (columns, rafters, girts, purlins, brace rods, etc.) which go together to make up the skeleton of a structure to which the covering can be applied.

Friction pile A bearing pile with supporting capacity produced by friction with the soil in contact with the pile.

Frost line The greatest depth to which ground may be expected to freeze.

Furring A light, nonstructural framework that is attached to a supporting surface to ensure a true, level, and even horizontal and plumb surface.

Gasket Washer-type device of plastic, rubber, or other pliable material used in faucets or other screwed joints to make a water or air tight seal. Hemp fibers wound around the threads of a screwed joint in a water pipe before it is tightened. When wet, hemp expands.

Glazing The process of placing glass in windows.

Glued laminated beam A solid wood structural member built up of laminations that have joined together with glue.

Glulam Trade name for glued laminated wood structural timbers.

Grade beam A horizontal load-bearing foundation member, end-supported like a standard beam, not ground-supported like the foundation wall, which forms a foundation for the walls of a superstructure.

Grading The process of designating the quality of a manufactured piece of wood.

Green lumber A term used by woodworkers when referring to timbers which still contain the moisture, or sap, of the tree from which the wood was cut. Lumber is said to be seasoned when the sap has been removed by natural processes of drying or by artificial drying in a kiln.

Ground water Water in the soil below the standing-water level.

Gutter A shallow channel or conduit of metal or wood set below and along the eaves of a house to catch and carry off rainwater. An eave trough.

Gypsum The basic cementing material in all gypsum plaster.

Gypsum lath A sheet of gypsum plaster with the surfaces covered with heavy paper to which a base coat of plaster is applied.

Gypsum wallboard A finish wallboard consisting of gypsum plaster core covered by paper or other sheet material. The standard width of the panel is 4 ft and lengths are available from 6 ft to 16 ft. Standard thicknesses are ⅜ in., ½ in., and ⅝ in.

Hand lay-up Fabrication process which has the advantage of almost complete freedom of fiber placement and tailoring the cross section. It is also easy to fabricate very thin sections.

Header In masonry, a brick or building stone laid across the thickness of a wall with one end toward face of wall.

Hinge A connection which allows swinging motion in one plane.

Hollow metal door A door constructed of cold-rolled sheet steel surfaces separated by sheet metal ribs. Both panel and flush types are available.

Hollow stem boring A drilling into the earth to bring up samples of the soil from various depths to determine the load-carrying capacity of the soil.

Hydration Formation of a compound by the combining of water with some other substance; in concrete, the chemical reaction between cement and water.

Ingot A large mass of metal cast in a mold.

Insulating glass A glass pane consisting of two or three parallel sheets of glass separated by a thin dehydrated air space.

Jetting A method of sinking piles when a pile hammer is not practical due to locality.

Joints In, masonry, the space between adjacent units.

Joist hanger A steel or sheet metal stirrup used to support and align the ends of joists which are to be flush with the girder.

Kiln dried Said of lumber which has been freed of excess moisture by heating in a kiln instead of open air.

Laitance A layer of weak and nondurable material containing cement and fines from aggregates, brought by bleeding water to the top of overwet concrete, the amount of which is generally increased by overworking or overmanipulating concrete at the surface, by improper finishing or by job traffic. This condition also exists in overtrowelled mortar.

Lamella roof A large-span vault built of wooden members joined by bolts or other means and connected in a diamond pattern.

Lift-slab construction A method of concrete construction in which floor and roof slabs are cast on or at ground level and hoisted into position by jacking; also a slab which is a component of such construction.

Liquid limit Water content, expressed as a percentage of the dry weight of the soil at which the soil passes from the plastic to the liquid state under standard test conditions; the minimum moisture content which will cause soil to flow if jarred slightly.

Lumber Any material, such as boards, planks, or beams cut from wood to a size and form suitable for marketing.

Masonry Construction composed of shaped or molded units, usually small enough to be handled by one man and composed of stone, ceramic brick or tile, concrete, glass, adobe, or the like.

Maximum dry density The dry density obtained by a specified amount of compaction of soil at the optimum moisture content.

Metal curtain wall A metal curtain wall is an exterior building wall that carries no roof or floor loads; it is fastened to the structural frame and acts solely as an enclosing envelope.

Metal lath An expanded or perforated sheet metal material onto which a base coat of plaster is applied.

Millwork Generally all building materials made of finished wood and manufactured in millwork plants and planning mills are included under the term millwork, such as doors, window and door frames, sash, blinds, porch work, mantels, panel work, stairways and special woodwork; does not include flooring, ceiling, or siding.

Model building codes Prepared by a regional agency to assist local municipalities establish minimum requirements for all types of construction.

Moisture-density curve A curve obtained by plotting the soil dry density for various moisture contents to determine which moisture content gives the maximum dry density or 100% compaction.

Moraines Ridges of rock fragments and particles formed from material picked up and redeposited by glacier movement.

Mortar A mixture of cement paste and sand; when used in masonry construction, the mixture may contain masonry cement, or ordinary hydraulic cement with lime, and possible other mixtures, to afford greater plasticity and durability than are attainable with ordinary hydraulic-cement paste.

Mud sill A plank, frame, or small footing on the ground used as base for a shore or post in formwork or to support framed construction.

Noise Any undesired sound which usually contains many frequency components over a wide range.

Occupancy Designated use for all or part of a building.

Open-web (trussed) joists Steel joists built up out of light steel shapes with an open latticed web. A bar joist or trussed joist.

Optimum moisture content The percent of moisture, at which, the greatest density of that particular soil can be obtained through compaction. Especially important in road construction.

Panel (framed) door A door consisting of stile and rail frames enclosing flat plywood or raised panel fillers.

Panic hardware Door hardware used on public buildings to ensure easy exit. Building codes specify that panic hardware shall have a push bar to release the locking mechanism and that the bar must extend across at least three-fourths of the door width.

Parging A thin coat of plastering applied to masonry walls for smoothing the surface or for dampproofing.

Particalboard A panel consisting of compressed wood chips, slivers, sawdust, and shavings combined with an adhesive.

Performance code This type of code requires a specified result rather than specific materials and methods.

Perlite A lightweight aggregate used to improve the fire-resistive and heat-insulating properties of plaster; a siliceous rock of volcanic origin.

Permeability Water vapor permeability is a property of a substance which permits passage of water vapor, and is equal to the permeance of a 1 inch thickness of the substance. When permeability varies with psychrometric conditions, the spot or specific permeability defines the property at a specific condition. Permeability is measured in perm-inches.

Pier foundation A concrete shaft, usually cylindrical in shape, extended to a dense material having the necessary bearing capacity.

Pig iron High-carbon crude iron from the blast furnace used as the main raw material for iron and steel making.

Pile cap A structural member placed on, and usually fastened to, the top of a pile or a group of piles and used to transmit loads to the pile or group of piles.

Pile footing   A footing supported by one or more piles.

Pile foundation   A foundation carried on piles to a denser supporting soil.

Pipe pile   A steel cylinder, usually between 10 and 24 inches in diameter, generally driven with open ends to firm bearing and then excavated and filled with concrete.

Pitch   The degree of inclination, as of a roof plane or a flight of stairs.

Plaster   A mixture of a cementing material, an inert fine aggregate, and water; used to finish ceiling and wall surfaces; usually the finish surfaces will have two or three coats of plaster applied.

Plastic   A material which contains as an essential ingredient an organic substance of large molecular weight, is solid in its finished state, and, at some time in its manufacture, can be shaped by flow.

Plastic limit   The water content at which a soil will just begin to crumble when rolled into a thread approximately ⅛ inch in diameter.

Plasticizer   A material added to increase the workability and flexibility of a resin.

Plate glass   A transparent, flat, relatively thin glass having plane polished surfaces and showing no distortion of vision when viewing objects through it at any angle.

Platform framing   System of wood frame house construction using wood studs one-story high finished with a platform consisting of the underflooring for the next story.

Plywood   A fabricated wood product constructed of veneer joined with glue, usually laid with grain of adjoining piles at right angles.

Portland cement   The product obtained by pulverizing clinker consisting essentially of hydraulic calcium silicates to which no additions have been made subsequent to calcination other than water or untreated calcium sulfate, or both, except that additions not to exceed 1.0% of other material may be interground with the clinker, at the option of the manufacturer, provided such materials in the amounts indicated have been shown not to be harmful.

Pozzolan   A siliceous, or siliceous and aluminous, material that in itself possesses little or no cementitious value but will, in finely divided form and in the presence of moisture, chemically react with calcium hydroxide at ordinary temperatures to form compounds possessing cementitious properties.

Precast concrete   A concrete member that is cast and cured in other than its final position.

Pressure bulb   A figure produced by plotting vertical soil pressures versus depth. Lines of equal magnitude are drawn to produce a bulb shape.

Pressure injected footing   A pile formed by driving a steel shell, open at the tip, then forcing concrete through the shell into the soil using pressure.

Prestressed concrete   Concrete in which internal stresses of such magnitude and distribution are introduced so that the tensile stresses resulting from the service loads are counteracted to a desired degree; in reinforced concrete the prestress is commonly introduced by tensioning the tendons.

Processed glass   Either plate or window glass that has had its transparency altered by a process of sand blasting or acid etching. Many degrees of transparency can be obtained from a frosted, almost opaque quality to a semi-polished, translucent appearance.

Pultrusion   A process in which a hot or cold semisoft solid material, such as metal or plastic, is pulled through the orifice of a die to produce a continuously formed piece in the shape of the desired product.

Quarrying   The operation of removing a natural deposit of stone.

Raft or mat foundation   A continuous slab of concrete, usually reinforced, laid over soft ground or where heavy loads must be supported to form a foundation.

Reinforced concrete   Concrete containing reinforcement and designed on the assumption that the two materials act together in resisting forces.

Relative humidity   The ratio of the quantity of water vapor actually present to amount present in a saturated atmosphere at a given temperature; expressed as a percentage.

Residual soil   A deposit of material which disintegrates in place, such as gravel.

Resilient flooring   Elastic flooring material of various kinds, including vinyl asbestos, cork, rubber, and vinyl plastic.

Revolving door   A door for entrance to public buildings, having four leaves pivoted at their inside stiles and enclosed in a circular vestibule.

Rigid frame   A term used in structural analysis to describe a rafter-to-column connection which is assumed to have sufficient rigidity to hold virtually unchanged the original angles between intersecting members.

Rise   The vertical height from the supports to the ridge of a roof.

Rivet   A round bar of steel, driven while red-hot into a hole through two pieces of steel which are to be joined. The head is held in position by a holder-up with a dolly while another worker strikes the end with a hand hammer, thus forming a head on it. The high-strength friction-grip bolt is much more convenient and quicker, making riveting obsolete for site work.

Rock   The hard, firm, and stable parts of earth's crust; any material which requires blasting before it can be dug.

Roll roofing A roofing material made of compressed fibers saturated with asphalt; supplied in rolls.

Rolling door A door that is supported on wheels which run on a track.

Roof deck That portion of the roof construction to which the roof covering material is applied and through which the loads on the roof are transmitted to supporting members.

Rubble Rough, broken stone used in uncoursed work of walls or for other fillings; rough broken stone direct from the quarry.

Runners A metal channel anchored to the floor and ceiling to support metal studs.

Safety glass A laminated glass built up of layers of glass between which are cemented layers of colorless transparency plastic. Chief uses are for automobiles, skylights, and windows of asylums.

Sandwich panel A noncomposite panel assembly used as covering; consists of an insulating core material with inner and outer skins.

Scratch coat The initial coat of plaster applied in a three coat plaster application. Its outer surface is usually scratched to improve the bond to the coat that follows.

Scuppers Outlets through a parapet wall to drain the roof of water.

Scuttle Horizontal doors or hatches that provide access through the roof by penetrating the roof itself.

Sealants An elastomeric material that is used to fill and seal the expansion joint. This material prevents the passage of moisture and allows horizontal and lateral movement at the expansion joint.

Seamless flooring A flooring material that features a unified, and unjointed surface. Usually a plastic material that can be applied by brush, roller, or trowel in thicknesses of ⅛ in. to ½ in.

Segregation The tendency, as concrete is caused to flow laterally, for coarse aggregate and drier material to remain behind and for mortar and wetter material to flow ahead; also occurs in a vertical direction when wet concrete is overvibrated or dropped vertically into the forms, the mortar and wetter material rising to the top; also called stratification.

Setting The layering of stones, lintels, bricks, etc., in a wall.

Shake A handsplit shingle widely used in the western states of the U.S.A.

Shear walls A wall which in its own plane carries shear resulting from wind, blast, or earthquake forces.

Shearing strength The angular displacement of a soil due to a force across it.

Sheet pile A pile, or sheeting, that may form one of a continuous interlocking line, or a row of timber, concrete, or steel piles, driven in close contact to provide a tight wall to resist the lateral pressure of water, adjacent earth, or other materials.

Sheeting A line of planks, often tongued and grooved on the sides, driven endwise into the ground to protect subgrade operations.

Shell pile A pile formed by driving a closed point sheet steel shell or casing into the ground and filling it with concrete.

Shell-less pile A pile formed by driving a shell with an inserted driving core; then withdrawing the core and filling the shell with concrete while withdrawing the shell.

Shingle Roof or wall covering of asphalt, asbestos, wood, tile, slate, or other material cut into stock lengths, widths, and thicknesses.

Shore A temporary support for formwork and fresh concrete or for recently built structures which have not developed full design strength; also called prop, tom, post, strut.

Shot drilling A method of drilling using chilled steel shot under a rotary bit.

Shrinkage limit The maximum water content at which a reduction in water content will not cause a decrease in volume of the soil mass.

Shrinking (shrinkage) Volume decrease caused by drying and chemical changes; a function of time but not of temperature or of stress due to external load; loss of bulk of soil when compacted in a fill; usually is computed on the basis of bank measure.

Single ply membrane roofing A roofing system employing a single membrane laid in sheets over the roof deck.

Skylight An opening in a roof or ceiling for admitting daylight; also, the window fitted into such an opening.

Slab A flat, usually horizontal, or nearly so, molded layer of plain or reinforced concrete usually of uniform thickness, but sometimes of variable thickness; the flat section of floor or roof either on the ground or supported by beams, columns or other framework.

Slab-band construction Concrete floor construction consisting of wide shallow beams, called bands, running continuously along each longitudinal row of columns and supporting one-way slabs spanning between bands and cast monolithically with them.

Sleeper A strip of wood laid over a rough concrete floor to which the finished wood floor is nailed.

Sliding door A door that is suspended on overhead tracks and operates on nylon rollers attached to the door.

Slip form A form which is pulled or raised as concrete is placed; may move in a generally horizontal direction to lay concrete evenly for highway paving or on slopes and inverts of canals, tunnels, and siphons; or vertically to form walls, bins, or silos of uniform cross section from bottom to top.

Slope The inclination of a surface expressed as one unit of rise or fall to so many horizontal units.

Slump test The procedure for measuring the slump of concrete.

Slurry trench A method of construction that uses a bentonite slurry in trench excavation to prevent the collapse of the trench walls.

Soil auger A tool used to bore holes in soil for soil testing.

Soldier beam A rolled steel section driven into the ground to carry the force of a horizontal sheeting earth bank.

Sound A rapid fluctuation of air pressure.

Sound masking A system to unobtrusively raise the background noise level in a room to provide acoustical privacy.

Sounding rod A steel rod or pipe about ¾ inch in diameter driven into soil with a maul or drop weight. The number of blows required to drive the rod indicates the nature of the underlying soil.

Spread footing A generally rectangular prism of concrete larger in lateral dimensions than the column or wall it supports, to distribute the load of a column or wall to the subgrade.

Spread foundation Any foundation where bearing over a sufficient area prevents undue settlement or rupture.

Stainless steel A hard, tough steel which retains polish; an alloy of steel which contains a high percentage of chromium, sometimes with the addition of nickel and copper. Has excellent resistance to corrosion.

Steel Iron compounded with other metals to increase strength, wearing or rust resistance, or to obtain other desired qualities.

Stone Individual blocks, masses, or fragments of rock taken from their original formation and considered for commercial use.

Stretcher A brick laid with the long face exposed.

Strip shingle A narrow or relatively long piece of roofing.

Strut A supporting piece; an inside brace resisting pressure along its length.

Suspended ceiling A ceiling that is suspended from the floor above. Often conceals electrical and mechanical distribution equipment. Metal runners are attached with wire hangers, and panels of ceiling material are placed on the runners.

Swelling Volume increase caused by wetting or chemical changes, or both; a function of time but not of stress due to external load.

Tempered glass A glass that has been heat-treated to increase its mechanical and thermal properties.

Tendon A steel element such as a wire, cable, bar, rod, or strand used to impart prestress to concrete when the element is tensioned.

Terrazzo A wearing surface for floors using concrete with a special aggregate of marble chip or other decorative material. The special aggregate is exposed by grinding after the concrete has set.

Test piles Foundation piles installed on the proposed construction site. Structural engineers then make load test on the piles to determine how many and what size piling are needed for the project.

Test pit An excavation to determine the nature of the material encountered or to disclose subsurface conditions.

Thickened slab A concrete slab whose thickness has increased under exterior and interior walls to serve as a foundation; placed integrally with the floor slab.

Tilt-up construction A method of concrete construction in which members are cast horizontally at a location adjacent to their eventual position, and tilted into place after removal of molds.

Timber Structural lumber usually 5 inches or more in the least dimension. In dimension joists and timbers, the strength, stiffness, and uniformity of size are of primary importance, appearance is secondary.

Total life cost A concept where lifetime ownership costs, rather than just first time construction, are the basis of comparison for alternate proposals.

Transmission loss The number of decibels that a sound loses in being transmitted through a wall or floor/ceiling.

Truss An assemblage of timbers, fastened together so as to mutually support each other and to prevent sagging or distortion of any kind; used as one of the principal supports of a roof.

Veneer A thin layer of selected wood for gluing to a support.

Vermiculite A lightweight aggregate used to improve the fire-resistive and heat-insulating properties of plaster; a micaceous mineral.

Void ratio The ratio of the volume of voids to the volume of the solids in a sample of aggregate or soil. The voids ratio for clay may have to be defined at a stated pressure since clay contracts with the rise in pressure.

Wale Long horizontal member, usually double, used to hold studs in position; also called waler or ranger.

Wall A vertical structure member which encloses, divides, supports, or protects a building or room.

Wash The slight slope of a top surface to shed water.

Wash boring A test hole from which samples are mixed with water; also, sinking a casing to bedrock by means of a jet of water inside it.

Water–cement ratio The ratio of the amount of water, exclusive only of that absorbed by the aggregates, to the amount of cement in a concrete or mortar mixture; preferably stated as a decimal by weight. The lower the water-cement ratio, the stronger the cement. It is usually expressed in terms of gallons of water per sack of cement.

Wearing surface   The top portion of the floor covering designed to absorb both traffic and wear.

Weathering steel   A bare unprotected steel that acquires a protective oxide coat that deters rust and corrosion. This steel soon acquires a sepia-toned patina that eventually weathers into a deep brownish-mauve color.

Weld   To build up or fasten together. A joint made by bringing surfaces heated to plasticity into close contact.

Well point   Perforated pipe sunk into sand to permit the pumping of ground water and excluding the sand.

Wind Bracing   Bracing provided to resist all lateral loads.

Window   An opening in a wall for light and ventilation, with all its appurtenances.

Wire Lath   A fabrication of wire woven or welded into a fabric, screen, or mesh, onto which a base coat of plaster is applied.

Wood   The cellulose substance inside the bark of trees, cut into lumber and veneer for many uses in building.

Wythe   The course or thickness of brick separating flues; each continuous vertical section, or thickness, of brick masonry.

REFERENCES AND TRADE ASSOCIATIONS

CHAPTER 1

References

American Insurance Association, *Fire Resistance Ratings,* New York. Copies of this publication will be sent on request.

Underwriters' Laboratories, Inc., *Building Materials List,* Chicago. Published annually.

International Conference of Building Officials, *Uniform Building Code,* 1985, Whittier, Calif. Published every three years.

American Insurance Association, *National Building Code,* New York.

Western Wood Products Association, *Product Use Manual,* 1984, Portland, Oreg.

Southern Building Code Congress, *Southern Standard Building Code,* Birmingham, Ala.

Building Officials Conference of America, Inc. (BOCA), *Basic Building Code,* Chicago.

Underwriters' Laboratories, Inc., *Standard for Fire Tests of Building Construction and Materials* UL 263, Chicago.

The Construction Specifications Institute, *Masterformat,* CSI Document MP-2-1, 1983, Washington, D.C.

Trade Associations

American Society for Testing and Materials, 1916 Race St., Philadelphia, PA 19103

Building Materials Research Institute, Inc., 15 E. 40th St., New York, NY 10016

Building Officials Conference of America, Inc., 1313 E. 60th St., Chicago, IL 60637

Building Research Advisory Board, 2101 Constitution Ave., N.W., Washington, DC 20418

Building Research Institute, 2101 Constitution Ave., N.W., Washington, DC 20418

Construction Specifications Institute, 1150 17th St., N.W., Washington, DC 20036

Federal Housing Administration, 451 Seventh St., S.W., Washington, DC 20411

International Conference of Building Officials, 50 S. Los Robles, Pasadena, CA 91101

National Bureau of Standards, Building Technology, Gaithersburg, MD 20234

Southern Building Code Congress, 1116 Brown Marks Bldg., Birmingham, AL 35203

Underwriters' Laboratories, Inc. 207 E. Ohio St., Chicago, IL 60611

CHAPTER 2

References

Ralph B. Peck, Walter E. Hanson, and Thomas H. Thornburn, *Foundation Engineering,* 2nd Ed., 1974, New York, John Wiley and Sons.

American National Standards Institute, *Building Code Requirements for Excavations and Foundations,* A56.1-1952, New York.

The Asphalt Institute, *Soils Manual,* 2nd Ed., College Park, Md.

Karl Terzaghi and Ralph B. Peck, *Soil Mechanics in Engineering Practice,* 2nd Ed., 1967, New York, John Wiley and Sons.

George B. Sowers and George F. Sowers, *Introductory Soil Mechanics and Foundations,* 1970, New York, Macmillan.

American Society for Testing and Materials, *ASTM Annual Book of Standards,* Part 11, 1971, Philadelphia, Pa.

American Society for Testing and Materials, *ASTM Annual Book of Standards,* Part 19, 1978, Philadelphia, Pa.

Trade Associations

American Society for Testing and Materials, 1916 Race St., Philadelphia, PA 19103

Asphalt Institue, Asphalt Institute Building, College Park, MD 20740

CHAPTER 3

References

American Iron and Steel Institute, *Pile Foundations,* 4th Ed., New York.

Catalog: Franki Foundation Specialists, Franki Foundation Company, New York, NY.

Catalog: Foster Vibro/Driver Extractors, L. B. Foster Co., Pittsburgh, Pa.

Catalog: Delmag Diesel Pile Hammers, The Foundation Equipment Corporation, Newscomerstown, Ohio.

Walter E. Lessey, *High Capacity Long Steel Piles,* American Iron and Steel Institute, New York

Catalog: Calweld Drilling Tools, Calweld Company, Santa Fe Springs, Calif.

M. J. Tomlinson, *Foundation Design and Construction,* 2nd Ed., 1969, New York, John Wiley and Sons.

Trade Associations

American Society of Landscape Architects, 200 K Street, N.W., Washington, DC 20005

Association of Drilled Shaft Contractors, P.O. Box 25704, Dallas, TX 75225

Deep Foundation Institute, P.O. Box 359, Springfield, NJ 07081

CHAPTER 4

References

American Concrete Institute, *Building Code Requirements for Reinforced Concrete* (ACI 318-85), 1985, Detroit.

American Society for Testing and Materials, *ASTM Annual Book of Standards,* Part 10, Philadelphia, Pa.

Concrete Reinforcing Steel Institute, *Manual of Standard Practice,* 3rd Ed., 1978 Chicago.

Portland Cement Association, *Design and Control of Concrete Mixtures,* 12th Ed., 1976, Skokie, Ill.

Sweet's Catalog, F. W. Dodge Corp., New York.

American Concrete Institute, *Formwork for Concrete,* Publication SP-4, 4th Ed., 1979, Detroit.

U.S. Department of the Interior, Bureau of Reclamation, *Concrete Manual,* 8th Ed., 1981, Denver, Colo.

American Concrete Institute, *Minimum Standard Requirements for Precast Concrete Floor and Roof Units,* Standard ACI 711-58, 1958, Detroit.

Trade Associations

American Concrete Institute, P.O. Box 4754, Redford Station, Detroit, MI 48219

American Concrete Pumping Association, 606 North Larchmont Blvd., Suite 4A, Los Angeles, CA 90004

American Plywood Association, 1119 A St., Tacoma, WA 98401

American Society of Concrete Constructors, 2510 Dempster St., Des Plaines, IL 60016

Concrete Pipe Association, Inc., 1501 Wilson Blvd., Arlington, VA 22209

Concrete Reinforcing Steel Institute, 228 N. LaSalle St., Chicago, IL 60601

Concrete Sawing and Drilling Association, 606 North Larchmont Blvd., Los Angeles, CA 90004

National Association of Reinforcing Steel Contractors, P.O. Box 225, 10533 Main St., Fairfax, VA 22030

National Crushed Stone Association, 1415 Elliot Pl., N.W., Washington, DC 20007

National Precast Concrete Association, 2201 E. 46th. St., Indianapolis, IN 46205

National Ready Mixed Concrete Association, 900 Spring St., Silver Spring, MD 20910

National Sand and Gravel Association, 900 Spring St., Silver Spring, MD 20910

Portland Cement Association, Old Orchard Rd., Skokie, IL 60076

Prestressed Concrete Institute, 205 W. Wacker Dr., Chicago, IL 60606

Reinforced Concrete Research Council, 5420 Old Orchard Rd., Skokie, IL 60076

Scaffolding and Shoring Institute, 2130 Keith Building, Cleveland, OH 44115

Wire Reinforcement Institute, 7900 West Park Dr., Suite 714, McLean, VA 22101

CHAPTER 5

References

Portland Cement Association, *Concrete Masonry Handbook,* 1976, Skokie, Ill.

Sweet's Catalog, F. W. Dodge Corp., New York.

Masonry Industry Advertising Committee, *Masonry Design Manual,* 1973, Los Angeles, Calif.

National Bureau of Standards, *Building Code Requirements for Reinforced Masonry,* American Standard A41.2-1960, Washington, D.C.

Structural Clay Products Institute, *Reinforced Brick Masonry,* Technical Notes on Brick and Tile Construction, Vol. 5, Nos. I to IV, January to April 1954, McLean, Va.

Structural Clay Products Institute, *Mortars for Clay Masonry,* Technical Notes on Brick and Tile Construction, No. 8, August 1961, McLean, Va.

Trade Associations

Brick Institute of America, 1750 Old Meadow Road, McLean, VA 22101

Expanded Shale, Clay & Slate Institute, 1041 National Press Bldg., Washington, DC 20004

Expansion Anchor Manufacturers Institute, Inc., 331 Madison Ave., New York, NY 10017

Indiana Limestone Institute of America, Inc., Suite 400, Stone City National Bank Bldg., Bedford, IN 47421

Institute of Masonry Research, 9013 Old Harford Rd., Baltimore, MD 21234

International Masonry Institute, 825 15th St., N.W., Washington, DC 20005

Marble Institute of America, 425 13th St., N.W., Washington, DC 20004

Mason Contractors Association of America, Inc., 208 S. La Salle St., Chicago, IL 60604

Masonry Institute of America, 2550 Beverly Blvd., Los Angeles, CA 90057

National Concrete Masonry Association, 1800 N. Kent St., Arlington, VA 22209

National Limestone Institute, Inc., 1315 16th St., N.W. Washington, DC 20036

Structural Clay Products Institute, 1750 Old Meadow Rd., McLean, VA 22101

Vermiculite Institute, Board of Trade Bldg., Chicago, IL 60604

CHAPTER 6

References

American Institute of Steel Construction, Inc., *Specifications for the Design, Fabrication and Erection of Structural Steel for Buildings,* Chicago.

Lincoln Electric Company, *Procedure Handbook of Arc Welding Design and Practice,* 1957, Cleveland, Ohio.

American Institute of Steel Construction, Inc., *Manual of Steel Construction,* 8th Ed., 1980, Chicago.

American Iron and Steel Institute, *The Picture Story of Steel,* Washington, D.C.

Metal Building Dealers Association, *Metal Building Systems,* 1980, Dayton, Ohio.

Trade Associations

Aluminum Association, 750 3rd Ave., New York, NY 10017

American Bureau of Metal Statistics, 420 Lexington Ave., New York, NY 10017

American Institute of Steel Construction, Inc., 400 N. Michigan Avenue, Chicago, IL 60611

American Iron & Steel Institute, 1000 16th Street, N.W., Washington, DC 20036

American Welding Society, Inc., 2501 N.W. Seventh St., Miami, FL 33125

Architectural Aluminum Manufacturers Association, 1 E. Wacker Dr., Chicago, IL 60601

Cast Iron Pipe Research Association, 1301 W. 22nd St., Suite 509, Oak Brook, IL 60521

Copper Development Association, Inc., 405 Lexington Ave., 57th Fl., New York, NY 10017

Metal Building Manufacturers Association, Keith Bldg., Cleveland, OH 44115

National Association of Architectural Metal Manufacturers, 228 N. LaSalle St., Chicago, IL 60601

National Ornamental Metal Manufacturers Association, 724 Ingleside Shore, Ingleside, IL 60041

Steel Deck Institute, P.O. Box 3812, St. Louis, MO 63122

Steel Joist Institute, 1703 Parham Road, Suite 204, Richmond, VA 23229

CHAPTER 7

References

Timber Engineering Co., *Typical Designs of Timber Structures,* Washington, D.C.

National Forest Products Association, *Manual for House Framing,* 1982, Washington, D.C.

National Forest Products Association, *Plank-and-Beam Framing for Residential Buildings,* Washington, D.C.

National Forest Products Association, *Heavy Timber Construction Details,* Washington, D.C.

Sweet's Catalog, F. W. Dodge Corp., New York.

American Institute of Timber Construction, *Timber Construction Manual,* 1984, John Wiley and Sons, New York.

German Gurfinkel, *Wood Engineering,* 2nd Ed., 1981, Southern Forest Products Association, New Orleans, La.

American Plywood Association, *Plywood Construction Systems,* 1984, Tacoma, Wash.

Western Wood Products, *Western Woods Use Book,* 1984, Portland, OR.

Edward B. Cooper, *Plastics in Building Construction,* Plastics in Building, 1955, Building Research Institute, Washington, D.C.

Small Homes Council, *Plastics as Building Materials,* Circular Series D.4.0, 1956, University of Illinois.

Trade Associations

American Institute of Timber Construction, 333 W. Hampden Ave., Englewood, CO 80110

American Walnut Manufacturers' Association Room 1729, 666 N. Lake Shore Dr., Chicago, IL 60611

American Plywood Association, P.O. Box 11700, Tacoma, WA 98411

American Wood Preservers Institute, 1651 Old Meadow Road, McLean, VA 22101

California Redwood Association, One Lombard Street, San Francisco, CA 94111

Fine Hardwoods Association, 666 N. Lake Shore Dr., Chicago, IL 60611

National Forest Products Association, 1619 Massachusetts Ave., N.W., Washington, DC 20036

National Hardware Lumber Association, 59 E. Van Buren St., Chicago, IL 60605

National Hardwood Lumber Association, 332 Michigan Ave., Chicago, IL 60604

National Lumber Manufacturers Association, 1619 Massachusetts Ave., N.W., Washington, DC 20036

Northeastern Lumber Manufacturers Association, 13 South St., Glen Falls, NY 12801

Plastics in Construction Council, 250 Park Ave., New York, NY 10017

Society of American Wood Preservers, Inc., 1501 Wilson Blvd., Suite 1004, Arlington, VA 22209

Society of the Plastics Industry, 355 Lexington Ave., New York, NY 10017

Southern Cypress Manufacturers Association, 805 Sterick Bldg., Memphis, TN 38103

Southern Forest Products Association, P.O. Box 52468, New Orleans, LA 70152

Southern Hardwood Lumber Manufacturers Association, 805 Sterick Bldg., Memphis, TN 38103

Southern Pine Inspection Bureau, P.O. Box 846, Pensacola, FL 32594

Timber Products Manufacturers, 951 E. 3rd Ave., Spokane, WA 99202

West Coast Lumber Inspector Bureau, P.O. Box 23145, Portland, OR 97223

Western Red & Northern White Cedar Association, P.O. Box 2786, New Brighton, MN 55112

Western Red Cedar Lumber Association, 700 Yeon Bldg., Portland, OR 97204

Western Wood Products Association, 1500 Yeon Bldg., Portland, OR 97204

CHAPTER 8

References

Insulation Board Institute, *Fundamentals of Building Insulation,* 1984, Chicago.

Sweet's Architectural Catalog File, F. W. Dodge Corp., New York. Published annually.

National Slate Association, *Slate Roofs,* 1953, New York.

Asphalt Roofing Manufacturers Association, *Residential Asphalt Roofing Manual,* 1984, Rockville, Md.

Donald H. Clark, *Manual of Handsplit Red Cedar Shakes,* Red Cedar Shingle & Handpsplit Shake Bureau, Seattle, Wash.

American Plywood Association, *Plywood Roof Systems,* 1979, Tacoma, Wash.

Trade Associations

Acoustical and Insulating Materials Association, 215 W. Touhy Ave., Park Ridge, IL 60068

Acoustical Society of America, 335 E. 45th St., New York, NY 10017

Adhesive & Sealant Council, 1410 Higgins Rd., Park Ridge, IL 60068

Asphalt Roofing Manufacturers Association, 6288 Montrose Road, Rockville, MD 20852

Building Waterproofers Association, 60 E. 42nd St., New York, NY 10017

National Council of Acoustical Consultants, 484 E. Main St., East Aurora, NY 14052

National Mineral Wool Insulation Association, 382 Springfield Ave., Summit, NY 07901

National Roofing Contractors Association, 1515 N. Harlem Ave., Oak Park, IL 60302

National Slate Association, 455 W. 23rd St., New York, NY 10011

Red Cedar Shingle & Handsplit Shake Bureau, 5510 White Bldg., Seattle, WA 98101

CHAPTER 9

References

Flat Glass Marketing Association, *Glazing Manual,* Topeka, Kans.

Sweet's Catalog Architectural File, F. W. Dodge Corp., New York. Issued annually.

Steel Door Institute, *Recommended Specifications for Standard Steel Doors and Frames,* SDI-100, Cleveland, Ohio.

National Association of Architectural Metal Manufacturers, *Metal Curtain Wall Manual,* 1960, Chicago.

National Woodwork Manufacturer's Association, *Industry Standard for Hardwood Veneered and Plastic Faced Flush Wood Doors,* IS 1, Park Ridge, Ill.

National Woodwork Manufacturer's Association, *Industry Standard for Wood Windows,* IS 2, Park Ridge, Ill.

Trade Associations

American Hardware Association, 20 N. Wacker Dr., Chicago, IL 60606

American Hardware Manufacturers Association, 2130 Keith Bldg., Cleveland, OH 44115

Builders Hardware Manufacturers Association, 60 E. 42nd St., New York, NY 10017

Flat Glass Marketing Association, 3310 Harrison Bldg., Topeka, KS 66611

National Builders Hardware Association, 1290 Avenue of the Americas, New York, NY 10019

National Sash & Door Jobbers Association, 20 N. Wacker Dr., Chicago, IL 60606

Stained Glass Association of America, 3600 University Dr., Fairfax, VA 22030

Steel Door Institute, 712 Lakewood Center North, Cleveland, OH 44107

Steel Window Institute, 2130 Keith Bldg., Cleveland, OH 44115

CHAPTER 10

References

American National Standards Institute, *American Standard Specifications for Portland Cement Stucco and Portland Cement Plastering,* ANSI A42.2 and A42.3, New York.

Gypsum Association, *Manual of Lathing and Plastering,* 1984, Evanston, Ill.

Portland Cement Association, *Plasterers Manual,* 1983, Skokie, Ill.

Sweet's Catalog, F. W. Dodge Corp., New York.

Gypsum Association, *Using Gypsum Board for Walls and Ceilings,* 1985, Evanston, Ill.

Maple Flooring Manufacturer's Association, *Design and Installation Guide for Hard Maple Flooring,* 1983, Chicago.

Trade Associations

American Hardboard Association, Suite 2236, 20 N. Wacker Dr., Chicago, IL 60606

American Institute of Interior Designers, 730 5th Ave., New York, NY 10019

Architectural Woodwork Institute, 5055 S. Chesterfield Rd., Arlington, VA 22206

Asphalt & Vinyl Asbestos Tile Institute, 101 Park Ave., New York, NY 10017

Carpet & Rug Institute, P.O. Box 2048 Holiday Dr., Dalton, GA 30720

Carpet Wool Council, Inc., 919 3rd Ave., New York, NY 10022

Ceramic Tile Institute, 3415 W. 8th St., Los Angeles, CA 90005

Gypsum Association, 1603 Orrington Ave., Evanston, IL 60201

International Association of Wall & Ceiling Contractors, 20 E. St., N.W., Washington, DC 20001

Maple Flooring Manufacturers Association, 8600 West Bryn Mawr Ave., Chicago, IL 60631

Metal Lath Association 221 N. LaSalle St., Chicago, IL 60601

National Association of Decorative Architectural Finishes, 112 N. Alfred St., Alexandria, VA 22314

National Bureau for Lathing & Plastering, 938 K St., N.W., Washington, DC 20001

National Ceramic Manufacturing Association, 53 E. Main St., Moorestown, NJ 20277

National Oak Flooring Manufacturers Association, 814 Sterick Bldg., Memphis, TN 38103

National Paint and Coatings Association, 1500 Rhode Island Ave., N.W., Washington, DC 20005

National Particleboard Association, 2306 Perkins Pl., Silver Springs, MD 20910

National Terrazzo & Mosaic Association, 3166 Des Plaines Ave., Des Plaines, IL 60018

National Woodwork Manufacturers Association, Inc., 400 W. Madison Ave., Chicago, IL 60606

Painting and Decorating Contractors of America, 7223 Lee Highway, Falls Church, VA 22046

Resilient Flooring & Carpet Association Inc., P.O. Box 11082, Oakland, CA 94611

Tile Contractors' Association of America, 112 N. Alfred, Alexandria, VA 22314

Tile Council of America, Inc., 360 Lexington Ave., New York, NY 10017

Wood & Synthetic Flooring Institute, 1441 Shermer Rd., Northbrook, IL 60062

INDEX

Page numbers in parentheses indicate tables; page numbers in brackets indicate illustrations.

411